CANADIAN EDITION

Third

Essentials of

Business

Communication

MARY ELLEN GUFFEY
LOS ANGELES PIERCE COLLEGE

BRENDAN NAGLE

Nelson
Thomson Learning™

Australia • Canada • Denmark • Japan • Mexico • New Zealand • Philippines
Puerto Rico • Singapore • South Africa • Spain • United Kingdom • United States

1120 Birchmount Road
Scarborough, Ontario M1K 5G4
www.nelson.com
www.thomson.com

Canadian Cataloguing in Publication Data

Guffey, Mary Ellen
        Essentials of business communication

3rd Canadian ed.
Includes bibliographical references and index.
ISBN 0-17-616759-5

1. Business writing. 2. English language – Business English. 3. Business communication.
I. Nagle, Brendan, 1958– . II. Title.

HF5718.3.G84 2000   808'.06665   C99-933103-5

Editorial Director	Evelyn Veitch
Acquisitions Editor	Nicole Gnutzman
Project Editor	Jenny Anttila
Production Editor	Natalia Denesiuk
Production Coordinator	Hedy Later
Marketing Manager	Don Thompson
Art Director	Angela Cluer
Cover Design	Liz Harasymczuk
Interior Design	Julie Greener
Compositor	Anita Macklin
Editor	Erika Krolman
Printer	Webcom

Printed and bound in Canada
    2   3   4   03   02   01   00

CONTENTS

UNIT 6

Communicating for Employment

PREFACE

Today's students will be working in environments that demand ever-increasing skill levels. They will be expected to collect information, solve problems, and make decisions independently. They will be working with global trading partners and collaborating with work teams in an increasingly diverse workplace. And they will be using sophisticated technology to communicate. *Essentials of Business Communication* has been thoroughly revised to help students and workplace communicators meet these challenges.

The Third Canadian Edition maintains the streamlined, efficient approach to communication that has equipped past learners with the skills needed to be successful in their work. It is most helpful to postsecondary and adult learners preparing themselves for new careers, planning a change in their current careers, or wishing to upgrade their writing and speaking skills.

The aim of this edition is to incorporate more of the comments, suggestions, and insights provided by adopters over the last few years. For those new to the book, some of the most popular features include the following:

TEXT-WORKBOOK FORMAT

The convenient text-workbook format presents an all-in-one teaching/learning package that includes concepts, workbook application exercises, writing problems, and a combination handbook/reference manual.

FOUR-STAGE SKILL DEVELOPMENT PLAN

Essentials of Business Communication, Third Canadian Edition, develops communication skills in a carefully designed four-stage plan.

Stage 1 (Chapter 1) presents the process of communication and considers the important effects of culture, workplace diversity, and technology on business communication. Stage 1 (Chapter 2) also introduces listening, nonverbal, and speaking skills. In Stage 1 instructors may elect to include an optional review of grammar, punctuation, usage, and style for business communicators.

Stage 2 (Chapters 3 and 4) develops basic and advanced writing techniques, including tips for using plain language, concise wording, conversational tone, parallelism, and many other "tricks of the trade."

Stage 3 (Chapters 5–10) teaches writing strategies and helps students apply these strategies in composing memos and e-mail messages, request and reply letters, negative news letters, persuasive messages, and special goodwill messages.

Stage 4 (Chapters 11–14) adapts basic communication strategies and techniques to a range of communication applications, including informal and formal reports, proposals, employment messages, and employment interviewing.

GRAMMAR/MECHANICS EMPHASIS

Each chapter includes instructions for a systematic review of the Grammar/Mechanics Handbook. Readers take a short quiz to review specific concepts, and they also proofread a business document that provides a cumulative review of all concepts previously presented. In this way students receive continual review and reinforcement of the fundamentals of correct writing.

WRITING PLANS, WRITING IMPROVEMENT EXERCISES, AND CRITICAL-THINKING CASES

Three unique features help readers develop writing skills. First, writing plans outline specific strategies so that students get started writing quickly. Second, writing improvement exercises break down the total writing process into simple components. Third, the first three or four problems in each of the memo- and letter-writing chapters provide documents and questions that guide students through the critical-thinking stages of creating a message. Many of these cases enable readers to revise realistic business messages. Writing plans and revision exercises are especially successful teaching-learning techniques for novice writers. Beginners get started quickly and confidently—without struggling to provide unknown details to unfamiliar, hypothetical cases.

CONCISE INSTRUCTIONAL PACKAGE

An important reason for the success of *Essentials of Business Communication* is that it practises what it preaches. The Third Canadian Edition follows the same strategy, concentrating on essential concepts presented without wasted words. This new edition still contains only 14 chapters, making it possible to cover the material in it easily in one term.

NEW AND CONTINUING FEATURES THAT MEET TODAY'S WORKPLACE CHALLENGES

Success in today's competitive, diverse, and global business environment requires flexible attitudes and special sensitivity to the effects of culture. Moreover, today's communicators must be able to think critically and must be familiar with on-line technology and the Internet. Many of the new features in the Third Canadian Edition address these special needs.

*   *Cross-Cultural Communication, Workplace Diversity, and Communication Technologies.* Now incorporated in Chapter 1, a discussion of the powerful effects of culture and workplace diversity prepares students to work and communicate with people from different cultures. This chapter also takes a look at emerging technologies in a typical work setting to give an overview of what students can expect in using the Internet and other on-line resources.

- *Communication Workshops.* End-of-chapter workshops focus on challenges related to ethics, diversity, the multicultural workplace, teamwork, and technology issues. Through tips, guidelines, discussion questions, activities, and applications, students develop new perspectives and tools that will enable them to thrive in an increasingly complex workplace.

- *Enhanced E-Mail Coverage.* Chapter 5 presents an extensive discussion of e-mail, including tips for effective use. And every chapter in the book now includes at least one e-mail activity to provide practice in using this pervasive communication technology. These activities are identified for you with the icon shown here.

- *Emphasis on the Internet, Including World Wide Web Resources.* Nearly every businessperson today is using or is affected by the Internet. Because business communicators must be familiar with on-line resources and operation, the Third Canadian Edition of *Essentials* presents Internet and on-line resources in many chapters. In selected problems we include Internet addresses for students to gain access to relevant Web sites for additional information.

Every chapter also includes at least one optional activity, identified by the icon shown here, requiring students to use the World Wide Web to gather information and solve problems.

- *Scannable Résumés and Links to On-Line Job Banks.* Many of today's job hunters use the Internet to post résumés and explore job openings. The Third Canadian Edition teaches students how to write computer-friendly résumés and also identifies the best on-line employment information currently available.

- *Expanded Coverage of Employment Interviewing.* Chapter 14 now describes screening and hiring interviews, provides advice for investigating prospective employers, and discusses how to fight interview fears. Most importantly, the chapter reveals all-time favourite interview questions and suggests strategies for answering them.

- *Electronic Citation Formats.* This edition's documentation appendix presents the latest formats for electronic citation of information.

- *Focus on Letter and Memorandum Writing.* Students learn to write letters and memos that request information, order goods, make claims, respond to inquiries, respond to claims, refuse requests, and refuse credit. They also learn to apply practical psychology in persuasive and sales letters, as well as learning how to develop goodwill with letters of appreciation, congratulation, sympathy, and recommendation. As in previous editions of *Essentials,* the Third Canadian Edition devotes an entire chapter to memos and e-mail messages, the main writing tasks of business communicators today.

- *Coverage of Formal and Informal Reports.* Two chapters develop functional report-writing skills. Chapter 11 concentrates on informal, short reports. Chapter 12 covers proposals and formal, long reports. This chapter includes a model proposal and long report, both of which are fully annotated.

- *New—Coverage of Nonverbal Communication.* Recognizing and understanding nonverbal messages helps successful communicators control the silent messages they send as well as interpret those they see. Chapter 2 discusses nonverbal communication, an important skill for all communicators.

- *Listening and Speaking Skills.* Good listening and speaking skills, in great demand by employers, are developed in Chapter 2. Students learn to recognize barriers to effective listening, and they study tips for active listening.

Moreover, they learn methods of organizing and delivering successful oral presentations. Because businesses are increasingly adopting a team approach to their work, students are also taught to plan and participate in productive and efficient business meetings.

- *Employment Communications Skills.* Successful résumés, letters of application, and other employment documents are among the most important topics in a good business communications course. In Chapter 13 the Third Canadian Edition shows chronological, functional, combination, and computer-friendly résumés. Chapter 13 also covers current job-search information, including tips for using on-line job banks and résumé services on the Internet. Moreover, this edition now includes an entirely new chapter (Chapter 14) devoted to employment interviewing.

- *New—End-of-Chapter Problems.* Over 50 percent of the problems and activities in the Third Canadian Edition are new. Many of the exercises relate to newsmaking situations and dilemmas requiring critical-thinking skills in solving realistic business problems facing today's communicators.

- *New—Models Comparing Effective and Ineffective Documents.* To facilitate speedy recognition of good and bad writing techniques and strategies, the Third Canadian Edition now demonstrates these techniques with many before-and-after documents. We've also added marginal notes to specific parts of model documents to draw students' attention to targeted strategies.

- *Diagnostic Test.* An optional grammar/mechanics diagnostic test helps students and instructors systematically pinpoint specific student writing weaknesses. Students may be directed to the Grammar/Mechanics Handbook for remediation.

- *Grammar/Mechanics Handbook.* A comprehensive Grammar/Mechanics Handbook supplies a thorough review of English grammar, punctuation, capitalization style, and number usage. Its self-teaching exercises may be used for classroom instruction or for supplementary assignments. The handbook also serves as a convenient reference throughout the course.

INSTRUCTOR SUPPORT

Essentials of Business Communication, Third Canadian Edition, includes extensive instructor support. A comprehensive instructor's manual is available, including solutions to the Grammar/Mechanics Challenges, additional lecture material, chapter-by-chapter lesson plans, evaluation suggestions for oral presentations and reports, and transparency masters. The package also contains a complete computerized test bank and a full set of PowerPoint presentation slides.

Your local Nelson Thomson Learning sales representative can provide more information about World Wide Web support resources.

ACKNOWLEDGMENTS

The Third Canadian Edition of *Essentials of Business Communication* has benefited from the input of professional communicators, educators, and students from across the country. As always, foremost appreciation and thanks go to Dr. Mary Ellen Guffey for providing an excellent foundation for the new edition and for her ongoing participation and support.

Many thanks go to the Canadian reviewers who went beyond the call of duty to provide detailed, insightful, and important additions to this edition. These dedicated professionals include: Madeleine J. Whitfield, Algonquin College; Carol Bolding, Grant MacEwan Community College; Phyllis Schmitt, Northern Alberta Institute of Technology; and Philip Walsh, Algonquin College.

The collaborative support of the staff at Nelson has added significantly to this edition as well. Thanks go to Nicole Gnutzman, Jenny Anttila, and Natalia Denesiuk.

As I assume the challenges that go with new directions, my network of willing volunteers, interested bystanders, and happy participants grows both in number and in importance. I would like to thank, in particular, Val MacPherson and her son Stephen for their contribution, the many colleagues and students who continue to provide their help and good humour, and Terry Klan for her patience and understanding.

BRENDAN NAGLE
Winnipeg, Manitoba

UNIT 1

LAYING COMMUNICATION FOUNDATIONS

1 FACING TODAY'S COMMUNICATION CHALLENGES

This century won't be like the last one. We will have the opportunity to work with new technologies in highly diverse work teams on projects that span the globe. Success will come for those who can communicate across cultural divides and who can bring together people with vastly different strengths and talents.[1]

STEPHEN LEAHEY, president, Manitoba Innovation Network

Learning Objectives

1. Examine the process of communication.
2. Understand the powerful effect culture has on communication.
3. Compare key North American cultural values with those of other cultures.
4. Describe methods for improving cross-cultural communication.
5. Discuss the effects of changing markets, work practices, and workforce diversity.
6. Identify specific techniques that develop effective communication among diverse workplace audiences.
7. Explain how computer technologies help business communicators collect information and process words.
8. Explain how electronic mail and presentation software enhance communication for businesspeople.

P eople with different backgrounds bring varied views to decision making. Stephen Leahey, of Manitoba Innovation Network, knows the value of such varied views. His organization builds networks of diverse individuals to create innovative products and services. The company relies on its employees' ability to work with a highly diverse group of people, who are located in many countries. The more effectively they work together, the more successful they are as a company.

Large and small companies alike collaborate and compete in world markets. Moreover, local markets are rapidly becoming more diverse. Success for businesses like Manitoba Innovation Network comes from having employees with a wide range of different outlooks, not from having lots of people with the same outlook.

Products and services for today's global, diverse markets require creative talents from a wide range of perspectives.

This book is about business communication. It will concentrate on writing, listening, nonverbal, and speaking skills. As a successful business communicator today, you will require more than these basic skills. That's because the world is changing rapidly, especially the work world.

As a good business communicator, you must also be aware of great changes in today's communication tools and technology. To help you meet the many challenges facing you, this first chapter presents an overview of (a) the communication process, (b) culture and communication, (c) workforce diversity, and (d) communication technologies.

EXAMINING THE COMMUNICATION PROCESS

Just what is *communication*? For our purposes communication is the *transmission of information and meaning from one individual or group to another*. The crucial element in this definition is *meaning*. Communication has as its central objective the transmission of meaning. The process of communication is successful only when the receiver understands an idea as the sender intended it. Both parties must agree not only on the information transmitted but also on the meaning of that information.

How does an idea travel from one person to another? Despite what you may have seen in science fiction movies, we can't just glance at another person and transfer meaning from mind to mind. Instead, we must engage in the sensitive process of communication. This process generally involves five steps, discussed here and depicted in Figure 1.1.

Communication is the transmission of information and meaning from one individual or group to another.

FIGURE 1.1

Communication Process

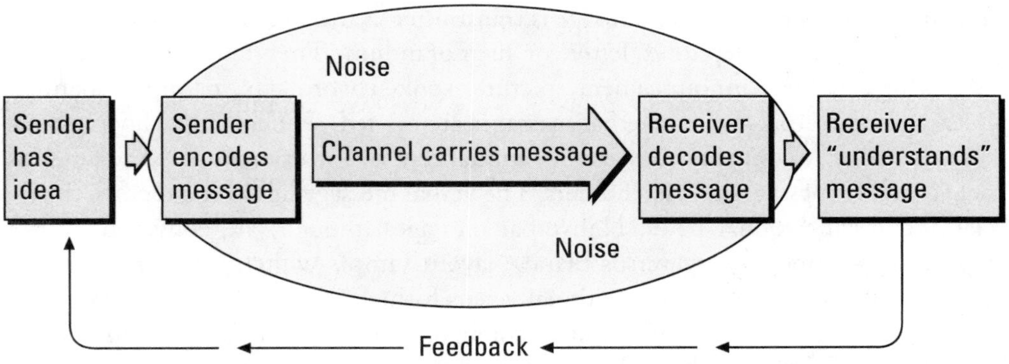

Communication barriers and noise may cause the communication cycle to break down.

SENDER HAS IDEA

The communication process begins when the sender has an idea. The form of the idea will be influenced by complex factors surrounding the sender. These factors include the sender's mood, frame of reference, background, culture, and physical makeup, as well as the context of the situation. The way you greet people at school, for example, depends on how you feel, the person you are addressing (a classmate,

The communication process has five steps: idea formation, message encoding, message transmission, message decoding, and feedback.

an instructor, a campus worker), and what your culture has trained you to say ("Hi," "How 'ya doing?" or "Good morning").

The form of the idea, whether a simple greeting or a complex idea, is shaped by assumptions the sender makes. Managers sending messages to employees assume they will be receptive. Direct-mail advertisers, on the other hand, assume that receivers will give their messages only a quick look. The ability to accurately predict how a message will affect its receiver is a key factor in successful communication. Equally important is skill in adapting that message to its receiver.

SENDER ENCODES IDEA IN MESSAGE

The next step in the communication process involves *encoding*. This means converting the idea into words or gestures that will convey meaning. A major problem in communicating any message verbally is that words have different meanings for different people. That's why skilled communicators try to choose familiar words with concrete meanings on which both senders and receivers agree. In selecting the best words and symbols for a message, senders must be alert to many factors. These factors include the receiver's communication skills, attitudes, background, experiences, and culture. How will the selected words affect the receiver? For example, a promotion for Irish Mist, an Irish whisky product, failed in Germany because the Irish managers had not done their homework. They had to change their product name after learning that, in German, *mist* means "manure." Because they start the exchange, senders have primary responsibility for communication success or failure. Choosing appropriate words or symbols is the first step.

MESSAGE TRAVELS OVER CHANNEL

The medium over which the message is transmitted is the *channel*. Messages may be sent by computer, telephone, letter, or memorandum. They may also be sent by means of a report, announcement, picture, spoken word, fax, or other channel. Because both verbal and nonverbal messages are carried, senders must choose channels carefully. A company may use its annual report, for example, as a channel to deliver many messages to shareholders. The verbal message lies in the report's financial and organizational news. Nonverbal messages, though, are conveyed by the report's appearance (glitzy versus bland), layout (ample white space versus tightly packed print), and tone (conversational versus formal).

Anything that disrupts the transmission of a message in the communication process is called *noise*. Channel noise ranges from static that disrupts a telephone conversation to spelling errors in an e-mail message. Such errors damage the credibility of the sender. Channel noise might even include the annoyance a receiver feels when the sender chooses an improper medium. For example, an announcement of a loan rejection sent on a postcard might upset a receiver.

RECEIVER DECODES MESSAGE

The person for whom a message is intended is the *receiver*. Translating the message from its symbol form into meaning involves *decoding*. Successful communication takes place only when a receiver understands the meaning intended by the sender.

Such success is often hard to achieve because no two people share the same background. Success is further limited because barriers and noise may disrupt the process.

Decoding can be disrupted internally by the receiver's lack of attention to or bias against the sender. It can be disrupted externally by loud sounds or illegible words. Decoding can also be sidetracked by misunderstood words or emotional reactions to certain terms. A memo that refers to all the women in an office as "girls," for example, may disturb its receivers so much that they fail to grasp the total message.

FEEDBACK TRAVELS TO SENDER

The verbal and nonverbal responses of the receiver create *feedback*, a vital part of the entire process. Feedback helps the sender know that the message was received and understood. Let's say you hear the message "How are you?" Your feedback might consist of words ("I'm fine") or body language (a smile or a wave of the hand).

Senders can encourage feedback by asking questions such as *Am I making myself clear?* and *Is there anything you don't understand?* Senders can further improve feedback by delivering the message at a time when receivers can respond. Senders should also provide only as much information as a receiver can handle. Receivers can improve the process by paraphrasing the sender's message. They might say, *Let me try to explain that in my own words* or *My understanding of your comment is . . .*

The best feedback is descriptive rather than evaluative. For example, here's a descriptive response: *I understand you want to launch a chocolate chip cookie business.* Here's an evaluative response: *Your business ideas are always weird.* An evaluative response is judgmental. It doesn't tell the sender if the receiver actually understood the message.

This brief look at the process of communication points out the complexities of transmitting meaning between receivers and senders. The communication process is even more complicated when people do not share the same culture.

To improve comprehension, skilled communicators provide opportunities for feedback during and after message delivery.

Descriptive feedback is more helpful than evaluative (judgmental) feedback.

UNDERSTANDING HOW CULTURE AFFECTS COMMUNICATION

Understanding the meaning of a message demands special sensitivity and skills when communicators are from different cultures. Negotiators for a Canadian company learned this lesson when they were in Japan looking for a trading partner. The Canadians were pleased after their first meeting with representatives of a major Japanese firm. The Japanese had nodded assent throughout the meeting and had not objected to a single proposal. The next day, however, the Canadians were stunned to learn that the Japanese had rejected the entire plan. In interpreting the nonverbal behavioural messages, the Canadians made a typical mistake. They assumed the Japanese were nodding in agreement, as fellow Canadians would. In this case, however, the nods of assent indicated comprehension—not approval.

Every country or region within a country has a unique culture or common heritage, joint experience, and shared learning that produce its culture. This background gives members of that culture a complex system of shared values and customs. It teaches them how to behave and conditions their reactions. Comparing Canadian values with those of other cultures will broaden your worldview. This comparison should also help you recognize some of the values that shape your actions and judgments of others.

COMPARING KEY CULTURAL VALUES

Canada is a country rich in separate and unique regions. Major urban areas such as Montreal, Toronto, and Vancouver boast multiple areas of distinct cultural identity. In most of Canada, a bilingual news release would mean that it appears in English and French. But in British Columbia's distinct society, Chinese language speakers make up the second largest linguistic group after anglophones. Roughly one-fifth of the population of B.C.'s lower mainland is made up of Chinese Canadians.[2] Life in the Prairie provinces differs significantly from that in the coastal provinces. In turn, the heritage and experiences of eastern Canadians differ from those of western Canadians.

While it may be difficult to define a typical Canadian, a *Maclean's* magazine poll found that Canadians are convinced that there is such a thing as a unique national identity—even though they are unable to agree on what the Canadian identity is. Asked what makes individual Canadians distinct, respondents highlighted the tendencies toward nonviolence and tolerance of others. As for what makes Canada distinct as a country, those asked said social programs and a nonviolent tradition were the two leading factors separating Canada from the United States and other countries.[3] Research also shows that, compared with Americans, Canadians tend to be more supportive of civil and political institutions.[4]

Despite the differences outlined above, however, most Canadians have habits and beliefs similar to those of Americans. It's impossible to fully cover the many facets of Canadian-American culture here, but we can look at some of the crucial habits and values that characterize a wider North American context (which, for the most part, here excludes Mexico) and, at the same time, give examples of cultures in which attitudes and values are at odds with these habits and values.

We'll focus on four dimensions to help you better understand some of the values that shape your actions and your judgment of others. These four are individualism, formality, communication style, and time orientation. Remember, though, that the following sections are based on generalizations, intended for the most part to help us form a broad perspective. They may not describe you or every member of another culture.

While North Americans value individualism and personal responsibility, other cultures emphasize group- and team-oriented values.

Individualism. One of the most identifiable characteristics of North American culture is its individualism. This is an attitude of independence and freedom from control. Canadian and American cultural traditions value initiative and self-assertion, and North Americans believe that these qualities lead to personal achievement. Individual action, self-reliance, and personal responsibility are very important; and a large degree of personal freedom is desirable. Other cultures emphasize membership in organizations, groups, and teams; they encourage acceptance of group values, duties, and decisions. In group-oriented Japan, for example, self-assertion and individual decision making are discouraged. "The nail that sticks up gets pounded down" is a common Japanese saying.[5] Business decisions are often made by all who have competence in the matter under discussion. Similarly, in China, managers also focus on the group rather than on the individual, preferring a "consultative" management style over an autocratic style.[6] Members of these cultures typically resist independence because it fosters competition and confrontation instead of consensus.

Formality. A second significant dimension of North American culture is the attitude toward formality. Canadians and Americans place less emphasis on tradition, ceremony, and social rules than do people in some other cultures. We dress casually and are soon on a first-name basis with others. Our lack of formality is often characterized by directness in our business dealings. Indirectness, we feel, wastes time, a valuable commodity. Formality levels also vary within North America. For instance, French Canadians may be less reserved—gesturing more expansively, requiring less personal space, and engaging in more touching—than English Canadians.[7]

North American informality and directness may be confusing abroad. In Mexico, for example, a typical business meeting begins with handshakes, coffee, and an expansive conversation about the weather, sports, and other light topics. An invitation to "get down to business" might offend a Mexican executive.[8] In Europe, first names are never used without an invitation. In Arab, South American, and Asian cultures, a feeling of friendship and kinship must be established before business can be transacted.

Communication Style. A third important dimension of North American culture relates to communication style. We value straightforwardness, are suspicious of evasiveness, and distrust people who might have a "hidden agenda" or who "play their cards too close to the chest."[9] North Americans also tend to be uncomfortable with silence and impatient with delays. Some Asian businesspeople have learned that the longer they drag out negotiations, the more concessions impatient North Americans are likely to make.

North Americans, moreover, tend to use and understand words literally. Hispanics, on the other hand, enjoy plays on words; and Arabs and South Americans sometimes speak with extravagant or poetic figures of speech that may be misinterpreted if taken literally. Nigerians prefer a quiet, clear form of expression; and Germans tend to be direct but understated.[10]

North Americans tend to be direct and to understand words literally.

Time Orientation. Canadians and Americans consider time a precious commodity, one to be conserved. We correlate time with productivity, efficiency, and money. Keeping people waiting for business appointments wastes time and is also rude. In other cultures, time may be perceived as an unlimited and never-ending resource to be enjoyed. Punctuality is an important Canadian value. Although French-speaking Canadians tend to have a more casual attitude toward time than English-speaking Canadians, individual francophone businesspeople vary.[11]

Although Asians are punctual, their need for deliberation and contemplation sometimes clashes with the typically North American desire for speedy decisions. They do not like to be rushed. A Japanese businessperson considering the purchase of North American appliances, for example, asked for five minutes to consider the salesperson's proposal. The potential buyer crossed his arms, sat back, and closed his eyes in concentration. A scant 18 seconds later, the American resumed his sales pitch to the obvious bewilderment of the Japanese customer.[12]

Figure 1.2 compares a number of cultural values for Americans, Japanese, and Arabs. Notice that belonging, group harmony, and collectiveness are very important to Japanese people, while family matters rank highest with Arabs. As we become aware of the vast differences in cultural values illustrated in Figure 1.2, we can better understand why communication barriers develop and how misunderstandings occur in cross-cultural interactions.

North Americans correlate time with productivity, efficiency, and money.

FIGURE 1.2

Comparison of Cultural Values Ranked by Priority

Americans	Japanese	Arabs
1. Freedom*	1. Belonging	1. Family security
2. Independence	2. Group harmony	2. Family harmony
3. Self-reliance	3. Collectiveness	3. Parental guidance
4. Equality	4. Age/Seniority	4. Age
5. Individualism	5. Group consensus	5. Authority
6. Competition	6. Cooperation	6. Compromise
7. Efficiency	7. Quality	7. Devotion
8. Time	8. Patience	8. Patience
9. Directness	9. Indirectness	9. Indirectness
10. Openness	10. Go-between	10. Hospitality

* "1." on each list represents the most important value.

Source: Used by permission. From *Multicultural Management 2000* by Farid Elashmawi, Ph.D. and Philip R. Harris, Ph.D. Copyright © 1998 by Gulf Publishing Company, Houston, Texas, 800-231-6275. All rights reserved. This is a revised edition. The first edition was published under the title *Multicultural Management*. Copyright © 1993 by Gulf Publishing Company.

CONTROLLING ETHNOCENTRISM AND STEREOTYPING

The process of understanding and accepting people from other cultures is often hampered by two barriers: ethnocentrism and stereotyping. These two barriers, however, can be overcome by developing tolerance, a powerful and effective aid to communication.

Ethnocentrism is the belief in the superiority of one's own culture and group.

Ethnocentrism. The belief in the superiority of one's own culture is known as *ethnocentrism*. This natural attitude is found in all cultures. If you were raised in Canada, the values just described as North American probably seem "right" to you, and you may wonder why the rest of the world doesn't function in the same sensible fashion. A Canadian businessperson in an Arab or Asian country might be upset at time spent over coffee or other social rituals before any "real" business is transacted. In these cultures, however, personal relationships must be established and nurtured before earnest talks may proceed.

Learning about other cultures and respecting other cultural values help you avoid ethnocentrism.

Ethnocentrism causes us to judge others by our own values. We expect others to react as we would, and they expect us to behave as they would. Misunderstandings naturally result. A Canadian who wants to set a deadline for completion of a deal is considered pushy by an Arab. That same Arab, who prefers a handshake to a written contract, is seen as naive and possibly untrustworthy by a Canadian. These ethnocentric reactions can be reduced through knowledge of other cultures and development of flexible, tolerant attitudes.

A *stereotype* is an oversimplified behavioural pattern applied to an entire group.

Stereotypes. Our perceptions of other cultures sometimes cause us to form stereotypes about groups of people. A stereotype is an oversimplified behavioural pattern applied to entire groups. For example, the Swiss are hard-working, efficient, and neat; Germans are formal, reserved, and blunt; Americans are loud, friendly, and impatient; Canadians are polite, trusting, and tolerant; Asians are gracious, humble, and inscrutable. These attitudes may or may not accurately describe cultural norms.

But when applied to individual business communicators, such stereotypes may create misconceptions and misunderstandings. Look beneath surface stereotypes and labels to discover individual personal qualities.

Tolerance. Working among people from other cultures demands tolerance and flexible attitudes. As global markets expand and as our multiethnic society continues to develop, tolerance becomes critical. Tolerance, here, does not mean "putting up with" or "enduring," which is one part of its definition. Instead, tolerance is used in a broader sense. It means having sympathy for and appreciating beliefs and practices different from our own.

One of the best ways to develop tolerance is by practising empathy. This means trying to see the world through another's eyes. It means being nonjudgmental, recognizing things as they are rather than as they "should be." It includes the ability to accept others' contributions to solving problems in a culturally appropriate manner. When Kal Kan Foods began courting the pets of Japan, for example, an Asian adviser suggested that the meat chunks in its Pedigree dog food be cut into perfect little squares. Why? Japanese pet owners feed their dogs piece by piece with chopsticks. Instead of insisting on what "should be" (feeding dogs chunky meat morsels), Kal Kan solved the problem by looking at it from another cultural point of view (providing neat small squares).[13]

Making the effort to communicate with sensitivity across cultures can be very rewarding in both your work life and your personal life. The suggestions in the box on page 10 provide specific tips for preventing miscommunication in oral and written transactions.

Developing intercultural tolerance means practicing empathy, being non-judgmental, and being patient.

CAPITALIZING ON WORKFORCE DIVERSITY

As global competition opens world markets, Canadian businesspeople will increasingly interact with customers and colleagues from around the world. At the same time, the Canadian workforce is also becoming more diverse in race, ethnicity, age, gender, national origin, physical ability, and countless other characteristics.

No longer, say the experts, will the workplace be predominantly male or oriented toward Western cultural values alone. The majority of new entrants to the workforce are women, First Nations peoples, and new Canadians, including visible minority group members. The Canadian workforce is getting older as the baby boom generation ages. By the year 2016 half of the Canadian population will be over 40, and 16 percent will be over 65. At the same time, the proportion of people under 15 will shrink to 19 percent from the current 25 percent.[14]

While the workforce is becoming more diverse, the structure of many businesses across North America is also changing. Called "flexible enterprises" by the OECD (Organization for Economic Cooperation and Development), these companies are adopting practices such as the following:

- Team-oriented management, where small groups of workers control projects.
- Employee empowerment with rank-and-file workers given authority to make decisions.
- Flattened organizations with fewer layers of management.
- Cooperative relationship building between companies and their external customers and competitors.

Global competition and an increasingly diverse local workforce require interaction among people who differ in race, ethnicity, gender, age, and in other ways.

Tips for Minimizing Oral and Written Miscommunication Among Cross-Cultural Audiences

Communication of oral or written ideas between people from different cultures often requires sensitivity and adjustment. Fortunately, much of today's global business is conducted in English; however, the level of proficiency may be limited. Remember that people who speak English as a second language don't always understand everything that is said in a conversation in English. The following tips may help you better understand and be understood in English:

Communicating Orally

- **Use simple English.** Speak in short sentences (under 15 words) with familiar, short words. Eliminate puns, sports and military references, slang, and jargon (special business terms). Be especially alert to idiomatic expressions that can't be translated, such as *burn the midnight oil* and *under the weather*.
- **Speak slowly and enunciate clearly.** Avoid fast speech, but don't raise your voice. Overpunctuate with pauses and full stops. Always write numbers for all to see.
- **Encourage accurate feedback.** Ask probing questions, and encourage the listener to paraphrase what you say. Don't assume that a yes, a nod, or a smile indicates comprehension or assent.
- **Check frequently for comprehension.** Avoid waiting until you finish a long explanation to request feedback. Instead, make one point at a time, pausing to check for comprehension. Don't proceed to B until A has been grasped.
- **Observe eye messages.** Be alert to a glazed expression or wandering eyes. These tell you the listener is lost.
- **Accept blame.** If a misunderstanding results, graciously accept the blame for not making your meaning clear.
- **Listen without interrupting.** Curb your desire to finish sentences or to fill out ideas for the speaker. Keep in mind that North Americans abroad are often accused of listening too little and talking too much.

- **Remember to smile!** Roger Axtell, an international behaviour expert, calls the smile the single most understood and most useful form of communication in either personal or business transactions.
- **Follow up in writing.** After conversations or oral negotiations, confirm the results and agreements with follow-up letters. For proposals and contracts, engage a translator to prepare copies in the local language.

Communicating in Writing

- **Adopt local styles.** Learn how documents are formatted and how letters are addressed and developed in the intended reader's country. Use local formats and styles.
- **Consider hiring a translator.** Engage a translator if (1) your document is important, (2) your document will be distributed to many readers, or (3) you must be persuasive.
- **Use short sentences and short paragraphs.** Sentences with fewer than 15 words and paragraphs with fewer than 5 lines are most readable.
- **Avoid ambiguous wording.** Include relative pronouns *(that, which, who)* for clarity in introducing clauses. Stay away from contractions *(Here's the problem)*. Avoid idioms *(once in a blue moon)*, slang *(my presentation really bombed)*, acronyms *(ASAP* for *as soon as possible)*, abbreviations *(CPM* for *cost per thousand)*, and jargon *(input, output, bottom line)*. Use action-specific verbs *(purchase a printer* rather than *get a printer)*.
- **Cite numbers and dates carefully.** In citing numbers, use figures *(15)* instead of spelling them out *(fifteen)*. Always convert dollar figures into local currency. Avoid using figures to express the month of the year. In North America, for example, *March 5, 2000*, might be written as *3/5/00*, while in Europe the same date might appear as *5.3.00*. For clarity, always spell out the month.

What does all this mean for you as a future business communicator? Simply put, your job may require you to interact with colleagues and customers from around the world. Your work environment will probably demand that you cooperate effectively with small groups of co-workers. And these co-workers will probably differ from you in race, ethnicity, gender, age, and other ways.

WHO BENEFITS FROM DIVERSITY?

Communicating in a diverse work environment will require new attitudes and skills for many North Americans. But acquiring these new employment skills is worth the effort because of the benefits that diversity brings to consumers, work teams, and business organizations.

Consumers. A diverse staff is better able to read trends and respond to the increasingly diverse customer base in local and world markets. Diverse consumers now want specialized goods and services tailored to their needs. Teams made up of different people with different experiences are better able to create the different products that these markets require. Consumers also want to deal with companies that respect their values. They are more likely to say, "If you're a company whose ads don't include me, or whose workforce doesn't include me, I won't buy from you."[15]

Work Teams. Employees today work in teams. Many are solving problems and making decisions that formerly were handled by middle and upper management. Instead of "top-down" authority, organizations are encouraging "bottom-up" control. Employees must work together harmoniously if they are to be productive.

Business Organizations. Organizations that set aside time and resources to cultivate diversity will suffer fewer discrimination complaints, fewer union clashes, and less interpersonal conflict. That's why today's diversity movement is viewed by a growing number of companies as a critical bottom-line business strategy to improve employee relationships and to increase productivity.[16]

New attitudes and skills will help consumers, work teams, and business organizations benefit from diversity.

TIPS FOR EFFECTIVE COMMUNICATION WITH DIVERSE WORKPLACE AUDIENCES

Capitalizing on workplace diversity is an enormous challenge for most organizations and individuals. Harmony and acceptance do not happen automatically when people who are dissimilar work together. The following suggestions can help you become a more effective communicator as you enter a rapidly evolving workplace with ethnically diverse colleagues and clients.

Understand the Value of Differences. Diversity makes an organization innovative and creative. Sameness fosters "groupthink," an absence of critical thinking sometimes found in homogeneous groups. Case studies, for example, of events like the U.S. invasion of Cuba and of the Challenger space shuttle disaster suggest that groupthink prevented alternatives from being considered.[17] Diversity in problem-solving groups encourages independent and creative thinking.

Don't Expect Conformity. Gone are the days when businesses could demand that new employees or customers simply conform to the existing organization's culture.

Successful communicators understand the value of differences, don't expect conformity, create zero tolerance for bias and stereotypes, and practise open-minded listening.

Stephen Leahey of Manitoba Innovation Network, who was introduced at the start of this chapter, stresses the value of people who bring new perspectives and ideas. But with those new ideas comes the responsibility to listen and to allow those new ideas to grow.

Create Zero Tolerance for Bias and Stereotypes. Cultural patterns exist in every identity group, but applying these patterns to individuals results in stereotyping. Assuming that African-Americans are good athletes, that women are poor at math, that French Canadians excel at hockey, or that European men are insensitive fails to admit the immense differences in people in each group. Check your own use of stereotypes and labels. Don't tell sexist or ethnic jokes at meetings. Avoid slang, abbreviations, and jargon that imply stereotypes. Challenge others' stereotypes politely but firmly.

Practise Focused, Thoughtful, and Open-Minded Listening. Much misunderstanding can be avoided by attentive listening. Listen for main points; take notes if necessary to remember important details. The most important part of listening, especially among diverse communicators, is judging ideas, not appearances or accents.

Invite, Use, and Give Feedback. As you learned earlier, a critical element in successful communication is feedback. You can encourage it by asking questions such as *Is there anything you don't understand?* When a listener or receiver responds, use that feedback to adjust your delivery of information. Does the receiver need more details? A different example? Slower delivery? As a good listener, you should also be prepared to give feedback. For example, summarize your understanding of what was said or agreed on.

Make Fewer Assumptions. Be careful of seemingly insignificant, innocent workplace assumptions. For example, don't assume that everyone wants to observe the holidays with a Christmas party and a decorated tree. Celebrating only Christian holidays in December and January excludes those who honour Hanukkah, Kwanza, and the Chinese New Year. Moreover, in workplace discussions don't assume that everyone is married or wants to be, or is even heterosexual, for that matter. For invitations, avoid phrases such as "managers and their wives." Spouses or partners is more inclusive. Valuing diversity means making fewer assumptions that everyone is like you or wants to be like you.

Learn About Your Cultural Self. Knowing your own cultural biases helps you become more objective and adaptable. Begin to recognize the stock reactions and thought patterns that are automatic to you as a result of your upbringing. Become more aware of your own values and beliefs. That way you can see them at work when you are confronted by differing values.

Learn About Other Cultures and Identity Groups. People are naturally threatened by the unknown. Consider the following proverb: "I saw in the distance what I took to be a beast, but when I came close, I saw it was my brother and my sister." The same error occurs in communities and work groups. From a distance an unknown person may appear to be threatening. But when the person is recognized or better known, our reactions change. Learning more about diverse groups and individuals helps you reduce the threat of the unknown. On the job, human resource development workshops and cultural discussion groups are good tools for expanding your horizons.

Seek Common Ground. Look for areas where you and others not like you can agree or share opinions. Be prepared to consider issues from many perspectives, all of which may be valid. Accept that there is room for different points of view to coexist peacefully. Although you can always find differences, it's much harder to find similarities. Professor Nancy Adler from McGill University offers three very useful methods to help diverse individuals find their way through conflicts made more difficult by cultural differences.[18] Her three methods are: (1) look at the problem from all participants' points of view; (2) uncover the interpretations each side is making based on their cultural values; and (3) create cultural synergy by working together on a solution that works for both sides. Looking for common ground and mutual goals can help you and those with whom you are dealing to reach your objectives even though you may disagree on how.

MEETING THE CHALLENGE OF TODAY'S COMMUNICATION TECHNOLOGIES

Today's communicators face increasing complexities in dealing with cross-cultural and diverse audiences. Moreover, they must become familiar with rapidly evolving technological communication tools. The good news is, however, that these amazing tools nearly always make communication easier, richer, and faster.

In her position as a product manager for a large beverage company, Tonya Lee provides a good example of how the different technologies can be used. Tonya helps promote PowerBurst, a sports drink that competes with Gatorade. In this position she monitors sales, keeps track of the competition, and seeks new ways to market PowerBurst. To enable her to complete these tasks, her company has given Tonya a powerful computer and some software. The four most important uses she makes of her computer are these: information collection, word processing, electronic mail, and presentations.

Amazing advances in technology make communication easier, richer, and faster.

INFORMATION COLLECTION

Two significant responsibilities for Tonya are monitoring sales and keeping track of the competition in the sports drink field. Tonya generally collects information from three electronic resources: (1) internal company databases, (2) commercial on-line services, and (3) the Internet, including the World Wide Web.

Internal Company Databases. Databases are electronic collections of information that may be sorted, cross-referenced, and retrieved easily. Tonya accesses her company's database for basic information about PowerBurst distributors. The database includes each distributor's company name, address, manager's name, telephone number, fax number, and date of most recent order, as well as beverages distributed and yearly volume of purchases. Tonya can add information about a distributor's special needs. All these data are stored in the distributor's file. Within the file, the entry for each distributor forms a record. Within each record are several columns, or *fields*, each for a single piece of information about that distributor.

Tonya can organize records in her distributor database in many ways to achieve her goals. Recently she planned to promote PowerBurst to industrial complexes where heavy physical labour was common. First, she located the addresses of large

Internal company databases store information that may be accessed and manipulated electronically.

logging, mining, and construction firms by searching a CD-ROM that classifies businesses by sector. Then she sorted her database to locate the records of PowerBurst distributors in the geographical areas of the targeted businesses. In this way, she could pinpoint her promotion effort to specific distributors.

On-Line Commercial Databanks and Networks. Tonya monitors the competition and checks trends in the sports drink field by using on-line commercial databases or networks. Two kinds of on-line commercial services are available: (a) pay-per-use research databases and (b) Internet service provider (ISP) on-line services.

Pay-per-Use Research Databases. One of the fastest ways for Tonya to locate specific information is through commercial database services such as Electric Library Canada, Intellisearch, Northern Light, InfoGlobe–Dow Jones Interactive, and NewScan. U.S. services include Lexis-Nexis, Dow Jones News/Retrieval Service, and DIALOG Information Retrieval Service. These services provide information from newspapers, magazines, journals, biographies, newsletters, directories, wire services reports, transcripts, and legal proceedings. Well-stocked and well-organized, these specialized collections formerly were frustrating and expensive to use. Tonya had to develop skill in selecting *keywords* (descriptors) as well as experience in exploring a particular database. Today, improved search tools enable even novice researchers to find answers to many business questions quickly. Tonya can quickly access and read at her computer monitor any publications mentioning, for example, the latest efforts of Coca-Cola and PepsiCo in the sports drink field.

Internet Service Providers' On-Line Services. Some companies do not subscribe to specialized information-retrieval services such as Lexis-Nexis because of the expense. Instead, they might use the generalized on-line services offered by their Internet service provider such as Sympatico, AOL Canada, or CompuServe Information Service. For a flat monthly fee these Internet service providers (ISPs) supply access to e-mail, news headlines, news articles, weather reports, sports results, travel news, and a variety of search engines.

The Internet. Tonya also uses the Internet to collect information. The Internet is a collection of voluntarily linked computer networks. It serves millions of registered users or "accounts" all over the world. Anyone who can connect to a network that's part of the Internet has access to the other networks as well. These loosely connected networks enable business organizations and people around the world to exchange information almost instantaneously. The fastest-growing segment of the Internet is the World Wide Web.

World Wide Web. The World Wide Web is a system for providing information through interoperating computer hardware, software, and networks worldwide. Tonya uses her Web browser to access documents on remote Web servers. Web documents are created using hypertext markup language (HTML). In addition to using HTML to create Web pages, Web page designers also use it to link one Web page with another. HTML and DHTML (dynamic hypertext markup language) allow Web designers to include imaginative graphics, realistic photographs, sound clips, and movies.

Web sites supply a wealth of information about companies and their products and services. But the Web is an unorganized mass of millions of Web sites, each containing potentially dozens of individual Web pages. Tonya explores the Web by using search engines; her current favourites are Canada.com (www.Canada.com) and Yahoo Canada (www.yahoo.ca). Search engines are programs that probe for Web sites that match your keywords. A major headache for users of the Web is the amount of time spent sorting through useless information. The information, however, is free; and sometimes Tonya discovers jewels. By searching on the word *Gatorade,* for example, Tonya turned up a surprising number of international athletic events sponsored by Gatorade. At the Gatorade site she found pages describing a Gatorade-sponsored basketball tournament as well as information about a variety of Gatorade products that can be purchased on-line. Such information enables her to keep in touch with her competitors' marketing strategies.

Search engines, such as Alta Vista, are necessary to locate information on the World Wide Web.

WORD PROCESSING

Tonya uses word processing software to write, edit, and format letters to distributors and reports to her manager. Some of the basic features of the word processing program she uses most are the following: cutting and pasting of text; blocking for underlining, moving, and copying; and searching and replacing of characters. Other word processing features include merge/sort for mass producing form letters and mailing labels; macros as shortcuts for often-used combinations; and page preview for seeing how a document looks before printing it. Many word processing programs also allow you to perform mathematics and to sort items into lists.

Word processing software enables business communicators to write, edit, and format business documents with professional results.

Dictionary and thesaurus programs help Tonya verify word meanings and locate synonyms for overused words. Spell checkers detect misspelled words, and grammar/style checkers flag some writing faults. Tonya, nevertheless, proofreads all of her documents because she knows that spell checkers and grammar/style checkers do not always catch correctly spelled words that are in the wrong place or that have been misused.

Word processing programs offer many extraordinary features. The most successful business communicators today can (1) use the important features of their word processing programs competently, and (2) compose at the keyboard comfortably.

ELECTRONIC MAIL

Tonya uses e-mail to send messages to salespeople, members of her department, other employees, and to her manager. She also exchanges e-mail messages with distributors throughout Canada and the United States, as well as around the world.

E-mail messages travel electronically over networks to receivers' computers where they remain stored until accessed.

Instead of sending memorandums printed on paper, increasing numbers of businesspeople like Tonya are communicating by e-mail. Messages travel electronically over networks connected by telephone lines and satellites. Almost instantly, a keyboarded message is delivered to another computer—whether to the next desk or halfway around the world. The message remains stored in the receiver's electronic mailbox until accessed. Then, the receiver may edit, store, delete, print, or forward the message.

E-mail has many advantages. It eliminates "telephone tag," where callers leave messages but cannot reach one another. E-mail improves response times and cuts telephone charges. It also allows you to digest a message and put more thought into its response. Moreover, e-mail reduces paper use, filing space, and printer use. Tonya especially likes the ease of responding to e-mail. Instead of retyping, she can clip important parts of the original message and merely add her comments. She also likes

Although e-mail messages are generally short, they still require planning and care.

being able to send messages across time zones without worrying. E-mail allows you to send messages at any time, 24 hours a day, 365 days a year.

A major disadvantage of e-mail, however, is information overload. It's not unusual for some managers to receive 50 to 150 messages daily, all demanding reading and response. Just a click of a key distributes a message to an entire organization. Thus, computer systems are increasingly clogged with hundreds of unsorted messages, some important and many not so important.

Currently, e-mail is most effective in delivering simple messages, such as that shown in Figure 1.3. Complex data should probably be sent in hard-copy documents. Although e-mail messages are usually short, they require the same planning and care as conventional communication. Chapter 5 provides suggestions for writing effective e-mail messages.

FIGURE 1.3

Electronic Mail Message

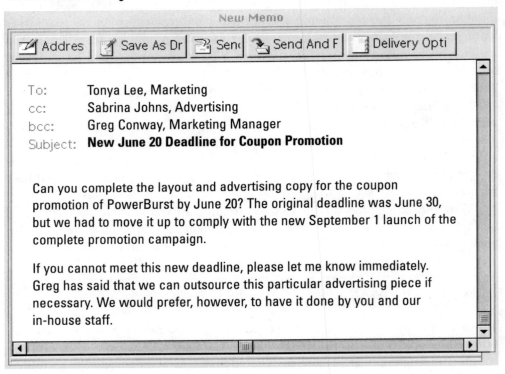

PRESENTATIONS

Occasionally, Tonya makes presentations to management, the marketing staff, sales reps, or distributors. She uses her computer and a Windows-based graphics program to prepare presentation "slides." This is the term used for each formatted frame, whether it takes the form of a transparency, 35mm slide, or computer screen. These slides may be displayed on a computer, an LCD (liquid crystal display) projection panel, or a TV monitor.

Most of the current presentation software programs such as Microsoft PowerPoint and Corel Presentations permit even amateurs to create special effects such as "wipes," "glitter," and "rain." Tonya uses templates to help her produce

Presentation software allows you to create professional "slide" shows for display on computers, LCD panels, or TV monitors.

pleasing colour combinations, heading styles, and bulleted points. The program she uses also enables her to print handouts and make speaker notes from the slides she is preparing. Tonya plans each presentation with an "outliner," a software feature that helps her divide a topic into main points and subpoints.

SUMMING UP AND LOOKING FORWARD

This chapter gave you an overview of the communication process. You learned that communication doesn't take place unless senders encode meaningful messages that can be decoded by receivers. Moreover, the chapter highlighted some of the major challenges you will face as a communicator in a rapidly changing business world. You studied culture and its effect on communication, and you looked at ways to capitalize on diversity in the workplace. You also examined some of the technologies that are changing the way we communicate. How well you meet these challenges will help determine how successful you are in your career.

The ability to communicate effectively is not inherited. Most of us require instruction, practice, supervision, and feedback to develop and improve communication skills. The remainder of this book focuses on developing your writing, listening, and speaking skills. In addition to techniques, you will learn to think critically in solving typical communication problems.

Communication skills are not inborn; they must be developed.

DISCUSSION

1. What should a businessperson know about the communication process?
2. Why is it important to recognize your own cultural values?
3. How is the Canadian workforce becoming more diverse?
4. Why are business organizations increasingly looking at diversity as a bottom-line value?
5. Describe how you might use four kinds of communication technology in your career.

CHAPTER REVIEW

6. Give a brief definition or explanation of the following words:
   a. Encode
   b. Channel
   c. Decode

7. Describe the concept of individualism. How does this concept set North American culture apart from some other cultures?

8. What is ethnocentrism, and how can it be reduced?

9. List seven suggestions for enhancing comprehension when you are talking with people for whom English is a second language. Be prepared to discuss each.

10. List at least eight suggestions for becoming a more effective communicator in a diverse workplace. Be prepared to discuss each.

11. What is an internal company database? Give an original example.

12. What is the World Wide Web?

13. What is Canada.com?

14. What should you be concerned about when using a word processor's spell checker?

15. How can a computer be used to make presentations?

ACTIVITIES AND CASES

1.1 Getting to Know You. Since today's work and classroom environments often involve cooperating in small groups, getting to know your fellow classmates is important. To learn something about the people in this class and to give you practice in developing your communication skills, your instructor may choose one of the following techniques:

a. For larger classes your instructor may divide the class into groups of four or five. Take one minute to introduce yourself briefly (name, major interest, hobbies, goals). Spend five minutes in the first group session. Record the first name of each individual you meet. Then informally regroup. In new groups, again spend five minutes on introductions. After three or four sessions, study your name list. How many names can you associate with faces?

b. For smaller classes your instructor may ask each student to introduce himself or herself in a two-minute oral presentation while standing before the class, answering questions such as Where are you from? What are your educational goals? What are your interests?

1.2 Collecting Want Ads. From the classified section of your local newspaper (or the newspaper of a larger city nearby), select five or more advertisements for positions that require good communication skills. Bring them to class for discussion.

Related Web Site: www.globecareers.com/

1.3 Analyzing Diversity: Hiring Your Friends. In a class discussion or in a short report, analyze the following diversity challenge. Cantech Industries grew from a $2 million-a-year manufacturing company into a $30-million industry powerhouse; as a result, new employees were needed on a daily basis. Cantech began hiring friends of staff members to fill the new positions. In a short time, Cantech had hired a workforce that shared many of the same characteristics. They were generally of the same age, sex, and ethnic origin, and had similar backgrounds and schooling. They shared many of the same values and attitudes—after all, they were friends! In what ways would Cantech benefit by diversifying its staff? What competitive advantages might it gain?

1.4 Alice in Wonderland Travels to Tokyo. Analyze the following cross-cultural incident. Jacques Guay is leader of a creative team representing a medium-sized Montreal company that builds circus sets and theme park attractions. The owners of a Japanese theme park asked Guay's team to develop a theme attraction for their Tokyo park. The Japanese were concerned about the new attraction and requested final approval over all designs. Jacques and his team recently travelled to Japan to make an important presentation to the owners. His team had worked for the past year developing the concept of an outdoor garden maze with a network of hedge passageways for children to wander through. The concept was based on *Alice in Wonderland*. The jobs of his entire team depended on selling the idea of this new attraction (including restaurants and gift shops) to the owners of the Tokyo park. Because the Japanese smiled and nodded throughout the presentation, Jacques assumed they liked the idea. When he pushed for final approval, the Japanese smiled and said that an outdoor garden attraction might be difficult in their climate. Jacques explained away that argument. He was hoping for a straightforward yes or no, but the Japanese answered, "We will have to study it very carefully." Thinking he had not made himself clear, Jacques began to review the strong points of the presentation. What cultural elements may be interfering with communication in this exchange?

1.5 Soup's On. Analyze the following cross-cultural incident. As a junior manager at McCain Foods Limited, you have been sent to Hong Kong to work on the development of new regional food varieties to appeal to 2 billion Asian consumers. The Chinese are among the highest per capita soup eaters in the world, consuming an average of one bowl a day. In the Hong Kong taste kitchen, you are currently working on cabbage soup, scallop broth, and a special soup that combines watercress and duck meat. You've even tested exotic ingredients like shark's fin and snake.[19] The supervisor of the taste kitchen understands English, but sometimes her eyes glaze over when you discuss procedures with her. What could you do to improve comprehension and minimize misunderstanding?

1.6 Translating Idioms. Explain in simple English what the following idiomatic expressions mean. Assume that you are explaining them to people for whom English is a second language.

    a. let the cat out of the bag
    b. take the bull by the horns
    c. he is a tightwad
    d. putting the cart before the horse
    e. to be on the road
    f. lend someone a hand
    g. with flying colours
    h. turn over a new leaf

1.7 Getting Along in Teams. Analyze the following incident and offer suggestions. Managers of a sports apparel company that manufactures sweatshirts, sweatsuits, T-shirts, headgear, and accessories are engaged in a sizeable program to hire a more diversified staff. The company is also restructuring so that small teams will develop and market new products. As a diversity consultant, you have been hired to advise management and supervisors. They want to know how to make the process of diversifying and reorganizing less traumatic and more effective. They know that communication is central to the success of their efforts. List at least eight suggestions that might help them and their employees work together harmoniously.

1.8 Technology in Your Field. Make an informal study of technology in your field. Talk with two or more individuals who are familiar with your career area. Ask them which business communication technologies they are using. What reactions do they have to the effectiveness of these technologies? What recommendations do they have for individuals training to enter the field? Be prepared to present your findings in an oral or written report.

1.9 Improving Your Writing. Discuss how word processing can improve the quality of a business communicator's writing. Consider content, format, and mechanics. What capabilities and software aid a writer? If you have no first-hand experience, team up with an experienced class member who can demonstrate some of the features of high-end word processing programs such as Word or WordPerfect.

1.10 Searching the Internet: Business Information. Using the Internet or your library's database of electronic sources, locate an article that

a. Appears in a business magazine or newspaper such as: *Canadian Business, The Globe and Mail Report on Business, National Post/Financial Post, Business Week,* or *The Economist.*
b. Was published within the past three years.
c. Covers a current business topic such as e-mail use or abuse, e-mail privacy, information overload, workforce diversity, multiculturalism on the job, the aging workforce, women in business, male/female communication styles, the glass ceiling, empowering people with disabilities, Internet growth, electronic commerce, or global marketing.
d. Contains anecdotes and information that would be helpful to business communicators.

Submit a copy of the article including its citation reference. Use a marker to underline the central points of the article.

1.11 Searching the Internet: Using Search Engines. From your personal computer or an available school or public library computer, select and use a search engine to conduct research. The following addresses will take you to some of the more common search engines:

www.canada.com, www.yahoo.ca, www.altavista.com, www.lycos.com, www.hotbot.com, www.infoseek.com.

For a more complete listing of search engines try www.sou.edu/library/cybrary/search.htm. You may wish to review www.albany.edu/library/internet/choose.html for some excellent tips on choosing a search engine.

Drawing on what you've learned so far, conduct the following two searches:
a. Choose a search engine and conduct a search for information about one of the topics discussed in this chapter. Try searching the same topic in several ways. For example, you might choose to search for information on word processing software. Your search engine should permit searches by category and

by keyword. By selecting "Computers" or a similar category link you will be searching by category. By entering a general keyword such as "software" you will be searching by keyword. Notice the difference between the two methods. Notice how many "hits" you receive from your general keyword search. Try narrowing your search by entering "word processing software." Record your findings. Which method seems more effective? Did the Web sites presented give you the information you needed? What kinds of searches would you recommend to other students? Submit your findings to your instructor.

b. Go to www.canadacareers.com/ and select one of the links to job-search engines. Find a listing for a job in which you might be interested. If possible, print the results of your search. If you cannot print, make notes on what you found and how you found it. Submit your findings to your instructor.

1.12 Connecting With E-Mail: Introducing Yourself. Send your instructor an e-mail message introducing yourself. See Chapter 5 for tips on preparing e-mail messages. In your message include the following:

a. Your reasons for taking this class.
b. Your career goals (both temporary and long-term).
c. A brief description of your employment, if any, and a list of your favourite activities.
d. An assessment and discussion of your current communication skills (excellent, average, need improvement).
e. A brief discussion of your familiarity with e-mail and the other communication technologies discussed in this chapter.

GRAMMAR/MECHANICS CHECKUP—1

Nouns

These checkups are designed to improve your control of grammar and mechanics. They systematically review all sections of the Grammar/Mechanics Handbook. Answers are given for odd-numbered statements; answers to even-numbered statements will be provided by your instructor.

Review Sections 1.01–1.06 in the Grammar/Mechanics Handbook. Then study each of the following statements. Underscore any inappropriate form, and write a correction in the space provided. Also, record the appropriate G/M section and letter to illustrate the principle involved. If a sentence is correct, write *C*. When you finish, compare your responses with those provided. If your answers differ, study carefully the principles shown in parentheses.

companies   (1.05e)
        Example: Two surveys revealed that many <u>companys</u> will move to the new industrial park.

_____   1. Her career has had many peaks and vallies.
_____   2. Counter business is higher on Saturday's, but telephone business is greater on Sundays.
_____   3. Some of the citys in Kevin's report offer excellent opportunities.
_____   4. Frozen chickens and turkies are kept in the company's lockers.
_____   5. All secretaries were asked to check supply inventorys.
_____   6. Only the Nashs and the Le Blancs brought their entire families.

7. In the 1980s profits grew rapidly; in the 1990's investments lagged.   _____
8. Both editor in chiefs instituted strict proofreading policies.   _____
9. Luxury residential complexes are part of the architect's plan.   _____
10. Trustees in three municipalitys are likely to approve increased school taxes.   _____
11. The instructor was surprised to find three Jennifer's in one class.   _____
12. André sent descriptions of two valleys in France to us via the Internet.   _____
13. How many copies of the statements showing your assets and liabilitys did you   _____
    make?
14. My monitor makes it difficult to distinguish between *o*'s and *a*'s.   _____
15. Both runner-ups complained about the winner's behaviour.   _____

---

1. valleys (1.05d)   3. cities (1.05e)   5. inventories (1.05e)   7. 1990s (1.05g)   9. complexes (1.05b)
11. Jennifers (1.05a)   13. liabilities (1.05e)   15. runners-up (1.05f)

GRAMMAR/MECHANICS CHALLENGE—1

Document for Revision

The following memo has many faults in grammar, spelling, punctuation, capitalization, word use, and number form. Study the guidelines provided in the Grammar/Mechanics Handbook to sharpen your skills. Then, use standard proofreading marks (see Appendix B) to correct the errors. When you finish, your instructor can show you the revised version of this memo.

Ineffective Writing

TO: Tran Nguyen   DATE: May 14, 200X

FROM: Rachel Stivers, Manager

SUBJECT: WORK-AT-HOME GUIDELINES

Since you will be completeing most of your work at home for the next 2 months.
Follow these guidelines;

1. Check your message bored daily and respond promptly, to those who are
   trying to reach you.

2. Call the office at least twice a week to pick up any telephone messages, return
   these calls promly.

3. Transmit any work you do, on the computer to Parmjit Singh in our computer
   services department, she will analyze each weeks accounts, and send it to the
   proper Departments..

4. Provide me with monthly reports' of your progress.

I know you will work satisfactory at home Tran. Following these basic guidelines
should help you accomplish your work, and provide the office with adequate contact
with you.

INTERACTING WITH PERSONS WITH DISABILITIES[20]

For people who are blind, learning the ropes in a new job can be particularly difficult. They rely on explanations and descriptions from sighted co-workers who are used to encoding their messages for other sighted people.

For visually impaired people, new objects, actions, and situations can seem foreign. Just imagine walking into a meeting where two people are talking, a radio is on, and an open window is letting in street noise. With imperfect vision, making sense of what is going on would be difficult. Accurate and concise verbal communication is very important. Here are some tips to help you know what to do.

COMMUNICATING ORALLY

- **Describe objects accurately.** Objects that are not easily categorized using hearing, touch, smell, or taste descriptions may be difficult for visually impaired people to fully understand. Think and describe objects in your workplace as if you are seeing them for the first time.
- **Give complete directions.** Finding the correct washroom or the right size of paper in the storeroom requires more specific directions than those you would give a sighted person.
- **Explain tasks completely.** To fully understand a new task, hands-on demonstrations can help. Keep it simple and give important information first. Speak slowly, using only a few key words, and try not to distract people with chat. Allow people time to feel and become familiar with the equipment to be used.

IMPROVING THE ENVIRONMENT

Life can be made much easier and safer for many people with visual disabilities by helping them use what sight they have, along with their other senses, usually hearing and touch.

- **Provide good lighting and high-contrast colours.** Most visually disabled people are not totally blind. Glare on the other hand, is not only distracting, but it also makes visually disabled people totally blind. Bright, contrasting colours enable people with low vision to see and find things, for example, a brown door against a white wall.
- **Reduce background noise.** Keeping background noise levels down allows people to identify important individual sounds and focus on their environment. Loud noise may make people insecure and jumpy.

- **Remove or indicate hazards.** Fixed hazards such as heat sources, electrical outlets, and extension cords need to be identified. Nonfixed hazards such as protruding notice boards, partly open doors, garbage cans, and bags or briefcases left in hallways can be avoided.
- **Use environmental sounds.** Sounds act like direction finders for someone who cannot see. They indicate location relative to windows, walls, and doors. The most useful sounds for this purpose are "fixed" sounds. You can use ticking clocks, fish tanks, sounds from other offices, (photocopy room, coffee room, etc.) or sounds from outside windows (traffic noise, etc.) to add information to your directions.
- **Remember to be patient.** Visually disabled people may take more time to learn some skills than sighted people, so resist the urge to "take over." Keep work-related information short, clear, and relevant.

Application. In teams, try giving "sound" directions to a well-known location in your school. Have one team member wear a blindfold while the others try to describe common objects. Record your experiences. If you are making a presentation before a group that includes some visually disabled people, what special provisions should you make? List all your suggestions. Then present them to the entire class or to your instructor.

Related Internet Resource: indie.ca/

CHAPTER 2 NONVERBAL, LISTENING, AND SPEAKING SKILLS

When it comes to your career, here is a simple fact—those who speak well in public are more likely to succeed than those who can't.[1]

JAN SPAK, past president of the Canadian Council of Human Resources Associations, vice-president of the North American Human Resources Management Association

Learning Objectives

1. Recognize how the eyes, face, body, and appearance can send nonverbal messages.
2. Identify barriers to effective listening.
3. Suggest techniques for becoming an active and effective listener.
4. Analyze the audience, organize the content, and plan visual aids for a good oral presentation.
5. Implement techniques for delivering a successful oral report.
6. Plan and participate in productive and efficient business meetings.

Effective writing, speaking, listening, and nonverbal communication skills are essential to the success of a business communicator.

Jan Spak sees the importance of well-developed speaking skills. Her experience with employees in the workplace constantly reinforces the idea that speaking, listening, and nonverbal skills are essential to success. Are you pleased with your ability to speak before groups? When it comes to listening, are you, like most people, working at only 25 percent efficiency? How well can you interpret the silent messages sent by nonverbal signals? In this chapter you'll be taught many techniques for developing your speaking and listening skills. You will also learn how to interpret nonverbal messages. The good news is that all of these skills can be greatly improved through study and practice.

IMPROVING NONVERBAL COMMUNICATION SKILLS

Understanding messages often involves more than merely listening to spoken words. Nonverbal clues, in fact, can speak louder than words. These clues include eye contact, facial expression, body movements, space, time, distance, and appearance. All these nonverbal clues affect how a message is interpreted, or decoded, by the receiver. In studies of interpersonal communication, researchers have found that only 7 percent of the "attitudinal" meaning of a message comes from the words spoken. An astounding 93 percent of the meaning results from nonverbal clues.[2]

Just what is nonverbal communication? It includes all unwritten and unspoken messages, whether intended or not. These silent signals have a strong effect on receivers. But understanding them is not simple. Does a downward glance indicate modesty? Fatigue? Does a constant stare reflect coldness? Dullness? Do crossed arms mean defensiveness? Withdrawal? Or do crossed arms just mean a person is cold?

Messages are even harder to decipher when the verbal and nonverbal codes do not agree. What would you think if Scott says he's not angry, but he slams the door when he leaves? What if Alicia assures the hostess that the meal is excellent, but she eats very little? The nonverbal messages in these situations speak more loudly than the words.

When verbal and nonverbal messages conflict, research shows that receivers put more faith in nonverbal cues. In one study speakers sent a positive message but averted their eyes as they spoke. Listeners perceived the total message to be negative. Moreover, they thought that averted eyes suggested lack of affection, superficiality, lack of trust, and nonreceptivity.[3]

When verbal and nonverbal messages clash, listeners tend to believe the nonverbal message.

Successful communicators recognize the power of nonverbal messages. Although it's unwise to attach specific meanings to gestures or actions, some cues broadcast by body language are helpful in understanding the feelings and attitudes of senders.

HOW THE EYES, FACE, AND BODY SEND SILENT MESSAGES

Words seldom tell the whole story. Indeed, some messages are sent with no words at all. The eyes, face, and body can convey a world of meaning without a single syllable being spoken.

Eye Contact. The eyes have been called the "windows to the soul." Even if they don't reveal the soul, the eyes are often the best predictor of a speaker's true feelings. Most of us cannot look another person straight in the eyes and lie. As a result, in North American culture we tend to believe people who look directly at us. Sustained eye contact suggests trust and admiration; brief eye contact signals fear or stress. Good eye contact enables the message sender to see if a receiver is paying attention, showing respect, responding favourably, or feeling distress. From the receiver's viewpoint, good eye contact reveals the speaker's sincerity, confidence, and truthfulness.

The eyes are thought to be the best predictor of a speaker's true feelings.

Since eye contact is learned, however, you should be aware that a steady gaze is viewed differently in other cultures. A department store manager in a U.S. city, for example, fired a young Hispanic clerk suspected of stealing. "She wouldn't meet my eyes when I questioned her," he told a union representative. "I knew she was lying." The union representative, himself Hispanic, explained, "What you don't understand is that a well-bred Hispanic girl will not make eye contact with a man who is not a relative. It's just considered too bold. . . . She'll look away or drop her eyes."[4]

Facial Expression. The expression on a person's face can be almost as revealing of emotion as the eyes. Experts estimate that the human face can display over 250,000 expressions.[5] To hide their feelings, some people can control these expressions and maintain "poker faces." Most of us, however, display our emotions openly. Raising or lowering the eyebrows, squinting, swallowing nervously, clenching the jaw, smiling broadly—all such voluntary and involuntary facial expressions can add to or entirely replace verbal messages.

Nonverbal messages often have different meanings in different cultures.

Posture and Gestures. A person's posture can convey anything from high status and self-confidence to shyness and submissiveness. Leaning toward a speaker suggests attraction and interest; pulling away or shrinking back denotes fear, distrust, anxiety, or disgust.

Similarly, gestures can communicate entire thoughts via simple movements. However, the meanings of these movements differ in other cultures. Unless you know local customs, they can get you into trouble. In Canada, for example, forming the thumb and forefinger in a circle means everything's OK. But in Germany and parts of South America, the OK sign is obscene. For most of the world nodding the head generally indicates agreement. In the Middle East, however, a single nod means no.[6] In England and Scotland tapping the nose says, "You and I are in on the secret." In Wales it means "You're really nosy." In Holland pointing a finger at your forehead means "How clever!" In the rest of Europe the same gesture means "You're crazy" or "That's a crazy idea!"[7]

People working with Bill Gates, CEO of Microsoft, the world's largest software company, have studied his body language to see if they can predict what the chief is thinking. Some observations: (1) if his hands are in his lap under the table, he is sceptical; (2) if he puts his elbows on the table, he is interested; and (3) if he covers his chin with his hand, he really likes what he is hearing.[8]

Tuning in on body language and other nonverbal messages requires that you be aware that they exist and that you value their importance. To take stock of the kinds of messages being sent by your body, ask a classmate to critique your use of eye contact, facial expression, and body movements. Another way to analyze your nonverbal style is to videotape yourself making a presentation and study your performance. This way you can make sure your nonverbal cues send the same message as your words.

How Time, Space, and Territory Send Silent Messages

People convey meaning in how they structure and organize time and in how they order the space around themselves.

In addition to nonverbal messages transmitted by your body, three external elements convey information in the communication process: time, space, and distance.

Time. How we structure and use time tells observers about our personality and attitudes. For example, when Heather Desrochers, a banking executive, gives a visitor a prolonged interview, she signals her respect for, interest in, and approval of the visitor or the topic to be discussed. Similarly, when Curtis Fraser twice arrives late for a meeting with a realtor, it could mean that the appointment is unimportant to Curtis, that the realtor has low status, that Curtis is a self-centred person, or that he has little self-discipline. These are assumptions that typical North Americans might make. In other cultures and regions, though, punctuality is viewed differently.

Space. How we order the space around us tells something about ourselves and our objectives. Whether the space is a bedroom, a dorm room, an office, or a department, people reveal themselves in the design and grouping of furniture within that space. Generally, the more formal the arrangement, the more formal and closed the communication environment. The way office furniture is arranged sends cues about how communication is to take place. An instructor who arranges chairs informally in a circle rather than in straight rows conveys her desire for a more open, egalitarian exchange of ideas. A manager who creates an open office space with few partitions separating workers' desks seeks to encourage an unrestricted flow of communication and work among areas.

The way we structure time and organize space sends silent messages about our personalities and goals.

Territory. Each of us has certain areas that we feel are our own territory, whether it's a specific spot or just the space around us. Family members may have a favourite living room chair; students sit in a chair at their first class and then return to that chair throughout the term; and veteran employees may feel that certain work areas and tools belong to them.

We all maintain zones of privacy in which we feel comfortable. Figure 2.1 categorizes the four zones of social interaction among North Americans, as formulated by anthropologist Edward T. Hall. Notice that North Americans are a bit stand-offish; only intimate friends and family may stand closer than about 45 cm (1.5 feet). If someone violates that territory, North Americans feel uncomfortable and defensive and may step back to reestablish their space.[9] Because the distance required for comfortable social interaction is largely controlled by culture, North Americans must be careful not to apply their norms universally.

The distance required for comfortable social interaction is controlled by culture.

FIGURE 2.1

Four North American Space Zones for Social Interaction

Zone	Distance	Uses
Intimate	0 to 45 cm (1.5 feet)	Reserved for members of the family and other loved ones.
Personal	45 cm to 123 cm (1.5 to 4 feet)	For talking with friends privately. The outer limit enables you to keep someone at arm's length.
Social	123 cm to 360 cm (4 to 12 feet)	For acquaintances, fellow workers, and strangers. Close enough for eye contact, yet far enough for comfort.
Public	360 cm and over (12 feet and over)	For use in the classroom and for speeches before groups. Nonverbal cues become important as aids to communication.

HOW APPEARANCE SENDS SILENT MESSAGES

The physical appearance of a business document, as well as the personal appearance of an individual, transmits immediate and important nonverbal messages.

The appearance of a message and of an individual can convey positive or negative nonverbal messages.

Appearance of Business Documents. The way a letter, memo, or report looks can have either a positive or a negative effect on the receiver. Envelopes—through their postage, stationery, and printing—can suggest routine, important, or junk mail. Letters and reports can look neat, professional, well organized, and attractive—or just the opposite. Sloppy, hurriedly written documents convey negative nonverbal messages regarding both the content and the sender. In succeeding chapters you'll learn how to create documents that send positive nonverbal messages through their appearance, format, organization, readability, and correctness.

Appearance of People. The way you look—your clothing, grooming, and posture—telegraphs an instant nonverbal message about you. Based on what they see, viewers make quick judgments about your status, credibility, personality, and potential. Because appearance is such a powerful force in business, some aspiring professionals are turning for help to image consultants. As one human relations specialist observes, "If you don't look and act the part, you will probably be denied opportunities."

TIPS FOR IMPROVING NONVERBAL SKILLS

Nonverbal communication can outweigh words in the way it influences how others perceive us. You can harness the power of silent messages by reviewing the following tips for improving nonverbal communication skills:

- *Establish and maintain eye contact.* Remember that in North America appropriate eye contact signals interest, attentiveness, strength, and credibility.
- *Use posture to show interest.* Encourage communication interaction by leaning forward, sitting or standing erect, and looking alert.
- *Improve your decoding skills.* Watch facial expressions and body language to understand the complete verbal and nonverbal message being communicated.
- *Probe for more information.* When you perceive nonverbal cues that contradict verbal meanings, politely seek additional clues (*I'm not sure I understand, Please tell me more about . . . ,* or *Do you mean that . . .*).
- *Avoid assigning nonverbal meanings out of context.* Make nonverbal assessment only when you understand a situation or a culture.
- *Associate with people from diverse cultures.* Learn about other cultures to widen your knowledge and tolerance of intercultural nonverbal messages.
- *Appreciate the power of appearance.* Keep in mind that the appearance of your business documents and your business space, and your own appearance send immediate positive or negative messages to receivers.
- *Observe yourself on videotape.* Ensure that your verbal and nonverbal messages agree by taping and evaluating yourself making a presentation.
- *Enlist friends and family.* Ask them to monitor your conscious and unconscious body movements and gestures to help you become a more effective communicator.

IMPROVING LISTENING SKILLS

Improving your communication skills not only involves being alert to nonverbal clues. It also means working on your listening skills.

Do you ever pretend to be listening when you're not?
Do you know how to look attentive in class when your mind wanders far away?
How about "tuning out" people when their ideas are boring or complex?
Do you find it hard to focus on ideas when a speaker's clothing or mannerisms are weird?

Most of us would answer yes to one or more of these questions because we have developed poor listening habits. In fact, some researchers suggest that we listen at only 25 percent efficiency. Such poor listening habits are costly in business. Letters must be rekeyed, shipments reshipped, appointments rescheduled, contracts renegotiated, and directions restated.

For many of us, listening is a passive, unconscious activity. We don't require our minds to work very hard at receiving sounds, and we don't give much thought to whether we're really listening. Only when a message is urgent do we perk up and try to listen more carefully. Then we become more involved in the communication process. We reduce competing environmental sounds; we concentrate on the speaker's words; we anticipate what's coming; we ask questions. Good listeners are active listeners. Passive listeners don't get involved; active listeners make a physical and mental effort to hear.

To improve listening skills, we must first recognize barriers that prevent effective listening. Then we need to focus on specific techniques that are effective in improving listening skills.

> Most individuals listen at only 25 percent efficiency.

BARRIERS TO EFFECTIVE LISTENING

As you learned in Chapter 1, barriers and noise can interfere with the communication process. Have any of the following barriers and distractions prevented you from hearing what's said?

- *Physical barriers.* You cannot listen if you cannot hear what is being said. Physical impediments include hearing disabilities, poor acoustics, and noisy surroundings. It's also difficult to listen if you're ill, tired, uncomfortable, or worried.

- *Psychological barriers.* As noted in Chapter 1, every person brings to the communication process a different set of cultural, ethical, and personal values. Each of us has an idea of what is right and what is important. If other ideas run counter to our preconceived thoughts, we tend to "tune out" the speaker and thus fail to hear. For example, if someone thinks his work is satisfactory, he might filter out criticism from his supervisor. Such selective listening results in poor communication and is unproductive for both the listener and the speaker.

- *Language problems.* Unfamiliar words can destroy the communication process because they lack meaning for the receiver. In addition, emotion-laden or "charged" words can adversely affect listening. If the mention of words like *abortion* or *overdose* has an intense emotional impact, a listener may be unable to pay attention to the words that follow.

- *Nonverbal distractions.* Many of us find it hard to listen if a speaker is different from what we view as normal. Unusual clothing, speech mannerisms, body twitches, or a radical hairstyle can cause enough distraction to prevent us from hearing what the speaker has to say.

- *Thought speed.* Because thought speed is more than three times as great as speech speed, listener concentration flags. Our minds are able to process thoughts much more quickly than speakers can say them. Therefore, we become bored and our minds wander.

- *Faking attention.* Most of us have learned to look as if we are listening even when we're not. Such behaviour was perhaps necessary as part of our socialization.

> Most North Americans speak at about 125 words per minute. The human brain can process information at least three times as quickly.

Faked attention, however, seriously threatens effective listening because it encourages the mind to flights of unchecked fancy. Those who practise faked attention often find it hard to concentrate even when they want to.

- *Grandstanding.* Would you rather talk or listen? Naturally, most of us would rather talk. Since our own experiences and thoughts are most important to us, we grab the limelight in conversations. We sometimes fail to listen carefully because we're just waiting politely for the next pause so that we can have our turn to speak.

HOW TO BECOME AN ACTIVE LISTENER

You can reverse the harmful effects of poor habits by making a conscious effort to become an active listener. This means becoming involved. You can't sit back and take in whatever a lazy mind happens to receive. The following techniques will help you become an active and effective listener.

- *Stop talking.* The first step to becoming a good listener is to stop talking. Let others explain their views. Learn to concentrate on what the speaker is saying, not on what your next comment will be.

To become a good listener, control your surroundings and your mindset.

- *Control your surroundings.* Whenever possible, remove competing sounds. Close windows or doors, turn off radios and noisy appliances, and move away from loud people or engines. Choose a quiet time and place for listening.
- *Establish a receptive mindset.* Expect to learn something by listening. Strive for a positive and receptive frame of mind. If the message is complex, think of it as mental gymnastics. It's hard work but good exercise to stretch and expand the limits of your mind.
- *Keep an open mind.* We all sift and filter information through our own biases and values. For improved listening, discipline yourself to listen objectively. Be fair to the speaker. Hear what is really being said, not what you want to hear.
- *Listen for main points.* Concentration is enhanced and satisfaction is heightened when you look for and recognize the speaker's central themes.
- *Capitalize on lag time.* Make use of the quickness of your mind by reviewing the speaker's points. Anticipate what's coming next. Evaluate evidence the speaker has presented. Don't allow yourself to daydream.
- *Listen between the lines.* Focus both on what is spoken and what is unspoken. Listen for feelings as well as for facts.
- *Judge ideas, not appearances.* Concentrate on the content of the message, not on its delivery. Avoid being distracted by the speaker's looks, voice, or mannerisms.
- *Hold your fire.* Force yourself to listen to the speaker's entire argument or message before reacting. Such restraint may enable you to understand the speaker's reasons and logic before you jump to false conclusions.

Listening actively may mean taking notes and providing feedback.

- *Take selective notes.* For some situations thoughtful note taking may be necessary to record important facts that must be recalled later. Select only the most important points so that the note-taking process does not interfere with your concentration on the speaker's total message.
- *Provide feedback.* Let the speaker know that you are listening. Nod your head and maintain eye contact. Ask relevant questions at appropriate times. Getting involved improves the communication process for both the speaker and the listener.

IMPROVING SPEAKING SKILLS

Listening and speaking make up a large part of the time you spend communicating. How much time you devote to speaking—and, more particularly, to making oral presentations and participating in meetings—depends on your occupation and on the level you reach in your career. Few businesspeople regularly deliver formal speeches. Instead, most of them communicate orally in informal conversations, small group discussions, and meetings.

Yet, any individual aspiring to a business career is well advised to develop speaking skills. A computer hardware sales representative pitches products before a group of potential customers. An accountant explains the financial position of an organization to management. A travel counsellor describes an excursion package to a single client or to a group. An office manager clarifies new office procedures, and a structural engineer explains load bearing to a land developer. In today's information society nearly all careers require speaking skills. And the higher you are promoted, the more you will have to express your ideas in writing and in speaking. It is no coincidence that most people promoted to high-level positions are effective writers and speakers. In this section you'll learn how to make oral presentations and how to participate in meetings.

As you advance in your career, the ability to express ideas orally takes on greater significance.

PREPARING AN ORAL REPORT

One of the most common speaking functions for businesspeople is the presentation of ideas in an oral report. Such a presentation is most frequently made informally to a manager or to a small group of colleagues. Only occasionally do businesspeople make formal speeches before large groups.

No matter the size of the audience, the best oral reports begin with planning. You will need to analyze the audience, organize the content, and plan visual aids.

ANALYZING THE AUDIENCE

Knowing about your audience helps you decide how to structure your report. The size of the audience affects the formality of your presentation: a large audience generally requires a more formal and less personalized approach. Other factors, such as age, sex, education, experience, and attitude toward the subject, also affect your presentation. Analyze these factors to decide on your strategy, vocabulary, illustrations, and level of detail. Your answers to specific questions will guide you in adapting the topic to your audience:

- How will this topic appeal to this audience?
- What do I want the audience to believe?
- What action do I want the audience to take?
- What aspects of the topic will be most interesting to the audience?
- Which of the following will be most effective in making my point: Statistics? graphic illustrations? demonstrations? case histories? analogies? cost figures?

ORGANIZING CONTENT

A precise statement of purpose helps you organize the content of your presentation.

Begin to organize your oral report by defining its purpose. Is your goal to inform? to persuade? to recommend? In describing your goal, write a statement of purpose.

For example, *the goal of this report is*

To inform all staff members of the benefits and options in the new dental care program.

To persuade the vice president of marketing that a consolidation of two sales territories would reduce costs and increase efficiency.

To recommend to the board of directors the establishment of a members' advisory committee that would encourage input from the employees of the organization.

Most presentations should focus on only two to four principal points.

After you have a firm statement of purpose, organize your report to reach your goal. Limit yourself to no more than four main points because this is about as much as listeners can absorb at one sitting. Once you know the main points, prepare an outline such as that shown in Figure 2.2.

FIGURE 2.2

Outline for an Oral Presentation

TITLE

Purpose:

I. INTRODUCTION
   A. Gain attention and involvement of audience
   B. Establish credibility as a speaker
   C. Preview main points
   Transition

II. BODY
   A. Main point
      1. Use data to illustrate, clarify, and contrast
      2.
      3.
      Transition
   B. Main point
      1. Use data to illustrate, clarify, and contrast
      2.
      3.
      Transition
   C. Main point
      1. Use data to illustrate, clarify, and contrast
      2.
      3.
      Transition

III. CONCLUSION
   A. Summarize main points
   B. Provide final focus
   C. Encourage questions

Oral presentations often contain three parts: an introduction, a body, and a conclusion. Experienced speakers explain the organization of speeches as follows: (1) tell them what you're going to tell them, (2) tell them what you have to say, and then (3) tell them what you've just told them. Such redundancy may seem boring, but repetition helps the audience retain information.

Another important point to remember about audiences is that they are not reading. They cannot control the rate of presentation or reread main points. It's easy for them to get lost. Therefore, good speakers help their listeners recognize the organization and main points in an oral report by emphasizing and repeating them. Good speakers also keep the audience on track by including helpful transitions, reviews, and previews.

Introduction. At the beginning of your report, identify yourself (if necessary) and your topic. Describe the goal of your report, its organization, and the main points you will cover. Also in your introduction make an effort to capture the attention of the audience with a question, startling fact, joke, story, quotation, or some other device. Make sure, of course, that your attention-getter is relevant to your topic. Some speakers involve the audience by opening with a question or a command that requires members to raise their hands or stand up.

> Help the listener follow your presentation by describing its organization (introduction, body, and conclusion).

To establish your credibility, you may need to describe your position, knowledge, or experience. What is it that qualifies you to speak? Try to connect with your audience. Listeners are particularly drawn to speakers who reveal something of themselves and identify with them. A consultant addressing office workers might reminisce about how she started as a clerk-typist; a CEO might tell a funny story in which the joke is on himself.

After capturing your audience's attention and establishing yourself, you'll want to preview the main points of your topic, perhaps with a visual aid. You might want to put off actually writing your introduction, however, until after you have organized the rest of the presentation.

Body. The biggest problem with most oral presentations is a failure to focus on a few principal ideas. Thus, the body of a short presentation (20 or fewer minutes) should include a limited number of main points, say, two to four. Develop each main point with adequate, but not excessive, explanation and detail. Too many details can obscure the main message, so keep your presentation simple and logical.

> Include verbal signposts so that listeners know where you've been and where you're heading in your presentation.

Remember that listeners have no pages to leaf back through if they should become confused. The best devices you can use to ensure that listeners don't get lost are verbal signposts. These tell where you've been and point to where you're going. Summarize each segment of your report with a statement such as the following:

> We see, then, that the two major problems facing management are difficulties in the delivery of raw material and high labour costs.

Or combine a review with a preview:

> Now that we've learned how sole proprietorships are different from partnerships, let's turn to corporations.

> I've described two good reasons for consolidating sales territories, but the final reason is most important.

Repeat main ideas as you progress. Indicate new topics or shifts in direction with helpful transitional expressions, such as *first, second, next, then, therefore, moreover, on the other hand, on the contrary*, and *in conclusion*.

Conclusion. You may end a presentation by reviewing the main themes of the talk, or you may round out the presentation by referring to your opening. Concentrate on the information that achieves your purpose. What do you want your listeners to believe? What action do you want them to take? When you finish, ask if audience members have any questions. If silence ensues, remark that you'll be happy to answer questions individually after the program is completed.

Conclude your presentation by emphasizing the information that you want your listeners to remember.

Planning Visual Aids

Oral reports are most successful when they show and tell.

Show and tell is effective not only for schoolchildren but also for adults. Some authorities suggest that we learn and remember 85 percent of all our knowledge visually. An oral report that incorporates visual aids is twice as likely to be understood and retained as a report lacking visual supplements. By appealing to the senses of both sight and sound, you can double the impact of a message.

When you incorporate visual aids into an oral report, keep a few points in mind:

- Use visual aids only for major points or for information that requires clarification.
- Keep the visual aids simple.
- Make sure the necessary equipment works properly. Have a backup ready.
- Ensure that everyone can see the visual aid.
- Talk to the audience, not to the visual aid.

In selecting ways to illustrate your oral report, you have a number of options, each with its particular uses, advantages, and disadvantages.

Visual aids are particularly useful for inexperienced speakers because the audience concentrates on the aids rather than on the speaker and because visual aids can jog the memory of the speaker.

- *Transparencies.* Easy and inexpensive to prepare, transparencies can be used to project a message on a screen in a lighted or unlighted room. They are popular in business and education because the masters can be printed or handwritten on plain paper. Masters are transferred onto transparent film using a photocopier. Transparencies can also be directly printed with laser printers. The transparency is then placed onto an overhead projector, which flashes the image onto a screen. Printed transparencies are useful because they can be made in advance, and they are easy to read when printed in a large font. They emphasize points for viewers while also prompting the speaker.
- *Flip charts.* Like a giant pad of paper, a flip chart consists of large sheets attached at the top. You may prepare the sheets in advance or write on them as you speak and flip through the pad. Flip charts are usually less visible than transparencies because they are propped on an easel on a level with the speaker and because the sheets are smaller than the images projected on a screen. Thus, they are less effective with larger audiences. However, flip charts require no special equipment, and they can be quite colourful if you use felt-tip markers.
- *Computer visuals.* With today's software programs (such as Microsoft PowerPoint and Corel Presentations) you can create colourful presentations with your PC. The output from these programs may be projected through a

data/video projector or an LCD (liquid crystal display) panel placed on an overhead projector. They can also be shown on a PC monitor, or on a TV monitor. With a little expertise and advanced equipment, you can create a multimedia presentation that includes stereo sound and videos. Many business speakers are switching to computer presentations because the visuals are easy to make, economical, and flexible. You can make changes right up to the last minute. Most important, though, such presentations make even amateurs look like real pros. For more information about presentation software, see the Communication Workshop on page 50.

- *Handouts.* To clarify and supplement their words, speakers often use handouts, on which they include such things as an outline, list of selected main points, illustration, flow chart, or table. Members of the audience appreciate these handouts because with them they have ready-made notes they can keep to remind them of the report. The major disadvantage of handouts is that audience members may read the handouts instead of listening to the speaker. For this reason some speakers distribute handouts only at the end of a presentation.

Experienced speakers distribute handouts when they conclude their presentations.

DELIVERING THE ORAL REPORT

Regardless of its excellent preparation and interesting content, a speech will be boring and fail in its purpose if delivered poorly. Good speakers choose an appropriate delivery method, and they practise techniques to hold the attention of the audience.

DELIVERY METHODS

Your audience will be most favourably impressed if your presentation is forceful but natural. Four delivery methods—memorized, reading, extemporaneous, and impromptu—are available:

Memorized Delivery. Inexperienced speakers often feel that they must memorize an entire report to be effective. Actually, unless you're a trained actor, a memorized delivery sounds wooden and unnatural. Also, forgetting your place can be disastrous. Therefore, memorizing an entire oral presentation is not recommended. However, memorizing important parts—the introduction, the conclusion, or a significant quotation—can be dramatic and impressive.

Reading Delivery. Reading a report to an audience creates a negative impression. It suggests that you don't know your topic very well, so that the audience loses confidence in your expertise. Reading also prevents you from maintaining eye contact with the audience. If you can't see their reactions, you can't benefit from feedback. Worst of all, reading is simply boring. If you must read your report, practise it enough so that you can look up occasionally as you present familiar sections.

If you read an oral presentation, you may put your audience to sleep.

Extemporaneous Delivery. The most effective method for presenting oral reports is the extemporaneous delivery. With this method you plan the report carefully and talk from notes containing key sentences. By practising with your notes, you can talk to

Speaking from notes extemporaneously is the best delivery method.

your audience in a conversational manner. Your notes should not consist of entire paragraphs, nor should they be single words. Instead, use complete sentences based on the major ideas in your outline. These key ideas will keep you on track and will jog your memory, but only if you have thoroughly practised the presentation.

Impromptu Delivery. An impromptu, or off-the-cuff, delivery is necessary if you are asked to give a spur-of-the-moment report. For example, you might be asked to report on the progress of a fundraising drive of which you are chairperson. Many activities in business require impromptu oral reports. Usually, you are very familiar with your topic, but you have little time to prepare your thoughts. Presenting accurate, coherent, persuasive, and well-organized information without adequate preparation is very difficult, even for the most experienced professional speakers. If you are asked to give an impromptu report, take a few moments to compose your thoughts and to jot down your main points.

DELIVERY TECHNIQUES

Nearly everyone experiences some degree of stage fright when speaking before a group. Such fears are quite natural. You can learn to control and reduce stage fright, as well as to incorporate techniques of effective speaking in your presentations, by studying suggestions from experts. Successful speakers use these techniques before, during, and after their reports.

BEFORE YOU SPEAK

Here are techniques that experts use before, during, and after delivering oral presentations.

- *Prepare thoroughly.* One of the most effective devices to reduce stage fright is ensuring that you know your topic well, which will give you confidence. Research your topic diligently and prepare a careful sentence outline. Those who are unprepared usually suffer the worst anxiety.
- *Rehearse repeatedly.* Practise your entire presentation, not just the first half. Place your outline sentences on separate cards. You may also wish to include transitional sentences to help you move to the next topic. Use these cards as you practise, and include your visual aids in your rehearsal. Record your rehearsal on tape so that you can hear how you sound.
- *Time yourself.* Try to deliver your presentation in no more than twenty minutes. Most audiences tend to get restless after this amount of time. Set a timer during your rehearsal to measure your speaking time.
- *Request a lectern.* Every beginning speaker needs the security of a high desk or lectern from which to deliver a presentation. It serves as a note holder and a convenient place to rest awkward hands and arms.
- *Check the room.* Make sure that a lectern has been provided. If you are using a computer, sound equipment, or a projector, make sure they are operational. Check electrical outlets and the position of the viewing screen. Ensure that the seating arrangement is appropriate to your needs.
- *Practise stress reduction.* If you feel tension and fear while you are waiting your turn to speak, use stress reduction techniques. Take very deep breaths. Inhale to a count of ten; hold this breath to a count of ten; exhale to a count of ten. Concentrate on your breathing, not on the audience awaiting you.

Deep-breathing exercises can significantly reduce stress.

DURING YOUR PRESENTATION

- *Begin with a pause.* When you first approach the audience, take a moment to adjust your notes and make yourself comfortable. Establish your control of the situation.
- *Present your first sentence from memory.* By memorizing your opening, you can immediately establish rapport with the audience through eye contact. You'll also sound confident and knowledgeable.
- *Maintain eye contact.* Look at your audience. If the size of the audience frightens you, pick out two individuals on the right and two on the left. Talk directly to these people.
- *Control your voice and vocabulary.* Speak in moderated tones but loudly enough to be heard. Eliminate verbal static, such as "ah," "er," and "uh." Silence is preferable to meaningless fillers when you are thinking of your next idea.
- *Put the brakes on.* Many novice speakers talk too rapidly, displaying their nervousness and making it very difficult for audience members to understand their ideas. Slow down and listen to what you're saying.
- *Move naturally.* Use the lectern to hold your notes so that you are free to move about casually and naturally. Avoid fidgeting with your notes, your clothing, or items in your pockets. Learn to use your body to express a point.
- *Use visual aids effectively.* Discuss and interpret each visual aid for the audience. Move aside as you describe it so that it can be seen fully. Use a pointer if necessary and face the audience as you point to items—don't turn to face the visual.
- *Avoid digressions.* Stick to your outline and notes. Don't suddenly include clever little anecdotes or digressions that occur to you as you speak. If it's not part of your rehearsed material, leave it out so that you can finish on time. Remember, too, that your audience may not be as enthralled with your topic as you are.

  Avoid digressions that occur to you as you speak.

- *Summarize your main points.* Conclude your presentation by repeating your main points or by emphasizing what you want the audience to think about or do. Once you have announced your conclusion, proceed to it directly. Don't irritate the audience by talking for five or ten more minutes.

AFTER YOUR PRESENTATION

- *Distribute handouts.* If you prepared handouts with data the audience will need to have after the presentation, pass them out when you finish.
- *Encourage questions.* If the situation permits a question-and-answer period, announce it at the beginning of your presentation. Then, when you finish, ask for questions. Set a time limit for questions and answers.
- *Repeat questions.* Although the speaker may hear the question, some people in the audience often do not. Begin each answer with a repetition of the question. This also gives you thinking time.
- *Answer questions directly.* Avoid becoming defensive or debating the questioner.
- *Keep control.* Don't allow one individual to take over. Keep the entire audience involved.

  Keep control of the question-and-answer period by repeating questions for the entire audience to hear and by involving the entire audience.

- *End gracefully.* To signal the end of the session before you take the last question, say something like "We have time for just one more question." After you answer the last question, express appreciation to the audience for the opportunity to talk with them.

DEVELOPING SUCCESSFUL MEETINGS AND CONFERENCES

Whether you like attending them or not, meetings and conferences are a necessary part of business today. These meetings can be more successful—and even enjoyable—if leaders and participants sharpen their listening and speaking skills.

Meetings and conferences consist of three or more individuals who meet for discussion. Meetings are called to gather information, clarify policy, seek consensus, and solve problems. Meetings are different from speeches, where one individual talks at an audience. In meetings individuals exchange ideas.

Meetings differ from conferences in that they are smaller and less formal. We'll concentrate on meetings in this discussion, although most of the advice holds for conferences as well. Meetings can be occasions for successful exchanges of information, or they can be boring time wasters.

WHY MEETINGS FAIL

Poor meetings are usually the result of poor planning or ineffective leadership.

Many failed meetings are the result of poor planning. Perhaps the meeting was unnecessary. Alternatives—such as personal conversations, e-mail messages, or telephone calls—might have served the purpose as well.

Poor leadership dooms some meetings. The leader fails to keep the group discussing target items. The discussion digresses or flounders in trivia, and no resolution is reached. Then the group must meet again, and no one enjoys additional meetings.

PLANNING MEETINGS

Successful meetings begin with planning. Decide first on a goal or an objective, and then determine whether a meeting is the best way to achieve the goal. If the goal is to announce a new policy regarding the scheduling of vacations, is a meeting the best way to inform employees? Perhaps an e-mail message would be better.

Agendas help prepare participants for meetings.

If a meeting is necessary, prepare an agenda of items to be discussed. The best agendas list topics, an estimate of time for each item, and an ending time. They may also include the names of individuals who are responsible for presenting topics or for performing some action. Send the agenda (and perhaps the minutes of the previous meeting) at least two days prior to the meeting. Notify only those people directly concerned with the business of this meeting. Plan to serve refreshments if you think the participants will need them.

CONDUCTING MEETINGS

Conducting good meetings requires real skill, which not every leader immediately has. Such skill comes with practice and with knowledge of the following pointers. To avoid wasting time and irritating the attendees, always start meetings on time—even if some participants are missing. Delaying sets a poor example. Individuals who came on time resent waiting for latecomers. Moreover, latecomers may fail to be on time for future meetings, knowing that the leader doesn't always start punctually.

Begin with a three- to five-minute introduction that includes the following: (1) goal and length of the meeting, (2) background of the problem, (3) possible solutions and constraints, (4) tentative agenda, and (5) procedures to be followed. At this point ask if participants agree with you thus far.

The most important part of a meeting is the first five to ten minutes when the leader introduces the topic and sets the tone.

Then assign one attendee to take minutes. It's impossible for the leader to direct a meeting and record its proceedings at the same time. Open the discussion, and from that point forward, say as little as possible. Adhere to the agenda and the time schedule. Keep the discussion on the topic by tactfully guiding speakers back to the main idea. You might say, "Jeff, I'm afraid I don't understand exactly how our sick leave policy relates to our vacation policy. Can you explain?" Encourage all individuals to participate. You can do this by occasionally asking for the opinions of the smart but silent participants. Try not to let one or two people monopolize the discussion. When the group seems to have reached a consensus, summarize it in your own words and look to see if everyone agrees. Finally, end the meeting at the agreed time. Announce that a report of the proceedings will be sent to all attendees.

PARTICIPATING IN MEETINGS

As a participant, you can get the most out of a meeting and contribute to its success by coming prepared. Read the agenda and gather any information necessary for your knowledgeable participation. One way to make yourself visible in an organization is to shine at meetings. Know the problem, its causes, possible solutions, alternatives, and how others have dealt with it. Careful preparation and wise participation at meetings often cause management to recognize upwardly mobile employees.

Making wise contributions at meetings can help employees be noticed by management.

Arrive at the meeting on time. Be ready to speak on an issue, but consider your timing. It may be smart to wait for others to speak first so that you can shape your remarks to best advantage. You can help the leader keep the discussion on target with remarks such as, "Can I add another option that we haven't considered yet? Manwin Manufacturers had a similar problem several years ago and they . . ."

Productive, enjoyable meetings result from good planning, skilful leadership, and active participation.

SUMMING UP AND LOOKING FORWARD

Nonverbal skills involve being aware of the silent messages sent by a person's eyes, face, body, and appearance. When verbal and nonverbal messages contradict each other, receivers are more likely to believe the silent message, so be aware of the nonverbal messages you are sending.

Improving your listening skills begins with recognizing that physical, psychological, language, and nonverbal barriers can destroy the communication process. Good listeners become actively involved by controlling the environment, keeping an open mind, listening for main points, capitalizing on lag time, and judging ideas instead of appearances. They also force themselves to hear an entire message before reacting, they take selective notes, and they provide feedback.

Before making an oral presentation, good speakers analyze the audience, define the purpose, organize the content, prepare an outline, and plan effective visual aids. In delivering an oral report, they speak from notes but have important sections memorized. After a presentation, they distribute handouts and answer questions, if appropriate.

Successful meetings are well planned and conducted by a leader who keeps the discussion on target, summarizes conclusions, and ends on time. Attendees can be most effective when they come prepared and speak to the issues.

You've now developed a solid communication foundation by studying nonverbal, listening, and speaking skills. The next ten chapters focus on writing skills, and the last two chapters teach you employment communication skills, including résumé writing and interviewing.

DISCUSSION

1. Why should businesspeople be sure that their verbal and nonverbal messages do not contradict each other?
2. Discuss seven barriers to effective listening and give an example of each from the business world.
3. Discuss the advantages and disadvantages of taking notes while you are listening. When would note taking be most effective?
4. Why do audiences prefer extemporaneous speakers?
5. Why is it necessary to keep the audience informed of the organization of an oral report?
6. Discuss the duties of a leader and the functions of a participant at business meetings and conferences.

CHAPTER REVIEW

7. What is nonverbal communication? Give several examples.

8. What percentage of the attitudinal meaning of a message comes from the words spoken?

9. Why is good eye contact important for North American communicators?

10. What should a listener do when the verbal and nonverbal messages of a speaker contradict each other?

11. How fast does the average North American speak?

12. List 11 ways to improve your listening skills. Be prepared to discuss each.

13. Name five characteristics that you should identify about your audience before preparing an oral report.

14. On how many main points should an oral report concentrate?

15. What is the first step in developing an oral report?

16. List the three parts of an oral report. Be prepared to discuss what goes in each part.

17. List four kinds of visual aids for oral reports. Be prepared to discuss each.

18. Notes for an oral report should consist of what?

19. What is an agenda, and what should it include?

20. Who takes the minutes of a meeting, and what is done with them?

ACTIVITIES AND CASES

2.1 Silent Messages. Analyze the kinds of silent messages you send your instructor, your classmates, and your employer. How do you send these messages? Group them into categories, as suggested by what you learned in this chapter. What do these messages mean? Be prepared to discuss them in small groups or in a memo to your instructor.

2.2 Body Language. What attitudes do the following body movements suggest to you? Do these movements always mean the same thing? What part does context play in your interpretations?

    a. Whistling, wringing hands
    b. Bowed posture, twiddling thumbs
    c. Steepled hands, sprawling sitting position
    d. Running hand through hair
    e. Open hands, unbuttoned coat
    f. Wringing hands, tugging ears

2.3 Universal Sign for "I Goofed." In an effort to reduce road rage on city streets, motorists submitted the following suggestions to a newspaper columnist.[10] In small groups or in a class discussion, consider the pros and cons of each of the following gestures, which are intended as an apology when a driver makes a mistake. Why would some fail?

    a. Lower your head slightly and bonk yourself on the forehead with the side of your closed fist.
    b. Make a temple with your hands, as if you were praying.
    c. Move the index finger of your right hand back and forth across your neck—as if you are cutting your throat.
    d. Flash the well-known peace sign. Hold up the index and middle fingers of one hand, making a "V."
    e. Place the flat of your hands against your cheeks, as children do when they've made a mistake.
    f. Clasp your hand over your mouth, raise your brows, and shrug your shoulders.
    g. Use your knuckles to knock on the side of your head. Translation: "Oops! Engage brain!"
    h. Place your right hand high on your chest and pat a few times, like a basketball player who drops a pass or a football player who makes a bad throw. This says, "I'll take the blame."
    i. Place your right fist over the middle of your chest and move it in a circular motion. This is universal sign language for "I'm sorry."
    j. Open your window and tap the top of your car roof with your hand.
    k. Smile and raise both arms, palms outward, which is a universal gesture for surrender or forgiveness.
    l. Use the military salute, which is simple and shows respect.
    m. Flash your biggest smile, point at yourself with your right thumb and move your head from left to right, as if to say, "I can't believe I did that."

2.4 Class Listening. Observe the listening habits in one of your classes for a week. Write a memo to your instructor describing your observations.

2.5 Self-Listening. Analyze your own listening habits. What are your strengths and weaknesses? Decide on a plan for improving your listening skills. Write a memo or e-mail message to your instructor including your analysis and your improvement plan.

2.6 Extra Credit Listening. You are a student in a business management or other class. Your instructor notices that you have good listening habits. Disturbed by the poor listening skills of some other class members, your instructor asks you to do research and to present a program (for extra credit) to help students improve their listening skills. For this presentation do the following:

a. Write a specific statement of purpose.
b. Prepare a complete outline.
c. Write the introduction.
d. List visual aids that would be appropriate and describe their content.

Related Web Site: www.smartbiz.com/sbs/arts/bly55.htm

2.7 In-Service Listening Training. If you are now employed or have been employed, adapt the assignment in Activity 2.6 to your work. Assume that your supervisor has asked you to present an in-service training workshop that helps employees improve listening skills. Respond to the instructions in items (a) through (d).

2.8 Critiquing a Speech. Select a speech from a book containing selected speeches in your library (if necessary, ask a librarian to help you find such a book) or from a federal government department Web site, or you might watch a Member of Parliament speak during a televised edition of Question Period. Write a memo report to your instructor in which you analyze the speech based on the following items:

a. Effectiveness of the introduction, body, and conclusion
b. Evidence of effective overall organization
c. Use of verbal signposts to create coherence
d. Emphasis of two to four main points
e. Effectiveness of supporting facts (use of examples, statistics, quotations, and so forth)

2.9 Summarizing a News or Feature Article. Make a five-minute oral presentation. Select a challenging news or feature article of interest to students preparing business careers. The article should contain at least 1000 words. Prepare a well-organized presentation that includes the following: (a) an attention-getting opening plus an introduction to the major ideas, (b) three to four main points that are easy for the audience to identify, and (c) a conclusion that reviews the main points and ends by asking for questions. Avoid self-conscious remarks such as "My report is about . . ." or "The article says . . ." or "I guess that ends it." Use one visual aid. Allow no more than three minutes for questions and answers. Your instructor may ask you to distribute copies of your article to the class one or two days prior to your presentation so that they may ask informed questions. Turn in an outline to your instructor before your presentation.

2.10 Making an Oral Presentation. Prepare a five- to ten-minute oral report. Use one of the following topics or a topic that you and your instructor agree on. You are an expert who has been called in to explain some aspect of the topic before a group of interested individuals. Since their time is limited, prepare a concise yet forceful report with effective visual aids.

a. The effective use of e-mail. Consider its uses and abuses. What problems are companies encountering? How are some organizations solving these problems?

b. Privacy rights of employees in regard to e-mail. Should the messages of employees be regarded as company property?

c. Information for future businesspeople. Introduce your classmates to some topic you feel they should know about. It could be internships to gain experience, on-line job hunting, the effect of e-mail in reducing face-to-face interaction, casual dress days in business, the glass ceiling, the language of annual reports, the value of customer feedback, ergonomic solutions to repetitive strain injuries, or environmental strategies of paper mill companies. You don't have to be an expert to be able to introduce a business-related topic to your classmates.

d. Rights of smokers and nonsmokers. Should smoking be banned in all public places, including restaurants, pubs, and nightclubs?

e. Dressing for an employment interview. Should one dress as current employees dress?

f. Economic outlook. What is the economic prospect for a given product (personal computers, shoes, women's apparel, domestic cars, TV sets, etc.) this year?

g. Franchise opportunities. What franchise would offer an entrepreneur the best chance for a profitable business in your area?

h. Best buys. What brands and models of computers and printers represent the best buys for home use today?

i. Career opportunities. What is the current employment outlook in three career areas of interest to you?

j. Interview persuasion. Why should you be hired for a position for which you have applied?

k. Company transportation. For its sales personnel, should your company rent automobiles, own them, or pay mileage costs on employee-owned vehicles?

l. Best convention site. Where should your professional organization hold its next convention?

m. Endangered species. What local plant or animal is endangered, and how can it be protected?

n. Looking good. How can your school (or company) improve its image?

o. Solving a problem. What measures could your school take to solve a problem? Consider the following: inadequate student parking, poor-quality snacks and food, long lines at registration, insufficient course offerings, excessive fees, lack of recreational facilities, poor bookstore service at busy times, inadequate computer laboratories, or poor appearance of grounds and buildings.

Related Web Site: www.toastmasters.org/tips/htm

2.11 Interviewing a Pro. Interview two or three individuals in your professional field. How is oral communication important in this profession? Does the need for oral skills change as one advances? What suggestions can this individual make for developing proficient oral communication skills among newcomers to the field? Discuss your findings with your class.

2.12 Planning a Meeting. Assume that at the next meeting of your students' organization you will discuss preparations for a careers day in the spring. The group will hear reports from committees working on speakers, business recruiters, publicity, reservations of school space, setup of booths, and any other matters you can think of. As president of your student organization, (a) prepare an agenda for the meeting and (b) compose your introductory remarks to open the meeting. Your instructor may ask you to submit these two documents or use them in staging an actual meeting in class.

2.13 Searching the Internet: Nonverbal Videos. As a research assistant in your department, you have been asked to locate educational videos about nonverbal communication. Use a search engine to search the World Wide Web. Submit a list of your findings to your instructor.

2.14 Connecting With E-Mail: Presentation Butterflies. Send an e-mail message to your instructor describing the fears or anxieties that you have experienced when presenting a speech, and then list the methods you plan to try in order to reduce your fears.

GRAMMAR/MECHANICS CHECKUP—2

Pronouns

Review Sections 1.07–1.09 in the Grammar/Mechanics Handbook. Then study each of the following statements. In the space provided, write the word that completes the statement correctly and the number of the G/M principle illustrated. When you finish, compare your responses with those provided. If your responses differ, carefully study the principles in parentheses.

Example: The Recreation and Benefits Committee will be submitting *(its, their)* report soon.

its   (1.09d)

1. I was expecting the manager to call. Was it *(he, him)* who left the message? _____
2. Every one of the members of the men's soccer team had to move *(his car, their cars)* before the game could begin. _____
3. A serious disagreement between management and *(he, him)* caused his resignation. _____
4. Does anyone in the office know for *(who, whom)* this stationery was ordered? _____
5. It looks as if *(her's, hers)* is the only report that cites electronic sources. _____
6. Mrs. Simmons asked my friend and *(I, me, myself)* to help her complete the work. _____
7. My friend and *(I, me, myself)* were also asked to work on Saturday. _____
8. Both printers were sent for repairs, but *(yours, your's)* will be returned shortly. _____
9. Give the budget figures to *(whoever, whomever)* asked for them. _____
10. Everyone except the broker and *(I, me, myself)* claimed a share of the commission. _____
11. No one knows that problem better than *(he, him, himself)*. _____
12. Investment brochures and information were sent to *(we, us)* shareholders. _____
13. If any one of the women tourists has lost *(their, her)* scarf, she should see the driver. _____

14. Neither the glamour nor the excitement of the position had lost *(its, it's, their)* appeal.
15. Any new subscriber may cancel *(their, his or her)* subscription within the first month.

---

1. he (1.08b)   3. him (1.08c)   5. hers (1.08d)   7. I (1.08a)   9. whoever (1.08j)   11. he (1.08f)
13. her (1.09c)   15. his or her (1.09b)

GRAMMAR/MECHANICS CHALLENGE—2

Document for Revision

The following short presentation abstract has faults in grammar, spelling, punctuation, capitalization, word use, number form, and proofreading. Study the guidelines in the Grammar/Mechanics Handbook and what you learned in the chapter. Then, use standard proofreading marks (see Appendix B) to correct the errors. When you finish, your instructor can show you the revised version of this abstract.

Ineffective Writing

Visual Aids

Before making a business presentation consider this wise proverb, "Tell me, I forget. Show me; I remember. Involve me; I understand." Your goals as a speaker are to make listeners understand remember and act on your ideas, include visual aides to get them interested and involved. 4 of the most popular visuals are: overhead transparencys, computer visuals, and handouts.

Overhead transparencies. Student and proffesional speakers alike rely on the overhead projecter for many reasons. Most meeting areas are equiped with projectors and screens. Moreover acetate transparencys for the overhead are inexpensive, they are easily prepared on a computer or copier; and they are simple to use.

Computer visuals. With todays greatly improved softwear programs, you can create multimedia presentations with your personel computer. One of the most popular presentation programs are PowerPoint. Slides may be projected on a PC monitor, a TV moniter, or a LCD (liquid crystal display panel. Presentation softwear are becoming very popular because they enable you and I to produce professional-looking programs. At a very low cost.

Slides. Slides deliver excelent resolution, creates an impression of professionalism, and they can be seen by large groups. Yet, their cost, inflexibility, and fairly difficult preparation off-set there advantages. Moreover, because they must be projected in a darkened room; speakers loose eye contact with the audience. He runs the risk of the problem of putting the viewers to sleep.

<u>Handouts.</u> You can enhance and compliment your presentations by distributing pictures, outlines, brochures, articals, charts, summarys, or other suppliments. Audience members apreciate handouts because it provides ready made notes. You should, however, hold in abeyance the distribution of handouts until such time as you are finished.

USING SOFTWARE TO MAKE PROFESSIONAL PRESENTATIONS

A powerful presentation may be the sizzle that sells the steak—whether convincing management to fund a project or pitching a new product to prospective buyers.

The latest presentation programs let even amateurs produce remarkable results. These programs contain sophisticated, though easy-to-use, tutorials and templates. You can add excitement by including special transition effects and simple animation. With a little advanced know-how and special equipment, you can add graphics, video, and sound to produce professional-quality slide shows. Moreover, you can print audience handouts and speaker notes from the slides you prepare.

Presentation software programs like Microsoft PowerPoint and Corel Presentations enable you to produce 35mm slides, black-and-white or colour printouts, and transparencies. These programs let you use automatic-build slides to add points one at a time for the most dramatic unveiling of your ideas.

USING AN OUTLINER

Most people plan a presentation with an "outliner," a feature that helps you divide your topic into main and subpoints. For example, a travel agency presentation might contain four main headings, two of which are (1) international tours and (2) domestic tours. The outliner would prompt you in developing each main heading. International tours might include three subheadings such as (a) cruise adventures, (b) horticultural explorations, and (c) excursions in the Orient.

BUILDING BULLET POINTS

You can easily translate an outline into headings and bullet points. Each main topic becomes a slide heading. Subheadings become bullet points. Experts recommend no more than five levels of subtopics for any presentation. Each bulleted item should contain no more than seven words. The bulleted text prompts you and emphasizes important points. Bullets also help audience members visualize the information to remember. Remember, though, that bullet points summarize; they don't tell the whole story.

MAKING MASTER SLIDES

Slide is the term for each formatted frame, whether it takes the form of a transparency, 35mm slide, or computer screen. A master slide can include your company name or logo or perhaps the name of the presentation. Select appropriate colours (usually from a template) for good contrast. Use recurring visual elements (colour combination, logo, and so forth) for all frames that develop the same subtopic.

Avoiding Information Overload

The best presentation slides contain no more than 30 five-digit numbers or 36 words arranged in no more than six lines. If you crowd the slide, the audience strains and the impact of the presentation dwindles. Information should fill two-thirds to three-fourths of the screen. Select solid fonts in a wide, bold style.

Application. Use a presentation program to prepare slides to illustrate a talk before your class. If you are unfamiliar with these software programs, visit your computer lab or a computer graphics class for a demonstration. If this is impossible, invite a businessperson, classmate, faculty member, friend, or vendor to make a presentation before your class with visual aids made from a software program. Evaluate the advantages and disadvantages of using presentation software in making business reports.

Related Web Site: www.yorku.ca/teachtec/archive/summer96/ppt/benefits.htm

UNIT 2

DEVELOPING WRITING TOOLS

CHAPTER 3

DEVELOPING BASIC WRITING TECHNIQUES

Plain language is a technique of organizing information in ways that make sense to the reader; thinking about your reader first and foremost and using language that is appropriate for your audience.[1]

CATHY CHAPMAN, past director of the National Literacy Secretariat and a key person in the Canadian government's plain-language implementation program

Learning Objectives

1. Make your writing more readable by using plain language and by substituting familiar words for unfamiliar words.
2. Achieve a forceful style by using precise verbs, concrete nouns, and vivid adjectives.
3. Recognize and avoid unnecessary jargon.
4. Recognize and avoid slang and clichés.
5. Eliminate repetitious words and redundancies.
6. Replace outdated expressions with more current expressions.
7. Develop a concise writing style by avoiding wordy prepositional phrases and long lead-ins.
8. Recognize and avoid needless adverbs and expletives.

One of the tasks assigned to the National Literacy Secretariat was to change the way governments in Canada communicate. The Government of Canada's official communications policy now requires public servants to use plain language to inform the public about government policies, programs, and services. Here's an example of the kind of hard-to-understand language the NLS is working to overcome:

> *Any statement contained in a document incorporated or deemed to be incorporated by reference herein shall be deemed to be modified or superseded for purposes of this document to the extent that a statement contained herein or in any other subsequently filed document which also is*

or is deemed to be incorporated by a reference herein modifies or supersedes such statement.[2]

Make any sense? Not to most people. Governments and leaders in the legal field alike have vowed to replace this kind of dense writing in documents with "plain language." But exactly what is plain language? Cathy Chapman, past director of the National Literacy Secretariat, puts it this way: "Plain language is a technique of organizing information in ways that make sense to the reader."[3]

In this book you'll learn how to communicate meaning, not befuddle readers. Plain language is clear, concise writing that enlightens the reader about your message. Good writers use many techniques to achieve this end. Most of these techniques revolve around the words you choose and the way you join them.

This chapter and the next provide many practical writing techniques that will help you write clearly. You'll learn to express your ideas with plain language, familiar words, and conciseness. You'll study how to use forceful words, precise verbs, concrete nouns, and vivid adjectives. You'll also be taught to avoid clichés, repetitious and redundant words, and outdated expressions.

PLAIN LANGUAGE

Good writers use plain language to express clear meaning. They do not use showy words and ambiguous expressions in an effort to dazzle or confuse readers. They write to express ideas, not to impress others.

In the past, business, legal, and government documents—as illustrated in the excerpt quoted above—were written in an inflated style that obscured meaning. This style of writing has been given various terms, such as *legalese, bureaucratese, doublespeak*, and the *official style*. It may be used intentionally to mask meaning. It may be an attempt to show off the writer's intelligence and education. Or it may result from lack of training. What do you think the manager's intention is in the following message?

> Personnel assigned vehicular space in the adjacent areas are hereby advised that utilization will be suspended temporarily Friday morning.

Employees will probably have to read that sentence several times before they understand that they are being advised not to park in the lot next door on Friday morning.

In an attempt to overcome this ambiguous style, the National Literacy Secretariat has published a guide for all government workers titled *Plain Language: Pure and Simple*. Many of its suggestions for writing clearly are covered in this chapter. In the United States, state governments are demanding that consumer disclosure statements and contracts be written in "plain English." This means a clear, simple style that uses everyday words. But the plain language movement goes beyond word choice. It also means writing that is easy to follow, well organized, and appropriately divided. A plain language document should include writing techniques you will study shortly—such as using familiar words, concise wording, active voice, parallel construction, and headings.

Don't be impressed by high-sounding language and legalese, such as *herein, thereafter, hereinafter, whereas*, and similar expressions. Your writing will be better understood if you use plain language.

Inflated, unnatural writing that is intended to impress readers more often confuses them.

FAMILIAR WORDS

Familiar words are more meaningful to readers.

Clear messages contain words that are familiar and meaningful to the receiver. How can we know what is meaningful to a given receiver? Although we can't know with certainty, we can avoid long or unfamiliar words that have simpler synonyms. Whenever possible in business communication, substitute short, common, simple words. Don't, however, give up a precise word if it says exactly what you mean.

Less Familiar Words	Simple Alternatives
ascertain	find out
conceptualize	see
encompass	include
hypothesize	guess
monitor	check
operational	working
option	choice
perpetuate	continue
perplexing	troubling
reciprocate	return
stipulate	require
terminate	end
utilize	use

PRECISE VERBS

Precise verbs make your writing forceful, clear, and lively.

Effective writing creates meaningful images in the mind of the reader. Such writing is sparked by robust, concrete, and descriptive words. Ineffective writing is often dulled by insipid, abstract, and generalized words. The most direct way to improve lifeless writing is through the effective use of verbs. Verbs not only indicate the action of the subject but also deliver the force of the sentence. Select verbs carefully so that the reader can visualize precisely what is happening.

General: Our sales representative will *contact* you next month.
Precise: Our sales representative will *(telephone, write, visit)* . . .

General: The vice president *said* that we should contribute.
Precise: The vice president *(urged, pleaded, demanded)* . . .

General: We must *consider* this problem.
Precise: We must *(clarify, remedy, rectify)* . . .

General: The newspaper was *affected* by the strike.
Precise: The newspaper was *(crippled, silenced, demoralized)* . . .

The power of a verb is diminished when it is needlessly converted to a noun. This happens when verbs such as *acquire, establish*, and *develop* are made into nouns *(acquisition, establishment,* and *development)*. These nouns then receive the central emphasis in the sentence. In the following pairs of sentences, observe how forceful the original verbs are compared with their noun forms.

Strong: The city *acquired* park lands recently. (Verb centred)
Weak: *Acquisition* of park lands was made recently by the city. (Noun centred)

Strong:	Mr. Miller and Mrs. Dueck *discussed* credit-card billing. (Verb centred)
Weak:	Mr. Miller and Mrs. Dueck had a *discussion* concerning credit-card billing. (Noun centred)
Strong:	Both companies must *approve* the merger. (Verb centred)
Weak:	Both companies must grant *approval* of the merger. (Noun centred)

CONCRETE NOUNS

Nouns name persons, places, and things. Abstract nouns name concepts that are difficult to visualize, such as *automation, function, justice, institution, integrity, form, judgment,* and *environment.* Concrete nouns name objects that are more easily imagined, such as *desk, car,* and *lightbulb.* Nouns describing a given object can range from the very abstract to the very concrete—for example, *object, motor vehicle, car, convertible,* and *Mustang.* All of these words or phrases can be used to describe a Mustang convertible. However, a reader would have difficulty envisioning a Mustang convertible when given just the word *object* or even *motor vehicle* or *car.*

In business writing, help your reader "see" what you mean by using concrete language.

Concrete nouns help readers visualize the meanings of words.

General	**Concrete**
a *change* in our budget	a *10 percent reduction* in our budget
that company's product	*NEC's Ultra Express pager*
a *person* called	*Mrs. Tomei, the administrative assistant,* called
we *improved* the assembly line	we *installed 26 advanced Unimate robots* on the assembly line

VIVID ADJECTIVES

Including highly descriptive, dynamic adjectives makes writing more vivid and concrete. Be careful, though, not to overuse them or to lose objectivity in selecting them.

A thesaurus (on your computer or in a book) helps you select precise words and increase your vocabulary.

General:	The report was on time.
Vivid:	The *detailed 12-page* report was submitted on time.
General:	Carlos needs a better truck.
Vivid:	Carlos needs a *rugged, four-wheel-drive* truck.
General:	We enjoyed the movie.
Vivid:	We enjoyed the *entertaining* and *absorbing* movie.
Overkill:	We enjoyed the *gutsy, exciting, captivating,* and *thoroughly marvellous* movie.

JARGON

Except in certain specialized contexts, you should avoid jargon and unnecessary technical terms. Jargon is special terminology that is peculiar to a particular activity or field. For example, geologists speak knowingly of *exfoliation, calcareous ooze*, and *siliceous particles*. Engineers are familiar with phrases such as *infrared processing flags, output latches*, and *movable symbology*. Telecommunications experts use such words and phrases as *protocol, mode*, and *asynchronous transmission*.

Every field has its own special vocabulary. Using that vocabulary within the field is acceptable and even necessary for accurate, efficient communication. Don't use specialized terms, however, if you have reason to believe that your reader may misunderstand them. Consider the following example: "Our team will need a bandwidth-intensive meeting with the folks in Marketing to get by the firewalls Engineering keeps putting up." The terms *bandwidth* and *firewall* are appropriate to the information technology field. But they are used inappropriately to describe an important meeting and problems or questions raised by a company's engineering department.

SLANG

Slang is composed of informal words with arbitrary and extravagantly changed meanings. Slang words quickly go out of fashion because they are no longer appealing when everyone begins to understand them. Consider the slang in the following "explanation" offered by a company spokesperson when asked why an announced business deal was being cancelled: "We have an awful lot of other things in the pipeline. This deal has more wiggle room so they put it on the back burner for now." The spokesperson added, however, that the partners will discuss the deal again since "there is no getting around this one." The meaning here, if the speaker really intended to impart any, is considerably obscured by the use of slang. Good communicators, of course, aim at clarity and avoid unintelligible slang.

CLICHÉS

Clichés are expressions that have become exhausted by overuse. These expressions lack not only freshness but also clarity. Some have no meaning for people who are new to our culture. The following partial list contains representative clichés you should avoid in business writing.

below the belt	last but not least
better than new	off the hook
beyond the shadow of a doubt	on the back burner
the big picture	outside the box
easier said than done	out to lunch
exception to the rule	pass with flying colours
fill the bill	riding high
first and foremost	shoot from the hip
hard facts	stand your ground
keep your nose to the grindstone	true to form

REPETITIOUS WORDS

Good communicators vary their words to avoid unintentional repetition. Observe how leaden and monotonous the following personnel announcement sounds:

> Employees will be able to elect an additional six employees to serve with the four previously elected employees who currently comprise the employees' board of directors. To ensure representation, swing-shift employees will be electing one swing-shift employee as their sole representative.

The unconscious repetition of words creates monotonous and boring reading.

In this example the word *employee* is used six times. In addition, the second sentence uses the word *representation* near its beginning and ends with the similar word *representative*. An easier-to-read version follows:

> Employees will be able to elect an additional six representatives to serve with the four previously elected members of the employees' board of directors. To ensure representation, swing-shift workers will elect their own board member.

In the second version synonyms *(representatives, members, workers)* replace *employee*. The second sentence has been reworked by using a pronoun *(their)* and by substituting *board member* for the repetitious *representative*. Variety of expression can be achieved by searching for appropriate synonyms and by substituting pronouns.

Good writers are also alert to the overuse of the articles *a, an*, and particularly *the*. Often the word *the* can simply be omitted.

Wordy: The deregulation of the telecommunications industry has caused a change in the cost of long-distance calling.

Improved: Telecommunications industry deregulation has changed long-distance calling costs.

REDUNDANT WORDS

Repetition of words to achieve emphasis or effective transition is an important writing technique, which is discussed in forthcoming chapters. The needless repetition, however, of words whose meanings are clearly implied by other words is a writing fault called *redundancy*. For example, in the expression *final outcome*, the word *final* is redundant and should be omitted, since *outcome* implies finality. Learn to avoid redundant expressions such as the following:

Redundant expressions (such as *combined together*) needlessly repeat their meanings.

absolutely essential	*final* outcome
adequate *enough*	*grateful* thanks
advance warning	*mutual* cooperation
basic fundamentals	*necessary* prerequisite
big *in size*	*new* beginning
combined *together*	*past* history
consensus *of opinion*	reason *why*
continue *on*	red *in colour*
each *and every*	refer *back*
exactly identical	repeat *again*
few *in number*	*true* facts

OUTDATED EXPRESSIONS

Replace outdated expressions with modern phrasing.

The world of business has changed greatly in the past century or two. Yet, some business writers continue to use antiquated phrases and expressions borrowed from a period when the "language of business" was exceedingly formal and flowery. In the 1800s, letter writers "begged to state" and "trusted to be favoured with" and assured their readers that they "remained their humble servants." Such language suggests quill pens, sealing wax, and sleeve guards. Avoid using stale expressions that linger from the past. Replace outdated expressions such as those shown here with more modern phrasing:

Outdated Expressions	Modern Phrasing
are in receipt of	have received
as per your request	at your request
attached hereto	attached
enclosed please find	enclosed is/are
kindly advise	please write (or fax or e-mail)
pursuant to your request	at your request
thanking you in advance	thank you
I trust that	I think, I believe
under separate cover	separately

CONCISE WORDING

Improve your writing by imagining that you will be fined $10 for every unnecessary word.

In business, time is indeed money. Applied to writing, this idea means that concise messages save reading time and, thus, money. In addition, messages that are written directly and efficiently are easier to read and comprehend. Say what you have to say and then stop.

Developing a concise writing style requires conscious effort. The scientist and philosopher Blaise Pascal once apologized for the length of a letter. He explained to his correspondent that the letter would have been shorter if he had had more time.

Taking the time to make your writing concise means that you look for other—shorter—ways to say what you intend. Examine every sentence that you write. Could the thought be conveyed in fewer words? In addition to eliminating repetitious words and redundant words, you should concentrate on shortening wordy phrases, deleting excessive prepositions, avoiding long lead-ins, omitting needless adverbs, and eliminating expletives.

Thomas Jefferson said, "The most valuable of all talents is that of never using two words when one will do."

Wordy	Concise	Wordy	Concise
at a later date	later	fully cognizant of	aware
at this point in time	now	in addition to the above	also
afford an opportunity	allow	in spite of the fact that	even though
are of the opinion that	believe	in the event that	if
at the present time	now, presently	in the amount of	for
despite the fact that	though	in the near future	soon
due to the fact that	because, since	in view of the fact that	because
during the time	while	inasmuch as	since
feel free to	please	more or less	about
for the period of	for	until such time as	until

WORDY PREPOSITIONAL PHRASES

Some wordy prepositional phrases may be replaced by single adverbs. For example, *in the normal course of events* becomes *normally* and *as a general rule* becomes *generally*.

Wordy:	Datatech approached the merger *in a careful manner.*
Concise:	Datatech approached the merger *carefully.*

Wordy:	The merger will *in all probability* be effected.
Concise:	The merger will *probably* be effected.

Wordy:	We have taken this action *in very few* cases.
Concise:	We have *seldom* taken this action.

LONG LEAD-INS

Delete unnecessary introductory words. The meat of the sentence often follows the words *that* or *because*.

Wordy:	*I am sending you this announcement to let all of you know that* the office will be closed Monday.
Concise:	The office will be closed Monday.

Wordy:	*You will be interested to learn that* you may now use the automatic banking machine at our Lynwood branch.
Concise:	You may now use the automatic banking machine at our Lynwood branch.

Wordy:	*I am writing this letter because* Professor Lydia Brunton suggested that your organization was hiring trainees.
Concise:	Professor Lydia Brunton suggested that your organization was hiring trainees.

NEEDLESS ADVERBS

Eliminating adverbs such as *very, definitely, quite, completely, extremely, really, actually, somewhat,* and *rather* streamlines your writing. Omitting these intensifiers also makes you sound more credible and businesslike.

Wordy:	We *actually* did not *really* give his plan a *very* fair trial.
Concise:	We did not give his plan a fair trial.

Wordy:	Professor Chiu offered an *extremely* fine course that students *definitely* appreciated.
Concise:	Professor Chiu offered a fine course that students appreciated.

EXPLETIVES

In the study of language, expletives are sentence fillers such as *there* and occasionally *it.* Avoid expletives that fatten sentences with excess words.

Wordy:	There are three vice presidents who report directly to the president.
Concise:	Three vice presidents report directly to the president.
Wordy:	It is the client who should apply for licensing.
Concise:	The client should apply for licensing.

SUMMING UP AND LOOKING FORWARD

In this chapter you learned basic techniques for writing simple, concise, and plain language. These writing techniques include substituting familiar words for unfamiliar ones, avoiding unnecessary jargon, and eliminating legalese and slang. You were encouraged to develop a forceful writing style by using precise verbs, concrete nouns, and vivid adjectives. Other key writing techniques include avoiding clichés, repetitive words, redundancies, and outdated expressions. Finally, you studied specific techniques for achieving conciseness by eliminating wordy prepositional phrases, long lead-ins, needless adverbs, and expletives.

The next chapter presents advanced writing techniques. You'll learn secrets for achieving conversational language, for emphasizing reader benefits, and for developing goodwill. You'll also study techniques for creating emphasis, unity, coherence, and parallelism.

DISCUSSION

1. What are the advantages of using plain language in business documents?
2. Because legal documents are written to be extremely precise, everyone should write like a lawyer. Discuss.
3. How can dull, lifeless writing be made forceful?
4. Because clichés are familiar and have stood the test of time, do they help clarify writing?
5. If your boss writes in a flowery, formal tone and relies on outdated expressions, should you also follow that style?

CHAPTER REVIEW

6. Why are verbs the most important words in sentences?

7. What happens when verbs are converted to nouns (for example, when *acquire* becomes *to make an acquisition*)?

8. Define *jargon*.

9. Provide at least three examples of jargon from your chosen field of specialization.

10. Define *slang*.

11. Give at least three examples of current slang.

12. Define *cliché* and provide at least one example (other than those provided in the chapter) that you have heard frequently.

13. What are articles, and what problem do they present to writers?

14. Define *redundant* and provide an example.

15. Define *expletive* and provide an example.

Writing Improvement Exercises

Familiar Words. Revise the following sentences using simpler language for unfamiliar terms. Assume that you are writing at a level appropriate for typical business communication. Use a dictionary if necessary.

Example: Please ascertain the extent of our fiscal liability.
Revision: Please find out how much we owe.

16. Profits are declining because our sales staff is not cognizant of our competitor's products.

17. He hypothesized that the vehicle was lacking in operational capacity because of a malfunctioning gasket.

18. We can change suppliers only after our contract with OfficePro reaches its termination.

19. The contract stipulates that management must perpetuate the present profit-sharing plan.

20. Numerous employee options are encompassed in the new benefits package.

Precise Verbs. Rewrite these sentences, centring the action in the verbs.

>   **Example:** Sabrina gave an appraisal of our office equipment.
>   **Revision:** Sabrina appraised our office equipment.

21. The engineer made an estimate of the project's duration.

22. Can you bring about a change in our company travel policy?

23. Streamlined procedures will produce the effect of reduction in labour costs.

24. An investigator made a determination of the fire damages.

25. The duty of the comptroller is verification of departmental budgets.

26. Please make a correction in my account to reflect my late payment.

Concrete Nouns and Vivid Adjectives. Revise the following sentences to include concrete and vivid language. Add appropriate words.

>   **Example:** They said it was a long way off.
>   **Revision:** Management officials promised that the merger would not take place for two years.

27. Our new copier is fast.

28. Liam's record indicates that he is a good worker.

29. An employee at my last place of employment was called about my recent job application at a new company.

30. Please contact them soon.

31. They said that the movie they saw was very interesting.

Jargon, Slang, and Clichés. Revise the following sentences using simpler language that would be clear to an average reader. Avoid jargon, slang, and clichés.

Example: Please get to the bottom line and stop beating around the bush.
Revision: Please get to the point and stop wasting time.

32. A glitch in the program caused the program to crash, but we should get back on-line in a flash.

33. Although there is little wiggle room in our budget, by keeping a tight ship we should have this project operational right on target.

34. With regard to our advertising budget, Mr. Singh says that TV is going down the tubes because audiences are being fractionalized into special interest groups.

35. This half-price promotional campaign sounds really gutsy, but I don't think we should touch it with a 10-foot pole.

36. Although she's no hacker, Rachel does like to surf the Net.

Repetition, Redundancy, and Outdated Expressions. Revise the following sentences to eliminate unnecessary repetition, redundancies, and outdated expressions.

Example: Because requests like yours are few in number, I will refer this matter back to the manager, pursuant to your request.
Revision: Because requests like yours are rare, I will refer this matter to our manager.

37. We extended our grateful thanks to the production manager who was able to prevent the oil damage from damaging the floor.

38. We are in receipt of your letter of October 3, and as per your request, we are sending you two complimentary passes to the conference.

39. The contract will be considered a valid contract if the terms of said contract receive the mutual approval of all parties who will sign the contract.

40. Attached please find instructions for completing the above-referenced claim.

41. First and foremost, we plan on emphasizing an instructional training program.

Concise Wording. Revise the following sentences to eliminate wordy phrases, wordy prepositional phrases, long lead-ins, imprecise words, and needless adverbs such as *really* and *quite*.

> **Example:** This is to notify you that our accountant actually couldn't find anything wrong with your report.
>
> **Revision:** Our accountant could find no fault with your report.

42. This memorandum is to inform you that all books and magazines borrowed from the library must be taken back to the library by June 1.

43. This is to let you know that you should feel free to use your credit card for the purpose of purchasing household items for a period of 60 days.

44. In view of the fact that we are at this point in time nearly ready to commence our advertising campaign, we must really insist that you submit your report.

45. In the normal course of events, we would wait until such time as we could actually check your credit.

Expletives and Review. Revise the following sentences to avoid expletives (including *there* and *it*). Also employ any other writing techniques you have learned.

> **Example:** Under ordinary circumstances, there are actually three technicians here to repair appliances.
>
> **Revision:** Ordinarily, three technicians are here to repair appliances.

46. There are really at least five advantages that computers have over a human decision maker.

47. As a general rule, there are multitudinous employers looking for qualified applicants.

48. Market researchers learned that in all probability there is no single factor causing the decline of interest in our product.

49. In very few cases is it necessary for us to revoke the privileges of our credit cards.

50. Due to the fact that there are private previews arranged for our preferred customers, the sale for the general public cannot really open until October 1.

51. In spite of the fact that there are four exactly identical movie theatres provided by Cinemax, patrons are complaining.

ACTIVITIES AND CASES

3.1 Locating Legalese, Bureaucratese, and Jargon. Find examples of legalese, bureaucratese, and jargon in newspapers, magazines, or other documents. Bring them to class for discussion. Continue to search for examples as your course continues.

Related Web Site: www.plainlanguagenetwork.org

3.2 Searching the Internet: Plain Language. You are the administrative assistant to a vice-president of a cellular telephone service. She has been given the task of simplifying the company's customer application for cellular telephone service. She asks you to find anything you can about plain language contracts in general and cellular telephone contracts in particular. You might first try the World Wide Web with keyword searches using expressions such as "plain language contract" or "plain language movement."

You might also try some of the links to on-line newspapers or magazines available through your school library's on-line search tools. If you find nothing on the Web, try using your library's other resources, such as CD-ROMs or newspaper or magazine databases. Print a copy of whatever you find and submit it to your instructor. Identify your findings carefully and tell how you found the references.

3.3 Connecting With E-Mail: Here's What I Learned. Your manager allowed you and three other members of your department to attend a seminar titled "Effective Writing Techniques for Business Communicators." You have just returned from the seminar, and your manager asks you to send her a brief message summarizing three of the most important techniques you learned. Select three techniques from this chapter. Send a message to your manager (your instructor, in this case) with your summary. Provide an original example of each.

GRAMMAR/MECHANICS CHECKUP—3

Verbs

Review Sections 1.10–1.15 in the Grammar/Mechanics Handbook. Then study each of the following statements. Underline any verbs that are used incorrectly. In the space provided write the correct form and the number of the G/M principle illustrated. If a sentence is correct, write *C*. When you finish, compare your responses with those provided. If your responses differ, study carefully the principles in parentheses.

Example: Our inventory of raw materials <u>were</u> presented as collateral for a short-term loan.	was (1.10c)

1. Located across town is a research institute and our product-testing facility.   _____
2. Can you tell me if a current list with all customers' names and addresses have been sent to marketing?   _____
3. The Bank of Montreal, along with the other large national banks, offer a variety of savings plans.   _____
4. Neither the plans that this bank offers nor the service just rendered by the customer service representative are impressive.   _____

_____ 5. Locating a bank and selecting a savings/chequing plan often require considerable research and study.

_____ 6. The budget analyst wants to know if the Equipment Committee are ready to recommend a printer.

_____ 7. Either of the printers that the committee selects is acceptable to the budget analyst.

_____ 8. If Mr. Catalano had chose the Maximizer Plus savings plan, his money would have earned maximum interest.

_____ 9. Although the applications have laid there for two weeks, they may still be submitted.

_____ 10. Mrs. Gebhardt acts as if she was the manager.

_____ 11. One of the reasons that our Yukon sales branches have been so costly are the high cost of living.

In the space provided write the letter of the sentence that illustrates consistency in subject, voice, and mood.

_____ 12. (a) If you read the instructions, the answer can be found.
(b) If you will read the instructions, you will find the answer.

_____ 13. (a) All employees must fill out application forms; only then will you be insured.
(b) All employees must fill out application forms; only then will they be insured.

_____ 14. (a) First, take an inventory of equipment; then, order supplies.
(b) First, take an inventory of equipment; then, supplies must be ordered.

_____ 15. (a) Select a savings plan that suits your needs; deposits may be made immediately.
(b) Select a savings plan that suits your needs; begin making deposits immediately.

---

1. *are* for *is* (1.10e)   3. *offers* for *offer* (1.10d)   5. C (1.10f)   7. C (1.10h)   9. *lain* for *laid* (1.15)
11. *is* for *are* (1.10c)   13. b (1.15c)   15. b (1.15c)

GRAMMAR/MECHANICS CHALLENGE—3

Document for Revision

The following memo has many faults in grammar, spelling, punctuation, capitalization, word use, and number form. Study the guidelines in the Grammar/Mechanics Handbook to sharpen your skills. Then, using standard proofreading marks (see Appendix B), correct the errors. When you finish, your instructor can show you a revised version of this memo.

Ineffective Writing

TO:	Jamal Williams, Vice-President	DATE: July 24, 200x
FROM:	Roxanne Crosley, Manager, Payroll	
SUBJECT:	Departmental Error	

This is to inform you that last month our central accounting department changed

it's computer program for payroll processing. When this computer change was

operationalized some of the stored information was not transfered to the new information database. As a consequence of this manoeuvre several errors occured in employee paycheques (1) parking payments were not deducted (2) pension deductions were not made and (3) errors occured in federal income tax calculations.

Each and every one of the employees effected have been contacted; and this error has been elucidated. My staff and myself has been working overtime to replace all the missing data; so that corrections can be made by the August 30th payroll run.

Had I made a verification of the true facts before the paycheques were ran this slip-up would not have materialized. To prevent such an error in the future I decided to take the bull by the horns. At this point in time I have implemented a rigorous new verification system. I am of the firm opinion that utilization of the new system will definitely prevent this perplexing event from reoccuring.

Communication Workshop: Ethics

MAKING ETHICAL DECISIONS

In your career you will doubtless face times when you are torn by conflicting loyalties. Should you tell the truth and risk your job? Should you be loyal to your friends even if it means bending the rules? Should you be tactful or totally honest? Is it your duty to help your company make a profit or should you be socially responsible?

Being ethical, according to the experts, means doing the right thing *given the circumstances*. Each set of circumstances requires analyzing issues, evaluating choices, and acting responsibly. Resolving ethical issues is never easy, but the task can be made less difficult if you know how to identify key issues. Asking yourself the following questions may be helpful.

- **Is the action you are considering legal?** No matter who asks you to do it or how important you feel the result will be, avoid anything that is prohibited by law. Giving a kickback to a buyer for a large order is illegal, even if you suspect that others in your field do it and you know that without the kickback you will lose the sale.

- **How would you see the problem if you were on the opposite side?** Looking at all sides of an issue helps you gain perspective. Consider the issue of mandatory drug testing among employees. From management's viewpoint such testing could stop drug abuse, improve job performance, and potentially lower workers' compensation costs. From the employees' viewpoint mandatory testing reflects a lack of trust of employees and constitutes an invasion of privacy. By weighing both sides of an issue, you can arrive at a more equitable solution.

- **What are the alternative solutions?** Consider all dimensions of other options. Would one alternative be more ethical than any of the others? Under the circumstances, is the alternative feasible? Can an alternative solution be implemented with a minimum amount of disruption and with a high degree of probable success?

- **Can you discuss the problem with someone whose opinion you value?** Suppose you feel ethically bound to report accurate information to a client, even though your boss has ordered you not to do so. Talking about your dilemma with a co-worker or with a colleague in your field might give you helpful insights and lead to possible alternatives.

- **How would you feel if your family, friends, employer, or co-workers learned of your action?** If the thought of revealing your action publicly produces fear, your choice is probably not a wise one. Losing the faith of your friends or the confidence of your customers is not worth whatever short-term gains might be realized.

Application. After six months of looking, recent graduate Kevin M. was offered a job with Company X. A week after starting to work, he received a better offer from Company Y. Kevin wants very much to leave Company X to accept Company Y's offer. In small groups or in a class discussion, apply the ethical guidelines suggested here. What action would you recommend for Kevin?

Related Web Site:
University of British Columbia Centre for Applied Ethics: ethics.ubc.ca/

APPLYING ADVANCED WRITING TECHNIQUES

Write naturally—the way you talk. Adding needless business jargon confuses readers more often than it impresses them. Conversational language works.[1]

CYNTHIA SELLEY, human resources manager,
Training and Development, Boeing Canada Technology

Learning Objectives

1. Distinguish between formal and conversational language.
2. Use positive language.
3. Recognize and develop reader benefits.
4. Use inclusive language and replace sexist terms.
5. Emphasize important ideas and de-emphasize unimportant ones.
6. Develop sentence unity by avoiding zigzag writing, mixed constructions, and misplaced modifiers.
7. Match sentence parts to achieve parallelism.
8. Use active- and passive-voice verbs strategically.
9. Achieve paragraph coherence.

Writing naturally, as Cynthia Selley advises, sounds easy. But it's not. It takes instruction and practice. You've already learned some techniques for writing naturally (using familiar words and plain language, and avoiding jargon, slang, clichés, and redundant words). This chapter presents additional writing tips that will help make your communication not only natural but also effective. These advanced writing techniques include how to use conversational language, express ideas positively, choose inclusive language, emphasize and de-emphasize ideas, and develop unity and coherence. Other important writing techniques covered in this chapter include parallelism, strategic use of active- and passive-voice verbs, and paragraph coherence.

CONVERSATIONAL LANGUAGE

Most business letters, memos, and reports replace conversation. Thus, they are most effective when they convey their message in an informal, conversational tone instead of a formal, pretentious one. Cynthia Selley and writing professionals recommend a casual, conversational tone in business writing. But achieving this tone is harder than one might think. Why?

Big words, complex sentences, and abstractions make writing sound formal and distant.

Many writers tend to become formal or distant when they put words on paper. They seem to undergo a personality change when they write. Perhaps this is a result of composition training in schools. Many students developed a writing style that impressed the instructor. They were rewarded when they used big words and complex sentences, even if their ideas were not altogether clear. After leaving school, some writers continue to use techniques learned long ago. Instead of writing as they speak, they construct long and complex sentences, and expressing their thoughts becomes confusing. Rather than using familiar pronouns such as *I*, *we*, and *you*, they depersonalize their writing by relying on third-person constructions such as *the undersigned, the writer,* and *the affected party*. Smart writers, by the way, use *I* sparingly and *you* liberally.

To develop a warm, friendly tone in your letters, imagine that you are sitting next to the reader. Talk to the reader with words that sound comfortable to you. Don't be afraid to use an occasional contraction such as *we're* or *I'll*. Avoid legal terminology, technical words, and formal constructions. Your writing will be easier to read and understand if it sounds like the following conversational examples:

You can develop a conversational tone in your written messages by using familiar words, occasional contractions, and first-person pronouns.

Formal:	All employees are herewith instructed to return the appropriately designated contracts to the undersigned.
Conversational:	Please return your contracts to me.
Formal:	Pertaining to your order, we must verify the sizes that your organization requires prior to consignment of your order to our shipper.
Conversational:	We'll send your order as soon as we confirm the sizes you need.
Formal:	The writer wishes to inform the above-referenced individual that subsequent payments may henceforth be sent to the address cited below.
Conversational:	Your payments should now be sent to us in Lakewood.

POSITIVE LANGUAGE

Readers learn more when you write positively.

The tone of a letter is considerably improved if you use positive rather than negative language. It's uplifting and pleasant to focus on the positive. Moreover, positive language generally conveys more information than negative language does. Positive wording tells what is and what can be done rather than what isn't and what can't be done. For example, *Your order cannot be shipped by January 10*, is not nearly so informative as *Your order will be shipped January 20*.

Analyze what you have to say, and then present it in positive language. Here are examples of statements in which the negative tone can be revised to reflect a positive impression.

Negative: We are unable to send your shipment until we receive proof of your payment.

Positive: We are happy to have your business and look forward to sending your shipment as soon as we receive your payment.

Negative: We are sorry that we must reject your application for credit at this time.

Positive: At this time we can serve you on a cash basis only.

Negative: If you fail to pass the exam, you will not qualify.

Positive: You'll qualify by passing the exam.

Negative: Although I've never had a paid position before, I have worked as an intern in an lawyer's office while completing my degree requirements.

Positive: My experience in a lawyer's office and my recent training in legal procedures and computer applications can be assets to your organization.

READER BENEFITS

Smart communicators know that the chance of success of any message is greatly improved by emphasizing reader benefits. This means making readers see how the message affects and benefits them personally.

It is human nature for individuals to be most concerned with matters that relate directly to themselves. This is a necessary condition of existence. If we weren't interested in attending to our own needs, we could not survive.

Most of us are also concerned with others. We are interested in their lives, and we care about their feelings. Individuals who are successful in the business world—and in their personal lives—often possess a trait called *empathy*. Empathy is the capacity to put yourself into another's position and experience that person's feelings.

Empathetic business writers care about readers and express that concern in their communication. They try to see the reader's viewpoint. Place yourself in the reader's position. How would you react? How would you feel? When you read a message, you're very likely thinking, consciously or unconsciously, "What's in it for me?" Now put the shoe on the other foot. When you create a message, say to yourself, "What's in it for the reader?" In what aspect of your message will the reader be most interested? How will it benefit the reader? Once you've answered these questions, write your message so that it emphasizes the benefits to the reader.

Be especially alert to the overuse of first-person pronouns such as *I, my, we,* and *our.* These words indicate that the writer is most interested in only one narrow view—the writer's. On the other hand, you should not sacrifice fluency, brevity, and directness to avoid an occasional *I* or *me.*

Compare the following sets of statements. Notice how first-person pronouns are de-emphasized and second-person pronouns *(you, your)* become more obvious when the focus shifts to the benefits and interests of the reader. Some experts refer to this technique as the *you* attitude.

Overuse of the pronouns *I* and *me* suggest that the writer's interests lie with the writer instead of with the reader.

I/we attitude:	I am pleased to offer my customers our Canada First investment program.
You attitude:	You are the first of our customers to be offered our Canada First investment program.
I/we attitude:	We have opened our new bank branch in Newton for your convenience.
You attitude:	You will now be able to use our new Newton branch for all your banking needs.
I/we attitude:	Before we can allow you to write cheques on your account, we request that you sign the enclosed signature card.
You attitude:	For your protection, please sign the enclosed signature card before you begin to write cheques on your account.

INCLUSIVE LANGUAGE

Alert and empathetic business communicators strive to create messages that include rather than exclude. Words, phrases, and images that reflect stereotypes reinforce mistaken assumptions about certain groups or individuals. They also inject bias into our communication. Women, Native people, people with disabilities, and racial or visible minorities have traditionally been most disadvantaged by the negative effects of stereotyping. Biased language not only hampers communication, it also alienates some individuals and excludes others entirely. All of your written, oral, electronic, and visual communication should be inclusive, unbiased, and fair to all individuals and groups.

In Canada, we strive for unbiased communication not just because we like precision, but also because it is the law. Human rights legislation across the country protects against toxic work environments. Biased communication may contribute to just such an environment and as such may violate provincial human rights codes.

Sensitive writers today try to use sex-neutral terms, such as letter carrier *instead of* mailman.

When creating your messages, identify or address people first as individuals, then mention the group to which they belong only if that information is relevant. Job titles should describe, not exclude. Using terms such as *manager, sales clerk,* or *flight attendant* does not suggest the inclusion of one group at the expense of another.

GENDER-INCLUSIVE LANGUAGE

The following suggestions, adapted from *Communicating Without Bias,*[2] will help you use gender-inclusive language in your writing. These suggestions can be used to ensure your language is inclusive for other groups as well.

- *Alternate word order in phrases that include both sexes.* Always putting men first in phrases such as *men and women, boys and girls, he or she, his and hers,* and *male and female* can give the impression that women are less important than men.
- *Identify women as individuals.* Identify a woman as someone's wife, mother, grandmother, or aunt only if it is appropriate in the context and men are or would be described in a similar way in this case.

- *Use generic nouns.* The nouns *fireman* and *mailman* suggest that only men hold these positions. Generic nouns such as *firefighter, letter carrier, salesperson, flight attendant, department head, committee chair, technician,* and *police officer* include both men and women.
- *Avoid feminine suffixes.* Words such as *manageress, waitress,* and *executrix* reinforce the idea that a women in a particular job is an exception and as such should be considered differently than a man in the same job. You can avoid offending your listener or reader by using neutral job titles or functions such as *manager, server,* or *executor*.
- *Use language that reflects equal respect for women and men.* Avoid using demeaning terms for adult women such as *girls, gals,* or *ladies* in situations where you would refer to men as *men.*
- *Use gender as an adjective only if relevant to your message.* The gender adjectives in terms such as *female physician, woman lawyer,* or *female deputy minister* are unnecessary and can suggest a biased attitude. Similarly, avoid using gender adjectives that stigmatize men, as in the term *male nurse.*
- *Use words or phrases that promote inclusivity.* For example, instead of saying *career woman,* consider using *professional, executive* or *businessperson.*
- *Avoid words or phrases that make assumptions about gender.* Phrases and words such as *feminine intuition, the fairer sex, his better half, women's work, ladylike,* and *manfully* assume certain characteristics based only on gender.
- *Describe similar behaviour using similar terms.* To describe men as aggressive or assertive, while describing women as strident or shrill for similar behaviour advances inappropriate stereotypes.
- *Use generic terms when referring to a general group of people.* Unless the intention is to refer only to men, terms such as *human beings, synthetic,* and *staff* or *employees* can replace *man, man-made,* and *manpower.*
- *Find alternatives for masculine pronouns.* When referring to persons whose gender has not been specified, use something other than *he, his,* or *him* to replace a noun that excludes women. Consider the following example:

A stereotype is a standardized, usually oversimplified opinion.

Noninclusive	Every lawyer has ten minutes for *his* summation. (This construction suggests that all lawyers are men.)
Inclusive	All lawyers have ten minutes for *their* summations. (Use a plural noun and plural pronoun.)
	Lawyers have ten minutes for summations. (Omit the pronoun entirely.)
	Every lawyer has ten minutes for *a* summation. (Use an article instead of a pronoun.)
	Every lawyer has ten minutes for *his* or *her* summation. (Use both a masculine and a feminine pronoun.)

Note, however, that the last alternative, which includes a masculine and a feminine pronoun, is wordy and awkward. Don't use it too frequently.

EMPHASIS

When you are talking with someone, you can emphasize your main ideas by saying them loudly, repeating them slowly, or even by pounding the table as you speak! You might raise your eyebrows or whisper in a low voice as well. But when you write, you must rely on other means to tell your readers which ideas are more important than others. Emphasis in writing can be achieved in two ways: mechanically or stylistically.

EMPHASIS THROUGH MECHANICS

Writers may emphasize their ideas by using mechanical or stylistic devices.

To emphasize an idea in print, a writer may use any of the following devices:

Underlining:	<u>Underlining</u> draws the eye to a word.
Italics and boldface:	You can use *italics* or **boldface** for special meaning and emphasis.
Font changes:	Changing from a large font to a small font or to a *different* font adds interest and emphasis.
All caps:	Printing words in ALL CAPS is like shouting them.
Dashes:	Dashes—if used sparingly—can be effective in capturing attention.
Tabulation:	Listing items vertically makes them stand out:

1. First item
2. Second item
3. Third item

Other means of achieving mechanical emphasis include the arrangement of space, colour, lines, boxes, columns, titles, headings, and subheadings. Today's word processors and printers provide a wonderful array of capabilities for setting off ideas.

EMPHASIS THROUGH STYLE

Although mechanical means are occasionally appropriate, more often a writer achieves emphasis stylistically. That is, the writer chooses words carefully and constructs sentences skilfully to emphasize main ideas and de-emphasize minor or negative ideas. Here are four suggestions for emphasizing ideas stylistically:

* *Use vivid words.* Vivid words, as you will recall from Chapter 3, are emphatic because they help the reader picture what's being described.

General:	One *business* uses *personal* selling techniques.
Vivid and emphatic:	*Avon* uses *face-to-face* selling techniques.
General:	A *customer said* that he wanted the contract returned *soon*.
Vivid and emphatic:	*Ms. Choquette* insisted that the contract be returned *by July 1.*

* *Label the main idea.* If an idea is significant, tell the reader.

Unlabeled:	Explore the possibility of leasing a site, but also hire a business consultant.
Labeled:	Explore the possibility of leasing a site; but, *more importantly,* hire a business consultant.

* *Place the important idea first or last in the sentence.* Ideas have less competition from surrounding words when they appear first or last in a sentence. Observe how the concept of productivity is emphasized in the first and second examples:

Emphatic:	*Productivity* is more likely to be increased when profit-sharing plans are linked to individual performance rather than to group performance.
Emphatic:	Profit-sharing plans linked to individual performance rather than to group performance are more effective in increasing *productivity.*
Unemphatic:	Profit-sharing plans are more effective in increasing *productivity* when they are linked to individual performance rather than to group performance.

- *Place the important idea in a simple sentence or in an independent clause.* Don't dilute the effect of the idea by making it share the spotlight with other words and clauses.

Emphatic:	You are the first trainee that we have hired for this program. (Use a simple sentence for emphasis.)
Emphatic:	Although we considered many candidates, you are the first trainee that we have hired for this program. (Independent clause contains main idea.)
Unemphatic:	Although you are the first trainee that we have hired for this program, we had many candidates and expect to expand the program in the future. (Main idea is lost in a dependent clause.)

De-emphasis

To de-emphasize an idea, such as bad news, try one of the following stylistic devices:

The word *stylistic* refers to literary or artistic style as opposed to content.

- *Use general words.*

Vivid:	Our records indicate that *you were recently fired.*
General:	Our records indicate that *your employment status changed recently.*

- *Bury the bad news in the middle of a sentence or in a dependent clause.* Instead of placing a negative point where it is conspicuous and perhaps painful to the reader, include it in a dependent clause.

Bad news can be made less painful by de-emphasizing its presentation.

Emphasizes bad news:	We cannot issue you credit at this time, but we do have a plan that will allow you to fill your immediate needs on a cash basis.
De-emphasizes bad news:	We have a plan that will allow you to fill your immediate needs on a cash basis since we cannot issue you credit at this time.

Additional tips and strategies for announcing bad news will be provided in Chapter 8.

Unity

Unified sentences contain thoughts that are related to only one main idea. The following sentence lacks unity because the first clause has little or no relationship to the second clause:

Unified sentences contain only related ideas.

| **Lacks unity:** | Our insurance plan is available in all provinces, and you may name anyone as your beneficiary. |
| **Revision:** | Our insurance plan is available in all provinces. What's more, you may name anyone as your beneficiary. |

Two ideas in a sentence are better expressed by separating the two dissimilar clauses and adding a connecting phrase. Three writing faults that destroy sentence unity are (a) zigzag writing, (b) mixed constructions, and (c) misplaced modifiers.

ZIGZAG WRITING

Zigzag sentences often should be broken into two sentences.

Sentences that twist or turn unexpectedly away from the main thought are examples of zigzag writing. Such confusing writing may result when too many thoughts are included in one sentence or when one thought does not relate to another. To rectify a zigzag sentence, revise it so that the reader understands the relationship between the thoughts. If that is impossible, move the unrelated thoughts to a new sentence.

Zigzag sentence:	I appreciate the time you spent with me last week, and I have purchased a computer and software that generate graphics.
Revision:	I appreciate the time you spent with me last week. As a result of your advice, I have purchased a computer and software that generate graphics.
Zigzag sentence:	The shareholders of a corporation elect a board of directors, although the chief executive officer is appointed by the board and the CEO is not directly responsible to the shareholders.
Revision:	The shareholders of a corporation elect a board of directors, who in turn appoints the chief executive officer. The CEO is not directly responsible to the shareholders.

MIXED CONSTRUCTIONS

Writers who fuse two different grammatical constructions destroy sentence unity and meaning.

Mixed construction:	The reason I am late is because my car battery is dead.
Revision:	The reason I am late is that my car battery is dead. (The construction introduced by *the reason is* should be a noun clause beginning with *that*, not an adverbial clause beginning with *because*.)
Mixed construction:	When the stock market index rose five points was our signal to sell.
Revision:	When the stock market index rose five points, we were prepared to sell. *Or,* Our signal to sell was an increase of five points in the stock market index.

MISPLACED MODIFIERS

Sentence unity can also be destroyed by the separation of phrases or clauses from the words that they modify.

Misplaced modifier:	We will be happy to send a park map for all motorists reduced to a smaller scale.
Revision:	We will be happy to send all motorists a park map reduced to a smaller scale.
Misplaced modifier:	Whether you travel for business or for pleasure, charge everything to your credit card in Canada or the United States.
Revision:	Whether you travel for business or for pleasure in Canada or the United States, charge everything to your credit card.

In each of the preceding examples, the sentence made sense once the misplaced phrase was moved closer to the words it modified.

Another modifier fault is called a *dangling modifier*. This results when an introductory verbal phrase is not followed immediately by a word that it can logically modify. Notice in each of the following revisions of dangling modifiers that the sentence makes sense once we place the logical modifier after the introductory phrase.

Keep phrases and clauses close to the words they describe.

Beware of introductory verbal phrases that are not immediately followed by the words they describe.

Dangling modifier:	To receive a degree, 120 credits are required. (This sentence reads as if *120 credits* are receiving a degree.)
Revision:	To receive a degree, a student must earn 120 credits.
Dangling modifier:	When filling out an employment application, the personnel manager expects each applicant to use ink. (The personnel manager is not filling out the application.)
Revision:	When filling out an employment application, each applicant is expected to use ink.

PARALLELISM

Parallelism is a writing technique that involves balanced writing. Sentences written so that their parts are balanced or parallel are easy to read and understand. To achieve parallel construction, use similar structures to express similar ideas. For example, the words *computing, coding, recording,* and *storing* are parallel because the words all end in *-ing*. To express the list as *computing, coding, recording,* and *storage* is disturbing because the last item is not what the reader expects. Try to match nouns with nouns, verbs with verbs, and clauses with clauses. Avoid mixing active-voice verbs with passive-voice verbs. Your goal is to keep the wording balanced by expressing similar ideas in the same way.

Balanced wording helps the reader anticipate your meaning.

Lacks parallelism:	The market for industrial goods includes manufacturers, contractors, wholesalers, and *those concerned with the retail function.*

Revision:	The market for industrial goods includes manufacturers, contractors, wholesalers, and *retailers.* (Parallel construction matches nouns.)
Lacks parallelism:	Our primary goals are to increase productivity, reduce costs, and *the improvement of product quality.*
Revision:	Our primary goals are to increase productivity, reduce costs, and *improve product quality.* (Parallel construction matches verbs.)
Lacks parallelism:	We are scheduled to meet in Toronto on January 5, we *are meeting in Montreal on the 15th of March,* and in Hamilton on June 3.
Revision:	We are scheduled to meet in Toronto on January 5, *in Montreal on March 15,* and in Hamilton on June 3. (Parallel construction matches phrases.)
Lacks parallelism:	Mrs. Horne audits all accounts lettered A through L; accounts lettered M through Z are audited by Mr. Faheem.
Revision:	Mrs. Horne audits all accounts lettered A through L; Mr. Faheem audits accounts lettered M through Z. (Parallel construction matches active-voice verbs in balanced clauses.)

All items in a list should be expressed in balanced constructions.

In presenting lists of data, whether setting them out horizontally or tabulating them vertically, be certain to express all the items in parallel form.

The three primary objectives of advertising are as follows:
1. Increase the frequency of product use
2. Introduce complementary products
3. Enhance the corporate image

ACTIVE AND PASSIVE VOICE

In sentences with active-voice verbs, the subject is the doer of the action. In passive-voice sentences, the subject is acted upon.

Active verb:	Mr. Wong *completed* the tax return before the April 30 deadline. (The subject, *Mr. Wong,* is the doer of the action.)
Passive verb:	The tax return *was completed* before the April 30 deadline. (The subject, *tax return,* is acted upon.)

Although active-voice verbs are preferred in business writing, passive-voice verbs perform useful functions.

In the first sentence, the active-voice verb emphasizes *Mr. Wong.* In the second sentence, the passive-voice verb emphasizes the *tax return.* In sentences with passive-voice verbs, the doer of the action may be revealed or left unknown.

Most writers prefer active verbs because such verbs tell the reader clearly what the action is and who or what is performing that action. On the other hand, passive verbs can be employed to perform certain necessary functions. They are helpful in at least three strategies:

1. Emphasizing an action or the recipient of the action *(You have been selected to represent us).*

2. De-emphasizing negative news *(Your watch has not been repaired)*.
3. Concealing the doer of an action *(A major error was made in the estimate)*.

In business writing, as well as in personal interactions, some situations demand tact and sensitivity. Instead of using a direct approach with active verbs, we may prefer the indirectness that passive verbs allow. Rather than making a blunt announcement with an active verb *(Jason made a major error in the estimate)*, we can soften the sentence with a passive construction *(A major error was made in the estimate)*.

How can you tell if a verb is active or passive? Identify the subject of the sentence and decide if the subject is doing the acting or if it is being acted upon. For example, in the sentence *An appointment was made for January 1*, the subject is *appointment*. The subject is being acted upon; therefore, the verb *(was made)* is passive. Another clue in identifying passive-voice verbs is that they generally include a *to be* helping verb, such as *is, are, was, were, being*, or *been*.

PARAGRAPH COHERENCE

A paragraph is a group of sentences with a controlling idea, which is usually stated first. Paragraphs package similar ideas into meaningful groups for readers. Effective paragraphs are coherent; that is, they hold together. But coherence does not happen accidentally. It is achieved through effective organization and skilful use of three devices:

Three ways to create paragraph coherence are (1) repetition of key ideas, (2) use of pronouns, and (3) use of transitional expressions.

- *Repetition of key ideas or key words.* Repeating a word or key thought from a preceding sentence helps guide a reader from one thought to the next. This redundancy is necessary to build cohesiveness into writing.

Effective repetition: Quality problems in production are often the result of inferior raw materials. Some companies have strong programs for ensuring the *quality of incoming production materials and supplies.*

The second sentence of the preceding paragraph repeats the key idea of *quality*. Moreover, the words *incoming production materials and supplies* refer to the *raw materials* mentioned in the preceding sentence. Good writers find similar words to describe the same idea, thus using repetition to clarify a topic for the reader.

- *Use of pronouns.* Pronouns such as *this, that, they, these*, and *those* promote coherence by connecting the thoughts in one sentence to the thoughts in a previous sentence. To make sure that the pronoun reference is clear, consider joining the pronoun with the word to which it refers, thus making the pronoun into an adjective.

Pronoun repetition: Xerox has a four-point program to assist suppliers. *This program* includes written specifications for production materials and components.

Be very careful, though, in using pronouns. A pronoun without a clear antecedent can be most annoying. That's because the reader doesn't know precisely to what the pronoun refers.

Faulty:	When company profits increased, employees were given a bonus, either a cash payment or company stock. *This* became a real incentive to employees.
Improved:	When company profits increased, employees were given a bonus, either a cash payment or company stock. *This profit-sharing plan* became a real incentive to employees.

- *Use of transitional expressions.* One of the most effective ways to achieve paragraph coherence is through the use of transitional expressions. These expressions act as road signs: they indicate where the message is headed and, so, help the reader anticipate what is coming. Here are some of the most effective transitional expressions. They are grouped according to use:

Time Association	Contrast	Illustration
before, after	although	for example
first, second	but	in this way
meanwhile	however	
next	instead	
until	nevertheless	
when, whenever	on the other hand	

Cause, Effect	Additional Idea
consequently	furthermore
for this reason	in addition
hence	likewise
therefore	moreover

Used appropriately, transitional expressions help the reader see how ideas and sentences are related, thus achieving paragraph coherence.

SENTENCE AND PARAGRAPH LENGTH

The average sentence contains between 15 and 20 words.

Generally, short sentences are more easily understood. The average sentence length is between 15 and 20 words. This doesn't mean that all sentences should have 15 to 20 words, however. Effective paragraphs contain a mixture of sentences, some shorter and some longer.

Just as shorter sentences are most readable, so are shorter paragraphs. As a writer, you can make your messages more engaging by controlling paragraph length. In business letters, first and last paragraphs are often very short (one to four typed lines). Other paragraphs in letters and in most reports should average about six lines, with ten lines being the maximum.

SUMMING UP AND LOOKING FORWARD

Cynthia Selley gives us good advice: write naturally. In this chapter you studied specific techniques for sounding natural, positive, and conversational. Because readers always want to know what's in it for them, you studied how to develop reader benefits. You learned how to use inclusive language, as well as how to emphasize important ideas and how to de-emphasize others. Other important writing techniques included avoiding zigzag writing, mixed constructions, and misplaced modifiers.

Finally, you studied techniques for developing parallelism, for using active- and passive-voice verbs strategically, and for achieving paragraph coherence.

In these opening chapters, you've learned many practical techniques for becoming an effective business communicator. Now, it's time for you to put these techniques to work. Chapter 5 introduces you to writing memorandums and e-mail messages, the most frequently used forms of communication for most business writers. Succeeding chapters present letters and reports.

DISCUSSION

1. Why is writing in a natural, conversational tone difficult for most people?
2. How do speakers and writers differ in the way they emphasize ideas?
3. Explain why and how empathic business writers try to see the reader's viewpoint.
4. Why is parallelism an important technique for writers to master?
5. Why are active-voice verbs preferred in business writing?

CHAPTER REVIEW

6. List three specific techniques for developing a warm, friendly, and conversational tone in business messages.

7. Why does positive language usually tell more than negative language? Give an original example.

8. Define *empathy*.

9. What is meant by *reader benefit*? Give an original example.

10. List five examples of pronouns and nouns that exclude.

11. List five techniques for achieving emphasis through mechanics.

12. List four techniques for achieving emphasis through style.

13. List two stylistic techniques for de-emphasizing an idea.

14. How can a writer achieve parallelism? Give an original example.

15. What is the average length of a sentence?

Writing Improvement Exercises

Conversational Language. Revise the following sentences to make the tone more conversational.

> **Example:** As per your recent request, the undersigned is happy to inform you that we are sending you forthwith the brochures you requested.
> **Revision:** I'm happy to send you the brochures you requested.

16. Kindly inform the undersigned whether or not your representative will be making a visitation in the near future.

17. Pursuant to your letter of the 12th, please be advised that your shipment was sent June 9, 200x.

18. Kindly be informed that your vehicle has been determined to require corrective work.

19. All students are herewith informed to send back to the undersigned the appropriately completed applications for parking.

20. The undersigned respectfully reminds affected individuals that employees desirous of investigating stock options must do so before December 30, 200x.

Positive Language. Revise the following sentences to use positive language. Add information if needed.

21. We regret to inform you that your order did not reach us immediately, so we cannot ship your bicycle headgear until August 1, 200x.

22. Parking is not permitted in any lot other than South Lot D.

23. We are sorry to inform you that you do not qualify for a credit account at this time.

24. Because your name was overlooked, you will not receive our introductory packet until we make our second mailing.

25. If you fail to pass the qualifying examination, you cannot be accepted.

Reader Benefit. Revise the following sentences to emphasize benefits to the reader.

Example:	We have just designed an amazing computer program that automatically computes income tax.
Revision:	You will be amazed by this computer program that automatically computes your income tax.

26. To prevent us from possibly losing large sums of money, our bank now requires verification of any large cheque presented for immediate payment.

27. Our extensive experience in investments enables us to find our customers the most profitable programs.

28. Our company policy demands that individuals who rent power equipment must demonstrate proficiency in the use of the item to be rented.

29. We are offering a new series of short-term loans that may be used for carrying accounts receivable and for stocking inventory.

30. For just $899 (Canadian) per person, we have arranged a three-day trip to Las Vegas that includes deluxe accommodation, the "City Lights" show, and selected meals.

Inclusive Language. Revise the following sentences to avoid biased expressions.

31. Every employee has the right to examine his personnel files.

32. The lady defence lawyer and the prosecutor agreed to the trial date.

33. The girl at the reception desk will be able to answer your questions.

Emphasis. For each of the following sentences, circle (a) or (b). Be prepared to justify your choice.

34. Which is more emphatic?
    (a) It is a good idea that we advertise more.
    (b) It is critical that we advertise heavily.

35. Which is more emphatic?
    (a) The committee was powerless to act.
    (b) The committee was unable to take action.

36. Which sentence places more emphasis on *product loyalty*?
    (a) Product loyalty is the primary motivation for advertising.
    (b) The primary motivation for advertising is loyalty to the product, although other purposes are also served.

37. Which is more emphatic?
    (a) We need a faster, more efficient distribution system.
    (b) We need a better distribution system.

38. Which sentence places more emphasis on the seminar?
    (a) An executive training seminar that starts June 1 will include four candidates.
    (b) Four candidates will be able to participate in an executive training seminar that we feel will provide a valuable learning experience.

39. Which sentence places more emphasis on the date?
    (a) The deadline is December 30 for applications for overseas assignments.
    (b) December 30 is the deadline for applications for overseas assignments.
40. Which is less emphatic?
    (a) Ms. Curtis said that her financial status had worsened.
    (b) Ms. Curtis said that she had lost her job and owed $2000.
41. Which sentence de-emphasizes the credit refusal?
    (a) We are unable to grant you credit at this time, but we will reconsider your application later.
    (b) Although we welcome your cash business, we are unable to offer you credit at this time; but we will be happy to reconsider your application later.
42. Which sentence gives more emphasis to *judgment*?
    (a) He has many admirable qualities, but most important is his good judgment.
    (b) He has many admirable qualities, including good judgment and patience.
43. Which is more emphatic?
    (a) Three departments are involved: (1) Legal, (2) Accounting, and (3) Distribution.
    (b) Three departments are involved:
        (1) Legal
        (2) Accounting
        (3) Distribution

Sentence Unity. The following sentences lack unity. Rewrite, correcting the identified fault.

> **Example:** (Dangling modifier) By advertising extensively, all the open jobs were filled quickly.
>
> **Revision:** By advertising extensively, we were able to fill all the open jobs quickly.

44. (Dangling modifier) To open a money market account, a deposit of $3000 is required.

45. (Mixed construction) The reason why Mr. Brasseur is unable to travel extensively is because he has family responsibilities.

46. (Misplaced modifier) Identification passes must be worn at all times in offices and production facilities showing the employee's picture.

47. (Misplaced modifier) The editor's rules were to be observed by all staff members, no matter how silly they seemed.

48. (Zigzag sentence) The business was started by two engineers, and these owners worked in a garage, which eventually grew into a million-dollar operation.

Parallelism. Revise the following sentences so that their parts are balanced.

49. (Hint: Match verbs.) Some of our priorities include linking employee compensation to performance, keeping administrative costs down, the expansion of computer use, and the improvement of performance-review skills of supervisors.

50. (Hint: Match active voice of verbs.) Sally Strehlke, of the Vancouver office, will now supervise our Western Division; and the Eastern Division will be supervised by our Ottawa office manager, David Haskins.

51. (Hint: Match nouns.) Word processing software is used extensively in the fields of health care, by lawyers, by secretaries in insurance firms, for scripts in the entertainment industry, and in the banking field.

52. If you have decided to cancel our service, please destroy your credit card and the notice card should be returned to us.

53. We need more laboratory space, additional personnel are required, and we also need much more capital.

54. The application for a grant asks for this information: funds required for employee salaries, how much we expect to spend on equipment, and what is the length of the project.

55. To lease an automobile is more expensive than buying one.

56. To use the copier, insert your ID card, the paper trays must be loaded, indicate the number of copies needed, and your original sheet should be inserted through the feeder.

Active-Voice Verbs. Business writing is more forceful if it uses active-voice verbs. Revise the following sentences so that verbs are in the active voice. Put the emphasis on the doer of the action. Add subjects if necessary.

> **Example:** The computers were powered up each day at 7 a.m.
> **Revision:** Yves powered up the computers each day at 7 a.m.

57. Initial figures for the bid were submitted before the June 1 deadline.

58. New spices and cooking techniques were tried by the Burger Barn to improve its hamburgers.

59. Substantial sums of money were saved by employees who enrolled early in our stock option plan.

60. A significant financial commitment has been made by us to ensure that our customers can take advantage of our discount pricing.

Passive-Voice Verbs. When indirectness or tact is required, use passive-voice verbs. Revise the following sentences so that they are in the passive voice.

> **Example:** Harprit did not submit the accounting statement on time.
> **Revision:** The accounting statement was not submitted on time.

61. Tran made a computational error in the report.

62. We cannot ship your order for ten monitors until June 15.

63. The government first issued a warning regarding the use of this pesticide over 15 months ago.

64. We will notify you immediately if we make any changes in your travel arrangements.

65. We cannot allow a cash refund unless you provide proof of purchase.

4.1 Searching the Internet: Humorous Computer Jargon. As a communication consultant, you are preparing to give a talk to employees of a large bank. Your topic is effective writing techniques. To enliven your talk, you need some humorous examples of computer jargon. Use a search engine to explore the World Wide Web to see what you can locate quickly. Find at least five examples of jargon. Print them or make notes describing them. Submit the examples to your instructor along with a written explanation of how you found them. If you get stuck, try the following URL: webvserver.maclab.comp.uvic.ca/writersguide

4.2 Connecting With E-Mail: Summary of Writing Techniques. You have just returned from the second part of the seminar titled "Effective Writing Techniques for Business Communicators." Once again, your manager asks you to submit a brief message summarizing three of the most important techniques you learned. Select three techniques from this chapter. Send a message to your manager (your instructor, in this case) with your summary.

GRAMMAR/MECHANICS CHECKUP—4

Adjectives and Adverbs

Review Sections 1.16 and 1.17 of the Grammar/Mechanics Handbook. Then study each of the following statements. Underscore any inappropriate forms. In the space provided write the correct form and the number of the G/M principle illustrated. You may need to consult your dictionary for current practice regarding some compound adjectives. If a sentence is correct, write *C*. When you finish, compare your responses with those provided. If your answers differ, study carefully the principles in parentheses.

live-and-let-live (1.17e)

Example: He was one of those individuals with a <u>live and let live</u> attitude.

_____ 1. Most of our long time customers have credit card accounts.
_____ 2. Many subscribers considered the $50 per year charge to be a bargain.
_____ 3. Other subscribers complained that $50 per year was exorbitant.
_____ 4. The computer supplied the answer so quick that we were all amazed.
_____ 5. He only had $1 in his pocket.
_____ 6. Some experts predict double-digit inflation will return.
_____ 7. Jeremy found a once in a lifetime opportunity.
_____ 8. Although the car was four years old, it was in good condition.
_____ 9. Of the two sample colours, which is best for the wall?
_____ 10. Professor Angela To is well known in her field.
_____ 11. Channel 12 presents up to the minute news broadcasts.
_____ 12. Lower tax brackets would lessen the after tax yield of some bonds.
_____ 13. The conclusion drawn from the statistics couldn't have been more clearer.
_____ 14. This new investment fund has a better than fifty fifty chance of outperforming the older fund.
_____ 15. If you feel badly about the transaction, contact your portfolio manager.

---

1. long-time (1.17e) 3. C (1.17e) 5. had only (1.17f) 7. once-in-a-lifetime (1.17e) 9. better (1.17a) 11. up-to-the-minute (1.17e) 13. couldn't have been clearer (1.17b) 15. bad (1.17c)

Document for Revision

The following letter has faults in grammar, punctuation, conversational language, outdated expressions, inclusive language, concise wording, long lead-ins, and many other problems. Drawing on the guidelines in the Grammar/Mechanics Handbook and what you learned in this chapter to sharpen your skills, use standard proofreading skills (see Appendix B) to correct the errors.

Ineffective Writing

Mr. Wing Chiang, Manager
Title Guaranty & Abstract Company
2430 Providence Avenue
Swift Current, SK S1R 2L3

Dear Wing:

Pursuant to our telephone conversation this morning, this is to advise that two (2) agent's packages will be delivered to you next week. Due to the fact that new forms had to be printed; we do not have them immediately available.

Although we cannot offer a 50/50 commission split, we are able to offer new agents a 60/40 commission split. There are two new agreement forms that show this commission ratio. When you get ready to sign up a new agent have her fill in these up to date forms.

When you send me an executed agency agreement please make every effort to tell me what agency package was assigned to the agent. On the last form that you sent you overlooked this information. We need this data to distribute commissions in an expeditious manner.

If you have any questions, don't hesitate to call on me.

Yours very truly,

Communication Workshop: Diversity

Examining the Gender Communication Gap

Do men and women have different communication styles? As increasing numbers of women enter the workforce and join management, an examination of communication styles becomes especially meaningful—for both women and men. An intense public debate has arisen over Deborah Tannen's book *Talking from 9 to 5: How Women's and Men's Conversational Styles Affect Who Gets Heard, Who Gets Credit, and What Gets Done at Work.* Let's consider some of the male/female communication differences, greatly simplified, as identified by Tannen and others.[3]

Men tend to approach business in a direct, results-oriented way. Women on the other hand tend to approach it in a more collaborative way. Collective action and responsibility assume greater importance than personal achievement. Team playing is natural, and the well-being of the individual is important. Tannen argues that girls playing in groups learn to blend in, be sensitive to one another's feelings, and avoid boasting. Boy groups, by contrast, are more competitive. Women want to be liked. Men want to be top dog.

In working together, men tend to be competitive and adversarial. Women are more collaborative, rewarding cooperation and valuing goodwill above measurable and immediate gain. For men, the goal is respect; for women, it's rapport.

Women's speech style is hesitant, ingratiating, and indirect. Women ask questions instead of making declarations, using "we" instead of "I." Women soften the effect of what they are saying for the sake of their listeners. Men speak more often, interrupt more, take up more meeting time, and turn up the volume when they speak.

In problem solving, men tend to go to the heart of the difficulty, stripping away all secondary considerations to resolve the issue. Women assemble options, looking at ramifications and implications. This approach is often seen as time-wasting and can be irritating to male colleagues.

In meetings women are often ignored or dismissed as weak. Since time is usually limited, discussion is frowned on when immediate solutions can be presented. Men use their bulk and aggressive body language to establish dominance.

In conversations men like to recount personal experiences and achievements. Women, by contrast, are more likely to discuss staff problems and personal matters. They analyze and internalize in situations where men are more likely to merely observe and report.

Application. In the next week listen carefully to conversations around you and to discussions in classrooms and at work. Do you hear evidence of differences in male/female communication styles? Notice examples of speech styles, problem-solving strategies, and teamwork. In your observations, do you find the distinctions described by Tannen and others valid, or are they merely examples of stereotyping? If you think some truth exists in the distinctions, should women in the work world change their style of communication to be more successful? How would you respond to the statement that contemporary business style is shifting toward the female collaborative mode? Be prepared to discuss these questions in class or to summarize your observations in a memo to your instructor.

UNIT 3

COMMUNICATING ROUTINE MESSAGES

MEMORANDUMS AND E-MAIL

5

It's a continual challenge for us to keep our product groups small enough so that they feel empowered to make their stuff happen, rather than feeling like cogs in some giant machine. At the same time, we need to maintain a larger sense of community and allow a wide range of smart people within the company to provide thoughts and suggestions about product plans. E-mail is a great tool in enabling that sort of communication. It permits us to share technical strategy and vision across the entire company.[1]

BILL GATES, CEO, Microsoft

Learning Objectives

1. Distinguish between direct and indirect writing strategies.
2. Recognize functions, characteristics, and kinds of internal messages.
3. Write memorandums and e-mail messages that deliver information.
4. Write memorandums and e-mail messages that make requests.
5. Apply techniques for emphasizing important points in lists.
6. Write memorandums and e-mail messages that respond to other documents.

Bill Gates, CEO at Microsoft, likes to be in constant contact with what's happening at his huge company. And he wants his 16,000-plus employees to be in touch with each other, exchanging information and ideas. He worries that Microsoft's size will work against excellence. But electronic mail has become an important tool in reducing barriers created by size and distance. Workers can almost instantly communicate with each other, whether they are working in separate rooms, in separate buildings, or on separate continents.

At many companies today internal communication has become increasingly important. Organizations are downsizing, flattening chains of command, forming work teams, and empowering rank-and-file employees. Given more power in making decisions, employees find that they need more information. They must collect, exchange, and evaluate information about the products and services they offer. Management also needs input from employees to respond rapidly to global market actions. This growing demand for information means increasing use of memorandums and e-mail.

Memos and e-mail are used to send messages within organizations.

Memorandums (memos) and electronic mail (e-mail) are used primarily for internal communication; that is, they deliver information within an organization. In many organizations more memos and e-mail messages are written than messages addressed to outsiders. Studies of executives, managers, and clerical personnel indicate that the memo is actually the workhorse of the office.[2] In fact, one expert reports that executives spend 22 percent of their time writing and reading memos.[3] This chapter focuses on the writing of e-mail messages and hard-copy memos that inform, request, and respond.

A WORD ABOUT STRATEGIES

Before we begin our discussion of internal communication, we need to consider writing strategies. Business messages usually follow one of two strategies: the direct plan or the indirect plan. How do you know which strategy to use? By analyzing your message and the anticipated reader reaction to that message, you can determine whether to use the direct or the indirect strategy. Most messages can be divided into three categories:

The anticipated reader reaction determines whether a message should be written directly or indirectly.

- *Positive or neutral messages.* Use the direct strategy because you can expect the reader to be pleased or at least not displeased.
- *Negative messages.* Use the indirect strategy because you can expect the reader to be displeased.
- *Persuasive messages.* Use the indirect strategy because you can expect the reader to be initially uninterested.

The direct strategy is most effective for positive or neutral messages. You will learn to apply the direct strategy in writing internal messages in this chapter. In Chapters 6 and 7 you will use the direct strategy for routine request letters and for routine replies. In Chapters 8 and 9 you will learn to use the indirect strategy for negative messages and for persuasive messages.

FUNCTIONS OF MEMOS AND E-MAIL MESSAGES

Memos and e-mail messages are a vital means of exchanging information within an organization. They explain policies, procedures, and guidelines. They make announcements, request information, and follow up conversations. They save time by relaying information to many people without the need for a meeting. They also ensure that all concerned individuals receive the same message, which would be unlikely if the message were transmitted orally. Moreover, printed copies of memos and e-mail messages provide a written record of decisions, telephone conversations, and meetings.

Memos and e-mail messages can save time and provide a written record.

Used judiciously, memos and e-mail messages are helpful. Misused, however, they waste time, energy, and resources. Don't send a message if a quick telephone call would function equally well. And don't send messages that are trivial or overly personal. Moreover, don't send copies to anyone who is not directly concerned.

As you might guess, e-mail is particularly susceptible to abuse. Its convenience, speed, and ease draw many people into overusing it. Consider the plight of Mario Juarez, manager of employee communication at Microsoft. He confesses that he has a love/hate relationship with his e-mail. He's thankful that he can be in touch with almost anyone in the company immediately. The downside, though, is that he receives hundreds of messages every day resulting in what he calls "absolute information overload."[4] Concerned about e-mail overuse and resulting lowered productivity, some companies are charging user fees and restricting the times when e-mail messages may be sent.[5] You'll learn more about smart e-mail practices later in this chapter.

Memos and e-mail messages have the following characteristics in common:

- They begin with *To, From, Date*, and *Subject*.
- They cover just one topic.
- They are informal.
- They are concise.

Memos and e-mail messages use an efficient standardized format, as shown in Figures 5.1 and 5.2. (See Appendix A for more information about formatting internal messages.) Use of the headings *To, From, Date*, and *Subject* produces two benefits. First, headings force senders to organize their thoughts in order to compose the subject of the message. Second, headings are invaluable aids for filing and retrieving messages. The subject line on an e-mail message is particularly important since it must capture the attention of busy readers.

FIGURE 5.1

Sample Hard-Copy Memorandum

Writers of memos usually sign their initials after their printed name.

Guide words identify important information and force writer to summarize topic.

Bullets, rather than numbers, are used to emphasize items that do not suggest a sequence.

Memos do not end with a complimentary closing such as *Sincerely yours.*

Laser Enterprises
Internal Memorandum

TO: Gerard Weykamp

FROM: Alisa Bowhay AB

DATE: February 6, 200x

SUBJECT: FORMATTING HARD-COPY MEMORANDUMS

Here is the information you requested regarding appropriate formatting for memorandums keyed at computers and printed on plain paper.

- Use 3-cm side margins.
- Leave a top margin of 3 cm to 5 cm.
- Type in all caps the headings TO, FROM, DATE, and SUBJECT.
- Single-space everything within paragraphs but double-space between paragraphs.

We prefer to make a master memo document with all the format settings. Then we read that command file into any new memo. Some programs use "wizards" to format memos quickly. Either method is fast and accurate.

If you'd like to discuss formatting computer memos further, please call me at Ext. 606.

FIGURE 5.2

E-mail Message

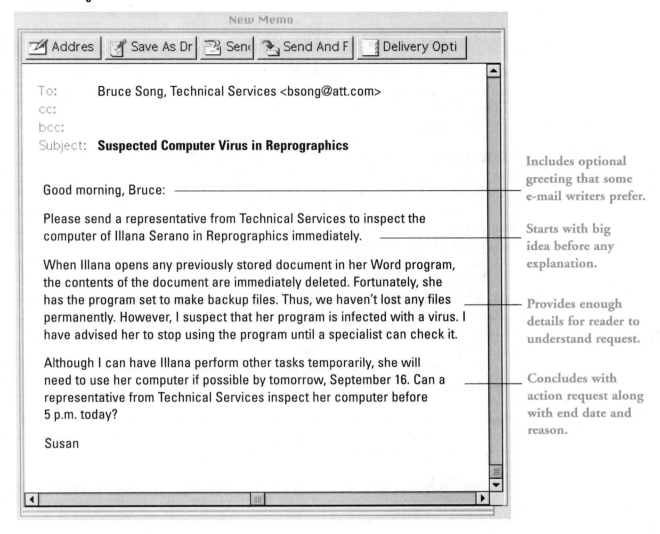

New Memo

| Addres | Save As Dr | Send | Send And F | Delivery Opti |

To: Bruce Song, Technical Services <bsong@att.com>
cc:
bcc:
Subject: **Suspected Computer Virus in Reprographics**

Good morning, Bruce: ——— *Includes optional greeting that some e-mail writers prefer.*

Please send a representative from Technical Services to inspect the computer of Illana Serano in Reprographics immediately. ——— *Starts with big idea before any explanation.*

When Illana opens any previously stored document in her Word program, the contents of the document are immediately deleted. Fortunately, she has the program set to make backup files. Thus, we haven't lost any files permanently. However, I suspect that her program is infected with a virus. I have advised her to stop using the program until a specialist can check it. ——— *Provides enough details for reader to understand request.*

Although I can have Illana perform other tasks temporarily, she will need to use her computer if possible by tomorrow, September 16. Can a representative from Technical Services inspect her computer before 5 p.m. today? ——— *Concludes with action request along with end date and reason.*

Susan

A memo or e-mail message normally covers only one topic. This facilitates action and filing. If a writer, for example, discusses in the same message both the faulty exhaust system on her company car and plans for a fitness program, the reader may place the printed message in a stack of paper relating to company cars and forget the details about the fitness program.

Memos and e-mail messages may be written somewhat more informally than letters addressed outside the organization. Because you usually know and work with the reader, you do not have to build goodwill or strive to create a favourable image. Like business letters, internal messages should sound like conversation. For example, *The undersigned takes pleasure in* is much more formal than *I'm happy to*. Which would you be more likely to say in conversation?

Although informality is appropriate in internal messages, the degree of informality depends on the relationship between the employees. When a close working relationship exists between the sender and the receiver, a warm personal tone is fitting.

To facilitate action and filing, memos and e-mail messages should cover a single topic only.

The techniques that you learned in Chapters 3 and 4 for writing concisely will help make your memos succinct. Remember, internal messages are more likely to be read and acted on if they are just long enough to say what is necessary.

FORMS OF INTERNAL MESSAGES

Internal messages in today's offices may appear in two forms: (1) hard-copy standard memos printed on paper or (2) e-mail memos sent over computer networks. Although many companies use e-mail networks, standard memos are still written for specific purposes.

Standard Memos. Some organizations provide stationery printed with the guide words *To, From, Date,* and *Subject.* Aligning the text that follows the guide words, however, can be difficult on today's computers and printers. Thus, individuals using computers generally prefer to skip the printed memo stationery and type in the guide words themselves. An alternative is to use a standardized memo template provided with your word processing software. When applied, the template automatically adds consistent and appropriate spacing, formatting, and heading styles.

The position of the date varies; it could appear at the top, in the middle, or after the subject line. Some memos, especially in large organizations, include additional guide words, such as *Routing, Department, Floor,* or *Reference File.* When memos are addressed to groups of people, their names may be listed under the word *Distribution* in the heading or in the lower left corner.

Unlike business letters, memos are usually unsigned. Instead, writers initial the *From* line. Close friends may add salutations *(Dear André)* and signatures to personalize their memos, but generally memos do not include these items. Senders of e-mail memos are encouraged to key their names at the ends of their messages. Personal identifiers that can be attached to a message such as electronic signatures or business cards may not be readable by every e-mail system.

Electronic Mail Memos. Instead of using paper to send memos, increasing numbers of businesspeople are turning to e-mail. E-mail uses computers, modems, and modem software to send messages electronically over networks connected by telephone lines and satellites.

Currently, e-mail is most effective in delivering simple messages, such as the one shown in Figure 5.2. Complex data should probably be sent in hard-copy documents. Because your future will undoubtedly include e-mail, the following tips will help you in composing electronic messages:

To be most successful with e-mail, follow these tips.

- *Upload your message.* Whenever possible, compose your message using word processing software then transfer it to your e-mail software. Most e-mail text editors are primitive. Word processing programs on the other hand are designed to edit text more efficiently. Moreover, you're less likely to "self-destruct" on your word processing program; you will be familiar with the save functions that will prevent your writing from being lost.
- *Provide a descriptive subject line.* Nearly all e-mail systems include a prompt for a subject. This subject often determines *whether* a message will be read and *when* it will be read. Thus, you'll want to make subject lines interesting, accurate, and informative. For example, instead of *Meeting,* try *Attend Urgent Meeting About Budget Cuts.*

- *Keep lines, paragraphs, and messages short.* Because computer monitors are small, lines under 65 characters in length are most readable. Paragraphs of no more than eight lines, with a blank line preceding a new paragraph, also enhance readability. Above all, keep your message short. E-mail is not an appropriate medium for lengthy discourse. Bill Gates at Microsoft is said to stop reading after three screens.
- *Don't automatically include the sender's message.* Most e-mail systems include a "Reply" capability that allows you to return the sender's entire message as you respond. Don't! If you must jog the sender's memory or if you don't want to rekey strategic wording, cut and paste the portions you need. But avoid irritating your recipients by returning their original messages when you respond.
- *Don't automatically "CC" your messages to a large distribution list.* Most e-mail systems include a "CC" capability that allows you to send copies of your message to numerous receivers at the same time. Send copies of your messages to those receivers who need copies. Routinely "copying" to many receivers is unnecessary and can cause clutter on the system.
- *Care about correctness.* Senders and receivers of e-mail tend to be casual about spelling, grammar, and usage. However, people are still judged by their writing, whether electronic or paper-based. Some businesspeople have been passed over for promotions as a result of sloppy e-mail messages. And some e-mail memos never intended for mass distribution have been downloaded into print and distributed through entire organizations. Correctness still counts.
- *Avoid sensitive messages.* Because e-mail is far from private, do not send sensitive, confidential, or potentially embarrassing messages. Moreover, think twice before transmitting inflammatory messages that you may later regret. E-mail does not disappear just because you hit the delete button. Your e-mail can survive on hard disks or backup storage tapes in your company's network. These storage systems can be searched easily and offending messages retrieved and downloaded.[6] Also, be aware that many organizations legitimately monitor e-mail work messages. Many Canadian companies now have written codes of ethics that limit privacy rights on company-owned computer equipment. They also provide employees with acceptable use policies for e-mail systems. That's why you should never send anything that could be viewed as evidence of malice or of treating an important issue (such as charges of sexual harassment) without due seriousness.[7]

DIRECT MEMOS

Whether you send hard-copy or electronic memos, the same writing principles apply. You'll want to use the direct strategy for neutral or positive messages.

DIRECT STRATEGY
- Main idea first
- Details or explanation
- Closing thought

The direct strategy gets right down to business quickly, with the main idea first. If your memo has a new procedure to announce, summarize that announcement in the first sentence. Don't explain why a new procedure is being introduced or what

The direct strategy starts with the main idea.

employee reactions to the new procedure might be. Save explanations and details for later.

Stating the main idea first has several advantages for senders and receivers:

- *It saves time for readers.* They don't have to skim the first part of the message quickly to find a key sentence that says what the message is about.
- *It enables readers to develop the proper mindset.* After they learn the main idea, readers comprehend the explanations and details that follow more readily. Everything makes sense because they anticipate what is coming.
- *It helps the writer organize the message logically.* Once the writer has stated the main idea, the rest of the message is easier to write.

Remember, however, that the direct strategy is useful only if you expect that the reader will not be displeased by the contents of the message. If the announcement of a new procedure might generate resistance, then persuasion is necessary and the indirect strategy (see Chapter 8) would be more effective.

DEVELOPING A MEMO-WRITING PLAN

A writing plan helps you organize a complete message.

Once you have decided on the strategy for your message, proceed to a writing plan. In this book you will be shown a number of writing plans appropriate for different messages. These plans provide a skeleton; they are the bones of a message. Writers provide the flesh. Simply plugging in phrases or someone else's words won't work. Good writers provide details and link together their ideas with transitions to create fluent and meaningful messages. However, a writing plan helps you get started and gives you ideas about what to include. At first, you will probably rely on these plans considerably. As you progress, they will become less important. Later in the book no plans are provided.

Here is a general writing plan for a message that is not expected to create displeasure or resistance.

WRITING PLAN FOR MEMOS AND E-MAIL MESSAGES

- *Subject line*—summarizes memo contents.
- *First sentence*—states the main idea.
- *Body*—provides background data and explains the main idea.
- *Closing*—requests action, summarizes message, or presents closing thought.

WRITING THE SUBJECT LINE

A subject line must be concise but meaningful.

Probably the most important part of a memo or an e-mail message is the subject line, which summarizes the contents in concise language. It should be brief, but not so brief that it makes no sense. The subject line *Revised Procedures* would probably be meaningless to a reader. An improved subject line might read, *Revised Procedures for Scheduling Vacations.* For memos addressed to busy executives, subject lines must also entice them to read further. If they don't see something that grabs their attention, they may not go beyond the subject line.

A subject line is like a newspaper headline. It should attract attention, create a clear picture, and present an accurate summary. It should not be a complete sentence and should rarely occupy more than one line. Here are some sample subject lines:

Subject: Saving Time and Money by Purchasing Reconditioned Copier
Subject: Funding Minority Internship Program
Subject: Recommendations for Securing Computers and Printers

BEGINNING WITH THE MAIN IDEA

Although an explanation occasionally must precede the main idea, the first sentence usually states the primary idea. An appropriate opening sentence for a message that announces new vacation procedures is as follows:

> Here are new guidelines for employees taking two- or three-week vacations between June and September.

Don't open a hard-copy memo by asking the reader to refer to a previous memo. Attach a copy of that document if necessary. Or provide a brief review of the relevant points. Asking the reader to dig out previous correspondence is inefficient and inconsiderate. E-mail users today often include the previous message when responding, but this practice is inefficient. A smarter practice involves "cutting" and "pasting" relevant portions of the previous message into the current message.

It's better to attach a copy of previous correspondence than to ask the reader to find it.

EXPLAINING CLEARLY IN THE BODY

In the body of the message, explain the main idea. If you are asking for detailed information, arrange the questions in logical order. If you are providing information, group similar information together. When considerable data are involved, use a separate paragraph for each topic. Work for effective transitions between paragraphs. Above all, make your message clear. You don't want to leave your readers scratching their heads, wondering what you are saying.

The tone of internal memos is informal. Don't be self-conscious about using contractions *(won't, didn't, couldn't)*, conversational language, and occasional personal pronouns *(I, me, we)*. Make an effort, though, to de-emphasize first-person pronouns. Concentrate on developing the *you* attitude.

Memos and e-mail messages are most effective when they are concise. For this reason they often include listed information. Lists condense information into readable and understandable forms.

CLOSING THE MEMO

End the memo with a request for action, a summary of the contents of the memo, or a closing thought. If action on the part of the reader is sought, spell out that action clearly. A vague request such as *Drop by to see this customer sometime* is ineffective because the reader may not understand exactly what is to be done. A better request might be: *Please make an appointment to see John Ayers before August 5.* Another way to close a memo is by summarizing its major points. This is particularly helpful if the memo is complicated.

If no action request is made and a closing summary is unnecessary, the writer may prefer to end the memo with a simple closing thought. Although it is unnecessary to conclude with goodwill statements such as those found in letters to customers, some closing statement is useful to prevent a feeling of abruptness. For example, a message might end with *I'll appreciate your assistance, I look forward to your response,* or *What do you think of this proposal?*

IMPROVING MEMO READABILITY WITH LISTS

Readers of memos are usually in a hurry. They want the important information to stand out. One of the best ways to improve the readability of any message is by listing items. Doing so is not difficult as the information in memos often lends itself to listing.

Lists make memos easier to read and review.

A list is a group or series of related items, usually three or more. Because lists require fewer words than complete sentences, they can be read and understood more quickly and easily. Listed information stands out; therefore, it's swiftly located and quickly reviewed.

You can write good lists by concentrating on two concepts: (1) the list itself and (2) the paragraph or sentence that introduces it.

Items in a List. Use lists only if the items that are related can be shown in the same form. If one item is a single word but the next item requires a paragraph of explanation, the items are not suitable for listing. Listed items must be balanced, or parallel, in construction. They must use similar grammatical form.

Instead of This	Try This
She likes sleeping, eating, and work.	She likes sleeping, eating, and working.
We are hiring the following: sales clerks, managers who will function as supervisors, and people to work in offices.	We are hiring the following: sales clerks, supervising managers, and office personnel.
Some of the most pressing problems are refunds that are missing, payments directed to the wrong place, and numerous lost documents.	These are the most pressing problems: missing refunds, misdirected payments, and lost documents.

A list of instructions snaps to attention if each item is a command starting with a verb. Bullets add further emphasis to items.

Here are instructions for using the copy machine:
- Insert your copy card into the slot.
- Load paper in the upper tray.
- Feed copies through the feed chute.

Some items are most efficiently shown with headings:

Date	City	Speaker
September 16	Regina	Dr. Roietta Fulgham
October 30	Saskatoon	Dr. Iva Upchurch

Items may be listed vertically, as shown previously, or integrated into sentences. Items shown vertically, obviously, stand out more—but they require more space. To use less space and to show less separation from the introduction, list items at the end of a sentence. Notice in the examples below that each item is followed by a comma and that the word *and* precedes the last item in the series. If the items are too long for incorporation in one sentence, use a vertical list or rewrite the material without a list. Using letters or numbers for listed items gives the items listed more importance and separation.

> Many individuals backslide on their resolutions regarding fitness. To keep exercising, you should (1) make a written commitment to yourself, (2) set realistic goals for each day's workout, and (3) enlist the support of your spouse or a friend.

> The health club has four sign-up months: January, May, August, and October.

Introductory Words. The introduction to a list must make sense in relation to each item in the list. It should be complete enough that the same words do not have to be repeated for each item.

Instead of This	**Try This**
Our goal	Our goal is to recruit sales reps who are
• Is to recruit intensely competitive sales reps	• Intensely competitive
• Is to use reps who are familiar with our products	• Familiar with our procedures
• Recruit intelligent reps who learn quickly	• Intelligent and learn quickly

Punctuating and Capitalizing Lists. Although some flexibility exists, most writers follow similar guidelines in punctuating and capitalizing words in lists.

- *Use a colon following the introduction to most lists.* However, do not use a colon if (1) the listed items follow a verb or preposition (*the colours are red, yellow, and blue*) or (2) another sentence precedes the list.
- *Omit punctuation after any item listed vertically.* Use a period only if the item is a complete sentence.
- *Capitalize the initial letter of any item listed vertically.* Even if the item does not form a complete sentence, capitalize the initial letter.

MEMOS AND E-MAIL MESSAGES THAT INFORM

You've now studied a basic plan for writing memos and e-mail messages, and you've learned how to highlight ideas with listing techniques. Now, you'll see how these techniques can be applied to specific situations. Most memos and e-mail messages can be divided into four groups: (1) those that inform, (2) those that request, (3) those that respond, and (4) those that persuade. In this chapter we will be concerned with the first three groups because they use the direct strategy. The fourth group, persuasive messages, uses the indirect strategy. They will be discussed in Chapter 9.

Memos that inform generally explain organization policies, procedures, and guidelines. As policy-making documents, these messages must be particularly clear and concise.

The memos shown in Figure 5.3 inform department managers of a change in job-hiring procedures. The ineffective version begins negatively with an explanation of what went wrong with a new hiring procedure. Instead of starting directly, this memo wanders through a maze of blame and incoherent explanation. The new

FIGURE 5.3

Effective and Ineffective Memos That Inform

Ineffective

TO: Susan Hsu, LaVerne McClellan, and Greg Medrano
FROM: Cynthia Chomsky
DATE: January 15, 200X
SUBJECT: PROBLEMS WITH CHANGES IN HIRING

Fails to pinpoint main idea in opening.

Rambling, negative explanation.

We had no idea last month when we implemented new hiring procedures that major problems would result. Due to the fact that every department is now placing newspaper advertisements for new-hires individually, problems occurred. This cannot continue. Perhaps we did not make it clear at that time, but all newly hired employees who are hired for a position should be requested through this office.

New procedure is hard to follow.

Uses threats instead of citing reader benefits.

Do not submit your advertisements for new employees directly to a newspaper. After writing them, they should be brought to Human Resources, where they will be centralized. You should discuss each ad with one of our counsellors. Then we will place the ad in an appropriate newspaper or other publication. If you do not follow these guidelines, chaos will result. You may pick up applicant folders from us the day after the closing date in the ad.

Effective

TO: Susan Hsu, LaVerne McClellan, and Greg Medrano

FROM: Cynthia Chomsky

DATE: January 15, 200x

SUBJECT: CHANGE IN JOB-ADVERTISING PROCEDURES

Effective today, all advertisements for departmental job openings should be routed through the Human Resources Department.

Summarizes main idea.

A major problem resulted from the change in hiring procedures implemented last month. Each department is placing newspaper advertisements for new-hires individually, when all such requests should be centralized in this office. To process applications more efficiently, please follow this procedure:

Explains why change in procedures is necessary.

1. Write an advertisement for a position in your department.

2. Let Human Resources place the ad in an appropriate newspaper.

3. Pick up applicant folders from Human Resources the day following the closing date provided in the ad.

Starts each listed item with a verb.

Following these guidelines will save you work and will also enable Human Resources to help you fill your openings more quickly. Call Ann Edmonds at Ext. 2505 if you have questions about this procedure.

Closes by reinforcing benefits.

procedure is stated negatively *(Do not submit your advertisements . . .)* and is hidden inside two paragraphs.

The effective version begins directly by telling readers immediately what the memo is about. The next paragraph explains why the change is necessary. A list enumerates step-by-step procedures, thus making it easy for the reader to understand and follow the steps. The final paragraph restates the primary benefits of the new procedure and tells how more information may be obtained if necessary.

MEMOS AND E-MAIL MESSAGES THAT REQUEST

Messages that make requests are most effective when they use the direct approach. The reader learns immediately what is being requested. However, if you have any reason to suspect that the reader may resist the request, then an indirect approach would probably be more successful.

Requests should be courteous and respectful, such as the one shown in Figure 5.4. They should not be demanding or dictatorial. The tone of the following request would likely antagonize its recipient:

> I want you to find out why the Davis account was not included in this report, and I want this information before you do anything else.

So that the intent of the message is not misunderstood, requests should be considered carefully and written clearly. What may seem clear to the writer may not always be clear to a reader. That's why it's always a good idea to have a fellow worker read important messages for clarity before they are sent out.

Whenever possible, the closing paragraph of a request should be *end dated*. An end date sets a deadline for the requested action and gives a reason for this action to be completed by the deadline. Such end dating prevents procrastination and allows the reader to plan a course of action to ensure completion by the date given. Notice in Figure 5.4 that the writer ends by asking that the responses be made before May 5 so that the information gathered can be used at a May 8 management meeting. Giving a reason adds credibility to a deadline.

> Please submit your order by December 1 so that sufficient labels will be on hand for mailing the year-end reports January 15.

The tone of a request message should encourage cooperation.

End dating includes a deadline and, if possible, a reason explaining the deadline.

MEMOS AND E-MAIL MESSAGES THAT RESPOND

Much office correspondence reacts or responds to memos, e-mail messages, and other documents. When responding to a document, follow these preparatory steps:

1. Collect whatever information is necessary.
2. Organize your thoughts.
3. Make a brief outline of the points you plan to cover. You may wish to make your outline or notes right on the document you are answering.

Begin the memo with a clear statement of the main idea, which often is a summary of the contents of the memo. Avoid wordy and dated openings such as *Pursuant to your request of January 20, I am herewith including the information you wanted*. Although many business messages actually sound like this, these kinds of messages waste time and say little.

Preparing to write a memo involves collecting and organizing information into an outline.

FIGURE 5.4

E-mail Message That Requests

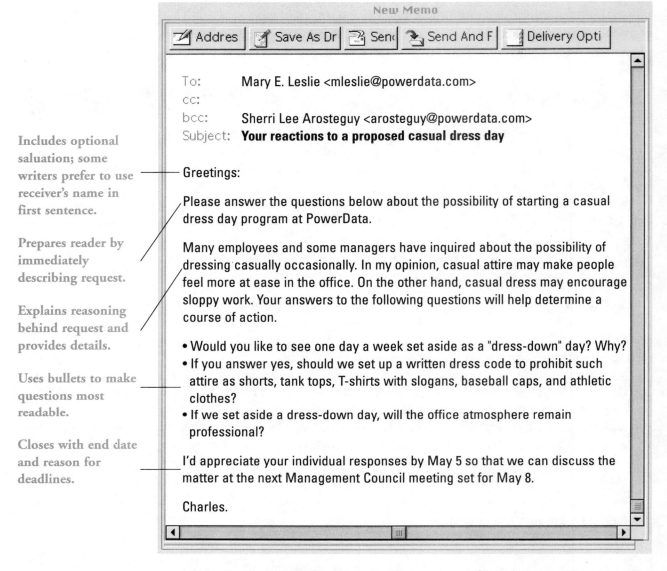

Includes optional salutation; some writers prefer to use receiver's name in first sentence.

Prepares reader by immediately describing request.

Explains reasoning behind request and provides details.

Uses bullets to make questions most readable.

Closes with end date and reason for deadlines.

(E-mail message shown in figure:)

New Memo

Addres | Save As Dr | Send | Send And F | Delivery Opti

To: Mary E. Leslie <mleslie@powerdata.com>
cc:
bcc: Sherri Lee Arosteguy <arosteguy@powerdata.com>
Subject: **Your reactions to a proposed casual dress day**

Greetings:

Please answer the questions below about the possibility of starting a casual dress day program at PowerData.

Many employees and some managers have inquired about the possibility of dressing casually occasionally. In my opinion, casual attire may make people feel more at ease in the office. On the other hand, casual dress may encourage sloppy work. Your answers to the following questions will help determine a course of action.

- Would you like to see one day a week set aside as a "dress-down" day? Why?
- If you answer yes, should we set up a written dress code to prohibit such attire as shorts, tank tops, T-shirts with slogans, baseball caps, and athletic clothes?
- If we set aside a dress-down day, will the office atmosphere remain professional?

I'd appreciate your individual responses by May 5 so that we can discuss the matter at the next Management Council meeting set for May 8.

Charles.

Notice in Figure 5.5 that Mary Leslie, manager of Legal Support Services, uses a straightforward opening in responding to her boss's request for information, referring to the request, announcing the information to follow, and identifying the date of the original message. Mary decides to answer with a standard hard-copy memo because she considers her reactions private and because she thinks that her boss will want to have a permanent record of each manager's reactions to take to the management council meeting. She also knows that she is well within the deadline set for a response.

The body of a response memo provides the information requested. Its organization generally follows the sequence of the request. In Mary's memo she answers the questions as her boss presented them. However, she further clarifies the information by providing summarizing headings in bold type. These headings emphasize the groupings and help the reader see immediately what information is covered. The memo closes with a summarizing and reassuring statement.

FIGURE 5.5

Memo That Responds

TO: Mabel Lam, Vice-President, Employee Relations

FROM: Mary E. Leslie, Manager, Legal Support Services

DATE: May 4, 200x

SUBJECT: REACTIONS TO PROPOSED CASUAL DRESS DAY PROGRAM

Here are my reactions to your inquiry about a casual dress day program made in your e-mail message of May 2.

> *Summarizes main idea and refers to previous message.*

- **Establish a casual dress day?** Yes, I would like to see such a day. In my department we now have a number of employees with flex schedules. They perform part of their work at home, where they can be as casual as they wish. Employees confined here in the office are a little resentful. I think a casual dress day could offer some compensation to those who come to the office daily.

- **Implement a dress code?** By all means! We definitely need a written dress code to establish company standards.

> *Arranges responses in order of original request and uses boldface headings to emphasize and clarify groupings.*

- **Professional office atmosphere?** I would hope that casual dress would not promote casual work attitudes as well. We must establish that professionalism is non-negotiable. For example, we can't allow two-hour lunches or entire afternoons spent gossiping instead of working. Moreover, I think we should be careful in allowing casual dress only on the designated day, once a week.

I think a casual attire program can be beneficial and improve morale. But we definitely need a dress code in place at the beginning of the program. Let me know if I may assist in implementing a casual dress day program.

> *Closes with reassuring remark and offer of further assistance.*

SUMMING UP AND LOOKING FORWARD

Memorandums and e-mail messages serve as vital channels of information within business offices. They use a standardized format to request and deliver information. In this chapter you learned to apply the direct strategy in writing messages that inform, request, and respond. You also learned to use bullets, numbers, and parallel form for listing information so that main points stand out. In the next chapter you will extend the direct strategy to writing letters that make requests.

DISCUSSION

1. Explain the functions of memos and e-mail messages within organizations.
2. Distinguish between the direct and indirect strategies.
3. How can memos and e-mail messages waste time, money, and resources?
4. Discuss this statement: Once you send a memo or an e-mail message, you have essentially published it.
5. Name four groups of memos and explain what strategy each should follow.

CHAPTER REVIEW

6. List three categories into which most messages can be grouped.

7. Explain what reader reaction you might expect for each of the three categories of messages you listed above.

8. What are the four guide words that appear at the top of most memos?

9. The use of a standardized memo format benefits whom?

10. Why should a memo or an e-mail message cover only one topic?

11. How do electronic mail and standard memos differ?

12. List five tips you could give to a person being introduced to the use of e-mail. Be prepared to discuss each.

13. List and describe briefly four parts of the writing plan for a memo.

14. Why are items listed vertically easy to read?

15. What is end dating?

Writing Improvement Exercises

Memo Openers and Organization. Compare the sets of message openers below. Circle the letter of the opener that illustrates a direct opening. Be prepared to discuss the weaknesses and strengths of each opener shown.

16. a. For some time now we have been thinking about the possibility of developing an in-service training program for some of our employees.

   b. Employees interested in acquiring and improving computer skills are invited to an in-service training program beginning October 4.

17. a. I am asking our Customer Relations Department to conduct a study and make recommendations regarding the gradual but steady decline of customer chequing accounts.

   b. We have noticed recently a gradual but steady decline in the number of customer chequing accounts. We are disturbed by this trend, and for this reason I am asking our Customer Relations Department to conduct a study and make recommendations regarding this important problem.

18. a. Some customer representatives in the field have suggested that they would like to key their reports from the field instead of coming back to the office to enter them in their computers. For this reason, we have made a number of changes. We would like you to use the following procedures.

   b. Customer representatives may now key their field reports using the following procedures.

Opening Paragraphs. The following opening paragraphs to memos are wordy and indirect. After reading each paragraph, identify the main idea. Then, write an opening sentence that illustrates a more direct opening. Use a separate sheet if necessary.

19. Some of our staff members are interested in computer software that might lessen our work here in Accounting. Several staff members asked if they could attend a seminar on February 11. This seminar previews accounting software that might be effective in our department. I am allowing the following employees to attend the seminar: Dave Neufeld, Tayreez Mushani, and Gail Switzer.

20. Your TechData Employees Association has secured for you discounts on auto repair, carpet purchases, travel arrangements, and many other services. These services are available to you if you have a Buying Power Card. All TechData employees are eligible for their own private Buying Power Cards.

Lists. Write lists as indicated below.

21. Use the following information to compose a sentence that includes an introductory statement and a list:

    Please follow in the plant at all times the following rules and restrictions. Hard hats should be worn at all times. Refrain from horseplay please. Smoking is prohibited for the good of all.

22. Use the following information to compose a bulleted vertical list with an introductory statement:

    To use the conventional Rollerblade heel brake, you should do these things. First, you should move one leg slightly forward. Then the ball of your foot should be lifted. Finally, the heel should be dragged to complete the braking action.

23. Use the following information to compose a sentence containing a list:

    Your lease is about to expire. When it does, you must make a decision. Three options are available to you. If you like, you may purchase the equipment at fair market value. Or the existing lease may be extended, again at fair market value. Finally, if neither of these options is appealing, the equipment could be sent back to the lessor.

Memo Format. Study memo formatting and parts in Appendix A. Then answer these questions:

24. Are standard memos usually single- or double-spaced?

25. Does a writer place his or her name at the end of a memo or e-mail message?

ACTIVITIES AND CASES

5.1 Memo That Informs: Sky-High Printing Bills. As Patricia Isaac, director of operations for DPI, a small software company, you are disturbed about some very large printing bills you've been receiving. Although all the bills seem high, a recent bill from PrintMasters is particularly suspicious. You don't want to blame anyone, but you do want to inform all staff members that no printing bills will be paid in the future without careful scrutiny. In talking it over with Sylvie Marchand, your colleague, you say, "We've got to make some changes. I can't plan my budget or control costs with these outrageous printing bills popping up." As a result of your discussion, you and Sylvie decide that DPI needs a standardized procedure for handling its printing requirements. Starting immediately, all departments must write out their exact specifications and then get two written estimates, which should be submitted to Sylvie for authorization, before they can order any outside printing job. The new procedures mean that DPI will probably get more competitive pricing and that departments will find better, more creative printing options. Now you must write a memo to the staff announcing the changes.

To help you organize your memo according to the principles you have learned in this chapter, read the options suggested here. Circle the most appropriate response for each question. Be prepared to discuss your reasoning for each choice.

1. What is the main idea in this memo?
   a. You are outraged at the high printing bills being received lately.
   b. You can't plan budgets or control costs when these unexpected bills keep coming in.
   c. The bill from PrintMasters is particularly suspicious.
   d. A new procedure for submitting requests for outside printing jobs is being instituted immediately.

2. An effective opening sentence for your memo might be
   a. Sylvie Marchand and I have been concerned about the high printing bills we have received lately.
   b. Please follow the new procedures listed below in submitting requests for outside printing jobs.
   c. Very large expenditures for printing jobs have been submitted recently, some of which are quite suspicious.
   d. Henceforth, no employee may send out a printing job without prior written approval.

3. The body of the memo should
   a. Explain why the new procedure is necessary and how to follow the new procedure.
   b. Recount the highlights of your conversation with Sylvie.
   c. Identify the most suspicious printing bills, particularly the one from PrintMasters.
   d. Identify the departments and employees who have been responsible for most of the high costs.

4. In explaining the new procedure, you will probably want to list each step. Which of the following statements illustrates the best form for listing the steps?
   a. Submission of all written estimates should be made to Sylvie Marchand.
   b. Written estimates should be submitted to Sylvie Marchand.
   c. Submit written estimates to Sylvie Marchand.
   d. Sylvie Marchand will expect all written estimates to be submitted to her.

5. An effective closing for your memo might be
   a. These procedures are effective immediately. Thank you for your cooperation in this matter.
   b. Following these new procedures, which are effective immediately, will result in more competitive pricing and perhaps may even provide you with new creative printing options. If you have any questions, call Sylvie Marchand at Ext. 556.

c. These procedures are effective immediately. By the way, don't forget to send me your ideas for equipping the new fitness centre.

d. If I may be of assistance to you in any way, do not hesitate to call me.

Use this memo for class discussion or as a writing assignment. If your instructor directs, compose the message as a standard memo addressed to all staff members or as an e-mail message addressed to your instructor.

5.2 Memo That Requests: Making the Best of Temps. Analyze the following poorly written memo and list at least five faults. Outline an appropriate plan for a memo that requests, then write an improved version of this memo.

Ineffective Writing

TO:	Department Managers
FROM:	Ryan Crawford, Manager
	Human Resources Department
DATE:	January 14, 200x
SUBJECT:	TEMPORARY WORKERS

This is to inform you that we have not been totally happy with the quality of the temporary workers we are getting. We have trouble budgeting for them, their selection is difficult, and so is the hiring of these extra workers.

Hoping to improve the problem, your help is requested. We need to know your past history in regard to the average number of temporary office workers in your department. This number would be based on how many you use each month. Your input is also requested in regard to the time a temporary worker remains in your employ. As a general rule, do you know the length of a temporary worker's work assignment? We're talking about your department only, of course. Another important bit of information revolves around the skills you need. To get you the best temps, your needs must be known. As a matter of fact, we also would like to know what temporary agencies you now use to supply temps to your department.

Pursuant to this request, we need your response by January 20. It would be advisable for you to write your answers on this sheet. Pending receipt of the return of this request, may we take the liberty of thanking you in advance. Through the use of the information you provide, we will make plans for an improved policy. That will help you fill your temporary employment needs pertaining to your department as efficiently as possible.

5.3 Memo That Responds: Management Council Speakers. Kimberly Kloss, secretary of the Management Council of DataTech, wrote a first draft of the following memo. Before mailing it, she attended a company workshop on improving communication techniques. Based on what she learned, she wrote comments to herself. Revise the memo using her suggestions.

TO: Martin Reid, Craig Joseph, Jacquie Laurendeau

Long-winded memo . . . wastes everyone's time!

FROM: Cynthia Chomsky

DATE: February 3, 199x

SUBJECT: Reminder   ← *really vague . . . must improve*

As you know, the Management Council is very concerned about our employee hiring techniques. This has become a problem in our company. I heard many of you say at our last meeting in January that you felt we had to improve our selection of employees. I understand that some new employees are hired for positions for which they are unsuited, and we don't seem to learn about the problem until it's too late. We really need to improve the entire personnel selection process, beginning with the writing of job specifications to the interviewing process. One area where we have been particularly lax is the checking of applicants' references.

this first ¶ is a real drag!

They already know all this stuff . . . condense or leave out

I was asked at our last meeting in January to find speakers. I spent a lot of time finding individuals who I thought would bring us valuable information about improving our interviewing and other hiring techniques. I think you're all really going to benefit from the programs I've arranged. Please be reminded that the Management Council meets at 2:30 p.m. in Conference Room C.   *need this?*

too much "I" – not enough "you"

move to end   *add end date*

If for some reason you cannot attend any of these meetings, you must call me. We also voted, if you will recall, to include outside guests at these last three sessions. So, if you would like to invite anyone, tell me his name so I can send him an invitation. — *by when?*

sexist!

Here are the three speakers I have arranged. The first is Norman J. Withers, from ABC Consultants. He will speak February 20 on the topic of "Job Specifications." Dr. Ann D. Seaman, University of Calgary, is the next speaker. She will speak on the topic of "The Interviewing Process," and her date is March 28. Last but not least is Erick Basil, from Smith & Burney, Inc. The title of his talk is "Reference Checking," set for April 30.

check spelling of names

arrange in list . . . use headings?

shorten entire memo!

cliché

5.4 Memo That Informs: What I Do on the Job. Write the following memo based on your own work or personal experience. Some employees have remarked to the boss that they are working more than other employees. Your boss has decided to study the matter by collecting memos from everyone and asks you to write a memo describing your current duties and the skills required for your position. If some jobs are found to be overly demanding, your boss may redistribute tasks or hire additional employees. Write a well-organized memo describing your duties, the time you spend on each task, and the skills needed for what you do. Provide enough details to make a clear outline of your job. Your boss or organization head appreciates brevity. Keep your memo under one page.

5.5 Memo That Informs: Party Time. As Wendy Nguyen, you have been asked to draft a memo to the office staff about the upcoming December holiday party. Decide what kind of party you would like. Include information about where the party will be held, when it is, what the cost will be, a description of the food to be served, whether guests are allowed, and whom to make reservations with.

5.6 Memo That Informs: Trading Obscenities. The Canadian Securities Commission (CSC) has been watching a recent initiative of the National Association of Securities Dealers in the United States. The NASD has sent a notice warning its member brokers against "the use of profane or obscene language." As more women become brokers, crude language has led to an increase in job-related harassment and toxic work environment complaints. To be fair, it should be noted that not all the complaints have come from women. Nevertheless, the new directive from NASD aims to require its members to police communication between brokers and their clients, and between traders. To ensure that this type of problem is addressed or avoided in Canada, the CSC wants its members to know about the NASD initiative.

As Mark Mandel, manager of a prestigious brokerage house in Toronto, you have just received a letter from the CSC advising you of the NASD initiative and the CSC's support for it. Write a memo to the numerous brokers on your staff informing them of the letter's concerns. Avoid blaming the entire staff for vulgar language. Though only a few of your brokers use obscenities regularly, you still have to emphasize the seriousness of the situation. Strive to gain everyone's cooperation.

5.7 Memo That Informs: It's a Dog-Eat-Pasta World. As Pamela Haas, marketing director for Premier Pet Products, you have just completed the planning stages of a campaign, organized by your advertising agency, The Wootton Group. The management council of Premier gave the go-ahead to Wootton for a unique effort to push pasta as an ideal food for pets. The most visible element of the campaign is a "Teach Your Dog to Say Pasta" contest. Dog owners will be encouraged to send in videotapes of their dogs barking "pasta." Sounds weird, but several dog owners swear that their dogs can do it. Sixty-second radio spots in several target markets across the country encourage contestants to call 1-800-PASTADG. Tied in with the promotion are product names such as Woof-A-Roni dog treats. Other promotional events will be held in grocery store "barking lots" in as many as 30 communities this summer. Hot dogs will be sold, of course, and dogs will participate in Frisbee games and costume contests. The promotions will end in August. The owner of the talking-dog contest winner will receive a two-week trip to Italy, where dogs are said to be crazy about pasta.

Your task is to inform Vice-President Matt Brooks of the details of the campaign that you and the advertising agency have developed. Prepare a well-organized memo listing the elements of the promotion.

5.8 Memo That Responds: What's New at Canada Post. Assume you are Leticia Boychuk and you work for MagicMedia Inc., a large software manufacturer. The office manager, Rachel Wilder, asks you to seek two kinds of information from Canada Post. First, she wants to learn exactly how envelopes should be addressed according to Canada Post guidelines. Second, she wants to know the air and surface rates for sending packages to the United States. She expects to be sending plenty of parcels to an American client in the spring. The easiest way to obtain this information is by visiting the Canada Post Web site; but, if that is impossible, go to a local postal outlet. Write a one-page memo summarizing your findings.

Related Web Site: www.canadapost.com

5.9 Memo That Requests: No More Paycheques. As Lindsay English, director of human resources, write a memo to all department managers of General Wheat, a large food company. The company has decided that to reduce costs employees will no longer receive a traditional paycheque. Instead, their pay will be electronically deposited into their bank accounts. Employees will receive a Summary of Pay Notice, which will indicate basic earnings and employee deductions such as income tax, and Canada Pension Plan and Employment Insurance deductions. Employees must provide the name and address of their local bank branch, their bank account number, and the bank branch transfer number. Explain why this is a good policy.

5.10 Memo That Responds: No More Paycheques. You are Bruni Comenic, manager of accounting services for General Wheat, responding to Ms. English's memo in the preceding problem. You could have called Ms. English, but you prefer to have a permanent record of this message. You are having difficulty collecting the required information from the departments. Department heads have told you that their employees are calling this initiative an invasion of privacy; as a result, very few employee account and transfer numbers have been forwarded to Accounting. This situation, if left unchecked, will mean the costs of issuing paycheques will go up (because the company will have to maintain both a paper-based cheque service and an electronic one) rather than down. Your staff is frustrated. You feel help from a higher authority is necessary. Appeal to Ms. English for solutions.

5.11 Memo That Informs: Wilderness Retreat. Assume you are Mark Peters, president of a small printing operation employing 25 workers. On Friday, June 7, your print shop employees will join you on an expense-paid, one-day retreat that you hope will improve teamwork among the workers. The retreat will be led by Wilderness Retreats, which offers companies outdoor team training designed to build employee trust, teamwork, and loyalty. Employees will meet at work at 8 a.m., and a Wilderness Retreats van will pick all of you up and take you to a nearby national park. Employees will spend the day on team-building activities, including a map-reading exercise that will require employee teams to find their way through a wooded area to a "home base." The group will return to work by 4 p.m. Since the print shop will be closed during the retreat, you consider the retreat a work day and expect all employees to attend. Write a memo to employees announcing the retreat.

5.12 Connecting with E-Mail: Memo That Informs: Sweet Rewards. The Candy Show in Vancouver is a "must attend" trade show for all manufacturers of sweets, including cereals and even fruit drinks. This year's main attractions were novelty and fat-free, natural items. "Nobody sells just candy anymore," observed one visitor. You need a gimmick, such as a connection with a cartoon character, a toy, or something high-tech. For example, Amural Confections featured a refillable "gumputer," available in three different flavours. Licensed merchandise, such as Golden Harvest Products' Mickey Mouse popcorn and sunflower seeds, is also very popular. Sports licences were also hot, such as an NHL gum bank. After novelty items, the most popular Candy Show items were natural or sugar- and fat-free products. Newman's Own, already well known for its salad dressings, showed off a new line of organic chocolate. Among the fat-free items, M&M/Mars introduced Starburst Jellybeans, bite-sized versions of the popular Fruit Chews candy. In the novelty area, Andes Candies is presenting its traditional mint thins in two new seasonal packages: a crystal twist pack containing a gift rose and a heart-shaped tin. Another big news item was "bigger bag" or bulk packaging. Nestlé is offering larger quantities of candy brands such as Arrow and Kit Kat in 200-gram bags, and Nestlé Crunch in 170-gram bags. These oversized options offer twice as much product and a definite price advantage over the regular Fun-Size bag. On its bulk packaging, Nestlé is looking for large profit margins of 30 to 80 percent with minimal decline in its smaller package candy sales.

As Peter Kim, assistant marketing director at a large Vancouver candy manufacturer, you have been sent to this year's Candy Show to observe what's hot. You are exhausted after visiting nearly all the exhibits in two days. But you must respond to your boss's request that you use your laptop computer to send her an e-mail message summarizing what you saw. She asked you to pick out three trends that could affect your company's product development. Describe each trend briefly. You'll give a full report when you return to the office.

5.13 Searching the Internet: Chocolates on the Web: Memo That Responds. Again act as Peter Kim, assistant marketing director at a large Vancouver candy manufacturer. Your boss asks you to check out a competitor's World Wide Web site. Godiva chocolates, according to your boss, has a much-acclaimed Web site. You are to go to the site, examine what it offers, and report your findings. Godiva is an upscale chocolatier offering its delights in the best department stores, as well as through its own stores and catalogue. Your boss wonders if a Web site might be a good investment for your company. In an e-mail message, report to your boss (your instructor, in this instance) on how Godiva uses the site and what it features.

Related Web Site: www.godiva.com/

GRAMMAR/MECHANICS CHECKUP—5

Prepositions and Conjunctions

Review Sections 1.18 and 1.19 in the Grammar/Mechanics Handbook. Then study each of the following statements. Write *a* or *b* to indicate the sentence in which the idea is expressed more effectively. Also record the number of the G/M principle illustrated. When you finish, compare your responses with those provided. If your answers differ, study carefully the principles shown in parentheses.

Example: (a) Raoul will graduate college this spring.   b   (1.18a)
           (b) Raoul will graduate from college this spring.

1. (a) DataTech enjoyed greater profits this year then it expected.   _____
   (b) DataTech enjoyed greater profits this year than it expected.
2. (a) I hate it when we have to work overtime.   _____
   (b) I hate when we have to work overtime.
3. (a) Dr. Simon has a great interest and appreciation for the study of robotics.   _____
   (b) Dr. Simon has a great interest in and appreciation for the study of robotics.
4. (a) Gross profit is where you compute the difference between total sales and the   _____
       cost of goods sold.
   (b) Gross profit is computed by finding the difference between total sales and
       the cost of goods sold.
5. (a) We advertise to increase the frequency of product use, to introduce comple-   _____
       mentary products, and to enhance our corporate image.
   (b) We advertise to have our products used more often, when we have comple-
       mentary products to introduce, and we are interested in making our corpo-
       ration look better to the public.
6. (a) What type computers do you prefer?   _____
   (b) What type of computers do you prefer?
7. (a) Many of our new products are selling better then we anticipated.   _____
   (b) Many of our new products are selling better than we anticipated.
8. (a) The sale of our Halifax branch office last year should improve this year's   _____
       profits.
   (b) The sale of our branch office in Halifax during last year should improve the
       profits for this year.
9. (a) Do you know where the meeting is at?   _____
   (b) Do you know where the meeting is?
10. (a) The cooling-off rule is a provincial government rule that protects consumers   _____
        from making unwise purchases at home.
    (b) The cooling-off rule is where the provincial government has made a rule
        that protects consumers from making unwise purchases at home.
11. (a) Meetings can be more meaningful if the agenda is stuck to, the time frame   _____
        is followed, and if someone keeps follow-up notes.
    (b) Meetings can be more meaningful if you stick to the agenda, follow the time
        frame, and keep follow-up notes.
12. (a) They printed the newsletter on yellow paper like we asked them to do.   _____
    (b) They printed the newsletter on yellow paper as we asked them to do.
13. (a) A code of ethics is a set of rules spelling out appropriate standards of behaviour.   _____
    (b) A code of ethics is where a set of rules spells out appropriate standards of
        behaviour.
14. (a) We need an individual with an understanding and serious interest in black-   _____
        and-white photography.
    (b) We need an individual with an understanding of and serious interest in
        black-and-white photography.
15. (a) The most dangerous situation is when employees ignore the safety rules.   _____
    (b) The most dangerous situation occurs when employees ignore the safety
        rules.

---

1. b (1.19d)   3. b (1.18e)   5. a (1.19a)   7. b (1.19d)   9. b (1.18b)   11. b (1.19a)   13. a (1.19c)
15. b (1.19c)

Document for Revision

The following memo has faults in grammar, punctuation, spelling, capitalization, number form, repetition, wordiness, and other areas. Use standard proofreading marks (see Appendix B) to correct the errors. When you finish, your instructor can show you the revised version of this memo.

Ineffective Writing

TO: Amy Mackenzie

FROM: Ira White

DATE: June 25, 200x

SUBJECT: COLLECTING DATA FOR ANNUAL REPORT

You have been assigned a special project, to collect information for next years annual report. You'll probably need to visit each department head personally to collect this information individually from them.

The Corporate Communications division which oversee the production of the annual report is of the opinion that you should concentrate on the following departmental data;

1. specific accomplishments of each department for the past year.

2. you must find out about goals of each department for the coming year.

3. in each department get names of interesting employees and events to be featured.

In view of the fact that this is a big assignment Maria Lukacz has been assigned to offer assistance to you. Inasmuch as the annual report must be completed by September first; please submit your data in concise narrative form to me by August fifth.

Communication Workshop: Technology

IS SOMEONE READING YOUR E-MAIL?

What happens when illegal or inappropriate information is found in an employee's computer? The University of British Columbia faced just such a situation. A student had asked a professor to review several e-mail messages containing course-related information. During the review, the professor discovered plagiarized materials on the student's computer. When confronted, the student admitted to saving the plagiarized material on his computer. He protested that the professor had no right to search other files on his computer. After a long and costly review process, the student failed the course. Shortly thereafter, the university drafted a code of ethics limiting privacy rights on school computers.[8]

Many people believe that electronic information is both private and temporary. They think that computers, whether company owned or not, are a secure place to store all sorts of information. After all, offensive or inappropriate electronic messages can be removed from a computer's hard drive with a simple stroke of the delete button. Or can they? Bill Gates, CEO of Microsoft, has found quite the opposite to be true. He has gained new respect for the lasting power of electronic documents and messages. Recently Microsoft found itself at the centre of a long antitrust trial in the United States. Most of the more than 3000 exhibits in the trial consisted of e-mail messages. The messages, some dating as far back as 1995, were recovered from the e-mail systems of the world's most successful software companies.[9] These messages formed the basis of the evidence used to support the claim that Microsoft was guilty of unfair business practices.

At the time the messages were sent, the senders had no idea their off-hand comments and informal replies would survive for so long. Nor did they know that these brief notes would become so important. But each should have been aware that e-mail is not private and that e-mail messages last.

Many corporations and institutions have developed acceptable-use policies for company-owned computers. They are trying to protect against the shock of legal action and to communicate to employees ethical and behavioural guidelines designed to protect both the employee and the employer. These policies focus on the privacy rights of employees and on the rights a company has over electronic information contained on company-owned computers. Many acceptable-use policies also include a clear statement of the employer's right to ensure that computer systems are used only for company purposes, even if that means monitoring messages and files.

Application. As the student representative on your school's Communications Committee, you have been asked to be a member of a subcommittee that will develop an acceptable-use policy for your school's computer system. In groups of three to five, discuss major areas the policy should address, such as using school equipment for playing games, downloading extremely large files, and sending private messages using the school e-mail system. Decide if e-mail should be monitored. Then individually or as a group, write a memo containing your suggestions and send it to the committee chair, Alicia Pena. Be explicit in outlining what constitutes appropriate use at your school. The following Web site provides a good appropriate-use policy example: www.cc.ubc.ca/appropriate-use/aup.html.

LETTERS THAT MAKE ROUTINE REQUESTS

We are committed to writing that uses plain language. Our internal messages and customer letters are becoming more reader-centred and a lot shorter.[1]

DENNICE M. LEAHEY, senior vice-president and ombudsman, Royal Bank Financial Group

Learning Objectives

1. Analyze letter content and select an appropriate writing strategy.
2. Write letters that request information concisely.
3. Write letters that order merchandise clearly and efficiently.
4. Identify and use appropriate salutations for letters.
5. Write letters that make justified claims.

Letters that fail to get to the point are a concern for senior management at the Royal Bank. A bank's livelihood depends on the quality of information it provides to its customers. Without clear messages that transmit information concisely, the Royal Bank risks alienating current customers and losing potential customers.

Messages that meander slowly toward their point have little appeal for most of us. Readers want to know why a message was written and how it involves them. And they want that information up front.

This chapter discusses written communication that travels outside an organization. Such communication generally takes the form of letters. Executives, managers, and supervisors at all levels of management, as well as nonmanagement employees, typically are called on daily to exchange information with customers and other organizations. Although information is also exchanged verbally, written communication in the form of letters is essential to provide a convenient, well-considered, and permanent communication record. This chapter examines letters that make routine requests, such as those requesting information, ordering merchandise, and making claims.

Like memos, letters are easiest to write when you have a plan to follow. The plan for letters, just as for memos, is fixed by the content of the message and its expected effect on the receiver. Letters delivering bad news require an indirect approach (Chapter 8). Most letters, however, carry good or neutral news. Because such letters will not produce a negative effect on their readers, they follow the direct strategy. You will recall that the main idea comes first in the direct strategy.

The content of a message and its anticipated effect on the reader determine the strategy you choose.

INFORMATION REQUESTS

The first kind of letter to be described in this chapter is the information request. Although the specific subject of each inquiry may differ, the similarity of purpose in routine requests enables writers to use the following writing plan.

WRITING PLAN FOR AN INFORMATION REQUEST

- *Opening*—asks the most important question first or expresses a polite command.
- *Body*—explains the request logically and courteously and asks other questions.
- *Closing*—requests a specific action with an end date, if appropriate, and shows appreciation.

OPENING DIRECTLY

Readers find the openings and closings of letters most interesting.

The most emphatic positions in a letter are the first and last sentences. Readers tend to look at them first. The writer, then, should capitalize on this tendency by putting the most significant statement first. The first sentence of an information request is usually a question or a polite command. It should not be an explanation or justification, unless resistance to the request is expected. When the information requested is likely to be forthcoming, immediately tell the reader what you want. This saves the reader's time and may ensure that the message is read. A busy executive who skims the mail, quickly reading subject lines and first sentences only, may grasp your request rapidly and act on it. A request that follows a lengthy explanation, on the other hand, may never be found.

Compare the two openings in the following inquiry about a computer program. The direct opening, expressed as a polite command, is far more effective because the reader knows immediately what is being requested.

> **Indirect Opening:** I read about the electronic tax filing program in the June 5 issue of *The Calgary Herald.* Because I have a business preparing tax returns primarily for construction contractors, I am very interested in this program. Would you please send me information about it.
>
> **Direct Opening:** Please send me information about your electronic tax filing program that was advertised in *The Calgary Herald* on June 5.

When a request seeks specific information, the first sentence of the inquiry letter will probably be a question:

> Will the electronic tax filing program advertised in *The Calgary Herald* run with Windows software?

Begin an information request letter with the most important question or a summarizing statement.

If several questions must be asked, use one of two approaches: (1) ask the most important question first, or (2) introduce the questions with a summary statement. The following example poses the most important question first, followed by other questions:

> Can the CMA's summer management institute be used as credit toward my certificate in human resources management?

Does the CMA issue an official education tax receipt for the institute?
If I register for the institute and then must cancel, may I receive a refund?

If you want to ask many questions that are equally important, begin with a summarizing statement:

Will you please answer the following questions about the CMA's summer institute in Quebec City.

Notice that the summarizing statement sounds like a question but has no question mark. That's because it's really a command disguised as a question. Rather than bluntly demanding information (*Answer the following questions*), we often prefer to soften commands by posing them as questions. Such statements (some authorities call them rhetorical questions) should not be punctuated as questions because they do not require answers.

DETAILS IN THE BODY

The body of a letter that requests information should provide necessary details and should be easy to read. Effective letters can be quickly scanned for the most important information. They use highlighting techniques such as bullets, numbered lists, and boldface print to make main points stand out. Highlighted text makes for fast reading and also for quick reference when the document is reviewed.

The body of a request letter may contain an explanation or a list of questions.

In the following example, the writer is after specific information from the local police association regarding their participation in a wellness fair. Notice that her bulleted questions are much easier to read than if the same information were written in paragraph form.

- How many officers will be able to participate in the Wellness Fair?
- Can you provide a list of their names?
- Do you want us to provide any equipment?
- What times are best for participating officers?

Items enumerated in a list are much easier to read than items bunched in a paragraph.

As you learned in Chapter 5, listed items are most effective when they are phrased similarly, that is, when they are parallel. Each of the questions posed should follow the same grammatical structure.

The quality of the information obtained from a request letter depends on the clarity of the inquiry. If you analyze your needs, organize your ideas, and frame your request logically, you are likely to receive a meaningful answer.

CLOSING WITH AN ACTION REQUEST

Use the final paragraph to ask for specific action, to set an end date if appropriate, and to express appreciation.

The ending of a request letter should tell the reader what you want done and when.

As you learned in working with memos, a request for action is most effective when an end date and reason for that date are supplied. If it's appropriate, use this kind of end dating:

Please answer the questions listed above and send me the information by October 15 so that we can ensure a successful event on October 30. We sincerely appreciate the contribution of your officers in this rewarding function.

It's always appropriate to end a request letter with appreciation for the action taken. However, don't fall into a cliché trap, such as *Thanking you in advance, I remain . . .* or the familiar *Thank you for any information you can send me.* Your appreciation will sound most sincere if you avoid mechanical, tired expressions. Here's a simple but sincere closing to a request for insurance information:

> I would appreciate it if you could send me this information by July 10, when I will be re-evaluating my entire insurance program.

ILLUSTRATING THE PLAN

The letter shown in Figure 6.1 requests information about conference accommodations and illustrates the writing plan you have learned. The letter has many questions to ask and begins with the most important one. The letter also illustrates the major parts of a business letter. Notice that it uses block style, the most popular letter style. For more information about letter formats and styles, see Appendix A.

ORDER REQUESTS

To order merchandise, you may occasionally have to write a letter.

The second category of letter to be presented in this chapter is the order request. Orders for merchandise are usually made by telephone, by fax, or by filling out an order form. On occasion, though, you may find it necessary to write a letter ordering merchandise. For example, if you had a merchandise catalogue but couldn't find its order forms, or if you were responding to an advertisement in a magazine, you'd have to write a letter to place an order.

Order requests use the direct strategy, beginning with the main idea.

WRITING PLAN FOR AN ORDER REQUEST

- *Opening*—authorizes purchase and suggests method of shipping.
- *Body*—lists items vertically; provides quantity, order number, description, and unit price; and shows total price of order.
- *Closing*—requests shipment by a specific date, tells method of payment, and expresses appreciation.

EFFECTIVE AND INEFFECTIVE ORDER LETTERS

A vague and confusing order letter, such as that shown at the top of Figure 6.2, is frustrating because it forces the reader to request additional information. Brent Royer wrote this letter in response to an advertisement featuring bargain prices for computer games. But the ad provided no toll-free number or order blank.

His first version is faulty for many reasons. Notice that the opening doesn't establish the message as an order. Moreover, the first sentence is 40 words long, making its meaning difficult to comprehend. Most sentences should average 15 to 20 words. Finally, this letter does not sufficiently describe the items being ordered, and it fails to mention a method of payment. The reader probably wonders if this is really an order.

FIGURE 6.1

Letter That Requests—Information-Block Style

GEOTECH ——————————————————— Letterhead
255 Cherry Street
Corner Brook NF
A2L 3W5

August 20, 200x ——————————————— Dateline

Ms. Jane Mangrum, Manager
Vancouver Hilton Hotel
6333 North Scottsdale Road —————————— Inside Address
Vancouver, BC   V5H 1W4

Dear Ms. Mangrum: ——————————————— Salutation

Can the Vancouver Hilton provide meeting rooms and accommodations for about
250 Geotech sales representatives from May 25 through May 29?

It is my responsibility to locate a hotel that offers both resort and conference facilities appropriate for the spring sales meeting of my company. Please answer these ———— Body
additional questions regarding the Vancouver Hilton:

1. Does the hotel have a banquet room that can seat 250?
2. Do you have at least four smaller meeting rooms, each to accommodate a maximum of 75?
3. Do you provide public address systems, audio-visual equipment, and ice water
   in each meeting room?
4. What is the nearest airport, and do you provide transportation to and from it?

I will be most grateful for answers to these questions and for any other information
you can provide about your resort facilities. May I please have your response by
September 1 so that I can meet with our planning committee September 4.

Sincerely yours, ——————————————————— Complimentary
                                                      close

Marlene Frederick

Marlene Frederick ——————————————— Author's name and
Corporate Travel Department   identification

MF: gdr ———————————————————————— Reference initials

An improved version of the order letter, also shown in Figure 6.2, begins with
specific order language, itemizes and describes the goods clearly, includes shipping
and payment information, and closes with an end date.

FIGURE 6.2

Order Letters

Outdated salutation

Unfocused opening fails to use order language.

Omits method of payment.

Ineffective

Dear Sirs:

I am writing this letter in response to your advertisement in which you show close-out prices on computer games including Fables and Friends, King Kong, Hugo's Horror House, and perhaps Wing Commander VI, which are now $25.95 and $24.95 each. Because you did not include an order blank or a toll-free number, I'm writing to you. Your prices really blew me away! I hope these items are for sale by mail.

I would be interested in two sets of each—one set for me and the others for gifts. Please send these as soon as possible.

Sincerely,

Effective

1302 North Plum Street
Steinbach, MB R3L 2N7
November 23, 200x

Discount Computer Sales
3981 East Street
Toronto, ON   M2T 1G5

MAIL ORDER FOR CLOSED-OUT COMPUTER GAMES

Please send by overnight mail the following items shown on page 38 in the December issue of *Video News:*

2	RVGA4.3	Fables and Friends	$25.95	$51.90
2	TVGA2.3	King Kong	36.95	73.90
2	EVGA4.2	Hugo's Horror House	22.95	45.90
2	WVGA3.2	Wing Commander VI	24.95	49.90
	Total			$221.60
	GST/PST			33.24
	Grand Total			$254.84

Because some of these games will be used as gifts, I would appreciate receiving them before December 15. Please charge my MasterCard account 4301-3390-8893-3201. Should you need to discuss any of these items, call me at (204) 420-3216.

Brent K. Royer

Brent K. Royer

Simplified style includes subject line but omits salutation.

Authorizes order.

Lists items clearly.

Establishes end date and identifies method of payment.

Omits complimentary close.

This letter illustrates simplified letter style, a wise choice when writing to companies or individuals whom you cannot address individually. By using this style, Tucker does not have to search for a suitable salutation. Notice that a subject line replaces the salutation, and the complimentary close is omitted. For more about the simplified style, see Figure A.4 in Appendix A. To learn more about choosing appropriate salutations, see the box below.

SIMPLE CLAIM REQUESTS

The third category of letters to be presented in this chapter is the simple claim request. A claim is a demand for something that is due or is believed to be due. A simple claim is one to which the writer believes the reader will agree—or should agree. For example, a purchaser has a legitimate claim for warranted products that fail, for goods that are promised but not delivered, for damaged products, or for poor service. When the writer feels that the claim is justified and that persuasion is not required, a claim request should follow the direct strategy.

The direct strategy is best for simple claims that require no persuasion.

WRITING PLAN FOR A SIMPLE CLAIM

- *Opening*—describes clearly the desired action.
- *Body*—explains the nature of the claim, tells why the claim is justified, and provides details regarding the action requested.
- *Closing*—ends pleasantly with a goodwill statement and includes end dating if appropriate.

Solving the Salutation Dilemma

Letters usually begin with a salutation, a greeting to the reader. This greeting is included to personalize a letter. If the name of the individual receiving the letter is known, the salutation is easy: *Dear Kevin* or *Dear Mr. Diegues* or *Dear Ms. Hayden.* But what should be used when no name is known? Grammar hotline services report that one of their most frequent inquiries concerns proper salutations.

In the past we used *Dear Sirs* or *Gentlemen* to address an organization and *Dear Sir* for anonymous individuals. With increasing numbers of women entering the workplace and a new sensitivity to the power of language developing, writers are avoiding the masculine salutations of the past.

Although no perfect all-purpose salutation has emerged, probably the best alternatives for business communicators are these:

- Use the name of an individual whenever possible in addressing letters. Many companies now have toll-free 800 numbers, making it easy for you to request the name, title, and department of anyone to whom you wish to write. Be sure to ask for the spelling of the name!
- When no name is available, use the simplified letter style (Figure 6.2), thus omitting a salutation.
- When no name is available and you cannot use simplified style, rely on *Dear Sir or Madam, Dear Madam or Sir,* or address your letter to a specific title such as *Dear Office Manager.*

OPENING WITH ACTION

In a simple claim request, tell the reader immediately what action you would like taken. Such directness may appear to be blunt, but actually it's businesslike and efficient. Don't begin a claim letter with an attempt to establish goodwill or with an explanation, such as that shown in the following indirect opening. Save the explanation for the body and the goodwill for the closing. Instead, in the opening sentence tell the reader what you want.

> **Indirect opening:** We've used Pentack tools for years and have always appreciated the quality product that you produce and the prompt service that we have received when we placed our orders.
>
> **Direct opening:** Please send us two metric socket sets to replace the two imperial sets sent with our order shipped October 23.

With this direct opening, the reader knows what you want and can read the remainder of the letter in the proper context.

JUSTIFYING IN THE BODY

Explain the reasons that justify your claim without becoming angry or emotional.

Here's where you explain why you feel your claim is justified. Provide the necessary details so that the problem can be rectified without misunderstanding. Avoid the tendency to fix blame. Instead of saying *You failed to send the items we ordered,* describe the situation objectively. Omit negative or angry words that offend the reader and may prevent compliance with your claim.

An objective explanation of the reason for replacing merchandise could read as follows:

> On October 10 we placed a telephone order requesting, among other things, two metric socket sets. When the order arrived yesterday, however, we noted that two imperial socket sets had been sent. Because we cannot use imperial sizes, we are returning the imperial sets by courier.

This unemotional presentation of the facts is more effective in achieving the writer's goal than an angry complaint.

After you have presented the circumstances of your claim objectively, you may wish to suggest alternatives to solving the problem; for example, *If it is impossible to send the metric socket sets, please credit our account.* When goods are being returned, you should inquire about the proper procedure. Some companies allow returns only with prior authorization.

CLOSING PLEASANTLY

End the claim letter pleasantly with an effort toward maintaining goodwill. If appropriate, include a date by which you want the claim satisfied.

> We realize that mistakes in ordering and shipping sometimes occur. Because we've been impressed by your prompt delivery in the past, we hope that you will be able to send the metric socket sets to us by November 1.

EFFECTIVE AND INEFFECTIVE CLAIM LETTERS

The claim letter shown at the top of Figure 6.3 is unlikely to achieve its goal. In demanding that a tire warranty be honoured, the writer failed to provide sufficient information. The account of what happened to the tire is incoherent, and the reader will be uncertain as to what action the writer wants. In addition, the tone of the letter is angry and harsh.

The improved version of the letter, shown at the bottom of Figure 6.3, takes a different tone and approach. In the first sentence this improved letter forthrightly asks for a refund under the tire warranty. The letter includes an unemotional, logical explanation of the problem. Its rational tone and sensible expression are more appealing to the reader, who needs to understand the problem before the organization can resolve it.

The improved version illustrates modified block style and mixed punctuation. Notice that the date is centred (although it may also be placed to end at the right margin), and the closing lines start at the centre of the page. Paragraphs may be blocked, as shown here, or indented five spaces. This letter also shows the company name in the closing lines. If included, it should appear in all capital letters two lines below the complimentary close. Leave enough space after it for the writer to sign the letter.

The claim letter shown in Figure 6.4 seeks permission to return a microcomputer to the manufacturer for repair. Normally, repairs are made locally, but this computer defies diagnosis. The letter writer does not angrily blame the local dealer for ineptness or criticize the manufacturer for producing a faulty product. Instead, the letter invites the manufacturer to help solve a "mystery." Notice that the letter opens by asking for instructions on how to return the computer rather than for permission to return the computer. The request for shipping instructions suggests the writer's confidence that the manufacturer will want to do the right thing and repair the malfunctioning computer.

This personal letter is shown with the return address typed above the date. Use this style when typing on paper without a printed letterhead.

SUMMING UP AND LOOKING FORWARD

In this chapter you learned to organize three types of request letters: information requests, order letters, and claim letters. All use the direct strategy. They open directly with the main idea first followed by details and explanations. In the next chapter you will learn to write response letters. You'll use the direct strategy in responding to information requests, order letters, and claim letters. The majority of all letters written in the business world either request information or respond to requests for it.

FIGURE 6.3

Claim Letters

Ineffective

Begins with emotional, illogical, and unclear demand.

Provides inadequate explanation of what happened.

Ends with threat instead of an attempt to establish goodwill.

Dear Goodday Tires:

What good is a warranty if it's not honoured? I don't agree with your dealer that the damage to my tire was cased by "road hazards." This tire was defective, and I am entitled to a refund.

My company purchased a GasSaver tire September 5, and it had been driven only 14,000 kilometres when a big bubble developed in its side. The gas station attendant said that its tread had separated from its body. But the dealer where my company bought it (Harbour Tire Company) refused to give us a refund. The dealer said that the damage was caused by "road hazards." They also said that they never give refunds, only replacements.

My company has always purchased GasSaver tires, but you can be sure that this is our last. Unless we get a refund, I intend to spread the word about how we were treated.

Yours truly,

Effective

Smith, Klein Industries
135 Fleet Street
Ottawa, Ontario K3W 2H5

March 4, 200x

Modified block style includes centred date and closing lines started at centre.

Ms. Michelle N. Jameson
Director, Customer Service
Goodday Tire Manufacturers
8401 Broad Street
Ottawa, ON K3L 2N2

Dear Ms. Jameson:

SUBJECT: WARRANTY REFUND ON GASSAVER TIRE

Please honour the warranty and issue a refund for one GasSaver radial tire that was purchased for my company car at Alliance Tire Centre on September 5.

Opens with direct request.

This whitewall tire cost $139.13 and carried a warranty for 42,000 kilometres. It had only 14,000 kilometres of wear when trouble developed. On a business trip to Montreal recently, I noticed that the tire made a strange sound. When I stopped the car and inspected the tire, it had an ugly bulge protruding from its rim. A service station attendant said that the tread had separated from the tire body. I was forced to purchase a replacement tire at considerably more than the price we paid for the GasSaver tire. When I returned the GasSaver tire to Alliance, it would not honour the warranty. Alliance said the tire was damaged by "road hazards" and that refunds could not be made.

Provides coherent, unemotional explanation.

My company generally purchases GasSaver tires, and we have been pleased with their quality and durability. Enclosed are copies of the sales invoice and the tire warranty for the tire in question. Also enclosed is a receipt showing that the defective tire was returned to Alliance Tire Company.

Supplies documentation of warranty.

I am confident that you will honour my request for a refund of the purchase price of $139.13 prorated for 14,000 kilometres of wear.

Ends courteously with specific request for action.

Sincerely yours,

SMITH, KLEIN INDUSTRIES

Carole Eustice

Carole Eustice
Vice President

Includes optional company name in capital letters above signature.

CE: prw
Enclosures

FIGURE 6.4

Effective Claim Letter—Personal Business Style

235 Providence Drive
Edmonton, AB T4L 2G5
August 14, 200x

Bravo Computers, Inc.
2308 Borregas Avenue
Sunnyvale, CA 94088-3565

Dear Sir or Madam:

SUBJECT: RETURN OF MALFUNCTIONING BRAVO COMPUTER

Please tell me how I may return my malfunctioning Bravo E654 computer to you for repair.

I am sure you can solve a problem that puzzles my local dealer. After about 45 minutes of normal activity, the screen on my Bravo suddenly fills with a jumble of meaningless letters, numbers, and symbols. Computers For You, the dealer from whom I purchased my Bravo, seems to be unable to locate or correct the malfunction.

Although I am expected to have my computer serviced locally, my dealer has been unable to repair it. I am confident that you can solve the mystery and that you will repair my Bravo quickly.

Sincerely yours,

Pauline LeBlanc

Pauline LeBlanc

Annotations:

Personal return address appears above date.

Opens confidently, requesting instructions for return of computer.

Describes malfunction coherently.

Closes pleasantly by expressing the belief that manufacturer will want to do the right thing.

DISCUSSION

1. How are letters like memos? How are they different?
2. Why should routine letters, such as inquiries and orders, follow the direct strategy?
3. Which is more effective in claim letters—anger or objectivity? Defend your position.
4. Why should the writer of a claim letter offer alternatives for solving the problem?
5. The quality of the information obtained from a request depends on the clarity of the inquiry. Discuss.

6. List three reasons for exchanging business information in letter form rather than in oral form.

7. When a request seeks specific information, the first sentence of the inquiry letter will probably be what?

8. Consider the following situations. Which strategy would be more effective? Write *Direct* or *Indirect* beside each to indicate your choice.
   a. You need information about skiing equipment advertised in a magazine.
   b. You want to convince your boss to change your assigned work schedule.
   c. You want a replacement for a CD player, still under warranty, that you ordered by mail.
   d. You want to find out how much it costs to rent a houseboat in the Lake of the Woods area for you and your family.
   e. As credit manager of a department store, you must deny a customer credit.
   f. You wish to order merchandise from a catalogue.

9. What are the two most emphatic positions in a letter?

10. What is the most popular letter style?

11. List two ways that you could begin an inquiry letter that asks many questions.

12. How does the simplified letter style solve the salutation dilemma?

13. What three elements are appropriate in the closing of a request for information?

14. The first sentence of an order letter should include what information?

15. The closing of an order letter should include what information?

Writing Improvement Exercises

Routine Request Openers. Revise the following openers from routine request letters so that they are more direct.

16. I am interested in your rental rates for a three-bedroom cabin on Lake of the Woods in August.

17. Recently I purchased a Country Manor linen tablecloth at the Bay. I haven't been pleased with it, and I am interested in a replacement.

18. The SmartSix camcorder that I ordered from you has arrived, and it seems to have a problem in the built-in microphone. I'm wondering if you can tell me where I may take it for repair.

19. Your spring sale catalogue shows a number of items in which I am interested. I would like the following items.

Order Request Letter. Analyze the following poorly written order letter and respond to the questions following it.

Ladies and Gentlemen:

We are interested in a number of items for our office overhead projectors used by our sales staff. Some of these items were shown in your fall catalogue. The primary item we need is four Overhead Projection Lamps (Order No. 108-559) priced at $25.99 each. I'm also interested in 3M Scotch Laser Printer Film (Order No. 172-822) at $20.79 a pack. We need five packs. Because we have many permanent transparencies, we want to try your frames that mount transparencies. I believe the 3M mounting frames (Order No. 179-392) are listed at $21.99 for a pack of 50. Send just one pack for us to try. While I'm at it, I might as well order six sets of Stabilo Marker Sets (Order No. 329-010), listed at $4.16 each. Please be sure that these are the water-soluble kind. I'll pay for this with MasterCard, and I need everything by September 1.

Sincerely,

Ineffective Writing

20. What does the opening lack?

21. Write an appropriate opening for this order letter.

22. How would you group the order information so that it is orderly and logical? Name five headings you could use.

23. Write an appropriate closing for this order request.

Letter Format. Read about letter formats and parts in Appendix A. Then answer the following questions.

24. If you are typing and printing a letter for yourself on plain paper, what items appear above the date?

25. How is simplified letter style different from block style, and why do some writers prefer simplified style?

26. In what two places could an attention line be typed?

27. If you write a letter to Software Enterprises Corp., what salutation would be appropriate?

28. When letters are addressed to individuals, should their names always contain a courtesy title, such as *Mr., Ms., Miss,* or *Mrs.*?

ACTIVITIES AND CASES

6.1 Information Request: Touring Europe on a Shoestring. You just saw a great TV program about cheap student travel in Europe, and you think you'd like to try it next summer. You decide to visit France, Spain, and Portugal (or any other countries you select). Begin planning your trip by gathering information from the country's tourist office. Many details need to be worked out. What about passports and entry visas?

How about inoculations (ouch!)? Since your budget will be limited, you need to stay in youth hostels whenever possible. Where are they? Are they private? Some hostels accept only people who belong to their organization. You really need to get your hands on a list of hostels for every country before departure. You are also interested in any special transport passes for students, such as a Eurail Pass. And while you are at it, you want to find out if there are any special guides for student travellers. Before writing a letter to a tourist office, which can provide all this information, answer the following questions:

1. What should you include in the opening of an information request?

2. What should the body of your letter contain?

3. How can questions be handled most effectively?

4. How should you close the letter?

Using the Internet, locate an address for information about a country of your choice. Write the letter using modified block style and plain paper. Because this is a personal business letter, include your return address above the date. See Appendix A.

Related Web Site: www.embpage.org

6.2 Claim Request: Weeping Walls. Play the role of Raj Bellary. On June 24 your company had the basement walls of its office building sealed with Modac II, an acrylic coating. This sealant was applied to reduce moisture in the basement so that you could store company files in this area. The contractor, Theo Friesen, promised that this product would effectively seal the walls and prevent moisture penetration, peeling, chalking, and colour fading for many years. He said that if you had any trouble, he might have to give it a second coat. After heavy rain in September, the walls of the basement leaked, making it necessary for you to remove the files stored there. Write a claim letter to Mr. Friesen asking that he correct the situation. Let him know that you want the basement effectively sealed by October 15 because you don't want this left over the winter.

Organize your letter according to the principles you studied in this chapter. To open this letter directly, decide what should be your most significant statement. In the body of the letter, consider which details are necessary to substantiate your claim. The ending of your claim request should describe what you want Mr. Friesen to do, and by what date.

If your instructor directs, write the entire letter to Mr. Theo Friesen, 4805 Grouse Road, Regina, Saskatchewan S3L 2N6. Add any information that you feel is necessary. Assume that you are writing this letter on company letterhead stationery. Use block style. (See Appendix A.)

6.3 Order Request: Camera Jumble. Analyze the following ineffective request for merchandise, and list at least five faults. Outline a writing plan for an order request. Then rewrite this request, using modified block style and placing your return address above the date. Send the letter to Cameratone, Inc., 140 Northern Boulevard, Swift Current, Saskatchewan S3R 2T5. Add any necessary information.

Ineffective Writing

Dear Sir:

I saw a number of items in your summer/fall catalogue that would fit my Lentax ME camera. I am particularly interested in your Super Zoom 55-200mm lens. Its number is SF39971, and it costs $139.95. To go with this lens I will need a polarizing filter. Its number is SF29032 and costs $22.95 and should fit a 52mm lens. Also include a 05CC magenta filter for a 52mm lens. That number is SF29036 and it costs $9.95. Please send also a Hikemaster camera case for $24.95. Its number is SF28355.

I am interested in having these items charged to my credit card. I'd sure like to get them quickly because my vacation starts soon.

Sincerely,

6.4 Order Letter: A Little Something Personal. Write a letter ordering items advertised in a magazine, newspaper, or catalogue. Assume that no order form is available. Attach the advertisement to your letter. Be sure to use an appropriate letter style for a personal business letter.

6.5 Claim Request: Gas Complaint. Analyze the following ineffective claim and list at least five faults. Outline a writing plan for an effective claim request. Then rewrite this request, adding any information you feel is needed for a complete claim. Use block style and address the letter to Susan Fowler, Manager, Customer Service, Apex Car Rentals, 6501 King Lawrence Road, Brandon, MB R5L 3T3.

Ineffective Writing

Dear Service Manager:

This is to inform you that you can't have it both ways. Either you provide customers with cars with full gas tanks or you don't. And if you don't, you shouldn't charge them when they return with empty tanks!

In view of the fact that I picked up a car in Brandon August 22 with an empty tank, I had to fill it immediately. Then I drove it until August 25. When I returned it to Winnipeg, I naturally let the tank go nearly empty, since that is the way I received the car in Brandon.

But your attendant in Winnipeg charged me to fill the tank—$42.50 (premium gasoline at premium prices)! Although I explained to him that I had received it with an empty tank, he kept telling me that company policy required that he charge for a fill-up. My total bill came to $445.50, which, you must agree, is a lot of money for a period of a three-day rental. I have the signed rental agreement and a receipt showing that I paid the full amount and that it included $42.50 for a gas fill-up when I returned the car.

Inasmuch as my company is a new customer and inasmuch as we had hoped to use your agency for our future car rentals because of your competitive rates, I trust that you will give this matter your prompt attention.

Sincerely,

6.6 Information Request: Backpacking Cuisine. Assume that you are Marc Vannault, manager of a health spa and also an ardent backpacker. You are organizing a group of hikers for a wilderness trip to the Yukon. One item that must be provided is freeze-dried food for the three-week trip. You are unhappy with the taste and quality of backpacking food products currently available. You expect to have a group of hikers who are older, affluent, and natural-food enthusiasts. You heard that Outfitters Inc., 1169 Willamette Street, Canmore, Alberta T0L 2P2, offers a new line of freeze-dried products. Write an inquiry letter to Outfitters to find out as much as possible about their products. Be specific with your questions.

6.7 Information Request: On-Line Microbrewery. Play the part of brewmaster Bill Antaya, owner of Crystal Ale Microbrewery, 7345 Post Road, Saskatoon, Saskatchewan S4L 2R3. Your Crystal Ale beers have won local taste awards. However, sales are dismal, perhaps because your beer is pricier than mass-produced beers and because you have a meagre advertising and sales budget.

Then you hear about the Canadian Beer Index, a Web site that promotes micro-brewed beer via the World Wide Web. When you visit the Web site, you find descriptions of beer from many microbreweries, along with images of their labels and contact information. You find other interesting information that you know will draw surfers to the site.

You wonder if you might include your product as part of the Canadian Beer Index, but you're not exactly sure how the service works. You have many questions! Write a letter to Peter Fahil, Webmaster, The Canadian Beer Index, 300 East Parkway Ave., Regina, Saskatchewan S3T 5Y6. You could also e-mail Mr. Fahil, but you may prefer a paper copy as permanent record of the correspondence.

Related Web Site: realbeer.com

6.8 Order Letter: Office Supplies to Go. You are William Vorstein, manager, Lasertronics Inc., 2004 Henrietta Road, Hamilton, Ontario L2N 4T1. You want to order some items from an office supply catalogue, but your catalogue is a year old and you have lost the order form. Rather than write for a new catalogue, you decide to take a chance and order items from the old (Fall 1998) catalogue, realizing that prices may be somewhat different. You want three Panasonic electric pencil sharpeners, one steel desktop organizer, two Roll-a-Flex files for 5- by 10-cm cards, and ten boxes of file folders. You would like to be invoiced for this purchase, and you prefer overnight courier delivery. Even though the prices may be somewhat higher, you decide to list the prices shown in your catalogue so that you have an idea of what the total order will cost. Write a letter to Monarch Discount Office Furniture, 2890 Monarch Road, Toronto, Ontario M2W 4T9.

6.9 Order Letter: N.W.T Request. Play the part of Terri Tran, who lives at 845 Wainee Street, Yellowknife, Northwest Territories X1L 2F3. When you were in California recently, you saw an unusual toy (use your imagination to describe it) at Toys-R-Us in San Dimas. Now that you're back in Yellowknife, you'd like to have that toy as a present for your nephew, but you have not been able to locate it. Write to Toys-R-Us and describe the toy. To save time, you want to order it and have it charged to your Visa credit card. You expect the toy to cost about $60, but you would go as high as $100 to purchase it. You would like to receive the toy within three weeks, and if they can't ship it immediately, you would like to know as soon as possible. Write to Toys-R-Us, 194 West Terrace Avenue, San Dimas, CA 91773, ordering the toy.

6.10 Claim Letter: Deep Desk Disappointment. Assume that you are Monica Keil, president of Keil Consulting Services, 423 E. Lawrence Avenue, Montreal, Quebec H5L 2E3. Since your consulting firm was doing very well, you decided to splurge and purchase a fine executive desk for your own office. You ordered an expensive desk described as "North American white oak embellished with hand-inlaid walnut cross-banding." Although you would not ordinarily purchase large, expensive items by mail, you were impressed by the description of this desk and by the money-back guarantee promised in the catalogue. When the desk arrived, you knew that you had made a mistake—it was not the high-quality product that you had anticipated. You are disappointed with the desk and decide to send it back, taking advantage of the money-back guarantee. You're not sure whether they will refund the freight charges, but it's worth a try. Supply any details needed. Write a letter to Big Spruce Wood Products, P.O. Box 488, Sandpoint, British Columbia V5N 7L8.

6.11 Claim Letter: Earth First Runs Dry. Assume that you are Megan Phillips, public relations assistant for a grassroots environmental organization, Earth First, 5314 River Road, Evergreen, New Brunswick E4L 2Y5. You are responsible for printing 250 flyers for an upcoming Earth First rally, but the ink cartridges for your two Stellar printers aren't working properly. Although the cartridges are clearly full, no ink is dispensing. When you tried to return the cartridges to your local office supply store, The Office Centre, the store refused to take them because you had purchased the cartridges more than 30 days ago. On the advice of the store manager, you purchase two new cartridges that enable you to print your flyers on time. However, you are frustrated about spending Earth First's meagre funds on faulty supplies. The store manager said that many customers recently had returned Stellar ink cartridges, which are the only cartridges on the market that use environmentally benign soy-based ink. Decide what will resolve your complaint: a cash refund of $126.50, replacement cartridges, or some other action. Send a claim letter, the cartridges, and a copy of your receipt to Stellar Printers, 908 East Street, Toronto, Ontario M4W 3T8.

6.12 Searching the Internet: River Rafting on the Web. As the program chair for the campus Ski Club, you have been asked to investigate river rafting. This is an active organization, and its members want to schedule a summer activity. A majority favoured rafting. Use a Web browser to search the World Wide Web for relevant information. Select five of the most promising Web sites offering rafting. If possible, print a copy of your findings to use as a reference. Then, summarize your findings in an e-mail message to your club president (your instructor in this instance). If any of the Web sites offer additional information through e-mail, request it. Your instructor may also ask you to compose a letter (to be sent via "snail mail") requesting additional information. Your letter would inquire about back-country exploration, jetboat trips, canoe support, and summer schedules.

GRAMMAR/MECHANICS CHECKUP—6

Commas 1

Review the Grammar/Mechanics Handbook Sections 2.01–2.04. Then study each of the following statements and insert necessary commas. In the space provided write the number of commas that you add; write *0* if no commas are needed. Also record the number of the G/M principle illustrated. When you finish, compare your responses with those provided. If your answers differ, study carefully the principles shown in parentheses.

Example: In this class students learn to write business letters, memos, and reports clearly and concisely.

<u>   2   (2.01)</u>

1. We do not as a rule allow employees to take time off for dental appointments. _____
2. You may be sure Mrs. Schwartz that your car will be ready by 4 p.m. _____
3. Anyone who is reliable conscientious and honest should be very successful. _____
4. A conference on sales motivation is scheduled for May 5 at the Plainsview Marriott Hotel beginning at 2 p.m. _____
5. As a matter of fact I just called your office this morning. _____
6. We are relocating our distribution centre from Peterborough Ontario to Des Moines Iowa. _____
7. In the meantime please continue to address your orders to your regional office. _____
8. The last meeting recorded in the minutes was on February 4 2000 in Fredericton. _____
9. Mr. Silver Mrs. Abuki and Ms. Esfahan have been selected as our representatives. _____
10. The package mailed to Ms. Leslie Holmes 3430 Larkspur Lane Regina Saskatchewan S5L 2E2 arrived three weeks after it was mailed. _____
11. The manager feels needless to say that the support of all employees is critical. _____
12. Eric was assigned three jobs: checking supplies replacing inventories and distributing delivered goods. _____
13. We will work diligently to retain your business Mr. Fuhai. _____
14. The vice-president feels however that all sales representatives need training. _____
15. The name selected for a product should be right for that product and should emphasize its major attributes. _____

1. (2) not, rule, (2.03)   3. (2) reliable, conscientious, (2.01)   5. (1) fact, (2.03)   7. (1) meantime, (2.03)   9. (2) Silver, Abuki, (2.01)   11. (2) feels, say, (2.03)   13. (1) business, (2.02)   15. (0)

GRAMMAR/MECHANICS CHALLENGE—6

Document for Revision

The following letter has faults in grammar, punctuation, spelling, number form, and wordiness. Use standard proofreading marks (see Appendix B) to correct the errors. When you finish, your instructor can show you the revised version of this letter.

March 3, 200x

FAX TRANSMISSION

Ms. Susan Petkowski, Manager

Customer Service Department

Steel Cabinets, Inc.

Calgary, AB   T2L 4F3

Dear Ms. Petkowski:

Please rush a shipment of twenty-three No. 36-440 verticle file cabinets to us, to replace those damaged in transit recently.

Ineffective Writing

We appreciate you filling our order for 100 of these file cabinets as shown on the accompanying Invoice. Twenty-three of them however were damaged in transit and cannot be sold in there present condition. Because of the fact that 2 transit companies handled the shipment of the file cabinets we cannot determine whom is responsable for the damage.

These verticle files were featured in our newspaper add and we expect to sell a good many in our presale which is scheduled to begin 3/15. Therefore we would appreciate you rushing these cabinets by Red Dog Freight before 3/12. Moreover please let us know what should be done with the damaged cabinets.

Sincerely,

Communication Workshop: Ethics

TECHNOLOGY AND ETHICS[2]

Computer technology is giving more employees greater access to larger amounts of personal and corporate information than ever before. As access increases, so too does the potential for misuse of confidential information. Canadian corporations see high-tech as the major source of potential ethical misconduct in their organizations. A survey sent to the CEOs of 1000 Canadian companies in both the private and public sectors found that misuse of proprietary knowledge and the security of internal communications were considered the two top risk areas for unethical behaviour. A third major risk area was the failure to report fraud or misconduct.

Why the concern over the misuse of information? According to James Hunter, head of KPMG's ethics and integrity practice, in the past employees in accounting departments did their work by hand, on paper. For a CEO to check the books now, she or he must also understand the computer system and software program used to create the books. In many organizations increasing reliance is being placed on the expert employee's sense of doing the right thing rather than on traditional rules and regulations.

Despite the potential for unethical behaviour, only about a third of Canadian companies have a formal system to allow employees to report misconduct without fear of reprisal. Almost one-quarter of companies have no system in place at all. This puts employees in a difficult ethical bind. If they tell the boss about unethical behaviour, they may betray a co-worker with whom they have worked for years.

In the United States, many companies have established toll-free hotlines so that employees can report questionable behaviour by superiors or fellow employees anonymously. So-called "snitch lines" have been slow to catch on in Canada.[3] Legal experts suggest that in Canada, company officers probably worry less about being sued than do those in the United States. However, like their U.S. counterparts, Canadian CEOs realize that no one is exempt from the effects of the toll-free lines.[4]

Application. In a class discussion consider these questions. What are the advantages and disadvantages of detailed ethical codes of conduct for employees? Should employees be encouraged to report what they suspect may be unethical behaviour on the part of fellow workers? Find examples of codes of ethics as well as information about hotlines, ethics training programs, or other methods used at Canadian companies or in government. Summarize your findings in a short report to your instructor. Indicate how specific companies get with their ethics codes. Do they get right down to describing individual prohibited deeds, or are they more general and thus more inclusive? How do they involve employees in the ethics of the company and how do they help employees who wish to report unethical behaviour?

Related Web Site: www.ethics.ubc.ca/rresources/business.html

LETTERS THAT RESPOND POSITIVELY

In today's business climate, there is an enormous vocabulary that helps us to define our work. We need to talk about complex material in simple ways. Our language must convey in simple and clear terms what we are trying to say so that the (reader) can understand and retain the information.[1]

ELIZABETH J. HUNT, director, The Voice Centre, a Canadian company specializing in speech training for corporate executives, politicians, teachers, broadcasters, and performers.

Learning Objectives

1. Apply the direct strategy in letters that respond positively.
2. Write clear and efficient letters and memos that deliver information.
3. Promote goodwill in acknowledging order requests.
4. Grant claims efficiently and effectively.

Clear writing is especially important in today's business world. As Elizabeth Hunt points out, business communicators can now choose from a vast business vocabulary when composing messages. The key, though, to writing effectively is to choose simple language so that the message is clear and understandable.

In this chapter you will continue to develop clear writing skills. These skills will be applied to letters that respond positively to requests and inquiries. Specifically, you'll learn to (a) respond to information requests, (b) acknowledge orders, and (c) agree to claims. This group of letters generally delivers good news that the reader expects and wants. Therefore, these messages follow the direct strategy with the main idea first.

RESPONDING TO INFORMATION REQUESTS

Use the direct strategy in responding to requests for information. The direct strategy follows this writing plan:

WRITING PLAN FOR AN INFORMATION RESPONSE

- *Subject line*—identifies previous correspondence.
- *Opening*—delivers the most important information first.

- *Body*—arranges information in a logical sequence, explains and clarifies, provides additional information, and builds goodwill.
- *Closing*—ends pleasantly.

SUBJECT LINE EFFICIENCY

Use the subject line to refer to previous correspondence.

Although it's not mandatory, a subject line is useful in responding to requests. It allows the writer to identify quickly and efficiently the previous correspondence. A subject line also jogs the reader's memory regarding the request. By putting identifying information in a subject line, the writer reserves the first sentence (one of the most important spots in a letter) for the main idea. Here's an effective subject line that responds to a request for information:

SUBJECT: YOUR NOVEMBER 3 LETTER ABOUT SUMMER INTERNSHIP PROGRAMS AT NYGARD INTERNATIONAL

OPENING STRENGTH

In a response letter, deliver good news early.

As the most emphatic position in the letter, the first sentence should carry the most important information. A response to a student's inquiry about summer internship opportunities at a large garment manufacturer should reveal the most important information immediately. Compare the direct opening shown here with the indirect and wordy one that follows it:

Direct opening: Summer internships are available at Nygard International for students who are enrolled in business administration and international business programs at Canadian colleges.

Indirect opening: We have received your letter of November 3 requesting information regarding our summer internship program here at Nygard International, and I am happy to respond to your inquiry.

If you are answering a number of questions, use one of two approaches. The most direct approach is to answer the most important question in the first sentence. Other answers may be supplied in the body of the letter. For example, the following response to a request from an airline customer with many questions begins directly:

On flights within Canada and between Canada and the United States, passengers are entitled to a total of three pieces of baggage, whether all are checked or one or two are carried on board.

A less direct approach starts with a summary statement that shows the reader you are complying with the request:

Here is the information you requested about passenger baggage aboard Atlantic Airlines.

This opening is followed by answers to the questions contained in the body of the letter. Either of these two approaches is superior to the familiar openings *Thank you for your letter of . . .* or *I have received your letter asking for . . .* These openings are indirect, overworked, and obvious. Stating that you received the customer's letter is obviously unnecessary, since you are answering it.

LOGIC IN THE BODY

Give explanations and additional information in the body of a letter that responds to an information request. If you are answering a number of questions or providing considerable data, arrange your information logically. It may be possible to enumerate information, as shown in this response to the inquiry about customer baggage. Notice that the writer offers a brief explanation of each restriction.

1. The largest and heaviest piece of baggage can weigh up to 35 kilograms. This restriction is based on the total capacity of our aircraft.

2. The length plus width plus height of the largest bag can total no more than 165 centimetres. These dimensions are based on what our people can physically handle in the confined work space of an aircraft belly.

3. Certain sporting equipment is carried free, when that equipment is counted as the largest bag. This category includes skis, fishing equipment, golf clubs, snow boards, and other sporting items.

A good way to answer questions is to number each answer.

If your response requires more information, devote an entire paragraph to each item.

In answering request letters from customers, you have an opportunity to build goodwill toward yourself and your organization by offering additional advice or data. Don't confine your response to the questions presented. If you recognize that other facts would be helpful, present them. For example, in the inquiry about Nygard International internships, the writer could describe the full-time internship program, which releases a student from classroom study for a semester (3 to 6 months), as well as the summer program. The writer also could offer helpful information regarding eligibility, application, deadlines, and rewards. This is information about which the student writer may not have known to inquire.

Build customer goodwill by offering additional information.

TAILOR-MADE CLOSING

To avoid abruptness, include a pleasant closing remark that shows your willingness to help the reader. Tailor your remarks to fit this letter and this reader. Since everyone appreciates being recognized as an individual, avoid form-letter closings such as *If we may be of any further assistance, do not hesitate to call upon us.* Improved closings are personalized:

> We appreciate your interest, Ms. Sullivan, in Nygard International's summer internship programs. The enclosed brochure describes the many departments within our organization that sponsor internships. Should you be interested in joining us, we would welcome your application.

ILLUSTRATIONS OF INFORMATION RESPONSES

The letter in Figure 7.1 responds to an inquiry from a reporter for information about a mediation services agency. This letter answers a number of frequently asked questions.

In responding to the reporter's inquiry, the writer uses a personalized salutation (*Dear Ms. McKenzie*) and a time-saving subject line. Although the first sentence does

FIGURE 7.1

Information Response Letter—Block Style

Identifies previous correspondence.

Answers each inquiry fully and logically in list form.

Builds goodwill by providing extra information.

Ends cordially without clichés.

TRG Mediation Services
930 Taylor Avenue, Regina, Saskatchewan S4A 2Y4

February 6, 200x

Ms. Irene McKenzie
The Regina Leader-Post
4980 Washington Avenue
Regina, Saskatchewan S4L 4W6

Dear Ms. McKenzie:

SUBJECT: YOUR FEBRUARY 1 LETTER REQUESTING INFORMATION FOR AN ARTICLE TO
APPEAR IN *THE REGINA LEADER-POST*

Here are answers to your questions about mediation services. We are eager to supply you with this information so that you can publish accurate news about the role mediators play in the labour–management relationship.

1. TRG is a mediation services company that provides assistance to businesses and individuals during labour disputes. Our professional mediators help both sides in labour–management disputes reach acceptable settlement terms. Without mediation services, many of these disputes would undoubtedly proceed to job action. Our mediators deal with disputes of all sorts, from harassment complaints to wage and contract negotiations.

2. We do not handle mediation services for person-to-person disputes such as those having to do with divorce or automobile accident insurance.

3. Many collective agreements include mediation as a required step in the negotiation process once contract talks have broken down. We do not, however, make decisions about the outcome of a settlement; this is part of the role of an arbitrator.

4. TRG uses the methods of principled negotiation, as articulated by the Harvard School of Business and others. Principled negotiation urges the participants in a dispute to search for ways whereby each participant can win rather than dwelling on win-lose scenarios. Our mediators are trained to help participants find the "win-win" solution.

Although you didn't ask, many people want to know what it is like to help groups of people who have reached an impasse move ahead. Helping people in this way can be very rewarding when mediation goes well. As is the case with most human activity, though, the job can be difficult when things don't go well.

You'll find additional information in the enclosed booklet, "Understanding and Using Mediation Services." To speak with me personally, just call (306) 598-2300. We look forward to seeing your article in print.

Sincerely,

Debbie Wills-Garcia

Debbie Wills-Garcia
Vice President

DWG:rio
Enclosure

not begin with an answer to a specific question, it does offer a summary statement introducing the responses. The body of the letter enumerates logically and in parallel form the information requested. Because the letter writer understands the reporter's need for complete explanations, she provides more than basic facts. Notice that the writer even answers a question the reporter did not ask (what the rewards of the job are). This letter builds goodwill by anticipating the needs of the inquirer, providing complete answers, and offering additional information. The cordial but concise closing avoids the usual clichés.

In contrast to this well-written letter, the ineffective information response shown at the top of Figure 7.2 suffers from a number of faults.

The first sentence of this ineffective letter uses dated language *(pursuant to)*, a wordy expression *(this is to advise you about)*, and needless repetition [*two (2)*]. In addition, the first sentence does not deliver the information requested. The second paragraph opens with *the writer*, a formal expression, instead of the more conversational *I*. Moreover, the tone of the body of the letter is rather harsh and negative, and the closing sounds insincere.

The information conveyed in the preceding message could be more effectively delivered by using the direct strategy and by improving the tone of the letter. Notice how the improved version at the bottom of Figure 7.2 achieves its objective.

RESPONDING TO ORDER REQUESTS

Many companies acknowledge orders by sending a printed postcard that merely informs the customer that the order has been received. Other companies take advantage of this opportunity to build goodwill and to promote new products and services. A personalized letter responding to an order is good business, particularly for new accounts, large accounts, and customers who haven't placed orders recently. An individualized letter is also necessary if the order involves irregularities, such as delivery delays, back-ordered items, or missing items.

Letters that follow up orders create excellent opportunities to improve the company image and to sell products.

Letters that respond to orders should deliver the news immediately; therefore, the direct strategy is most effective. Here's a writing plan that will achieve the results you want in acknowledging orders.

WRITING PLAN FOR AN ORDER RESPONSE

- *Opening*—tells when and how shipment will be sent.
- *Body*—explains details of shipment, discusses any irregularities in the order, includes resale information, and promotes other products and services if appropriate.
- *Closing*—builds goodwill and uses friendly, personalized closing.

GIVING DELIVERY INFORMATION IN THE OPENING

Customers want to know when and how their orders will be sent. Since that news is most important, put it in the first sentence. It is unnecessary to say that you have received an order. An inefficient opener such as *We have received your order dated June 20* wastes words and the reader's time by providing information that could be inferred from more effective openers. Even a seemingly courteous opening such as *Thank you for your recent order* does not really tell readers what they want to know.

The first sentence should tell when and how an order will be sent.

FIGURE 7.2

Ineffective and Effective Information Responses

Opens indirectly and uses legalese.

Sounds harsh and needlessly formal.

Uses tired, insincere-sounding closing.

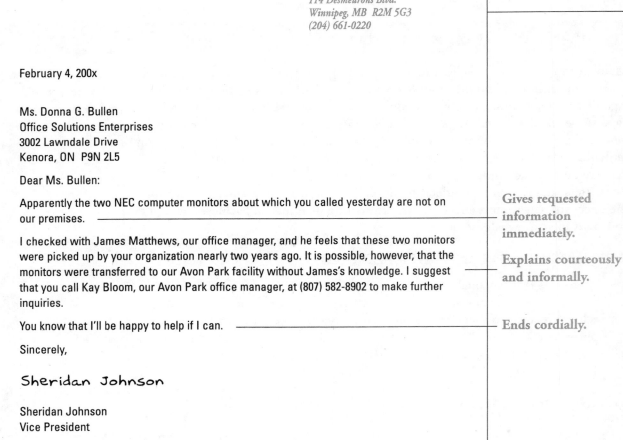

Ineffective

Dear Ms. Bullen:

Pursuant to our telephone conversation of yesterday morning, this is to advise you about the two (2) NEC computer/monitors in which you are interested.

The writer has been in contact with James Matthews, our office manager, and he has no record of these monitors. These monitors are not now on our premises. He is convinced that someone from your organization (he knows not whom) picked these monitors up two years ago.

It is my hope that this answers your question. If I may be of further assistance, please let me know.

Sincerely,

Sheridan Johnson

Effective

STRATEGIC SYSTEMS, INC.

114 Desmeurons Blvd.
Winnipeg, MB R2M 5G3
(204) 661-0220

February 4, 200x

Ms. Donna G. Bullen
Office Solutions Enterprises
3002 Lawndale Drive
Kenora, ON P9N 2L5

Dear Ms. Bullen:

Apparently the two NEC computer monitors about which you called yesterday are not on our premises.

I checked with James Matthews, our office manager, and he feels that these two monitors were picked up by your organization nearly two years ago. It is possible, however, that the monitors were transferred to our Avon Park facility without James's knowledge. I suggest that you call Kay Bloom, our Avon Park office manager, at (807) 582-8902 to make further inquiries.

You know that I'll be happy to help if I can.

Sincerely,

Sheridan Johnson

Sheridan Johnson
Vice President

Gives requested information immediately.

Explains courteously and informally.

Ends cordially.

Instead of stating that an order has been received, imply it in a first sentence that provides delivery details. Here's an example:

> We are sending your cheques and invoice forms by Z Express air freight service, and these forms should arrive by February 8.

This opening sentence provides delivery information, and it is certainly superior to the two perfunctory openers shown previously. However, it could still be improved. Notice that it emphasizes "we" instead of "you." Because this letter is primarily a goodwill effort, its effect can be enhanced by presenting its message from the viewpoint of the reader. Notice how the following version suggests reader benefits and emphasizes the *you* attitude:

A perfunctory opening is routine, superficial, and mechanical.

> Your cheques and invoice forms were sent by Z Express air freight service. They should reach you by February 8—two days ahead of your deadline.

PUTTING DETAILS IN THE BODY

You should include details relating to an order in the body of a letter that acknowledges the order. You will also want to discuss any irregularities about the order. If, for example, part of the order will be sent from a different location or prices have changed or items must be back-ordered, present this information.

The body of an order response is also the appropriate place to include resale information. *Resale* refers to the process of reassuring customers that their choices were good ones. You can use resale in an order letter by describing the product favourably. You might mention its features or attributes, its popularity among customers, and its successful use in certain applications. Perhaps your competitive price recommends it. Resale information confirms the discrimination and good judgment of your customers and encourages repeat business. After an opening statement describing delivery information, resale information such as the following is appropriate:

When a sales clerk tells you how good you look in the new suit you just purchased, the clerk is practising "resale."

> The multipurpose cheques you have ordered have several different cheque formats, including one for accounts payable and payroll. Customers tell us that these formatted cheques are the answer to their cheque-writing problems.

Order acknowledgment letters are also suitable vehicles for sales promotion material. An organization often has other products or services that it wishes to highlight and promote. For example, a computer supply company might include the following sales feature:

Resale emphasizes a product already sold; promotion emphasizes additional products to be sold.

> Another good buy from Quill is our popular Zip disk available in our "mini" bulk pack of 10 disks at only $13.95 each. And we will send you free a desk storage tray for your Zip disks.

Use sales promotion material, however, in moderation. Too much can be a burden to read and therefore irritating.

SHOWING APPRECIATION IN THE CLOSING

The closing should be pleasant, forward-looking, and appreciative. Above all, it should be personalized. That is, it should relate to one particular letter. Don't use all-

The best closings are personalized; they relate to one particular letter.

purpose form-letter closings such as *We appreciate your interest in our company* or *Thank you for your order* or *We look forward to your continued business.*

Notice that each personalized closing in the following list refers to the customers personally and to their current orders:

> You may be certain that your cheques and invoice forms will reach you before your February 10 deadline. We genuinely appreciate your business and look forward to serving you again.

> We appreciate the payment you enclosed with your order. It is always a pleasure to do business with your organization.

> You have our appreciation for this order and our assurance, Ms. Nystrom, that your future orders will be processed as efficiently and as promptly as this one.

> We are confident that you will be pleased with the quality and durability of your Super-Grip 4-ply tires. Your satisfaction with our products and our service, Mr. Steiner, is our primary concern. We hope it will be our privilege to serve you again.

SKILFUL AND FAULTY RESPONSES TO ORDERS

Companies responding to customers' orders have a unique opportunity to build goodwill and promote new products. Some order responses, such as the one shown at the top of Figure 7.3, totally miss the mark. Notice its wordy and outdated style, a form of writing some businesspeople still use. It starts out poorly with an impersonal salutation. It continues to progress slowly in the first sentence by stating obvious information that could be implied. It also gives the reader no hint of when the books will arrive. The second paragraph of the letter is unnecessarily negative. Instead of capitalizing on the popularity of the books ordered, the writer uses negative language *(sorry to report, we will be forced)*, implying that the shipment might be delayed. The letter contains a number of outdated and wordy expressions *(pursuant to your request, every effort will be made, attached please find)*. The writer does not use resale or sales promotion to encourage repeat orders. Finally, the closing is wordy and overly formal.

The improved version of this letter, shown at the bottom of Figure 7.3, is written in an upbeat style that promotes good feelings between the writer and the customer. Notice that the letter contains a personal salutation, and the first sentence reveals immediately when the books should arrive. The body of the letter confirms the wise selection of the reader by mentioning the successful sales of the books ordered. To promote future sales, this letter includes sales promotion information. It closes with sincere appreciation that ties in directly with the content of the letter. Notice throughout the letter the emphasis on the *you* attitude and benefits to the reader. The first letter sounds tired and negative. The second sounds professional and positive.

RESPONDING TO CLAIMS

A claim is usually bad news to the organization receiving it. A claim means that something went wrong—goods were not delivered, a product failed to perform, a shipment was late, service was poor, or billing was fouled up. Large organizations

FIGURE 7.3

Order Acknowledgment Letters

Fails to address receiver by name.

Opens with obvious statement.

Uses negative language.

Misses chance to promote products.

Ineffective

Dear Customer:

We are in receipt of your Purchase Order No. 2980 under date of March 15.

I'm sorry to report that the books you have ordered are selling so quickly that we cannot keep up with orders. Therefore, we will be forced to send them from our Toronto distribution centre. Pursuant to your request, every effort will be made to ship them as quickly as possible.

Attached please find a list of our contemporary issues. May I take the liberty to say that we thank you for allowing us to serve your book needs.

Sincerely,

Charles Bailey

Effective

Chartwell Publishers
1050 Birchmont Road
Scarborough, Ontario MIK 5G4

(416) 752-8900 FAX (416) 752-3966
Internet: www.chartwell.com

March 20, 200x

Ms. Sheila Miller
2569 Notre Dame Avenue
Winnipeg, MB R3H 0J9

Dear Ms. Miller:

SUBJECT: YOUR MARCH 15 BOOK ORDER NO. 2980

The books requested in your Order No. 2980 will be shipped from our Toronto distribution centre and should reach you by April 1.

The volumes you have ordered are among our best-selling editions and will certainly generate good sales for you at your spring book fair.

For your interest we are enclosing a list of contemporary issues recently released. If you place an order from this list or from our general catalogue, you will be eligible for special terms that we are offering for a limited time. For each $100 worth of books ordered at full list price, we will issue a $10 credit toward the purchase of additional books—as long as all the books are ordered at the same time.

We are genuinely pleased, Ms. Miller, to be able to help supply the books for your fair. Please take advantage of our special terms and place your next order soon.

Sincerely,

Charles Bailey

Charles Bailey
Marketing Division

CB:wuh
Enclosure

Addresses receiver by name.

Opens with information the reader wants most.

Includes resale by reassuring reader of wise selections and providing sales promotion information.

Ties in appreciation for order with content of letter.

have customer service departments that handle most claims. Smaller organizations respond individually to customer claims.

An individual who writes letters responding to claims has three goals:

- To rectify the wrong, if one exists
- To regain the confidence of the customer
- To promote future business

When a claim is received, you must first gather information to determine what happened and how you will respond. Some organizations automatically comply with customer claims—even when the claim may be unjustified. They comply merely to maintain good public relations.

Once you have gathered information, you must decide whether to grant the claim. If you respond positively, your letter will represent good news to the reader. Use the direct strategy in revealing the good news. If your response is negative, arrange the message indirectly (Chapter 8). Here's a writing plan for responding favourably to a claim.

WRITING PLAN FOR GRANTING A CLAIM

- *Subject line (optional)*—identifies the previous correspondence.
- *Opening*—grants the request or announces the adjustment immediately, and includes resale or sales promotion if appropriate.
- *Body*—provides details about how you are complying with the request, tries to regain the customer's confidence, and includes resale or sales promotion if appropriate.
- *Closing*—ends positively with a forward-looking thought, expresses confidence in future business relations, and avoids referring to unpleasantness.

STREAMLINING REFERENCE IN THE SUBJECT LINE

A subject line streamlines the reference to the reader's correspondence. Although it is optional, a subject line enables you to reserve the first sentence for announcing the most important information. Here are examples of subject lines that effectively identify previous correspondence:

SUBJECT: YOUR JUNE 3 INQUIRY ABOUT INVOICE 3569

SUBJECT: REQUEST FOR EXTENSION OF WEAREVER TIRE WARRANTY

SUBJECT: YOUR DECEMBER 7 LETTER ABOUT YOUR SNO-FLAKE ICE CRUSHER

REVEALING GOOD NEWS IN THE OPENING

Since you have decided to comply with the reader's claim, reveal the good news immediately. The following openings for various letters illustrate how to begin a message with good news.

A second shipment of toner cartridges for your printers has been sent by courier and should reach you by April 25.

We agree with you that the warranty on your Turbo programmable calculator Model AI 25C should be extended for six months.

You may take your Sno-Flake ice crusher to Ben's Appliances at 310 First Street, Moose Jaw, where it will be repaired at no cost to you.

The enclosed cheque for $325 demonstrates our desire to satisfy our customers and earn their confidence.

In announcing that you will grant a claim, do so without a grudging tone—even if you have reservations about whether the claim is legitimate. Once you decide to comply with the customer's request, do so happily. Avoid half-hearted or reluctant responses such as the following:

Although the Sno-Flake ice crusher works well when it is used properly, we have decided to allow you to take yours to Ben's Appliances for repair at our expense.

Don't begin your letter with an apology such as *We are sorry that you are having trouble with your Sno-Flake ice crusher*. This negative approach reminds the reader of the problem and may rekindle the heated emotions or unhappy feelings experienced when the claim was written. Also, such an opening is indirect. It doesn't tell the reader the good news first.

EXPLAINING COMPLIANCE IN THE BODY

In responding to claims, most organizations sincerely want to correct a wrong. They want to do more than just make the customer happy. They want to stand behind their products and services; they want to do what's right.

In the body of the letter, then, explain how you are complying with the claim. In all but the most routine claims, you should also seek to regain the confidence of the customer. You might reasonably expect that a customer who has experienced difficulty with a product, with delivery, with billing, or with service has lost faith in your organization. Rebuilding that faith is important for future business. How to rebuild lost confidence depends on the situation and the claim. If procedures need to be revised, explain what changes will be made. If a product has defective parts, tell how the product is being improved. If service is faulty, describe genuine efforts to improve it. Sincere and logical explanations do much to reduce hard feelings.

Sometimes the problem is not with the product but with the way it's being used. In other instances customers misunderstand warranties or inadvertently cause delivery and billing mix-ups by supplying incorrect information. Again, rational and sincere explanations will do much to regain the confidence of unhappy customers.

In your explanation avoid using negative words that convey the wrong impression. Words such as *trouble, regret, misunderstanding, fault, defective, error, inconvenience*, and *unfortunately* carry connotations of blame and wrongdoing. Try to use as few negative words as possible. Keep your message positive and upbeat.

Whether to apologize is debatable. Some writing experts argue that apologies remind customers of their complaints and are therefore negative. Instead, these experts say, letter writers should, in their letters, focus on how they are satisfying the customer. Real letters that respond to customers' claims, however, often include apologies.[2] If you feel that your company is at fault and that an apology is an appropriate goodwill gesture, by all means include it. Be careful, though, not to admit negligence. You'll learn more about responding to negative letters in Chapter 8.

Most businesses comply with claims because they want to promote customer goodwill.

Because negative words suggest blame and fault, avoid them in letters that attempt to build customer goodwill.

In regaining the confidence of the reader, it may be appropriate to include resale information. If a customer is unhappy with a product, explain its features and applications in an effort to resell it. Depending on the situation, new product information could also be promoted.

SHOWING CONFIDENCE IN THE CLOSING

End your letter by looking ahead positively.

End positively by expressing confidence that the problem has been resolved and that continued business relations will result. You might mention the product in a favourable light, suggest a new product, express your appreciation for the customer's business, or anticipate future business. It's often appropriate to refer to the desire to be of service and to satisfy customers. Do the following closings achieve the objectives suggested here?

> Your Sno-Flake ice crusher will help you remain cool and refreshed this summer. For your additional summer enjoyment, consider our Smoky Joe tabletop gas grill shown in the enclosed summer catalogue. We genuinely value your business and look forward to your future orders.

> We hope that this refund cheque convinces you of our sincere desire to satisfy our customers. Our goal is to earn your confidence and continue to justify that confidence with quality products and matchless service.

> You were most helpful in telling us about this situation and giving us an opportunity to correct it. We sincerely appreciate your cooperation.

> In all your future dealings with us, you will find us striving our hardest to merit your confidence by serving you with efficiency and sincere concern.

EFFECTIVE AND INEFFECTIVE RESPONSES TO CLAIMS

The letter shown at the top of Figure 7.4 is a response to an angry letter from Jeremy Garber of Sound Inc. who did not receive a shipment of electronic equipment from Electronic Warehouse. Mr. Garber wants his shipment sent immediately. When Amy Hopkins of Electronic Warehouse investigated, she found that the order was sent to the address shown on the Sound Inc. stationery on which the order was placed. The claim letter sent by the customer, however, was written on Sound Inc. stationery with a different address. The customer, Mr. Garber, seems to be unaware of the discrepancy.

This response gets off to a bad start by failing to address the customer personally. Then, instead of revealing when the customer might expect this shipment, the opening sentence blames the customer for providing an erroneous address.

The body of the letter does not promote goodwill. It continues to criticize Sound Inc. for the shipping problem, and it sounds sarcastic. Any reader of this letter would probably feel defensive. Moreover, the reader would have difficulty understanding whether another shipment is coming.

The claim from Sound Inc. does represent a problem to Electronic Warehouse. Ms. Hopkins must decide if a second shipment is justified. If so, who should pay the shipping and restocking fee? In this instance Ms. Hopkins decides to promote goodwill by sending a second shipment and by having her company absorb the extra

FIGURE 7.4

Claim Letter Responses

Ineffective

Fails to reveal good news immediately. Blames customer.

Creates ugly tone with negative words and sarcasm.

Sounds grudging and reluctant in granting claim.

Gentlemen:

In response to your recent complaint about a missing shipment, it's very difficult to deliver merchandise when we have been given an erroneous address.

Our investigators looked into your problem shipment and determined that it was sent immediately after we received the order. According to the shipper's records, it was delivered to the warehouse address given on your stationery: 3590 University Avenue, Saint John, New Brunswick E2M 1G7. Unfortunately, no one at that address would accept delivery, so the shipment was returned to us. I see from your current stationery that your company has a new address. With the proper address, we probably could have delivered this shipment.

Although we feel that it is entirely appropriate to charge you shipping and restocking fees, as is our standard practice on returned goods, in this instance we will waive those fees. We hope this second shipment finally catches up with you.

Sincerely,

Amy Hopkins

Effective

Electronic Warehouse
930 Abbot Park Place
Saint John, New Brunswick E3L 047

February 21, 200x

Mr. Jeremy Garber
Sound Inc.
2293 Second Avenue
Saint John, New Brunswick   E3M 2R5

Dear Mr. Garber

SUBJECT: YOUR FEBRUARY 18 LETTER ABOUT YOUR PURCHASE ORDER

You should receive by February 25 a second shipment of the speakers, VCRs, headphones, and other electronic equipment that you ordered January 20.

The first shipment of this order was delivered January 28 to 3590 University Avenue, Saint John, NB. When no one at that address would accept the shipment, it was returned to us. Now that I have your letter, I see that the order should have been sent to 2293 Second Avenue, Saint John, New Brunswick E3M 2R5. When an order is undeliverable, we usually try to verify the shipping address by telephoning the customer. Somehow the return of this shipment was not caught by our normally painstaking shipping clerks. You can be sure that I will investigate shipping and return procedures with our clerks immediately to see if we can improve existing methods.

As you know, Mr. Garber, our volume business allows us to sell wholesale electronics equipment at the lowest possible prices. However, we do not want to be so large that we lose touch with our customers. Over the years it is our customers' respect that has made us successful, and we hope that the prompt delivery of this shipment will earn yours.

Sincerely,

Amy Hopkins

Amy Hopkins
Distribution Manager

c David Cole
   Shipping Department

Uses customer's name in salutation.

Announces good news immediately.

Regains confidence of customer by explaining what happened and by suggesting plans for improvement.

Closes confidently with genuine appeal for customer's respect.

costs. Once this decision is made, the good news should be announced immediately and positively.

The bottom portion of Figure 7.4 shows a much-improved version of the response. In this letter the writer explains what happened to the first shipment. She also graciously accepts blame for the incident, even though the customer is probably equally guilty for not providing the proper shipping address.

Notice in the improved letter how effectively Amy Hopkins achieves two of the three goals of an adjustment letter. She rectifies the wrong suffered by the customer and strives to regain his confidence. She treats the third goal—promoting future business—tactfully in the closing, without the use of resale or sales promotion.

Some claims involve minimal loss of customer confidence. In the letter shown in Figure 7.5, Bravo Computers responds to Pauline LeBlanc. (Her request letter, shown in Chapter 6, Figure 6.4, asked Bravo to solve her computer's mystery malfunction.) In responding to her request, Bravo could merely have sent the instructions for packing and shipping the computer. Instead, it took this opportunity to maintain and promote customer goodwill with a friendly letter explaining its service policy. Notice that the letter avoids mentioning negatives, such as the malfunctioning computer. The closing does not dwell on the loss of her computer while it's being repaired. Rather, the letter emphasizes the customer's happiness with her computer by referring to her dependence on it. The letter ends with a forward-looking promise of the computer's speedy return.

FIGURE 7.5

Claim Response Letter

Announces good news in first sentence.

Explains company procedures and how company is complying with request.

Ends confidently and promises quick return of computer.

Dear Ms. LeBlanc:

We are indeed intrigued by your Bravo computer mystery and authorize you to send your Bravo E654 to our Diagnostic Department for inspection.

Normally, we try to have our computers repaired locally to minimize transportation costs and to reduce stress to internal parts. However, your mystery case may require our special attention. We are enclosing a return authorization slip with instructions on how to pack your computer for shipping.

Most users find that they can't get along without their computers for even a day. We will do our best to have your Bravo E654 on its way back to you within four working days of its receipt here in Sunnyvale. We hope that this speedy service indicates to you our sincere interest in satisfying our customers.

Sincerely,

SUMMING UP AND LOOKING FORWARD

In this chapter you learned to write letters that respond favourably to information requests, orders, and claims. These messages employ the direct strategy, so they begin directly with the primary idea. But not all letters will carry good news. Occasionally, you must deny requests and deliver bad news. In the next chapter you will learn to use the indirect strategy in conveying negative news.

DISCUSSION

1. Why is it advisable to use a subject line in responding to requests?
2. Since brevity is valued in business writing, is it ever wise to respond with more information than requested? Discuss.
3. Why is it a good business practice to send a personalized acknowledgment of an order?
4. Distinguish between resale and sales promotion.
5. Discuss the policy of granting all customer claims, regardless of merit.

CHAPTER REVIEW

6. What is the most important position in a letter?

7. Name two ways to open a letter that responds to multiple questions.

8 Name three instances in which sending a personalized order acknowledgment is particularly appropriate.

9. What do customers want to know first about their orders?

10. Give an example of resale.

11. List five situations in which claim letters might be written by customers.

12. What are three goals a writer strives to achieve in responding to customer claims?

13. Name at least five negative words that carry impressions of blame and wrong-doing.

14. What should be included in the subject line of a response to a claim?

15. Why do some business writers avoid apologies in responding to unhappy customers?

Writing Improvement Exercises

Subject Lines. Write effective subject lines for the following messages that appeared in this chapter:

16. Information response letter addressed to Ms. Bullen in Figure 7.2.

17. Claim response addressed to Ms. LeBlanc in Figure 7.5.

Direct　　**Indirect**

Letter Openers. Place a check mark in the appropriate column to indicate whether the following letter openers are direct or indirect. Be prepared to explain your choices.

_____ 18. Thank you for your letter of December 2 in which you inquired about the availability of No. 19 bolts of fabric.

_____ 19. We have an ample supply of No. 19 bolts in stock.

_____ 20. This will acknowledge receipt of your letter of December 2.

_____ 21. Yes, the Princess Cruise Club is planning a 15-day Mediterranean cruise beginning October 20.

_____ 22. I am pleased to have the opportunity to respond to your kind letter of July 9.

_____ 23. Your letter of July 9 has been referred to me because Mr. Halvorson is away from the office.

_____ 24. We sincerely appreciate your recent order for plywood wallboard panels.

_____ 25. The plywood wallboard panels that you requested were shipped today by Coast Express and should reach you by August 12.

Opening Paragraph

26. Revise the following opening paragraph of a response to a request for information. Use a separate sheet of paper.

Thank you for your letter of March 3 inquiring about the RefreshAire electronic air cleaner. I am pleased to have this opportunity to provide you with information. You asked how the RefreshAire works and specifically if it would remove pollen from the air. I can assure you that the RefreshAire removes pollen from the air—and smoke and dust as well. It then recirculates clean air. We think it makes offices, conference rooms, and cafeterias cleaner and more healthful for everyone.

Closing Paragraph

27. The following concluding paragraph to a claim letter response suffers from faults in strategy, tone, and emphasis. Revise and improve it on a separate sheet of paper.

As a result of your complaint of June 2, we are sending a replacement shipment of laser printers by Atlantic Express. Unfortunately, this shipment will not reach you until June 5. We hope that you will not allow this troubling incident and the resulting inconvenience and lost sales you suffered to jeopardize our future business relations. In the past we have been able to provide you with quality products and prompt service.

ACTIVITIES AND CASES

7.1 Response to Information Request: Scannable Résumés. Analyze the following poorly written letter from an athletic shoe manufacturer to a prospective job applicant, Michael Madzar, 382 Dufresne Road, Laval, Quebec H7E 1Y7. List at least five major faults. Outline a writing plan for a response to an information request. Then rewrite this message, rectifying the faults. Use block style.

Dear Mr. Madzar:

Your letter of April 11 has been referred to me for a response. We are pleased to learn that you are considering employment here at ABI Footwear, and we look forward to receiving your résumé, should you decide to send same to us.

Ineffective Writing

You ask if we scan incoming résumés. Yes, we certainly do. Actually, we use SmartTrack, an automated résumé-tracking system. SmartTrack is wonderful! You know, we sometimes receive as many as 300 résumés a day, and SmartTrack helps us sort, screen, filter, separate, process, organize, and record all of these résumés. Some of the résumés, however, cannot be scanned, so we have to return those—if we have time.

The reasons that résumés won't scan may surprise you. Some applicants send photocopies or faxed copies, and these can cause misreading, so don't do it. The best plan is to send an original copy. Some people use coloured paper. Big mistake! White paper (8 1/2- by 11-inch) printed on one side is the best bet. Another big problem is unusual type fonts, such as script or fancy gothic or antique fonts. They don't seem to realize that scanners do best with plain, readable font such as Helvetica or Univers in a 10- to 14-point size.

Other problems occur when applicants use graphics, shading, italics, underlining, horizontal and vertical lines, parentheses, and brackets. Scanners like plain "vanilla" résumés! Oh yes, staples can cause misreading. And folding of a résumé can also cause the scanners to foul up. To be safe, don't staple or fold, and be sure to use wide margins and a quality printer (no dot matrixes!!).

When a hiring manager within ABI Footwear decides to look for an appropriate candidate, he is told to submit key words to describe the candidate he has in mind for his opening. We tell him (or sometimes her) to zero in on nouns and phrases that best describe what they want. Thus, my advice to you is to try to include those words that highlight your technical and professional areas of expertise.

If you do decide to submit your résumé to ABI Footwear, be sure you don't make any of the mistakes described herein that would cause the scanner to misread it.

Sincerely,

7.2 Response to Claim: Doors That Won't Stretch. You are Jay Brandt, manager of Custom Wood Inc., a firm that manufactures quality precut and custom-built doors and frames. You have received a letter dated August 3 from Julie Chen, 3282 Richmond Road, Vancouver, BC V1L 2E6. Ms. Chen is an interior designer, and she complains that the oak French doors she ordered for a client recently were made to the wrong dimensions.

Although they were the wrong size, she kept the doors and had them installed because her clients were without outside doors. However, her carpenter charged an extra $455.50 to install them. She claims that you should reimburse her for this amount, since your company was responsible for the error. You check her July 2 order and find that she is right. Instead of measuring a total of 3.13 square metres, the doors were made to measure 3.23 square metres. Normally, your Quality Control Department carefully monitors custom jobs. You resolve to review personally the plant's custom product procedures.

Ms. Chen is a successful interior designer and has provided Custom Wood with a number of orders. You value her business and decide to send her a cheque for the amount of her claim. You want to remind her that Custom Wood has earned a reputation as the manufacturer of the finest wood doors and frames on the market. You have a new line of greenhouse windows that are available in three sizes. Include a brochure describing these windows.

Review the writing plan for granting a claim. Use this letter for class discussion or write a response to Ms. Chen on a separate sheet. Use block style.

7.3 Response to Order: Fitness Feedback. Analyze the following poorly written message following up on an order of fitness equipment for a health training centre. List at least five major faults in the letter. Outline a writing plan for an order response, then rewrite the message, rectifying its faults. Use block style. Address your revision to Mrs. Helen Dumont, Manager, Health and Fitness Trends, 5839 Victory Drive, Kingston, ON K7S 2L4.

Ineffective Writing

Gentlemen:

We have received your kind order under date of November 14. Permit me to say that most of the order will be shipped shortly.

Only the FlexDeck treadmills will be delayed. We've had quite a run on these treadmills, and we just can't keep them in stock. Therefore, they will be sent separately from the factory in Buffalo, New York, and will probably arrive sometime around December 15. All the other items (the exercise bikes, the stairclimber, and the health riders) are being sent today by Midland Express and will, in all probability, reach you by December 5.

We also have some new items that your fitness centre might like. One item is especially interesting. It's the LifeCycle 5500 recumbent aerobic trainer, which can burn over 750 calories per hour while providing a wide contoured seat and lower back support. Attached please find a brochure describing it and some of our other newer items.

If we can be of further service, do not hesitate to call upon us.

Sincerely,

7.4 Response to Information Request: Tell Me About Your Major. A friend in a distant city is considering moving to your area for more education and training in your field. This individual wants to know about your program of study. Write a letter describing a program in your field (or any field you wish to describe). What courses must be taken? Toward what degree, certificate, or employment position does this program lead? Why did you choose it? Would you recommend this program to your friend? How long does it take? Add any additional information you feel would be helpful.

7.5 Response to Claim: You're Right! Assume that you are a manager in the business in which you now work (or one about which you have some knowledge). Imagine that a customer, colleague, or employee has made a legitimate claim against your organization. Write a letter granting the claim. Make the letter as realistic and factual as possible.

7.6 Response to Information Request: Backpacking Cuisine. As Karie Osborne, owner of Outfitters Inc., producer of freeze-dried backpacking foods, answer the inquiry of Marc Vannault (described in Chapter 6, Activity 6.6). You are eager to have Mr. Vannault sample your new, all-natural line of products containing no preservatives, sugar, or additives. You want him to know that you started this company two years ago after you found yourself making custom meals for discerning backpackers who rejected typical camping fare. Along with a complete list of dinner items and the suggested retail prices, you will also send him your "Saturday Night on the Trail" product sampler. All your food products are made from choice ingredients in sanitary kitchens that you personally supervise and are flash frozen in a new vacuum process that you patented. Your products are currently available at High-Country Sports Centre, 19605 Rocky Mountain Highway, Calgary, AB T8L 1Z8. Write a response to Marc Vannault, 322 East Drive, Penticton, BC V2A 1T2.

7.7 Response to Information Request: The Canadian Beer Index On-Line. As Peter Fahil, Web master for the Canadian Beer Index, respond to a letter from a potential customer, microbrewer Bill Antaya (see Chapter 6, Activity 6.7). In addition to answering Mr. Antaya's questions, you hope to gain his company, Crystal Ale Microbrewery, as a new customer by highlighting the benefits of the Canadian Beer Index. Of course, you want to clarify for Mr. Antaya that the Canadian Beer Index doesn't brew beer; it simply advertises and promotes Canadian producers on its Web site. The cost is determined by relative sales, based on local or regional distribution.

Although you can't predict how many customers each brewer will gain through the Canadian Beer Index, you do know that over the past six months there have been approximately 45,000 visitors to the Canadian Beer Index site.

Small brewers appreciate the Canadian Beer Index site because it brings in customers, reducing the need for expensive advertising campaigns and enabling brewers to maintain reasonable beer prices. Consumers particularly appreciate the site's product write-ups and beer articles by well-known brewmasters. The Canadian Beer Index includes 50 breweries and about 250 beers.

Gaining new customers hasn't been easy, so the site now offers short-term contracts to brewers new to the service. Brewers may call you personally at (306) 756-1456 for more information

Write to Bill Antaya, Crystal Ale MicroBrewery, 7345 Post Road, Saskatoon, Saskatchewan S4L 2R3. Answer the questions in his inquiry (Activity 6.7). Along with your reply, send him your brochure "The Canadian Beer Index."

Related Web Site: realbeer.com

7.8 Response to Order: Office Supplies to Go. Respond to the order placed by William Vorstein, manager, Lasertronics Inc. 2004 Henrietta Road, Hamilton, Ontario L2N 4T1 (described in Chapter 6, Activity 6.8). Yes, all of the prices listed in your old catalogue have increased. That's the bad news. The good news is that you have in stock everything he ordered, except the desktop organizer, which will be shipped from the manufacturer in Pittsburgh, Pennsylvania, within three weeks. Lasertronics might be interested in your new line of office supply products at discount prices. Send him a new catalogue and call his attention to the low, low price on continuous-form computer paper.

7.9 Response to Order: N.W.T. Request. As the customer relations manager at Toys-R-Us, you are responding to a letter from Terri Tran. (Her request was described in Chapter 6, Activity 6.9. If you wrote that request, respond to it in this problem naming the toy you described. If you did not write that letter, use the "Wild Mantis" toy identified here.) You think that the toy she has described is the "Wild Mantis," a battery-operated, four-wheel-drive toy racing car (your store's Item No. 825990-2). Wild Mantis has operating headlights, forward/reverse gears, and controlled steering. It costs $84.97, plus tax and shipping. It should arrive within her three-week deadline. Tell her that you are sending Wild Mantis and that you have charged the total amount (figure it out) to her Visa card. Write this order response to Terri Tran, 845 Wainee Street, Yellowknife, Northwest Territories X1L 2F3.

7.10 Response to Claim: Deep Desk Disappointment. As Rodney Harding, sales manager, Big Spruce Wood Products, it is your job to reply to customer claims, and today you must respond to Monica Keil, president, Keil Consulting Services, 423 E. Lawrence Avenue, Montreal, Quebec, H5L 2E3 (described in Chapter 6, Activity 6.10). You are disappointed that she is returning the executive desk (Invoice No. 3499), but your policy is to comply with customer wishes. You want her to give Big Spruce Wood Products another chance. Since she is apparently furnishing her office, send her another catalogue and invite her to look at the traditional conference desk on page 10-E. This is available with a matching credenza, file cabinets, and accessories. She might be interested in your furniture-leasing plan, which can produce substantial savings. You promise that you will personally examine any furniture she may order in the future. Write her a letter granting her claim.

7.11 Response to Claim: Earth First Runs Dry. As Antonio Garcia, customer service manager for Stellar Printers, 908 East Street, Toronto Ontario M4W 3T8, reply to a claim letter from Megan Phillips, public relations assistant, Earth First, 5314 River Road, Evergreen, New Brunswick, E4L 2Y5 (see Chapter 6, Activity 6.11). Explain to Ms. Phillips that Stellar Printers will refund to Earth First $126.50 for the two faulty cartridges it purchased. The cartridges were apparently made with a new type of protective tape, which worked well in manufacturing and was much cheaper for Stellar to use. Unfortunately, when printer owners removed the protective tape as instructed, residue from the tape clogged the cartridges' ink holes, causing the cartridges to malfunction even though they were still full of ink. In February, Stellar stopped using the defective tape. Instead, it returned to its original protective tape to seal cartridges. Write a letter granting the claim.

7.12 Connecting With E-Mail: Going to Comdex? As a management trainee for Compuware Inc., you have received an e-mail message from one of Compuware's customers, Mahmud Hasan. Mr. Hasan wants to know if Compuware will have a booth at this year's Comdex show in Toronto on November 18–25. This is the biggest computer trade show in the world, with over 210,000 people attending. Yes, of course, Compuware will be at the show, which is being held at the Toronto Convention Centre, with a display at Booths 120 and 121. In addition to its full line of computer components and accessories, Compuware is really pushing its Graphics Pro Turbo program that creates TV-quality multimedia presentations. Send an e-mail message to Mahmud Hasam (in care of your instructor) answering his inquiry.

7.13. Searching the Internet: Getting Up to Speed on Web Copyright Law. Your boss wants to add some new content to the company's Web site. She's thinking of adding interesting articles she has found at other sites, but she's not sure about what is and is not protected by copyright law. Can she just copy and use any information appearing on a public site? Can she cut and paste parts of other sites' articles into articles already on the company site? She asks you to research the question and report what you find in an e-mail message to her. One site your boss recommends is www.smithlyons.ca/it/tcii/index.htm. You might wish to browse other sites as well. Report your findings in an e-mail message to your boss (your instructor in this instance).

GRAMMAR/MECHANICS CHECKUP—7

Commas 2

Review the Grammar/Mechanics Handbook Sections 2.05—2.09. Then study each of the following statements and insert necessary commas. In the space provided write the number of commas that you add; write *0* if no commas are needed. Also, record the number of the G/M principle(s) illustrated. When you finish, compare your responses with those provided. If your answers differ, study carefully the principles shown in parentheses.

1 (2.06a)

Example: When businesses encounter financial problems, they often reduce their administrative staffs.

_____

_____

_____

_____

_____

_____

_____

_____

_____

_____

1. As stated in the warranty this printer is guaranteed for one year.
2. Today's profits come from products currently on the market and tomorrow's profits come from products currently on the drawing boards.
3. Companies introduce new products in one part of the country and then watch how the product sells in that area.
4. One large automobile manufacturer which must remain nameless recognizes that buyer perception is behind the success of any new product.
5. The imaginative promising agency opened its offices April 22 in Cambridge.
6. The sales associate who earns the highest number of recognition points this year will be honoured with a bonus vacation trip.
7. Darren Wilson our sales manager in the Cedar Falls area will make a promotion presentation at the June meeting.
8. Our new product has many attributes that should make it appealing to buyers but it also has one significant drawback.
9. Although they have different technical characteristics and vary considerably in price and quality two or more of a firm's products may be perceived by shoppers as almost the same.
10. To motivate prospective buyers we are offering a cash rebate of $20.

Review of Commas 1 and 2

_____

_____

_____

_____

_____

11. When you receive the application please fill it out and return it before Monday January 3.
12. On the other hand we are very interested in hiring hard-working conscientious individuals.
13. In March we expect to open a new branch in Concord which is an area of considerable growth.
14. As we discussed on the telephone the ceremony is scheduled for Thursday June 9 at 3 p.m.
15. Dr. Adams teaches the morning classes and Mrs. Wilder is responsible for evening sections.

---

1. (1) warranty, (2.06a)   3. (0) (2.05)   5. (1) imaginative, (2.08)   7. (2) Wilson, area, (2.09)
9. (1) quality, (2.06a)   11. (2) application, Monday, (2.06a, 2.04a)   13. (1) Concord, (2.06c)
15. (1) classes, (2.05)

GRAMMAR/MECHANICS CHALLENGE—7

Document for Revision

The following letter has faults in grammar, punctuation, spelling, number form, and negative words. Use standard proofreading marks (see Appendix B) to correct the errors. When you finish, your instructor can show you the revised version of this letter.

May 3, 200x

Mr. Ragu Raghavan

Medical Supplies, Inc.

P.O. Box 489

North York, Ontario M3J 3K1

Dear Mr. Raghavan:

You will be recieving shortly the rubbermaid service and utility carts you ordered along with 5 recycling stack bins. Unfortunately, the heavy duty can crusher is not available but it will be sent from the factory in Albany New York and should reach you by May 31st.

You may place any future orders, by using our toll free telephone number (1-800-577-9241), or our toll free fax number (1-800-577-2657). If you need help with any items ask for one of the following sales represenatives, Bill Small, Susan Freed, or Rick Woo. When the items you order are in our currant catalogue it will be shipped the same day you place you're order. For products to be custom imprinted please provide a typed or printed copy with your order.

Remember we are the only catalogue sales company that guarantees your full satisfaction. If you are not pleased we'll arrange for a prompt refund, credit or replacement. We'll also refund or credit all shipping costs associated with the returned items. We want your business!

Yours truly,

Communication Workshop: Multicultural

ADAPTING STRATEGIES FOR MULTICULTURAL AND INTERNATIONAL CORRESPONDENCE

The letter-writing suggestions you've been studying work well for correspondence in North America. You may wish, however, to modify the organization, format, and tone of letters going abroad.

Canadian businesspeople appreciate efficiency, straightforwardness, and conciseness in letters more than do writers from other countries. Moreover, Canadian business letters tend to be more informal and conversational. International correspondents, however, may look upon such directness and informality as inappropriate, insensitive, and abrasive. Letters in Japan, for example, may begin with deference, humility, and references to the changing seasons and nature:

> Allow us to open with all reverence to you. The season for cherry blossoms is here with us and everybody is beginning to feel refreshed. We sincerely congratulate you on becoming more prosperous in your business.[3]

Mexican culture stresses the importance of family and relationships. Establishing and winning trust is an essential part of any written document. Letters in Mexico often begin with a comment about family or mutual friends:

> It is a great privilege for me to address such a successful businessman as you. It is also a true honour for me to learn that you are one of the direct descendants of . . .[4]

Letters in Germany commonly start with a long, formal lead-in, such as *Referring to your kind inquiry from the 31st of the month, we take the liberty to remind you with this letter.*[5] French correspondents would consider it rude to begin a letter with a request before it is explained. French letters typically include an ending with this phrase (or a variation of it): *I wish to assure you [insert reader's most formal title] of my most respectful wishes [followed by the writer's title and signature].*

International letters are also more likely to include passive-voice constructions *(your letter has been received)*, exaggerated courtesy *(great pleasure, esteemed favour)*, and obvious flattery *(your eminent firm)*.

Letters from other countries may also use different formatting techniques. Whereas Canadian business letters are printed and single-spaced, in other countries they may be handwritten and single- or double-spaced. Because the placement and arrangement of letter addresses and closing lines vary greatly, you should always research local preferences before writing. For important letters going abroad, it's wise to have someone familiar with local customs read and revise the message.

Application. Assume your company must send a letter requesting a favour from one of its American suppliers. Outline the writing plan for a favour request letter. How might the writing plan be modified for a Japanese supplier? Mexican supplier? French supplier? German supplier? Encourage class members to bring foreign business letter examples to class. You might ask foreign students, your campus admissions office, or local export/import companies if they would be willing to share business letters from other countries. Compare letter styles, formats, tone, and development with typical North American business letters. Discuss their similarities and differences.

UNIT 4

CONVEYING NEGATIVE, PERSUASIVE, AND SPECIAL MESSAGES

CHAPTER 8

LETTERS AND MEMOS THAT CARRY NEGATIVE NEWS

A going concern . . . is how to give internal and external customers bad news yet maintain goodwill. Everyone agrees this is a difficult task and something we all need to get better at.[1]

VERA M. HELD, Toronto-based communications coach, speaker, and writer

Learning Objectives

1. Identify the need for indirectness in delivering bad news.
2. Recognize six components in an effective indirect strategy.
3. Apply skilful writing techniques in refusing requests.
4. Retain goodwill while refusing claims.
5. Demonstrate tact in refusing credit requests.

Letters and memos that carry negative news can have a significant impact on a company's success. In fact, as Vera Held suggests, they are the kind of messages that concern business owners and managers because of their potential to damage customer relationships. Although many of the letters you will write will involve positive messages, occasionally you will have to write messages that convey negative news both externally to customers and internally to co-workers. These messages must be written in a way that explains the bad news but retains goodwill at the same time.

As you learned earlier, the first step in writing a business message is analyzing the effect it will have on the reader. If the message will antagonize, disappoint, upset, hurt, or anger the recipient, an indirect strategy may be more effective than the direct strategy. In this chapter you will learn why plenty of thought goes into writing bad-news messages. In learning to apply the indirect strategy, you'll discover that it does require more effort than does sending good news.

Examples of letters that deliver disappointing news are those that deny requests, refuse claims, reveal price increases, decline invitations, announce shipping delays, turn down job applicants, discontinue services, or deny credit. In this chapter we'll be applying the indirect method to bad-news messages.

If your message delivers bad news, consider using the indirect method.

ANALYZING THE MESSAGE

Recipients of good news like to learn the news quickly. That's why the direct strategy is most effective. Directness, however, is not so effective for bad news. Most writers feel that blurting out bad news at the beginning of a message is inconsiderate and upsetting. The reader is then in a poor frame of mind to receive the remainder of the message. Or, worse yet, the bad news may cause the reader to stop reading altogether. Reasons for the refusal and explanations that follow may never be seen. The principal goal of the indirect strategy is presenting reasons and explanations before revealing any bad news.

The indirect method allows the writer to explain before announcing the bad news.

KNOWING WHEN TO BE DIRECT WITH BAD NEWS

The indirect strategy, which we will discuss shortly, is generally better for negative news—but not always. Some people prefer frankness and directness. If you know the receiver well, the direct strategy may be appropriate even for negative messages. For example, assume that David Li, a good customer with whom you are friendly, must be told that his company will no longer be receiving a pricing discount. You know that David is a no-nonsense, up-front fellow who values candour. For him the direct strategy is entirely appropriate. He doesn't like "beating around the bush."

Some readers, however, may prefer to have bad news announced directly.

Other occasions may also call for directness. Let's say you have been unsuccessful in getting your message across by writing one or more messages using the indirect strategy. You may decide that bluntness is needed. The direct approach, for example, might be appropriate in responding to Ashley Clark. She has been told twice, in memos using an indirect strategy, that she does not qualify for a promotion because she lacks sufficient college training in her field. She applied for the promotion a third time and still had not enrolled in the necessary courses. This time her superior wrote a direct memo that spelled out the denial immediately and then explained the reasons for the denial.

Typically, though, we try to soften the blow of bad news by delaying it until after we have explained the reasons justifying it. Delaying the bad news is just one part of an overall strategy that has proved effective in delivering messages with negative news. The indirect strategy includes the following six elements.

INDIRECT STRATEGY

- Buffer
- Transition
- Explanation
- Bad news
- Alternative(s)
- Goodwill closing

APPLYING THE INDIRECT STRATEGY

The indirect strategy gives you a general outline for presenting negative news. Before implementing it, however, you need to analyze each step and study illustrations that show how these steps are used in writing letters and memos. After you have examined the steps, you'll learn how to put them together in writing letters for common

Before applying the indirect strategy, analyze the reasons underlying the bad news.

business situations that involve delivering negative news. By developing skill in using this strategy in the most common situations, you should be able to adapt it to similar business problems.

We'll discuss the indirect strategy in the order shown, but the thinking process actually follows a slightly different order. Skilful writers first decide whether their message will likely elicit a positive or negative reaction from the reader. If a request must be denied or a claim refused, they analyze their reasons for refusing. If they don't have good reasons, they can't write convincing letters. Thus, the explanation shapes the rest of the letter and determines the content and tone. Although the letter begins with a buffer, the thinking process begins much earlier—with the reasons for delivering the bad news.

DEVELOPING A GOOD BUFFER

A buffer is a device that reduces shock. In denying a request or delivering other bad news, we can reduce the shock a reader may suffer by opening with a buffer paragraph. This opening should put the reader in a receptive frame of mind. Our objective, remember, is to induce the recipient to read the entire letter. We want the reader to understand our reasons and explanations before we disclose the bad news.

An effective buffer is neutral, upbeat, and relevant.

An effective buffer is generally neutral, upbeat, and relevant. A buffer is neutral when it does not signal the bad news that is to follow nor falsely suggests that good news will be forthcoming. A buffer is upbeat if it emphasizes something positive for the reader. The positive element could be resale material that relates to a product, a compliment or praise for the reader, or a statement that builds goodwill. A buffer is relevant if it refers to the situation at hand. A buffer statement that describes the unusually good weather may be neutral and upbeat, but it has no relation to the bad news.

Here are a number of buffer statements for negative letters. The first is the opening statement for a letter delivering the news that a candidate did not receive a job for which he was interviewed. The buffer refers to the interview positively but does not suggest that the candidate will be hired:

> I enjoyed talking with you last week about your background and the excellent business administration program at the University of Western Ontario.

A letter denying a request for credit for merchandise that a customer wishes to return employs a resale buffer:

Try not to forecast bad news nor falsely imply good news.

> Your selection of an Ambassador top-grain pigskin leather attaché case is a smart one because these cases combine fashionable styling with high-quality leathers.

A letter refusing an invitation to speak at an awards banquet begins with a compliment to the reader:

> You have done a splendid job of organizing the program for the October 5 Ducks Unlimited awards banquet.

A letter denying an adjustment to a customer's account opens with a warm statement regarding the customer's past payment record:

> We genuinely appreciate the prompt payments you have always made in response to our monthly billings.

BUILDING A SMOOTH TRANSITION

After the opening buffer statement, use a transition that guides the reader to the explanation that follows. Avoid problem words such as *but, unfortunately,* and *however* because they clearly suggest that bad news is to come.

Experienced writers try to plant a keyword or idea in the buffer or transition that leads the reader naturally to the reasons for the refusal. In this next example a business must refuse a request for campaign contributions from a candidate running in a civic election. Notice how the keywords *candidate* and *contribution* form a link between the buffer and the explanation for refusing the request:

> Your efforts to build a campaign chest for city council candidate Gladys Harris are commendable. This candidate deserves the support of civic-minded businesses and individuals who are able to make *contributions*.

> Your *candidate*, if elected, will help administer funds to municipal departments and offices. As you may know, a significant portion of our business involves providing supplies for city offices. City council members who have accepted campaign contributions from vendors supplying city accounts may be accused of conflict of interest. Rather than place your candidate in this awkward position, our lawyer advises us to avoid making financial contributions to the campaigns of city council candidates. Although we are unable to provide financial support, many of our employees will be contributing their time and efforts to work personally for the election of your candidate.

> We hope that the participation of our staff will contribute to a successful campaign for Gladys Harris.

Reference to a keyword or idea builds a transition between the buffer and the following explanation.

Buffer

Transition

Explanation

Bad news

Alternative

Goodwill closing

PRESENTING THE EXPLANATION BEFORE THE BAD NEWS

In the preceding example, keywords in the buffer and transition lead the reader smoothly to the explanation. As you know, the explanation is the most important part of a negative letter. Without sound reasons for denying a request or refusing a claim, the letter will fail, no matter how cleverly it is written. The explanation is, after all, the principal reason for using the indirect method. We want to be able to explain before refusing.

In the explanation, as in the transition, don't let problem words *(but, however, unfortunately)* signal the refusal. Your explanation should show that you have analyzed the situation carefully. Tell clearly why a refusal is necessary: an item is no longer under warranty or was never warrantied in the first place, or a cash refund cannot be granted for an item that cannot be resold, or a product failed because it was misused. In some instances, such as the denial of credit or the refusal to allow damaged goods to be returned, the explanation can emphasize reader benefits. The reader, along with other customers, benefits from lower prices if a business is able to avoid unnecessary credit costs and unfair returns.

Strive to project an unemotional, objective, and helpful tone. Don't lecture or patronize *(If you will read the operating instructions carefully. . .),* avoid sounding presumptuous *(I'm sure the salesperson who demonstrated this unit explained that . . .),* and don't hide behind company policy *(Our company policy prevents us from granting your*

The success of a negative letter depends on how well the explanation is presented.

request). Explain specifically why the company policy is necessary. If you have more than one reason for refusing, begin with the strongest reason. Present the bad news, and then continue with additional reasons for refusing.

BREAKING THE BAD NEWS

You can soften the blow of bad news by using some of these seven techniques.

In Chapter 4 you learned stylistic techniques for de-emphasizing ideas. Now we will expand on those techniques and apply them as you learn to break bad news.

- *Avoid the spotlight.* Don't put the bad news in a conspicuous position. The most emphatic positions in a letter are the first and last sentences. Other conspicuous spots are the beginnings and ends of sentences and paragraphs. The reader's attention is drawn to these positions and lingers there. Strategically, then, these are not good places for announcing bad news. To give the least emphasis to an idea, place it in the middle of a sentence or in the middle of a paragraph partway through your letter.

- *Use a long sentence.* Short sentences emphasize content. Since you want to de-emphasize bad news, avoid short, simple sentences *(We cannot ship your goods)*. Longer sentences diffuse the bad news and also give you a chance to explain the bad news or offer alternatives.

Be selective in applying these techniques whenever you break bad news.

- *Put the bad news in a subordinate clause.* Grammatical attention in a sentence is always focused on the independent clause. To de-emphasize an idea, then, put it in a less conspicuous spot, such as a subordinate clause *(Although your credit application cannot be approved at this time, we welcome your cash business)*. The bad news is subordinated in the dependent clause *(Although your credit application)* where the reader is less likely to dwell on it.

- *Use the passive voice.* The active voice, recommended for most business writing, is direct and identifies the subject of a sentence *(I cannot allow you to examine our personnel files)*. To be less direct and to avoid drawing unnecessary attention to yourself as writer, use the passive voice *(Examination of our personnel files cannot be permitted because . . .)*. The passive voice focuses attention on actions rather than personalities; it helps you be impersonal and tactful.

- *Be clear but not overly graphic.* Bad news is best received when it is clear but not painfully vivid. For example, the following refusal is unnecessarily harsh because it provides too many details:

  We will not pay for your freelance services in cash, as you request. Such payments violate our accepted company policy and create the opportunity for you to avoid paying taxes. We pay for all of our freelance services only by cheque and only upon receipt of an invoice.

  This refusal would be more tactful if it were less direct and less graphic:

  We pay our freelancers by cheque once we receive their invoices.

- *Imply the refusal.* In certain instances a refusal does not have to be stated directly. In the preceding example the tactful revision does not actually say *We cannot pay you in cash*. Instead, the refusal is implied. Recall the letter refusing campaign funds:

Rather than place your candidate in this awkward position, our lawyer advises us to avoid making financial contributions to the campaigns of city council candidates.

Instead of hammering home the bad news *(Therefore, we cannot contribute to this campaign)*, the author spared the feelings of the reader by implying the refusal.

Here's another example of an implied refusal. Instead of refusing an invitation to speak at a campus job symposium, a business executive writes:

Although my appointment schedule is completely booked during the week of your employment symposium, I wish you success with this beneficial event.

Implying a refusal is not quite as devastating as an explicit denial. Such subtlety saves the feelings of both the writer and the reader. Be very careful, however, in using this technique. It is imperative that the reader understand the refusal. Don't be so vague that additional correspondence is required to clarify the refusal.

Implied refusals are effective only if they are not so subtle that the reader misses the point.

- *Offer an alternative.* If appropriate, suggest some recourse to the reader. You might offer a compromise, a substitute, or an alternative offer:

For security reasons visitors are never allowed inside Building J. It is possible, however, to tour our assembly facility in the fall during our Open House.

My schedule prevents me from speaking to your group, but I have asked a colleague, Dr. Susan Rehwaldt, to consider addressing your conference.

Alternatives are an important means of maintaining good relations with consumers. Many customer-focused companies authorize their staff to use a variety of alternatives in responding to disappointed consumers. Some send coupons, gift boxes, or even T-shirts. Others provide discounts or special offers to unsatisfied customers.

CLOSING WITH GOODWILL

After explaining the bad news clearly and tactfully, shift to an idea that renews good feelings between the writer and the reader. In the letter refusing to pay a freelancer in cash, the closing regains her confidence:

Provide a courteous, pleasant, and forward-looking closing that doesn't refer directly to the bad news.

We hope that we may continue to use your services as a freelancer in the future.

If you are presenting an alternative, make it easy to accept:

Dr. Rehwaldt is an excellent speaker, and I'm sure your group would enjoy her presentation. I am including Dr. Rehwaldt's address so that you may write her directly.

When writing to customers, encourage continued business relations. Resale or sales promotional material may be appropriate:

I am enclosing a sample of a new imported fragrance and a coupon to save you $15 on your initial purchase. We look forward to serving you soon.

For the most effective closings, avoid the following traps:

- *Don't refer to the bad news.* Focus on positive, friendly remarks. Don't needlessly revive the reader's emotions regarding the bad news.

Irony is the use of
words to express
something other
than, and especially
opposite to, the
literal meaning.

- *Don't conclude with clichés.* Remarks such as *If we may be of further service* or *Thank you for understanding our position* sound particularly insincere and ironic in messages delivering negative news.
- *Don't invite further correspondence.* Expressions such as *If you have any further questions* or *If you would like to discuss this further* suggest that the matter is still open for discussion. Don't encourage a pen-pal relationship. Your decision is fair and final.

REFUSING REQUESTS

When you must refuse a request and you feel that the refusal is likely to antagonize, upset, hurt, or anger the reader, use an indirect approach, such as the following writing plan illustrates.

WRITING PLAN FOR REFUSING A REQUEST OR CLAIM

- *Buffer* —identifies previous correspondence incidentally or in a subject line and begins with neutral statement on which both the reader and the writer can agree.
- *Transition* —plants key idea or word that leads naturally to the explanation.
- *Explanation* —presents valid reasons for refusal, avoids problem words that forecast bad news, and includes resale or sales promotion material if appropriate.
- *Bad news* —softens the blow by de-emphasizing the refusal.
- *Alternative* —suggests a compromise, alternative, or substitute if possible.
- *Closing* —renews good feelings with a positive statement, avoids referring to the bad news, and looks forward to continued business.

EXPERT AND FAULTY LETTERS THAT REFUSE REQUESTS

Two versions of a request refusal are shown in Figure 8.1. A magazine writer requested salary information for an article, but this information could not be released. The ineffective version begins with needless information that could be implied. The second paragraph creates a harsh tone with such negative words as *sorry, must refuse, violate,* and *liable.* Since the refusal precedes the explanation, the reader probably will not be in a receptive frame of mind to accept the reasons for refusing. Notice, too, that the bad news is emphasized by its placement in a short sentence at the beginning of a paragraph. It stands out here and adds more weight to the rejection already felt by the reader.

Moreover, the refusal explanation is overly graphic, containing references to possible litigation. The tone at this point is threatening and unduly harsh. Then, suddenly, the author throws in a self-serving comment about the high salary and commissions of his salespeople. Instead of offering constructive alternatives, the ineffective version reveals only tiny bits of the desired information. Finally, the closing sounds syrupy and quite insincere.

In the more effective version of this refusal, the opening reflects the writer's genuine interest in the request. But it does not indicate compliance. The second sen-

FIGURE 8.1

Refusing a Request

States obvious information.

Sounds harsh, blunt, and unnecessarily negative.

Switches tone.

Ineffective

Dear Ms. Marcus:

I have your letter of October 21 in which you request information about the salaries and commissions of our top young salespeople.

I am sorry to inform you that we cannot reveal data of this kind. I must, therefore, refuse your request. To release this information would violate our private employee contracts. Such disclosure could make us liable for damages, should any employee seek legal recourse. I might say, however, that our salespeople are probably receiving the highest combined salary and commissions of any salespeople in this field.

If it were possible for us to help you with your fascinating research, we would certainly be happy to do so.

Sincerely yours,

Effective

CANON ELECTRONICS

115 Bloor Street West
Toronto, Ontario M4A 1W5
(416) 593-1098

January 15, 200x

Ms. Sylvia Marcus
1305 Elmwood Avenue
Peterborough, Ontario K6N 1Y5

Dear Ms. Marcus:

The article you are now researching for *Business Management Weekly* sounds fascinating, and we are flattered that you wish to include our organization. We do have many outstanding young salespeople, both male and female, who are commanding top salaries.

Each of our salespeople operates under an individual salary contract. During salary negotiations several years ago, an agreement was reached in which both sales staff members and management agreed to keep the terms of these individual contracts confidential. Although specific salaries and commission rates cannot be released, we can provide you with a ranked list of our top salespeople for the past five years. Three of the current top salespeople are under the age of thirty-five.

Enclosed is a fact sheet regarding our top salespeople. We wish you every success with your article, and we hope to see our organization represented in it.

Cordially,

Lloyd Kenniston

Lloyd Kenniston
Executive Vice President

LK:je
Enclosure: Sales Fact Sheet

Buffer shows genuine interest, and transition sets up explanation.

Explanation gives good reasons for refusing request.

Refusal is softened by substitute.

Closing is pleasant and forward looking.

tence acts as a transition by introducing the words *salespeople* and *salaries*, which are repeated in the following paragraph. Reasons for refusing this request are objectively presented in an explanation that precedes the refusal. Notice that the refusal *(Although specific salaries and commission rates cannot be released)* is a subordinate clause in a long sentence in the middle of a paragraph. To further soften the blow, the letter offers an alternative. The cordial closing refers to the alternative, avoids mention of the refusal, and looks to the future.

It's always easier to write refusals when alternatives can be offered to soften the bad news. But often no alternatives are possible. The refusal shown in Figure 8.2 involves a delicate situation in which a manager has been asked by her superiors to violate a contract. Several of the lawyers for whom she works have privately asked her to make copies of a licensed software program for them. They apparently want this program for their personal computers. Making copies is forbidden by the terms of the software licensing agreement, and the manager refuses to do this. Rather than saying no to each lawyer who asks her, she sends all staff computer users the e-mail message shown in Figure 8.2.

The opening tactfully avoids suggesting that any lawyer has actually asked to copy the software program. These professionals may prefer not to have their private requests made known. A transition takes the reader to the logical reasons against copying. Notice that the tone is objective, and neither preaching nor condemning. The refusal is softened by being linked with a positive statement *(Although this program must not be copied, we look forward to using it for many of your projects here . . .)*. To divert attention from the refusal, the memo ends with a friendly, off-the-subject remark.

REFUSING CLAIMS

All businesses offering products or services will receive occasional customer claims for adjustments. Claims may also arise from employees. Most of these claims are valid, and the customer or employee receives a positive response. Even unwarranted claims are sometimes granted because businesses genuinely desire to create a good public image and to maintain friendly relations with employees.

Some claims, however, cannot be approved because the customer or employee is mistaken, misinformed, unreasonable, or possibly even dishonest. Letters responding to these claims deliver bad news. And the indirect strategy breaks bad news with the least pain. It also allows the writer to explain why the claim must be refused before the reader realizes the bad news and begins resisting.

EFFECTIVE LETTER THAT REFUSES CLAIM

In the letter shown in Figure 8.3, the writer denies a customer's claim for the difference between the price the customer paid for speakers and the price he saw advertised locally (which would have resulted in a cash refund of $151). While Premier Sound Sales does match any advertised lower price, the price-matching policy applies only to the same models. This claim must be rejected because the advertisement the customer submitted shows a different, older speaker model.

The letter to Jim Vandermark opens with a buffer that agrees with a statement in the customer's letter. It repeats the key idea of product confidence as a transition

FIGURE 8.2

Refusing a Request and Offering No Alternative

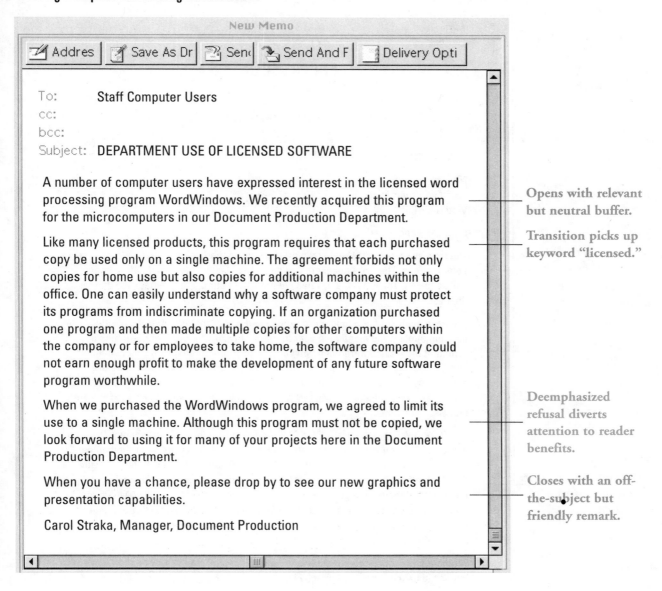

New Memo

Addres | Save As Dr | Send | Send And F | Delivery Opti

To: Staff Computer Users
cc:
bcc:
Subject: DEPARTMENT USE OF LICENSED SOFTWARE

A number of computer users have expressed interest in the licensed word processing program WordWindows. We recently acquired this program for the microcomputers in our Document Production Department.

Like many licensed products, this program requires that each purchased copy be used only on a single machine. The agreement forbids not only copies for home use but also copies for additional machines within the office. One can easily understand why a software company must protect its programs from indiscriminate copying. If an organization purchased one program and then made multiple copies for other computers within the company or for employees to take home, the software company could not earn enough profit to make the development of any future software program worthwhile.

When we purchased the WordWindows program, we agreed to limit its use to a single machine. Although this program must not be copied, we look forward to using it for many of your projects here in the Document Production Department.

When you have a chance, please drop by to see our new graphics and presentation capabilities.

Carol Straka, Manager, Document Production

Opens with relevant but neutral buffer.

Transition picks up keyword "licensed."

Deemphasized refusal diverts attention to reader benefits.

Closes with an off-the-subject but friendly remark.

to the second paragraph. Next comes an explanation of the price-matching policy. The writer does not assume that the customer is trying to pull a fast one. Nor does she suggest that the customer didn't read or understand the price-matching policy. The safest path is a neutral explanation of the policy along with precise distinctions between the customer's speakers and the older ones. The writer also gets a chance to resell the customer's speakers and demonstrate what a quality product they are. By the end of the third paragraph, it's evident to the reader that his claim is unjustified.

Notice how most of the components in an effective claim refusal are woven together in this letter: buffer, transition, explanation, and pleasant closing. The only missing part is an alternative, which was impossible in this situation.

FIGURE 8.3

Refusing a Claim

PREMIER SOUND SALES
3091 Geddes Road
Vancouver, BC V5S 1E4
Phone: (604) 499-2341 Fax: (604) 499-5904

May 24, 200x

Mr. Jim Vandermark
4205 Evergreen Avenue
Victoria, BC V1L 2W4

Dear Mr. Vandermark:

Begins with neutral statement on which both reader and writer can agree.

You're absolutely right! We do take pride in selling the finest products at rock-bottom prices. The Boze speakers you purchased last month are premier concert hall speakers. They're the only ones we present in our catalogue because they're the best.

Explains price-matching policy.

We have such confidence in our products and prices that we offer the price-matching policy you mention in your letter of May 20. That policy guarantees a refund of the price difference if you see one of your purchases offered at a lower price for 30 days after your purchase. To qualify for that refund, customers are asked to send us an advertisement or verifiable proof of the product price and model. As our catalogue states, this price-matching policy applies only to the same models.

Without actually saying no, shows why claim can't be honoured.

Our Boze AM-5 II speakers sell for $749. You sent us a local advertisement showing a price of $598 for Boze speakers. This advertisement, however, described an earlier version, the Boze AM-4 model. The AM-5 speakers you received have a wider dynamic range and smoother frequency response than the AM-4 model. Naturally, the improved model you purchased costs a little more than the older AM-4 model that the local advertisement describes. Your speakers have a new three-chamber bass module that virtually eliminates harmonic distortion. Finally, your speakers are 20 percent more compact than the AM-4 model.

Renews good feelings by building confidence in wisdom of purchase.

You bought the finest compact speakers on the market, Mr. Vandermark. If you haven't installed them yet, you may be interested in ceiling mounts, shown in the enclosed catalogue on page 48. We value your business and invite your continued comparison shopping.

Sincerely yours,

Melanie Tang

Melanie Tang
Enclosure

REFUSING CREDIT

Banks, other financial institutions, and businesses often deny credit by using impersonal form letters. These letters may list a number of possible reasons for the credit rejection, such as insufficient credit references, irregular employment, delinquent credit obligations, insufficient income, inadequate collateral, temporary residence, or inability to verify income.

Form letters are convenient for the writer, but they often antagonize the reader because they are unclear, inappropriate, or insensitive. Even when individuals are poor credit risks, they may be hurt by tactless and blunt form letters. Form-letter refusals or poorly written letters not only hurt the feelings of the reader but also ignore an opportunity to promote future business. An individual or business that is a poor credit risk today may become a good credit risk and a potential customer in the future.

An effective plan for writing a credit refusal follows the principles of the indirect strategy.

Credit refusals use a five-part strategy to break the bad news.

WRITING PLAN FOR A CREDIT REFUSAL

- *Buffer*—expresses appreciation for an order or a credit application, and includes resale information if appropriate.
- *Transition*—moves from buffer to explanation logically and repeats key idea or word if possible.
- *Explanation*—shows concern for the reader, explains objectively why credit must be refused, and doesn't preach or hide behind company policy.
- *Bad news*—implies refusal or states it respectfully, offers alternatives, and suggests possible extension of credit in the future.
- *Closing*—projects an optimistic look to the future and includes resale or sales promotion material.

CREDIT REFUSALS THAT RETAIN BUSINESS

As much as companies want business, they can extend credit only when payment is likely to follow. Credit applications, from individuals or from businesses, are generally approved or disapproved on the basis of the applicant's credit history. After reviewing the applicant's record, a credit manager applies the organization's guidelines and approves or turns down the loan.

If you must deny credit to a prospective customer, here are four tips for conveying the refusal:

- Avoid language that causes hard feelings.
- Include only factually correct information. Avoid adding your opinions or suggestions.
- Strive to retain customers on a cash basis.
- Prepare for possible future credit—without raising false expectations.

Credit applicants often will continue to do business with an organization even if they are denied credit. Naturally, you'll want to do everything possible to encourage that patronage. Thus, keep the refusal respectful, sensitive, and upbeat. Some organizations give no explanation of the reasons for the refusal. Instead, they provide the name of the credit-reporting agency and suggest that inquiries be directed to it.

Keeping the customer's goodwill is the primary goal of a credit refusal.

The credit refusal shown in Figure 8.4 strives to retain the business represented by a customer's order. It opens with a buffer that discusses good qualities of the product ordered. This buffer/introduction sets up a transition *(Because we'd like to see this fine product distributed by your full-service dealership . . .)* before the explana-

FIGURE 8.4

Refusing Credit

COMMUNICATION
SYSTEMS

4317 54th Avenue S.E.
Calgary, Alberta T2C 2A2
Phone: (403) 279-1698 FAX: (403) 236-1401

January 19, 200x

Mr. Greg Sargema
Empress Sound Suppliers
5920 Jasper Boulevard
Edmonton, Alberta T2C 2A6

Dear Mr. Sargema:

You've come to the right place for cordless phone systems, and we appreciate your February 14 order. The Nomad 400 model that you have ordered offers outstanding features, including two-way paging, pulse dialling, and intercom capabilities.

Because we'd like to see this fine product distributed by our full-service dealership, we submitted your credit application to Equilan Services. After reviewing their report, we find that credit cannot be extended at this time. To learn more about your record, you may call Equilan at (403) 369-3211. When your firm's financial situation improves, we would sincerely like to serve you on a credit basis.

In the meantime, please consider this plan. Order one dozen of the Nomad 400 units today. By paying for this reduced order with cash, you would receive a 2 percent cash discount. After you have sold these fast-moving units, place another cash order through our toll-free order number. We promise to deliver your items immediately so that your inventory is never depleted. In this way, you can obtain the units you want now, enjoy cash discounts, and replace your inventory almost instantaneously.

We're proud of our quality products and our competitive prices. If we can do business with you now or in the future, please call us at 1-800-896-3320.

Yours truly,

Margaret Gormann

Margaret Gormann, Manager
Marketing Unit One

MG:fty

Opens confidently with resale and sets up transition.

De-emphasizes denial by using passive voice.

Suggests alternative plan for cash purchase.

Looks forward optimistically to future business.

tion, which follows. Actually, not much explaining has to be done. Most companies today do not try to interpret a bad credit report; they simply refer the applicant to the reporting agency.

This letter then suggests an alternative whereby the customer can obtain the desired merchandise on a cash basis. Notice how the writer emphasizes the *you* view and shows reader benefits. The conclusion is pleasant and looks forward to future business.

Retaining the reader's goodwill is the goal in any credit refusal. And tone is the key to keeping that goodwill. Notice in Figure 8.4 how respectful and objective the words sound. It's not easy to say no and remain friends; but it can be done, as this letter illustrates.

ETHICS AND THE INDIRECT STRATEGY

You may worry that the indirect organizational strategy is unethical or manipulative because the writer deliberately delays the main idea. But consider the alternative. Breaking bad news bluntly can cause pain and hard feelings. How many times have you heard the comment "I didn't mind the news so much as the way I was told."

By delaying bad news, you soften the blow somewhat, as well as ensure that your reasoning will be read while the receiver is still receptive. Your motives are not to deceive the reader or to hide the news. Rather, your goal is to be a compassionate, yet effective communicator.

The key to ethical communication lies in the motives of the sender. Unethical communicators intend to deceive. For example, Victoria's Secret, the clothing and lingerie chain, once offered free $10 gift certificates. However, when customers tried to cash the certificates, they found that they were required to make a minimum purchase of $50 worth of merchandise.[2] For this misleading, deceptive, and unethical offer, the chain paid a $100,000 fine. The indirect strategy provides a setting in which to announce bad news; it does not avoid or misrepresent the truth.

> Ethical communicators using the indirect strategy do not intend to deceive.

ADAPTING THE INDIRECT STRATEGY

The strategy of giving reasons first makes sense in refusing requests, refusing claims, and denying credit. The same general principles of indirectness are appropriate whenever bad news must be delivered. For example, a company announcement reducing extended health benefits for employees would certainly represent bad news to the employees. The indirect strategy would be best for such an announcement. News that a supplier is out of a needed item or that a product is no longer manufactured or that its price has risen are all messages that will be irritating to a customer. That's why the indirect strategy is probably most effective when announcing this kind of news.

We have applied this strategy only to written business messages. The strategy is, however, also appropriate in oral communication and in interpersonal relations. If you must tell a friend that you can't fulfil a promise, a good explanation preceding the refusal may help you retain the friendship. If you must tell your brother that you dented the fender of his car, the indirect strategy will help you announce the bad news. Now that you've learned this strategy, you'll be able to adapt it to many situations beyond the letter- and memo-writing plans illustrated here.

> Application of the principles of indirectness is often successful in solving personal problems.

SUMMING UP AND LOOKING FORWARD

When faced with delivering bad news, you have a choice. You can announce it immediately, or you can delay it by presenting a buffer and reasons first. Many business communicators prefer the indirect strategy because it tends to preserve goodwill. In this chapter you learned to apply the indirect strategy in request refusals, claim refusals, and credit denials. This same strategy is appropriate when you make persuasive requests or when you try to sell something. Chapter 9 discusses how to apply the indirect strategy to persuasive and sales messages.

DISCUSSION

1. Discuss at least five situations in which the indirect strategy would be appropriate for delivering a negative message.
2. Does the indirect strategy represent an effort to manipulate the reader?
3. Discuss the idea that organization and development of a message delivering negative news begin with the explanation.
4. Analyze the effectiveness of the following opening statements for negative-news letters:
   a. Unfortunately, we would like to approve your credit application but we cannot.
   b. I enjoyed talking with you last week when you came in to be interviewed for the position of assistant to the registrar.
   c. The weather recently has certainly been pleasant for this time of the year, hasn't it?
5. Analyze the effectiveness of the following closing statements for negative letters:
   a. Once again, please let me say that we would like to grant your request but we cannot allow outsiders to use our confidential company files even for such worthy research as you describe.
   b. If you have any further questions about this matter, please remember that I am available to serve you.
   c. Although we regret very much any inconvenience our shipping error has caused you, we trust that you will understand our position in this matter.

CHAPTER REVIEW

6. The indirect strategy should be used when you expect what kind of reader reaction?

7. List in proper sequence the six elements involved in organizing a negative message according to the indirect strategy.

8. What is a buffer, and when should it be used?

9. What are three characteristics of a good buffer?

10. How can a writer develop a transition between the opening of a letter and an explanation that follows?

11. List seven ways to de-emphasize bad news. Be prepared to discuss each.

12. List three ways that you should not close a negative message.

13. Name three problem words that signal refusal in a letter.

14. Write *passive* or *active* beside the following sentences to indicate the voice of the verbs in each of them:
    a. We cannot refund the full purchase price.
    b. The full purchase price cannot be refunded.
    c. The shipment of your order has been delayed.
    d. Our delivery service has delayed shipment of your order.

15. Name four emphatic positions in a letter.

Writing Improvement Exercises

Subordinate Clauses. You can soften the effect of bad news by placing it in a subordinate clause that begins with *although, since,* or *because.* The emphasis in a sentence is on the independent clause. Instead of saying *We cannot serve you on a credit basis,* try *Since we cannot serve you on a credit basis, we invite you to take advantage of our cash discounts and sale prices.*

Revise the following refusals so that the bad news appears in a subordinate clause.

16. We no longer manufacture the Model SF-7. However, we now make a substitute, the Model SF-9, which we would like to send you.

17. We hope to have our plant remodelling completed by October. We cannot schedule tours of the bottling plant until after we finish remodelling.

18. Island Airways cannot accept responsibility for expenses incurred indirectly from flight delays. However, we do recognize that this delay inconvenienced you.

Passive-Voice Verbs. Passive-voice verbs may be preferable in breaking bad news because they enable you to emphasize actions rather than personalities. Compare these two refusals:

Active voice: I cannot authorize you to take three weeks of vacation in July.
Passive voice: Three weeks of vacation in July cannot be authorized.

Revise the following refusals so that they use passive-voice instead of active-voice verbs.

19. We cannot refund cash for the items you purchased on credit.

20. I have already filled my schedule on the date you wish me to speak.

21. We do not examine new patients until we have reviewed their medical history.

Implied Refusals. Bad news can be de-emphasized by implying a refusal instead of stating it directly. Compare these refusals:

Direct refusal: We cannot send you a price list nor can we sell our lawn mowers directly to customers. We sell only through dealers, and your dealer is HomeCo Inc.
Implied refusal: Our lawn mowers are sold only through dealers, and your dealer is HomeCo Inc.

Revise the following refusals so that they are implied.

22. We cannot open a credit account for you because your application states that you have no regular employment. This allows us to serve you only as a cash customer.

23. I find it impossible to contribute to the fundraising campaign this year. At present all the funds of my organization are needed to lease new equipment and offices for our new branch in Richmond. I hope to be able to support this fund in the future.

24. We cannot ship our fresh fruit baskets c.o.d. Your order was not accompanied by payment, so we are not shipping it. We have it ready, though, and will rush it to its destination as soon as you call us with your credit card number.

ACTIVITIES AND CASES

8.1 Favour Refusal: Nix to Mountain Biking Support. As Ron Levin, president of CyclePro, you must refuse a request from the Mid Continental Biking Association. This group wants your company to become a major sponsor of the Prairies regional event leading to the first annual North American Mountain Bike Championship—to the tune of $5000. You applaud the MCBA for its proactive stance in encouraging families to participate in the sport of mountain biking and you'd like to support the new North American Mountain Bike Championship.

But you are a small Winnipeg company, and all your current profits are being ploughed into an expensive new program for clearing new mountain biking trails in Whiteshell Provincial Park. You don't have the kind of money the MCBA wants. However, you wouldn't mind taking an ad in the program or contributing $500 toward trophies.

Consider how you will develop the refusal letter. Analyze the following options in relation to the indirect strategy. Circle the letters representing the most appropriate possibilities for this letter.

1. To open this letter appropriately, you might
   a. Take advantage of this opportunity to complain about the MCBA's track record for upkeep of biking trails.
   b. Explain your financial difficulties and your need to invest all profits in business-related activities.

c. Congratulate the Mid Continental Biking Association on its accomplishments in bringing nationally recognized competitive events to the local area.

d. Promote your company and image by describing your new products.

2. A logical transition might

   a. Describe how your company is also working to improve the sport of mountain biking with your investment in trail development.

   b. Warn the MCBA that trail development is an increasingly important issue in the sport. Without committed trail-developing programs, the sport will die in this region.

   c. Ask if other manufacturers have been asked to support this event and how much they are contributing.

   d. Comment on the selection of Morden as the venue for this event.

3. In explaining why you cannot become a major sponsor, you might

   a. Promote your new products by describing each one in detail.

   b. Suggest that the MCBA work for government support of trail-developing programs rather than waste its time on bike races.

   c. Assert that if you didn't have to spend so much time and money developing trails, you might be able to offer major support.

   d. Explain that your heavy investment in trail development prevents you from making a large contribution.

4. Which of the following sentences softens the refusal most effectively?

   a. We cannot become a major sponsor because of our heavy trail development expenses, but we could donate up to $500 for trophies or program costs.

   b. Although we cannot be a major sponsor because of our heavy trail development expenses, we could donate up to $500 for trophies or program costs.

   c. If we didn't have to spend so much on trail development, we could probably become a major sponsor.

   d. Although we would like to become a major sponsor, we are unable to do so at this time.

Use this problem for discussion. At the option of your instructor, write the entire letter (individually or as a class project) to Craig Van Wijk, Executive Director, Mid Continental Biking Association, 6423 North Broadway, Regina, Saskatchewan S3R 2T4. You may wish to incorporate some of the sentences you selected here, but consider this a skeleton. Flesh out your letter with explanations, examples, appropriate connecting thoughts, and a goodwill closing. Use modified block style.

8.2 Request Refusal: Bad Time for Conference. Analyze the following poorly written message and list at least five of its major faults. Outline a writing plan for refusing a request. Then rewrite the message, rectifying the faults.

Ineffective Writing

TO:	Gina Caracas, Records Manager	DATE: May 30, 200x
FROM:	Deanna Finch, President	
SUBJECT:	CONFERENCE	

Please be informed that I have taken under advisement your request to be allowed to attend the conference of the Association of Records Managers and Administrators in Montreal. Unfortunately, this conference is six days long and comes in September, a very critical time for us.

I'm sorry to have to deny your request, because it looks like a worthwhile conference. It would afford an opportunity for records management personnel, like you, to learn more about current procedures and technologies. You've been doing an outstanding job of helping us begin the conversion of our files to microforms.

But to have you gone for a period of six days in September, when, as you know, we complete our budget requests for the following fiscal year is out of the question. We need you at our budget planning meetings, particularly since you have proposed the purchase of computer equipment that will generate micrographs directly. Another reason that you can't go in September, in spite of the fact that I would like to see you go, is that Tiffany Norris, in your department, has requested the months of August through October for her maternity leave. Your absence, together with hers, would put us in a real bind.

For these reasons, I cannot allow you to leave in September. However, if there is a suitable conference at some other time in the year when your absence would be less critical, I would be happy to let you go. I'm sorry about this matter, Gina. This is certainly little thanks for the excellent progress you are making in the massive task of converting our filing system.

8.3 Credit Refusal: GodMother Wants to Cater. Analyze the following poorly written credit refusal and list at least five major faults. Outline a writing plan for refusing credit. Then rewrite the message, rectifying its faults. Address the letter to Ms. Abina Senna, GodMother Enterprises, 905 North Bay Drive, Thunder Bay, Ontario P2W 3R7.

Dear Ms. Senna:

Thank you for your recent order. However, we are unable to fill this order because of the bad credit record you have on file at Atlantic Credit Information Services.

Ineffective Writing

We understand that you are opening a new gourmet catering business called "The GodMother." Our sales rep left us one of your sample menus, and I must say that we were all impressed with your imaginative international selections, including duck lasagna and chicken fettuccine verde. Although we are sure your catering business will be a success, we cannot extend credit because of your current poor credit rating.

Did you know that you can find out what's in your credit file? If you would like to see what prevented you from obtaining credit from us, you may contact Atlantic Credit Information Services, 11856 Beach Boulevard, Halifax, Nova Scotia B3P 1L4 (902-532-9145).

We are truly sorry that we cannot fill your initial order totalling $1430. We pride ourselves on serving most of Thunder Bay's restaurants and catering services. We would be proud to add The GodMother to our list of discerning customers. Perhaps the best way for you to join that select list is with a smaller order to begin with. We would be happy to serve you on a cash basis. If this plan pleases you, do let me know.

Sincerely,

8.4 Claim Refusal: Depressed Mattress. For class discussion analyze the following poorly written message. Discuss its major faults, and suggest a writing plan for refusing the claim. Then, at the option of your instructor, rewrite the message, rectifying its faults. Address the letter to Mrs. Shannon Kearney, 1176 53rd Street South, Calgary, AB T1L 0G7. Use modified block style.

Ineffective Writing

Dear Mrs. Kearney:

We have your letter of May 23 demanding repair or replacement for your newly purchased BeautyTest mattress. You say that you enjoy sleeping on it; but in the morning when you and your husband get up, you claim that the mattress has body impressions that remain all day.

Unfortunately, Mrs. Kearney, we can neither repair nor replace your mattress because those impressions are perfectly normal. If you will read your warranty carefully, you will find this statement: "Slight body impressions will appear with use and are not indicative of structural failure. The body-conforming coils and comfort cushioning materials are beginning to work for you and impressions are caused by the natural settling of these materials."

When you purchased your mattress, I'm sure your salesperson told you that the BeautyTest mattress has a unique, scientifically designed system of individually pocketed coils that provide separate support for each person occupying the bed. This unusual construction, with those hundreds of independently operating coils, reacts to every body contour, providing luxurious comfort. At the same time, this system provides firm support. It is this unique design that's causing the body impressions that you see when you get up in the morning.

Although we never repair or replace a mattress when it merely shows slight impressions, we will send our representative out to inspect your mattress, if it would make you feel better. Please call for an appointment at (800) 322-9800. Remember, on a BeautyTest mattress you get the best night's rest possible.

Cordially,

8.5 Request Refusal: Strikeout for Expanded Office Teams. Assume you are Hank James, vice president of human resources at Tissue Mills Paper Co., 508 W. Inverary Road, Kingston, Ontario K2G 1V8. Recently several of your employees requested that their spouses or friends be allowed to participate in Tissue Mills's intramural sports teams. Over 100 employees currently participate in the eight co-ed volleyball, softball, and tennis teams, which are open to company employees only. The teams were designed to improve employee friendships and to give employees a regular occasion to have fun together. If teams were restructured to allow nonemployees to participate, you're afraid that some team members might not enjoy it and that employee interaction would be limited as a result. Furthermore, the company would have to create additional teams if many nonemployees joined, and you don't want the administrative or equipment costs of more teams. Besides, the company already sponsors a family holiday party and an annual company picnic, both of which nonemployees are welcome to attend. Write a memo to the staff denying the request of several employees to include nonemployees on Tissue Mills's intramural sports teams.

8.6 Request Refusal: Turning Down Software Training. As Victor Cortez, marketing director, Trinity Software Systems, 111 Parliament Street, Toronto, Ontario M5N 2E8, you are confronted with the task of denying a favour to a potential customer. Ava Brown, principal, Heritage School, 3201 Eglinton Avenue East, Toronto, Ontario, M4L 3F9, is interested in purchasing your educational software system, but she wants training from Trinity for 65 Heritage teachers and staff. The training costs would be extensive, but the real problem is that Trinity doesn't have the personnel for this huge task. Instead, Trinity would like to train one or two Heritage teachers as on-site trainers. Trinity also would provide training videotapes and a training program guide. Schools that use Trinity software enjoy having their own "experts" on hand. Because Trinity maintains an ongoing relationship with them, teacher-trainers are informed of software updates and can get help if they need it. Write a letter to Mrs. Brown denying her request but keeping her as a potential customer. Send her a package that will answer all her questions about your program. She can reach you at 921-1489.

8.7 Request Refusal: Saying No to Under-21 Crowd on Carnival Cruises. The world's largest cruise line finds itself in a difficult position. Carnival climbed to the No. 1 spot by promoting fun at sea and pitching its appeal to younger customers who were drawn to on-board discos, swim-up bars, and hassle-free partying. But apparently the partying of high school and college students has gotten out of hand. Roving bands of teens have virtually taken over some cruises in recent years. Mike Driscall, editor of *Cruise Week,* describes "drunken, loud behaviour" in reporting the complaints of travel agents. To crack down, Carnival raised the drinking age from 18 to 21 and instituted a new policy whereby anyone under 21 must be accompanied by an adult over 25.

As Eric Rivera, a Carnival marketing manager, you must respond to the inquiry of April Corcoran of Constant Travel, an Edmonton travel agency that features special spring- and summer-break packages for college and high school students. Constant Travel has been an excellent Carnival customer over the years; however, you must refuse the request of Ms. Corcoran to help set up student tour packages because of the aforementioned problems with unaccompanied youth and because your real market is family packages. You must write to Constant and break the bad news. Write to April Corcoran, Constant Travel Agency, 520 West Road, Edmonton, AB T2L 3H5. Send her a schedule for spring and summer Caribbean cruises. Tell her you will call during the week of January 5 to help her plan special family tour packages.[3]

Related Web Site: www.bvt-usa.com/cruises/c-expect.html

8.8 Claim Refusal: Wilted Landscaping. As Cassandra Powell, owner of Town & Country Landscaping, you must refuse the following request. Mr. and Mrs. Paul Alexander have asked that you replace the landscaping in the home they recently purchased in Canmore. You had landscaped that home nearly a year ago for the former owner, Mrs. Hunter, installing a sod lawn and many shrubs, trees, and flowers. It looked beautiful when you finished, but six months later, Mrs. Hunter sold the property and moved to Calgary. Four months elapsed before the new owners moved in, and during that time, the newly installed landscaping suffered. You guarantee all your work but you do not feel justified in complying with the Alexanders' request because the yard was not maintained by the property owner who had the contract with you.

You would like to retain the goodwill of the new owners, since this is an affluent neighbourhood, but you can't afford to replace the materials invested in this job. You would be happy to inspect the property and offer suggestions to the new owners. In reality, you wonder if the Alexanders might not have a claim against the former owner or the owner's real estate agent for failing to maintain the property. Clearly, however, the claim is not against you. Write to Mr. and Mrs. Paul Alexander, 3318 Clearview Drive, Canmore, AB T2N 3E4.

8.9 Credit Refusal: The Sports Connection. As manager of The Sports Connection, you must refuse the application of Wendy Takahashi for an extended membership in your athletic club. This is strictly a business decision. You liked Wendy very much when she applied, and she seems genuinely interested in fitness and a healthful lifestyle. However, your "extended membership" plan qualifies the member for all your testing, exercise, aerobics, and recreation programs. This multiservice program is necessarily expensive and requires a solid credit rating. To your disappointment, however, you learned that Wendy's credit rating is decidedly negative. Her credit report indicates that she is behind in payments to four businesses, including Holiday Health Spa, your principal competitor. You do have other programs that offer the use of available facilities, like the racquetball and handball courts and aerobics classes, on a cash basis. Refuse her credit application and suggest that she make an inquiry to TRS Information Services to learn about her credit report. Write to Wendy Takahashi, Mountain View Apartments No. 16E, 1406 North Face Road, Vancouver, BC, V5N 3L4.

8.10 Connecting With E-Mail: Refusing Christmas. In the past your office has always sponsored a Christmas party at a nice restaurant. As your company has undergone considerable downsizing and budget cuts during the past year, you know that no money is available for holiday entertaining. Moreover, as the staff becomes more diverse, you decide that it might be better to celebrate a "holiday" party instead of a Christmas event. As executive vice president, respond to the e-mail request of Dana Gillian, office manager. Dana has asked for permission to make restaurant reservations for this year's Christmas party. Refuse Dana, but offer some alternatives. Send your response to Dana via your instructor's e-mail address.

8.11 Searching the Internet: Refusing Request to Evict Noisy Neighbour. As Arman Aryai, you must deny the request of Robert Brockway, one of the tenants in your three-storey office building. Mr. Brockway, a CA, demands that you immediately evict a neighbouring tenant who plays loud music throughout the day, interfering with Mr. Brockway's conversations with clients and with his concentration. The noisy tenant, Ryan McInnis, seems to operate an entertainment booking agency and spends long hours in his office. You know you can't evict Mr. McInnis immediately because of his lease. Moreover, you hesitate to do anything drastic because paying tenants are hard to find. Although you need more information, you don't want to engage an expensive lawyer. On the Internet you find The Law Student's Legal Advice Program (www.lslap.bc.ca/1400main.htm). The section titled "Landlord and Tenant Law" gives you some ideas about dealing with this situation. Decide on a course of action. Then write to Robert Brockway, CA, Suite 203, Pico Building, 1405 Bower Boulevard, Vancouver, BC V6L 1Y3. Deny his request but tell him how you plan to resolve the problem.

Related Web Site: www.lslap.bc.ca/1400main.htm

Commas 3

Review the Grammar/Mechanics Handbook Sections 2.10–2.15. Then study each of the following statements and insert necessary commas. In the space provided write the number of commas that you add; write *0* if no commas are needed. Also record the number of the G/M principle(s) illustrated. When you finish, compare your responses with those provided. If your answers differ, study carefully the principles shown in parentheses.

Example: It was Ms. Jeffreys, not Mr. Simpson, who was assigned the Madison account.   2   (2.21)

1. "The choice of a good name" said President Gordon "cannot be overestimated." _____
2. Lois A. Wagner Ph.D. and Durva S. Peshwar M.B.A. were hired as consultants. _____
3. Their August 15 order was shipped on Monday wasn't it? _____
4. Brand names are important in advertising specialty goods such as refrigerators and television sets. _____
5. The bigger the investment the greater the profit. _____

Review Commas 1, 2, 3

6. As you requested your order for ribbons file folders and envelopes will be sent immediately. _____
7. We think however that you should re-examine your networking system and that you should consider electronic mail. _____
8. Within the next eight-week period we hope to hire Sue Richards who is currently working in private industry. _____
9. Our convention will attract more participants if it is held in a resort location such as San Diego Miami or Las Vegas. _____
10. If everyone who applied for the position were interviewed we would be overwhelmed. _____
11. Our main goal is to provide quality products backed by prompt efficient service. _____
12. In the past ten years we have employed over 30 well-qualified individuals many of whom have selected banking as their career. _____
13. Your shipment has been charged to your new account which we were pleased to open on the basis of your excellent credit. _____
14. Steven Sims who spoke to our class last week is the author of a book entitled *Writing Winning Résumés*. _____
15. Mrs. Hartung uses market research extensively and keeps a close watch on her own operations her competition and the market in order to identify the latest trends. _____

1. (2) name," Gordon, (2.14a)   3. (1) Monday, (2.14b)   5. (1) investment, (2.12)   7. (2) think, however, (2.03)   9. (2) Diego, Miami, (2.01, 2.15)   11. prompt, (2.08, 2.15)   13. (1) account, (2.06c, 2.15)   15. (2) operations, competition, (2.01)

Document for Revision

The following memo has faults in grammar, punctuation, spelling, number form, wordiness, and negative words. Use standard proofreading marks (see Appendix B) to correct the errors. When you finish, your instructor can show you the revised version of this memo.

Ineffective Writing

DATE: August 5, 200x

TO: Jason Su, Vice President

FROM: Roger Franco, Market Research

SUBJECT: ANALYSIS OF GATORADE XL

Here is a summery of the research of James Willis' and myself. Regarding the reduced sugar sports drink being introduced by our No. 1 compititor, Gatorade.

In just under a years time Gatorade developed this new drink, it combines together a mixture of 50 percent sugar and 50 percent artificial sweetener. Apparently Gatorade plans to spend over $8 million to introduce the drink in North America, and to assess consumers reactions to it. It will be tested on the shelfs of convience stores grocerys and other mass merchants in five citys in Canada and the United States.

The companys spokesperson said, "The 'X' stands for excelent taste, and the 'L' stands for less sugar." Aimed at young adult's who don't like the taste of sweetener but who want to control calories. The new sports drink is a hybrid sugar and diet drink. Our studys show that simular drinks tryed in this country in the 1980's were unsucessful. On the other hand a 50 calorie low sugar sports drink introduced in Canada two year ago was well received, similarly in Japan a 40 calorie soda is now marketed sucessfully by Coca-Cola.

However our research in regard to trends and our analysis of Gatorade XL fails to indicate that the North American consumers will be interested in a midcalorie sports drink. Financial analysts response to Gatorades announcement of it's new drink was not unfavourable.

In view of the foregoing the writer and his colleague are of the opinion that we should take a wait and see attitude. Toward the introduction of our own low sugar sports drink.

Communication Workshop: Diversity

JUST WHAT IS SEXUAL HARASSMENT?

In today's workplace, employees are becoming more aware of their words and actions. Men and women are learning that appropriate behaviour is professional behaviour. Pats, hugs, and neck rubs are out. Sexual stereotyping, sexual jokes, and sexual visual materials do not belong in the professional workplace. In fact, these kinds of behaviours can become the basis for a complaint to the Canadian Human Rights Commission. Consider the following examples from *Sexual Harassment in Employment in New Brunswick:*[4]

Mary's boss often asks her to join him for a drink to "discuss her career." He keeps saying that he "could really help her if she was a little friendlier." Mary doesn't like her boss's approach but knows that if she doesn't show up, she may not be promoted.

Susan works with five men who often make remarks such as "This is a man's job" or "Women should be at home doing dishes and washing." Sometimes they brush up against her, grab her or pinch her.

Both Mary and Susan are being sexually harassed. Sexual actions, comments, or requests are harassment if they are unwelcome or if the decisions affecting employees or job applicants are based on submission to or rejection of sexual conduct. This definition extends to conduct occurring any time even after work and away from the workplace.

Sexual harassment directed at men or women is illegal in Canada under the Canadian Human Rights Act. Each province also maintains its own human rights legislation that further defines harassment. Even a single incident can be harassment. Examples of sexual harassment include:

- Degrading remarks about either sex
- Unwelcome pinching, hugging, brushing up against, and patting
- Unwelcome sexual requests, remarks, jokes, or gestures
- Unfair evaluations or reprimands, reduced working hours, overwork, dismissals, discipline, or refusals to hire or to promote, when those actions are in retaliation for refusing to submit to sexual harassment.

In a broader sense, according to communication experts, sexual harassment is anything that a victim believes is sexual harassment. The most notable case of alleged sexual harassment came in the U.S. Senate confirmation hearings for Supreme Court Justice Clarence Thomas. Attorney and law professor Anita Hill, a former colleague of Judge Thomas, testified that Thomas's sexual jokes and discussions of pornographic films at the office constituted sexual harassment.

It's wise to remember that different people perceive behaviour differently. Some may think a touch on the hand or arm is an innocent act between colleagues. Others may view it as an action that is both inappropriate and unnecessary for the effective performance of the job.

Application. Suppose office worker Greg says to Lisa, his colleague, "That dress looks great on your body." Although Greg meant to compliment Lisa's fitness and her taste in clothes, Lisa considers it a sexual comment and complains to her superior. Using the guidelines presented here, should Greg's superior consider this incident sexual harassment? What lessons can be learned from this incident? Discuss your response in a memo to your instructor or in small groups.

Related Web Site: www.gov.nb.ca/hrc-cdp/e/sexharas.htm

LETTERS AND MEMOS THAT PERSUADE

The same need exists in almost every organization. In our search for more business, selling is becoming everyone's responsibility. Thus communications skills—both verbal and written—have become essential. To advance . . . you must make communication skills one of your top priorities.[1]

PETER URS BENDER, management consultant and one of
Canada's top business speakers and presenters

Learning Objectives

1. Use the indirect strategy to persuade.
2. Write convincing claim request letters.
3. Request favours persuasively.
4. Present new ideas in persuasive memos.
5. Analyze techniques used in sales letters.
6. Compose carefully planned sales letters.

The ability to persuade or to sell an idea is a key factor in the success you achieve in your business messages, in your career, and in your interpersonal relations. As Peter Urs Bender points out, persuasive individuals are highly valued in today's successful organizations. He suggests that everyone make persuasive communication skills a priority. Persuasive individuals become decision makers, managers, executives, and entrepreneurs because their ideas generally prevail. This chapter will examine techniques for presenting ideas persuasively.

The ability to use persuasion skilfully is a primary factor in personal and business success.

PERSUASIVE REQUESTS

Persuasion is necessary when resistance is anticipated or when ideas require preparation before they can be presented effectively. For example, if Kim Owens purchased a new Ford and the transmission repeatedly required servicing, she might be forced to write to Ford's head office asking that the company install a new transmission in her car. Kim's claim letter should be persuasive; she must convince Ford that replacement, not repair, is needed. Routine claim letters, such as those you wrote in Chapter 6, are straightforward and direct. Persuasive requests, on the other

Use persuasion when you must change attitudes or produce action.

hand, are generally more effective when they are indirect. Reasons and explanations should precede the main idea. To overcome possible resistance, the writer lays a logical foundation before the request is delivered. A writing plan for a persuasive request requires deliberate development.

WRITING PLAN FOR A PERSUASIVE REQUEST

- *Opening*—obtains the reader's attention and interest.
- *Persuasion*—explains logically and concisely the purpose of the request and proves its merit.
- *Closing*—asks for a particular action and shows courtesy and respect.

CLAIM REQUEST

The most important parts of a claim letter are the sections describing the desired action and the proof that such action is reasonable.

The organization of an effective persuasive claim centres on the closing and the persuasion. First, decide what action you want taken to satisfy the claim. Then, decide how you can prove the worth of your claim. Plan carefully the line of reasoning you will follow in convincing the reader to take the action you request. If the claim is addressed to a business, the most effective appeals are generally to the organization's pride in its products and its services. Refer to its reputation for integrity and your confidence in it. Show why your claim is valid and why the company will be doing the right thing in granting it. Most organizations are sincere in their efforts to produce quality products that gain consumer respect.

Anger and emotional threats toward an organization do little to achieve the goal of claim letters. Claims are usually referred to a customer service department. The claims adjuster answering the claim probably had nothing to do with the design, production, delivery, or servicing of the product. An abusive letter may serve only to offend the claims adjuster, thus making it hard for the claim to be evaluated rationally.

Claim letters should avoid negative and emotional words, and should not attempt to fix blame.

The most effective claim quickly captures the reader's attention in the opening and sets up the persuasion that follows. In the body of the claim, convincing reasons should explain and justify the claim. Try to argue without overusing negative words, without fixing blame for the problem, and without becoming emotional. That's not easy to do. You'll be most successful if you arrange objective reasons in an orderly manner with appropriate transitions to guide the reader through the persuasion.

Following the persuasion, spell out clearly the desired action in the closing. Remember, the best claims show respect and courtesy.

Observe how the claim letter shown in Figure 9.1 illustrates the preceding suggestions. The opening statements secure the reader's attention and at the same time set up the description of events and persuasive arguments to follow. Notice the absence of rancour and harsh words, although the writer was probably rather upset over these events. Notice, too, how the closing rounds out the letter by referring to the opening statement.

FAVOUR REQUEST

Asking for a favour implies that you want someone to do something for nothing—or for very little. Common examples are requests for the donation of time, money, and energy, or for someone's name, resources, talent, skills, or expertise. On

FIGURE 9.1

Claim Request—Block Style

AMS LIMITÉE

4439 rue de la Morenie, Sherbrooke, Quebec J1H 4E6 (819) 358-3319

January 23, 200x

D. Gerard, Inc.
3350 avenue Montmorency
Montreal, Quebec H2L 2E9

Dear Sir or Madam:

SUBJECT: BUTONE MODEL 150 HOT-WATER HEATING SYSTEM

Your Butone hot-water heating system appealed to my company for two reasons. First, it promised high-efficiency heat with a 36 percent savings in our oil-heating system costs. Second, your firm has been in the heating business for forty years, and such a record indicates that you have a tradition of concern for your customers.

Gains attention with favourable comments about the company.

We think that we were right about your heating system. Now we wonder if we're right about your concern for your customers.

Last September we purchased a Butone oil-fired Model 150 and had it installed in our eight-room office building by your dealer, Chauffage Saint-Laurent. For two weeks it heated our offices comfortably. One morning, though, we arrived and found our rooms cold. We called Chauffage Saint-Laurent, and its technician came out to inspect our system. He reported that the automatic ignition device had failed. He replaced it, and the system worked well for two days. Then, on the third day after this repair, a fire developed in the combustion area of the heating unit, destroying the circulating pump and its motor. Technicians from Chauffage Saint-Laurent returned immediately and replaced the entire heating unit.

Explains events in orderly, logical fashion.

We assumed this replacement was covered by the system's 5-year warranty. That's why we were surprised two days ago to receive from Chauffage Saint-Laurent a bill for $255.92 covering installation of the new unit. In a telephone conversation, Monique Denis, of Chauffage Saint-Laurent, said that the warranty covers only replacement of the unit. The cost of the installation is extra.

We feel that this charge is unjustified. The fire that destroyed the unit resulted from either a defective unit or faulty servicing by Chauffage Saint-Laurent. Since we feel responsibility for neither of these conditions, we believe that we should bear no charges. Our insurance carrier shares this view.

Argues convincingly that the charge is unjustified.

Please pay the attached bill or instruct Chauffage Saint-Laurent to cancel it. This would indicate to us that we were right both about your product and about your reputation.

Closes with action request that ties in with opening.

Sincerely,

Reva A. Alexander

Reva A. Alexander
Office Manager

Attachment

occasion, everyone needs to ask a favour. Small favours, such as asking a co-worker to lock up the office for you on Friday, can be straightforward and direct. Little resistance is expected. Larger favours, though, require careful planning and an indirect strategy. A busy executive is asked to serve on a committee to help disabled children. A florist is asked to donate table arrangements for a charity fundraiser. A well-known author is asked to speak before a local library group. In each instance persuasion is necessary to overcome natural resistance.

The letters shown in Figure 9.2 illustrate two versions of a favour request. In a nutshell, an organization without funds hopes to entice a well-known authority to speak before its regional conference. Such a request surely requires indirectness and persuasion, but the ineffective version begins with a direct appeal. Even worse, the reader is given an opportunity to refuse the request before the writer has a chance to present reasons for accepting. Moreover, this letter fails to convince the reader that she has anything to gain by speaking to this group. Finally, the closing suggests no specific action to help her accept, should she be so inclined.

A favour request is doomed to failure if the writer does not consider its effect on the reader. In the more effective version, notice how the writer applies the indirect strategy. The opening catches the reader's interest and makes her want to read more regarding the reaction to her article. By showing how Dr. Kasdorf's interests are related to the organization's, the writer lays a groundwork of persuasion before presenting the request. The request is then followed by reasoning that shows Dr. Kasdorf how she will benefit from accepting this invitation. This successful letter concludes with an action closing.

PERSUASIVE MEMO

Presenting reasons first avoids premature rejection of new idea.

Within an organization the indirect strategy is useful when persuasion is needed in presenting new ideas to management or to colleagues. It's also useful in requesting action from employees and in securing compliance with altered procedures. Whenever resistance is anticipated, a sound foundation of reason should precede the main idea. This foundation prevents the idea from being rejected prematurely.

You should expect new ideas to create resistance. It doesn't matter whether the ideas are moving downward as orders from management, moving upward as suggestions to management, or moving laterally among co-workers. Resistance to change is natural. When asked to perform differently or to try something new, some individuals resist because they are lazy. Others resist because they fear failure. Still others resist because they feel threatened—the proposed changes may encroach on their status or threaten their security. Some people resist new ideas because they are jealous of the person making the proposal.

Offering counter-arguments helps overcome resistance.

Whatever the motivation, resistance to new ideas and altered procedures should be expected. You can prepare for this resistance by anticipating objections, offering counter-arguments, and emphasizing benefits. Don't assume that the advantages of a new plan are obvious and therefore may go unmentioned. Use concrete examples and familiar illustrations in presenting arguments.

In the memo shown in Figure 9.3, Megan Wong, supervisor, argues for the purchase of new equipment and software. She expects the director to resist this purchase because the director knows little about computing and because the budget is already overextended. Megan's memo follows the writing plan for a persuasive request. It begins by describing a costly problem in which Megan knows the reader is

FIGURE 9.2

Ineffective and Effective Favour Requests

Provides easy excuse for refusal.

Sounds writer-centred instead of reader-centred.

Closes negatively and fails to tell how to respond.

Ineffective

Dear Dr. Kasdorf:

Although your research, teaching, and consulting must keep you extremely busy, we hope that your schedule will allow you to be the featured speaker at the Canadian Association of Human Resources Managers' regional conference in Vancouver on March 23.

We are particularly interested in the article that appeared in the *Harvard Business Review*. A number of our members indicated that your topic, "Cost/Benefit Analysis for Human Resources," is something we should learn more about.

We have no funds to pay you, but we would like to invite you and your spouse to be our guests at the banquet following the day's sessions. We hope that you will be able to speak before our group.

Sincerely,

Effective

Canadian Association of Human Resource Managers
196 West 4th Avenue, Vancouver, BC V6R 3T4 (604) 543-8922

January 4, 200x

Professor Beverly J. Kasdorf
University College of the Cariboo
200 Mountain Way
Kamloops, BC V1L 2R4

Dear Dr. Kasdorf:

Cost/benefit analysis applied to human resources is a unique concept. Your recent article on that topic in the *Harvard Business Review* ignited a lively discussion at the last meeting of the Vancouver chapter of the Canadian Association of Human Resources Managers.

Many of the managers in our group are experiencing the changes you describe. Functions in the personnel area are now being expanded to include a wide range of salary, welfare, benefit, and training programs. These new programs can be very expensive. Our members are fascinated by your cost/benefit analysis that sets up a formal comparison of the costs to design, develop, and implement a program idea against the costs the idea saves or avoids.

The members of our association have asked me to invite you to be the featured speaker on March 23, when we hold our annual Pacific Region Conference in Vancouver. About 150 human resource specialists will attend the all-day conference at the Parkland Hotel. We would like you to speak at 2 p.m. on the topic of "Applying Cost/Benefit Analysis in Human Resources Today." Although we cannot offer you an honorarium, we can offer you an opportunity to help human resources managers apply your theories in solving some of their most perplexing problems. You will also be able to meet managers who might be able to supply you with data for future research into personnel functions. In addition, the conference includes two other sessions and a banquet, to which you and a guest are invited.

Please call me at (604) 543-8922 to allow me to add your name to the program as the featured speaker before the Canadian Association of Human Resource Managers on March 23.

Respectfully yours,

Joanne Northern

Joanne Northern
Executive Secretary

Grabs attention of reader by appealing to her interests.

Persuades reader that her expertise is valued.

Softens negative aspects of request with reader's benefits.

Ends confidently with specific action to be taken.

interested. To convince the director of the need for these purchases, Megan must first explain the background of her request. Instead of using generalities, she cites specific examples of how the new scanner and software would function in their company and how much money it would save. Megan also anticipates the limitations of the purchases and discusses their effect on the proposal. In the closing Megan asks for a specific action and provides support documentation to speed her request. She also includes end dating, which prompts the director to act by a certain date.

FIGURE 9.3

Successful Persuasive Memo

Captures attention of reader by describing a costly problem.

Explains background and rationale before making proposal.

Tells exactly what is needed.

Anticipates objections and answers them.

Summarizes benefits in a list.

Delays mention of price until after convincing arguments are presented.

Ends with explicit request and provides end dating.

TO: Maria Franklin, Director, Operations
DATE: April 7, 200x
FROM: Megan Wong, Supervisor, Central Services   MW
SUBJECT: REDUCING OVERTIME AND IMPROVING TURNAROUND TIME

Last month we paid nearly $5400 in overtime to word processing specialists who were forced to work 50- and 60-hour weeks to keep up with the heavy demand for printed documents. Despite this overtime the average turnaround time for documents submitted to Central Services is now five working days.

Many of the documents submitted to us are already keyed or are in print and must be rekeyed into our word processing system by our operators. For example, some of the engineers in Systems Design bring us rough-draft proposals they have produced on their computers, but their programs are not compatible with ours. Hence, we are forced to rekey the material.

I estimate that we could eliminate at least 40 percent of our overtime and also reduce turnaround time on documents by two days if our operators had two items: (a) a scanner and (b) conversion software. A scanner is an optical character reader that converts printed images to electronic forms. Conversion software makes different word processing programs compatible.

Although these two items will not solve all our problems, they could offer considerable relief. Scanners can read most printed material accurately, but 100 percent accuracy cannot be guaranteed. Some hard-to-read fonts and dark paper backgrounds reduce scanning accuracy. Software conversion programs, too, are not perfect. Only the most popular word processing programs can be converted to our system. Despite these limitations I believe that the addition of a scanner and conversion software promises three significant benefits:

1. Savings of at least $2700 in overtime each month by reducing rekeying of printed documents.

2. Reduction of turnaround time from five days to a maximum of three days.

3. Improved morale of word processing specialists.

For these reasons, I recommend that we purchase a Quad Turbo Scanner, Model 2000, along with Software Labs' "Disk Magic" conversion software. The purchase price of these two items, approximately $5000, will be recovered within two months, as a result of reduced overtime payments.

Enclosed are details of the recommended scanner and conversion software. Please give me authorization to submit a purchase order for these two items by June 1 so that Central Services may improve turnaround time before we are asked to begin work on the fiscal reports in July.

SALES LETTERS

Direct-mail selling is a rapidly growing, multibillion-dollar industry. The professionals who specialize in direct-mail marketing have made a science of analyzing a market, developing an appropriate mailing list, studying the product, preparing a comprehensive presentation that appeals to the needs of the target audience, and motivating the reader to act. This carefully orchestrated presentation typically concludes with a sales letter accompanied by a brochure, a sales list, illustrations of the product, testimonials, and so forth.

We are most concerned here with the sales letter: its strategy, organization, and appeals. You'll want to learn the secrets of these messages for many reasons. Although the sales letters of big organizations are usually written by professionals, many smaller companies cannot afford such specialized services. Entrepreneurs and employees of smaller businesses may be called on to write their own sales messages. For example, one recent graduate started a graphics/secretarial service and immediately had to write a convincing letter offering her services. Another graduate went to work for a small company that installs security systems. Because of his recently earned degree (other employees weren't as sure of their skills), he was asked to draft a sales letter outlining specific benefits for residential customers.

From a broader perspective nearly every letter we write is a form of sales. We sell our ideas, our organizations, and ourselves. Learning the techniques of sales writing will help you be more effective in any communication that requires persuasion and promotion. Moreover, recognizing the techniques of selling will enable you to respond to such techniques more rationally. You'll be a better-educated consumer of ideas, products, and services if you understand how sales appeals are made.

Recognizing and applying the techniques of sales writing can be helpful even if you never write an actual sales letter.

The following writing plan for a sales letter attempts to overcome anticipated reader resistance by creating a desire for the product and by motivating the reader to act.

WRITING PLAN FOR A SALES LETTER

- *Opening*—captures the attention of the reader.
- *Body*—emphasizes a central selling point, appeals to the needs of the reader, creates a desire for the product, and introduces price strategically.
- *Closing*—stimulates the reader to act.

ANALYZING THE PRODUCT AND THE READER

Before implementing the writing plan, it's wise to study the product and the target audience so that you can emphasize features with reader appeal.

To sell a product effectively, learn as much as possible about its construction, including its design, raw materials, and manufacturing process. Study its performance, including ease of use, efficiency, durability, and applications. Consider warranties, service, price, and special appeals. Know your own product but also that of your competitor. In this way, you can emphasize your product's strengths against the competitor's weaknesses.

Both the product and the reader require careful analysis before a successful sales letter can be written.

If a product is being developed and marketed for consumers in different cultures, learn as much as possible about the targeted cultures. Although companies would like to use the same products and advertising campaigns as they push into global markets, most find that a "one size fits all" approach falls flat. They may think globally, but they must execute locally. For example, in producing and selling dishwasher soap and fabric softeners in Europe, Unilever discovered amazing differences in cultural preferences. Germans demanded products that were gentle on lakes and rivers. Spaniards wanted cheaper products that made shirts white and soft. And Greeks asked for smaller packages that kept the cost of each store visit low.[2] When Heinz tried to sell its ketchup in France, it ran a TV ad featuring an American cowboy on horseback in the desert lassoing a Heinz ketchup bottle. Sales results were disappointing. Later market research showed that youngsters would be more receptive to the product than their elders in France. Thus, Heinz launched a new ad featuring a sprightly teenager who places an open jar of ketchup on the edge of a rooftop and runs downstairs in time to catch the spilling ketchup on a hot dog.[3]

In Britain consumers are put off by "hard sell" ads. Instead, they prefer to be approached gently, entertained, and charmed. Products destined for international markets should use persuasive strategies that are crafted for specific cultural groups. (See the Communication Workshop at the end of this chapter for more discussion of persuasion and multicultural issues.)

A target audience is preselected for characteristics that make it a good market for a particular product.

Knowing the audience and adapting your message to it is important for any communication. But it's especially true for sales letters. That's why the most effective sales letters are sent to targeted audiences. Mailing lists for selected groups can be purchased or compiled. For example, the manufacturer of computer supplies would find an appropriate audience for its products in the mailing list of subscribers to a computer magazine. By using a selected mailing list, a sales letter writer is able to make certain assumptions about the readers. Readers may be expected to have similar interests, abilities, needs, income, and so forth. The sales letter, then, can be adapted to appeal directly to this selected group. In working with a less specific audience, the letter writer can make only general assumptions and must use a shotgun approach, hoping to find some appeal that motivates the reader.

CAPTURING THE READER'S ATTENTION

Attention-getting devices are especially important in unsolicited sales letters.

Gaining the attention of the reader is essential in unsolicited or uninvited sales letters. In solicited sales letters, individuals have requested information; thus, attention-getting devices are less important.

Provocative messages or unusual formats may be used to attract attention in unsolicited sales letters. These devices may be found within the body of a letter or in place of the inside address.

Offer:	Your free calculator is just the beginning!
Product feature:	Your vacations—this year and in the future—can be more rewarding thanks to an exciting new book from *Canadian Geographic*.
Inside-address opening:	We Wonder, Mrs. Crain, If You Would Like to Know How to Retire in Style with Mutual Funds.
Startling statement:	Extinction is forever. That's why we need your help in preserving many of the world's endangered species.

Story: On a beautiful late spring afternoon, twenty-five years ago, two young men graduated from the same college. They were very much alike, these two young men . . . Recently, these men returned to their college for their class's 25th reunion. They were still very much alike . . . But there was a difference. One of the men was manager of a small department of [a manufacturing company]. The other was its president.

Other effective openings include a bargain, a proverb, a solution to a problem, a quote from a famous person, an anecdote, and a question.

APPEALING TO THE READER

Persuasive appeals generally fall into two broad groups: emotional appeals and rational appeals. Emotional appeals are those associated with the senses; they include how we feel, see, taste, smell, and hear. Strategies that arouse anger, fear, pride, love, and satisfaction are emotional.

Rational strategies are those associated with reason and intellect; they appeal to the mind. Rational appeals include references to making money, saving money, increasing efficiency, and making the best use of resources. Generally, use rational appeals when a product is expensive, long-lasting, or important to health and security. Use emotional appeals when a product is inexpensive, short-lived, or nonessential.

Banks selling chequing and savings services frequently use rational appeals. They emphasize saving money in chequing fees, earning interest on accounts, receiving free personalized cheques, and saving time in opening the account. In contrast, a travel agency selling a student tour to Mexico uses an emotional strategy by describing the "sun, fun, rockin', and partying" to be enjoyed. Many successful selling campaigns combine appeals, emphasizing perhaps a rational appeal while also including an emotional appeal in a subordinated position.

> Emotional appeals relate to the senses; rational appeals relate to reasoning and intellect.

EMPHASIZING CENTRAL SELLING POINTS

Although a product may have a number of features, concentrate on just one or two of those features. Don't bewilder the reader with too much information. Analyze the reader's needs and tailor your appeal directly to the reader. The letter selling a student tour to Mexico emphasized two points:

> In sales letters develop one or two central selling points and stress them.

1. *We see to it that you have a great time.* Let's face it. By the end of the term, you've earned your vacation. The books and jobs and stress can all be shelved for a while.

2. *We keep our trips cheap.* Mazatlan 1A is again the lowest-priced adventure trip offered in Canada.

The writer analyzed the student audience and elected to concentrate on two appeals: (1) an emotional appeal to the senses (having a good time) and (2) a rational appeal to saving money (paying a low price).

CREATING A DESIRE FOR THE PRODUCT

Create a desire for a product through reader benefits, concrete and objective language, product confidence, or testimonials.

In convincing readers to purchase a product or service, you may use a number of techniques:

- *Reader benefit.* Discuss product features from the reader's point of view. Show how the reader will benefit and how the product's features meet the needs of the reader.

  You'll be able to extend your summer swim season by using our new solar pool cover.

- *Concrete language.* Use concrete words instead of general or abstract language:

  Our Mexican tour provides more than just a party. Maybe you've never set eyes on a giant saguaro cactus . . . or parasailed high above the Pacific Ocean . . . or watched a majestic golden sunset from your own private island.

- *Objective language.* Avoid language that sounds unreasonable. Overstatements using words like *fantastic, without fail, foolproof, amazing, astounding,* and so forth do not ring true. Overblown language and preposterous claims may cause readers to reject the entire sales message.

- *Product confidence.* Build confidence in your product or service by assuring customer satisfaction. You can do this by offering a free trial, money-back guarantee, free sample, or warranty. Another way to build confidence is to associate your product with respected references or authorities:

  Our concept of economical group travel has been accepted and sponsored by five city recreation departments. In addition, our program has been featured in *Maclean's,* the *Toronto Star,* the *Globe and Mail,* and the *National Post.*

- *Testimonials.* The statements of satisfied customers are effective in creating a desire for the product or service:

  A student returning from Mazatlan's cruise last year said, "I've just been to paradise."

INTRODUCING PRICE STRATEGICALLY

Introduce price early if it is a sales feature; otherwise, delay mentioning it.

If product price is a significant sales feature, use it early in your sales letter. Otherwise, don't mention price until after you have created the reader's desire for the product. Some sales letters include no mention of price; instead, an enclosed order form shows the price. Other techniques for de-emphasizing price include the following:

Price can be de-emphasized by using one of these five techniques.

- *Show the price in small units.* For instance, instead of stating the total cost of a year's subscription, state the magazine's price when calculated per issue. Or describe insurance premiums by their cost per day.

- *Show how the reader is saving money by purchasing the product.* In selling solar heating units, for example, explain how much the reader will save on heating bills.

- *Compare your prices with those of competitors.* Describe the savings to be realized when your product is purchased.
- *Make your price a bargain.* For instance, point out that the special introductory offer is one third off the regular price. Or say that the price includes a special discount if the reader acts immediately.
- *Associate the price with reader benefits.* Note, for example, that "for as little as $3 a month, you'll enjoy emergency road and towing protection, emergency trip-interruption protection, and nine other benefits."

Notice in Figure 9.4 how price is directly linked to customer benefits. New Western Bank opens its promotional letter by telling the reader how much money can be saved on its chequing account. This central selling feature is then emphasized throughout the letter, although other selling points are also mentioned.

STIMULATING ACTION

The closing of a sales letter has one very important goal: stimulating the reader to act. A number of techniques help motivate action:

- *Make the action clear.* Use specific language to tell exactly what is to be done:

  Fill out the enclosed postage-paid card.
  Call this toll-free number.
  Send the enclosed reservation card along with your cheque.

- *Make the action easy.* Highlight the simple steps the reader needs to take:

  Just fill in your credit card number and indicate the amount of your gift. Drop the postage-paid order form in the mail, and we'll handle the details.

- *Offer an inducement.* Encourage the reader to act while low prices remain in effect. Offer a gift or a rebate for action:

  Now is a great time to join the Can-West Travel Club. By joining now, you'll receive a handsome black and gold-tone electronic calculator and a quartz pen-watch.

- *Limit the offer.* Set a specific date by which the reader must act in order to receive a gift, a rebate, benefits, low prices, or a special offer:

  Act quickly, because I'm authorized to make this special price on solar greenhouses available only until May 1.

- *Make payment easy.* Encourage the reader to send a credit card number or to return a card and be billed later.

The sales letter for the Workplace Equity Institute shown in Figure 9.5 sounds quite casual. However, it actually required considerable planning on the part of the writer. This letter announces a newsletter containing tips to help managers avoid conduct that might result in unfair treatment of employees. The letter concentrates on a central selling point (the need for current and useful information) as it leads up to the action to be taken (returning a reservation form). Notice how the writer uses both emotional and rational appeals. Emotional appeals refer to a fear that managers might accidentally stumble into messy situations leading to claims against the

You can encourage the reader to act by applying one or more of these methods.

FIGURE 9.4

Effective Sales Letter—Modified Block Style

New Western Bank
3200 Portage Avenue, Winnipeg, MB R2H 8L9

Diane Ladd
AVP & Manager
Personal Financial Centre

April 3, 200x

Mr. Chen Xian
1045 Cuthbert Street
Winnipeg, MB R3L 2H3

Dear Mr. Xian:

Captures attention with appealing offer.

Why pay $50, $100, or even $150 a year in chequing account service charges when New Western has the right price for chequing—FREE!

Emphasizes central selling point but also introduces other services.

At New Western Bank we want your business. That's why we're offering "Totally Free Chequing." Compare the cost of your present chequing account. We know you'll like the difference. We also have six other personalized chequing plans, one of which is certain to be right for you.

Focuses on rational appeals.

Suggests specific reader benefits.

In addition to the best price on chequing accounts, we provide a variety of investment opportunities and two hassle-free credit-line programs. Once you qualify, you can use your credit line at any time without applying for a new loan each time you need money. With one of our credit-line programs, you can write a cheque for just about anything, including a vacation, home improvements, major purchases, unexpected bills, or investment opportunities.

If you have not yet heard about New Western Bank, you'll find that we have eight convenient locations to serve you.

Makes it easy for reader to open account.

Check out the details of our services described in the enclosed pamphlets. Then check us out by stopping in to open your free chequing account at one of our eight convenient locations. You can also open your account by simply filling out the enclosed postage-paid card and returning it to us.

Offers incentive for action before given date.

If you open your New Western chequing account before June 15, we'll give you 200 free cheques and we'll buy back any unused cheques you have from your present chequing account. Act now to start saving money. We look forward to serving you.

Sincerely yours,

Diane Ladd

Diane Ladd
Accounts Vice President

DL:egh
Enclosures

FIGURE 9.5

Successful Sales Letter—Modified Block Style

WORKPLACE EQUITY INSTITUTE INC.
533 Winfield Road   Kelowna, BC   V1L 2H4

February 13, 200x

Mr. C. D. Avery, President
Avery Enterprises Inc.
2043 Fraser Street
Vancouver, BC V5L 2E2

Dear Mr. Avery:

If you had told me a couple of years ago that any time I hired, fired, or appraised an employee I could be facing review from the Human Rights Commission, I'd have said you were crazy.

Attracts attention with startling statement.

Just last October, though, I read about an employee who claimed that he had been fired because he had complained that his company had not kept its promises to him. He filed a complaint with the Commission and was later awarded either reinstatement or a year's severance pay for wrongful dismissal! You're probably as concerned as I am about how difficult it is in today's world to ensure that your company practises fair treatment for all its employees. Issues like discrimination, wrongful dismissal, sexual harassment, and employee testing are becoming more and more common. Employees are taking action to ensure that their rights are protected. Now more than ever employers need to know and protect the rights of everyone in their workplaces.

Builds interest with emotional appeals.

As a business owner, you may be aware of what constitutes fair treatment. But what about all the managers in your company who aren't as knowledgeable? How can you train them to avoid stumbling accidentally into improper—or even worse, illegal—behaviour?

The best way to prepare your managers is with our easy-to-read newsletter called the MANAGER'S UPDATE. Twice a month, this four-page letter delivers valuable advice to the managers you pick. They will learn to focus on positive behaviours and avoid those "red flag" promises, practices, and actions that lead to claims of unfair treatment. And with legal fees starting at $200 and $300 an hour, you know how costly it is to defend against any claim. That's where MANAGER'S UPDATE can save you thousands of dollars—and at a cost of less than 85 cents an issue.

Announces product and creates desire.

Associates price with reader benefit.

To start your protection immediately, just sign the enclosed reservation form. Fill in the number of copies you want, and return the form in the postage-paid envelope. I'll take care of the rest.

Makes it easy to respond.

Sincerely,

Paul Cerilli

Paul Cerilli, President

PC:rjt

P.S. Respond within ten days and we'll rush you at no charge THE EMPLOYER'S OBLIGATION, a special reference book selling for $39.95 in bookstores.

Motivates action with free gift.

company. Rational appeals centre on the cost of lawyers' fees compared with the low cost of the newsletter. The price of the newsletter subscription is linked with reader benefits, followed by a satisfaction guarantee. In the closing the writer requests action and makes it easy to take. A strategic postscript offers a final incentive: a free gift for prompt action. This letter typifies successful sales letters. It sounds conversational, it offers reader benefits, and it motivates action.

SUMMING UP AND LOOKING FORWARD

The ability to persuade is a powerful and versatile communication tool. In this chapter you learned to apply the indirect strategy in writing claim letters, making requests, writing sales letters, and overcoming resistance to new ideas. The techniques suggested here will be useful in many other contexts beyond the writing of these business documents. You will find that logical organization of arguments is also extremely effective in expressing ideas orally.

In coming chapters you will learn how to modify and generalize the techniques of direct and indirect strategies in preparing goodwill messages as well as writing short and long reports.

DISCUSSION

1. Why is the ability to persuade a significant trait in both business and personal relations?
2. The organization of a successful persuasive claim centres on the reasons and the closing. Why?
3. Should favour requests be written directly or indirectly? Discuss.
4. Why do individuals resist change?
5. Some individuals will never write an actual sales letter. Why is it nevertheless important for them to learn the techniques for doing so?
6. How is a sales letter like a persuasive claim letter? How is it different?

CHAPTER REVIEW

7. In the indirect strategy, what should precede the main idea?

8. List at least four examples of favour requests.

9. Name at least eight items a salesperson should know about a product before attempting to sell it.

10. The most effective sales letters are sent to what kind of audience?

11. What is an unsolicited sales letter? Give an example.

12. What is a solicited sales letter? Give an example.

13. List at least five ways to gain a reader's attention in the opening of a sales letter.

14. In selling a product, when are rational appeals most effective?

When are emotional appeals most effective?

15. Name six writing techniques that stimulate desire for a product.

Writing Improvement Exercises

Strategies. For each of the following situations, check the appropriate writing strategy.

	Direct Strategy	Indirect Strategy
16. An appeal for a contribution to Children's World, a charity		
17. An announcement that in the future all dental, health, and life insurance benefits for employees will be reduced		
18. A request to another company for verification of employment regarding a job applicant		
19. A letter to a painting contractor demanding payment for replacing ceramic floor tiles damaged by sloppy painters		
20. A request for information about an oak desk and computer workstation		
21. A letter to a grocery store asking for permission to display posters advertising a school fundraising car wash		
22. A request for a refund of the cost of a computer program that does not perform the functions it was expected to do		
23. A request for a refund of the cost of a hair dryer that stopped working after a month's use (the hair dryer carries a one-year warranty)		
24. An invitation to a prominent author to speak before a student rally		
25. A memo to employees describing the schedule and selections of a new mobile catering service		

ACTIVITIES AND CASES

9.1 Persuasive Request Letter: A Copier That's Nothing But Trouble. Analyze the following poorly written persuasive claim and list at least five major faults. Outline an appropriate writing plan for a persuasive claim. After class discussion, your instructor may ask you to rewrite this message, rectifying its faults. Address your letter to International Copy Services, 1506 Fourth Street S.W., Calgary, AB T7L 2E3. Assume that you are writing on your company's letterhead. Use block style.

Ineffective Writing

Gentlemen:

Our Regal compact system copier SP-270F has caused us nothing but trouble since it was installed. It was purchased in September, and repairs have been needed no less than five times since September. This means that we have been without our copier at times when we desperately needed it. Therefore, we want you to replace this copier that won't work and bring us a new unit—or you can refund the amount that it cost when it was purchased.

Just after it was installed, the automatic document feeder jammed. Your technician, after our telephone call, came out to promptly fix it. But we still lost almost a day of copier use. It wasn't long before another repair was needed. In October the document feeder jammed again, and our copies were looking light in appearance. On October 12 your technician made a replacement of parts in the document assembly; the toner apparatus was also cleaned by him. This worked fine for five days. Next the collator jammed. We tried different paper, as recommended by your technician, but it still doesn't work well. In just four months of ownership, that copier has required five repair calls. That means that we have been without a copier a lot of the time. And we are very angry about the time and energy required to have it serviced.

We selected the Regal SP-270F copier because it promised automatic document feeding, that two-sided copies could be made at once and it had automatic collation and fast speed.

Attached please find a copy of our service record with this SP-270F copier. We believed your advertisement that said that Regal made "tough copiers for tough customers." Now I'm getting tough. Call me at 469-2900 immediately because I want action by February 1.

Angrily,

9.2 Persuasive Request Memo: Promoting Your Hotel. As Christine Harris, group sales manager of The Riverfront Hotel, it's your job to promote the hotel to convention planners. You have a potential customer in the Active Living Alliance, an organization for people living with disabilities. It wants to host its July 9–15 convention in your hotel. To host the convention, the hotel must ensure that all of Riverfront's facilities are accessible to people with disabilities, which will mean some upgrading to restrooms and the front-desk area. The hotel's in-room, televised information system will also have to be upgraded to include sound. The staff, furthermore, will need refresher training in customer service techniques for people with disabilities.

The benefits of hosting the convention would be many. Like most meetings for individuals with disabilities, this convention would yield higher-than-average returns. The Active Living Alliance convention would last six days—twice as long as most at The Riverfront. Moreover, the organization has promised to schedule most evening meals at the hotel. The total convention revenues, including payment for rooms, meals, meeting rooms, and equipment, could reach nearly $700,000. And if the convention went well, the organization would likely book future conventions at The Riverfront. The Riverfront could develop a niche market for clientele with special needs, which would bolster its lagging convention business.

Write a memo to the hotel's general manager, James Stockbridge, persuading him to consider hosting the Active Living Alliance convention. Get a commitment from Mr. Stockbridge to meet on September 1 with Carol Martin, president of the Active Living Alliance. You'll also need to get permission to secure a cost estimate for the hotel alterations from The Design Group. The contractor has experience building to hotel specifications, and the $3000 estimate fee can be applied to the alteration bill. If you schedule the cost estimate before September 15, you will have plenty of time to reply to the Active Living Alliance. Its deadline is November 15. Once Mr. Stockbridge has talked with the organization president and costs have been established, you feel certain he will agree to the alterations.

9.3 Sales Letter: Fitness at Crown Pizza.

Assume you are Robert Bushie, sales representative, Fitness Associates, 135 East Stokely Blvd., Dartmouth, Nova Scotia B2V 1S4. Fitness Associates sells fitness equipment and personal training services to businesses. You need to write a letter that generates new sales, and Crown Pizza looks especially promising. Through a friend, you've learned that Crown is striving to reduce employee sick days. Recent statistics from their 12 outlets in the Dartmouth/Halifax area show a dramatic decrease in productivity and irregular staffing levels. You hope to convince the company that it would benefit from a company-wide fitness plan. Health research shows that a healthy lifestyle contributes significantly to employee satisfaction on the job, while reducing absenteeism by up to 40 percent in some companies. Studies show that moderately sized centres coupled with motivational and training programs yield the greatest success. For just $30,000, Fitness Associates will provide exercise equipment including stationary bikes, weight machines, and treadmills. Their fitness experts will design a fitness room, set up the fitness equipment, and design appropriate programs. Best of all, the one-time cost is usually offset by cost savings within one year of centre installation. For additional fees FA can also provide fitness consultants for employee fitness assessments. Write a sales letter to Ms. Kathleen Stewart, Human Resources Vice President, Crown Pizza Company, 145 South Superior Street, Dartmouth, Nova Scotia, B2L 3H5, asking for an appointment. Send her a brochure detailing the products and services that Fitness Associates provides. As an incentive, offer free fitness assessments for all employees if Crown Pizza installs a fitness facility by December 1.

9.4 Sales Letter: Analyzing Its Pitch.

Select a one-page sales letter that you or a friend has received. (If you are unable to find one, your instructor may be able to help.) Read the letter carefully. Then answer the following questions.

1. At what audience is the letter aimed?

2. Is the appeal emotional or rational? Is the appeal effective? Explain.

3. What techniques capture the reader's attention?

4. Is the opening effective? Explain.

5. Is a central selling point emphasized? Explain.

6. Does the letter emphasize reader benefits? Explain.

7. Is concrete language used?

8. How is confidence in the product or service developed?

9. How is price introduced?

10. What action is to be taken, and how is the reader motivated to take that action?

After a class discussion of the various ways the members of your class answered these ten questions, your instructor may ask you to write an improved version of the sales letter you analyzed. Implement suggestions from this chapter.

9.5 Claim Request: Excessive Legal Fees. You are the business manager for McConnell's, a producer of gourmet ice cream. McConnell's has 12 ice cream parlours in the Edmonton area and a reputation for excellent ice cream. Your firm was approached by an independent ice cream vendor who wanted to use McConnell's name and recipes for ice cream to be distributed through grocery stores and drugstores. As business manager you worked with a law firm, Lancomb, Pereigni, and Associates, to draw up contracts regarding the use of McConnell's name and quality standards for the product. When you received the bill from Louis Lancomb, you couldn't believe it. McConnell's was charged for 38 hours of preparation time by a lawyer and for 55 hours of paralegal assistance. At $450 per hour and $100 per hour, respectively, the charges seemed excessively high. The bill also showed $415 for telephone calls, which might be accurate because Mr. Lancomb had to converse with McConnell's owners, who were living in Ireland at the time. Write a persuasive letter to Mr. Lancomb. You doubt that an experienced attorney would require 38 hours to draw up the contracts in question. Moreover, you have checked with other businesses and found that excellent legal advice can be obtained for $300 per hour. McConnell's would like to continue using the services of Lancomb, Pereigni, and Associates for future legal business. Such future business is unlikely if an adjustment is not made to this bill. Write a persuasive request to Louis Lancomb, Legal Counsel, Lancomb, Pereigni, and Associates, 2690 Whyte Avenue, Edmonton, AB T2A 1L5.

9.6 Persuasive Favour Request: Inviting a Winner.
As program chair of the Women in Business Association, a national group of businesswomen, you must persuade Joann R. Schulz to be the speaker at your annual conference on April 14 in Toronto. Ms. Schulz was recently named Small Business Person of the Year by the Canadian Association of Independent Business.

After her 44-year-old husband died of a heart attack, Ms. Schulz threw herself into their fledgling company and eventually transformed it from a small research company into an international manufacturer of devices for the treatment of eye problems. Under her leadership, her Vancouver company grew from 3 to 75 employees in six years. It now sells more than $5 million worth of artificial lenses annually in 22 countries.

Although you can offer Ms. Schulz only $1000, you have heard that she is eager to encourage female entrepreneurs. You feel she might be receptive to your invitation. Invite Ms. Joann R. Schulz, President, NBR Industries, 3450 West 16th Avenue, Vancouver, BC V1N 3E5.

9.7 Persuasive Favour Request: Cultivating an Internship.
Your school has no formal work experience program in your field. You realize that work experience is invaluable both to acquaint you with the field and also to help you find employment. You confirm with your department head a suitable number of credit hours for the experience. Although you're taking a full load of courses, you decide to write to The Selby Group, asking this company to take you on as a part-time work experience employee. By arranging the hours around your existing class schedule, you feel you could work 12 to 15 hours per week for one semester. You're interested in functioning in a specific capacity at Selby's, but you are also open to working wherever the company can accommodate you. Of course, you don't expect to get paid, but you will be receiving up to three credits toward completion of your program if The Selby Group can take you for one semester. Write a persuasive letter to Jerry Cohen, Manager, Human Resources, The Selby Group, 190 Royal Road, Prince George, British Columbia V2N 2E6.

9.8 Personal Persuasive Memo: We Need a Change.
In your own work or organization experience, identify a problem for which you have a solution. Should a procedure be altered to improve performance? Would a new or different piece of equipment help you perform your work better? Could some tasks be scheduled more efficiently? Are employees being used most effectively? Could customers be better served by changing something? Do you want to work other hours or perform other tasks?

Once you have identified a situation requiring persuasion, write a memo to your boss or organization head. Use actual names and facts. Employ the concepts and techniques outlined in this chapter to help you convince your boss that your idea should prevail. Include concrete examples, anticipate objections, emphasize reader benefits, and end with a specific action to be taken.

9.9 Persuasive Memo: Overusing Overnight Shipments. As office manager of Cambridge Software, write a memo persuading technicians, engineers, programmers, and other employees to reduce the number of overnight or second-day mail shipments. Your courier costs and other shipping bills have been sky high, and you feel that staff members are overusing these services.

Encourage employees to send messages by fax. Sending a fax costs only about 35 cents a page to most long-distance areas and nothing to local areas. There's a whopping difference between 35 cents and $15 for an overnight courier service! Whenever possible, staff members should obtain the courier service account number of the recipient and use it for charging the shipment. If staff members plan ahead and allow enough time, they can use regular mail service, which takes three to five days.

You'd like to reduce overnight delivery services voluntarily by 50 percent over the next two months. Unless a sizable reduction occurs, you're afraid there may be significant consequences. Address the memo to all employees.

9.10 Persuasive Favour Request: Celebrity Auction. As treasurer of your school's Associated Students Organization, you have a big job. You must find ways to raise money for your institution's pledge to aid the United Way's adult literacy program in your community. The Adult Literacy Campaign, which is the fundraising element of this program, has estimated that 10,000 people in your city need reading and writing skills instruction. The ASO is planning the usual bake sales, car washes, and gathering and selling of recyclables (bottles, cans, newspapers) to raise funds. But you have a brilliant idea for an additional funding source: a celebrity raffle. At a spring ASO rally, items or services from local and other celebrities could be auctioned. The ASO approves your idea and asks you to begin by writing a letter persuading your institution president to donate one hour of tutoring in a subject he or she chooses.

9.11 Sales Letter: It's Personal. Identify a situation in your own job or a previous job in which a sales letter is needed. Using suggestions from this chapter, write an appropriate sales letter. Promote a product or service. Use actual names, information, and examples. Make your sales letter as realistic as possible.

 9.12 Connecting With E-Mail: Project H.E.L.P. As employee relations manager of Western Life Insurance Company, one of your tasks is to promote Project H.E.L.P. (Higher Education Learning Program), an on-the-job learning opportunity. Project H.E.L.P. is a combined effort of major corporations and the Association of Canadian Community Colleges. You must recruit 12 employees who will volunteer as instructors for 20 or more students. The students will spend four hours a week at the company's head office earning three units of credit a semester. This semester the students will be serving in the following departments: Claims, Word Processing, Corporate Media Services, Marketing, Communications, Library, and Administrative Support. Your task is to write an e-mail memo to the employees in these departments to encourage them to volunteer. They will be expected to supervise and instruct the students. Employees will receive two hours of release time per week to work with the students. The program has been very successful thus far. School officials, students, and employees alike express satisfaction with the experience and the outcomes. Write a persuasive memo with convincing appeals that will bring you 12 volunteers to work with Project H.E.L.P.

9.13 Searching the Internet: Persuading Your Member of Parliament Via "Snail Mail." Assume you are interested in an issue of national importance, and you want your MP to know your position. Choose an issue about which you feel strongly: student loans, pension reform, human rights in other countries, environmental protection, the federal debt, employment insurance, or some other area regulated by the federal government. Obtain your MP's address by visiting the federal government's Internet site (www.parl.gc.ca/36/sm-e.htm). The e-mail address, if available, is included as well. However, although e-mail messages are fast, they don't carry as much influence as personal letters. Therefore, it's better to write a persuasive letter to your MP outlining your feelings. For best results, consider these tips. (1) Use the proper form of address, such as *The Honourable John Smith, Dear Minister Smith,* if you are writing to a cabinet minister, and *The Honourable Joan Doe, Dear Ms. Doe,* if you are writing to an MP. (See www.pch.gc.ca/ceremonial-symb/english/prt_address_2.html for a full discussion of correct forms of address.) (2) Identify yourself as a member of his or her riding. (3) Immediately state your position *(I urge you to support/oppose . . . because)*. (4) Present facts and illustrations, and say how they affect you personally. If legislation were enacted, how would you or your organization be better off or worse off? Avoid generalities. (5) Offer to provide further information. (6) Keep the letter polite, constructive, and brief (one page tops).

GRAMMAR/MECHANICS CHECKUP—9

Semicolons and Colons

Review Sections 2.16-2.19 in the Grammar/Mechanics Handbook. Then study each of the following statements. Insert any necessary punctuation. Use the delete sign (✐) to omit unnecessary punctuation. In the space provided indicate the number of changes you made and record the number of the G/M principle(s) illustrated. (When you replace one punctuation mark with another, count it as one change.) If you make no changes, write *0*. This exercise concentrates on semicolon and colon use, but you will also be responsible for correct comma use. When you finish, compare your responses with those provided. If your responses differ, study carefully the specific principles shown in parentheses.

Example:	The job of Mr. Wellworth is to make sure that his company has enough cash to meet its obligations ; moreover , he is responsible for locating credit when needed.	<u>2</u> (2.16a)

1. Short-term financing refers to a period of less than one year long-term financing on the other hand refers to a period of ten years or more. _____
2. Cash resulting from product sales does not come in until December therefore our cash flow becomes critical in October and November. _____
3. We must negotiate short-term financing during the following months September October and November. _____
4. Some of the large corporations that have important overseas sales are: MacMillan Bloedel, Nortel Hydro-Quebec and Spar Aerospace. _____
5. Although some firms rarely, if ever, need to borrow short-term money many businesses find that they require significant credit to pay for current production and sales costs. _____

6. A supermarket probably requires no short-term credit, a greeting card manufacturer however typically would need considerable short-term credit.

7. We offer three basic types of credit open-book accounts promissory notes and trade acceptances.

8. Speakers at the conference on credit include the following businesspeople Sheridan Black financial manager Lytton Industries Miriam Minkoff comptroller Royal Bank and Mark Kendall legal counsel Bank of Montreal.

9. The prime interest rate is set by the Bank of Canada and the Bank's director accomplishes this by varying the amount of cash the chartered banks must deposit with it.

10. Most banks are in business to lend money to commercial customers for example retailers service companies manufacturers and construction firms.

11. Avionics, Inc., which is a small electronics firm with a solid credit rating recently applied for a loan but Maple Leaf Trust refused the loan application because of the company's poor business plan.

12. When Avionics, Inc., was refused by Maple Leaf Trust its financial managers submitted applications to Fidelity Trust, Farmers Credit Union, and Mountain Financial.

13. The cost of financing capital investments at the present time is very high therefore Avionics' managers may elect to postpone certain expansion projects.

14. If interest rates reach as high as 15 percent the cost of borrowing becomes prohibitive and many businesses are forced to reconsider or abandon projects that require financing.

15. Several investors decided to pool their resources then they could find attractive investments.

---

1. (3) year; financing, hand, (2.03, 2.16b)   3. (3) months: September, October, (2.01, 2.17a)
5. (1) money, (2.06a, 2.16b)   7. (3) credit: accounts, notes, (2.01, 2.17a)   9. (1) Canada, (2.05)
11. (2) rating, loan; (2.06c, 2.16c)   13. (2) high; therefore, (2.16)   15. (1) resources; (2.16b)

GRAMMAR/MECHANICS CHALLENGE—9

Document for Revision

The following letter has faults in grammar, punctuation, spelling, number form, wordiness, and repetition. Drawing on the guidelines provided in the Grammar/Mechanics Handbook and what you learned in the chapter, use standard proofreading marks (see Appendix B), to correct the letter.

Ineffective Writing

October, 23 200x

Ms. Christie Young

637, rue St-Urbain

Montreal, PQ H3A 1A3

Dear Ms. Young:

Enclosed are copies of this years Sportour ski brochure. This year, in addition to our charter program (which include all our charter trips to the rockies and Europe and the United States we are introducing a new program in conjunction with western airlines.

The combination of these 2 programs, offer our customers the most complete ski package we have every created. Value, flexability and variety are all amalgamated in this years program.

Due to the fact that many dates and destinations are all ready begining to fillup please select your trip and complete and fill out the reservation form included in the brochure. Send your deposit of two hundred dollars and forward to the Sportours Main Office as soon as possible.

We invite you to ski with us this comming season, and look forward to serving you, as a special incentive we're taking fifty dollars off the complete package price against the first 25 people who send in there reservations.

Sincerely,

Cultural Arrogance and Persuasive Strategies

As the world becomes one big marketplace, many companies are learning the hard way that not all people think and act the same. Some companies have even been accused of "cultural arrogance" in marketing abroad because they insist on reusing persuasive appeals originally designed for their local market. They wrongly assume that these persuasive appeals can easily cross cultural borders. These companies are finding that insensitive persuasive strategies result in products that fail to sell in other cultures.

Take, for instance, U.S.-based Procter & Gamble's first attempt to sell Pampers diapers in Japan, the world's second-largest consumer market. Japanese consumers found the diapers too fat, bulky, and expensive. It turns out that Japanese mothers change their babies' diapers about 14 times a day. Thus, Japanese mums preferred thinner and cheaper disposable diapers.[4]

There are many more examples of companies that did not consider how a persuasive advertising campaign or product name would be interpreted by another culture. Canon, the Japanese multinational, experienced problems with its OES camera in Finland. The camera had been successful in North America; however, in Finland the acronym *OES* stands for "I cannot say" or "I don't know." Canon's marketing of the OES name created indecision in the minds of Finns.

Similar problems arose for the British maker of Schweppes Tonic Water. Used in an Italian sales promotion campaign, this product name's translation was "Schweppes Toilet Water." A Scandinavian company had a problem when it tried to sell its bathroom tissue in the United Kingdom. The company called its product "Crapp." It was unsuccessful for obvious reasons.[5]

Rubbermaid, the maker of kitchen, bath, office, and kids' products, experienced significant challenges when it tried to expand into European markets. Rubbermaid's North American customers liked the selections of neutral blues or almond colours. But southern Europeans preferred red containers. Customers in Holland chose white. And although Rubbermaid sold millions of open-top waste baskets across North America, Europeans didn't like them. They favoured holders with tight lids so that no garbage peeked out.[6]

Although many companies have had to learn the hard way when they expand into other countries and cultures, Yogen Früz is not one. This Canadian company, the largest seller of frozen yogurt in the world, has customers in 80 countries, including Bosnia, El Salvador, Colombia, and Guatemala. Part of its successful strategy has been to learn about a country's culture before beginning operations in that country. For example, at the grand opening of their first franchise in Guatemala, a country with a strong religious tradition, the company ensured that a priest was on hand to give the store his blessing.[7]

Application. In a class discussion or in a memo to your instructor, react to the following questions. What do you think is meant by "cultural arrogance"? Is it influenced by ethnocentrism (see Chapter 1)? Was it exemplified by Procter & Gamble, Rubbermaid, Schweppes, and Canon? What could each of these organizations have done to ensure a better reception for its products in the targeted culture? What key persuasion and selling considerations were missed in these marketing ventures?

CHAPTER 10 GOODWILL AND SPECIAL MESSAGES

There are no economic constraints that prevent you from thanking people for their efforts. But keep in mind that a mere thank you, accompanied by general comments, is pretty hollow . . . Specificity, warmth, and sincerity are as important as the difference between a personal note and a computerized form letter.[1]

ANDREW S. GROVE, CEO, Intel Corporation,
the world's largest computer chip manufacturer

Learning Objectives

1. Recognize opportunities for writing goodwill messages.
2. Appreciate how special messages can build goodwill.
3. Write letters of appreciation, congratulations, and sympathy.
4. Write letters of recommendation and introduction.
5. Write form and guide letters.

This chapter presents a diverse group of goodwill and special messages that require you to adapt the strategies and writing techniques you have learned in previous chapters. Some of the messages convey personal goodwill, and others carry business information of a special nature. Generally, they do not have specific writing plans. You will find, as you progress in your development of the craft of writing, that you are less dependent on writing plans to guide you. Although you will not be provided with detailed writing plans here, we will point out similarities between situations and make suggestions regarding appropriate strategies. This chapter will be helpful not only for its opportunities to adapt strategies but also for the models provided.

GOODWILL MESSAGES

Letters that convey social approval satisfy deep human needs for both the sender and the receiver.

Goodwill messages carry good wishes, warm feelings, and sincere thoughts to friends, customers, and employees. These are messages that do not *have* to be written—and often are not written for a number of reasons. Because these messages are not urgent and because words do not come readily to mind, it's easy for writers to procrastinate. Writers may feel an urge to express thanks or congratulations or sympathy, but they put it off until the moment passes. Then it's too late. Yet, nearly everyone appreciates receiving sincere thanks or words of congratulations. Human nature creates within us a desire for social approval: we want to be accepted, remembered, consoled, appreciated, and valued. Although busy or unsure business writers may avoid writing goodwill messages, these letters and memos are worth the effort because they gratify both senders and receivers, and because they fulfil important human needs.

Greeting cards and commercial thank-you notes provide ready-made words, but these messages cannot express your own personal thoughts. When you receive a card, what do you read first—the printed words of the card maker or the penned-in remarks of the sender? The personal sentiments of the sender are always more expressive and more meaningful to the reader than is the printed message.

Goodwill messages are most effective when they are immediate, spontaneous, sincere, and personal. They should follow a direct strategy:

- Identify the situation.
- Include specific details and personal thoughts.
- Close with a forward-looking thought or a concluding remark.

MESSAGES OF APPRECIATION

Extend thanks and show appreciation when someone has done you a favour or whenever an action merits praise. Letters of appreciation may also be written to customers for their business, as shown in Figure 10.1. Relationships with customers and suppliers are the cornerstone of successful enterprises. Common business wisdom dictates sending letters of appreciation, cards, and sometimes gifts during the December holiday period. But it's also important to express appreciation all year round. Notice that the message in Figure 10.1 begins by identifying the situation. The body provides specific details, while the closing looks forward to continued profitable dealings.

Letters of appreciation should be written when someone has done you a favour. The letter to Ellen D'Sousa in Figure 10.2 expresses the gratitude of a class for a guided tour of a corporate communication centre. Thanks and compliments fill the opening, body, and closing of this message. It's no secret that readers rarely tire of sincere praise, so be sure to include many specific references to the reader and to the service rendered. Notice that a copy (expressed by *c*) of this thank-you letter was sent to Ms. D'Sousa's boss. In this way, the letter becomes more than a routine thank you. Not only is her boss made aware of her excellence, but the letter will probably also be placed in the employee's personnel file and be useful in future performance evaluations and promotions.

In expressing appreciation, remember that thanks and compliments are more powerful when they are written rather than spoken. People know that it takes much more effort to sit down and write a note. And written messages are tangible and lasting. The receiver might hang your letter or note prominently as a continuing reminder of your thoughtfulness.

Letters or notes of appreciation for hospitality are generally handwritten, but they may also be printed, particularly if one's handwriting is not terrific. Two versions of a thank-you letter for a dinner at a professor's home are shown in Figure 10.3. The ineffective message fails because of its generalities and its overemphasis on *I*. Thank-you letters and notes should be about the reader, not the writer.

A good letter of appreciation for a dinner generally refers to the (1) fine food, (2) warm hospitality, and (3) pleasant company. Notice in the more effective thank

Thank-you letters generally refer to the fine food, warm hospitality, and good company provided.

FIGURE 10.1

Appreciation for a Customer's Business

STAFFING RESOURCE NETWORK
302 N.E. Third Avenue
Charlottetown, PE C1A 2E4
Phone: (902) 320-4491 FAX: (902) 320-3591
Web Site: www.staffresource.com

January 3, 200x

Ms. Rhonda Fontaine, Vice President
Budget Recycling and Reuse
549 Mirth Centre
Charlottetown, PE C1D 4R3

Dear Ms. Fontaine:

Expresses appreciation immediately.

Staffing your organization with temporary office workers for the past six years has been our pleasure, and we are grateful for your business.

Reminds and assures customer of services.

As we begin the new year, I want you to know that you may continue to count on us for temporary staff members who are as productive as your permanent personnel. As a regular user of our services, you know how cost-effective it is to keep a lean staff, calling on us to help you fill in with temporaries during peak periods and for special projects.

Closes with forward-looking thought.

Thank you for allowing us to send you our qualified temporaries. We appreciate the confidence you have shown in our agency these past six years, and we look forward to at least six more years of mutually profitable dealings.

Sincerely,

Allan Contois

Allan Contois
President

you in Figure 10.3 that the writer includes all three of these elements. And he makes his appreciation especially meaningful by remembering a number of specifics, such as delicious trout dinner and superb chocolate mousse. By highlighting specifics, the writer not only personalizes the letter but also decreases the use of *I*.

Although many goodwill letters and notes are handwritten, they may be printed—particularly if your handwriting is poor.

MESSAGES OF CONGRATULATION

Messages of congratulation deliver recognition for a special event, such as a promotion, appointment, award, graduation, or significant honour. They also mark per-

FIGURE 10.2

Appreciation for Favour

SUCCESS COLLEGE

40 Red Oak Lane
Windsor, ON   N5L 2T4

February 18, 200x

Ms. Ellen D'Sousa, Manager
Information Support Services
Atlas Labs
6398 Darien Boulevard
Windsor, ON N4H 1E7

Dear Ms. D'Sousa:

Your excellent guided tour of the Communications Services Centre at Atlas Labs was the highlight of the term for our class.

Your lucid description of the Centre's operations and equipment enabled our business communication class to better understand some of the technology being used in this field. We very much appreciated learning how work groups compose and edit reports using software to keep track of individual comments and multiple versions of report drafts. Equally interesting was your explanation and demonstration of desktop videoconferencing. Your careful preparation for our group and your painstaking organization of the tour schedule allowed our class to see numerous operations in a short time. Many students commented on your enthusiastic and knowledgeable presentation.

Our trip to Atlas was entertaining and instructive. We enjoyed the modern interior design, the "urban Eden" of indoor plants and trees, the colourful artwork and furniture, and the lovely employee lounges. Most important, though, we appreciated your tour because it helped bridge the gap between classroom information and real-world applications in the field of communications. On behalf of our entire class, I thank you.

Sincerely,

Robin A. Gottesman

Robin A. Gottesman
Student, Communication 202 Class

c Mr. Raymond T. LaManna
  Vice President, Information Services

Opens with enthusiastic appreciation for favour.

Recalls details and specifics for personal touch.

Summarizes and highlights most important reason for appreciation.

---

sonal events, such as an engagement, marriage, anniversary, or birth. These messages should contain warmth, approval, and praise. Avoid mechanical phrases such as *Congratulations on your promotion. You certainly deserve it.* Try to include personal references and specific details that make your thoughts different from the bland and generalized expressions in greeting cards. Often brief and conversational, congratulatory letters may be handwritten or keyboarded. If a news clipping announced the good news, it's a nice touch to attach the article to your congratulatory letter. Smart managers know that they can lift employee morale with recognition in the form of awards, words of encouragement, and notes, such as the following memo congratulating an employee on her promotion.

FIGURE 10.3

Ineffective and Effective Appreciations of Hospitality

Fails to name event. ——

Vagueness suggests little thought went into message. ——

Ineffective

Dear Professor and Mrs. Brighton:

I want to thank you very much for inviting me. It was great.

I know everyone else enjoyed it as much as I did. I certainly appreciate your invitation.

Sincerely,

John Courchene

Effective

4029 Lewiston Drive
Brandon, MB R4H 2L4
May 12, 200x

Professor Cliff Brighton and Mrs. Anne Brighton
340 Overlook Avenue
Brandon, MB R4L 3T1

Dear Professor and Mrs. Brighton:

Thanks for inviting the other members of our business club and me to your home for dinner last Saturday.

The warm reception you gave us made the evening very special. Your gracious hospitality, the delicious trout dinner and that superb chocolate mousse, and the lively discussion following dinner all served to create an enjoyable evening that I will long remember. Perhaps we did not resolve the issue of exorbitant executive salaries, but we certainly thrashed it out.

I appreciate the opportunity you provided for us students to become better acquainted with each other and with you.

Cordially,

John Courchene

John Courchene

Quckly identifies reason for thanks.

Personalizes thank you with specifics.

Tells why hospitality was important to writer.

TO: Pam Peterson   DATE: January 25, 200x
FROM: Robert Buckley
SUBJECT: CONGRATULATIONS!

Your promotion to the position of supervisor of Document Services, Pam, is wonderful news! It seems only yesterday that you were an inexperienced part-time assistant who came to my office with excellent skills, bubbling enthusiasm, and a desire to succeed.

We missed you when you left our department, but we take great pride in your accomplishments and wish you every success in your new position.

Congratulations should be sent promptly, and they should focus on the reader.

MESSAGES OF SYMPATHY

Grief is easier to bear when we know others care. Whatever the misfortune, show your concern with sympathetic words. Depending on the situation, express the loss that you feel, console the reader, and extend your willingness to help in any way possible. You'll want to recognize virtues in the loved one and assure the reader that he or she is not alone in this unhappy moment. If you need ideas regarding what to say in a message of sympathy, examine the model here. Inspiration can also be gleaned from the thoughts expressed in commercially prepared cards. Study the cards, adopt some of the ideas, and then write your own individual message. The handwritten note in Figure 10.4 shows a note written by a manager to an administrative assistant who lost her husband.

A letter of sympathy should console the reader, point out virtues in the loved one, and express willingness to help.

FIGURE 10.4

Message of Sympathy

Dear Jane,

We were deeply saddened to learn of your loss. Although words are seldom adequate to express sympathy, I want you to know that I count myself among your many friends who share your grief and understand the profound loss that you are experiencing.

Henry's kind nature, his patience, and his devotion to you were apparent to all. He will be missed. If there is any way that we may ease your sorrow, you know that we are here and eager to assist.

Sincerely,

Christopher

SPECIAL INFORMATION LETTERS

A group of special information letters that you may be expected to write as a businessperson includes messages that ask for or offer recommendations. Other special messages include form and guide letters. All these letters employ the direct strategy and the same emphasis on specifics that you learned in writing goodwill messages.

FIGURE 10.5

Letter Requesting Recommendation

3219 Crest Hill Drive
Medicine Hat, AB T1A 0P8
May 19, 200x

Professor Pat McMahon
Western School of Business and Technology
1580 South Drive
Medicine Hat, AB T2L 3E9

Dear Professor McMahon:

Opens with compliment and explanation.

Your course in office information technology was my introduction to the field, and your instruction provided an excellent background in this career area. Because you know this field well and because you also know my work as a student, may I use your name as a reference when I apply for employment?

Provides information to help reader comply with request.

As I will complete my course work at Western School of Business and Technology in June, I will be looking for employment shortly. Being able to list your name as a reference would assist my efforts greatly. Enclosed is a fact sheet listing information that may be helpful to you when you write about me.

Expresses appeciation and supplies postcard for quick reply.

I am grateful to you for the excellent foundation you provided in office technology and for any help you can provide in my job search. Please indicate your willingness to serve as a reference by mailing the enclosed postage-paid card.

Sincerely yours,

Natalie Kienzler

Natalie Kienzler

Enclosures

LETTERS REQUESTING RECOMMENDATION

When you apply for employment, for admission to special programs, or for acceptance to some social organizations, you may need to request letters of recommendation.

Always ask permission before listing someone as a reference.

Naturally, before you list anyone as a reference, you will ask for permission. This is not only courteous but also prudent. By offering the opportunity to accept or refuse, you can find individuals who will write favourable recommendations.

A letter asking for permission to list an instructor as a reference, such as that shown in Figure 10.5, should be persuasive. Notice that the writer provides explanations and kind words before announcing her request. The writer also makes it easy for the receiver to agree to the request by including an addressed postcard.

If an instructor or someone else agrees to write a recommendation, you can assist that person by supplying a résumé, data sheet, or fact sheet. If you know the position for which you are applying, furnish specifics about what the job requires and what you would like the recommender to cover. Your recommender wants to help you succeed. Give that person details about the job requirements and your qualifications. For example, if the job description states "must have strong interpersonal skills and excellent written and oral communication skills," tell your recommenders of these specifications. Also provide concrete examples explaining how you feel that you meet the specifications so that your recommenders can write a targeted recommendation.

Help your recommender by supplying data about the job and about you.

LETTERS OF RECOMMENDATION

A letter of recommendation evaluates an individual. Recommendations may be written to nominate people for awards and for membership in organizations. Most often, however, they are written by employers to appraise the performance of current or past employees. As you progress in your career into supervisory and management roles, you can expect to write such recommendations.

You'll be expected to write recommendations as you progress in your career.

Writers of recommendations, of course, must be truthful. Even though recommendations are expected to show an applicant in a positive way, they should not be false or deceptive. Nor should they be discriminatory. The accompanying box, "Danger Zone: Letters of Recommendation," describes some of the problems and provides specific guidelines that every business writer should follow.

If you decide to write a letter of recommendation for a job applicant, ask the candidate to supply you with personal and professional information. Request a data sheet or a résumé, and ask what information the applicant wants emphasized.

Recommendations often have three parts: opening, body, and conclusion. In the opening of an employment recommendation, you should give the name of the candidate and the position sought, if it is known. State that your remarks are confidential, and suggest that you are writing at the request of the applicant. Describe your relationship with the candidate, as shown here:

The opening of a recommendation names the candidate, states that the message is confidential, and describes your relationship.

> Mr. Wai Leung, whom your organization is considering for the position of media trainer, requested that I submit confidential information on his behalf. Mr. Leung worked under my supervision for the past two years in our Video Training Centre.

Letters that recommend individuals for awards may open with more supportive statements, such as *I'm very pleased to nominate Robert Walsh for the Employee-of-the-Month award. For the past sixteen months, Mr. Walsh served as staff accountant in my division. During that time he distinguished himself by . . .*

The body of an employment recommendation letter should describe the applicant's job performance and characteristics. Employers are particularly interested in such traits as communication, organizational, and people skills. They're also eager for comments about ability to work both with a team and independently, honesty, dependability, ambition, loyalty, and initiative. In describing these traits, though, be sure to back them up with evidence. One of the biggest weaknesses in letters of recommendation is that writers tend to make global, nonspecific statements *(He was careful and accurate* versus *He completed eight financial statements monthly with about 99 percent accuracy).* Employers prefer definite, task-related descriptions:

The body describes the applicant's job performance and employment traits.

Danger Zone: Letters of Recommendation

Many companies today are making sure their managers know how to write equitable, nondiscriminatory recommendation letters. Employers know that discriminatory letters of recommendation could damage reputations, prevent employees from gaining employment, and result in a complaint to the Human Rights Commission. Managers are learning to include only information that is clearly related to the job performed, such as dates of employment, positions held, and measurable successes and failures.

The Canadian Human Rights Commission defines discrimination as treating people differently, negatively, or adversely without a good reason. Discrimination also means making a distinction about an individual based on prohibited grounds, of which the Commission describes 12: race, national or ethnic origin, colour, religion, age, sex (including pregnancy and childbirth), marital status, family status, mental or physical disability (including previous or present drug or alcohol dependence), pardoned conviction, or sexual orientation.

Even if your intention is to be supportive, comments referring to prohibited grounds are illegal. Notice how the following statements are reworded to remove the prohibited references:

Avoid: Miriam Gunther, recently arrived from Germany, quickly became an important addition to our staff.

Improved: Miriam Gunther started with us June 5, 1998, and quickly became an important addition to our staff.

Avoid: Once Wendy had her second child, her work really improved.

Improved: In her last six months, Wendy's number of returns dropped by 30 percent.

Avoid: Even though Bill is gay, he had no trouble fitting in with the other staff.

Improved: Bill communicated his ideas effectively to other staff.

Businesspeople today recognize the importance of conveying personnel information in a positive, bias-free way. They know that accurate, equitable recommendation letters provide a service to both employee and employer. Yet, those who write recommendation letters are cautious, fearing the charge that the letter is unfair—that it, for example, withholds information about a prospective employee's flaws, exaggerates his or her positive qualities, or unintentionally defames her or his character by telling only a partial truth. The following guidelines can help you write effective, fair recommendation letters:

- **Write only in response to requests.** Don't volunteer information, particularly if it's negative.
- **Omit discriminatory remarks.** Leave out any and all comments regarding race, nationality, religion, and sexual orientation.
- **Provide only job-related information.** Avoid commenting on behaviour or activities away from the job.
- **Avoid vague or ambiguous statements.** Imprecise or poorly explained remarks (she left the job suddenly) may be made innocently but could be interpreted quite differently.
- **Supply specific evidence for any negatives.** Support any damaging information with verifiable facts.
- **Stick to the truth.** Avoid making any doubtful statements.

As a training development specialist, Mr. Leung demonstrated superior organizational and interpersonal skills. He started as a Specialist I, writing scripts for interactive video modules. After six months he was promoted to team leader. In that role he supervised five employees who wrote, produced, evaluated, revised, and installed 14 computer/videodisc training courses over a period of eighteen months.

Be especially careful to support any negative comments with verification (not *He was slower than other customer service reps* but *He answered 25 calls an hour, while most service reps average 40 calls an hour*). In reporting deficiencies be sure to describe behaviour *(Her last two reports were late and had to be rewritten by her supervisor)* rather than evaluate it *(She is unreliable and her work is careless)*.

Examples should accompany any negative comments.

In the final paragraph of a letter of recommendation, you should offer an overall evaluation. Indicate how you would rank this person in relation to others in similar positions. Many managers add a statement indicating whether they would rehire the applicant, given the chance. If you are strongly supportive, summarize the candidate's best qualities. In the closing you might also offer to answer questions by telephone. Such a statement, though, could suggest that the candidate has weak skills and that you will make damaging statements orally but not in print. Here's how our sample letter might close:

Provide an overall evaluation in the conclusion.

Mr. Leung is one of the most productive employees I have supervised. I would rank him in the top 10 percent of all the media specialists with whom I have worked. Were he to return to Bridgeport, we would be pleased to rehire him. If you need additional information, call me at (517) 443-9902.

General letters of recommendation, written when the candidate has no specific position in mind, often begin with the salutation *TO PROSPECTIVE EMPLOYERS*. More specific recommendations, to support applications to known positions, address an individual. When the addressee's name is unknown, consider using the simplified letter format, shown in Figure 10.6, which avoids a salutation.

Figure 10.6 illustrates a complete letter of recommendation for employment. After naming the applicant and the position sought, the letter describes the applicant's present duties. Instead of merely naming positive qualities *(personable, superior people skills, works well with a team, and creative)*, the writer demonstrates these attributes with specific examples and details.

The following list summarizes suggestions for writing effective letters of recommendation for employment. Notice how many of these items are covered in the letter of recommendation in Figure 10.6.

- Identify the reason for writing.
- Suggest the confidentiality of the recommendation.
- Establish your relationship with the applicant.
- Identify the length of employment and job duties, if relevant.
- Describe the applicant's professional and personal qualities.
- Describe the applicant's relations with others.
- Include specific details and examples that illustrate the applicant's personality and performance.
- Compare the applicant with others in his or her field.
- Offer an overall rating of the applicant.
- Summarize the significant attributes of the applicant.
- Draw a conclusion regarding the recommendation.

FIGURE 10.6

Letter of Recommendation for Employment—Simplified Style

St. Elizabeth's Hospital
423 Clark Street
London, ON N6G 3R5

January 9, 200x

Director, Human Resources
Health Services Centre
5440 Memorial Boulevard
Toronto, ON M5A 2T4

RECOMMENDATION OF TANI PUROHIT

At the request of Tani Purohit, I submit this confidential information in support of her application for the position of assistant director of your Human Resources Department. Ms. Purohit served under my supervision as assistant director of Patient Relations at St. Elizabeth's Hospital for the past four years.

Ms. Purohit was in charge of many patient service programs for our 550-bed hospital. A large part of her job involved monitoring and improving patient satisfaction. Because of her personable nature and superior people skills, she got along well with fellow employees, patients, and physicians. Her personnel record includes a number of "Gotcha" citations, given to employees caught in the act of performing exemplary service.

Ms. Purohit works well with a team, as evidenced by her participation on the steering committee to develop our "Service First Every Day" program. Her most significant contributions to our hospital, though, came as a result of her own creativity and initiative. She developed and implemented a patient hotline to hear complaints and resolve problems immediately. This enormously successful telephone service helped us improve our patient satisfaction rating from 7.2 last year to 8.4 this year. That's the highest rating in our history, and Ms. Purohit deserves a great deal of the credit.

We're sorry to lose Ms. Purohit, but we recognize her desire to advance her career. I am confident that her resourcefulness, intelligence, and enthusiasm will make her successful in your organization. I recommend her without reservation.

Suzanne M. Lindsey

SUZANNE M. LINDSEY, SUPERVISOR, PATIENT RELATIONS
SML:egi

Identifies applicant, cites confidentiality, and explains relationship of writer.

Supports general qualities with specific details.

Describes and interprets accomplishments.

Summarizes main points and offers evaluation.

FORM AND GUIDE LETTERS

Form letters are prewritten, printed messages used to deliver repetitious and routine information. To save the expense of composing, evaluating, revising, and printing individual letters, many organizations prepare standardized form letters for recurring situations.

Form letters contain blanks to be filled in.

Form letters can be personalized with blanks for such variables as names and addresses, dates, balances, and other specific data. These letters are efficient for sales messages, personnel policy announcements, procedural explanations for customers and suppliers, order acknowledgments, and other repetitive information.

Guide letters use prewritten sentences and paragraphs. Insurance companies, for example, send thousands of guide letters to policyholders to answer routine questions regarding their coverage. Rather than compose individual responses, company representatives select appropriate paragraphs from a database of ready-made answers and use word processing software to organize these paragraphs to form a letter.

Form and guide letters unquestionably save time and money. Well-written, repetitive messages used appropriately are expedient and accepted by readers. Poorly written or misused letters, on the other hand, are doubly offensive. Readers' feelings are hurt because they are treated mechanically, and they are also confused because a letter did not apply to them or did not answer their questions.

When used properly, form and guide letters are efficient and cost-effective.

Word processing software makes the preparation and processing of form and guide letters simple. If you decide to use this means of delivering messages, follow these guidelines:

- Be certain that your form and guide letters are appropriate to the situation for which they will be used.
- Compose your letters so that they are responsive and yet require insertion of a minimum number of variables.
- Test your form and guide letters over a long period to see if they are effective.
- Revise your letters based on reader reactions.

Personalized form letters, such as that shown in Figure 10.7, can be tailored to individual circumstances by inserting variable data in the places provided. Word processing software merges a shell or main document with variable data to produce individually printed letters quickly and economically.

SUMMING UP AND LOOKING FORWARD

Goodwill and special messages can be among the most important that you write because they build solid relationships with employees, clients, and suppliers. To be effective, they should be written immediately, sound sincere, and include specifics about the reader. Letters of recommendation should describe performance objectively and be honest. Form and guide letters are special messages that deliver routine, repetitious information. They can save time and effort for companies, but each one must be written carefully so that it is responsive to the situation.

Now that you have completed your instruction in writing letters and memos, you're ready to learn about writing reports. Chapter 11 introduces informal reports, and Chapter 12 discusses formal reports.

DISCUSSION

1. Why do we frequently put off writing goodwill letters?
2. Why write a letter of sympathy or congratulation when a greeting card would accomplish the same end?
3. How are goodwill messages important to a manager's career?
4. Why should an applicant ask permission before listing an individual's name as a reference?
5. As a means of screening candidates, are letters of recommendation a valid source of information?

FIGURE 10.7

Personalized Form Letter——Block Style

Word processing software enables you to merge main document with mailing list.

Variable data fields provide individual information for each message.

CONNECTIONS INTERNATIONAL
1821 Ferry Road, Fredericton, NB E3B 2L4
Voice: (506) 455-9328 FAX: (506) 458-3321

{Current date}

{Title} {First name} {Last name}
{Street address}
{City} , {Province} {Postal code}

Dear {Title} {Last name}:

We appreciate your interest in our Canadian Studies program offered to Japanese students. The enclosed pamphlet describes the program in detail and shows pictures of students who have participated in the past.

In brief, our organization, Connections International, supplies transportation, tours, and cultural/social programs for Japanese students coming to Canada to study the English or French language and Canadian business and culture.

Our next group is scheduled to arrive {date}, and the tentative cost is {price} per student per week. This payment covers transportation, travel, and entertainment as outlined in the enclosed pamphlet. An advance payment of {deposit} is required at least three weeks before departure. This deposit is necessary to set the program in operation, retain proper vehicles, and make necessary hotel and lodging reservations. The amount will be deducted from the total payment for the group.

Thank you very much for considering the cultural immersion programs of Connections International. We look forward to providing warm and rewarding experiences for your students.

Sincerely yours,

CONNECTIONS INTERNATIONAL

Melissa M. Hashimoto
Senior Coordinator

Enclosure

CHAPTER REVIEW

6. In goodwill messages the writer typically follows the direct strategy and includes what in the opening, body, and close?

7. Name three instances when letters of appreciation are appropriate.

8. Why should a copy of a letter of appreciation be sent to an employee's supervisor?

9. What four kinds of information or topics can you include in a letter of sympathy?

10. Name three instances when letters of recommendation, other than for employment, might be written.

11. What six guidelines can help you stay out of dangerous territory in writing employment letters of recommendation?

12. List eleven suggestions regarding information to be included in a letter of recommendation.

13. How can the writer of a letter of recommendation avoid generalities?

14. When are form letters useful?

15. Name four guidelines for preparing the most helpful form and guide letters.

ACTIVITIES AND CASES

10.1 Employment Recommendation: Sorry to See You Go. Assume that you are Ross Neil, manager of Builder's City. Alan B. Khory, one of your favourite department managers, has now completed his college diploma and will be leaving the store. Mr. Khory asks you to write a recommendation for him to enter a management trainee program for a large retailer. You know that he is a quiet, unassertive individual; but he has been an excellent hardware manager for you these past three years.

Mr. Khory started as a clerk and became department manager at the Wadena store within six months, while at the same time working toward a college diploma. His department has five employees. He solved some problems within his department, which increased sales and, of course, increased profits. His department integrated the new computerized inventory system into its operations long before some others.

You feel that Mr. Khory has been one of your most enterprising and responsible department managers. In your letter you want to show that he has those traits that are necessary to be a good manager. Although you want to show that Mr. Khory demonstrates initiative and problem-solving abilities, you feel that you should also mention that Mr. Khory is quiet. But, you will add, he gets along well both with customers and with those employees that he supervises.

Before you begin writing this letter of recommendation, outline a plan. The information presented here is unorganized and poorly expressed. Improve it. Add any realistic data necessary to create a good letter. Conclude your letter with a statement regarding the potential success of Mr. Khory. Use block style. Address your letter to Ms. Jane Bennett, Director, Human Resource Services, Federated Stores Inc., 390 Portage Avenue, Winnipeg, MB R3H 2E3.

10.2 Letter of Appreciation: Thanks for Your Care. You are genuinely appreciative of the care shown by Robert Chu, R.N., for your bedridden mother over the past two years. You decide to send him a box of chocolates and a letter that expresses your gratitude and also lets his employer know what an outstanding employee he is.

Here are some facts you should include in your letter. Nurse Chu not only took care of your mother's medical needs but also taught you how to care for your mother. He was enthusiastic and always had lots of cheerful conversation; everyone felt better when he visited. He made suggestions and even gave you demonstrations of professional techniques for easing your mother's discomfort. The entire family appreciated Mr. Chu's compassion and concern for your mother. He visited for two years. During that time your mother's condition improved, and now it has stabilized. You feel that he is an extraordinary nurse and an excellent representative of his employer, HomeCare Inc.

Write the letter to Robert Chu, R.N., HomeCare Inc., 2310 Eglinton Avenue E., Scarborough, Ontario M2W 3E6. Use modified block style. Add any necessary information. Be sure that his employer, Dr. Chandler H. Alexander, President, HomeCare Inc., is informed of your praise.

10.3 Letter of Sympathy: For a Friend. Assume that the spouse of a colleague or friend has died. Write a letter of sympathy. Include enough detail to make your letter significantly different from greeting card messages.

10.4 Letter of Appreciation: For Your Boss. Write a letter of appreciation to your boss (supervisor, manager, vice president, president, or chief executive officer) and his or her spouse. Assume that you and other members of your immediate staff were entertained at an elegant dinner during the winter holiday season. Include specific details that make your letter personal, sincere, and concrete.

10.5 Request for Recommendation: For You. Write to an instructor or a previous employer asking for permission to use that individual as a reference.

10.6 Letter of Recommendation: By You. You are about to leave your present job. When you ask your boss for a letter of recommendation, to your surprise he tells you to write it yourself and then have him sign it. [Actually, this is not an unusual practice today. Many businesspeople find that employees are very perceptive and accurate when they evaluate themselves.] Use specifics from a current or previous job. If you have not worked, interview a fellow student. Assume that you are the student's instructor; write a letter of recommendation for the student.

10.7 Letter of Appreciation: Thanks for Speaking. As program chair of the Women in Business Association (see Chapter 9, Activity 9.6), you must send a thank-you letter to Ms. Joann R. Schulz, President, NBR Industries, 3450 West 16th Avenue, Vancouver, BC V1N 3E5. She gave the keynote address at your annual conference on April 14 in Toronto. Provide details. Send her a copy of the Women in Business Association's *Entrepreneur News,* in which a story about her appeared, along with a picture of her delivering her speech before your group.

10.8 Letter of Congratulation: For Employee. Shinya Ouchi, a part-time worker in the Human Resources Department for the past three years, has just completed the requirements for a bachelor's degree in computer science. As manager of the department, write him a letter of congratulations. Although he will probably be leaving, you are very happy for him.

10.9 Letter of Recommendation: For Employee. As office manager of the law firm of Ernst, Katz, and Ernst, you have been asked to write a letter describing the service of Wendy White, who is moving to another city with her husband. Wendy has been a fine legal secretary, and you are happy to accommodate her. Since she has not asked you to address the letter to a specific individual, write an undirected letter of recommendation.

10.10 Letter of Appreciation: To Instructor. After finishing the course of instruction at your school, you have taken a job in your field. One of your instructors was especially helpful to you when you were a student. This instructor also wrote an effective letter that was instrumental in helping you obtain your job. Write a letter thanking your instructor.

10.11 Form Letter: To Students. Write a personalized form letter to selected students at your school. These students have filled out applications to graduate, but a computer search of their records indicates that they are missing some requirements. Leave a blank space to fill in the missing requirement(s). Tell these students that a mistake may have been made; perhaps their records have an error or are not up to date. Regardless, the students must come in for a conference with a records officer. Since time is limited, the conferences have already been scheduled. Leave a blank space for the date of the conference to be filled in for each student.

10.12 Connecting with E-Mail: Letter of Recommendation. One of your instructors has been nominated for a teaching award. Selected students have been asked to write letters in support of the nomination. However, the deadline for submitting the letters is just one day away. Thus, the chairperson of the teaching committee asks you to send your recommendation by e-mail, with a hard copy to follow later. Write an e-mail message recommending an instructor of your choice. Send it to your instructor.

10.13 Searching the Internet: *Globe and Mail's Report on Business.* You are the editor/publisher of a newsletter for accounting firms. You provide the major articles and interesting items, but each firm puts its name on your newsletter and circulates it among its clients for advertising and promotion purposes. You're always looking for sources of articles and tidbits of news that would fill your pages. Jeffrey Cohen, one of the CAs subscribing to your service, suggests that you take a look at the *Globe and Mail's Report on Business* Web site. You do, and you find useful articles and financial information for your newsletter. Write a letter of appreciation to Jeffrey Cohen, Suite 201, 7041 South Street, Lethbridge AB T1K 2E3. Be sure to visit the *Globe and Mail's Report on Business* Web site and check out the "Money and Markets" information so that you will have details to describe.

Related Web site: www.globeandmail.ca/lmanual/robhub.html

GRAMMAR/MECHANICS CHECKUP—10

Possessives

Review Sections 2.20–2.22 in the Grammar/Mechanics Handbook. Then study each of the following statements. Underscore any inappropriate form. Write a correction in the space provided and record the number of the G/M principle(s) illustrated. If a sentence is correct, write *C*. When you finish, compare your responses with those provided. If your answers differ, study carefully the principles shown in parentheses.

years'   (2.20b)   **Example:** In just two <u>years</u> time, the accountants and managers devised an entirely new system.

_____ 1. Two supervisors said that Mr. Wilsons work was excellent.
_____ 2. In less than a years time, the offices of both lawyers were moved.
_____ 3. None of the employees in our Electronics Department had taken more than two weeks vacation.
_____ 4. All the secretaries agreed that Ms. Lanhams suggestions were practicable.
_____ 5. After you obtain your boss approval, send the application to Human Resources.
_____ 6. We tried to sit at our favourite waitress station, but all her tables were filled.
_____ 7. Despite Aldo objecting, his wife selected mutual funds not stocks for her investments.
_____ 8. The apartment owner requires two months rent in advance from all applicants.
_____ 9. Four companies buildings were damaged in the fire.
_____ 10. In one months time we hope to be able to complete all the address files.
_____ 11. Only one womans car had its engine running.

12. One secretaries desk will have to be moved to make way for the computer.
13. Several sellers permits were issued for two years.
14. Marks salary was somewhat higher than David.
15. Lisas job in accounts receivable ends in two months.

_____

1. Mr. Wilson's (2.20a)   3. weeks' (2.20b)   5. boss's (2.20b)   7. Aldo's (2.22)   9. companies'
(2.20b)   11. woman's (2.20a)   13. sellers' (2.20b)   15. Lisa's (2.20a)

GRAMMAR MECHANICS CHALLENGE—10

Document for Revision

The following letter has faults in grammar, punctuation, spelling, number form, wordiness, and word use. Use standard proofreading marks (see Appendix B) to correct the errors.

October 4, 200x

Ms. Nathalie Boudreau

Human Resources Department

Travellers Investment Corporation

1010 Overlook Drive

Victoria, BC V1L 2T3

Ineffective Writing

Dear Ms. Boudreau:

This is to inform you that Mr. Darrell Dix who you are considering for a systems' programmer position, ask me to submit confidential information, on his behalf.

I had responsibility for supervision of Mr. Dix for the passed two years, when he worked as a part time computer technician in our computer users centre. In assisting our employees who use computers solve their computing problems; his computer expertise and creativity were demonstrated.

Mr. Dix excepted direction easily, but could also work independent when necessary. For example when I ask him to bring about the organization of our software storage; he did a good job with no supervision whatsoever.

Of all the technicians we have employed Mr. Dix ranks among the top 1/3. Its a pleasure to reccomend him; and I feel certain that he will be successful as a systems programer.

Sincerly,

ARE "SMILEYS" APPROPRIATE FOR BUSINESS E-MAIL MESSAGES?

"Smileys" or emoticons are a kind of visual shorthand used in e-mail to help receivers interpret the tone of a message. Because e-mail messages lack voice inflection and body language, they can easily be misunderstood. That's why senders sometimes add a symbol to express a facial expression.[2] Trouble is, the symbols all face sideways. But once you get used to them, they add a dimension of humour to a message, and they soften what might otherwise result in hard feelings. Created from keyboard characters, they usually follow the punctuation at the end of a sentence.

:-)	Smiling, joking	%-)	Confused but happy
:-(	Frowning, bummer	%-(	Confused, unhappy
;-)	Wink, pun, or sly joke	:`-(	Crying
:-o	Shocked, yelling	:-&	Tongue-tied
:-()	Gabby	:-<	Really upset
:-D	Delighted	8-)	Wide-eyed
:-]	Sarcastic, smirking	>:-)	Devilish

Feeling the need for smileys but not satisfied with the Western symbols, the Japanese have developed their own versions.[3] Theirs are upright and somewhat ambiguous.

(^_^)	Regular smile	(^o^;>)	Excuse me
(^.^)	Girl's smile (mouth closed)		(scratching side of head)
(^o^)	Happy	(^^;)	Cold sweat
(*^o^*)	Excited		

Notice that a sad face is missing? Perhaps to avoid offending, Japanese people rarely use face marks showing anger or sadness. The regular smile is most popular. Why a special symbol for a girl's smile? In Japan it's considered impolite for a woman to show her teeth when smiling; thus the closed-mouth smile is for women.

Admittedly, smileys are fun to use. But some experts think they are inappropriate for business communication. David Angell and Brent Heslop, authors of *The Elements of E-Mail Style*, contend that smileys are the equivalent of e-mail slang and should not be used in formal business e-mail messages.[4]

Application. Compare the Japanese and Western smileys. Are the Japanese symbols an improvement? On either side of the Pacific, do smileys serve an important function in e-mail messages? Why would they be any more necessary for e-mail than for hard-copy messages such as letters or memos? Are they appropriate for any business communication? In an e-mail or hard-copy memo to your instructor, discuss your answers.

UNIT 5

REPORTING DATA

INFORMAL REPORTS

I now create three layers of reports. An extremely detailed one goes to the Board of Directors. The next layer of management receives a version . . . directed more to issues that need resolving. The third report contains inside information of interest to employees and comes with a covering letter. Now these three reports are the cornerstone in [the company's] chemistry. Everyone is informed.[1]

TERENCE H. MATTHEWS, chairman of the board and
CEO, Newbridge Networks Corporation

Learning Objectives

1. Identify seven kinds of informal reports and four report formats.
2. Define a report project and gather data.
3. Organize report data using effective headings.
4. Present data objectively to gain credibility.
5. Write information and recommendation reports.
6. Write justification and progress reports.
7. Write formal and informal minutes of meetings.
8. Write summaries and to-file reports.

> Informal reports are relatively short (under ten pages) and are usually written in memo or letter format.

Companies like Newbridge Networks thrive because of good reports. Terence Matthews makes sure that everyone in his company has the facts presented simply and understandably. Collecting information and organizing it clearly into meaningful reports are skills that all successful businesspeople today require. In this age of information, reports play a significant role in helping decision makers like Terence Matthews solve problems. You can learn to write good reports by examining basic techniques and by analyzing appropriate models. In this chapter we'll concentrate on informal reports. These reports tend to be short (usually under ten pages), personal in tone, and use memo or letter format.

SEVEN KINDS OF INFORMAL REPORTS

> Reports that provide data are informational; reports that draw conclusions and make recommendations are analytical.

We'll consider seven categories of informal reports frequently written in business. In many instances the boundaries of the categories overlap; distinctions are not always clear-cut. Individual situations, goals, and needs may make one report take on some characteristics of a report in another category. Still, these general categories, presented here in a brief overview, are helpful to beginning writers. Later in the chapter the reports will be illustrated and discussed in more detail.

- *Information reports.* Reports that collect and organize information are informative or investigative. They may record routine activities, such as daily, weekly, and monthly reports of sales or profits. They may investigate options, performance, or equipment. Although they provide information, they do not analyze that information.

- *Recommendation reports.* Recommendation reports are similar to informative reports in that they present information. However, they offer analysis in addition to data. They attempt to solve problems by evaluating options and offering recommendations. These reports are solicited; that is, the writer has been asked to investigate and report.
- *Justification reports.* Like recommendation reports, justification reports attempt to solve problems. However, they are unsolicited; that is, the writer generates the report on his or her own. She or he observes a problem, analyzes alternatives, and describes a potential solution.
- *Progress reports.* Progress reports monitor the headway of unusual or non-routine activities. For example, progress reports would keep management informed about a committee's preparations for a trade fair 14 months from now. Such reports usually answer three questions: (1) Is the project on schedule? (2) Are corrective measures needed? (3) What activities are next?
- *Minutes of meetings.* A record of the proceedings of a meeting is called "the minutes." This record is generally kept by the designated meeting secretary. Minutes may be kept for groups that convene regularly, such as the monthly meeting of a club, or for groups that meet irregularly, such as committees.
- *Summaries.* A summary condenses the primary ideas, conclusions, and recommendations of a longer report or publication. Employees may be asked to write summaries of technical reports. Students may be asked to write summaries of periodical articles or books to sharpen their writing skills.
- *To-file reports.* Reports prepared to document an idea or action are called "to-file" reports. These useful reports provide a written record of conversations, directives, and decisions. In today's often complex business world, such reports are becoming increasingly important.

REPORT FORMATS

How should a report look? The following four formats are frequently used.

- *Letter format* is appropriate for informal reports prepared by one organization for another. These reports are much like letters except that they are more carefully organized, using headings and lists where appropriate.
- *Memo format* is common for informal reports written for circulation within an organization. These internal reports follow the conventions of memos that you learned in Chapter 5—with the addition of headings.
- *Report format* is used for longer and somewhat more formal reports. Printed on plain paper (instead of letterhead or memo forms), these reports begin with a title followed by carefully displayed headings and subheadings. (For an illustration of report format, see Figure 11.7, which shows the formal minutes of a meeting.)
- *Prepared forms* are useful in reporting routine activities, such as police arrest reports or merchandise inventories. Standardized headings on these forms save time for the writer; forms also make similar information easy to locate.

Today's reports and other business documents are far more sophisticated than the typewritten documents of the past. If you've worked with a computer and a laser printer, you know how easy it is to make your documents look as if they were professionally printed. In fact, reports are no longer typed; today, they are designed. You must learn to use type sizes, fonts, margins, and a host of word processing capabilities to fashion attractive documents. The accompanying box, "Ten Tips for Designing Better Documents," offers suggestions to make sure you avoid common traps.

GUIDELINES FOR WRITING INFORMAL REPORTS

DEFINING THE PROJECT

Begin a report by formulating a statement of purpose: Why are you writing this report?

Begin the process of report writing by defining your project. This definition should include a statement of purpose. Ask yourself: Am I writing this report to inform, to analyze, to solve a problem, or to persuade? The answer to this question should be a clear, accurate statement identifying your purpose. In informal reports the statement of purpose may be only one sentence; that sentence usually becomes part of the introduction. Notice how the following introductory statement describes the purpose of the report:

> This report presents data regarding in-service training activities coordinated and supervised by the Human Resources Department between the first of the year and the present.

After writing a statement of purpose, analyze who will read your report. If your report is intended for your immediate supervisors and they are supportive of your project, you need not include extensive details, historical development, definition of terms, or persuasion. Other readers, however, may require background data and persuasive strategies.

The expected audience for your report influences your writing style, your research method, your vocabulary, your areas of emphasis, and your communication strategy. Remember, too, that your audience may consist of more than one set of readers. Reports are often distributed to secondary readers who may need more details than the primary reader.

Ten Tips for Designing Better Documents

Desktop publishing packages, word processing programs, and laser printers now make it possible for you to turn out professional-looking documents. The temptation, though, is to overdo it by incorporating too many features in one document. Here are ten tips for applying good sense and good design principles in "publishing" your documents:

- **Analyze your audience**. Sales brochures and promotional letters can be flashy—with colour print, oversized type, and fancy borders—to attract attention. But such effects are out of place for most conservative business documents. Also consider whether your readers will be reading painstakingly or merely browsing. Lists and headings help those readers who are in a hurry.

- **Choose an appropriate type size**. For most business memos, letters, and reports, the body text should be 10 to 12 points. Larger type looks amateurish, and smaller type is hard to read.
- **Use a consistent type font**. Although your software may provide a variety of fonts, stay with a single family of type within one document—at least until you become more expert. The most popular fonts are Times Roman and Helvetica. For emphasis and contrast, you may vary the font size and weight with **bold**, *italic*, ***bold italic***, and other selections.
- **Generally, don't justify right margins**. Textbooks, novels, newspapers, magazines, and other long works are usually set with justified (even) right margins. However, for shorter works ragged-right margins are recommended because such margins add white space and help readers locate the beginnings of new lines. Slower readers find ragged-right copy more legible.
- **Separate paragraphs and sentences appropriately**. The first line of a paragraph should be indented or preceded by a blank line. To separate sentences, typists have traditionally left two spaces. This spacing is still acceptable for most business documents. If you are preparing a newsletter or brochure, however, you may wish to adopt printers' standards, leaving one space after end punctuation.
- **Design readable headlines**. Presenting headlines and headings in all caps is generally discouraged because solid blocks of capital letters interfere with recognition of word patterns. To further improve readability, select a sans serif typeface (one without cross strokes or embellishment), such as Helvetica.

- **Strive for an attractive page layout**. In designing title pages or visual aids, provide for a balance between print and white space. Also consider placing the focal point (something that draws the reader's eye) at the optical centre of a page—about three lines above the actual centre. Moreover, remember that the average reader scans a page from left to right and top to bottom in a Z pattern. Plan your visuals accordingly. Most word processing software includes templates and wizards to help in the design of attractive title pages.
- **Use graphics and clip art with restraint**. Images such as drawings, photographs, and clip art can easily be imported into documents. Spreadsheets, organization charts, and flow charts can also be created and inserted into documents. Use such images, however, only when they are well drawn, relevant, and purposeful.
- **Avoid amateurish results**. Many beginning writers, eager to display every graphic device a program offers, produce busy, cluttered documents. Too many typefaces, ruled lines, oversized headlines, and images will overwhelm readers. Strive for simple, clean, and forceful effects.
- **Develop expertise**. Learn to use the templates, wizards, and other page layout features of your current word processing software. Or you could investigate desktop publishing programs such as Corel Ventura or Adobe PageMaker. These programs help you produce professional-looking documents, newsletters, brochures, announcements, and promotional literature. Graphic designers create graphics from scratch using programs like CorelDraw or Adobe PhotoShop. Although the learning curve for many of these programs is steep, such effort is well spent if you need to extend the graphics or layout capabilities of your word processing software.

GATHERING DATA

The facts for reports
are often obtained
from company
records, observation,
surveys, interviews,
and research.

A good report is based on solid, accurate, verifiable facts. Typical sources of factual information for informal reports include (1) company records; (2) observation; (3) surveys, questionnaires, and inventories; (4) interviews; and (5) research.

Company Records. Many business-related reports begin with analysis of company records and files. From these records you can observe past performance and methods used to solve previous problems. You can collect pertinent facts that will help determine a course of action.

Observation. Another logical source of data for many problems lies in personal observation and experience. For example, if you were writing a report on the need for additional computer equipment, you might observe how much the current equipment is being used and for what purpose.

Surveys, Questionnaires, and Inventories. Data from groups of people can be collected most efficiently and economically by using surveys, questionnaires, and inventories. For example, if you were part of a committee investigating the success of a campus recycling program, you might begin by using a questionnaire to survey use of the program by students and faculty.

Interviews. Talking with individuals directly concerned with the problem produces excellent first-hand information. Interviews also allow for one-on-one communication, thus giving you an opportunity to explain your questions and ideas while eliciting the most accurate information.

Electronic and Other Research. An extensive source of current and historical information is available electronically through computer databases and other on-line resources. From a home, office, or library computer you can obtain access to vast amounts of information provided by governments, newspapers, magazines, and companies from all over the world. Be careful, though: searching through the massive amounts of electronic information available can be time consuming. For short, informal reports the most usable data will probably be found in periodicals. Chapter 12 contains more detailed suggestions about using on-line resources such as the Internet and especially the World Wide Web.

DETERMINING ORGANIZATION

Like correspondence, reports may be organized inductively (indirectly) or deductively (directly). Placement of the main idea (recommendations or conclusions) is delayed in the inductive approach. Figures 11.1 and 11.2 show the same material for a report organized two different ways.

In Figures 11.1 and 11.2 you find only the skeleton of facts representing a complex problem. However, you can see the effects of organization. The inductive approach brings the reader through the entire process of analyzing a problem. It mirrors our method of thinking: problem, facts, analysis, recommendation. As you learned earlier, this strategy is successful when persuasion is necessary. It's also useful when the reader lacks knowledge and must be informed. However, busy executives

FIGURE 11.1

Inductive Organization

Inadequate student parking on campus during prime class times.	Problem
10,000 permits sold for 3000 parking spaces; some parking lots unusable in bad weather; large numbers of visitors without permits fill parking spaces; no land for new lots.	Facts
Carpool? Try shuttles from distant parking lots? Enforce current regulations more strictly? Charge premium for parking in prime locations or during prime times? Build multistorey parking structures? Restrict visitors?	Discussion
Short-term: begin shuttle program. Long-term: solicit funds for improving current lots and building new multistorey structures.	Recommendations

FIGURE 11.2

Deductive Organization

Inadequate student parking on campus during prime class times.	Problem
Short-term: begin shuttle program. Long-term: solicit funds for improving current lots and building new multistorey structures.	Recommendations
10,000 permits sold for 3000 parking spaces; some lots unusable in bad weather; large numbers of visitors without permits fill spaces; no land for new lots.	Facts
Carpool? Try shuttles from distant parking lots? Enforce current regulations more strictly? Charge premium for parking in prime locations or during prime times? Build multistorey parking structures? Restrict visitors?	Discussion

or readers already familiar with the problem may want to get to the point more quickly.

The deductive approach is more direct; recommendations and conclusions are presented first so that readers have a frame of reference for reading the discussion and analysis that follow. Business reports are commonly organized deductively. Analyze your audience and purpose to determine the best overall strategy.

> The difference between the inductive and the deductive strategy is the placement of conclusions and recommendations.

USING EFFECTIVE HEADINGS

Good headings are helpful to both the report reader and the writer. For the reader they serve as an outline of the text, highlighting major ideas and categories. They also act as guides for locating facts and in pointing the way through the text. Moreover, headings provide resting points for the mind and for the eye, breaking up large chunks of text into manageable and inviting segments. For the writer, headings force organization of the data into meaningful blocks.

Functional heads (such as *Problem, Summary,* and *Recommendations*) help the writer outline a report. But talking heads (such as *Students Perplexed by Shortage of Parking* or *Short-Term Parking Solutions*) provide more information to the reader. Many of the examples in this chapter use functional heads for the purpose of instruction. It's sometimes possible to make headings both functional and descrip-

> Functional headings show the outline of a report; talking heads provide more information.

tive, such as *Recommendations: Shuttle and New Structures*. Whether your heads are talking or functional, keep them brief and clear.

Most informal reports are simple, requiring only one level of heading. Longer, more formal reports demand subdividing the topic into levels of headings (see Chapter 12).

Here are general tips on displaying headings effectively:

- *Strive for parallel construction.* Use balanced expressions such as *Visible Costs* and *Invisible Costs* rather than *Visible Costs* and *Costs That Don't Show*.
- *Don't enclose headings in quotation marks.* Quotation marks are appropriate only for marking quoted words or words used in a special sense, such as slang. They are unnecessary in headings.
- *Don't use headings as antecedents for pronouns* such as *like, this, that, these,* and *those*. For example, if the heading reads *Laser Printers*, don't begin the next sentence with *These are often used with desktop publishing software.*

BEING OBJECTIVE

Reports are more believable when the author is impartial, separates fact from opinion, uses moderate language, and cites sources.

Reports are convincing only when the facts are believable and the writer is credible. You can build credibility in a number of ways:

- *Present both sides of an issue.* Even if you favour one possibility, discuss both sides and show through logical reasoning why your position is superior. Remain impartial, letting the facts prove your point.
- *Separate fact from opinion.* Suppose a supervisor wrote, *Our department works harder and gets less credit than any other department in the company.* This opinion is difficult to prove, and it damages the credibility of the writer. A more convincing statement might be, *Our productivity has increased 6 percent over the past year, and I'm proud of the extra effort my employees are making.* After you've made a claim or presented an important statement in a report, ask yourself, Is this a verifiable fact? If the answer is no, rephrase your statement to make it sound more reasonable.
- *Be sensitive and moderate in your choice of language.* Don't exaggerate. Instead of saying *most people think . . .* it might be more accurate to say *some people think . . .* Obviously, avoid using labels and slanted expressions. Calling someone a *turkey,* an *egghead,* or an *elitist* demonstrates bias. If readers suspect that a writer is prejudiced, they may discount the entire argument.
- *Cite sources.* Tell your readers where the information came from. For example, *In a telephone interview with Blake Spence, director of transportation, October 15, he said . . .* or *the Vancouver Sun (August 10, p. 40) reports that . . .* By referring to respected sources, you lend authority and credibility to your statements. Your words become more believable and your argument, more convincing.

INFORMATION REPORTS

Information reports usually contain three parts: *introduction, findings,* and *summary*.

Writers of information reports provide information without drawing conclusions or making recommendations. Some information reports are highly standardized, such as police reports, hospital admittance reports, monthly sales reports, or statistical reports on government program use. Many of these are fill-in reports using prepared forms for recurring data. Other information reports are more personalized, as illustrated in Figure 11.3. They often include these sections:

INTRODUCTION

This part may also be called *Background*. In this section do the following: (1) explain why you are writing, (2) describe what methods and sources were used to gather information and why they are credible, (3) provide any special background information that may be necessary, (4) give the purpose of the report, if known, and (5) offer a preview of your findings.

FINDINGS

This section may also be called *Observations, Facts, Results,* or *Discussion.* Important points to consider in this section are organization and display. Since information reports generally do not include conclusions or recommendations, inductive or deductive organization may be less appropriate. Instead, consider one of these methods of organization: (1) chronological, (2) alphabetical, (3) topical, or (4) most to least important.

To display the findings effectively, number the paragraphs, underline or boldface the key words, or indent the paragraphs. Be sure that words used as headings are parallel in structure. If the findings require elaboration, either include this discussion with each segment of the findings or place it in a separate section entitled *Discussion.*

SUMMARY

This section is optional. If it is included, use it to summarize your findings objectively and impartially.

The information report shown in Figure 11.3 supplies information from an investigator about names available for a new recording series. The writer, an information specialist and consultant, used functional headings *(Introduction, Discussion of Findings,* and *Summary).* These headings immediately announce the report's organization, but they give no hint of what the sections actually reveal.

Notice how easy this information report is to read. Short paragraphs, ample use of headings, white space, concise writing, and an enumerated list all contribute to improved readability.

RECOMMENDATION REPORTS

Recommendation reports present information and analysis intended to solve a problem. They are usually written in response to requests by superiors. Writers are expected to analyze data, draw conclusions, and make recommendations. These reports may be arranged inductively or deductively, depending on the problem, audience, and purpose. To arrange a report deductively, place the conclusions and recommendations near the beginning. For an inductive arrangement, place them toward the end.

Unlike information reports, recommendation reports include conclusions and recommendations.

FIGURE 11.3

Information Report—Letter Format

S E R V I C E S   S T E F F I N S   I N C .
392, rue Sainte-Catherine
Montreal, Quebec H4J 2E8
(514) 571-3302

August 4, 200x

Ms. Karen Dumoulin, Promotions Manager
Disques Cargo Inc.
703 boul. Saint-Laurent
Montreal, Quebec H2S 3J4

Dear Ms. Dumoulin:

SUBJECT: AVAILABILITY OF NAMES FOR NEW RECORDING SERIES

Here is the report you requested regarding the availability of names for use in a new recording series under the Disque Cargo label.

Introduction

The following information is based on a review of the Canadian Intellectual Property Office, the Canadian Trademarks Database, the Canadian Techsource database, as well as the family of TRADEMARKSCAN databases, which facilitates searches of Canadian, U.S., British and European trademarks. The U.S. Patent and Trademark Office, the Copyright Office, and several other sources of patent data within the music industry were also reviewed. Using on-line databases, my staff conducted a full search of the five names you submitted. Of the group, we find that two names are possible for your use.

Discussion of Findings

Below are summaries of the results of our electronic search of the five specific titles you suggested.

1. Gold Label. Our research disclosed one recording company using the "Gold Label" name, and this causes us some concern. However, our outside counsel advises us that the name "Gold Label" is available for Disque Cargo's use in light of the trademark registrations for "Gold Note," currently owned by your affiliated companies.

2. The Master Series. Several registrations containing the word "Master" appear in the Canadian Intellectual Property Office. Since many registrations exist, no one can assert exclusive rights to that word. Therefore, Disque Cargo's use of the name "The Master Series" is not precluded.

Identifies report and authorization.

Discusses research methods.

Enumerates research findings.

The recommendation report shown in Figure 11.4 presents information about procedures for hiring and using temporary employees. Organized inductively, this report begins with a description of the background and problem. Conclusions and recommendations follow. Because the writer thought the reader would require persuasion, she arranged the report to follow logical thought processes.

In addition to illustrating inductive organization, the recommendation report in Figure 11.4 shows the memo format. This report was internal; therefore, it used company memo stationery.

FIGURE 11.3   Continued

Ms. Karen Dumoulin   Page 2   August 4, 200x

3. <u>Heavenly Voices</u>. Our search of copyright records disclosed that approximately seven songs were recorded in 1995 on the "Heavenly Voices" record label, with an address in Memphis, Tennessee. Repeated attempts to reach this business have been unsuccessful.

4. <u>Celestial Sounds</u>. A record label using this name produced 12 titles in 1996. Apparently, the recording company is now defunct, but the trademark registration, No. 1,909,233, persists.

5. <u>Cherubim</u>. This name has at least one currently operating outstanding trademark, Trademark Registration No. 2,109,900 for "Cherubim Music."

<u>Summary</u>

Of the five names discussed here, the first two appear to be open to you: "Gold Label" and "The Master Series." The names "Heavenly Voices" and "Celestial Sounds" require additional research. Since "Cherubim" is trademarked, it is unavailable for your consideration.

Should you have any other names you would like us to check, please call me at (514) 571-3302. It's always a pleasure to serve you.

Sincerely,

Ellie Steffins

Ellie Steffins
President

ES:jer

Underlines headings to improve readability.

Summarizes significant findings.

The headings in this report include *Background, Problem, Conclusions, Recommendations,* and *Limitations.* Other possible section headings for a recommendation report follow:

Introduction	Analysis of Facts
Background	Options
Problem	Rejected Alternatives
Method of Collecting Data	Limitations
Findings	Conclusions
Presentation of Facts	Recommendations

FIGURE 11.4

Recommendation Report—Memo Format

PYRAMID INDUSTRIES   Internal Memorandum

TO: Ken Ogata, Director   DATE: June 3, 200x
           Human Resources Services

FROM: Laurie Glaze, Manager   *Laurie*
           Information Services

SUBJECT: DEVELOPING PROCEDURES FOR USING TEMPORARY EMPLOYEES

At your request I am submitting this report detailing my recommendations for improving the use of temporary employees in all departments within Pyramid. My recommendations are based on my own experience with hundreds of temporary employees in my department, on interviews and an informal survey with other managers, on a brief review of related articles, and on informal discussions with human resources personnel at Rescom International.

Background

Pyramid has increased its number of service accounts from 58 to 97 over the past three years. During that same period the number of permanent employees has increased only 12 percent. Because we have not been able to find qualified individuals to hire as full-time employees, we have been forced to rely on temporary employees more heavily than ever before. During the past year Pyramid has required the services of 189 temporary employees.

Joe Pittarelli in Human Resources Services reports that he does not expect the employment picture to improve in the future. He feels that Pyramid will probably continue to hire large numbers of temporary employees for at least the next two years.

Problem

Temporary employees are hired by department managers who have little experience in acquiring temps, planning their work, or supervising them. As a result, the productivity of the temps is not always as great as it could be. Moreover, we sometimes hire expensive, highly skilled individuals for routine tasks. These workers are bored with their assigned tasks and dissatisfied with their experience at Pyramid; hence they refuse to return.

Findings

A survey of our department managers and supervisors revealed an almost unanimous desire for a standard set of procedures relating to temporary employees. Department managers were especially concerned with defining their needs and managing temps effectively. Many human resources managers use prepared forms to help department managers define their needs. One study indicated that prepared forms improved the quality of hiring in 70 percent of companies that used them. These marked improvements were supported in informal discussions with human resources personnel at Rescom International.

Includes signature here rather than at end.

Announces report and establishes sources of data.

Presents facts that suggest significance of problem.

Provides details that justify need for change.

JUSTIFICATION REPORTS

Justification reports are unsolicited; that is, the idea originates with the writer.

Justification reports include information, analysis, and recommendations. Unlike recommendation reports, however, they are *unsolicited*—that is, the idea for a justification report starts with the writer instead of with a superior. The writer may wish to purchase equipment, change a procedure, or revise existing policy. Typically, the

FIGURE 11.4 Continued

Ken Ogata   Page 2   June 3, 200x

To address the issue of effective management of temps, Don Swerski, author of *The Art and Practice of Management,* maintains that productivity of new employees increases when their supervisors are provided with management guidelines to follow. My contacts at Rescom International say that since establishing managerial guidelines covering new employees, Rescom has seen a 42 percent drop in new employee turnover.

Conclusions

Pyramid could improve the productivity and effectiveness of its temporary employees by instituting changes in two areas: (1) establishing and communicating standardized procedures for department managers requesting temps and (2) introducing techniques for department managers to follow when temps first arrive.

Recommendations

System for Requesting Temps. I recommend that Human Resources Services prepare a form that supervisors complete when they need temporary employees. The form will require department managers to indicate precisely what skills are required for the tasks to be completed. Requests for temps should then be channelled through one office, such as Human Resources Services.

Procedures for Introducing Temps to Workforce. I recommend that Human Resources Services, in consultation with the supervisors most directly involved, develop management guidelines that will incorporate the following checklist items:

1. Work to be completed.
2. Tasks explained.
3. Supplies and operating equipment available.
4. Feedback forms for temps.

Limitations

The success of these recommendations is limited by two factors. First, Human Resources Services must agree to assume the task of regulating the hiring of all temporary employees. Second, the new procedures must reflect departmental needs for the new managers to use them. To ensure the success of this initiative, several workshops should be provided to develop the new procedures and to instruct managers in using the procedures effectively.

Draws conclusions from preceding facts.

Itemizes specific actions to solve problem.

Gains credibility by acknowledging limitations of recommendations.

desired change will be obvious to the reader. Therefore, persuasion should not be a primary goal. Start directly with the proposal or problem. Follow this with some or all of the following headings: *Present System, Proposed System, Advantages, Cost and Savings, Methods or Procedures, Conclusion,* and *Discussion.* Figure 11.5 shows a justification report produced within AMP Products.

FIGURE 11.5

Justification Report—Memo Format

MEMORANDUM

TO: Joseph Lukowski, Vice President   DATE: June 11, 200x
Operations Division

FROM: Sally Stouder, Office Manager   SS
Accounting Department

SUBJECT: INSTALLATION OF FLAT, UNDERCARPET WIRING TO UPDATE CURRENT
ELECTRICAL, DATA PROCESSING, AND COMMUNICATION WIRING
SYSTEM

Presents main idea (proposal) immediately.

<u>Proposal</u>

Because AMP Products needs a flexible, economical wiring system that can accommodate our ever-changing electrical, communication, and data processing needs, I propose that we install a flat, undercarpet wiring system.

Describes problem, emphasizing current deficiencies.

<u>Present System</u>

At present our department has an outdated system of floor ducts and power poles and a network of surface wiring that is overwhelmed by the demands we are now placing on it. The operation of 27 pieces of equipment (including computers, printers, modems, faxes, and copiers), plus 34 telephones requires extensive electrical circuits and cabling. In addition, our overhead lighting, consisting of fluorescent fixtures in a drop ceiling structure, contains excessive wiring above the drop ceiling.

We have outgrown our present wiring system, and future growth is contingent on the availability of power. Since AMP Products' goal is to have a computer terminal and modem at every workstation, we must find a better way to service our power needs than through conventional methods.

Shows how new system would solve problems.

<u>Advantages of Proposed System</u>

Power, telephone, and data cables are now available in a flat form only .01 cm thick. This flat, flexible cable can be installed underneath existing carpeting, thus preventing costly and disruptive renovation necessary for installing additional round cables. Because flat cables can be moved easily, an undercarpet system would provide great flexibility. Whenever we move a computer or add a printer or a fax machine, we can easily make necessary changes in the wiring.

PROGRESS REPORTS

Progress reports describe the headway of unusual or nonroutine projects. Most progress reports include these four parts: (1) the purpose and nature of the project; (2) a complete summary of the work already completed; (3) a thorough description of work currently in progress, including personnel, methods, obstacles, and attempts to remedy obstacles; and (4) a forecast of future activities in relation to the sched-

FIGURE 11.5   Continued

Vice President Lukowski   Page 2   June 11, 200x

Undercarpet wiring would allow us to eliminate all power poles. These poles break up the office landscaping and create distracting shadows about which employees complain.

Offers convincing arguments for undercarpet wiring.

Installation of an undercarpet wiring system in the Accounting Department would enable AMP Products to evaluate the system's effectiveness before considering it for other areas, such as sales, customer services, and field warehousing.

Cost and Savings

Wireco Corporation estimates that undercarpet wiring for the Accounting Department would cost about $29,000. If we were to use conventional methods to install round wiring, we would have to renovate our entire department at a cost of over $200,000. Undercarpet wiring, then, would save AMP Products over $170,000. Equally important, however, are the savings to be realized in productivity and employee satisfaction, which would deteriorate if renovation were required.

Relates costs to savings and benefits.

uled completion date, including recommendations and requests. In Figure 11.6 Maria Robinson explains the construction of a realty company branch office. She begins with a statement summarizing the construction progress in relation to the expected completion date. She then updates the reader with a brief recap of past progress. She emphasizes the present status of construction and concludes by describing the next steps to be taken.

FIGURE 11.6

Progress Report

> **MEMORANDUM**
>
> TO: Dorothy Prevatt, President   DATE: April 20, 200x
>
> FROM: Maria Robinson, Development Officer   MR
>
> SUBJECT: CONSTRUCTION PROGRESS OF MISSISSAUGA BRANCH OFFICE
>
> Summary
>
> Construction of Prevatt Realty's Mississauga branch office has entered Phase 3. Although we are one week behind the contractor's original schedule, the building should be ready for occupancy August 15.
>
> Past Progress
>
> Phase 1 involved development of the architect's plans; this process was completed February 5. Phase 2 involved submission of the plans for county building department approval. The plans were then given to four contractors for estimates. The lowest bidder was Holst Brothers Contractors. This firm began construction on March 25.
>
> Present Status
>
> Phase 3 includes initial construction procedures. The following steps have been completed as of April 20:
>
> 1. Demolition of existing building at 273 Lakeshore Blvd.
> 2. Excavation of foundation footings for the building and for the surrounding wall.
> 3. Installation of steel reinforcing rods in building pad and wall.
> 4. Pouring of concrete foundation.
>
> The contractor indicated that the project was one week behind schedule for the following reasons. The building inspectors required additional steel reinforcement not shown on the architect's blueprints. Further, excavation of the footings required more time than the contractor anticipated because the Number 4 footings were all below grade.
>
> Future Schedule
>
> Despite some time lost in Phase 3, we are substantially on target for the completion of this office building by August 1. Phase 4 includes framing, drywalling, and plumbing.

Introduces report; the heading Summary *could be omitted.*

Describes completed work concisely.

Itemizes current activities.

Projects future activities.

FORMAL MINUTES

Minutes provide a summary of the proceedings of meetings. Formal, traditional minutes, illustrated in Figure 11.7, are written for large groups and legislative bodies. The following items are usually included in the sequence shown:

FIGURE 11.7

Minutes of Meeting, Traditional—Report Format

Canadian Association of Occupational Therapists
Planning Committee Meeting
October 23, 200x, 10 a.m.
Conference Room A, Century Towers

Present: Marilyn Andrews, Bob Schmidt, June Gonzales, Brendan Miller, Yves Pariseau, Nakima Sakami

Absent: Amy Costello

The meeting was called to order by Chair Marilyn Andrews at 10:05 a.m. Minutes from the June 22 meeting were read and approved.

Old Business

Brendan Miller and Nakima Sakami reviewed the information distributed at the last meeting about hotels being considered for the Vancouver conference. Brendan said that the Hilton Regency has ample conference rooms and remodelled interiors. Nakima reported that the Embassy Suites Vancouver also has excellent banquet facilities, adequate meeting facilities, and rooms at $82 per night. Bob Schmidt moved that we hold the convention at the Embassy Suites Vancouver. Brendan Miller seconded the motion. The motion passed 5–1.

New Business

Marilyn Andrews announced three possible themes for the convention, all of which focused on technology and the changing role of the occupational therapist. June Gonzales suggested the following possible title: "The New, the Tried and True, and the Unusual." Nakima Sakami suggested a communication theme. Several other possibilities were discussed. Marilyn appointed a subcommittee of June and Nakima to bring two or three concrete theme ideas to the next committee meeting.

Reports

Brendan Miller reported on convention exhibits and expressed his desire to involve more companies and products. Discussion followed regarding how this might be accomplished. Brendan moved that the Association's office staff develop a list of possible exhibitors. Marilyn Andrews seconded the motion. It passed 6–0.

The meeting was adjourned at 11:45 by Marilyn Andrews.

Yves Pariseau
Yves Pariseau, Secretary

Shows attendees and absentees.

Describes disposition of previous minutes and old business.

Summarizes new business and announcements.

Records discussion, motions, votes, and action taken.

Shows name and signature of person recording minutes.

- Name of group, date, time, place, name of meeting
- Names of people present; names of absentees, if appropriate
- Disposition of previous minutes
- Old business, new business, announcements, reports
- Motions, votes, action taken
- Name and signature of individual recording minutes

INFORMAL MINUTES

The minutes of business meetings and small organizations may be recorded informally, as illustrated in Figure 11.8. These minutes are usually shorter and easier to read than formal minutes. Informal minutes place less emphasis on the conventions of reporting and do not attempt to record the exact wording of individual statements. Instead, informal minutes concentrate on the following:

- Summaries of important discussions
- Decisions reached
- Items on which action must be taken, including people responsible and due dates

SUMMARIES

A summary condenses the primary ideas, conclusions, and recommendations of a longer publication.

A summary compresses essential information from a longer publication. Employees are sometimes asked to write summaries that condense technical reports, periodical articles, or books so that their staffs or superiors may grasp the main ideas quickly (see Figure 11.9). Students are often asked to write summaries of articles, chapters, or books to sharpen their writing skills and to confirm their knowledge of reading assignments. A summary includes primary ideas, conclusions, and recommendations. It usually omits examples, illustrations, and references. Organized for readability, a summary often includes headings and bulleted or enumerated lists. It may include the reactions of the reader.

TO-FILE REPORTS

To-file reports provide a record of conversations for future reference.

To-file reports document oral decisions, directives, and discussions. They create a concise, permanent record that may be important for future reference. Because individuals may forget, alter, or retract oral commitments, a written record should often be established. However, to-file reports should not be made for minor events.

To-file reports typically include the names and titles of involved individuals, along with a summary of the decision. A copy of the report is sent to involved individuals so that corrections or amendments may be made before the report is filed. Figure 11.10 shows a to-file report in memo format.

SUMMING UP AND LOOKING FORWARD

The seven types of reports discussed and illustrated in this chapter are representative of commonly seen reports in business transactions. All of the examples in this chapter are considered relatively informal. Longer, more formal reports are necessary for major investigations and research. These reports, along with suggestions for research methods, are presented in Chapter 12.

DISCUSSION

1. How do business reports differ from business letters?

FIGURE 11.8

Minutes of Meeting, Informal— Report Format

GRAND BEACH HOMEOWNERS' ASSOCIATION

Board of Directors Meeting
April 12, 200x

MINUTES

Directors Present: J. Weinstein, A. McGraw, J. Carson, C. Stefanko, A. Pettus
Directors Absent: P. Hook

<u>Summary of Topics Discussed</u>

- Report from Architectural Review Committee. Copy attached.

- Landscaping of centre divider on P.T.H. 59. Three options considered: hiring private landscape designer, seeking volunteers from community, assigning association custodian to complete work.

- Collection of outstanding assessments. Discussion of delinquent accounts and possible actions.

- Use of beach club by film companies. Pros: considerable income. Cons: damage to furnishings, loss of facility to homeowners.

- Nomination of directors to replace those with two-year appointments.

<u>Decisions Reached</u>

- Hire private landscaper to renovate and plant centre divider on P.T.H. 59.

- Attach liens to homes of members with delinquent assessments.

- Submit to general membership vote the question of renting the beach club to film companies.

<u>Action Items</u>

Item	Responsibility	Due Date
1. Landscaping bid	J. Carson	May 1
2. Attorney for liens	P. Hook	April 20
3. Creation of nominating committee	A. Pettus	May 1

Summarizes discussion.

Capsulizes decisions rather than showing motions and voting.

Highlights items for action.

---

2. Of the reports presented in this chapter, discuss those that require inductive development versus those that require deductive development.
3. How are the reports that you write for your courses similar to those presented here? How are they different?
4. Compare and contrast traditional and informal minutes of meetings. Why would some organizations require traditional minutes?
5. Compare and contrast justification reports and proposals.

FIGURE 11.9

Summary of Article—Memo Format

MEMO TO: Professor Valerie Evans   DATE: November 18, 200x

FROM: Edwin Huong EH

SUBJECT: ANALYSIS OF COMPUTER MAINTENANCE ARTICLE

Introduces report.

In response to your request, here is an analysis of "Taking the Sting Out of Computer Repair," which appeared in the July 1999 issue of *Office Administration and Automation.*

Major Points

Summarizes primary ideas and conclusions.

The author, Michael B. Chamberlain, discusses three alternatives available to computer users seeking service. Each has advantages and disadvantages.

• <u>Factory service</u>. The user sends the equipment back to the factory for repairs. Expert service is provided, but generally the time required is impossibly long.

• <u>Customer self-service</u>. Large companies may maintain in-house repair departments, but their technicians find it difficult to keep abreast of changing hardware and software.

• <u>Third-party service</u>. Independent computer maintenance organizations offer convenience, but they can't always handle multivendor systems.

Omits examples, illustrations, and references.

The author favours the third option and provides many tips on how to work with third-party maintenance companies. Before choosing such an organization, he warns, make sure that it has experts who can work with your particular configuration.

Strengths and Weaknesses

Provides evaluation of article.

The strength of this article lies in the discussion of how to choose a service organization. The author also provides helpful preventive maintenance tips.

This article had two weaknesses. First, the author failed to support his choice of third-party maintenance companies effectively. Second, the article was poorly organized. It was difficult to read because it was not developed around major ideas. Better headings would have helped readers recognize significant data.

CHAPTER REVIEW

6. List seven kinds of short reports. Be prepared to describe each.

FIGURE 11.10

To-File Report—Memo Format

INFORMATICS INC.

Internal Memo

TO: Kimberlee Bartel   DATE: February 4, 200x
        Chief Counsel

FROM: Judith Bynum JB
        Operations Manager

SUBJECT: DISPOSTION OF UNORDERED MERCHANDISE

This confirms our telephone conversation today in which you advised me regarding the disposition of unordered merchandise sent to my office by vendors. It is my understanding that I am under no obligation to return this merchandise since its delivery was unauthorized. I further understand that after reasonable time has elapsed, we may use this merchandise or dispose of it as we see fit.

Please respond by February 10 if this record of our conversation is inaccurate.

Provides record of conversation.

Repeats major ideas.

Requests correction if necessary.

---

7. List four formats suitable for reports. Be prepared to discuss each.

8. From the lists that you made above, select a report category and appropriate format for each of the following situations.
   a. Your supervisor asks you to read a long technical report and tell him or her the important points.

b. You want to tell management about an idea you have for improving a procedure that you think will increase productivity.

c. You just completed a telephone conversation with a union representative detailing your rights in a disagreement you had with your supervisor.

d. You are asked to record the proceedings of a meeting of your school's student association.

e. As Engineering Department office manager, you have been asked to describe your highly regarded computer system to another department.

f. As a police officer, you are writing a report of an arrest.

g. At a mail-order catalogue company, your boss asks you to investigate ways to reduce the time that customers are kept waiting for service representatives to take their telephone orders. He wants your report to examine the problem and offer solutions.

9. If you were about to write the following reports, where would you gather information? Be prepared to discuss the specifics of each choice.
   a. You are a student representative on a curriculum committee. You are asked to study the course requirements for your major and make recommendations.

   b. As department manager, you must write job descriptions for several new positions you wish to establish in your department.

   c. You are proposing to management the replacement of a copier in your department.

   d. You must document the progress of a 12-month campaign to alter the image of Levi's jeans.

10. What three questions do progress reports typically address?

11. What one factor distinguishes reports developed inductively from those developed deductively?

12. What is the purpose of a to-file report?

13. Information reports generally contain what three parts?

14. Why are informal minutes usually easier to read than traditional minutes?

15. An article summary that your employer asks you to write should include what items?

ACTIVITIES AND CASES

11.1 Information Report: Describing Your Job. Your instructor wants to learn about your employment. Select a position you now hold or one that you have held in the past. (If you have not been employed, choose an organization to which you belong.) Write an information report describing your employment. As an introduction describe the company and its products or services, its ownership, and its location. As the main part of the report, describe your position, including its tasks and the skills required to perform these tasks. Summarize by describing the experience you gained. Your memo report should be single-spaced and one to two pages long.

11.2 Information Report: Learning About a Position. Gather information about a position for which you might be interested in applying. Learn about the nature of the job and what kinds of experience are required. Describe the working conditions in the field, typical entry-level salaries, and who might be successful in this field.

If your instructor wishes to make this an extended report, collect information about two companies where you might apply. Investigate each company fully. Describe the functions of an employee working in the position you have investigated. You might interview one or more individuals who are working in the position to gather information. You can make this into a recommendation report by drawing conclusions and making recommendations.

11.3 Recommendation Report: Retaining Employees. An employer for whom you worked last year regarded you highly. Although you are no longer employed there, this individual called to ask your candid opinion on how to retain employees. He is concerned about the high rate of turnover. What advice can you offer? How do similar businesses recruit and retain their employees? Using actual experiences, write a letter report responding to this request.

11.4 Recommendation Report: Expanding the Company Library. Despite the interest in on-line publications, managers and employees at your company still like to browse through magazines in the company library. Bonnie Finley, the company librarian, wants to add business periodicals to the library subscription list and has requested help from various company divisions. You've been assigned to recommend four periodicals in your particular specialty (accounting, marketing, or whatever). Visit your library and use appropriate indexes and guides to select four periodicals to recommend. Write a memo report to Ms. Finley describing the particular readership, usual contents, and scope of each periodical. To judge each adequately, you should examine several issues. Explain why you think each periodical should be ordered and who would read it. Convince the librarian that your choices would be beneficial to your department.

11.5 Justification Report: Evaluating Your Curriculum. You have been serving as a student member of a college curriculum advisory committee. Examine the course requirements for a degree, diploma, or certificate in your area. Are the requirements realistic and practical? What improvements can you suggest? Interview other students and faculty members for their suggestions. Write to the head of your faculty or department proposing your suggestions.

11.6 Justification Report: Purchasing New Equipment. In your work or your training, identify equipment that needs to be purchased or replaced (computer, printer, modem, VCR, copier, camera, etc.). Write a justification report comparing two or more brands.

11.7 Progress Report: Making Headway Toward Your Educational Goal. You made an agreement with your parents (or spouse, relative, or partner) that you would submit a progress report at this time describing your headway toward your educational goal (employment, certificate, diploma, degree). Write that report in memo format.

11.8 Minutes: Recording the Proceedings of a Meeting. Attend an open meeting of an organization at your school or elsewhere. Record the proceedings in formal or informal minutes.

11.9 Summary: Condensing an Article About E-Mail Privacy. Your boss, Richard A. Morrisey, is worried because the company has no formal e-mail policy. Should employees be allowed to use e-mail for personal messages? May management monitor the messages of employees? He asks you to research this topic (or another topic on which you and your instructor agree). Find a good article (at least 1000 words) in a magazine, journal, or electronic database. Write a one- or two-page memo summary for Mr. Morrisey.

11.10 To-File Report: Remembering a Decision. You just saw the vice president of operations in the hall and reminded her that your department needs a new copier. She told you to go ahead and get estimates from three sources. You know what a faulty memory she has, and you don't want her to forget or renege on this decision. Write her a to-file report.

11.11 Longer Report: Solving a Problem. Choose a business or organization with which you are familiar and identify a problem such as poor quality, indifferent service, absenteeism at organization meetings, uninspired cafeteria food, outdated office equipment, arrogant management, lack of communication, underappreciated employees, wasteful procedures, and so forth. Describe the problem in detail. Assume you are to report to management (or to the leadership of an organization) about the nature and scope of the problem. Decide which kind of report to prepare (information, recommendation, justification), and choose the format. How would you gather data to lend authority to your conclusions and recommendations? Determine the exact topic and report length after consultation with your instructor.

11.12 Searching the Internet: Reporting on Codes of Ethics. Your boss, Judith R. Helgason, wants to know what other companies are doing to develop codes of ethics. She asks you to search the Internet to locate at least two good examples of company codes of ethics. Compare and contrast the two codes. Summarize your findings in an information report to Ms. Helgason.

Related Web Site: www.ethics.ubc.ca/resources/business/codes.html

11.13 Connecting With E-Mail: Progress Report. Send your instructor a report detailing the progress you are making on a report (one that you may be writing for either this chapter or Chapter 12). Discuss (a) the purpose of the report, (b) the work already completed, (c) the work currently in progress, and (d) your schedule for completing the report.

GRAMMAR/MECHANICS CHECKUP—11

Other Punctuation

Although this checkup concentrates on Sections 2.23–2.29 in the Grammar/Mechanics Handbook, you may also refer to other punctuation principles. Insert any necessary punctuation. In the space provided, indicate the number of changes you make and record the number of the G/M principle(s) illustrated. Count each mark separately; for example, a set of parentheses counts as 2. If you make no changes, write *0*. When you finish, compare your responses with those provided. If your responses differ, study carefully the specific principles shown in parentheses.

Example: (De-emphasize.) The consumption of Mexican food products is highest in certain provinces (Ontario and British Columbia), but this food trend is spreading to other parts of the country.
     <u>2</u>   (2.27)

1. (Emphasize.) The convention planning committee has invited three managers Jim Lowey, Frank Beyer, and Carolyn Wong to make presentations.   _____
2. Would you please Ms. Seniuk use your computer to recalculate these totals   _____
3. (De-emphasize.) A second set of demographic variables see Figure 13 on page 432 includes nationality, religion, and race.   _____
4. Because the word recommendation is frequently misspelled we are adding it to our company style book.   _____
5. Recruiting, hiring, and training these are three important functions of a human resources officer.   _____
6. The office manager said, "Who placed an order for 15 dozen ribbon cartridges"   _____
7. Have any of the research assistants been able to locate the article entitled How Pension Reform Will Affect You   _____
8. (Emphasize.) The biggest grain-producing provinces Manitoba, Saskatchewan, and Alberta are experiencing severe weather problems.   _____
9. Have you sent invitations to Mr Jose E Pereira, Miss Michelle Hale, and Ms Sylvia Perillo   _____
10. Dr. Y. W. Yellin wrote the chapter entitled Trading on the Options Market that appeared in a book called Securities Markets.   _____
11. Rafael said, "I'll be right over" however he has not appeared yet.   _____
12. In business the word liability may be defined as any legal obligation requiring payment in the future.

13. Because the work was scheduled to be completed June 10; we found it necessary to hire temporary workers to work June 8 and 9.
14. Did any c o d shipments arrive today
15. Hooray I have finished this checkup haven't I

_____

1. (2) managers— Wong— (2.26a)   3. (2) (see Figure 13 on page 432) (2.27)   5. (1) training— (2.26c)   7. (3) "How You"? (2.28e, 2.28f)   9. (4) Mr. E. Ms. Perillo? (2.23b 2.24)   11. (2) over"; however, (2.16, 2.28f)   13. (1) June 10, (2.06)   15. (3) Hooray! checkup, I? (2.24, 2.25)

GRAMMAR/MECHANICS CHALLENGE—11

Document for Revision

The following progress report has faults in grammar, punctuation, spelling, number form, wordiness, and word use. Use standard proofreading marks (see Appendix B) to correct the errors.

Ineffective Writing

TO: Jon Peterson   DATE: January 6, 200x

FROM: Vicky Lee

SUBJECT: SITE FOR "CEDAR BAY" TELEFILM

This memo describes the progress of my exploration for an appropriate rustic home to be used in connection with the fishing village sequences in the telefilm "Cedar Bay".

Work Completed: To prepare for this assignment several sites in the Rushing River area were visited. Possible locations include turn of the century estates, victorian mansions and rustic farmhouses. One acceptional cite is the sea shanty inn a 97 year old hotel situated close to the wharf with a breath taking view of the ocean, beaches, and distant mountains.

Work to Be Completed: In the next 5 days I'll search the coast north of the rushing river area including the villages of Deep Bay, Cabot cove, and Hidden Bay. Many of the old village's contain charming structures that may present exactly the degree of atmosphere and mystery we seek, these villages have the added advantage of easy acess.

My final report in regards to the 3 most promising locations are nearly completed. You will in all probability be able to visit these cites January 21st.

Communication Workshop: Collaboration

LAYING THE GROUNDWORK FOR TEAM WRITING PROJECTS

The chances are that you can look forward to some kind of team writing in your future career. You may collaborate voluntarily (seeking advice and differing perspectives) or involuntarily (through necessity or by assignment). Working with other people can be frustrating, particularly when some team members don't carry their weight or when conflict breaks out. Team projects, though, can be harmonious and productive when members establish ground rules at the outset and adhere to guidelines such as the following.

Preparing to work together. Before you discuss the project, talk about how your group will function.

- Limit the size of your team, if possible, to three or four members. Larger groups have more difficulties. An odd number is usually preferable so that ties in voting are avoided.
- Name a meeting leader (to plan and conduct meetings), a recorder (to keep a record of group decisions), and an evaluator (to determine if the group is on target and meeting its goals).
- Decide whether your team will be governed by consensus (everyone must agree) or by majority rule.
- Compare schedules of team members, and set up the best meeting times. Plan to meet often. Avoid other responsibilities during meetings.
- Discuss the value of conflict. By bringing conflict into the open and encouraging confrontation, your team can prevent personal resentment and group dysfunction. Confrontation can actually create better final documents by promoting new ideas and avoiding "group think."
- Discuss how you will deal with members who are not pulling their share of the load.

Planning the document. Once you've established ground rules, you're ready to discuss the project and resulting document. Be sure to keep a record of the following decisions your team makes.

- Establish the document's specific purpose and identify the main issues involved.
- Decide on the final form of the document. What parts will it have?
- Discuss the audience(s) for the document and what appeal would help it achieve its purpose.
- Develop a work plan. Assign jobs. Set deadlines.

- Decide how the final document will be written: individuals working separately on assigned portions, one person writing the first draft, the entire group writing the complete document together, or some other method.

Collecting information. The following suggestions help teams gather accurate information.

- Brainstorm for ideas as a group.
- Decide who will be responsible for gathering what information.
- Establish deadlines for collecting information.
- Discuss ways to ensure the accuracy of the information collected.

Organizing, writing, and revising. As the project progresses, your team may wish to modify some of its earlier decisions.

- Review the proposed organization of your final document, and adjust it if necessary.
- Write the first draft. If separate team members are writing segments, they should use the same word processing program to facilitate combining files.
- Meet to discuss and revise the draft(s).
- If individuals are working on separate parts, appoint one person (probably the best writer) to coordinate all the parts, striving for a consistent style and format.

Editing and evaluating. Before the document is submitted, complete these steps.

- Give one person responsibility for finding and correcting grammatical and mechanical errors.
- Meet as a group to evaluate the final document. Does it fulfil its purpose and meet the needs of the audience?

Application. Select a report topic from this chapter or Chapter 12. In teams of three to five, prepare a report as a collaborative effort. Implement the suggestions included here. Your instructor may assign grades not only on the final report but also on your team effectiveness and your individual contribution, as determined by fellow team members.

PROPOSALS AND FORMAL REPORTS

Every detail of a project must be scrutinized before it leaves this place. A bid could be thrown out after months of work, all over a minor item costing a few cents.[1]

TERRY LAMBDEN, vice-president of engineering, procurement, and construction, Propak Systems Ltd., an Alberta-based international oil and gas processing systems manufacturer

Learning Objectives

1. Identify and explain the parts of informal and formal proposals.
2. Describe the preparatory steps for writing a formal report.
3. Collect data from both primary and secondary sources, including company data, library resources, and on-line data.
4. Distinguish among five organizational strategies for reports.
5. Outline topics and use appropriate heading format.
6. Illustrate data, using tables, charts, and graphs.
7. Sequence 13 parts of a formal report.

P roposals are written offers to solve problems, provide services, or sell equipment. Many companies like Propak earn a sizable portion of their income from sales resulting from proposals. That's why creating effective proposals is especially important today. Let's say that sports shoe manufacturer Nike wants to upgrade the computers and software in its human resources department. If it knows exactly what it wants, it would prepare a request for proposal (RFP) specifying its requirements. It then publicizes this RFP, and companies interested in bidding on the job submit proposals.

Both large and small companies are increasingly likely to use RFPs to solicit competitive bids on their projects. This enables them to compare "apples to apples." That is, they can compare prices from different companies on their projects. They also want the legal protection offered by proposals, which are legal contracts.

In writing proposals, the most important thing to remember is that proposals are sales presentations. They must be persuasive, not merely mechanical descriptions of what you can do. You may recall from Chapter 9 that effective persuasive sales messages (1) emphasize benefits for the reader and (2) make it easy for the reader to understand and respond. In addition to these features, proposals promote the person making the proposal. In other words, when you write a proposal, you will detail your expertise and accomplishments in the proposal.

Proposals may be informal or formal; they differ primarily in length and format.

Proposals are persuasive offers to solve problems, provide services, or sell equipment.

Both large and small companies today often use requests for proposals (RFPs) to solicit competitive bids on projects.

Informal proposals are often presented in two- to four-page letters. Sometimes called *letter proposals*, they contain six principal parts: introduction, background, proposal, staffing, budget, and authorization. The informal letter proposal shown in Figure 12.1 illustrates all six parts of a letter proposal. This proposal is addressed to a Calgary dentist who wants to improve patient satisfaction.

INTRODUCTION

Effective proposal openers "hook" readers by promising extraordinary results or resources or by identifying key benefits, issues, or outcomes.

Most proposals begin by briefly explaining the reasons for the proposal and by highlighting the writer's qualifications. To make your introduction more persuasive, you need to provide a "hook" to capture the reader's interest. One proposal expert suggests these possibilities:[2]

- Hint at extraordinary results with details to be revealed shortly.
- Promise low costs or speedy results.
- Mention a remarkable resource (well-known authority, new computer program, well-trained staff) available exclusively to you.
- Identify a serious problem (worry item) and promise a solution, to be explained later.
- Specify a key issue or benefit that you feel is the heart of the proposal.

For example, Dana Swensen, in the introduction of the proposal shown in Figure 12.1, focused on a key benefit. In this proposal to conduct a patient satisfaction survey, Dana thought that the client, Dr. Larocque, would be most interested in specific recommendations for improving service to her patients. But Dana didn't hit on this hook until after the first draft had been written. Indeed, it's often a good idea to put off writing the introduction to a proposal until after you have completed other parts. For longer proposals the introduction also describes the scope and limitations of the project, as well as outlining the organization of the material to come.

BACKGROUND, PROBLEM, PURPOSE

The background section identifies the problem and discusses the goals or purposes of the project. Your aim is to convince the reader that you understand the problem completely. Thus, if you are responding to an RFP, this means repeating its language. For example, if the RFP asks for the *design of a maintenance program for high-speed mail-sorting equipment*, you would use the same language in explaining the purpose of your proposal. This section might include segments entitled *Basic Requirements, Most Critical Tasks*, and *Most Important Secondary Problems*.

PROPOSAL, PLAN, SCHEDULE

The proposal section must give enough information to secure the contract but not so much detail that the services are not needed.

In the proposal section itself, you should discuss your plan for solving the problem. In some proposals this is tricky because you want to disclose enough of your plan to secure the contract without giving away so much information that your services aren't needed. Without specifics, though, your proposal has little chance, so you

FIGURE 12.1

Informal Proposal

SWENSEN RESEARCH ASSOCIATES

One Providence Plaza, Calgary, Alberta T1A 4E5   (403) 628-3011

May 16, 200x

Dr. Marie Larocque
1789 Clarkston Avenue
Calgary, AB T1L P5G

Dear Dr. Larocque:

I enjoyed talking with you several days ago about your successful general dentistry practice. Swensen Research Associates is pleased to submit the following proposal outlining our plan to analyze your patients' levels of satisfaction and suggest ways to improve your service to them.

Background and Purposes

We understand that you have been incorporating a total quality management system in your practice. Although you have every reason to believe your patients are pleased with the service you provide, you would like to give them an opportunity to discuss what they like and possibly don't like about your service. Specifically, your purposes are to survey your patients to (1) determine the level of their satisfaction with you and your staff, (2) elicit their suggestions for improvement, (3) learn more about how they discovered you, and (4) compare your "preferred" and "standard" patients.

Proposed Plan

On the basis of our experience in conducting many local and national customer satisfaction surveys, Swensen Research proposes the following plan.

Survey. We will develop a short but thorough questionnaire probing the data you desire. The questionnaire will measure patient reactions to such elements as courtesy, professionalism, accuracy of billing, friendliness, and waiting time. After you approve it, the questionnaire will be sent to a carefully selected sample of 300 patients whom you have separated into groupings of "preferred" and "standard."

Analysis. Data from the survey will be analyzed by demographic segments, such as patient type, age, and gender. Our experienced team of experts, using state-of-the-art computer systems and advanced statistical measures, will study the (a) degree of patient satisfaction, (b) reasons for satisfaction or dissatisfaction, and (c) relationship between responses of your "preferred" and "standard" patients. Moreover, our team will report to you specific suggestions for making patient visits more pleasant.

Report. You will receive a final report with the key findings clearly spelled out. Our expert staff will also draw conclusions based on these findings. The report will include tables summarizing all responses.

Uses opening paragraph in place of introduction.

Grabs attention with "hook" that focuses on key benefit.

Identifies four purposes of survey.

Announces heart of proposal.

Divides total plan into logical segments for easy reading.

must decide how much to reveal. Tell what you propose to do and how it will benefit the reader. Remember, too, that a proposal is a sales presentation. Sell your methods, product, and "deliverables"—items that will be left with the client. In this section some writers specify how the project will be managed and how its progress will be audited. Most writers also include a schedule of activities or timetable showing when events will take place.

FIGURE 12.1 Continued

<table>
<tr><td>Dr. Marie Larocque</td><td>Page 2</td><td>May 16, 200x</td></tr>
</table>

Uses past-tense verbs to show that work has already started on the project.

Schedule. With your approval, the following schedule has been arranged for your patient satisfaction survey:

Questionnaire development and mailing	June 1–6
Deadline for returning questionnaire	June 24
Data tabulation and processing	June 24–26
Completion of final report	July 1

Staffing

Builds credibility by describing outstanding staff and facilities.

Swensen Research Associates is a nationally recognized, experienced research consulting firm specializing in survey investigation. I have assigned your customer satisfaction survey to Dr. Kelly Miller, our director of research. Dr. Miller was trained at Queen's University and has successfully supervised our research program for the past nine years. Before joining SRA, she was a marketing analyst with Procter & Gamble Company. Assisting Dr. Miller will be a team headed by James Wilson, our vice president for operations. Mr. Wilson earned a bachelor's degree in computer science and a master's degree in marketing from the University of Calgary, where he graduated with honours. Within our organization he supervises our computer-aided telephone interviewing (CATI) system and manages our 30-person professional interviewing staff.

Budget

Itemizes costs carefully because a proposal is a contract offer.

	Estimated Hours	Rate	Total
Professional and administrative time			
Questionnaire development	3	$150/hr.	$ 450
Data processing and tabulation	16	40/hr.	640
Analysis of findings	15	150/hr.	2250
Preparation of final report	5	150/hr.	750
Mailing costs			
300 copies of questionnaire			120
Postage and envelopes			270
Total costs			$4480

Authorization

Closes by repeating key qualifications and main benefits.

Makes response easy and provides deadline.

We are convinced, Dr. Larocque, that our professionally designed and administered client satisfaction survey will enhance your efforts to implement a total quality management system in your practice. Swensen Research Associates can have specific results for you by July 1 if you sign the enclosed duplicate copy of this letter and return it to us with a retainer of $2300. The prices in this offer are in effect only until September 1.

Sincerely,

Dana H. Swensen

Dana H. Swensen, President

DHS:pem
Enclosure

STAFFING

The staffing section of a proposal describes the credentials and expertise of the project leaders. It may also identify the size and qualifications of the support staff, along with other resources such as computer facilities and special programs for analyzing statistics. In longer proposals, résumés of key people may be provided. The staffing or personnel section is a good place to endorse and promote your staff.

BUDGET

A central item in most proposals is the budget, a list of project costs. You need to prepare this section carefully because it represents a contract; you can't raise the price later—even if your costs increase. You can—and should—protect yourself with a deadline for acceptance. In the budget section some writers itemize hours and costs; others present a total sum only. A proposal to install a complex computer system might, for example, contain a detailed line-by-line budget. In the proposal shown in Figure 12.1, Dana Swensen felt that she needed to justify the budget for her firm's patient satisfaction survey, so she itemized the costs. But the budget included in a proposal to conduct a one-day seminar to improve employee communication skills might be a lump sum only. Your analysis of the project will help you decide what kind of budget to prepare.

Because a proposal is a legal contract, the budget must be carefully researched.

AUTHORIZATION

Informal proposals often close with a request for approval or authorization. In addition, the closing should remind the reader of key benefits and motivate action. It might also include a deadline date beyond which the offer is invalid.

FORMAL PROPOSALS

Formal proposals differ from informal proposals not in style but in size and format. Formal proposals respond to big projects and may range from 5 to 200 or more pages. To facilitate comprehension and reference, they are organized into many parts. In addition to the six basic parts just described, formal proposals contain some or all of the following additional parts: copy of the RFP, letter of transmittal, abstract and/or executive summary, title page, table of contents, figures, and appendix.

Formal proposals respond to big projects and may contain 200 or more pages.

Well-written proposals win contracts and business for companies and individuals. In fact, many companies depend entirely on proposals to generate their income. Large companies such as Hewlett-Packard and IBM employ staffs of people that do nothing but prepare proposals to compete for new business.

FORMAL REPORTS

Formal reports, whether they offer only information or whether they also analyze that information and make recommendations, typically have three characteristics: formal tone, traditional structure, and lengthiness. Although formal research reports in business are infrequently seen, they serve a very important function. They provide management with vital data for decision making. In this section we will consider the entire process of writing a formal report: preparing to write; collecting, documenting, organizing, and illustrating data; and presenting the final report.

The primary differences between formal and informal reports are tone, structure, and length.

PREPARING TO WRITE

Like proposals and informal reports, formal reports begin with a definition of the project. Probably the most difficult part of this definition is limiting the scope of the report. Every project has limitations. Decide at the outset what constraints influence the range of your project and how you will achieve your purpose. How much time do you have for completing your report? How much space will you be allowed for reporting on your topic? How accessible are the data you need? How thorough should your research be? For example, if you are writing about low morale among swing-shift employees, how many of your 475 employees should you interview? Should you limit your research to company-related morale factors, or should you consider external factors over which the company has no control? In investigating variable-rate mortgages, should you focus on a particular group, such as first-time homeowners in a specific area, or should you consider all mortgage holders? The first step in writing a report, then, is determining the precise boundaries of the topic.

Once you have defined the project and limited its scope, write a statement of purpose. The statement of purpose should describe the goal, significance, and limitations of the report. Notice how the following statement pinpoints the research and report:

> The purpose of this report is to explore employment possibilities for entry-level health records technicians in the city of St. John's. It will consider typical salaries, skills required, opportunities, and working conditions. This research is significant because of the increasing number of job openings in the health records field. This report will not consider health care sector secretarial employment, which represents a different employment focus.

The planning of every report begins with a statement of purpose explaining the goal, significance, and limitations of the project.

COLLECTING DATA

Effective reports, whether formal or informal, are founded on accurate data. Data collected for business reports or proposals, as shown in Figure 12.2, may be gathered from two sources, primary and secondary. Primary information is obtained from first-hand observation and experience. Secondary information comes from reading what others have observed or experienced.

PRIMARY SOURCES

Because they generally seek to solve current problems, formal business reports rely heavily on primary source material. Four logical sources of primary information for a report are (1) observations, (2) interviews, (3) surveys, and (4) experiments.

Primary data are facts that have not already been collected and recorded by someone else.

Observations. In business reports personal observation often provides essential data. For example, if Jasbir Mangat, a marketing manager, were writing a report recommending changes in sales territories, he would probably begin by carefully observing the current territories and analyzing sales coverage. If Samantha Jones, a student, were reporting on employment possibilities, she might begin by observing classified ads in a local newspaper.

Interviews. Collecting information by talking with individuals gives the researcher immediate feedback and provides a chance for explanation of questions if necessary. If the information collected is to be used scientifically or systematically, the interviewer should follow an interview schedule—that is, the same questions, stated identically, should be addressed to all interviewees.

FIGURE 12.2

Primary and Secondary Data Sources

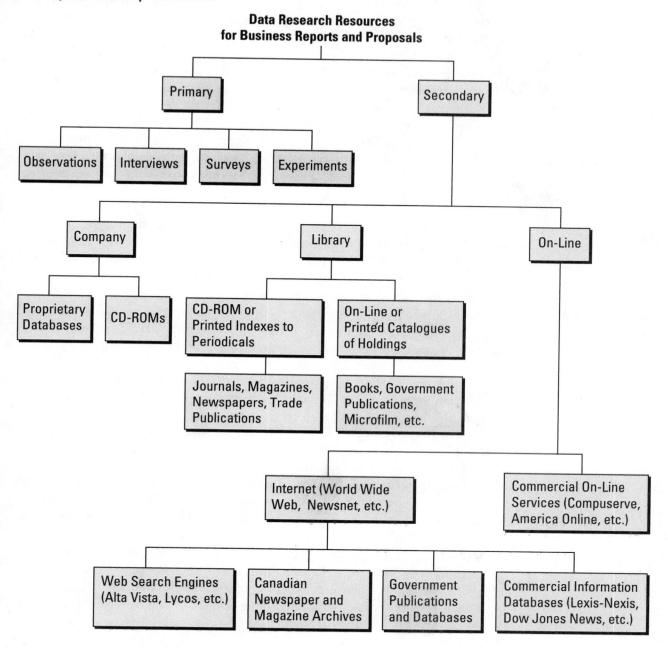

Surveys. If many questions need to be asked of a large group of individuals and if costs must be kept down, then surveys may be used to collect data. Good surveys, however, cannot be conducted casually. Questions should be carefully written and tested on sample groups before actually being administered. Thought should be given to how the results will be tabulated and interpreted.

Experiments. Although experimentation is more common to the physical and social sciences, decision makers in business may also use this technique to gather information. In promoting a new product, for example, a business might experiment with an ad in two different newspapers and compare the results.

SECONDARY SOURCES

The most important information in formal business reports usually comes from first-hand, primary sources. Yet, the research process for every business report or proposal should begin with secondary sources. Why? Beginning with a search of secondary sources provides an overview of the project. Often, something has already been written about your topic. Reviewing secondary sources can save you time and effort and prevent you from "reinventing the wheel."

As a researcher of secondary sources today, you have many more options available to you than ever before. Figure 12.2 shows rich veins of secondary information ready for you to mine. With your computer, for example, you can find information on just about any subject, but only if you know where to look and only if you have search skills. Our discussion will concentrate on secondary data in three main areas: company records, libraries, and on-line sources.

Many formal business reports require company, library, and/or on-line research to provide background data.

Company Data. Business reports generally seek to solve company problems, such as how to reduce expenses, how to serve customers better, and how to sell more of the company's products. Report writers often consult proprietary databases to collect vital internal data. These databases hold vast amounts of in-house information, such as customer files, which can be searched by product line, sales potential, and demographics (age, gender, and income, for example). Companies also may have purchased business CD-ROMs, such as *World Marketing Data & Statistics*, and indexes listing company profiles, addresses, earnings, and industry groupings. Some CD-ROM databases even have spreadsheet and charting functions that can be incorporated directly into a report. Much of the business information formerly available only in print or on CD-ROM is now available on the World Wide Web where it is immediately available either free or at a cost.

Library Data. When you go to a library today, you'll probably use (a) indexes to periodicals and/or (b) an on-line catalogue to books. Magazines, pamphlets, and journals are called periodicals because of their recurrent publication. Journals are compilations of scholarly articles. Journals and other periodicals generally provide the most up-to-date information on a topic. Most libraries today have all their indexes included in an on-line catalogue, which lets you look up books, journals, business magazines, videos, and other items available on their shelves. If you need historical, in-depth data on a subject, consult your library's holdings in its on-line catalogue. Your library's network also offers access to a vast array of electronic periodical indexes and abstracts, full-text journal databases, electronic encyclopedias, and sources of statistical data not available on their shelves. Library computers usually offer Internet access as well.

For many business reports, books are inadequate because the information they contain is outdated. Recent issues of periodicals are generally more timely and should be consulted first. To locate articles in business, industrial, and trade magazines and journals, consult the *Canadian Business Periodicals Index, Business Source Elite, Canadian Newsdisc, CBCA Fulltext Reference,* or business directories such as *Canadian Business Directories, Canadian Who's Who,* or *Small Business Profiles Index.*

On-Line Data. By using computers with dial-up connections or computers with network connections, business researchers can gather information from (a) commercial on-line services and (b) the Internet.

Commercial On-Line Services. U.S.-based CompuServe, Prodigy, and America Online are examples of companies that provide generalized on-line services, as discussed in Chapter 1. In Canada, companies such as Sympatico and America Online Canada offer similar services with a distinctly Canadian focus. Business researchers would probably be most interested in the databases. These services offer revealing profiles and financial data on thousands of public companies. As well, Lexis-Nexis, Dow Jones News, and many other information-retrieval services have Web sites that provide direct access to business-related materials. For a subscription fee, these retrieval services provide information from newspapers, magazines, journals, directories, legal proceedings, and a wide range of other sources.

The Internet. With its global connections and millions of users, the Internet has been called the world's biggest electronic library. And it has revolutionized the way we collect information. Let's say you are writing a report about start-up companies. You could use Web search engines to find not only government articles with how-to information but also statistics on successes and failures in industry groups. Archived (preserved) articles available at the Web sites of Canadian and world newspapers and magazines could provide valuable background data. You could even go to the Web sites of specific start-up companies to see how they are structured. And if you wanted to ask questions of an expert, you could probably locate one in a Usenet discussion group available on the Internet. (To see the Web sites of a number of Internet sites of interest to frugal business researchers, look at the Chapter 12 Communication Workshop on page 311.) Basic information at many Web sites is free. For more comprehensive data, businesses generally subscribe to commercial information services such as Lexis-Nexis (www.lexis-nexis-canada.com), Infoglobe-Dow-Jones Interactive Canada (ip.dowjones.com/canada), or Dun & Bradstreet Canada (www.dnb.ca).

SEARCH STRATEGIES

To give formal reports credibility and authority, researchers generally rely on a certain amount of secondary data obtained in print or electronically. You can be most effective in searching for that data by observing the following suggestions.

- *Become acquainted with your library's resources, both print and electronic.* It pays to discuss your project with a reference librarian. By the way, several years ago a *Wall Street Journal* poll revealed that librarians are among the friendliest, most approachable people in the working world.

- *Learn to use your computer to conduct research.* An amazing number of information resources are now available on-line and with CD-ROMs. Access to Web resources is gained by using Web search engines. Some of the most commonly used search engines are Yahoo.ca, Hotbot.ca, and Canada.com. Each of these engines allows you to limit your search to Canadian sites only or broaden your search to include the entire Web. Other general search engines are: AltaVista, Infoseek, Excite, Web Crawler, and Lycos.

- *Don't allow yourself to become a victim of information overload.* You can't read everything that's been written about your subject. Look up only relevant and current references. Be selective.

- *Be resourceful and persevering when searching for data.* For example, if you're looking for information about speaking skills for businesspeople, you might look under such descriptors as *speech, communication, language, public relations,* and *conversation.* Don't forget to ask your librarian for help with key words.

- *Keep excellent notes.* Make a record of each reference on a separate printout sheet or card. You'll need the author's name, title of the article or book, and complete publication information, in addition to your notes regarding the reference content. If possible, print out complete bibliographic information, including URLs (uniform resource locators) for on-line references.

CITING SOURCES

If you use data from secondary sources, the data must be documented; that is, you must indicate where the data originated. Using the ideas of someone else without giving credit is called *plagiarism* and is unethical. Even if you paraphrase (put the information in your own words), the ideas must be documented. In citing sources, you should use direct quotations sparingly. Good writers use the exact words of another writer only to (1) emphasize opinions because of the author's status as an expert; (2) duplicate the exact wording before criticizing; or (3) repeat identical phrasing because of its precision, clarity, or aptness.

Not many writers enjoy the task, but most take pains nevertheless to properly document report data—for many reasons. Citing sources strengthens a writer's argument. Acknowledging sources also shields writers from charges of plagiarism. Moreover, good references help readers pursue further research. Fortunately, word processing programs have taken much of the pain out of documenting data, so the task is no longer so tedious. In Appendix C you will find additional information about preparing the Notes and Bibliography sections of a formal report.

ORGANIZING AND OUTLINING DATA

Once you've collected the data for a report and recorded that information on notes or printouts, it must be organized into a coherent plan of presentation. First, you should decide on an organizational strategy, and then you'll want to outline the report following your plan.

ORGANIZATIONAL STRATEGIES

The overall presentation of a topic may be inductive or deductive, while parts of the report are chronological (such as the background) or topical (such as discussion of findings).

The readability of a report is greatly enhanced by skilful organization of the facts presented. You have already studied numerous strategies or plans of organization for shorter documents. Here is a brief overview of possible plans for the organization of formal reports:

- *Deductive strategy.* As you recall from earlier instruction, the deductive strategy presents main ideas first. In formal reports that would mean beginning with proposals, recommendations, or findings. For example, if you were studying five possible locations for a proposed shopping centre, you would begin with the recommendation of the best site and follow with a discussion of other sites. Use this strategy when the reader is supportive and knowledgeable.
- *Inductive strategy.* Inductive reasoning presents facts and discussion first, followed by conclusions and recommendations. Since formal reports generally

seek to educate the reader, this order of presentation is often most effective. Following this sequence, a study of possible locations for a shopping centre would begin with data regarding all proposed sites followed by analysis of the information and conclusions drawn from that analysis.

- *Chronological sequence.* Information sequenced along a time frame is arranged chronologically. This plan is effective for presenting historical data or for describing a procedure. A description of the development of a multinational company, for example, would be chronological. A report explaining how to obtain federal funding for a project might be organized chronologically. Often topics are arranged in a past-to-present or present-to-past sequence.

- *Geographical or spatial arrangement.* Information arranged geographically or spatially is organized by physical location. For instance, a report analyzing a company's national sales might be divided into sections representing different geographical areas such as the Atlantic region, Central Canada, the Prairie region, and the Pacific region.

- *Topical or functional arrangement.* Some subjects lend themselves to arrangement by topic or function. A report analyzing changes in the management hierarchy of an organization might be arranged in this manner. First, the report would consider the duties of the CEO followed by the function of the general manager, business manager, marketing manager, and so forth.

In organizing a formal report, you may find that you combine some of the preceding plans. However it's done, you must break your topic into major divisions, usually three to six. These major divisions then can be partitioned into smaller subdivisions. To identify these divisions, you may use functional heads (such as *Introduction, Findings, Discussion, Conclusions, Recommendations*) or talking heads that explain the contents of the text. You may wish to review the suggestions for writing effective headings that appeared in Chapter 11, pages 251 to 252.

OUTLINING FOR CLARITY

Most writers agree that the clearest way to show the organization of a report topic is by recording its divisions in an outline. Although the outline is not part of the final report, it is a valuable tool of the writer. It reveals at a glance the overall organization of the report. Figure 12.3 shows an abbreviated outline of a report about forms of business ownership. Rarely is a real outline so perfectly balanced; some sections are usually longer than others. Remember, though, not to put a single topic under a major component. If you have only one subpoint, integrate it with the main item above it or reorganize. Use details, illustrations, and evidence to support subpoints.

The format of your report headings is closely related to your outline. You may choose to format your headings automatically by using one of your word processing program's report templates. Or, you may wish to customize your report headings. Figure 12.4 discusses and illustrates levels of headings.

ILLUSTRATING DATA

Tables, charts, graphs, illustrations, and other visual aids can play an important role in clarifying, summarizing, and emphasizing information. Numerical data become

FIGURE 12.3

Outline Format

FORMS OF BUSINESS OWNERSHIP

I. Sole proprietorship (first main topic)
   A. Advantages of sole proprietorship (first subdivision of Topic I)
      1. Minimal capital requirements (first subdivision of Topic A)
      2. Control by owner (second subdivision of Topic A)
   B. Disadvantages of sole proprietorship (second subdivision of Topic I)
      1. Unlimited liability (first subdivision of Topic B)
      2. Limited management talent (second subdivision of Topic B)

II. Partnership (second main topic)
   A. Advantages of partnership (first subdivision of Topic II)
      1. Access of capital (first subdivision of Topic A)
      2. Management talent (second subdivision of Topic A)
      3. Ease of formation (third subdivision of Topic A)
   B. Disadvantages of partnership (second subdivision of Topic II)
      1. Unlimited liability (first subdivision of Topic B)
      2. Personality conflicts (second subdivision of Topic B)

The tips presented here for generating and implementing graphics in formal reports are useful in other presentations as well.

meaningful, complex ideas are simplified, and visual interest is provided by the appropriate use of graphics. Here are general tips for making the most effective use of visual aids:

- Clearly identify the contents of the visual aid with meaningful titles and headings.
- Refer the reader to the visual aid by discussing it in the text and mentioning its location and figure number.
- Locate the table close to its reference in the text.
- Strive for vertical placement of visual aids. Readers are disoriented by horizontal pages in reports.
- Give credit to the source if appropriate.

TABLES

Probably the most frequently used visual aid in reports is the table. A table presents quantitative information in a systematic order of columns and rows. Be sure to identify columns and rows clearly. In Figure 12.5 *Maritime* represents a row heading; *1st Qtr.* represents a column heading.

CHARTS AND GRAPHS

A chart or graph clarifies data by showing the relationship between one variable and another. Pie charts, line charts, bar charts, and organization charts most frequently appear in formal reports.

FIGURE 12.4

Levels of Headings in Reports

REPORT, CHAPTER, AND PART TITLES

The title of a report, chapter heading, or major part (such as CONTENTS or NOTES) should be centred in all caps. If the title requires more than one line, arrange it in an inverted triangle with the longest lines at the top. Begin the text a triple space (two blank lines) below the title, as shown here.

First-Level Subheading

Headings indicating the first level of division are centred and underlined. Capitalize the first letter of each main word. Whether a report is single-spaced or double-spaced, most typists triple-space (leaving two blank lines) before and double-space (leaving one blank line) after a first-level subheading.

Every level of heading should be followed by some text. For example, we could not jump from "First-Level Subheading," shown above, to "Second-Level Subheading," shown below, without some discussion between.

Good writers strive to develop coherency and fluency by ending most sections with a lead-in that introduces the next section.

Second-Level Subheading

Headings that divide topics introduced by first-level subheadings are under-lined and begin at the left margin. Use a triple space above and a double space below a second-level subheading. If a report has only one level of heading, use either a first- or second-level subheading style.

Always be sure to divide topics into two or more subheadings. If you have only one subheading, eliminate it and absorb the discussion under the previous major heading. Try to make all headings within a level grammatically equal. For example, all second-level headings might use verb forms *(Preparing, Organizing,* and *Composing)* or noun forms *(Preparation, Organization,* and *Composition).*

Third-Level subheading . Because it is part of the paragraph that follows, a third-level subheading is also called a "paragraph subheading." Capitalize only the first word and proper nouns in the subheading. Underline the subheading and end it with a period. Do not underline the period. Double-space before a paragraph subheading.

Centre first-level subheadings, capitalize initial letters of main words, and initial letters of second elements of hyphenated words if they are nouns.

Start second-level subheadings at left margin and capitalize initial letters of main words.

Indent third-level subheadings as part of paragraph and capitalize first letter.

Pie Chart. Pie, or circle, charts help readers visualize a whole and the proportions of its components, as shown in Figure 12.6. Pie charts are particularly useful in showing percentages. In preparing pie charts, arrange the largest portion to begin at the 12 o'clock position. It's helpful to include both a description and the actual per-cent of the total with each segment. To avoid visual clutter, group a number of small components into one segment. All segments should total 100 percent. Labels are easiest to read when typed horizontally outside the segments.

FIGURE 12.5

Table

DYNAMO PRODUCTS
Number of Computers Sold, 1998

Region	1st Qtr.	2nd Qtr.	3rd Qtr.	4th Qtr.	Yearly Totals
Maritime	13 302	15 003	15 550	16 210	60 065
Central	12 678	11 836	10 689	14 136	49 339
Mountain	10 345	11 934	10 899	12 763	45 941
Pacific	9 345	8 921	9 565	10 256	38 087
Total	45 670	47 694	46 703	53 365	193 432

FIGURE 12.6

Pie Chart

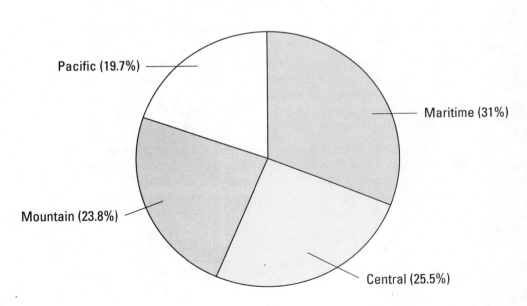

Dynamo Products
1998 Sales

Pacific (19.7%)
Maritime (31%)
Mountain (23.8%)
Central (25.5%)

Line Chart. Line charts are useful in showing changes in quantitative data over time. Like many visual aids, line charts cannot show precise data; instead, they give an impression of a trend or movement. Notice in Figure 12.7 that the time variable (years) is shown horizontally and the quantitative variable (tonnes of candy bars produced) is shown vertically. The trend shows strong growth in milk chocolate bars and decline in the production of granola bars.

FIGURE 12.7

Line Chart

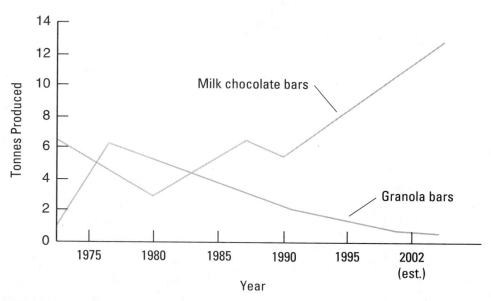

Trends in Candy Bar Production

FIGURE 12.8

Bar Chart

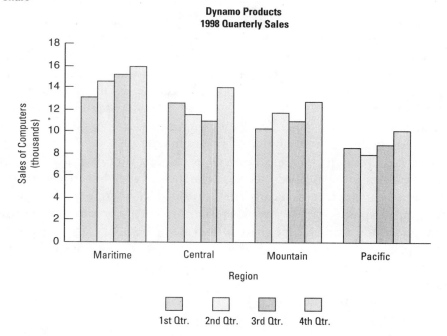

Bar Chart. A bar chart uses horizontal bars or vertical columns to compare information. Figure 12.8 shows a company's quarterly sales by regions of the country.

Organization Chart. An organization chart shows management structure and lines of authority. The chart in Figure 12.9 defines the hierarchy of authority from the board of directors to individual managers.

In making bar charts, start with graph paper or draw your own grid, marking off even segments before you make the first column

FIGURE 12.9

Organization Chart

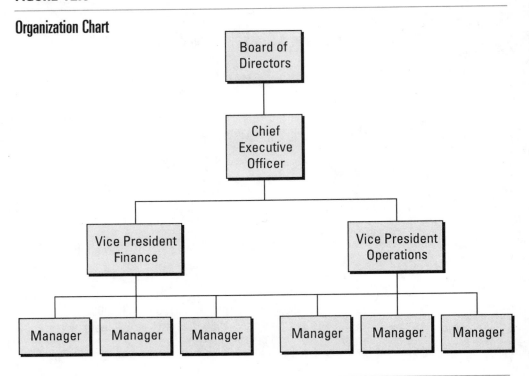

USING YOUR COMPUTER TO PRODUCE CHARTS

Designing effective bar charts, pie charts, figures, and other graphics is easy with today's software. Spreadsheet programs—such as Lotus 1-2-3, Excel, and QuattroPro—as well as presentation graphics programs—such as Harvard Graphics, Microsoft PowerPoint, and Lotus Freelance Graphics—allow even nontechnical people to design quality graphics. These graphics can be printed directly on paper for written reports or used for transparency masters and slides for oral presentations. The benefits of preparing visual aids on a computer are near-professional quality, shorter preparation time, and substantial savings in costs.

To prepare a computer graphic, begin by assembling your data, usually in table form (such as that in Figure 12.5). Next, choose what type of chart you want: pie chart, grouped bar chart, vertical bar chart, horizontal bar chart, organization chart, or some other graphic. To make a pie chart, key in the data or select the data from an existing file. Add a title for the chart, as well as any necessary labels. For a bar or line chart, indicate the horizontal and vertical axes (reference lines or beginning points). Most programs will automatically generate legends for figures.

The finished chart can be printed on paper or imported into your word processing document to be printed with your finished report.

PRESENTING THE FINAL REPORT

Long reports are generally organized into three major divisions: (a) prefatory parts, (b) body, and (c) supplementary parts. Below (text continues on page 299) is a description of the order and content of each part. Refer to the model formal report in Figure 12.10 for illustration of most of these parts.

FIGURE 12.10

Model Formal Report
Title Page

ECONOMIC IMPACT OF ROXBURY INDUSTRIAL PARK
ON THE CITY OF WINNIPEG

Includes report title in all caps with longer line above shorter line.

Prepared for
The Standing Policy Committee on Property and Development
Winnipeg City Council
Winnipeg, Manitoba

Highlights name of report recipient.

Prepared by
Diana Del Rio
Senior Research Consultant
Monroe, Del Rio Industrial Consultants

Identifies report writer.

January 10, 200x

Omits page number.

The title page is usually arranged in four evenly balanced areas. If the report is to be bound on the left, move the left margin and centre point .5 cm to the right. Notice that no page number appears on the title page, although it is counted as page i. In designing the title page, be careful to avoid anything unprofessional—such as too many type fonts, italics, oversized print, and inappropriate graphics. Keep the title page simple and professional.

FIGURE 12.10 Continued

Letter of Transmittal

MONROE, DEL RIO INDUSTRIAL CONSULTANTS
588 Main Street
Winnipeg, MB R2L 1E6

January 12, 200x

Councillor Richard Moody
Chairperson
The Standing Policy Committee on Property and Development
City of Winnipeg
Winnipeg, MB R2L 1E6

Dear Councillor Moody:

Announces report and identifies authorization.

The attached report, requested by the Standing Policy Committee on Property and Development in a letter dated May 20, describes the economic impact of Roxbury Industrial Park on the city of Winnipeg. We believe you will find the results of this study useful in evaluating future development of industrial parks within the city limits.

Gives broad overview of report purposes.

This study was designed to examine economic impact in three areas:

(1) Current and projected tax and other revenues accruing to the city from Roxbury Industrial Park

(2) Current and projected employment generated by the park

(3) Indirect effects on local employment, income, and economic growth

Describes primary and secondary research.

Primary research consisted of interviews with 15 Roxbury Industrial Park tenants and managers, in addition to a 1999 survey of over 500 RIP employees. Secondary research sources included the Annual Budget of the City of Winnipeg, other government publications, periodicals, books, and on-line resources. Results of this research, discussed more fully in this report, indicate that Roxbury Industrial Park exerts a significant beneficial influence on the Winnipeg metropolitan economy.

Offers to discuss report; expresses appreciation.

I would be pleased to discuss this report and its conclusions with you at your request. My firm and I thank you for your confidence in selecting our company to prepare this report.

Sincerely,

Diana Del Rio

Diana Del Rio
Senior Research Consultant

DDR:mef
Attachment

A letter or memo of transmittal announces the report topic and explains who authorized it. It briefly describes the project and previews the conclusions, if the reader is supportive. Such messages generally close by expressing appreciation for the assignment, suggesting follow-up actions, acknowledging the help of others, or offering to answer questions. The margins for the transmittal should be the same as for the report, about 3 cm on all sides.

FIGURE 12.10 Continued

Table of Contents and List of Figures

Uses leaders to guide eye from heading to page number.

Indents secondary headings to show levels of outline.

Includes tables and figures in one list for simplified numbering.

Because the table of contents and the list of figures for this report are small, they are combined on one page. Notice that the titles of major report parts are in all caps, while other headings are a combination of upper- and lowercase letters. The style duplicates that within the report. Applying a template from your word processing program will enable you to generate a contents page automatically, including leaders and accurate page numbering—no matter how many times you revise.

FIGURE 12.10 Continued

Executive Summary

EXECUTIVE SUMMARY

Opens directly with major research findings.

Winnipeg can benefit from the development of industrial parks like the Roxbury Industrial Park. Both direct and indirect economic benefits result, as shown by this study conducted by Monroe, Del Rio Industrial Consultants. The study was authorized by the Standing Policy Committee on Property and Development when Goldman-Lyon & Associates sought City Council's approval for the proposed construction of a G-L industrial park. The City Council requested evidence demonstrating that an existing development does actually benefit the city.

Identifies data sources.

Our conclusion that Winnipeg benefits from industrial parks is based on data supplied by a survey of 500 Roxbury Industrial Park employees, personal interviews with managers and tenants of RIP, city documents, and professional literature.

Summarizes organization of report.

Analysis of the data revealed benefits in three areas:

(1) Revenues. The City of Winnipeg earned nearly $1 million in tax and other revenues from the Roxbury Industrial Park in 1998. By 2002 this income is expected to reach $1.7 million (in constant 2000 dollars).

(2) Employment. In 1998 RIP businesses employed a total of 735 workers, who earned an average wage of $28,719. By 2002 RIP businesses are expected to employ directly nearly 1500 employees who will earn salaries totalling over $45 million.

(3) Indirect benefits. Because of the multiplier effect, by 2002 Roxbury Industrial Park will directly and indirectly generate a total of 3836 jobs in the Winnipeg area.

Condenses recommendations.

On the basis of these findings, it is recommended that development of additional industrial parks be encouraged to stimulate local economic growth.

An executive summary or abstract highlights report findings, conclusions, and recommendations. Its length depends on the report it summarizes. A 100-page report might require a ten-page summary. Shorter reports may contain one-page summaries, as shown here. Unlike letters of transmittal (which may contain personal pronouns and references to the writer), summaries are formal and impersonal. They use the same margins as the body of the report.

FIGURE 12.10 Continued

Page 1

ECONOMIC IMPACT OF ROXBURY INDUSTRIAL PARK

PROBLEM

This study was designed to analyze the direct and indirect economic impact of Roxbury Industrial Park on the city of Winnipeg. Specifically, the study seeks answers to these questions:

(1) What current tax and other revenues result directly from this park? What tax and other revenues may be expected in the future?

(2) How many and what kind of jobs are directly attributable to the park? What is the employment picture for the future?

(3) What indirect effects has Roxbury Industrial Park had on local employment, incomes, and economic growth?

BACKGROUND

The Standing Policy Committee on Property and Development commissioned this study of Roxbury Industrial Park at the request of Winnipeg City Council. Before authorizing the development of a proposed Goldman-Lyon industrial park, the City Council requested a study examining the economic effects of an existing park. Members of Council wanted to determine to what extent industrial parks benefit the local community, and they chose Roxbury Industrial Park as an example.

For those who are unfamiliar with it, Roxbury Industrial Park is a 40-acre industrial park located in Winnipeg about 2 kilometres from the centre of the city. Most of the area lies within a specially designated area known as Redevelopment Area No. 2, which is part of the Winnipeg Capital Region Development Commission's planning area. Construction on Roxbury Industrial Park started in 1990.

Lists three problem questions.

Describes authorization for report and background of study.

The first page of a formal report contains the title printed 5 cm from the top edge. Titles for the major parts of a report (such as *PROBLEM, BACKGROUND, FINDINGS,* and *CONCLUSIONS*) are centred and are all caps. First-level headings (such as *Employment* on page 295) are underscored and printed with upper- and lowercase letters. Second-level headings (such as *Distribution* on page 295) begin at the side. See Figure 12.4 for an illustration of heading formats.

FIGURE 12.10 Continued

Page 2

Provides specifics for data sources.

Previews organization of report.

Places figure close to textual reference.

The park now contains 14 building complexes with over 25,000 square metres of completed building space. The majority of the buildings are used for office, research and development, marketing and distribution, or manufacturing purposes. Approximately five acres of the original area are yet to be developed.

Data for this report came from a 1999 survey of over 500 Roxbury Industrial Park employees, interviews with 15 RIP tenants and managers, the Annual Budget of the City of Winnipeg, current books, articles, and on-line resources. Projections for future revenues resulted from analysis of past trends and "Estimates of Revenues for Debt Service Coverage, Redevelopment Project Area 2."

DISCUSSION OF FINDINGS

The results of this research indicate that major direct and indirect benefits have accrued to the city of Winnipeg and surrounding municipal areas as a result of the development of Roxbury Industrial Park. The research findings presented here fall into two categories: (a) revenues, and (b) employment.

Revenues

Roxbury Industrial Park contributes a variety of tax and other revenues to the city of Winnipeg. Figure 1 summarizes revenues.

Figure 1

REVENUES RECEIVED BY THE CITY OF WINNIPEG FROM ROXBURY INDUSTRIAL PARK

Current Revenues and Projections to 2002

	1998	2002
Property taxes	$604,140	$1,035,390
Revenues from licences	126,265	216,396
Business Taxes	75,518	129,424
Provincial service receipts	53,768	92,134
Licenses and permits	48,331	82,831
Other revenues	64,039	111,987
Total	$972,061	$1,668,162

Source: City of Winnipeg Standing Committee on Finance, *Annual Report.* Winnipeg: City Clerk's Office, 1999, 103.

2

Notice that this formal report is single-spaced. Many businesses use this space-saving format. However, some organizations prefer double-spacing, especially for preliminary drafts. Page numbers may be centred, 2.5 cm from the bottom of the page, or they may be placed 2.5 cm from the upper right corner at the margin. Strive to leave a minimum of 2.5 cm for top, bottom, and side margins.

FIGURE 12.10 Continued

Page 3

Sales and Use Revenues

As shown in Figure 1, the city's largest source of revenues from RIP is property tax. Revenues from this source totalled $604,140 in 1998, according to figures provided by the City of Winnipeg Standing Committee on Finance.[1] Property taxes accounted for more than half of the park's total contribution to the city of $972,061.

Other Revenues

Other major sources of city revenues from RIP in 1998 include revenues from licences such as motor vehicle in lieu fees, trailer coach licences ($126,265), business taxes ($75,518), and provincial service receipts ($53,768).

Projections

Total city revenues from RIP will nearly double by 2002, producing an income of $1.7 million. This projection is based on an annual growth rate in sales of 8 percent in constant 2000 dollars.

Employment

One of the most important factors to consider in the overall effect of an industrial park is employment. In Roxbury Industrial Park the distribution, number, and wages of people employed will change considerably in the next five years.

Distribution

A total of 735 employees currently work in various industry groups at Roxbury Industrial Park, as shown in Figure 2. The largest number of workers (58 percent) is employed in manufacturing and assembly operations. In the next largest category, the computer and electronics industry employs 24 percent of the workers. Some overlap probably exists because electronics assembly could be included in either group. Employees also work in publishing (9 percent), warehousing and storage (5 percent), and other industries (4 percent).

Although the distribution of employees at Roxbury Industrial Park shows a wide range of employment categories, it must be noted that other industrial parks would likely generate an entirely different range of job categories.

3

Continues interpreting figures in table.

Sets stage for next topics to be discussed.

Only the most important research findings are interpreted and discussed for readers. The depth of discussion depends on the intended length of the report, the goal of the writer, and the expectations of the reader. Because the writer wants this report to be formal in tone, she avoids *I* and *we* in all discussions.

FIGURE 12.10 Continued

Page 4

Pie chart shows proportion of a whole.

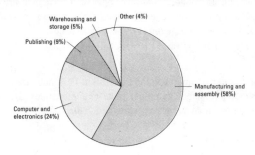

Figure 2

EMPLOYMENT DISTRIBUTION OF INDUSTRY GROUPS

Warehousing and storage (5%)
Other (4%)
Publishing (9%)
Manufacturing and assembly (58%)
Computer and electronics (24%)

Source: 1999 survey of RIP employees.

<u>Wages</u>

In 1998 employees at RIP earned a total of $21.1 million in wages, as shown in Figure 3. The average employee in that year earned $27,920. The highest average wages were paid to employees in white-collar fields, such as the computer and electronics ($36,800) and publishing ($30,300) industries. Average wages for workers in blue-collar fields ranged from $26,400 in manufacturing and assembly to $24,200 in warehousing and storage.

Figure 3

AVERAGE ANNUAL WAGES BY INDUSTRIAL GROUPS

Roxbury Industrial Park, 1998

Industry Group	Employees	Annual Wages	Total
Manufacturing and assembly	463	$26,400	$12,223,200
Computer and electronics	157	36,800	5,777,600
Publishing	62	30,300	1,878,600
Warehousing and storage	30	24,200	726,000
Other	23	21,900	503,700
	735	$27,920	$21,109,100

Source: 1999 Survey of RIP employees.

Table condenses complex data into readable and understandable form.

4

If you use figures or tables, be sure to introduce them in the text (for example, *as shown in Figure 3*). Although it's not always possible, try to place them close to the spot where they are first mentioned. To save space, you can print the title of a figure at its side. Because this report contains few tables and figures, the writer named them all "Figures" and numbered them consecutively.

FIGURE 12.10 Continued

Page 5

Projections

By 2002 Roxbury Industrial Park is expected to more than double its number of employees, bringing the total to over 1500 workers. The total payroll in 2002 will also more than double, producing over $45 million (using constant 2000 dollars) in salaries to RIP employees. These projections are based on an 8 percent growth rate,[2] along with anticipated increased employment as the park reaches its capacity.

Future development in the park will influence employment and payrolls. One RIP project manager stated in an interview that much of the remaining 5 acres is planned for medium-rise office buildings, garden offices, and other structures for commercial, professional, and personal services.[3] Average wages for employees are expected to increase because of an anticipated shift to higher-paying white-collar jobs. Industrial parks often follow a similar pattern of evolution.[4]

Clarifies information and tells what it means in relation to original research questions.

CONCLUSIONS AND RECOMMENDATIONS

Summarizes conclusions and recommendations.

Analysis of tax revenues, employment data, personal interviews, and professional literature leads to the following conclusions and recommendations about the economic impact of Roxbury Industrial Park on the city of Winnipeg:

1. Property tax and other revenues produced nearly $1 million in income for the city of Winnipeg in 1998. By 2002 revenues are expected to produce $1.7 million in income.

2. RIP currently employs 735 employees, the majority of whom are working in manufacturing and assembly. In 1998 the average wage per employee was $27,920.

3. By 2002 RIP is expected to employ more than 1500 workers, producing a total payroll of over $45 million.

4. Employment trends indicate that by 2002 more RIP employees will be engaged in higher-paying white-collar positions.

On the basis of these findings, we recommend that the City Council of Winnipeg authorize the development of additional industrial parks to stimulate local economic growth.

5

After discussing and interpreting the research findings, the writer articulates what she considers the most important conclusions and recommendations. Longer, more complex reports may have separate sections for conclusions and resulting recommendations. In this report they are combined. Notice that it is unnecessary to start a new page for the conclusions.

FIGURE 12.10 Continued

Notes and Bibliography

NOTES

1. City of Winnipeg Standing Committee on Finance, *Annual Report* (Winnipeg: City Clerk's Office, 1999), 103.

2. Arthur M. Miller, "Estimates of Revenues for Debt Service Coverage, Redevelopment Project Area No. 2," *Miller and Schroeder Municipals* (Winnipeg: Rincon Press, 1998), 78–79.

3. Ivan M. Novak, interview by author, 30 September 1999.

4. Masood A. Badri, "Infrastructure, Trends, and Economic Effects of Industrial Parks," *Industry Week*, 1 April 1998, 38–45, in ABI/INFORM [on-line database] [cited 15 December 1998]; available from melvyl.ucop.edu.

BIBLIOGRAPHY

Badri, Masood A. 1998. "Infrastructure, Trends, and Economic Effects of Industrial Parks." *Industry Week*, 1 April, 38–45. In ABI/INFORM [on-line database]. [cited 15 December 1997]. Available from melvyl.ucop.edu.

Census of Canada. 1996. "Travel to Work Characteristics for the 10 Largest Metropolitan Areas by Population in Canada: 1996 Census." [cited 15 December 1998]. Available from www.statCan.ca.

City of Winnipeg. 1998. *Annual Budget*. Winnipeg: City Clerk's Office.

City of Winnipeg Standing Committee on Finance. 1999. *Annual Report*. Winnipeg: City Clerk's Office.

Cohen, Allen P. 1998. "Industrial Parks Invade Suburbia." *The New York Times*, 10 December, 1.

Miller, Arthur M. 1998. "Estimates of Revenues for Debt Service Coverage, Redevelopment Project Area No. 2," *Miller and Schroeder Municipals*. Winnipeg: Rincon Press.

Novak, Ivan M. 1999. Interview with author. 30 September.

6

Documents references in order of appearance in text.

Lists all sources alphabetically in hanging indented form.

A bibliography may be omitted if few sources are cited.

All references cited within the text are listed in the Notes. For more information about documenting sources, see Appendix C. Notes entries are arranged as they appear in the text, while bibliography entries are alphabetical. Some writers include all works they investigated in the bibliography. Most word processing software programs today automatically update notes within the text and print a complete list for you, thus making documentation almost painless.

PREFATORY PARTS (PARTS PRECEDING THE BODY)

- *Title fly.* A single page with the title begins a formal report. In less formal reports, the title fly is omitted. Our model report does not include this optional part. Compose the title of your report carefully so that it shows immediately what the report covers and what it does not cover.

- *Title page.* In addition to the title, the title page shows the author, the individual or organization who authorized the report, the recipient of the report, and the date.

- *Letter of authorization.* If a letter or memo authorized the report, it may be included in the prefatory material. This optional part is omitted from the model in Figure 12.10.

- *Letter of transmittal.* This is the first impression the reader receives of the report; as such, it should be given serious consideration. Use the direct strategy and include some or all of the suggestions here:

  1. Deliver the report ("Here is the report you authorized").
  2. Present an overview of the report.
  3. Suggest how to read or interpret it.
  4. Describe limitations, if they exist.
  5. Acknowledge those who assisted you.
  6. Suggest follow-up studies, if appropriate.
  7. Express appreciation for the assignment.
  8. Offer to discuss the report personally.

- *Table of contents.* Identify the name and location of every part of the report except the title fly, title page, and table of contents itself. Use spaced periods (leaders) to join the part with its page number.

- *Executive summary, abstract, or synopsis.* A summary condensing the entire report may carry any of these names. This time-saving device summarizes the purpose, findings, and conclusions.

BODY OF REPORT

- *Introduction or background.* After the prefatory parts, begin the body of the report with an introduction that includes any or all of the following items:

  1. Explanation of how the report originated and why it was authorized
  2. Description of the problem that prompted the report and the specific research questions to be answered
  3. Purpose of the report
  4. Scope (boundaries) and limitations or restrictions of the research
  5. Sources and methods of collecting data
  6. Summary of findings, if the report is written deductively
  7. Preview of the major sections of the report to follow, thus providing coherence and transition for the reader

- *Discussion of findings.* This is the main section of the report and contains numerous headings and subheadings. It is unnecessary to use the title *Discussion of Findings;* many business report writers prefer to begin immediately with the major headings into which the body of the report is divided. As with short reports, you may organize the body deductively, inductively, chronologically, geographically, or topically. Present your findings objectively, avoiding the use of first-person pronouns *(I, we)*. Include tables, charts, and graphs if necessary to illustrate findings. Analytic and scientific reports may include another section entitled *Implications of Findings*, in which the findings are analyzed and related to the problem. Less formal reports contain the author's analysis of the research findings within the *Discussion* section.

- *Summary, conclusions, recommendations.* If the report has been largely informational, it ends with a summary of the data presented. If the report analyzes research findings, then it ends with conclusions drawn from the analyses. An analytic report frequently poses research questions. The conclusion to such a report reviews the major findings and answers the research questions. If a report seeks to determine a course of action, it may end with conclusions and recommendations. The recommendations regarding a course of action may be placed in a separate section or incorporated with the conclusions.

SUPPLEMENTARY PARTS OF REPORT

- *Footnotes or endnotes.* See Appendix C for details on how to document sources. In the footnote method the source notes appear at the foot of each page. In the endnote method they are displayed immediately after the text on a page with the heading *Notes*.
- *Bibliography.* Most formal reports will include a bibliography that lists all sources consulted in the report research—whether they were actually cited in notes or not. See Appendix C regarding the bibliography.
- *Appendix.* The appendix contains any supplementary information needed to clarify the report. Charts and graphs illustrating significant data are generally part of the report proper. However, extra information that might be included in an appendix are such items as a sample questionnaire, a questionnaire cover letter, correspondence relating to the report, maps, other reports, and optional tables.

SUMMING UP AND LOOKING FORWARD

Proposals are offers to solve problems, provide services, or sell equipment. Both small and large businesses today write proposals to generate income. Informal proposals may be as short as two pages; formal proposals may be 200 pages or more. Regardless of the size, proposals contain standard parts that must be developed persuasively.

Formal reports present well-organized information systematically. The information may be collected from primary or secondary sources. All ideas borrowed from others must be documented. Good reports contain appropriate headings and illustrations.

You've now completed the unit on report writing. Next you'll study communication for employment, including interviewing and writing résumés and other employment messages.

DISCUSSION

1. Why is the writing of proposals an important function in many businesses?
2. How are proposals different from other business reports?
3. How is the process of writing a formal report similar to that of writing an informal report?
4. Distinguish between primary and secondary data. Which data are more likely to be useful in a business report?
5. Should every long, formal report have graphic aids? Explain.

CHAPTER REVIEW

6. What are the six principal parts of an informal proposal? Be prepared to explain each.

7. How are formal proposals different from informal proposals?

8. What is the first step in writing a formal report?

9. Do formal business reports generally rely more heavily on primary or secondary data?

10. List three sources of secondary information, and be prepared to discuss how each might be useful in writing a formal report about updating your company's accounting procedures.

11. Describe five types of data resources available through the Internet.

12. List four levels of headings, and explain how they are different.

13. Pie charts are most helpful in showing what?

   Line graphs are most effective in showing what?

14. If you've never used a library or an electronic database, where should you begin?

15. List the parts of a formal report. Be prepared to discuss each.

ACTIVITIES AND CASES

12.1 Outlining. Construct an outline using the following data gathered initially to write a report. Include a title. Assume that you will collect more data later. After you complete the outline, indicate what level of heading each line of the outline would require.

The operation of a business would be very risky without some form of property insurance. Most fire insurance policies protect against loss to buildings and their contents. Wooden buildings, of course, would cost more than brick buildings to insure. The contents of buildings are valued separately. Insurance experts believe that nearly one-third of all business-related fires may be caused by arson. Another form of property insurance is marine insurance. Ocean marine insurance is the oldest form of insurance in the country. It protects the ship and its cargo. Inland marine insurance, strangely enough, protects against damage to property being transported in three areas: goods transported by ship, truck, or train—that is, goods being moved by any of these three means may be covered with inland marine insurance.

Nearly 3 million automobile accidents occur each year in Canada. Automobile insurance is a form of property insurance. It covers many areas, including bodily injury, medical payment coverage (to protect policyholders, their family members, and any passengers in the car), and uninsured motorist coverage. Auto insurance also includes property damage. This pays the cost of damage to other people's property (such as buildings and cars). Collision insurance is different. It pays for damage to the policyholder's car. You can have full coverage or deductible ($100 to $500).

12.2 Organizing. As a research consultant with Search, Inc., you have been asked to find a sales and distribution site in the Winnipeg area for Farrell Electrical Components, 3450 Hastings Street, Vancouver, British Columbia V8N 1L4. Farrell seeks office space, a conference/display area, and 700 square metres of heated warehouse space. If sales are successful, Farrell may need an additional 500 square metres of warehouse space in the future. Farrell needs access to major transportation facilities and main thoroughfares in an area zoned for light industry. Farrell wants to lease for at least two years with possible renewal. It needs to make a decision within three weeks. If no space is available, it will delay until next year.

You have been assigned the task of researching this assignment and then writing a report that includes a recommendation for Farrell based on your findings.

a.   Who is the audience for this long report? Should you include extensive background data explaining why the report is being written? Explain.

b.   Would you rely on primary or secondary research? How would you gather data for this report?

c.   What constraints will limit your research?

d.· What visual aids would enhance this report?

e.   On a separate sheet write a statement of purpose that could become part of the introduction to your report. Include Farrell's requirements.

f.   You have narrowed the choices to five locations near Winnipeg International Airport. On a separate sheet make a table from the following rough notes. Include a title and subtitle, as well as appropriate columnar headings.

(1)   The site at 3348 Quebec Street has 400 m^2 of office space and 725 m^2 of warehouse space with an option for additional space. Cost: $2200 per month with a 1-year minimum lease.

(2)   A space in the Aurora Industrial Park offers only 300 m^2 of office space but it has 825 m^2 of warehouse space. Cost: $2750 per month with a 3-year lease preferred.

(3)   A warehouse at 2280 Monaco Street has 700 m^2 of warehouse space with an option to expand. It rents for $1950 per month with 280 m^2 for offices. Minimum 1-year lease.

(4)   30 Colfax Centre offers 300 m^2 of office space and 750 m^2 of warehouse space but cannot guarantee additional warehouse space in the future. Cost: $3000 per month, with a 2-year lease.

(5)   A building at 3340 Montview Avenue will lease for only $1500 per month. It has a total of 775 m^2, of which 200 m^2 is office space, and the rest is warehousing. Two-year lease. Additional warehouse space is available.

g.   Compose a lead-in sentence that introduces the preceding table in your report.

h.   What strategy would you follow in organizing this report? Why?

12.3 Visual Aids. From *Maclean's, Canadian Business, Business Week*, a textbook, or some other publication, locate one example of a table, a pie chart, a line chart, a bar chart, and an organization chart. Bring copies of these visual aids to class. How effectively could the data have been expressed in words, without the graphics? Is the appropriate graphic form used? How is the graphic introduced in the text? Your instructor may wish you to submit a memo discussing visual aids.

12.4 Library Recommendation. Assume that you have been asked to recommend a library to fellow students who have little library experience. Visit your school or public library. Observe its resources, method of operation, shelf lists, electronic capabilities, and personnel. Write a one-page memo report describing your findings.

12.5 Bibliography. Select a business topic that interests you. Prepare a bibliography of at least five current magazine articles, three books, and five other references that contain relevant information regarding the topic. Your instructor may ask you to divide your bibliography into sections: *Books, Periodicals, Other Resources*. You may also be asked to annotate your bibliography, that is, to compose a brief description of each reference, such as this:

> Rush, William. "Dawn of the Dead Ed." *Modern Instruction*, January 2000, 137–140. This article discusses the explosion of computer-based training systems and the expectation that these so-called expert systems will replace teachers.

 12.6 Computer Databases. Compose a list of computer information sources available on line. What, if any, are the charges for receiving data? What is the procedure for using the services? Write a memo describing your findings. Include one or more visual aids to illustrate your data.

12.7 Proposal: Outsourcing. Businesses today are doing more "outsourcing" than ever before. This means that they are going outside to find specialists to handle some aspect of their business, such as billing, shipping, or advertising. They're also hiring experts with special training and equipment to solve problems for which they lack the necessary talent and staff. For a business where you have worked or an organization you know, select a problem. Here are some possible problems: poor handling of customer orders, inefficient payroll practices, inadequate computer equipment or software, unsatisfactory inventory control, poor use of sales staff, bad scheduling of employees, poorly trained employees, sexual harassment on the job, e-mail misuse, and poor telephone techniques. Assume the boss has asked you as a consultant to either solve the problem or study it and tell the organization what to do. Prepare an informal proposal describing your plan to solve the problem or perform a service. Decide how much you will charge and what staff you will need. Send your letter proposal to your boss (in this case, your instructor).

12.8 Proposal: Profiting from Someone Else's Mistakes. Your company, Dominion Transport Services (DTS), offers solutions, especially for businesses without a transportation specialist on staff. Specifically, you and your staff of nine check all shipping charges to ensure that trucking companies are charging the correct rates. You also give advice on how to get the lowest shipping rates. Because of your expertise and research capabilities, you can advise any company about the most financially stable and reliable truckers.

In addition to auditing shipments, you file freight claims for your clients and fight wrongful claims against them. Your fee is one-half of whatever you save clients on their shipping transactions. They pay nothing if you don't save them money. Write a letter proposal to Steve Rubin, President, Club Enterprises, 468 Industry Avenue, Markham, ON L3S 3H5 proposing your services. Club Enterprises makes a security device for locking the steering column of a car. Club ships out 2 million units annually, and it receives .75 million tonnes of raw materials—most of it by truck. Steve Rubin has heard of your service and asks you to submit a proposal to him, although he has prepared no formal RFP.[3]

12.9 Formal Report: Readability of Insurance Policies. The 21st Century Insurance Company is concerned about the readability of its policies. Customers are complaining they can't understand their insurance policies. As part of its quality assurance program, 21st Century hires you as a consultant to study its standard policy and make recommendations.

Examine a life, home, or automobile insurance policy that you or a friend or relative holds. Study the policy for jargon and confusing language, and evaluate its physical format for readability. Does it have an index or glossary?

In addition to the data you collect from your own examination of the policy, 21st Century gives you the data shown in Figure 12.11 from a recent policyholder survey. Prepare a report for Heather St. Amant, vice president, 21st Century Insurance Company, discussing your analysis, conclusions, and recommendations for improving its basic policy.

FIGURE 12.11

21st Century Insurance Company Policyholder Survey

Response to statement: "I am able to read and understand the language and provisions of my policy.".

Age Group	Strongly Agree	Agree	Undecided	Disagree	Strongly Disagree
18–34	2%	9%	34%	41%	14%
35–49	2	17	38	33	10
50–64	1	11	22	35	31
65+	1	2	17	47	33

12.10 Formal Report: Fast-Food Checkup. Select a fast-food franchise in your area. Assume that the national franchising headquarters has received complaints about the service, quality, and cleanliness of the unit.

You have been sent to inspect and to report on what you see. Visit on two or more occasions. Make notes on how many customers were served, how quickly they received their food, and how courteously they were treated. Observe the number of employees and supervisors working. Note the cleanliness of observable parts of the restaurant. Inspect the restroom as well as the exterior and surrounding grounds. Sample the food. Your boss is a stickler for details; he has no use for general statements like *The restroom was not clean.* Be specific. Draw conclusions. Are the

CHAPTER 12   Proposals and Formal Reports

305

complaints justified? If improvements are necessary, make recommendations. Address your report to Lawrence C. Shymko, President.

12.11 Collaborative Formal Report: Intercultural Communication.
North American businesses are expanding into foreign markets with manufacturing plants, sales offices, and branch offices abroad. Unfortunately, many North Americans have little knowledge of or experience with people from other cultures. To prepare for participation in the global marketplace, collect information for a report focused on a Pacific Rim, Latin American, or European country where English is not a first language. Before selecting the country, though, consult your campus international program for volunteers who are willing to be interviewed. Your instructor may make advance arrangements seeking international student volunteers.

In teams of three to five, collect information about your target country from the library and other sources. Then invite an international student representing your target country to be interviewed by your group. In your primary and secondary research, investigate the topics listed in Figure 12.12. Confirm what you learn in your secondary research by talking with your interviewee. When you complete your research, write a report for the CEO of your company (make up a name and company). Assume that your company plans to expand its operations abroad. Your report should advise the company's executives of social customs, family life, attitudes, religions, education, and values in the target country. Remember that your company's interests are business-oriented; don't dwell on tourist information. Write your report individually or in teams.

12.12 Formal Report: Consumer Product Investigation.
Study a consumer product that you might consider buying. Are you (or your family) interested in purchasing a VCR, computer, camera, microwave, car, van, camcorder, or some other product? Your investigation should include primary data collected from interviews with users, owners, salespersons, service technicians, and so forth. You'll also find rich resources in sales brochures and pamphlets. Conduct secondary research by studying (and citing) magazine articles in such publications as *Consumer Reports*. Be sure to narrow your topic by setting boundaries on your search. For example, are you interested in an economy van with good mileage that will be driven 80 kilometres daily? Are you in the market for an economical auto-focus camera?

In the introduction, discuss why you selected this product and for whom it is intended (for example, a VCR for a middle-class family that would use it primarily for watching rented videocassettes and for recording television programs). Perhaps provide some background data about the product gleaned from your reading. In the *Findings* section you might discuss such topics as price, warranty, specific features, and service reputation. Draw conclusions from your data, and make a recommendation. Address the report to your instructor. Your instructor may ask you to work in pairs on this project.

12.13 Formal Report: Communication Skills on the Job.
Collect information regarding communication skills used by individuals in a particular career field (accounting, management, marketing, office administration, paralegal, and so forth). Interview three or more individuals in a specific occupation in that field. Determine how much and what kind of writing they do. Do they make oral presentations? How much time do they spend in telephone communication? Do they use e-mail? If so, how much and for what? What recommendations do they have for training for this position? What

FIGURE 12.12

Intercultural Interview Topics and Questions[4]

Social Customs

1. How do people react to strangers? Friendly? Hostile? Reserved?
2. How do people greet each other?
3. What are the appropriate manners when you enter a room? Bow? Nod? Shake hands with everyone?
4. How are names used for introductions? Is it appropriate to inquire about one's occupation or family?
5. What are the attitudes toward touching?
6. How does one express appreciation for an invitation to another's home? Bring a gift? Send flowers? Write a thank-you note? Are any gifts taboo?
7. Are there any customs related to how or where one sits?
8. Are any facial expressions or gestures considered rude?
9. How close do people stand when talking?
10. What is the attitude toward punctuality in social situations? In business situations?
11. What are acceptable eye contact patterns?
12. What gestures indicate agreement? Disagreement?

Family Life

1. What is the basic unit of social organization? Basic family? Extended family?
2. Do women work outside of the home? In what occupations?

Housing, Clothing, and Food

1. Are there differences in the kind of housing used by different social groups? Differences in location? Differences in furnishings?
2. What occasions require special clothing?
3. Are some types of clothing considered taboo?
4. What is appropriate business attire for men? For women?
5. How many times a day do people eat?
6. What types of places, food, and drink are appropriate for business entertainment? Where is the seat of honour at a table?

Class Structure

1. Into what classes is society organized?
2. Do racial, religious, or economic factors determine social status?
3. Are there any minority groups? What is their social standing?

Political Patterns

1. Are there any immediate threats to the political survival of the country?
2. How is political power manifested?
3. What channels are used for expression of popular opinion?
4. What information media are important?
5. Is it appropriate to talk politics in social situations?

Religion and Folk Beliefs

1. To which religious groups do people belong? Is one predominant?
2. Do religious beliefs influence daily activities?
3. Which places have sacred value? Which objects? Which events?
4. How do religious holidays affect business activities?

Economic Institutions

1. What are the country's principal products?
2. Are workers organized in unions?
3. How are businesses owned? By family units? By large public corporations? By the government?
4. What is the standard work schedule?
5. Is it appropriate to do business by telephone?
6. Is participatory management used?
7. Are there any customs related to exchanging business cards?
8. How is status shown in an organization? Private office? Secretary? Furniture?
9. Are businesspersons expected to socialize before conducting business?

Value Systems

1. Is competitiveness or cooperation more prized?
2. Is thrift or enjoyment of the moment more valued?
3. Is politeness more important than factual honesty?
4. What are the attitudes toward education?
5. Do women own or manage businesses? If so, how are they treated?
6. What are your people's perceptions of Canadians? What has been hardest for you to adjust to in Canada? How could Canadians make this adjustment easier for you?

conclusions can you draw from your research? What recommendations would you make for individuals entering this field? Your instructor may wish you to study the perception of businesspeople over the past ten years regarding the communication skills of employees. To gather such data, conduct library or on-line research.

12.14 Searching the Internet: Proposal for Setting up a Web Site. As a consultant, you have been asked to investigate the cost of setting up a World Wide Web site for Arni Einarsson, who owns a travel agency (or a florist shop, party-planning service, secretarial service, automotive parts store, teddy bear gift shop, car dealership, or any other reasonable community organization or business). Use search engines on the Internet to locate information. Investigate the characteristics of a Web site, how to create and promote a site, and Web server maintenance. Mr. Einarsson wants a low-cost but high-quality site. Develop cost figures. Draw conclusions and make recommendations in a letter proposal to Mr. Einarsson.

12.15 Connecting With E-Mail: Reporting on Your Report. Send an e-mail message to your instructor summarizing your report topic, outlining your work plan, and showing your work schedule. Be concise but specific.

GRAMMAR/MECHANICS CHECKUP—12

Capitalization

Review Sections 3.01–3.16 in the Grammar/Mechanics Handbook. Then study each of the following statements. Circle any lowercase letter that should be capitalized. Draw a slash (/) through any capital letter that you wish to change to lowercase. Indicate in the space provided the number of changes you made in each sentence and record the number of the G/M principle(s) illustrated.* If you made no changes, write *0.* When you finish, compare your responses with those provided. If your responses differ, study carefully the principle(s) in parentheses.

<u>4</u>   (3.01, 3.06a)   **Example:** After consulting our /awyers for /egal advice, /ice President Mills signed the /ontract.

1. All canadian passengers from Flight 402 must pass through Customs Inspection at Gate 17 upon arrival at Pearson international airport.
2. Personal tax rates for japanese citizens are low by International standards; rates for japanese corporations are high, according to Iwao Nakatani, an Economics Professor at Osaka university.
3. In the end, Business passes on most of the burden to the Consumer: What looks like a tax on Business is really a tax on Consumption.
4. Lisa enrolled in courses in History, Sociology, French, and Computer Science.
5. Did you see the *Maclean's* article entitled "Careers in horticulture are nothing to sneeze at"?
6. Although I recommend the Minex Diskettes sold under the brand name Maxidisk, you may purchase any Diskettes you choose.
7. According to a Federal Government report, any development of Provincial waterways must receive an environmental assessment.
8. The prime minister of canada said, "this country continues to encourage Foreign investment."

9. The Comptroller of Ramjet International reported to the President and the Board of Directors that revenue canada was beginning an investigation of their Company. _____

10. My Mother, who lives near St. John's, reports that protecting your car from the corrosive effect of road Salt is particularly important in the East. _____

11. Our Managing Editor met with Leslie Hawkins, Manager of the Advertising Sales Department, to plan an Ad Campaign for our special issue. _____

12. In the fall, Editor in Chief Porter plans an article detailing the astounding performance of the austrian, german, and italian automobile industries. _____

13. To reach Mount Royal park, which is located on an Island in the St. Lawrence river, tourists pass over the Jacques Cartier bridge. _____

14. On page 6 of the catalogue you will see that the computer science department is offering a number of courses in programming. _____

15. Please consult figure 3.2 in chapter 5 for statistics canada figures regarding non-english-speaking residents. _____

---

1. (5) Canadian, customs inspection, International Airport (3.01, 3.02, 3.07)   3. (4) business, consumer, business, consumption (3.01, 3.13)   5. (5) Horticulture, Are, Nothing, Sneeze, At (3.12)   7. (3) federal government, provincial (3.10)   9. (7) comptroller, president, board of directors, Revenue Canada, company (3.01, 3.04, 3.06e)   11. (5) managing editor, manager, ad campaign (3.02, 3.06d, 3.06e, 3.09)   13. (4) Park, island, River, Bridge (3.01, 3.03)   15. (5) Figure, Chapter, Statistics Canada, English (3.02, 3.04, 3.07)

* Note: G/M principles are listed in ascending order.

GRAMMAR/MECHANICS CHALLENGE—12

Document for Revision

The following report abstract has faults in grammar, punctuation, spelling, number form, wordiness, and word use. Use standard proofreading marks (see Appendix B) to correct the errors.

Ineffective Writing

ABSTRACT

On the date of November 10th Dennis W. Wilbur, Director, Human Resources development authorized a study to ascertain whether or not workplace equity guidelines for women was being met at Globex Enterprises.

A research program was developed to make inquiry into each divisions hiring practices. Data in regard to the employment of 23,102 past and present employees was searched by the program to make a determination of the date of employment, division, and sex. Statistics Canada data were also examined in way of comparison.

The following findings in regard to the aforementioned study, resulted;

• Vancouver is 5% above the figure for compliance for the 5 year period

• Toronto is 7% below the compliance figure for the 5 year period

On the basis of these findings the Workplace Equity Committee (1) reccomend the developement of an intensive recruiting program to search for and bring qualified females into the Toronto division and (2) the developement of a training program to train females for drafting and design positions in Toronto. This will bring Toronto in compliance.

CONDUCTING WEB RESEARCH ON A SHOESTRING

The World Wide Web is bursting with information, but not all of it is free. Often one must subscribe to a service to obtain more than a sample of its archived (preserved) data. For business researchers on a tight budget, the following Web sites provide free information that could be helpful in verifying facts, discovering relevant statistics, locating an expert, finding illustrations, or gathering evidence for a report.

- Hoover's Online **www.hoovers.com** This site provides free information capsules on over 10,000 companies. Each capsule includes a company address and telephone number, names of officers, recent sales figures, and often a Web site address. For more extensive company profiles, you must subscribe.
- Canadian government information: Statistics Canada's site at **www.statCan.ca** provides survey data, statistics, and articles on topics ranging from Canadian census information to international trade. The official Government of Canada site at **www.canada.gc.ca** is an excellent location to find plenty of information on business and economic development.
- Strategis: Canada's Business Information Site at **www.strategis.ic.gc.ca** is a one-stop location for up-to-the-minute statistics, company information, research, and analysis.
- Canada/Provincial Business Service Centres: **www.cbsc.org** Each province has its own site offering advice on starting, financing, and expanding a business. These sites also provide business resource information important to local entrepreneurs.
- Canadian news and magazine archives: **www.canbus.com**, **www.globeandmail.ca**, and **www.nationalpost.com** Here you'll find not only breaking business news but also a rich collection of archived and searchable articles of interest to business researchers.
- The Electric Library **www.elibrary.com** This is a good place to investigate magazines, reference works, and news wires. You must subscribe to use the service.
- Deja News Research Service **www.dejanews.com** This site has a large index of archived Usenet news articles. Checking the Usenet groups may help you find experts who could answer questions.
- Web search engines such as **ca.yahoo.com** and **www.canada.com** index a huge number of Web sites. Both of these engines search Canadian sites. Other general search engines include Google, AltaVista, Northern Light, InfoSeek, Lycos,

HotBot, Excite, WebCrawler, and Snap. URL's for these sites are created by entering "www." then the name of the engine, then ".com" in the Go To window of your browser.

- Web meta search engines search the Internet and the listings of other search engines. Some of these are AskJeeves, SavvySearch, Internet Sleuth (**www.isleuth.com**), ProFusion, MetaCrawler (**www.go2net.com**), Inference Find (**www.infind.com**), Dogpile, Cyber411, Mamma, and HotSheet. All URLs not listed are created in the same way as outlined above.

Application. Select a company (such as Reebok, Coca-Cola, Investors Group, Corel Corp, or Bombardier) to research. Visit at least three of the previously listed Web sites to locate (a) the exact name and address of the company; (b) the name of the CEO or president; (c) the addresses of two or more specific Web sites devoted to the company; (d) recent company announcements, news, or products; (e) and possible newspaper or Usenet comments about the company and its products. In an e-mail message or memo to your instructor, describe your findings.

Related Web Site: www.sou.edu/library/cybrary/search.htm

UNIT 6

COMMUNICATING FOR EMPLOYMENT

13 THE JOB SEARCH, RÉSUMÉS, AND COVER LETTERS

Today's business environment is so competitive that most résumés receive an initial 15-second glance.[1]

MARC BELAICHE, consultant with Toronto office of Creative Financial Staffing (CFS), one of the world's fastest growing accounting and financial placement companies

Learning Objectives

1. Prepare for employment by identifying your interests, evaluating your qualifications, choosing a career path, and searching the job market.
2. Compare and contrast chronological, functional, and combination résumés.
3. Organize, format, and produce a persuasive résumé.
4. Recognize strategies for making your résumé computer friendly.
5. Write a persuasive cover letter to introduce your résumé.

After a decade of downsizing, businesses are again hiring but many experienced people are looking for jobs. In the face of this heavy competition, finding a good job requires an early start and a determined effort. If you are a serious job seeker, you should expect to devote as much time to job hunting as you would to a full-time job. And be prepared to use some high-tech tools in your search.

Whether you are applying for your first permanent position, competing for promotion, or changing careers, you'll be more successful if you understand employment strategies and how to promote yourself with a winning résumé. As Marc Belaiche suggests, a successful résumé makes an impact almost instantly. This chapter provides expert current advice in preparing for employment, searching the job market, writing a persuasive résumé, and developing an effective cover letter.

PREPARING FOR EMPLOYMENT

Today's job market is vastly different from that of a decade ago. Instead of picking and choosing among jobs, candidates must now find ways to stand out from stiff competition. The jobs are there, but only the most focused and persevering candidates will be successful. Today's job hunter will also find many new technological avenues leading to employment, along with hot computer resources to aid a job search. You can start the employment process by (1) identifying your interests, (2) evaluating your qualifications, and (3) searching the job market.

IDENTIFYING YOUR INTERESTS

The employment process begins with introspection. This means looking inside yourself to analyze what you like and dislike so that you can make good employment choices. Career counsellors charge large sums for helping individuals learn about themselves. You can do the same kind of self-examination—without spending a dime. For guidance in choosing a field that eventually proves to be satisfying, answer the following questions. If you have already chosen a field, think carefully about how your answers relate to that choice.

Finding the perfect job demands examining your interests, your qualifications, and the job market.

- Do I enjoy working with people, data, or things?
- How important is it to be my own boss?
- How important are salary, benefits, and job stability?
- How important are working environment, colleagues, and job stimulation? Would I rather work for a large or small company?
- Must I work in a specific city, geographical area, or climate?
- Am I looking for security, travel opportunities, money, power, or prestige?
- What do I consider to be the perfect job, boss, and co-workers?

EVALUATING YOUR QUALIFICATIONS

In addition to your interests, you must take a hard look at your qualifications. Employers want to know what assets you have to offer them. Your responses to the following questions will target your thinking as well as prepare a foundation for your résumé. Remember, though, that employers seek more than empty assurances; they will want proof of your qualifications.

Answering specific questions about your interests and qualifications helps you choose a career.

- What skills have I acquired in school, on the job, or through other activities? How can I demonstrate these skills?
- Do I work well with people? What evidence can I offer from extracurricular activities, clubs, and jobs?
- Am I a leader, self-starter, or manager? What examples can I suggest?
- Do I learn quickly? Am I creative? How can I demonstrate these characteristics?
- Do I communicate well in speech and in writing? How can I verify these talents?
- Do I speak, write, or understand another language?
- Do I have up-to-date computer skills? What evidence can I offer?

CHOOSING A CAREER PATH

As a result of job trends and personal choices, the average Canadian can expect to change careers at least three times and change jobs at least seven times in a lifetime. Some of you probably have not yet settled on your first career choice; others are returning to school to retrain for a new career. You'll make the best career decisions when you can match your interests and qualifications with the requirements of and

Career information can be obtained at campus career centres and libraries, in classified ads, through interviews, on the Internet, and from professional organizations.

rewards from specific careers. But where can you get specific career data? Consider the following possibilities:

- *Visit your school career or counselling centre.* Most have literature, inventories, software programs, and on-line services that allow you to investigate such fields as accounting, finance, office administration, hotel management, and so forth.

- *Search the Internet.* Amazing resources are becoming available on the Internet. With your computer you can access Web sites that provide career-planning advice, career development manuals, job directories, and information about career paths. An easy place to start your career information search is at the Youth Resource Network site (www.youth.gc.ca/jobinfo_e.shtml).
- *Use your library.* Several publications are especially helpful. Consult the latest editions of the *Dictionary of Occupational Titles, Occupational Outlook Handbook*, and *Job Futures* for information about career duties, qualifications, salaries, and employment trends. Canada WorkInfoNet is an online clearinghouse for information about careers and labour markets (www.workinfonet.ca/cwn/english/main.html). The site provides up-to-date information on available jobs, occupation descriptions, and labour market information.
- *Take a summer job or part-time position in your field.* Trying out a career by actually working in it or in an allied area is the best way to learn about that career. Students are increasingly seeking cooperative work/learn programs because relevant experience is especially important in today's competitive job market.
- *Interview someone in your chosen field.* People are usually flattered when asked to describe their careers. Inquire about needed skills, required courses, financial and other rewards, benefits, working conditions, future trends, and entry requirements.
- *Monitor the classified ads.* Early in your education career, begin scanning want ads in your chosen field. Check job availability, qualifications sought, duties, and salary range. Don't wait until you're about to graduate to see how the job market looks.
- *Join professional organizations in your field.* Frequently, these organizations offer student membership status and reduced rates. You'll have an inside track on issues, career news, and possibly jobs.

SEARCHING THE JOB MARKET

A mistake many job hunters make is not looking hard enough for a job. A successful candidate today must mount an aggressive job-search campaign, and such a campaign includes some or all of the following steps:

- *Study classified ads in local and national newspapers.* Classified ads are a good beginning place, but be aware that they represent only about one-third of all jobs available. Nearly two-thirds, representing the "hidden" job market, are unadvertised.
- *Learn to network.* To locate jobs in the "hidden" market, tell everyone you know that you are looking for a job. Ask questions like "Do you know anyone who might have an opening for a person with my skills?" If they don't, ask, "Do you know anyone else who might know of someone who would?" If not,

A job-search campaign involves studying classified ads and announcements in professional publications, checking on-line job listings, investigating companies, and developing a network of contacts.

"Do you know someone who knows lots of people?" Develop contacts; talk with these contacts. Ask the most promising contacts how a person with your background and skills might get started in the field.

- *Check on-line job listings.* Many large and diverse databases of job listings are available on the Internet. Links to the most popular governmental and nongovernmental on-line services can be found at www.youth.gc.ca/jobopps/jobban_e.shtml. Here you can begin your search through almost 50 different Canadian and international job banks.

- *Contact companies in which you're interested, even if you know of no current opening.* Write an unsolicited letter and include your résumé. Follow up with a telephone call. A good way to learn about an organization is to visit its Web site. Try some of the research sites listed in the Chapter 12 Communication Workshop to learn Web addresses and other information about many public companies.

- *Sign up for school interviews with visiting company representatives.* On-campus recruiters may open your eyes to exciting jobs and locations.

- *Ask for advice from your instructors.* They often have contacts and ideas for expanding your job search.

THE PERSUASIVE RÉSUMÉ

After learning about the employment market and developing job leads, your next step is writing a persuasive résumé. Such a résumé does more than merely list your qualifications. It packages your assets into a convincing advertisement that sells you for a specific job. The goal of a persuasive résumé is winning an interview. Even if you are not in the job market at this moment, preparing a résumé now has advantages. Having a current résumé makes you look well organized and professional should an unexpected employment opportunity arise. Moreover, preparing a résumé early helps you recognize weaknesses and might give you two or three years in which to bolster your credentials.

CHOOSING A RÉSUMÉ STYLE

Your qualifications and career goal will help you choose from among three résumé styles: chronological, functional, and combination.

Chronological. Most popular with recruiters is the chronological résumé, shown in Figure 13.1. It lists work history job by job, starting with the most recent position. Recruiters favour the chronological style because such résumés quickly reveal a candidate's work stability and promotion record. The chronological style works well for candidates who have experience in their fields of employment and for those who show steady career growth.

> Chronological résumés focus on employment history; functional résumés focus on skills.

Functional. The functional résumé shown in Figure 13.2 focuses attention on a candidate's skills rather than on past employment. Like a chronological résumé, the functional résumé begins with the candidate's name, address, telephone number, job objective, and education. [The next five pages illustrate résumés. The text continues on page 323.]

FIGURE 13.1

Chronological Résumé

SIMONE AYOTTE

32 Gurnett Drive
Hamilton, Ontario L9C 7K1

Voice (905) 445-2101
E-mail: sayotte@aol.com

Includes detailed objective in response to advertisement.

OBJECTIVE Position with financial services organization installing accounting software and providing user support, where computer experience and proven communication and interpersonal skills can be used to improve operations.

Uses present-tense verbs for current job.

EXPERIENCE **Accounting software consultant**, Financial Specialists, Hamilton, Ontario
June 1998 to present
• Design and install accounting systems for businesses like 21st Century Real Estate, Healthco Insurance, Aurora Lumber Company, and others.
• Provide ongoing technical support and consultation for regular clients.
• Help write proposals, such as recent one that won $250,000 contract.

Office manager (part-time), Post Premiums, Toronto, Ontario
June 1997 to May 1998
• Conceived and implemented improved order processing and filing system.
• Managed computerized accounting system; trained new employees to use it.
• Worked with team to develop local area network. Was complimented by Vice President Rogers as a team player and one who takes initiative.

Chronological format arranges jobs and education by dates.

Bookkeeper (part-time), Sunset Avionics, Hamilton, Ontario
August 1996 to May 1997
• Kept books for small airplane rental and repair service.
• Performed all bookkeeping functions including quarterly internal audit.

EDUCATION **Mohawk College**, Hamilton, Ontario
Working toward a diploma in accounting; 25 out of 40 credits completed.

Humber College, Toronto, Ontario. Certificate in bookkeeping, 1998
GPA 3.6/4.0

Computer Associates training seminars, summer and fall 1997
Certificates of completion
Seminars in consulting ethics, marketing, and ACCPAC accounting software

Creates open look with white space around headings

SPECIAL SKILLS • Proficient in WordPerfect, PageMaker, Lotus 1-2-3, and Excel.
• Skilled in ACCPAC Plus, MAS90, and Solomon IV accounting software.
• Trained in technical writing, including proposals and documentation.
• Experienced in using Internet and Web resources in problem solving.
• Fluent in French.

HONOURS AND ACTIVITIES Dean's list, 3 semesters
Member, Beta Alpha Gamma (business student honorary)
Member, Academic Affairs Advisory Committee, Mohawk College, 1999–2000

Simone Ayotte uses a chronological résumé to highlight her work experience, most of which is directly related to the position she seeks. Although she is a recent graduate, she has accumulated experience in two part-time jobs and one full-time job. If she had wished to emphasize her special skills (which is not a bad idea considering her heavy computer expertise), she could have placed the special skills section just after her objective.

FIGURE 13.2

Functional Résumé

Jon Penner

5 Pinecroft Drive, Winnipeg, MB R4L 2H7   (204) 995-3301

OBJECTIVE

Position in sales or marketing with opportunity for advancement and travel.
Proven Internet, customer service, consumer sales, presentations, and oral and written communication skills; demonstrated take-charge, leadership qualities.

SALES/MARKETING SKILLS
- Learned to be customer-oriented in demonstrating lawn-care equipment at trade shows in central and western Canada.
- Achieved product sales amounting to 120 percent of forecast through aggressive sales effort in competitive field.
- Developed Internet skills in comparative study of products marketed at World Wide Web sites for lawn-care equipment.
- Used persuasive skills in personally generating over $25,000 in telephone subscriptions as part of President's Task Force for the Millennium Foundation at the University of Manitoba.
- Successfully served 40 or more retail customers daily as high-energy clerk in electrical appliance department of hardware store.

COMMUNICATION SKILLS
- Developed analytic and writing skills by conducting survey, analyzing results, and writing 20-page report about developing a recycling program at the University of Manitoba.
- Polished speaking skills by giving talks before selected classes and organizations encouraging students to support recycling program.
- Honed presentation skills as part of award-winning team at Youth United Nations meeting.

ORGANIZATIONAL/MANAGEMENT SKILLS
- Demonstrated leadership capabilities by conceptualizing, organizing, and conducting highly successful school campaign to raise funds for a local health awareness program.
- Scheduled events and arranged weekend student retreat for Newman Club.
- Trained and supervised two counter employees at Pizza Bob's.
- Organized courses, extracurricular activities, and part-time employment to graduate in two years with a 3.4 grade-point average (4.0 = A).

EDUCATION

University of Manitoba, Winnipeg, MB, Bachelor of Arts, 1998
Major: Business Administration with marketing emphasis. GPA in major: 3.6

EMPLOYMENT

1999–2000, MacDan Industries, Steinbach, MB
Summer 1998, Pizza Bob's, Winnipeg, MB
Summer 1997, Bellefonte Manufacturers Representatives, Winnipeg, MB

Annotations:

Adds skills summary to objective for immediate visibility.

Mentions Internet and World Wide Web skills, hot items for recruiters.

Emphasizes relevant skills for sales and marketing position.

De-emphasizes meagre employment history.

Jon Penner, a recent graduate, chose this functional format to de-emphasize his limited work experience and to emphasize his potential in sales and marketing. His objective is general but he combines it with a summary of his qualifications for maximum impact. Notice how he uses action verbs to introduce keyword nouns that may be picked up by résumé scanners. Note, too, how he weaves his educational achievement in with his work accomplishments.

FIGURE 13.3

Combination Résumé

Omits job objective to keep all options open.

Focuses on skills and aptitudes that employers seek.

Arranges employment by job title for easy reading.

Combines activities and awards to fill out section.

Includes references because local employers expect them (most résumés omit them).

AMANDA B. THORSON
564 Fairfield Rd.
Victoria, BC W1L 2W3

Residence: (604) 935-3196

Messages: (604) 935-4399

SKILLS AND CAPABILITIES
- Experienced with e-mail, Word, Microsoft Office, Lotus, Excel, File Maker Pro.
- Type 70 wpm on computer or electronic typewriter.
- Take symbol shorthand at 90 wpm with accurate transcription.
- Skilled in the production of legal documents and correspondence.
- Competent in producing mailable copy from machine transcription.
- Able to perform office tasks and interact as a team player using excellent written and oral communication skills.

EXPERIENCE

Word Processing Operator 1, Limited-term employee
Camosun College, Victoria, BC V5L 2N5, May 1999 to August 1999
- Transcribed confidential letters, memos, reports, and other documents from machine dictation using Microsoft Word for Windows.
- Proofread documents for other operators, marking grammar and content errors. Commended by supervisor for zero error tolerance.

Student Assistant
Camosun College, Victoria, BC V5L 2N5, Summer 1998
- Typed memos and input financial aid data on terminal to mainframe; printed and verified monthly report for $90,000 budget.
- Screened incoming telephone calls for supervisor and counsellors.

Part-time Cook and Cashier
Souprrr Subs, Victoria, BC V5R 3T4, May 1997 to May 1998
- Prepared menu items, accepted customer payments, balanced cash drawer.

EDUCATION
Camosun College, Victoria, BC V5L 2N5
Major: Office assistant and word processing specialist programs
Administrative Assistant Diploma expected May 2000. GPA in major: 3.6 (4.0 = A)

ACTIVITIES, AWARDS
- Received the Fennimore Award from the Camosun College Foundation for academic excellence and contribution to campus life.
- Developed leadership qualities as secretary of Business Professionals of North America Club and as representative of the Pacific chapter at national competitions.

REFERENCES

Ms. Shirley A. Yost	Professor Lois Wagner	Mr. James W. Loy
Faculty of Science	Camosun College	Camosun College
University of Victoria	Highway 18 East	Highway 18 East
Victoria, BC V4L 3E6	Victoria, BC V5L 2N5	Victoria, BC V5L 2N5
(604) 390-4491	(604) 822-8931	(604) 822-8749

Because Amanda Thorson wanted to highlight her skills and capabilities along with her experience, she combined the best features of functional and traditional résumés. This style is becoming increasingly popular. Notice that she mentions qualities employers value: communication, computer, leadership, and team-player skills. Although it's not standard practice, she also includes references because employers in her area expect them.

FIGURE 13.4

Combination Résumé

TRAN M. NGUYEN
923 Queen Street West, Toronto, Ontario, M5R 3Y2 (416) 857-3301

OBJECTIVE
Word processing   Secretarial   Administrative   General Office

SUMMARY OF QUALIFICATIONS
- Up-to-date computer training, including WordPerfect, Word for Windows, Lotus, spreadsheets, PowerPoint, e-mail, World Wide Web, and Internet
- Keyboard 60 wpm accurately
- On-the-job experience in machine transcription, editing, and proofreading
- Proven ability to budget time, perform under stress, follow instructions, adapt quickly to a challenge, and follow through on assignments
- Certificate of excellence for written communication skills

EMPLOYMENT
- Province of Ontario, Department of Justice, Law Courts Building, Toronto, Ontario, January 2000 to May 2000
  Administrative intern
  File memos, find and copy cases from law books, type letters and memos, maintain office supplies, enter cases on computer, send and receive e-mail. Successfully perform all duties in an atmosphere where accuracy and ability to follow detailed instructions are essential. Cleared three-month backlog in five weeks.

- Save-On Drugs, Toronto, Ontario, June 1996 to August 1999
  Part-time pharmacy clerk
  Accepted and processed prescriptions on computer. Cheerfully answered approximately 40 telephone calls daily. Enjoyed serving up to 50 customers daily. Commended by Manager Dick Thomas for attention to detail and multitasking ability.

- Office Technology Department, George Brown College, Toronto, Ontario, September 1998 to June 1999
  Student secretary, work-study program
  Served as personal secretary to department chair. Created, revised, and retrieved letters, memos, files, and reports using WordPerfect. Organized department computer files so that hundreds of files could be located logically and efficiently. Assisted in developing World Wide Web resource brochure.

- Ross Department Stores, Scarborough, Ontario, June 1996 to July 1997
  Floor sales associate
  Developed interpersonal and customer skills by assisting customers in sales selections. Worked as part of a successful team that surpassed its national sales goal. Promoted to assistant manager after six months.

EDUCATION
George Brown College, Toronto, Ontario, Executive Assistant Diploma expected June 2000
Specialization in Office Technology

Annotations (right margin):
- Expands opportunities with broad objective.
- Places skills necessary for targeted job at top for maximum visibility.
- Includes testimonial to humanize résumé.
- Uses bullets, boldfacing, and white space to achieve emphasis and readability.

By moving her skills and capabilities to the top of her résumé, Tran Nguyen puts them in the spotlight. Although she has no paid experience in her field, she capitalizes on student experiences and an internship. The combination résumé style allows her to present her employment chronologically while emphasizing the important skills she offers in her field. Notice how she includes both interpersonal and technical skills throughout her résumé.

FIGURE 13.5

Combination Résumé

KEITH M. DAVIES

498 Mountain View Avenue
Surrey, BC V4L 1E6
(604) 479-1982
E-mail: Kdavies@msn.com

Objective: Position as Staff Accountant with progressive firm, where my technical, computer, and communication skills will be useful in managing accounts and acquiring new clientele.

SKILLS AND CAPABILITIES

Accounting
- Ability to journalize entries accurately in general and specialized journals.
- Proficient in posting to general ledger, preparing trial balance, and detecting discrepancies.
- Trained in preparing and analyzing balance sheet and other financial statements.

Computer
- Experienced in using Lotus 1-2-3, dBASE III1, and WordPerfect, Windows.
- Comfortable with MS-DOS, mainframes, networks, and Internet.
- Ability to learn new computer programs and applications with little instruction.

Communication and Interpersonal
- Enjoy working with details and completing assignments accurately and on time.
- Demonstrate sound writing and speaking skills acquired and polished in business letter writing, report writing, and speech classes.
- Interact well with people as evidenced in my successful sales, volunteer, and internship work.

EXPERIENCE

Tax Preparer, Volunteer Income Tax Assistance program (VITA)
Sponsored by Revenue Canada and Kwantlen University College, Surrey. Prepared federal tax returns for individuals with incomes under $25,000. Conducted interviews with over 50 individuals to elicit data regarding taxes. Determined legitimate tax deductions and recorded them accurately. (Tax seasons, 1997 to present)

Accounting Intern, Software Inc., Accounting Department, Vancouver, BC
Assisted in analyzing data for weekly accounts payable aging report. Prepared daily cash activity report for sums up to $10,000. Calculated depreciation on 12 capital asset accounts with a total valuation of over $900,000. Researched and wrote report analyzing one division's budget of $150,000. (Spring 1999)

Salesperson, Wal-Mart, Vancouver, BC
Helped customers select gardening and landscaping supplies. Assisted in ordering merchandise, stocking the department, and resolving customer problems. (Summers 1997, 1998)

EDUCATION

Kwantlen University College, Surrey, BC. Business Administration Diploma expected June 2000
Major: Business Accounting
Specialization: Accounting Theory and Practice. GPA: 3.2 (A = 4.0)
Participated as member of Accounting Club for two years.
University of British Columbia. B.A. June 1998
Major: Philosophy. GPA: 3.4 (A = 4.0)
Received Award of Merit for volunteer work as orientation guide and peer tutor.

Keith Davies' résumé responds to an advertisement specifying skills for a staff accountant. He uses the combination format to allow him to highlight the skills his education and limited experience have provided. Notice how he highlights his Internet and World Wide Web computer skills. Whenever possible, he quantifies his achievements to make them more forceful.

Instead of listing jobs, though, the functional résumé groups skills and accomplishments in special categories, such as *Supervisory and Management Skills, Retailing and Marketing Experience, Organizational Skills, Project Coordination, Communication and Public Relations*, and *Computer Experience*. This résumé style highlights accomplishments and can de-emphasize a negative employment history. People who have changed jobs frequently or who have gaps in their employment records may prefer the functional résumé. Recent graduates with little experience also find the functional résumé useful.

Combination. The combination résumé style, shown in Figures 13.3 through 13.5, draws on the best features of the chronological and functional résumé styles. This style emphasizes a candidate's capabilities while also including a complete job history. The combination résumé is another good choice for recent graduates.

ARRANGING THE PARTS

Although résumés have standard parts, their arrangement and content must be strategically planned. The most persuasive résumés emphasize skills and achievements aimed at a particular job or company. They show a candidate's most important qualifications first, and they de-emphasize any weaknesses. "Most people are probably guilty of underselling themselves on the résumé," reports a recruiter who reads hundreds of résumés every week. During interviews he often found that applicants had more to offer than their résumés revealed.[2] Your task is to analyze your experience and skills so that you don't miss any opportunities to emphasize those qualities needed for the targeted job. Yet, to avoid a cluttered look, you must arrange the parts of your résumé with no more than six headings.

Most résumé writers study models and adapt a style they like. A word of warning, though: you'll probably be disappointed in your result if you use a typewriter, computer, or printer with standard draft spacing. You need proportional spacing or scalable fonts to fit more words, spaces, and lines on a page. No two résumés are alike, but most job hunters consider the following parts.

Main Heading. Your résumé should always begin with your name, address, telephone number, and e-mail address (if available). If possible, include a number where messages may be left for you. Prospective employers tend to call the next applicant when no one answers. Adding your e-mail address makes contacting you more convenient. Avoid showing both permanent and temporary addresses; some specialists say that dual addresses immediately identify about-to-graduate students. Keep the main heading as uncluttered and simple as possible. And don't include the word *résumé;* it's like putting the word *letter* above correspondence.

Career Objective. Opinion is divided on the effect of including a career objective on a résumé. Recruiters think such statements indicate that a candidate has made a commitment to a career. Moreover, career objectives make the recruiter's life easier by quickly classifying the résumé. But such declarations can also disqualify a candidate if the stated objective doesn't match a company's job description. As Marc Belaiche warns, "vague, general resumes often get lost among the crowd. It is important to tailor objectives to highlight specific industry experience."[3]

You have three choices regarding career objectives. One option is to include a career objective when applying for a specific, targeted position. For example, the fol-

Résumés targeted to specific positions have the best chance of being read.

Generally, include a specific career objective for targeted jobs only.

lowing responds to an advertised position: *Objective: To work in the health care industry as a human resources trainee with exposure to recruiting, training, and benefit administration.* A second choice—one that makes sense if you are preparing an all-purpose résumé—is to omit the career objective. A third possibility involves using a general statement, such as, *Objective: Challenging position in urban planning,* or *Job Goal: Position in sales/marketing.* Some consultants warn against using the words *entry-level* in your objective, because such words emphasize lack of experience.

Many aggressive job applicants today prepare individual targeted résumés for each company or position sought. Thanks to word processing, the task is easy.

Education. The next component is your education—if it is more noteworthy than your work experience. In this section you should include the names and locations of schools, dates of attendance, major fields of study, and degrees, diplomas, and certificates received. Your grade point average and/or class ranking are important to prospective employers. One way to enhance your GPA is to calculate it in your major courses only (for example, *3.6/4.0 in major*). A list of completed courses makes dull reading; refer to courses only if you can relate them to the position sought. When relevant, include certificates earned, seminars attended, and workshops completed. Because employers are interested in your degree of self-sufficiency, you might wish to indicate the percentage of your education for which you paid. If your education is incomplete, include such statements as, *B.A. degree expected September 2000,* or *80 credits completed in 120-credit program.* Entitle this section *Education, Academic Preparation,* or *Professional Training.*

> Educational achievements should precede employment history on a résumé only when the education section is more noteworthy.

Work Experience. Anyone seeking a job today must recognize the value of experience. When asked what advice she had for people with little experience, résumé expert Yana Parker replied, "Get some!"[4] She suggests internships, part-time jobs, or even volunteer work in your career area.

If your work experience is significant and relevant to the position sought, this information should appear before the education category. List your most recent employment first and work backwards, including only those jobs that you think will help you win the targeted position. A job application form may demand a full employment history, but your résumé may be selective. (Be aware, though, that time gaps in your employment history will probably be questioned in the interview.) For each position show the following:

- Employer's name, city, and province
- Dates of employment, including month and year
- Most important job title
- Significant duties, activities, accomplishments, and promotions

Describe your employment achievements concisely but concretely. Avoid generalities such as *Worked with customers.* Be more specific, with statements such as *Served 40 or more retail customers a day, Successfully resolved problems about custom stationery orders,* or *Acted as intermediary among customers, printers, and suppliers.* If possible, quantify your accomplishments, such as *Conducted study of equipment needs of 100 small businesses in Edmonton, Personally generated orders for sales of $90,000 annually, Keyboarded all the production models for a 250-page employee procedures manual,* or *Assisted editor in layout, design, and news writing for 12 issues of division newsletter.*

In addition to technical skills, employers seek individuals with communication, management, and interpersonal capabilities. This means you'll want to select work experiences and achievements that illustrate your initiative, dependability, responsibility, resourcefulness, and leadership. Employers also want people who can work together in teams. Thus, include statements such as *Collaborated with interdepartmental team in developing 10-page handbook for temporary workers* and *Headed student government team that conducted most successful volunteer program in school history.*

Statements describing your work experience become forceful and persuasive by using action verbs, such as those listed in Figure 13.6 and demonstrated in Figure 13.7. These verbs should introduce nouns that a manager might use to describe the skills and traits needed for your targeted job.

Capabilities and Skills. Recruiters want to know specifically what you can do for their companies. Therefore, list your special skills, such as *Proficient in preparing correspondence and reports using WordPerfect.* Include your ability to use computer programs, office equipment, other languages, or sign language. Describe proficiencies you have acquired through training and experience, such as *Trained in computer accounting, including general ledger, accounts receivable, accounts payable, and payroll.* Use expressions like *competent in, skilled in, proficient with, experienced in,* and *ability to;* for example, *Competent in typing, editing, and/or proofreading reports, tables, letters, memos, manuscripts, and business forms.* If you are current with today's technology, you might say, *Experienced in Internet navigation, including World Wide Web search skills.* Be sure to incorporate nouns such as those used in a job description for the position you want.

Emphasize the skills and aptitudes that recommend you for a specific position.

You'll also want to highlight exceptional aptitudes, such as working well under stress and learning computer programs quickly. If possible, provide details and evidence that back up your assertions—for example, *Mastered the Barrister computer program in 25 hours with little instruction.* Search for examples of your writing, speaking, management, organizational, and interpersonal skills—particularly those talents that are relevant to your targeted job.

For recent graduates this section can be used to give recruiters evidence of your potential. Instead of *Capabilities*, the section might be called *Skills and Abilities, Highlights of Skills,* or *Skills Summary.*

Awards, Honours, and Activities. If you have three or more awards or honours, highlight them by listing them under a separate heading. If not, put them with activities. Include awards, scholarships (financial and other), fellowships, honours, recognition, commendations, and certificates. Be sure to identify items clearly. Your reader may be unfamiliar, for example, with organizations that have Greek names (such as fraternities and sororities), honorariums, and awards; tell what they mean. Instead of saying *Recipient of Star award,* give more details: *Recipient of Star award, given by Red River College to outstanding graduates who combine academic excellence and extracurricular achievement.*

Awards, honours, and activities are appropriate for résumés; most personal data are not.

It's also appropriate to include school, community, and professional activities. Employers are interested in evidence that you are a well-rounded person. This section provides an opportunity to demonstrate leadership and interpersonal skills. Strive to use action statements. For example, instead of saying *Treasurer of business club,* explain more fully: *Collected dues, kept financial records, and paid bills while serving as treasurer of 35-member business management club.*

FIGURE 13.6

Action Verbs for Persuasive Résumés

Management Skills	Communication Skills	Research Skills	Technical Skills	Teaching Skills
administered	addressed	clarified	assembled	adapted
analyzed	arbitrated	collected	built	advised
consolidated	arranged	critiqued	calculated	clarified
coordinated	collaborated	diagnosed	computed	coached
delegated	convinced	evaluated	designed	communicated
developed	developed	examined	devised	coordinated
directed	drafted	extracted	engineered	developed
evaluated	edited	identified	executed	enabled
improved*	explained	inspected	fabricated	encouraged
increased	formulated	interpreted	maintained	evaluated
organized	interpreted	interviewed	operated	explained
oversaw	negotiated	investigated	overhauled	facilitated
planned	persuaded	organized	programmed	guided
prioritized	promoted	summarized	remodeled	informed
recommended	publicized	surveyed	repaired	instructed
scheduled	recruited	systematized	solved	persuaded

* The underlined words are especially good for pointing out accomplishments.

Experts don't agree on including references on a résumé.

Personal Data. You needn't include information such as birth date, marital status, height, weight, and religious affiliation. Such information doesn't relate to genuine occupational qualifications, and employers and recruiters are legally barred from asking for such information. Some job seekers do, however, include hobbies or interests (such as skiing or photography) that might grab the employer's or recruiter's attention or serve as conversation starters. You should also indicate your willingness to travel or to relocate, since many companies will be interested.

References. Listing references on a résumé is favoured by some recruiters and opposed by others. Such a list takes up valuable space. Moreover, it is not normally instrumental in securing an interview—few companies check references before the interview. Instead, they prefer that a candidate bring to the interview a list of individuals willing to discuss her or his qualifications. If you do list them, use parallel form. For example, if you show a title for one person (*Professor, Dr., Mrs.*), show titles for all. Include complete addresses with postal codes and telephone numbers with area codes.

Whether or not you include references on your résumé, you should have their names available when you begin your job search. Ask three to five previous employers or instructors whether they will be willing to answer inquiries regarding your qualifications for employment. Be sure, however, to provide them with an opportunity to refuse. No reference is better than a negative one. Do not include personal or character references, such as friends or neighbours, because recruiters rarely consult them. Companies are more interested in the opinions of objective individuals.

FIGURE 13.6 Continued

Financial Skills	Creative Skills	Helping Skills	Clerical or Detail Skills	More Verbs for Accomplishments
administered	acted	assessed	approved	achieved
allocated	conceptualized	assisted	catalogued	expanded
analyzed	created	clarified	classified	improved
appraised	customized	coached	collected	pioneered
audited	designed	counselled	compiled	reduced (losses)
balanced	developed	demonstrated	generated	resolved (problems)
budgeted	directed	diagnosed	inspected	restored
calculated	established	educated	monitored	spearheaded
computed	founded	expedited	operated	transformed
developed	illustrated	facilitated	organized	
forecasted	initiated	familiarized	prepared	
managed	instituted	guided	processed	
marketed	introduced	motivated	purchased	
planned	invented	referred	recorded	
projected	originated	represented	screened	
researched	performed		specified	

Source: Reprinted with permission from *The Damn Good Résumé Guide*, p. 62. Copyright © 1996 by Yana Parker, Ten Speed Press, P.O. Box 7123, Berkeley, CA, 94707. Available from your local bookseller or call 800-841-2665. Or visit us at www.tenspeed.com.

Testimonials. Although references are usually not listed, some candidates today are including brief testimonials to humanize their résumés and to provide a competitive edge. "After you've cited an achievement, you can follow up with a short flattering quote from your boss or a client," advises Joyce Lain Kennedy.[5]

> Updating and troubleshooting DOS computer systems for 250 students and faculty. Dr. Brian Wilson, lab director, said, "Jeffrey is the glue that holds this computer lab together. He's definitely our computer guru."

> Keyboarded selected articles and proofread 12 issues of departmental newsletter. "You're the best proofreader we've ever had. Now we all must live up to your very high standards," said Deborah Cook, office manager and newsletter editor.

Another way to handle testimonials is to list them in a section called *Complimentary Quotations* included at the end of your résumé. This is a good section to fill out a second page of a résumé that won't fit on one page. Remember, testimonials work. Think of how many you've heard in advertisements or seen in TV commercials.

PREPARING FOR RÉSUMÉ SCANNING

Thus far we've aimed our résumé advice at human readers. However, the first reader of your résumé may well be a computer. Increasingly, hiring companies use scanners to digitize all incoming résumés. This technology creates a database that employers can search with keywords. Hiring managers identify the skills, traits, and experience

FIGURE 13.7

Using Action Verbs to Introduce Statements with Keywords for Scanners

Developed organizational and research skills by **identifying** weaknesses in internship program and recommending five alternative programs.

Demonstrated time management skills by **reducing** delivery delays an average of three days per order.

Helped set priorities and **streamline** office work so that staff could be reduced from five to three employees.

Organized team to study marketing possibilities through a company World Wide Web site.

Took initiative in **creating** a 12-point checklist for managers to use when requesting temporary workers.

Designed five posters announcing new employee suggestion program.

Calculated shipping charges for overseas deliveries and **recommended** most economical rates.

Managed 24-station computer network linking data and employees in three departments.

Distributed and **explained** summer job application forms to over 500 students.

---

required for an open position; and these words become search terms for the résumé database. Only résumés containing these keywords are selected for review. Don't panic, though! Computers don't do the hiring. After selection, résumés are reviewed by humans, so your résumé must satisfy both the computer and the hiring manager.

How can you know whether a company will scan your résumé? The easiest way is to call any company where you plan to apply. Ask if it scans résumés electronically. Some companies even solicit résumés over the Internet and provide instructions on how to submit your résumé electronically. Visit a company's Web site for on-line advice.

Making Your Résumé Computer Friendly. A scannable résumé must sacrifice many of the graphics possibilities that writers have been learning to employ. Computers are not impressed by graphics. Computers prefer "clean" résumés—free of graphics and fancy fonts. To make a computer-friendly "clean" résumé, such as that shown in Figure 13.8, you'll want to apply the following suggestions:

- *Avoid small print and unusual typefaces.* Because touching letters or unusual fonts are likely to be misread, use a familiar font, such as Helvetica or Times Roman. Type size should be at least 12 points.
- *Avoid graphics and vertical lines.* Scanners gag on graphics such as arrows or vertical lines. Most scanners, however, can read asterisks, bullets, and bold type. Italics and underlining are acceptable to many scanners but not to all.
- *Use smooth white paper, black ink, and a quality printer.* Avoid coloured and textured papers as well as dot-matrix printers. Don't fold or staple a résumé intended for scanning.
- *Be sure that your name is the first line on the page.* Don't use fancy layouts that may confuse a scanner. Scanners look for names first.

FIGURE 13.8

Computer-Unfriendly and Computer-Friendly Résumés

Fancy font, graphic, and failure to place name first prevent scanner from reading name accurately.

Fails to include keywords relating to job sought.

Vertical lines cause scanner to misread this section.

Vague job description contains few key words for scanner to pick up.

Computer Unfriendly

CLJ *Casandra L. Johnson*

3340 Bay Drive
Regina, SK S2R 3L3
(306) 742-4490

Objective
　　Position with progressive firm where experience, skills, and hard work are rewarded.

Strengths

Accounting software	Persuasive
Banking CRT experience	Communicative
EXCEL spreadsheet	Open-minded
WordPerfect	Customer-oriented
Learn new programs quickly	Hard working

Experience
　　National Bank, Regina, SK S1L 2W3
　　July 1998 to present
　　Customer Service Representative
　　　　Responsible for counter work, customer interaction, handling money.

Computer Friendly

Casandra L. Johnson
3340 Bay Drive
Regina, SK S2R 3L3
(306) 742-4490

OBJECTIVE
Position in operations department of bank, including operations officer, or customer service representative. Proven skills in bookkeeping, accounting, payables, receivables, management. Demonstrated customer-service, communication, organizational skills. Computer skills, including spreadsheets and Internet navigation. Bachelor of Business Administration in progress.

EXPERIENCE
National Bank, Regina, SK S1L 2W3
July 1998 to present
Customer Service Representative
- Cheerfully greet customers, make deposits and withdrawals, accurately enter on computer. Balance up to $10,000 in cash with computer journal tape daily within 15-minute time period.
- Solve customer problems and answer questions patiently. Issue cashier's cheques, savings bonds, and traveller's cheques. Commended for accuracy and ability to work under pressure.

Ames Aviation Maintenance Company, Regina, SK S3S 2L4
June 1995–June 1998
Bookkeeper
- Managed all bookkeeping functions including accounts payable, accounts receivable, payroll, and tax reports for small business.

EDUCATION
University of Saskatchewan, Regina SK. Completing Bachelor of Business Administration.

STRENGTHS
Computer:　　Accounting software, banking CRT experience, EXCEL spreadsheet, Word, Windows, Internet. Learn new programs quickly.
Interpersonal:　Persuasive, communicative, open-minded. Selected to represent our branch on company Diversity Committee. Able to set priorities and follow through. Maintain 3.2 GPA while working nearly full time to pay for college.

Plain font, name first on line by itself enable scanner to read lines accurately.

Expanded objective features many keywords relating to job sought, skills, and experience.

Specifics in job description include many nouns for scanner to match.

Uses at least a 12-point font for best scanning.

Goes on to second page, which is not unusual in computer-friendly résumés. Be sure to put name at top of second page.

- *Provide white space.* To ensure separation of words and categories, leave plenty of white space. For instance, instead of using parentheses to enclose a telephone area code, insert blank spaces or periods, as in *204 799.5542*.
- *Emphasize keywords.* Keywords are usually nouns that describe what an employer wants. Notice in Figure 13.8 that the expanded objective in the computer-friendly résumé includes many possible job titles for the position sought. It also features nouns and phrases identifying important employment traits and skills. How can you know what nouns to include? Take a look at job advertisements and job descriptions to see what employers are requiring. When you have these skills, be sure to spotlight them. See Figure 13.9 for a list of the most requested interpersonal keywords.

E-Mail and Internet Transmission. If you don't have an e-mail address, think seriously about getting one. The easiest way is to subscribe to a commercial on-line service such as AOL Canada, CompuServe, or Sympatico. Some services such as Canada.com offer free Web-based e-mail. E-mail lets you communicate around the world instantly. And from your own computer (don't use your employer's), you can send your résumé for a quick response to an ad or on-line posting. Moreover, you'll be demonstrating your computer skills. Some job hunters submit their résumé to on-line posting services such as the National Graduate Register (www.WorkLinkNGR.com) or the Electronic Labour Exchange (ele.engenia.com)—or even post their résumé on a personal Web page.

FIGURE 13.9

Interpersonal Keywords Most Requested by Employers Using Résumé-Scanning Software*

Ability to delegate	Innovative
Ability to implement	Leadership
Ability to plan	Multitasking
Ability to train	Open communication
Accurate	Open minded
Adaptable	Oral communication
Aggressive work	Organizational skills
Analytical ability	Persuasive
Assertive	Problem solving
Communication skills	Public speaking
Competitive	Results oriented
Creative	Safety conscious
Customer oriented	Self-accountable
Detail minded	Self-managing
Ethical	Setting priorities
Flexible	Supportive
Follow instructions	Takes initiative
Follow through	Team building
Follow up	Team player
High energy	Tenacious
Industrious	Willing to travel

*Reported by Resumix, a leading producer of résumé-scanning software.
Source: *Electronic Résumé Revolution,* p. 70, Joyce Lain Kennedy and Thomas J. Morrow, Copyright © 1994. Reprinted by permission of [Wiley-Liss, Inc., a subsidiary of] John Wiley & Sons, Inc.

APPLYING THE FINAL TOUCHES

Because your résumé is probably the most important message you will ever write, you'll revise it many times. With so much information in concentrated form and with so much riding on its outcome, your résumé demands careful polishing, proofreading, and critiquing.

As you revise, be certain to verify all the facts, particularly those involving your previous employment and education. Don't be caught in a mistake, or worse, a distortion of previous jobs and dates of employment. These items likely will be checked. And the consequences of puffing up a résumé with deception or flat-out lies are simply not worth the risk.

As you continue revising, look for other ways to improve your résumé. For example, consider consolidating headings. By condensing your information into as few headings as possible, you'll produce a clean, professional-looking document. Study other résumés for valuable formatting ideas. Ask yourself what graphics highlighting techniques you can use to improve readability: capitalization, underlining, indenting, and bulleting. Experiment with headings and styles to achieve a pleasing, easy-to-read message. Moreover, look for ways to eliminate wordiness. For example, instead of *Supervised two employees who worked at the counter*, try *Supervised two counter employees*. Review Chapters 3 and 4 for more writing tips.

Above all, make your résumé look professional. Avoid anything humorous or "cute," such as a help-wanted poster with your name or picture inside. Eliminate the personal pronoun *I*. The abbreviated, objective style of a résumé precludes the use of personal pronouns. Use white, off-white, or buff-coloured heavy bond paper (24-pound).

After revising, proofread, proofread, and proofread again: for spelling and mechanics, for content, and for format. Then, have a knowledgeable friend or relative proofread it again. This is one document that must be perfect.

Studying the model résumés in Figures 13.1 to 13.5 should give you many ideas for your own. Notice that the models illustrate the qualifications of job seekers with little experience as well as some with more experience. Remember, you'll get the best results if you use a computer and a good printer.

Finally, be sure to write your résumé yourself because no one knows you as well as you. Don't delegate the task to a résumé-writing service. Such services tend to produce eye-catching, elaborate documents with lofty language, fancy borders, and fuzzy thinking. Here's an example: "Objective: An entry-level position that will allow me to use my academic skills to gain hands-on experience while providing for career-development opportunities." Save your money and buy a good interview suit instead.

In addition to being well written, a résumé must be carefully formatted and meticulously proofread.

THE PERSUASIVE COVER LETTER

To accompany your résumé, you'll need a persuasive cover letter (also called a *letter of application*). A survey of U.S. business executives revealed that 60 percent of them considered the cover letter as important as, if not more critical than, the résumé itself.[6]

The cover letter has three purposes: (1) introducing the résumé, (2) highlighting ways in which your strengths benefit the reader, and (3) gaining an interview. In many ways your cover letter is a sales letter; it sells your talents and tries to beat the

Cover letters introduce résumés, relate writer strengths to reader benefits, and seek an interview.

competition. It will, accordingly, include many of the techniques you learned for sales letters (Chapter 9).

Human resource professionals disagree on how long to make the cover letter. Many prefer short letters with no more than four paragraphs; instead of concentrating on the letter, these readers focus on the résumé. Others desire longer letters that supply more information, thus giving them a better opportunity to evaluate a candidate's qualifications. The latter human resource professionals argue that hiring and training new employees is expensive and time-consuming; therefore, they welcome extra data to guide them in making the best choice the first time. Follow your judgment as to whether to write a brief or a lengthier cover letter. If you feel, for example, that you need space to explain in more detail what you can do for a prospective employer, do so.

Regardless of its length, a cover letter should have three primary parts: (1) an opening that gains attention, (2) a body that builds interest and reduces resistance, and (3) a closing that motivates action.

GAINING ATTENTION IN THE OPENING

Check the spelling of the receiver's name and organization.

The first step in gaining the interest of your reader is addressing that individual by name. Rather than sending your letter to the "Human Resources Manager" or "Human Resources Department," try to identify the name of the appropriate individual. Make it a rule to call the organization for the correct spelling and the complete address. This personal touch will distinguish your letter and demonstrate your serious interest.

How you open your cover letter depends largely on whether the application is solicited or unsolicited. If an employment position has been announced and applicants are being solicited, you can use a direct approach. If you do not know whether a position is open and you are prospecting for a job, use an indirect approach. Whether direct or indirect, the opening should attract the attention of the reader. Strive for openings that are more imaginative than *Please consider this letter an application for the position of . . .* or *I would like to apply for . . .*

Openings for solicited jobs may refer to an employee.

Openings for Solicited Jobs. Here are some of the best techniques to open a cover letter for a job that has been announced:

- *Refer to the name of an employee in the company.* Remember that employers always hope to hire known quantities rather than complete strangers:

  Mitchell Sims, a member of your Customer Service Department, recently informed me that DataTech is seeking an experienced customer service representative. The attached summary of my qualifications demonstrates my preparation for this position.

  At the suggestion of Ms. Claudette Guertin of your Human Resources Department, I submit my qualifications for the position of personnel assistant.

- *Refer to the source of your information precisely.* If you are answering an advertisement, include the exact position advertised and the name and date of the publication. For large organizations it's also wise to mention the section of the newspaper where the ad appeared:

Your advertisement in Section C-3 of the June 1 *Vancouver Sun* for a junior accountant greatly appeals to me. With my accounting training and computer experience, I believe I could serve DataTech well.

The September 10 issue of the *National Post* reports that you are seeking a mature, organized, and reliable administrative assistant with excellent communication skills.

Susan Butler, placement director at Carleton University, told me that DataTech has an opening for a technical writer with knowledge of desktop publishing techniques.

- *Refer to the job title and describe how your qualifications fit the requirements.* Human resources managers are looking for a match between an applicant's credentials and the job needs:

  Will an honours degree in recreation studies and two years of part-time experience developing wellness activities for a retirement community qualify me for the position of activity director . . . ?

  Because of my specialized training in computerized accounting at Simon Fraser University, I feel confident that I have the qualifications you described in your advertisement for an accountant trainee.

Openings for Unsolicited Jobs. If you are unsure whether a position actually exists, you may wish to use a more persuasive opening. Since your goal is to convince this person to read on, try one of the following techniques:

Openers for unsolicited jobs show interest in and knowledge of the company, as well as spotlighting reader benefits.

- *Demonstrate interest in and knowledge of the reader's business.* Show the human resources manager that you have done your research and that this organization is more than a mere name to you.

  Since the Canadian Automobile Association is organizing a new information management team for its recently established group insurance division, could you use the services of a well-trained business administration graduate who seeks to become a professional underwriter?

- *Show how your special talents and background will benefit the company.* Human resources managers need to be convinced that you can do something for them:

  Could your rapidly expanding publications division use the services of an editorial assistant who offers exceptional language skills, an honours degree from Brandon University, and two years' experience in producing a school literary publication?

In applying for an advertised job, Mabel Lam wrote the solicited cover letter shown in Figure 13.10. Notice that her opening identifies the position and the newspaper completely so that the reader knows exactly what advertisement Mabel means. More challenging are unsolicited cover letters, such as Jon Penner's shown in Figure 13.11. Because he hopes to discover or create a job, his opening must grab the reader's attention immediately. To do that, he capitalizes on company information appearing in the newspaper. Notice, too, that Jon purposely kept his cover letter short and to the point because he anticipated that a busy executive would be unwilling to read a long, detailed letter.

Jon's unsolicited letter, Figure 13.11, "prospects" for a job. Some job candidates feel that such letters may be even more productive than efforts to secure advertised jobs, since "prospecting" candidates face less competition.

FIGURE 13.10

Solicited Letter of Application

1770 Hawthorne Place
Red Deer, AB T4R 3L2
May 23, 200x

Mr. William A. Caldwell
Director, Human Resources
Del Rio Enterprises
Calgary, AB T2A 3L4

Dear Mr. Caldwell:

Identifies position and exact place where advertisement appeared.

Since I have focused my education and training on sales and marketing, your advertisement for an assistant product manager, which appeared on May 22 in Section C of the *National Post*, immediately caught my attention.

Shows how her qualifications match those in the ad.

Your ad states that the job includes "assisting in the coordination of a wide range of marketing programs as well as analyzing sales results and tracking marketing budgets." A recent internship at Ventana Corporation introduced me to similar tasks. I assisted the marketing manager in analyzing the promotion, budget, and overall sales success of two products Ventana was evaluating. My ten-page report examined the nature of the current market, the products' life cycles, and their sales/profit return. In addition to this research, I helped formulate a product merchandising plan and answered consumers' questions at a local trade show. This brief but challenging introduction to product management convinced me that I could be successful and happy in a marketing career.

Highlights training, computer skills, and experience.

Intensive coursework in marketing and management, as well as proficiency in spreadsheets, databases, and the Internet, has given me the kind of marketing and computing training that Del Rio demands in a product manager. Moreover, I have had retail sales experience and have been active in school organizations. I'm confident that my academic preparation, my marketing experience, and my ability to work well with others qualify me for this position.

Ties in request for interview with review of major qualifications.

After you have examined the enclosed résumé for details of my qualifications, I would be happy to answer questions. Please call me to arrange an interview at your convenience so that we may discuss how my marketing, computing, and interpersonal skills could contribute to Del Rio Enterprises.

Sincerely,

Mabel Lam

Mabel Lam
Enclosure

BUILDING INTEREST IN THE BODY

The body of a cover letter should build interest, reduce resistance, and discuss relevant personal traits.

Once you have captured the attention of the reader, you can use the body of the letter to build interest and reduce resistance. Keep in mind that your first goal is to relate your remarks to a specific position. If you are responding to an advertisement, you'll want to explain how your preparation and experience fill the stated requirements. If you are prospecting for a job, you may not know the exact requirements. Your employment research and knowledge of your field, however, should give you a reasonably good idea of what is expected for this position.

FIGURE 13.11

Unsolicited Letter of Application

5 Pinecroft Drive,
Winnipeg, MB R4L 2H7
May 29, 200x

Mr. Arthur P. Minsberg
Vice President, Operations
Sports World Inc.
490 Portage Avenue
Winnipeg, MB R2G 1L7

Dear Mr. Minsberg:

Today's *Winnipeg Free Press* reports that your organization plans to expand its operations to include national distribution of sporting goods, and it occurs to me that you will be needing highly motivated, self-starting sales representatives and marketing managers. I have these significant qualifications to offer:

- Four years of formal training in business administration, including specialized courses in sales management, retailing, marketing promotion, and consumer behaviour.

- Practical experience in demonstrating and selling consumer products, as well as successful experience in telemarketing.

- A strong interest in most areas of sports and good communication skills (which helped me become a sportscaster at the University of Manitoba radio station CLQW).

I would like to talk with you about how I can put these qualifications, and others summarized in the enclosed résumé, to work for Sports World as it develops its national sales force. I'll call during the week of June 5 to discuss your company's expansion plans and the opportunity for an interview.

Sincerely yours,

Jon Penner

Jon Penner

Enclosure

Shows knowledge of company and resourcefulness.

Focuses on three most important qualities.

Takes initiative for follow-up.

It's also important to emphasize reader benefits. In other words, you should describe your strong points in relation to the needs of the employer. In one employment survey many human resources professionals expressed the same view: "I want you to tell me what you can do for my organization. This is much more important to me than telling me what courses you took in college or what 'duties' you performed on your previous jobs."[7] Instead of *I have completed courses in business communication, report writing, and technical writing,* try this:

Courses in business communication, report writing, and technical writing have helped me develop the research and writing skills required of your technical writers.

Spotlighting reader benefits means matching personal strengths to employer needs.

Choose your strongest qualifications and show how they fit the targeted job. And remember, students with little experience are better off spotlighting their education and its practical applications, as these candidates did:

Because you seek an architect's apprentice with proven ability, I am enclosing a drawing of mine that won second place in the Algonquin College drafting contest last year.

Successfully transcribing over 100 letters and memos in my college transcription class gave me experience in converting the spoken word into the written word, an exacting communication skill and one that is demanded of your administrative assistants.

In the body of your letter, you'll also want to discuss relevant personal traits. Employers are looking for candidates who, among other things, are team players, take responsibility, show initiative, and learn easily. Notice how the following paragraph uses action verbs and key traits to paint a picture of a promising candidate:

In addition to developing technical and academic skills at St. Francis Xavier University, I gained interpersonal, leadership, and organizational skills. As vice president of the university's business students' organization, I helped organize and supervise two successful fundraising events. These activities involved developing concepts, motivating others to help, scheduling work sessions, and coordinating the efforts of 35 diverse students in reaching our goal. I look forward to applying such experience in your management trainee program.

Finally, in this section or the next, you should refer the reader to your résumé. Do so directly or as part of another statement, as shown here:

Please refer to the attached résumé for additional information regarding my education, experience, and references. As you will notice from my résumé, I will graduate in June with a bachelor's degree in business administration.

MOTIVATING ACTION IN THE CLOSING

The closing of a cover letter should include a request for an interview.

After presenting your case, you should conclude with a spur to action. This is where you ask for an interview. If you live in a distant city, you may request an employment application or an opportunity to be interviewed by the organization's nearest representative. However, never ask for the job. To do so would be presumptuous and naive. In requesting an interview, suggest reader benefits or review your strongest points. Sound sincere and appreciative. Remember to make it easy for the reader to agree by supplying your telephone number and the best times to call you. And keep in mind that some human resources managers prefer that you take the initiative and call them. Here are possible endings:

I hope this brief description of my qualifications and the additional information on my résumé indicate to you my genuine desire to put my skills in accounting to work for you. Please call me at (416) 488-2291 before 10 a.m. or after 3 p.m. to arrange an interview.

To add to your staff an industrious, well-trained word processing specialist with proven communication skills, call me at (604) 492-1433 to arrange an interview. I can meet with you at any time convenient to your schedule.

Next week, after you have examined the attached résumé, I will call you to discuss the possibility of arranging an interview.

FINAL TIPS

As you revise your cover letter, notice how many sentences begin with *I*. Although it's impossible to talk about yourself without using *I*, you can reduce "I" domination with this writing technique: Make activities and outcomes, and not yourself, the subjects of sentences. For example, rather than *I took classes in word processing and desktop publishing*, say *Classes in word processing and desktop publishing prepared me to* . . . Instead of *I enjoyed helping customers*, say *Helping customers taught me to be patient under stress*.

Like the résumé, your cover letter must look professional and suggest quality. This means using a traditional letter style, such as block or modified block. Also, be sure to print it on the same bond paper as your résumé. And, as with your résumé, proofread it several times yourself; then, have a friend read it for content and mechanics.

> A cover letter should look professional and suggest quality.

SUMMING UP AND LOOKING FORWARD

In today's tough job market, an employment search begins with identifying your interests, evaluating your qualifications, and choosing a career path. Finding the perfect job will mean a concentrated effort devoted to checking classified advertisements, networking, and studying on-line job possibilities. In applying for jobs, you'll want to submit a persuasive résumé that sells your skills and experience. Whether you choose a chronological, functional, or combination résumé style, you'll tailor your assets to fit the position sought. If you think your résumé might be scanned, emphasize keywords and keep the format simple. A persuasive cover letter should introduce your résumé and describe how your skills and experiences match those required.

Now, if your résumé and letter of application have been successful, you'll proceed to the employment interview, one of life's most nerve-wracking experiences. The last chapter in this book provides helpful suggestions for successful interviewing and follow-up communication.

DISCUSSION

1. What kinds of questions should you ask yourself before choosing a career?
2. Why is the résumé the most important document you may ever write?
3. What are the advantages and disadvantages to including a job objective on a résumé?
4. Why are companies increasingly using scanning devices for incoming résumés?
5. What are the three parts of a cover letter, and what is the goal of each part?

6. How are most jobs likely to be found? Through classified ads? Employment agencies? Networking? The Internet?

7. What is the goal of a résumé?

8. Describe a chronological résumé and discuss its advantages.

9. Describe a functional résumé and discuss its advantages.

10. When does it make sense to include a career objective on your résumé?

11. In addition to technical skills, what traits and characteristics do employers seek?

12. What are the three purposes of a cover letter?

13. How can you make your résumé computer friendly?

14. In an unsolicited cover letter, what techniques can you use to persuade a receiver to read your letter?

15. In a cover letter, how can you avoid starting too many sentences with *I*? Give an example.

13.1 Cover Letter. Analyze each section of the following cover letter.

Dear Human Resources Manager:

Ineffective Writing

(1) Please consider this letter as an application for the position of staff accountant that I saw advertised in the *Saskatoon Star Phoenix* on April 27. Accounting has been my major in college, and although I have had no paid work experience in this field, I believe that I could be an asset to Meyers & Jacoby.

(2) For four years I have studied accounting, and I am fully trained for full-charge bookkeeping as well as computer accounting. I have taken 36 credits in college accounting and courses in electronic data processing. I have also taken other courses that may help me in business, including business communication, human relations, report writing, and economics.

(3) In addition to my course work, during the tax season I have been a student volunteer for VITA. This is a project to help individuals in the community prepare their income tax returns, and I learned a lot from this experience. I have also received some experience in office work and working with figures when I was employed as an office assistant for Copy Quick, Inc.

(4) I am a competent and responsible person who gets along pretty well with others. I have been a member of some college and social organizations and have even held elective office.

(5) I feel that I have a strong foundation in accounting as a result of my course work and my experience. Along with my personal qualities and my desire to succeed, I hope that you will agree that I qualify for the position of staff accountant with Meyers & Jacoby.

Sincerely,

Make specific suggestions to the writer of this letter for improving each of the five paragraphs.

13.2 Learning About Employment in Your Field. Visit your school or local library. Photocopy a page from the *Dictionary of Occupational Titles* that describes a position for which you could apply in two to five years. Print pages from the on-line version or photocopy pages from the hard copy of the *Occupational Outlook Handbook*. Focus on information that describes employment in the area in which you are interested. Save these copies to attach to your letter of application.

Related Web Site: www.workinfonet.ca/cwn/english/main.html

13.3 Clipping Classifieds. Clip a job advertisement from the classified section of a local or national newspaper. Select an ad describing the kind of employment you will seek now or when you complete your program. (If you can find no advertisement, write one. Construct an advertisement for a legitimate position that could possibly have appeared in an advertisement.) Save this advertisement to attach to your résumé when you submit it.

13.4 The Perfect Candidate. Using information you have gathered from your research and from other sources, describe the successful candidate for the position in Activity 13.3. What education will this individual have? Experience? Skills? Personal qualities? Physical abilities? Appearance?

13.5 Career Objectives. In preparation for writing your résumé, write two career objectives for yourself. Write one that is broad, encompassing both short- and long-term goals. Write another that is narrow and aimed at a specific job.

13.6 Inventorying Your Assets. On a separate sheet prepare for writing your résumé by completing inventory lists:

- *Education.* List degrees, certificates, and training accomplishments. Include courses, seminars, and skills that are relevant to the job you seek.
- *Experience.* Begin with your most recent job. For each position list the following information: employer, your job title, dates of employment, and three to five accomplishments. Use active verbs and strive to quantify your achievements. Don't merely list duties. Focus on keywords that employers might use as search words.
- *Awards, honours, activities.* List awards, recognition, honours, or activities that recommend you for the targeted job. Look over the examples in this chapter.
- *Skills, strengths.* Think about skills, talents, or characteristics you possess that relate to the targeted job. Decide whether to use this category or one of the others shown in the models in this chapter. Write statements that demonstrate traits and skills employers seek. Be sure to include computer skills.

13.7 Writing Your Résumé. Using the data you have just developed, write your résumé. Revise until it is perfect. Attach a copy of the advertisement from Activity 13.3.

13.8 Writing a Scannable Résumé. Make another version of your résumé that is computer friendly. Because you should use a larger font, your résumé may require two pages. Be sure to place your name at the top of the second page.

13.9 Posting a Résumé on the Web. Visit the following Web site to familiarize yourself with the methods of preparing an on-line or hypertext version of your résumé:

www.eresumes.com. At the option of your instructor, you may develop a hypertext résumé that includes expanded sections describing your experience, education, and strengths. Some job candidates use hyptertext résumés as they would use a portfolio, displaying samples of work and letters of recommendation. Once you complete your on-line or hypertext résumé, you may post it on your own Web site. Print a copy for your instructor.

Related Web Site: www.worklinkNGR.com

13.10 Writing a Solicited Cover Letter. Write a cover letter for your résumé. Attach the photocopies from Activity 13.2.

13.11 Writing an Unsolicited Cover Letter. Write an unsolicited letter seeking a part-time or summer position with an actual firm in your area.

13.12 Searching the Internet: Job Hunting in Cyberspace. Study the list of Internet resources available for job hunters in the Communication Workshop at the end of this chapter. Visit at least three of the sites and select two or more jobs in which you might be interested. If possible, print copies of the job listings to submit to your instructor. Also learn how to list a résumé with one of the résumé banks.

13.13 Connecting With E-mail: Recommending Job Banks and Résumé Banks. Using what you've learned in completing Activity 13.12, send an e-mail message to your instructor, recommending the best job site on the Web and the best résumé bank for college students. Be specific in explaining why you recommend these two sites.

GRAMMAR/MECHANICS CHECKUP—13

Number Style

Review Sections 4.01–4.13 in the Grammar/Mechanics Handbook. Then study each of the following pairs. Assume that these expressions appear in the context of letters, reports, or memos. Write *a* or *b* in the space provided to indicate the preferred number style and record the number of the G/M principle illustrated. When you finish, compare your responses with those provided. If your responses differ, study carefully the principles in parentheses.

Example: (a) six investments	(b) 6 investments	a	(4.01a)

1. (a) sixteen credit cards	(b) 16 credit cards	_____
2. (a) Fifth Avenue	(b) 5th Avenue	_____
3. (a) 34 newspapers	(b) thirty-four newspapers	_____
4. (a) July eighth	(b) July 8	_____
5. (a) twenty dollars	(b) $20	_____
6. (a) on the 15th of June	(b) on the fifteenth of June	_____
7. (a) at 4:00 p.m.	(b) at 4 p.m.	_____
8. (a) 8 sixty-four page books	(b) eight 64-page books	_____
9. (a) over 18 years ago	(b) over eighteen years ago	_____
10. (a) 2,000,000 residents	(b) 2 million residents	_____
11. (a) fifteen cents	(b) 15 cents	_____
12. (a) a thirty-day warranty	(b) a 30-day warranty	_____

_____	13. (a) 2/3 of the books
_____	14. (a) two telephones for 15 employees
_____	15. (a) 6 of the 130 letters

13. (a) 2/3 of the books   (b) two-thirds of the books
14. (a) two telephones for 15 employees   (b) 2 telephones for 15 employees
15. (a) 6 of the 130 letters   (b) six of the 130 letters

1. b (4.01a)   3. a (4.01a)   5. b (4.02)   7. b (4.04)   9. b (4.08)   11. b (4.02)   13. b (4.12)
15. a (4.06)

GRAMMAR/MECHANICS CHALLENGE—13

Document for Revision

The following résumé (shortened for this exercise) has faults in grammar, punctuation, spelling, number form, verb form, wordiness, and word use. Use standard proofreading marks (see Appendix B) to correct the errors. When you finish, your instructor can show you the revised version of this résumé.

Ineffective Writing

MEGAN A. Kozlov

245 Topsail Road

St. John's, Newfoundland A1B 3Z4

EDUCATION

Memorial University, St. John's, Newfoundland. Bachelor of Arts Degree expected in June 2000. Major English.

EXPERIENCE:

- Administrative Assistant. Host Systems, St. John's. 1997 too pressent Responsible for entering data on Macintosh computer. I had to insure accuracy and completness of reports that were to be entered. Another duty was maintaining a well-organized filing system. I also served as Office Courier.

- Lechter's Housewares. Outlook Newfoundland. 2nd Asst. Mgr I managed store in absence of mgr. and asst. mgr. I open and close registers. Ballanced daily reciepts. Ordered some mds. I also had to supervise 2 employes, earning rabid promotion.

- Clerk typist. Sunshine Travel Outlook Nfld. 1994–95. (part time) Entered travel information on IBM PC. Did personalized followup letters to customer inquirys. Was responsible for phones. I also handled all errands as courier.

STRENGTHS

IBM PC, transcription, poofreading.

Can type 50 words/per/minute.

I am a fast learner, and very accurate.

Word-perfect, Lotus, InterNet

LOOKING FOR JOBS ON THE INTERNET: SUCCESS IN CYBERSPACE

The Internet can be a highly effective search tool for students looking for jobs and recruiters looking for employees. A job seeker can get free access to millions of worldwide job postings 24 hours a day, 7 days a week. Recruiters are scouring cyberspace for just the right employee. But be careful—a random Internet job search can turn into a "black hole" that burns up hours of time while returning few serious leads. How can you make effective use of the vast array of excellent on-line resources without getting overwhelmed by information? The following tips will help you plan an effective on-line job search.

- **Use the Net as a part of your total job search plan.** Continue to cultivate the tried-and-true strategies for job searching including networking and studying classified advertisements. Experts refer to the "law of diminishing returns" when talking about time spent on-line. Eventually, your time invested in searching far exceeds the returns you may be getting.[8]

- **Use the Net to narrow your search.** The Net has lots of information designed to help you select a career and target your search before you hit the job banks. For example, are you interested in working with a larger company or smaller firm, in a professional setting or as a technician or technologist? Do you plan to be in a field related to computers? Will you need to move to find employment or will something be available locally? Answering these questions will help you refine your search once you start to browse job banks.

- **Use the Net's full resources.** Use the Internet for more than just access to job banks. Through the Net you can network with potential employers; learn about labour market information and trends; review local, national, and international newspapers; visit potential employers' sites for job opportunities as well as pre-interview preparations; and participate in newsgroups to get targeted job listings and specific industry contacts.

- **Use the Net to demonstrate your computer skills to potential employers.** Select several job banks that meet your needs and post your résumé. Often this can be done at no cost. You may even wish to create an electronic résumé for your own site that acts like a portfolio of your computer skills.

To get started on your Internet job search, visit the following Web sites. They offer a wide range of services from job searching via Human Resources Development Canada to listings of useful U.S. and international services.

- Canada WorkInfoNet (www.workinfonet.ca) is an internet directory (like a telephone book) providing useful links to all HRDC sites, government job postings, subsidized jobs and internships, job-related newsgroups, and job-finding clubs.
- Campus WorkLink: NGR (www.WorkLinkNGR.com) is a joint site provided by the Canadian Association of Career Educators and Employers and Industry Canada's National Graduate Register. Billed as Canada's largest on-line job search tool, this site provides a wide variety of services and features enabling job seekers and employers to select the job search tools that work for them.
- Canada Job Bank (jb-ge.hrdc-drhc.gc.ca) provides a listing of job orders placed by employers with Human Resources Development Canada.
- The Bridges Initiative Inc. (www.bridges.com), Canadian Jobs Catalogue (www.kenevacorp.mb.ca), and the Canadian Employment Search Network (www.canjobs.com) are just three examples of the many private-sector on-line employment services offering a full range of tools to browsers and subscribers.

Application. Explore one of the Web sites discussed here. Print the descriptions of two jobs in which you would be interested. Submit these to your instructor along with a memo describing briefly the pros and cons of using the Web to find a job. What advice would you give to other students who may be job searching on the Internet for the first time?

EMPLOYMENT INTERVIEWING AND FOLLOW-UP MESSAGES

Nothing delights interviewers more than candidates who have done their homework. They want to know that a candidate has done a little research on the company and understands the challenges it is facing. As a bonus, the most heartwarming candidates have actually given a little thought to the job they are applying for.[1]

MICHAEL STERN, president, Michael Stern Associates Inc.,
an executive search firm headquartered in Toronto

Learning Objectives

1. Distinguish between screening interviews and hiring/placement interviews.

2. Identify information resources in investigating target employers.

3. Explain how to prepare for employment interviews.

4. Recognize how to control nonverbal messages and how to fight interview fears.

5. Be prepared to answer favourite interview questions and know how to close an interview.

6. Itemize topics and behaviours to be avoided in interviews.

7. Write follow-up letters and other employment messages.

Job interviews, for most of us, are intimidating; no one enjoys being judged and, possibly, rejected. Should you expect to be nervous about an upcoming job interview? Of course! Everyone is uneasy about being scrutinized and questioned. But think of how much more nervous you would be if you had no idea what to expect in the interview and if you were unprepared.

This chapter presents different kinds of interviews and shows you how to prepare for them. You'll learn how to gather information about an employer, as well as how to reduce nervousness, control body language, and fight fear during an interview. You'll pick up tips for responding to recruiters' favourite questions and how to cope with illegal questions and salary matters. Moreover, you'll receive pointers on significant questions you can ask during an interview. Finally, you'll learn what you should do as a successful follow-up to an interview.

Yes, you can expect to be nervous. But you can also expect to ace an interview when you know what's coming and when you prepare thoroughly. Remember, it's often the degree of preparation that determines who gets the job.

SUCCEEDING IN VARIOUS KINDS OF EMPLOYMENT INTERVIEWS

Job applicants generally face two kinds of interviews: screening interviews and hiring/placement interviews. You must succeed in the first to proceed to the second.

SCREENING INTERVIEWS

Screening interviews by telephone are intended to eliminate those who fail to meet minimum requirements.

Screening interviews do just that—they screen candidates to eliminate those who fail to meet minimum requirements. Telephone conversations, sometimes as short as five minutes, are often used for screening interviews. The important thing to remember about screening interviews is to be prepared!

- Keep a list near the telephone of positions for which you have applied.
- Have your résumé, references, a calendar, and a notepad handy.
- If caught off guard, ask if you can call back in a few minutes from the telephone in your office. Organize your materials and yourself.
- Sell your qualifications and sound enthusiastic.

HIRING/PLACEMENT INTERVIEWS

In hiring/placement interviews, recruiters try to uncover negative information while candidates try to minimize faults and emphasize strengths.

Although these interviews are the real thing, in many ways they are like a game. Trained interviewers try to uncover any negative information that will eliminate a candidate. The candidate, of course, tries to minimize faults and emphasize strengths to avoid being eliminated. Like most games, the more practice you get, the better you perform because you know what to expect. Conducted in depth, hiring/placement interviews may take many forms.

- *One-to-one interviews* are most common. You can expect to sit down with a company representative and talk about the job and your qualifications. If the representative is the hiring manager, questions will be specific and job related. If the representative is from human resources, the questions will probably be more general.
- *Sequential and group interviews* are common with companies that rule by consensus. You may face many interviewers in sequence, all of whom you must listen to carefully and respond to positively. In group interviews, the employer may be looking for signs of leadership. Strive to stay focused, summarize important points, and ask good questions.
- *Stress interviews* are meant to test your reactions. If asked rapid-fire questions from many directions, take the time to slow things down. For example, *I would be happy to answer your question, Ms. X, but first I must finish responding to Mr. Z.* If greeted with silence, another stress technique,

you might say, *Would you like me to begin the interview? Let me tell you about myself.* Or ask a question such as *Can you give me more information about the position?*

INVESTIGATING THE TARGET

One of the most important steps in winning the interview game is gathering information about a prospective employer. In learning about a company, you may uncover information that convinces you that this is a company where you would prefer not to work. It's always better to learn about negatives early in the process. More likely, though, the information you collect will help you tailor your application and interview responses to the organization's needs. As Michael Stern suggests, recruiters are impressed by candidates who have done their homework.

Researching an organization enlightens candidates and impresses recruiters.

For companies that are publicly held, you can generally learn a great deal from annual reports and financial disclosure reports. Company information is also available from Dun and Bradstreet Canada (www.dnb.ca), the *Blue Book of Canadian Business* (www.bluebook.ca), the *Financial Post* (www.nationalpost.com), Hoover's company information handbooks (www.hoovers.com), Moody's Financial Information Services, publisher of Moody's Manuals (www.fisonline8.fisonline.com), and *Standard and Poor's Registry of Corporations* (standardpoor.com). All of these resources and many others are available on the Internet. And many big and small companies today maintain Web sites bursting with juicy information. Another way to learn about an organization is to call their office or the interviewer directly. Ask what you can read to prepare you for the interview. Here are some specifics to research:

- Find out all you can about company leaders. Their goals, ambitions, and values often are adopted by the entire organization—including your interviewer.
- Investigate the business philosophy of the leaders, including their priorities, strategies, and managerial approaches. Are you a good match with your target employer? If so, be sure to let the employer know that there is a correlation between their needs and your qualifications.
- Learn about the company's accomplishments and setbacks. This information should help you determine where you might make your best contribution.
- Study the company's finances. Are they so shaky that a takeover is imminent? If so, look elsewhere.
- Examine its products and customers. What excites you about this company?
- Check out the competition. What are its products, strengths, and weaknesses?
- Analyze the company's advertising, including sales and marketing brochures. One candidate, a marketing major, spent a great deal of time poring over brochures from an aerospace contractor. During his initial interview, he shocked and impressed the recruiter with his knowledge of the company's guidance systems. The candidate had, in fact, relieved the interviewer of his least-favourite task—explaining the company's complicated technology.[2]

Study company leaders, organizational strategies, finances, products, customers, competition, and advertising.

For smaller companies and those that are not publicly owned, you'll probably have to do a little more footwork. You might start with the local library. Ask the reference librarian to help you locate information. Newspapers might contain stories or press releases with news of an organization. Visit your local Better Business

Bureau to discover if the company has had any difficulties with other companies or consumers. Try your local Canada Business Service Centre for company information and annual reports. Investigate the chamber of commerce to see what you can learn about the target company.

Talking with company employees is always a good idea, if you can manage it. They are probably the best source of inside information. Try to be introduced to someone who is currently employed—but not working in the immediate area where you wish to be hired. Seek someone who is discreet.

You know how flattered you feel when an employer knows about you and your background. That feeling works both ways. Employers are pleased when job candidates take an interest in them. Be ready to put in plenty of effort in investigating a target employer because this effort really pays off at interview time.

The best source of inside information is company employees.

PREPARING AND PRACTISING

After you have learned about the target organization, study the job description. It not only helps you write a focused résumé but also enables you to match your education, experience, and interests with the employer's position. Finding out the duties and responsibilities of the position will help you practise your best response strategies.

One of the best ways to prepare involves itemizing your (a) most strategic skills, (b) greatest areas of knowledge, (c) strongest personality traits, and (d) key accomplishments. Write this information down and practise relating these strengths to the kinds of questions frequently asked in interviews. Here are some specific tips for preparation:

Practise telling stories that emphasize your most strategic skills, areas of knowledge, strongest personality traits, and key accomplishments.

- Practise, practise, practise. Recite answers to typical interview questions in a mirror, with a friend, while driving in your car, or in spare moments. Keep practising until you have the best responses down pat.
- Consider videotaping or tape recording a practice session to see and hear how you really come across. Do you look and sound enthusiastic?
- Expect to explain problem areas on your résumé. For example, if you have little or no experience, you might emphasize your recent training and up-to-date skills. If you have gaps in your résumé, be prepared to answer questions about them positively and truthfully.
- Try to build interviewing experience with less important jobs first. You will become more confident and better able to sell your strengths with repeated interviewing exposure. Think of it as a game that requires practice.

SENDING POSITIVE NONVERBAL MESSAGES

What comes out of your mouth and what's written on your résumé are not the only messages an interviewer receives about you. Nonverbal messages also create powerful impressions on people. Here are suggestions that will help you send the right nonverbal messages during interviews.

- Arrive on time or a little early. If necessary, find the location on a trial run a few days before the interview so that you know how much time it will take to arrive at the interview location.
- Be courteous and congenial to everyone. Remember that you are being judged

not only by the interviewer but by the receptionist and anyone else who sees you before and after the interview. They will notice how you sit, what you read, and how you look.

- Introduce yourself to the receptionist and wait to be invited to sit.
- Dress professionally. Even if some employees in the organization dress casually, you should look qualified, competent, and successful. Dress the part!
- Greet the interviewer confidently. Extend your hand, look him or her directly in the eye, and say, "I'm pleased to meet you, Mr. X. I am Z." In this situation a firm, not crushing, handshake sends a nonverbal message of poise and assurance.
- Wait for the interviewer to offer you a chair. Make small talk with upbeat comments, such as "This is a beautiful headquarters. How many employees work here?" Don't immediately begin rummaging in your briefcase for your résumé. Being at ease and unrushed suggest that you are self-confident.
- Control your body movements. Keep your hands, arms, and elbows to yourself. Don't lean on a desk. Sit erect, leaning forward slightly. Keep your feet on the floor.
- Make eye contact frequently but don't get into a staring contest. A direct eye gaze, at least in North America, suggests interest and trustworthiness.
- Smile enough to convey a positive attitude. Have a friend give you honest feedback on whether you generally smile too much or not enough.
- Sound enthusiastic and interested—but sincere.

> Send positive nonverbal messages by arriving on time, being courteous, dressing professionally, greeting the interviewer confidently, controlling your body movements, making eye contact, and smiling.

FIGHTING FEAR

Expect to be nervous. It's natural! Other than public speaking, employment interviews are the most dreaded events in people's lives. One of the best ways to overcome fear is to know what happens in a typical interview. Figure 14.1 describes how a recruiter usually structures an interview. You can further reduce your fears by following these suggestions.

- Practise interviewing as much as you can—especially with real companies. The more times you experience the interview situation, the less nervous you will be.
- Prepare 110 percent! Know how you will answer the most frequently asked questions. Be ready with success stories. Rehearse your closing statement. One of the best ways to reduce butterflies is to know that you have done all you can to be ready for the interview.
- Take deep breaths, particularly if you feel anxious while waiting for the interviewer. Deep breathing makes you concentrate on something other than the interview and also provides much-needed oxygen.
- Remember that the interviewer isn't the only one who is gleaning information. You have come to learn about the job and the company. In fact, during some parts of the interview, you will be in charge. This should give you courage.

> Fight fear by practising, preparing 110 percent, breathing deeply, and knowing that you are in charge for part of the interview.

ANSWERING QUESTIONS

The way you answer questions can be almost as important as what you say. Use the interviewer's name and title from time to time when you answer. *Ms. Lyon, I would*

FIGURE 14.1

Steps in an Employment Interview From a Recruiter's Perspective

1. Before interview, review candidate's résumé. Look for patterns of growth and outstanding accomplishments. Note items to pursue. Check career objective.
2. Greet candidate, introduce self, make candidate feel comfortable.
3. Describe open position; confirm candidate's interest in it.
4. Using résumé, probe for evidence of relevant skills and traits.
5. Give brief overview of organization.
6. Solicit questions from candidate.
7. Close interview.
8. Fill out evaluation form.

> Your question-answering technique can be as important as your answers.

be pleased to tell you about . . . People like to hear their own names. But be sure you are pronouncing the name correctly!

Occasionally it may be necessary to refocus and clarify vague questions. Some interviewers are inexperienced and ill at ease in the role. You may even have to ask your own question to understand what was asked, *By _____ do you mean _____?*

Consider closing out some of your responses with *Does that answer your question?* or *Would you like me to elaborate on any particular experience?*

> Stay focused on the skills and traits that employers seek; don't reveal weaknesses.

Always aim your answers at the key characteristics interviewers seek: expertise and competence, motivation, interpersonal skills, decision-making skills, enthusiasm for the job, and a pleasing personality. Employers are looking for these skills and traits. And remember to stay focused on your strengths. Don't reveal weaknesses, even if you think they make you look human. You won't be hired for your weaknesses, only for your strengths.

Use good English and enunciate clearly. Remember, you will definitely be judged by how well you communicate. Avoid slurred words such as *gonna* and *din't*, as well as slangy expressions such as *yeah, like,* and *you know*. Also eliminate verbal static *(ah, and, uhm)*. As you practise answering expected interview questions, it's always a good idea to make a tape recording. Is your speech filled with verbal static?

You can't expect to be perfect in an employment interview. No one is. But you can avert sure disaster by avoiding certain topics and behaviours such as those described in Figure 14.2.

ALL-TIME FAVOURITE QUESTIONS WITH SELECTED ANSWERS

> You can anticipate 90 to 95 percent of all questions you will be asked in an interview.

Employment interviews are all about questions. And most of the questions are not new. You can actually anticipate 90 to 95 percent of all questions that will be asked before you ever walk into an interview room.[3]

The following questions represent all-time favourites asked of recent graduates and other job seekers. You'll find get-acquainted questions, experience and accomplishment questions, crystal-ball questions, and squirm questions. To get you thinking about how to respond, we've provided an answer or discussion for the first question in each group. As you read the remaining questions in each group, think about how you could respond most effectively.

FIGURE 14.2

A Checklist of Interview Don'ts

- Don't ask for the job. It's naive, undignified, and unprofessional. Wait to see how the interview develops.
- Don't trash your previous employer, supervisors, or colleagues. The tendency is for interviewers to wonder if you would speak about their companies similarly.
- Don't be a threat to the interviewer. Avoid suggesting directly or indirectly that your goal is to become head honcho, a path that might include the interviewer's job.
- Don't be late or too early for your appointment. Arrive five minutes before you are scheduled.
- Don't discuss controversial subjects, and don't use profanity.

- Don't smoke unless the interviewer smokes.
- Don't emphasize salary or benefits. If the interview goes well and these subjects have not been addressed, you may mention them toward the end of the interview.
- Don't be negative about yourself or others. Never dwell on your liabilities.
- Don't interrupt. It is not only impolite but also prevents you from hearing a complete question or remark.
- Don't accept a job immediately after getting an offer. Take time to think over this important decision.
- Don't accept an offer until you have completed all your interviews.

QUESTIONS TO GET ACQUAINTED

1. Tell me about yourself.

   Experts agree that you must keep this answer short (1 to 2 minutes tops) but on target. Try practising using this formula: "My name is _____. I have completed _____ degree with a major in _____. Recently I worked for _____ as a _____. Before that I worked for _____ as a _____. My strengths are _____ (interpersonal) and _____ (technical)." Try rehearsing your response in 30-second segments devoted to your education, your work experience, and your qualities/skills.

2. Tell me about your educational experience at college and why you chose your major.
3. If you had it to do over again, would you choose the same way? Why?
4. Do you prefer to work by yourself or with others? Why?
5. What are your key strengths?
6. What are some things you do in your spare time? Hobbies? Sports?
7. How did you happen to apply for this job?
8. What particular qualifications do you have for this job?
9. Do you consider yourself a team player? Describe your style as a team player.

Prepare for get-acquainted questions by practising a short formula response.

QUESTIONS ABOUT YOUR EXPERIENCE AND ACCOMPLISHMENTS

10. Why should we hire you when we have applicants with more experience or better credentials?

Employers will hire candidates with less experience and fewer accomplishments if they can demonstrate the skills required.

In answering this question, remember that employers often hire people who present themselves well instead of others with better credentials. Emphasize personal strengths that could be an advantage with this employer. Are you a hard worker? How can you demonstrate it? Have you had recent training? Some people have had more years of experience but actually have less knowledge because they have done the same thing over and over. Stress your experience using the latest methods and equipment. Be sure to mention your computer training and use of the Internet and Web. Emphasize that you are open to new ideas and learn quickly.

11. Tell me about your part-time jobs, internships, or other experience.
12. What were your major accomplishments in each of your past jobs?
13. Why did you change jobs?
14. What was a typical workday like?
15. What job functions did you enjoy most? Least? Why?
16. Who was the toughest boss you ever worked for and why?
17. What were your major achievements in school?

CRYSTAL BALL GAZING AND QUESTIONS ABOUT THE FUTURE

Show ambition and interest in succeeding with this company.

18. Where do you expect to be five years from now?

It's a sure kiss of death to respond that you'd like to have the interviewer's job! Instead, show an interest in the current job and in making a contribution to the organization. Talk about the levels of responsibility you'd like to achieve. One employment counsellor suggests showing ambition but not committing to a specific job title. Suggest that you will have learned enough to have progressed to a position where you will continue to grow.

19. If you got this position, what would you do to complement the team environment?
20. What if your supervisor gave you an assignment and then left town for two weeks. What would you do?
21. This is a large (or small) organization. Do you think you would like that environment?
22. If you were aware that a co-worker was falsifying data, what would you do?
23. If your supervisor was dissatisfied with your work, and you thought it was acceptable, how would you resolve the conflict?
24. Do you plan to continue your education?

QUESTIONS TO MAKE YOU SQUIRM

Strive to convert discussion of your weaknesses to topics that show your strengths.

25. What are your key weaknesses?

It's amazing how many candidates knock themselves out of the competition by answering this question poorly. Actually, you have many choices. You can present a strength as a weakness *(Some people complain that I'm a workaholic or too attentive to detail)*. You can mention a corrected weakness *(I found that I really needed to learn about the Internet, so I took a course . . .)*. You could cite an unrelated skill *(I really need to brush up on my French)*. You can cite a learning objective *(One of my long-term goals is to learn more about international management. Does your company have any plans to expand overseas?)* Another possibility is to reaffirm your qualifications *(I have no weaknesses that would affect my ability to do this job)*.

26. If you could change one thing about your personality, what would it be and why?
27. What would your former boss say about you?
28. What do you want the most from your job? Money? Security? Power?
29. How did you prepare for this interview?
30. Do you feel you achieved the best grade point average of which you were capable in your education?
31. Relate an incident in which you faced an ethical dilemma. How did you react? How did you feel?
32. If your supervisor told you to do something a certain way and you knew that way was dead wrong, what would you do?

QUESTIONS ABOUT MONEY

33. How much money are you looking for?

    One way to handle salary questions is to ask politely to defer the discussion until it's clear that a job will be offered to you. *(I'm sure when the time comes, we'll be able to work out a fair compensation package. Right now, I'd rather focus on whether we have a match.)* Another possible response is to reply candidly that you can't know what to ask for until you know more about the position and the company. If you continue to be pressed for a dollar figure, give a salary range. Be sure to do research before the interview so that you know what similar jobs are paying. For example, check the full-time earnings estimates published at Job Futures (www.hrdc-drhc.gc.ca/JobFutures).

    > Defer discussion of salary until later in the interview when you know more about the job and whether it will be offered.

34. How much are you presently earning?
35. How did you finance your education?
36. How much money do you expect to earn at age _____?

QUESTIONS FOR YOU TO ASK

At some point in the interview, you will be asked if you have any questions. Your questions should not only help you gain information, but they should also impress the interviewer with your thoughtfulness and interest in the position. Remember, though, that this interview is a two-way street. You must be happy with the prospect of working for this organization. You want a position for which your skills and personality are matched. Use this opportunity to find out whether this job is right for you, by asking questions such as these:

> Your questions should impress the interviewer but also elicit valuable information about the job.

1. What will my duties be (if not already discussed)?
2. Tell me what it's like working here in terms of the people, management practices, work loads, expected performance, and rewards.
3. Why is this position open? Did the person who held it previously leave?
4. What training programs are available from this organization? What specific training will be given for this position?

5. What are the possibilities for promotion from this position?
6. Who would be my immediate supervisor?
7. What is the organizational structure, and where does this position fit in?
8. Is travel required in this position?
9. How is job performance evaluated?
10. Assuming my work is excellent, where do you see me in five years?
11. How long do employees generally stay with this organization?
12. What are the major challenges for a person in this position?
13. What can I do to make myself more employable to you?
14. What is the salary for this position?
15. When will I hear from you regarding further action on my application?

FIELDING ILLEGAL QUESTIONS

You may respond to an illegal question by asking tactfully how it relates to the responsibilities of this position.

Because human rights legislation protects job applicants from discrimination, interviewers may not ask questions such as those in the following list. Nevertheless, you may face an inexperienced or unscrupulous interviewer who does ask some of these questions. How should you react? If you find the question harmless and if you want the job, go ahead and answer it. If you think that answering it would damage your chance to be hired, try to deflect the question tactfully with a response such as, *Could you tell me how my marital status relates to the responsibilities of this position?* Or, you could use the opportunity to further emphasize your strengths. An older worker responding to a question about age might mention experience, fitness, knowledge, maturity, stability, or extensive business contacts. You might also wish to reconsider working for an organization that sanctions such procedures.

Here are some illegal questions that you may or may not wish to answer:

1. Are you married, divorced, separated, single, or living common-law?
2. Is your spouse subject to transfer in his/her job? Tell me about your spouse's job. (But, it is legal to mention travel requirements and ask whether you can meet those requirements.)
3. What is your corrected vision? (But it is legal to ask about quality of vision if visual acuity is directly related to safety or some other factor of the job.)
4. Do you have any disabilities? Do you drink or take drugs? Have you ever received psychiatric care or been hospitalized for emotional problems? Have you ever received worker's compensation? (But it is legal to ask if you have any condition that could affect your ability to do the job or if you have any condition that should be considered during selection.)
5. Have you ever been arrested? Have you ever been convicted of a crime? Do you have a criminal record? (But if bonding is a requirement of the job, it is legal to ask if you are eligible.)
6. How old are you? What is your date of birth? Can I see your birth certificate? (But it is legal to ask *Are you eligible to work under Canadian laws pertaining to age restrictions?*)
7. In what other countries do you have a current address? (But it is legal to ask *What is your current address, and how long have you lived there?*)
8. What is your maiden name? (But it is legal to ask *What is your full name?*)
9. What is your religion? How often do you attend church? Would you work on a specific religious holiday? Can you provide a reference from clergyperson or religious leader?

10. Do you have children? What are your child care arrangements? (But it is legal to ask *Can you work the required hours?* and *Are you available for overtime work?*)
11. Where were you born? Were you born in Canada? Can you provide proof of citizenship? (But it is legal to ask *Are you legally entitled to work in Canada?*)
12. Were you involved in military service in another country? (But it is legal to ask about Canadian military service where preference is given to veterans by law.)
13. What is your mother tongue? Where did you receive your language training? (But it is legal to ask if you understand, read, write, and/or speak the language(s) required for the job.)
14. How much do you weigh? How tall are you?
15. What is your sexual orientation?
16. Are you under medical care? Who is your family doctor? Are you receiving therapy or counselling? (But it is legal to make offers of employment conditional on successful completion of a medical exam.)

CLOSING THE INTERVIEW

After the recruiter tells you about the organization and after you have asked your questions, the interviewer will signal the end of the interview, usually by standing up or by expressing appreciation that you came. If not addressed earlier, you should at this time find out what action will follow. Too many candidates leave the interview without knowing their status or when they will hear from the recruiter.

You may learn that your résumé will be distributed to several departments for review. If this is the case, be sure to ask when you will be contacted. When you are ready to leave, briefly review your strengths for the position and thank the interviewer for telling you about the organization and for considering you for the position. Ask if you may leave an additional copy of your résumé or your list of references. If the recruiter fails to give you a firm date for notification, ask if you may call in one week to learn of the status of your candidacy.

After leaving the interview, make notes of what was said in case you are called back for a second interview. Also note your strengths and weaknesses so that you can work to improve in future interviews. Be sure to alert your references (whom you prepared in advance with a copy of your résumé, highlighted with sales points). Finally, write a thank-you letter, which will be discussed shortly.

If you don't hear from the recruiter within five days (or at the specified time), call him or her. Practise saying something like, "I'm wondering what else I can do to convince you that I'm the right person for this job."

End the interview by thanking the interviewer, reviewing your strengths for this position, and asking what action will follow.

FOLLOW-UP LETTERS AND OTHER EMPLOYMENT DOCUMENTS

Although the résumé and cover letter are your major tasks, other important letters and documents are often required during the employment-seeking process. You may need to make requests, write follow-up letters, or fill out employment applications. Because each of these tasks reveals something about you and your communication skills, you'll want to put your best foot forward. These documents often subtly influence company officials to extend an interview or offer a job.

APPLICATION REQUEST LETTER

Some organizations consider candidates only when they submit a completed application form. To secure a form, write a routine letter of request. But provide enough information about yourself, as shown in the following example, to assure the reader that you are a serious applicant:

Dear Mr. MacEachern:

Because you expect a positive response, announce your request directly.

Include end date and reason.

Please send me an application form for work in your Human Resources Department. In June I will be completing my studies in psychology and communications at the University of Western Ontario in London, Ontario. My program included courses in public relations, psychology, and communications.

I would appreciate receiving this application by May 15 so that I may complete it before making a visit to your city in June. I'm looking forward to beginning a career in human resources management.

APPLICATION OR RÉSUMÉ FOLLOW-UP LETTER

If your letter or application generates no response within a reasonable time, you may decide to send a short follow-up letter like the one below. Doing so (1) jogs the memory of the human resources officer, (2) demonstrates your serious interest, and (3) allows you to emphasize your qualifications or to add new information. Avoid any accusations that might make the reader defensive.

Dear Mrs. Massicotte:

Opens by reminding the reader of your interest.

Reviews your strengths or adds new qualifications.

Closes by looking forward positively.

Please know that I am still interested in becoming an administrative assistant with DataTech Inc.

Since I submitted an application in May, I have completed my schooling and have been employed as a summer replacement for office workers in several downtown offices. This experience has honed my word processing and communication skills. It has also introduced me to a wide range of office procedures.

Please keep my application in your active file and let me know when I may put my formal training, technical skills, and practical experience to work for you.

INTERVIEW FOLLOW-UP LETTER

After a job interview you should always send a brief letter of thanks. This courtesy sets you apart from other applicants (most won't bother). Your letter also reminds the interviewer of your visit, as well as suggesting your good manners and genuine enthusiasm for the job.

Follow-up letters are most effective if sent immediately after the interview.[4] In your letter refer to the date of the interview, include the exact job title for which you were interviewed, and perhaps include a brief discussion of specific topics discussed. Avoid worn-out phrases, such as *Thank you for taking the time to interview me*. Be careful, too, about overusing *I*, especially to begin sentences. Most important, show that you really want the job and that you are qualified for it. Review your major selling points for the position. Notice how the following letter reminds the interviewer of the applicant's key strengths while conveying enthusiasm and confidence:

Dear Ms. Su:

Talking with you Thursday, May 23, about the graphic designer position was both informative and interesting.

Thanks for describing the position in such detail and for introducing me to Ms. Thomas, the senior designer. Her current project designing the annual report in four colours on a Macintosh sounds fascinating as well as quite challenging.

Now that I've learned in greater detail the specific tasks of your graphic designers, I'm more than ever convinced that my computer and creative skills can make a genuine contribution to your graphic productions. My training in design and layout using Photoshop ensures that I could be immediately productive on your staff.

In addition to my technical skills, you will find me an enthusiastic and hard-working member of any team effort. I'm eager to join the graphics staff at your Halifax headquarters, and I look forward to hearing from you soon.

Mentions the interview date and specific position.

Shows appreciation, good manners, and perseverance.

Reminds the reader of interpersonal skills and enthusiasm for this job.

Highlights specific skills for the job.

REJECTION FOLLOW-UP LETTER

If you didn't get the job and you think it was perfect for you, don't give up. Employment consultant Patricia Windelspecht advises, "You should always respond to a rejection letter. . . . I've had four clients get jobs that way." In a rejection follow-up letter, it's okay to admit you're disappointed. Be sure to add, however, that you're still interested and will contact them again in a month in case a job opens up. Then follow through for a couple of months—but don't overdo it. "There's a fine line between being professional and persistent and being a pest," adds consultant Windelspecht.[5] Here's an example of an effective rejection follow-up letter:

Dear Mr. Flett:

Although I'm disappointed that someone else was selected for your accounting position, I appreciate your promptness and courtesy in notifying me.

Because I firmly believe that I have the technical and interpersonal skills needed to work in your fast-paced environment, I hope you will keep my résumé in your active file. My desire to become a productive member of your staff remains strong.

I enjoyed our interview, and I especially appreciate the time you and Mr. Garcia spent describing your company's expansion into international markets. To enhance my qualifications, I've enrolled in a course in international accounting at Sheridan College.

Should you have an opening for which I am qualified, you may reach me at (905) 719-3901. In any case, I will call you in a month to discuss employment possibilities.

Subordinates disappointment to appreciation at being notified promptly.

Emphasizes continuing interest and confidence in meeting job requirements.

Refers to specifics of interview; tells how skills are being improved.

APPLICATION FORM

Some organizations require job candidates to fill out job application forms, such as that in Figure 14.3, instead of submitting résumés. This practice permits them to compile standardized data about each applicant. Here are some tips for filling out such forms:

FIGURE 14.3

Sample Employment Application

TO OUR APPLICANTS: Please answer all questions completely. If you need help in completing this application, please request assistance from a member of this office. We will be pleased to serve you.

NAME: Last	First	Middle	TODAY'S DATE

PRESENT ADDRESS: No. Street City Province Postal Code

HOME TELEPHONE:
(   )

WORK TELEPHONE:
(   )

SOCIAL INSURANCE NUMBER:

POSITION APPLIED FOR: SALARY EXPECTED DATE OPEN FOR HIRE

WOULD YOU WORK –
☐ Full-time? ☐ Part-time?

REFERRED BY:

WERE YOU PREVIOUSLY EMPLOYED BY US?
☐ Yes ☐ No

IF "YES," WHEN?

DO YOU HAVE THE LEGAL RIGHT TO BE EMPLOYED IN CANADA?
☐ Yes ☐ No

VISA NUMBER (IF ANY) EXPIRATION DATE:

PERSON TO BE NOTIFIED IN CASE OF ACCIDENT OR EMERGENCY: NAME

ADDRESS: TELEPHONE NUMBER:
(   )

HAVE YOU SERVED IN THE CANADIAN ARMED FORCES?
☐ Yes ☐ No

IF "YES," WHEN?

HAVE YOU EVER BEEN CONVICTED OF A CRIMINAL OFFENCE?
☐ Yes ☐ No

ON THE LINES BELOW, PLEASE LIST ANY FRIENDS OR RELATIVES WHO ARE STUDENTS HERE OR WHO ARE WORKING FOR US.
   Name   Relationship

1.

2.

EDUCATION

NAME AND LOCATION OF HIGH SCHOOL: DID YOU GRADUATE?
☐ Yes ☐ No

Name of College, University, or Vocational School	Location	Major Subjects	Degrees or Certificates

SKILLS/ABILITIES

Please list any skills or abilities you have that you think may be used in your employment here. Any craft, trade, office, clerical, professional, or administrative skills or abilities may be included. Also list any skills or abilities you gained doing volunteer work, household duties, or while pursuing a hobby.

Skill/Ability	Duration of Training	Length of Experience

TYPING SPEED: SHORTHAND SPEED: WORD PROCESSING PROGRAMS:

OTHER SOFTWARE PROGRAMS:

In filling out an employment application, always read the entire application form before you begin filling in answers. For salary questions, it's wise to respond with "Open" or "Negotiable." Remember that an employment application is a legal document. Errors or lying can result in dismissal if discovered after an applicant is hired.

FIGURE 14.3 Continued

EMPLOYMENT / EXPERIENCE				
Please list all jobs and activities for the past ten years or since attending school as a full-time student. Include part-time employment and self-employment. Include experience gained doing volunteer work or community service work. Begin with the most recent employment and activities first.				

NAME OF EMPLOYER | **YOUR JOB TITLE**

ADDRESS OF EMPLOYER | **DESCRIBE WORK YOU PERFORMED**

SUPERVISOR'S NAME, JOB TITLE, AND TELEPHONE NUMBER

DATE STARTED	DATE ENDED	DURATION	PAY	REASON FOR LEAVING

NAME OF EMPLOYER | **YOUR JOB TITLE**

ADDRESS OF EMPLOYER | **DESCRIBE WORK YOU PERFORMED**

SUPERVISOR'S NAME, JOB TITLE, AND TELEPHONE NUMBER

DATE STARTED	DATE ENDED	DURATION	PAY	REASON FOR LEAVING

NAME OF EMPLOYER | **YOUR JOB TITLE**

ADDRESS OF EMPLOYER | **DESCRIBE WORK YOU PERFORMED**

SUPERVISOR'S NAME, JOB TITLE, AND TELEPHONE NUMBER

DATE STARTED	DATE ENDED	DURATION	PAY	REASON FOR LEAVING

NAME OF EMPLOYER | **YOUR JOB TITLE**

ADDRESS OF EMPLOYER | **DESCRIBE WORK YOU PERFORMED**

SUPERVISOR'S NAME, JOB TITLE, AND TELEPHONE NUMBER

DATE STARTED	DATE ENDED	DURATION	PAY	REASON FOR LEAVING

REFERENCE CHECKS	
MAY WE ASK YOUR PRESENT OR PREVIOUS EMPLOYERS ABOUT YOU? ☐ Yes ☐ No	NOT UNTIL I GIVE NOTICE ON (date):

DRIVER'S LICENCE NUMBER:	CLASS	PROVINCE ISSUED

SIGNATURE X	DATE:

By my signature above, I certify that all answers and statements on this application are true and complete to the best of my knowledge. I understand that should an investigation disclose untruthful or misleading answers, my application may be rejected, my name removed from consideration, or my employment terminated.

Pay particular attention to statements like the one following the signature above. Many employers thoroughly check all information shown on an employment application. Make sure it is accurate.

- Carry a card summarizing those vital statistics not included on your résumé. If you are asked to fill out an application form in an employer's office, you will need a handy reference to the following data: social insurance number; graduation dates; beginning and ending dates of all employment; salary history; full names, titles, and present work addresses of former supervisors; and full names, occupational titles, occupational addresses, and telephone numbers of persons who have agreed to serve as references.
- Look over all the questions before starting. Fill out the form neatly, printing if your handwriting is poor.
- Answer all questions. Write *Not applicable* if appropriate.
- Be prepared for a salary question. Unless you know what comparable employees are earning in the company, the best strategy is to suggest a salary range or to write *Negotiable* or *Open*.
- Ask if you may submit your résumé in addition to the application form.

SUMMING UP

Whether you face a screening interview or a hiring/placement interview, you must be well prepared. You can increase your chances of success and reduce your sweaty palms considerably by knowing how interviews are typically conducted and by investigating the target company thoroughly. Practise answering typical questions, including legal and illegal ones. Consider tape recording or videotaping a mock interview so that you can check your body language and improve your answering techniques.

Close the interview by thanking the interviewer, reviewing your main strengths for the position, and asking what the next step is. Follow up with a thank-you letter and a call back, if appropriate.

You have now completed 14 chapters of rigorous instruction aimed at developing your skills so that you can be a successful business communicator in today's rapidly changing world of information. Remember that this is but a starting point. Your skills as a business communicator will continue to grow on the job as you apply the principles you have learned and expand your expertise.

DISCUSSION

1. Is it normal to be nervous about an employment interview, and what can be done to overcome this fear?
2. Why are good interviewing skills as important as a good résumé?
3. What can you do to improve the first impression you make at an interview?
4. Why is it important to avoid discussing salary early in an interview?
5. Why should a job candidate write a thank-you letter after an interview?

CHAPTER REVIEW

6. If you have sent your résumé to many companies, what information should you keep near your telephone and why?

7. Your first interview is with a small local company. What kind of information should you seek about this company and where could you expect to find it?

8. Name at least two ways in which you can practise for the interview and receive feedback on your performance.

9. Name at least six interviewing behaviours you can exhibit that send positive nonverbal messages.

10. What is your greatest fear of what you might do or what might happen to you during an employment interview? How can you overcome your fears?

11. Should you be candid with an interviewer when asked about your weaknesses?

12. How can you clarify vague questions that may be asked by recruiters?

13. How should you respond if you are asked why a company should hire you when it has applicants with more experience or better credentials?

14. How should you respond to questions you feel are illegal?

15. What kind of follow-up letters might a job candidate write?

ACTIVITIES AND CASES

14.1 Researching an Organization. Select an organization where you would like to be employed. Assume you've been selected for an interview. Using resources described in this chapter, locate information about the organization's leaders and their business philosophy. Find out about the organization's accomplishments, setbacks, finances, products, customers, competition, and advertising. Prepare a summary report documenting your findings.

Related Web Site: www.cbsc.org

14.2 Building Interview Skills. Consider a position you are eligible for now or one for which you will be eligible when you complete your education. Identify the skills and traits necessary for this position. In addition to computer and communication skills, employers generally want to know if a candidate works well with a team, accepts responsibility, solves problems, is efficient, meets deadlines, shows leadership, saves time and money, and is a hard worker. If you prepared a résumé in Chapter 13, be sure that it addresses these areas. Now prepare interview worksheets listing at least ten technical and other skills or traits you think a recruiter will want to discuss in an interview for your targeted position.

14.3 Preparing Success Stories. Using the worksheets you prepared in Activity 14.2, prepare success stories that show how you have developed the skills or traits required. Select three to five stories to develop into answers to potential interview questions. For example, here's a typical question: "How does your background relate to the position we have open?" A possible response: "As you know, I have just completed an intensive training program in _____. In addition, I have over three years of part-time work experience in a variety of business settings. I developed responsibility and customer-service skills in filling orders efficiently, resolving shipping problems, and monitoring key accounts. I also inventoried and organized products worth over $200,000. When the owner returned from a vacation to Florida, I was commended for increasing sales and was given a bonus in recognition of her gratitude." People relate to and remember stories. Try to shape your answers into memorable stories.

14.4 Polishing Answers to Interview Questions. Select 3 questions from each of the 5 question categories discussed in this chapter. Write your answers to these 15 questions. Try to incorporate skills and traits required for the targeted position. Polish these answers and your delivery technique by practising in front of a mirror or into a tape recorder.

14.5 Knowing What to Ask. Decide on three to five questions that you would like to ask during an interview. Write these questions out and practise asking them so that you sound confident and sincere.

14.6 Practising Interviewing with a Partner. Choose a partner in your class. Make a list of five employment questions from those presented in this chapter. In front of the class or in one-on-one sessions, you and your partner will role-play an interview. One acts as interviewer; the other is the candidate. Prior to the interview, the candidate tells the interviewer what job and company she or he is applying to. For the interview, the interviewer and candidate should dress appropriately and sit in chairs facing each other before the class. The interviewer greets the candidate and makes him or her comfortable. The candidate gives the interviewer a copy of her or his résumé. The interviewer asks three (or more depending on your instructor's time schedule) questions from the list of questions. The interviewer may also ask follow-up questions if appropriate. When finished, the interviewer ends the meeting graciously. After one interview, reverse roles and repeat.

14.7 Videotaping an Interview. One of the best ways to develop interviewing skills is by videotaping a mock interview. Your instructor may act as interviewer or an outside businessperson may be asked to conduct mock interviews in your classroom. Engage a student or campus specialist to videotape each interview. Review your performance and critique it looking for ways to improve. Your instructor may ask class members to offer comments and suggestions on individual interviews.

14.8 Handling Illegal Interview Questions. Assume you are being interviewed at one of the top companies on your list of potential employers. The interviewing committee consists of a human resources manager and the supervising manager of the department where you would work. At various times during the interview the supervising manager has asked questions that made you feel uncomfortable. For example, he asked if you were married. You know this question is illegal, but you saw no harm in answering it. But then he asked how old you were. Since you started college early and graduated in a year and a half, you are worried that you may not be considered mature enough for this position. But you have most of the other qualifications required and you are convinced you could succeed on the job. How should you answer this question?

14.9 Requesting an Application Form. You decide to apply for a position with KillerAp Software, 2443 Pacific Grove Drive, White Rock, BC V2L 3E5. Send a letter addressed to Doug Tyson, human resources manager, requesting an employment application.

14.10 Filling Out an Application Form. Take the time to fill in all the necessary information required in the application form in Figure 14.3. Once you've filled it out, you can remove the form and carry it with you as a reference when you apply for employment.

14.11 Saying Thanks for the Interview. You've just completed an exciting employment interview with Electronic Data Sources, 132 Maplegrove Plaza, Montreal, QC H1L 2W4 (or a company of your choice). Write a follow-up thank-you letter to Ronald T. Ranson, Human Resources Development, who interviewed you.

14.12 Refusing to Take No for an Answer. After an excellent interview with Electronic Data Sources, 132 Maplegrove Plaza, Montreal, QC H1L 2W4 (or a company of your choice), you're depressed to learn that they hired someone else. Because you really want to work for EDS, write a follow-up letter to Ronald T. Ranson, who wrote the rejection letter to you.

14.13 Searching the Internet: Playing Hot Seat, the Mock Job Interview Game. You can find wonderful, free, and sometimes entertaining information about job-search strategies, career tips, and interview advice on the Internet. Use a search engine to locate a site, such as Kaplan's Career Center, which offers tips for successful employment interviewing. If you visit Kaplan and if it's still available, play "The Hot Seat: Mock Job Interview" game to see if you qualify for a regular paycheque and benefits—or to see if you're shown to the door! From any Web site featuring careers, make a list of at least five good interview pointers—ones that were not covered in this chapter.

Related Web Site: www.kaplan.com/career/

14.14 Connecting With E-Mail: Reporting Employment Tips. Visit an Internet career site, such as the one mentioned in Activity 14.13, and send a report of your findings in an e-mail message to your instructor. Describe what is available at the site and list at least five employment tips not mentioned in this chapter.

GRAMMAR/MECHANICS CHECKUP—14

Punctuation Review

Review Sections 1.17 and 2.01–2.29 in the Grammar/Mechanics Handbook. Study each of the following statements and insert any necessary punctuation. In the space provided, indicate the number of marks that you added and record the number of the G/M principle(s) illustrated. When you finish, compare your responses with those provided. If your responses differ, study carefully the specific principles shown in parentheses.

<u> 1 </u>   <u> (2.05) </u>   **Example:** Regina has never been much of a financial mecca , but suddenly it has attracted some new insurance companies.

1. A Toronto based law firm Sanders & Dempsey has been promoting Regina's location.
2. Saskatchewan may have fewer restrictions therefore many smaller insurance companies are rushing to apply for full service and limited service privileges.
3. By April the following four companies had applied to open Regina branches Independent Life, Mutual Life, Canada Assurance, and Trustco Inc.
4. What the companies seem to be hoping is that Saskatchewans liberal restrictions will permit their limited service insurance companies to offer services forbidden elsewhere.
5. George Hancock who is now an attorney with Sanders & Dempsey formerly worked in the Comptrollers office.
6. During his time with the agency Mr. Hancock interpreted local provincial and federal insurance laws and regulations.
7. He was as a matter of fact aware of additional banking opportunities not just those in Regina.
8. When interviewed recently he said "No one really knows how far a company can go because the law has never been fully tested."
9. A limited service insurance company can acquire other institutions more easily than a full service company its purchases need no approval by the federal government.
10. (Emphasize.) Three major insurance companies Independent Life, Mutual Life, and Canada Assurance now have branches in Regina.
11. When the interest payments began local officials became concerned but they did not act until April.

12. An article entitled Companies Rush to Set Up Shop in Regina appeared in the _____
    Regina Leader Post

13. Regina City Council on the other hand hopes to establish permanent far _____
    reaching regulations.

14. Acting on behalf of the Council Mayor Mary Reese said that Regina may have _____
    to examine contractors applications more carefully.

15. Insurance companies must now meet new requirements for example they must _____
    offer $50 million in the form of investment capital to local businesses.

---

1. (2) Toronto-based firm, Dempsey, (1.17e, 2.09)   3. (1) branches: (2.17)   5. (3) Hancock, Dempsey, Comptroller's (2.09, 2.20a)   7. (3) was, fact, opportunities, (2.03, 2.12)   9. (3) limited-service full-service company; (1.17e, 2.16b)   11. (2) began, concerned; (2.06a, 2.16c)   13. (4) Council, hand, permanent, far-reaching (1.17e, 2.03, 2.08)   15. (2) requirements; example, (2.16)

GRAMMAR/MECHANICS CHALLENGE—14

Document for Revision

The following interview thank-you letter has faults in grammar, punctuation, spelling, wordiness, and word use. Use standard proofreading marks (see Appendix B) to correct the errors.

Ineffective Writing

420 Harrison Road

Charlottetown, PE C1A 3T6

June 4, 200x

Mr. Anthony R. Masters

Human Resources Department

Biolage Enterprises

7246 South Bay Avenue

Charlottetown, PE C1A 4L1

Dear Mr. Master:

I appriciate the opportunity for the interview yesterday for the newly-listed Position

of Sales Trainee. It was really a pleasure meeting yourself and learning more about

Biolage Enterprises, you have a fine staff and a sophisticated approach to mar-

keting.

You're organization appears to be growing in a directional manner that parralels my

interests' and career goals. The interview with yourself and your staff yesterday

confirmed my initale positive impressions of Biolage Enterprises and I want to reit-

erate my strong interest in working with and for you. My prior Retail sales experi-

ence as a sales associate with Sears; plus my recent training in Microsoft Word and Excel would enable me to make progress steadily through your programs of training and become a productive member of your sales team in no time at all.

Again, thank-you for your kind and gracius consideration. In the event that you need any additional information from me, all you have to do is give me a call me at (902) 391-7792.

Sincerly yours,

Communication Workshop: Ethics

ARE INFLATED QUALIFICATIONS WORTH THE RISK?

Job candidates are expected to highlight their strengths and minimize their weaknesses when they present their qualifications in résumés and interviews. But some candidates step over the line that separates honest self-marketing from deceptive half-truths and flat-out lies. Most oganizations have mechanisms in place for checking out important contentions made by job candidates. As one recruiter put it, "Lies tend to trip you up over time. In one search we completed, two candidates each supplied different figures when we asked them their salary in successive interviews. They were trying to squeeze more out of our client, of course, but neither of them had bothered to remember their first lie."[6]

No matter how much you want a job, distorting facts on a résumé or in an interview is unethical. Lying is illegal. And either practice can destroy a career. No job seeker wants to be in the unhappy position of explaining or defending misrepresentation. Avoiding the following common problems can keep you off the hot seat:

- **Inflated education, grades, or honours.** Some job candidates claim diplomas or degrees from colleges or universities when in fact they merely attended classes. Others increase their grade point averages or claim fictitious honours. Any such dishonest reporting is grounds for dismissal when discovered.
- **Enhanced job titles.** Wishing to elevate their status, some applicants misrepresent their titles. For example, one technician called himself a "programmer" when he had actually programmed only one project for his boss. A mail clerk who assumed added responsibilities conferred upon herself the title of "supervisor." Even when the description seems accurate, it's unethical to list any title not officially granted. If you feel that a job title inaccurately describes your real duties, check with your supervisor to see if you could use a better title.
- **Puffed-up accomplishments**. Some job seekers inflate their employment experience or achievements. One clerk, eager to make her photocopying duties sound more important, said that she assisted the vice president in communicating and distributing employee directives. In addition to puffery, guard against taking sole credit for achievements that required many people.
- **Altered employment dates.** Some candidates extend the dates of employment to hide unimpressive jobs or to cover periods of unemployment or illness. Let's say that several years ago Cindy was unemployed for fourteen months between working for Company A and being hired by Company B. To improve her

employment history, she adds seven months to her tenure with Company A and seven months to Company B. Now her history has no gaps. But she has laid a potential booby trap for herself.

Today more than ever, you want to be accurate in making statements describing your qualifications. You can expect that companies will check your background. Employers can't afford the loss in productivity that comes with hiring the wrong person. It pays for them to thoroughly check facts with previous employers and your references.

Giving deceptive information to potential employers can endanger your entire employment future. If your honest qualifications aren't good enough to get you the job you want, start working now to improve them.

Application. As a class, discuss the difference between honest self-marketing and deception. What are some examples from your experience? Where could college students go wrong in preparing résumés or in interviewing? Is a new employee "home free" when inflated statements are not caught in the selection or interviewing process? How do you feel about signing a release statement allowing a hiring organization to investigate your background? How can candidates improve their qualifications so that they don't feel the necessity to puff them up? Your instructor may ask you to write a memo summarizing the conclusions of this discussion and identifying implications for job candidates.

REFERENCE GUIDE TO DOCUMENT FORMATS

Business documents carry two kinds of messages. Verbal messages are conveyed by the words chosen to express the writer's ideas. Nonverbal messages are conveyed largely by the appearance of a document. If you compare an assortment of letters and memos from various organizations, you will notice immediately that some look more attractive and more professional than others. The nonverbal message of the professional-looking documents suggests that they were sent by people who are careful, informed, intelligent, and successful. Understandably, you're more likely to take seriously documents that use attractive stationery and professional formatting techniques.

To ensure that your documents carry favourable nonverbal messages about you and your organization, you'll want to give special attention to the appearance and formatting of your letters, envelopes, memos, and fax cover sheets.

APPEARANCE

To ensure that a message is read and valued, you need to give it a professional appearance. Two important elements in achieving a professional appearance are stationery and placement of the message on the page.

STATIONERY

Most organizations use high-quality stationery for business documents. This stationery is printed on select paper measured by weight. Office stationery is usually in the 16- to 24-pound range. Lighter 16-pound paper is generally sufficient for internal documents, including memos. Heavier 20- to 24-pound paper is used for printed letterhead stationery. Paper is also judged by its cotton-fibre content. Good-quality stationery contains 25 percent or more cotton fibre.

SPACING

In preparing business documents on a typewriter or word processor, follow accepted spacing conventions. When using a typewriter, double-space after all end punctuation marks (period, question mark, exclamation point). With most of today's word processing software, a single space is sufficient. Colons used in the expression of time should appear without spacing, as shown here:

Two appointments are available: 2:30 and 4:15.

JUSTIFICATION

Many word processing programs automatically justify right margins, a print feature you'll want to avoid for letters and memos. Justification adds extra space between words to make all lines of text end evenly (as here). If you have a printer with proportional spacing, these extra spaces are distributed evenly. But many printers lack this capacity, thus resulting in awkward spacing gaps. Moreover, experts tell us that justified right margins make documents more difficult to read, since the eye cannot easily see where individual lines end. Natural resting points for the eye are removed. And justified business letters look computer-generated and thus less personal. This is why smart communicators use ragged (unjustified) right margins for business letters and memos.

Justified right margins, however, are appropriate for special documents, such as formal reports, brochures, newsletters, and announcements. Writers with laser printers and scalable fonts (which permit a variety of type faces and sizes) include justification as one of many techniques to create print-quality output.

LETTER PARTS

Professional-looking business letters are arranged in a conventional sequence with standard parts. Following is a discussion of how to use these letter parts properly. Figure A.1 illustrates the parts in a block-style letter. (See Chapters 6 and 7 for additional discussion of letters and their parts.)

LETTERHEAD

Most business organizations use $8\frac{1}{2}$- by 11-inch paper printed with a letterhead displaying their official name and address, telephone and fax numbers, and the organization's Web site address. The letterhead may also include a logo and an advertising message such as *EBank: A new way to bank.*

RETURN ADDRESS

If you type a letter on paper without a printed letterhead, place your address immediately above the date (see Figure A.1). Do not include your name here; you will type your name at the end of your letter. In typing your return address, avoid abbreviations except for the province's name, which appears as a two-letter code (see Figure A.6). If your return address contains two lines, begin typing it on line 11 so that the date appears on line 13. For letters prepared in the block style, type the return address at the left margin. For modified block-style letters, start the return address at the centre to align with the complimentary close.

DATELINE

On letterhead paper you should place the date two line spaces below the last line of the letterhead or 5 cm from the top edge of the paper (line 13). On plain paper place the date immediately below your return address. Since the date goes on line 13, start the return address an appropriate number of lines above it. The most common dateline format is as follows: *June 9, 2000.* Don't use *th* (or *rd*) when writing the date this way. For European or military correspondence, use the following dateline format: *9 June 2000.* Notice that no commas are used.

ADDRESSEE AND DELIVERY NOTATIONS

Delivery notations such as *FAX TRANSMISSION, OVERNIGHT DELIVERY, CONFIDENTIAL,* or *CERTIFIED MAIL* are typed in all capital letters two line spaces above the inside address.

FIGURE A.1

Block and Modified Block Letter Styles

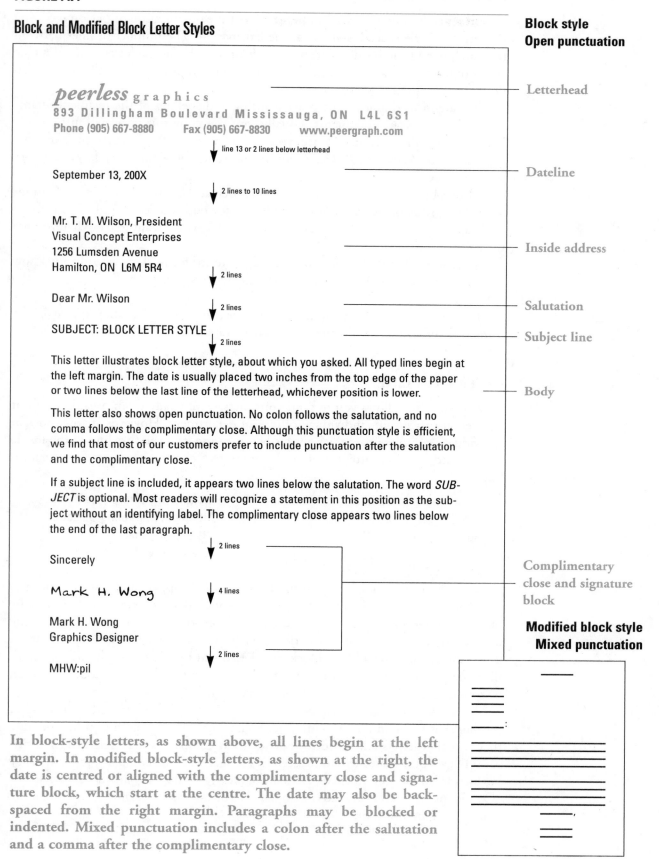

Block style
Open punctuation

peerless graphics
893 Dillingham Boulevard Mississauga, ON L4L 6S1
Phone (905) 667-8880   Fax (905) 667-8830   www.peergraph.com

↓ line 13 or 2 lines below letterhead

——————— Letterhead

September 13, 200X

↓ 2 lines to 10 lines

——————— Dateline

Mr. T. M. Wilson, President
Visual Concept Enterprises
1256 Lumsden Avenue
Hamilton, ON L6M 5R4

↓ 2 lines

——————— Inside address

Dear Mr. Wilson

↓ 2 lines

——————— Salutation

SUBJECT: BLOCK LETTER STYLE

↓ 2 lines

——————— Subject line

This letter illustrates block letter style, about which you asked. All typed lines begin at the left margin. The date is usually placed two inches from the top edge of the paper or two lines below the last line of the letterhead, whichever position is lower.

——————— Body

This letter also shows open punctuation. No colon follows the salutation, and no comma follows the complimentary close. Although this punctuation style is efficient, we find that most of our customers prefer to include punctuation after the salutation and the complimentary close.

If a subject line is included, it appears two lines below the salutation. The word *SUBJECT* is optional. Most readers will recognize a statement in this position as the subject without an identifying label. The complimentary close appears two lines below the end of the last paragraph.

↓ 2 lines

Sincerely

↓ 4 lines

Mark H. Wong

——————— Complimentary
close and signature
block

Mark H. Wong
Graphics Designer

↓ 2 lines

MHW:pil

Modified block style
Mixed punctuation

In block-style letters, as shown above, all lines begin at the left margin. In modified block-style letters, as shown at the right, the date is centred or aligned with the complimentary close and signature block, which start at the centre. The date may also be backspaced from the right margin. Paragraphs may be blocked or indented. Mixed punctuation includes a colon after the salutation and a comma after the complimentary close.

INSIDE ADDRESS

Type the inside address—that is, the address of the organization or person receiving the letter—single-spaced, starting at the left margin. The number of lines between the dateline and the inside address depends on the size of the letter body, the type size (point or pitch size), and the length of the typing lines. Generally, two to ten lines are appropriate.

Be careful to duplicate the exact wording and spelling of the recipient's name and address on your documents. Usually, you can copy this information from the letterhead of the correspondence you are answering. If, for example, you are responding to *Jackson & Perkins Company*, don't address your letter to *Jackson and Perkins Corp.*

Always be sure to include a courtesy title such as *Mr., Ms., Mrs., Dr.,* or *Professor* before a person's name in the inside address—for both the letter and the envelope. Although many women in business today favor *Ms.,* you'll want to use whatever title the addressee prefers.

Remember that the inside address is not included for readers (who already know who and where they are). It's there to help writers accurately file a copy of the message.

In general, avoid abbreviations (such as *Ave.* or *Co.*) unless they appear in the printed letterhead of the document being answered.

ATTENTION LINE

An attention line allows you to send your message officially to an organization but to direct it to a specific individual, officer, or department. However, if you know an individual's complete name, it's always better to use it as the first line of the inside address and avoid an attention line. Here are two common formats for attention lines:

MultiMedia Enterprises
931 Calkins Road
Toronto, ON M3W 1E6

ATTENTION MARKETING DIRECTOR

MultiMedia Enterprises
Attention: Marketing Director
931 Calkins Road
Toronto, ON   M3W 1E6

Attention lines may be typed in all caps or with upper- and lowercase letters. The colon following *Attention* is optional. Notice that an attention line may be placed two line spaces below the address block or printed as the second line of the inside address. You'll want to use the latter format if you're composing on a word processor because the address block may be copied to the envelope and the attention line will not interfere with the last-line placement of the postal code. (Mail can be sorted more easily if the postal code appears in the last line of a typed address.)

Whenever possible, use a person's name as the first line of an address instead of putting that name in an attention line. Some writers use an attention line because they fear that letters addressed to individuals at companies may be considered private. They worry that if the addressee is no longer with the company, the letter may be forwarded or not opened. Actually, unless a letter is marked "Personal" or "Confidential," it will very likely be opened as business mail. Figure A.2 shows more examples of attention lines.

FIGURE A.2

Letter Addressees and Salutations

Addressee	Salutation	Explanation
Individual Mr. Leslie Lanham, CEO Atlantic Associates, Inc. 2320 Park Avenue Halifax NS B3P 2L5	Dear Mr. Lanham: Dear Leslie:	For specific individuals use a courtesy title (such as *Mr.* or *Ms.*) and the person's last name. For friends use a first-name greeting. When you are unsure of an addressee's gender, include the full name *(Dear Leslie Lanham)*. A helpful alternative is the simplified letter style, which omits a salutation.
Organization Pacific Builders Association Whistler Building, Suite 303 105 Redwood Boulevard Vancouver, BC V0L 2E3	Ladies and Gentlemen: Gentlemen: Ladies:	When women are part of management or if you are unsure, use *Ladies and Gentlemen*. If you know a company has only male managers, use *Gentlemen*. For a company with only female managers, use *Ladies*. An alternative that avoids this dilemma is the simplified letter style, which omits a salutation.
Individual Within Organization Windsor Fabricators Attention: Ms. Lisa Jonas 3038 North Jennings Windsor, ON N8S 4E8	Ladies and Gentlemen:	Although an attention line is included here, the message is addressed to the organization—hence the salutation *Ladies and Gentlemen*. However, when you know an individual's name, as in this case, it's better to use that name on the first line of the address without *Attention*. Then the salutation would be *Dear Ms. Jonas*.
Position or Department Within Organization Magnaflex Enterprises, Inc. Attention: Sales Manager 200 Main Street Winnipeg, MB R4T 1P7	Ladies and Gentlemen:	When a letter is addressed to an organization for the attention of an individual in a specific position, the salutation should address the organization. If this salutation sounds awkward, use the simplified letter style and avoid a salutation.
Group of People Customers or individuals from a large database	Dear Customer: Dear Policyholder:	When you are sending form letters to a large group and cannot use individual salutations, use an appropriate general salutation.

SALUTATION

For most letter styles place the letter greeting, or salutation, two lines below the last line of the inside address or the attention line (if used). If the letter is addressed to an individual, use that person's courtesy title and last name *(Dear Mr. Lanham)*. Even if you are on a first-name basis *(Dear Leslie)*, be sure to add a colon (not a comma or a semicolon) after the salutation. Do not use an individual's full name in the salutation (not *Dear Mr. Leslie Lanham*) unless you are unsure of gender *(Dear Leslie Lanham)*.

For letters with attention lines or those addressed to organizations, the selection of an appropriate salutation has become more difficult. Formerly, *Gentlemen* was used generically for all organizations. With increasing numbers of women in business management today, however, *Gentlemen* is problematic. Because no universally acceptable salutation has emerged as yet, you'll probably be safest with *Ladies and Gentlemen* or *Gentlemen and Ladies*.

One way to avoid the salutation dilemma is to address a document to a specific person. Another alternative is to use the simplified letter style (see Figure A.4), which conveniently omits the salutation (and the complimentary close). Figure A.2 discusses and illustrates letter addresses and appropriate salutations.

SUBJECT AND REFERENCE LINES

Although experts suggest placing the subject line two line spaces below the salutation, many businesses actually place it above the salutation. Use whatever style your organization prefers. Reference lines often show policy or file numbers; they generally appear two lines above the salutation.

BODY

Most business letters and memorandums are single-spaced, with double line spacing between paragraphs. Very short messages may be double-spaced with indented paragraphs.

COMPLIMENTARY CLOSE

Typed two line spaces below the last line of the letter, the complimentary close may be formal *(Very truly yours)* or informal *(Sincerely* or *Respectfully)*. The simplified letter style omits a complimentary close.

SIGNATURE BLOCK

In most letter styles the writer's typed name and optional identification appear three to four lines below the complimentary close. The combination of name, title, and organization information should be arranged to achieve a balanced look. The name and title may appear on the same line or on separate lines, depending on the length of each. Use commas to separate categories within the same line, but not to conclude a line. Women may choose to include *Ms., Mrs.,* or *Miss* before their names. Parentheses are optional. Men do not use *Mr.* before their names.

Sincerely,   Respectfully,

Jeremy M. Wood, Manager   Sandra Baker-Murillo
Technical Sales and Services   Executive Vice President

Some organizations include their names in the signature block. In such cases the organization name appears in all caps two lines below the complimentary close, as shown here.

Sincerely,

LITTON COMPUTER SERVICES

Ms. Celine A. Saverin
Executive Assistant

REFERENCE INITIALS

If used, the initials of the typist and writer are typed two line spaces below the writer's name and title. Generally, the writer's initials are capitalized and the typist's are lowercased, but this format varies.

ENCLOSURE NOTATION

When an enclosure or attachment accompanies a document, a notation to that effect appears two line spaces below the reference initials. This notation reminds the typist to insert the enclosure in the envelope, and it reminds the recipient to look for the enclosure or attachment. The notation may be spelled out *(Enclosure, Attachment)*, or it may be abbreviated *(Enc., Att.)*. It may indicate the number of enclosures or attachments, and it may also identify a specific enclosure *(Enclosure: Form 1099)*.

COPY NOTATION

If you make copies of correspondence for other individuals, you may use *cc* to indicate carbon copy, *pc* to indicate photocopy, or merely *c* for any kind of copy. A colon following the initial(s) is optional.

SECOND-PAGE HEADING

When a letter extends beyond one page, use plain paper of the same quality and colour as the first page. Identify the second and succeeding pages with a heading consisting of the name of the addressee, the page number, and the date. Use either of the following two formats:

Ms. Rachel Ruiz   2   May 3, 200x

Ms. Rachel Ruiz
Page 2
May 3, 200x

Both headings appear on line 7 followed by two blank lines to separate them from the continuing text. Avoid using a second page if you have only one line or the complimentary close and signature block to fill that page.

LETTER STYLES

Business letters are generally prepared in one of three formats. The most popular is the block style, but the simplified style has much to recommend it.

BLOCK STYLE

In the block style, shown in Figure A.1, all lines begin at the left margin. This style is most favoured because it is easy to format.

MODIFIED BLOCK STYLE

The modified block style differs from block style in that the date and closing lines appear at the centre, as shown at the bottom of Figure A.3. The date may be (1) centred, (2) begun at the centre of the page (to align with the closing lines), or (3) backspaced

FIGURE A.3

Letter on Plain Paper, Modified Block Style

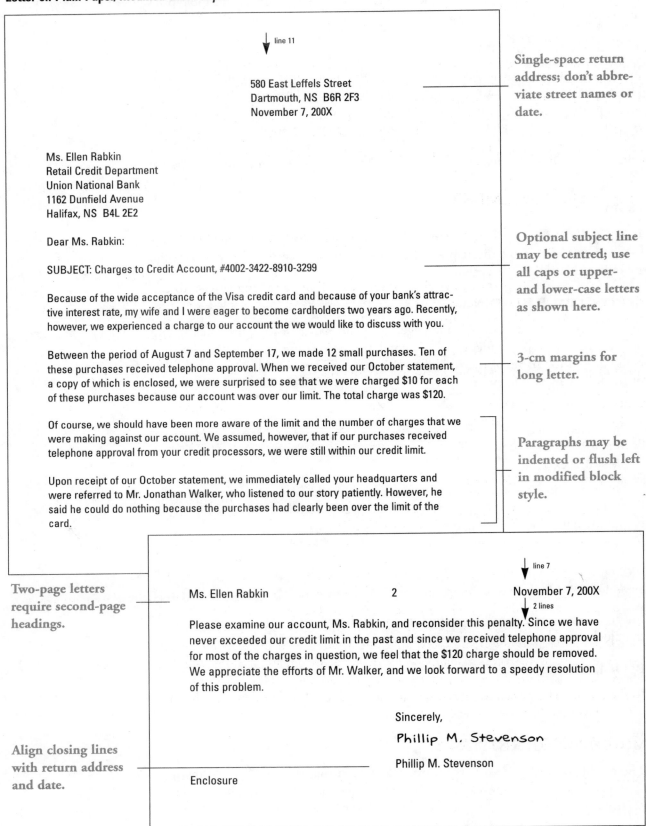

line 11

580 East Leffels Street
Dartmouth, NS B6R 2F3
November 7, 200X

Single-space return address; don't abbreviate street names or date.

Ms. Ellen Rabkin
Retail Credit Department
Union National Bank
1162 Dunfield Avenue
Halifax, NS B4L 2E2

Dear Ms. Rabkin:

SUBJECT: Charges to Credit Account, #4002-3422-8910-3299

Optional subject line may be centred; use all caps or upper- and lower-case letters as shown here.

Because of the wide acceptance of the Visa credit card and because of your bank's attractive interest rate, my wife and I were eager to become cardholders two years ago. Recently, however, we experienced a charge to our account the we would like to discuss with you.

Between the period of August 7 and September 17, we made 12 small purchases. Ten of these purchases received telephone approval. When we received our October statement, a copy of which is enclosed, we were surprised to see that we were charged $10 for each of these purchases because our account was over our limit. The total charge was $120.

3-cm margins for long letter.

Of course, we should have been more aware of the limit and the number of charges that we were making against our account. We assumed, however, that if our purchases received telephone approval from your credit processors, we were still within our credit limit.

Upon receipt of our October statement, we immediately called your headquarters and were referred to Mr. Jonathan Walker, who listened to our story patiently. However, he said he could do nothing because the purchases had clearly been over the limit of the card.

Paragraphs may be indented or flush left in modified block style.

Two-page letters require second-page headings.

Ms. Ellen Rabkin   2   November 7, 200X

line 7

2 lines

Please examine our account, Ms. Rabkin, and reconsider this penalty. Since we have never exceeded our credit limit in the past and since we received telephone approval for most of the charges in question, we feel that the $120 charge should be removed. We appreciate the efforts of Mr. Walker, and we look forward to a speedy resolution of this problem.

Sincerely,

Phillip M. Stevenson

Phillip M. Stevenson

Align closing lines with return address and date.

Enclosure

from the right margin. The signature block—including the complimentary close, writer's name and title, or organization identification—begins at the centre. The first line of each paragraph may begin at the left margin or may be indented five or ten spaces. All other lines begin at the left margin.

SIMPLIFIED STYLE

Many organizations today prefer the simplified letter style, shown in Figure A.4. Like the block style, all lines begin at the left margin. A subject line appears in all caps three lines below the inside address and three lines above the first paragraph. The salutation and complimentary close are omitted. The signer's name and identification appear in all caps five lines below the last paragraph. This letter style is efficient and avoids the problem of appropriate salutations and courtesy titles.

LETTER PLACEMENT

Business letters should be typed so that they are framed by white space. You can set margins using the following chart, or you can use the standard or default margins, discussed after the chart.

The following chart shows margins for short, medium, and long letters. To use the chart, first estimate the number of words in the body of your letter (excluding the inside address and closing lines). Then set the appropriate margins. Notice that a short letter (under 100 words) requires 5-cm margins while a long letter (over 200 words) uses margins of 2.5 to 3 cm. Your goal is to place your message in the middle of a page surrounded by a balanced frame of white space.

Letter Length	Words in Body	Side Margins	Blank Lines After Date
Short	Under 100	5 cm	7 to 11 (12 pitch) 6 to 8 (10 pitch)
Medium	100 to 200	3 cm	2 to 8 (12 pitch) 2 to 3 (10 pitch)
Long	Over 200	2.5 to 3 cm	2 to 8 (12 pitch) 2 to 3 (10 pitch)

Some companies prescribe standard margins, usually 2.5 to 3 cm (1 to 1.5 inches). This practice is convenient and efficient because many word processing programs use these standard margins as their defaults. Letter writers don't have to change their margins. However, standard margins often result in unbalanced documents, particularly for short messages. Find out whether your organization prefers adjusting margins to accommodate the length of a document or using standard default margins. Remember, too, that you can always adjust the number of blank lines after the date to balance a document on the page.

PUNCTUATION STYLES

Two punctuation styles are commonly used for letters. Open punctuation, shown with the block-style letter in Figure A.1, contains no punctuation after the salutation

FIGURE A.4

Simplified Letter Style

Identifies method of delivery.

Replaces salutation with subject line.

Leaves two blank lines above and below subject line.

Omits complimentary close.

Highlights writer's name and identification with all caps.

Identifies copy.

ABC ● ***Automation Business Consultants***
2682 Roefield Street
Calgary AB T2N 6C5
(403) 369-1109

July 19, 200X

FAX TRANSMISSION

Ms. Sara Hendricks, Manager
Western Land and Home Realty
17690 Anscomb Boulevard
Edmonton, AB T5L 9R4

SIMPLIFIED LETTER STYLE

You may be interested to learn, Ms. Hendricks, that some years ago the Administrative Management Society recommended the simplified letter format illustrated here. Notice the following efficient features:

1. All lines begin at the left margin.

2. The salutation and complimentary close are omitted.

3. A subject line in all caps appears 3 lines below the inside address and 3 lines above the first paragraph.

4. The writer's name and identification appear 5 lines below the last paragraph.

In addition to its efficiency, this letter style is helpful in dealing with the problem of appropriate salutations. Since it has no salutation, your writers need not worry about which to choose. For many reasons we recommend this style to your staff.

Holly Higgins

HOLLY HIGGINS, MANAGER, OFFICE DIVISION

HH:tb

c John Fox

or complimentary close. Mixed punctuation, shown with the modified block style letter in Figure A.3, requires a colon after the salutation and a comma after the complimentary close. Many business organizations prefer mixed punctuation, even in a block-style letter.

If you choose mixed punctuation, be sure to use a colon—not a comma or semicolon—after the salutation. Even when the salutation is a first name, the colon is appropriate.

ENVELOPES

An envelope should be printed on the same quality and colour of stationery as the letter it carries. Because the envelope introduces your message and makes the first impression, you need to be especially careful in addressing it. Moreover, how you fold the letter is important.

RETURN ADDRESS

The return address is usually printed in the upper left corner of an envelope, as shown in Figure A.5. In large companies some form of identification (the writer's initials, name, or location) may be typed above the company name and return address. This identification helps return the letter to the sender in case of non-delivery.

On an envelope without a printed return address, single-space the return address in the upper left corner. Beginning on line 3 on the fourth space (approximately 12mm or 1/2 inch) from the left edge, type the writer's name, title, company, and mailing address.

MAILING ADDRESS

On legal-sized No. 10 envelopes (10.5 cm by 24 cm), begin the address on line 13 about 11.5 cm from the left edge, as shown in Figure A.5. For small No. 8 envelopes (7.5 cm by 15 cm), begin typing on line 12 about 6.2 cm from the left edge.

FIGURE A.5

Envelope Formats

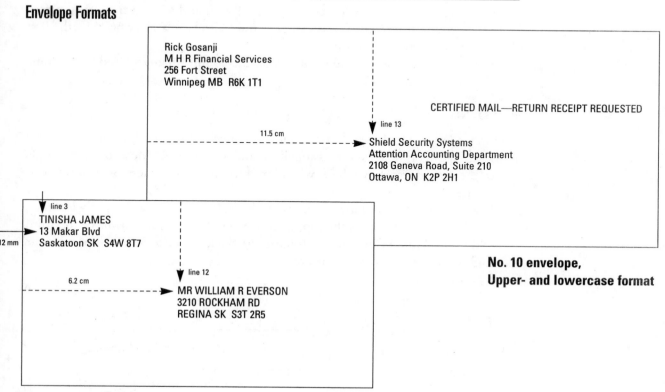

No. 10 envelope,
Upper- and lowercase format

No. 8 envelope,
Canada Post uppercase format

Canada Post recommends that addresses be typed in all caps without any punctuation. This style, shown in the small envelope in Figure A.5, was originally developed to facilitate scanning by optical character readers. Today's OCRs, however, are so sophisticated that they scan upper- and lowercase letters easily.

Many companies today prefer to use the same format for the envelope as for the inside address. If the same format is used, writers can take advantage of word processing programs to "copy" the inside address to the envelope, thus saving keystrokes and reducing errors. Having the same format on both the inside address and the envelope also looks more professional and consistent. For these reasons you may choose to use the familiar upper- and lowercase combination format. But you will want to check with your organization to learn its preference.

Since Canada Post's sorting equipment scans the address from bottom to top, they recommend placing information not needed to deliver the envelope such as *ATTENTION* above the address block. Canada Post also recommends the following format for addresses:

RECIPIENT'S NAME AND/OR TITLE
DEPT./BUILDING NAME
ORGANIZATION NAME
STREET ADDRESS / UNIT OR APARTMENT NUMBER
MUNICIPALITY OR CITY / PROVINCE / POSTAL CODE

In addressing your envelopes for delivery in this country or in the United States, use the two-letter province and state abbreviations shown in Figure A.6. Notice that these abbreviations are in capital letters without periods. The postal code is essential and should appear on the same line as the municipality and province, be separated from the province by two spaces, and always appear in capital letters. The postal code must appear in an area located between 19 mm and 45 mm from the bottom edge of an envelope or card. The postal code must also have a space between the first three characters and the last three.

For letters addressed outside of Canada, the country name should stand alone at the bottom of the address block.

FOLDING

The way a letter is folded and inserted into an envelope sends additional nonverbal messages about a writer's professionalism and carefulness. Most businesspeople follow the procedures shown here, which produce the least number of creases to distract readers.

For large No. 10 envelopes, begin with the letter face up. Fold slightly less than one third of the sheet toward the top, as shown below. Then fold down the top third to within 6 to 7 mm of the bottom fold. Insert the letter into the envelope with the last fold toward the bottom of the envelope.

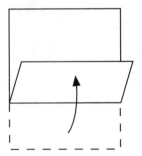
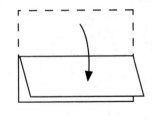

FIGURE A.6

Abbreviations of Provinces, Territories, and States

Province or Territory	Two-Letter Abbreviation
Alberta	AB
British Columbia	BC
Labrador	LB
Manitoba	MB
New Brunswick	NB
Newfoundland	NF
Northwest Territories and Nunavut	NT
Nova Scotia	NS
Ontario	ON
Prince Edward Island	PE
Quebec	QC
Saskatchewan	SK
Yukon Territory	YT

State or Territory	Abbreviation	State or Territory	Abbreviation
Alabama	AL	Montana	MT
Alaska	AK	Nebraska	NE
Arizona	AZ	Nevada	NV
Arkansas	AR	New Hampshire	NH
California	CA	New Jersey	NJ
Canal Zone	CZ	New Mexico	NM
Colorado	CO	New York	NY
Connecticut	CT	North Carolina	NC
Delaware	DE	North Dakota	ND
District of Columbia	DC	Ohio	OH
Florida	FL	Oklahoma	OK
Georgia	GA	Oregon	OR
Guam	GU	Pennsylvania	PA
Hawaii	HI	Puerto Rico	PR
Idaho	ID	Rhode Island	RI
Illinois	IL	South Carolina	SC
Indiana	IN	South Dakota	SD
Iowa	IA	Tennessee	TN
Kansas	KS	Texas	TX
Kentucky	KY	Utah	UT
Louisiana	LA	Vermont	VT
Maine	ME	Virgin Islands	VI
Maryland	MD	Virginia	VA
Massachusetts	MA	Washington	WA
Michigan	MI	West Virginia	WV
Minnesota	MN	Wisconsin	WI
Mississippi	MS	Wyoming	WY
Missouri	MO		

For small No. 8 envelopes, begin by folding the bottom up to within 6 to 7 mm of the top edge. Then fold the right third over to the left. Fold the left third to within 6 to 7 mm of the last fold. Insert the last fold into the envelope first.

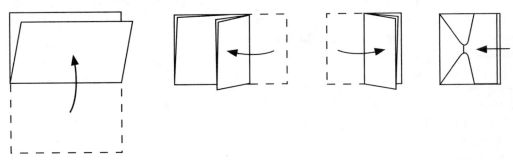

MEMORANDUMS

As discussed in Chapter 5, memorandums deliver messages within organizations. Some offices use memo forms imprinted with the organization name and, optionally, the department or division names, as shown in Figure A.7. Although the design and arrangement of memo forms vary, they usually include the basic elements of *TO, FROM, DATE*, and *SUBJECT*. Large organizations may include other identifying headings, such as *FILE NUMBER, FLOOR, EXTENSION, LOCATION*, and *DISTRIBUTION*.

Because of the difficulty of aligning computer printers with preprinted forms, many business writers use a standardized memo template provided with word processing software. This template automatically provides attractive headings with appropriate spacing and formatting. Other writers store their own preferred memo formats. Either method eliminates alignment problems.

If no printed forms or computer templates are available, memos may be typed on company letterhead or on plain paper, as shown in Figure A.8. On a full sheet of paper, start on line 13; on a half sheet, start on line 7. Double-space and type in all caps the guide words: *TO:, FROM:, DATE:, SUBJECT:*. Align all the fill-in information two spaces after the longest guide word *(SUBJECT:)*. Leave three lines after the last line of the heading and begin typing the body of the memo. Like business letters, memos are single-spaced.

Memos are generally formatted with side margins of 3.5 cm ($1\frac{1}{4}$ inches), or they may conform to the printed memo form. (For more information about memos, see Chapter 5.)

E-MAIL MESSAGES

Because e-mail is a developing communication medium, formatting and use are still fluid. The following suggestions, illustrated in Figure A.9, may guide you in setting up the parts of an e-mail message, but always check with your organization to observe its practices.

TO LINE

Include the receiver's e-mail address after *To*. Some writers personalize the line somewhat by naming the receiver first, followed by that person's e-mail address in angle brackets, such as *Marilyn Lammers <mlammers@accountpro.com>*.

FIGURE A.7

Printed Memo Forms

Mercantile Bank of Canada
Loans Division

Interoffice
Memorandum

TO:

FROM:

DATE:

SUBJECT:

PYRAMID, INC.
Internal Memo

TO: DATE:

FROM: FILE:

SUBJECT:

FIGURE A.8

Memo on Plain Paper

↓ line 13

MEMO

3.5 cm →   TO: Dawn Stewart, Manager   DATE: February 3, 200X
                        Sales and Marketing   *DS*

            FROM: Jay Murray, Vice President
                        Operations

            SUBJECT: TELEPHONE SERVICE REQUEST FORMS

↓ 3 lines

To speed telephone installation and improve service within the Bremerton facility, we are starting a new application procedure.

Service request forms will be available at various locations within the three buildings. When you require telephone service, obtain a request form at one of the locations that is convenient for you. Fill in the pertinent facts, obtain approval from your division head, and send the form to Brent White. Request forms are available at the following locations:

FIGURE A.9

Typical E-Mail Message

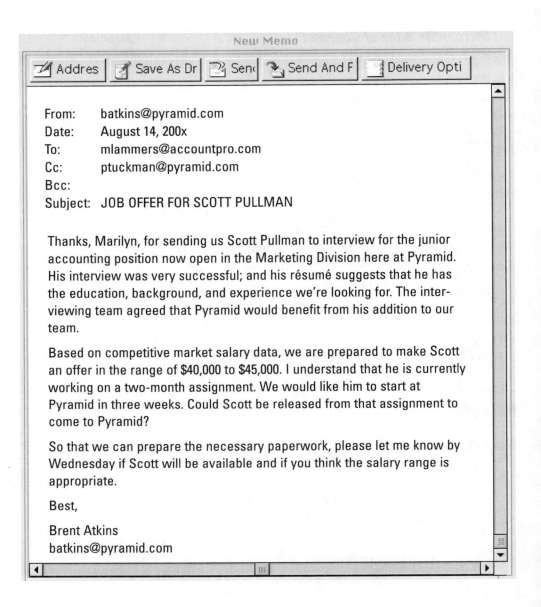

New Memo

Addres | Save As Dr | Send | Send And F | Delivery Opti

From: batkins@pyramid.com
Date: August 14, 200x
To: mlammers@accountpro.com
Cc: ptuckman@pyramid.com
Bcc:
Subject: JOB OFFER FOR SCOTT PULLMAN

Thanks, Marilyn, for sending us Scott Pullman to interview for the junior accounting position now open in the Marketing Division here at Pyramid. His interview was very successful; and his résumé suggests that he has the education, background, and experience we're looking for. The interviewing team agreed that Pyramid would benefit from his addition to our team.

Based on competitive market salary data, we are prepared to make Scott an offer in the range of $40,000 to $45,000. I understand that he is currently working on a two-month assignment. We would like him to start at Pyramid in three weeks. Could Scott be released from that assignment to come to Pyramid?

So that we can prepare the necessary paperwork, please let me know by Wednesday if Scott will be available and if you think the salary range is appropriate.

Best,

Brent Atkins
batkins@pyramid.com

FROM LINE

Most systems automatically include your name and e-mail address after *From*.

CC

Insert the e-mail address of anyone who is to receive a copy of the message. *Cc* stands for carbon copy or courtesy copy. Don't be tempted, though, to send needless copies just because it's so easy.

BCC

Include here the e-mail address of anyone who is to receive a copy of the message without the addressee's knowledge. *Bcc* stands for blind carbon copy. However, sending blind carbon copies is dangerous because you just might make an address error, and the addressee could learn of the intended *bcc*.

SUBJECT

Identify the subject of the memo briefly. Be sure to include enough information to be clear and compelling. Many people archive their e-mail so a subject line in an e-mail can be as important for filing purposes as the subject line of a paper memo.

SALUTATION

Include a brief greeting, if you like. Some writers use a salutation such as *Dear Lisa* followed by a comma or a colon; others are more informal with *Hi, Lisa!* Some start with *Good morning* or *Greetings.* Others prefer to skip a salutation; instead, they include the name of the receiver in the first line, as shown in Figure A.9. Practice seems to be divided over whether to treat e-mail messages more like letters (with salutations) or memos (without salutations).

MESSAGE

Cover just one topic in your message, and try to keep your total message as brief as you would for a paper memo. To assist you, many e-mail systems have text-editing features such as cut, copy, paste, and word-wrap.

CLOSING

Conclude an external message, if you like, with *Cheers* or *Best* followed by your name. If the recipient is unlikely to know you, it's not a bad idea to include your title and organization. Most e-mail packages allow users to include a signature file or personal electronic business card that includes important identifying and contact information. Writers of e-mail messages sent within organizations may omit closings and even skip their names at the ends of messages because receivers recognize them from identification in the opening lines.

FAX COVER SHEET

Documents transmitted by fax are usually introduced by a cover sheet, such as that shown in Figure A.10. As with memos, the format varies considerably. Important items to include are (1) the name and fax number of the receiver, (2) the name and fax number of the sender, (3) the number of pages being sent, and (4) the name and telephone number of the person to notify in case of unsatisfactory transmission.

When the document being transmitted requires little explanation, you may prefer to attach an adhesive note (such as a Post-it™ fax transmittal form) instead of a full cover sheet. These notes carry essentially the same information as shown in the printed fax cover sheet in Figure A.10. They are perfectly acceptable in most business organizations and can save considerable paper and transmission costs.

FIGURE A.10

Fax Cover Sheet

FAX TRANSMISSION

DATE: _____   FAX NUMBER: _____

TO: _____
_____
_____

FROM: _____   FAX NUMBER: _____
_____
_____

NUMBER OF PAGES TRANSMITTED INCLUDING THIS COVER SHEET: _____

MESSAGE:

If any part of this fax transmission is missing or not clearly received, please call:

NAME: _____

PHONE: _____

PROOFREADING MARKS

PROOFREADING MARK		DRAFT COPY	FINAL COPY
═	Align horizontally	/Lisa Kim TO:/	TO: Lisa Kim
‖	Align vertically	‖166.32 132.45	166.32 132.45
≋	Capitalize	Coca-cola runs on ms-dos	Coca-Cola runs on MS-DOS
◯	Close up space	meeting at 3 p. m.	meeting at 3 p.m.
⅃ ⅄	Centre	⅃ Recommendations ⅂	Recommendations
ℓ	Delete	in my ~~final~~ judgement	in my judgment
∧	Insert word(s)	Ellen Mary ∧Guffey	Mary Ellen Guffey
∨	Insert apostrophe	our company's product	our company's product
∧	Insert comma	you will∧of course∧	you will, of course,
≈	Insert dash	perhaps∧but	perhaps—but
∧	Insert semicolon	value∧therefore, we feel	value; therefore, we feel
∧	Insert hyphen	tax∧free income	tax-free income
⊙	Insert period	Ms⊙ Holly Hines	Ms. Holly Hines
∨	Insert quotation mark	shareholders receive a ∨bonus∨	shareholders receive a "bonus"
#∧	Insert space	word∧processing program	word processing program
/	Lowercase (remove capitals)	the /Vice /President H/UMAN R/ESOURCES	the vice president Human Resources
⊏	Move to left	⊏I. Labour costs	I. Labour costs
⊐	Move to right	A. Findings of a study ⊐	A. Findings of a study
◯	Spell out	aimed at ②depts	aimed at two departments
¶	Start new paragraph	¶Keep the screen height at eye level.	Keep the screen height at eye level.
.....	Stet (leave as original)	officials talked ~~openly~~	officials talked openly
∼	Transpose	accounts recievable only talked about	accounts receivable talked only about
∿	Use boldface	Conclusions	**Conclusions**
—	Use italics	(ital)The Perfect Résumé	*The Perfect Résumé*

Appendix C

DOCUMENTATION FORMATS

Although business writers are careful to document their sources, they do not all follow the same formatting style. Many organizations have developed their own in-house styles for showing references. In this discussion we shall be concerned only with suggestions for the writers of long business reports. We shall not try to present a comprehensive treatment of documentation, including all the exceptions and procedures appropriate for authors of books, doctoral dissertations, and master's theses.

Documenting sources in a business report can be done using the traditional formats suggested in *The Chicago Manual of Style*, 14th edition (Chicago: University of Chicago Press, 1993, pp. 487–635). Or, you may choose to use the parenthetic method of citation favoured by the Modern Language Association (in *The MLA Handbook for Writers of Research Papers*, 4th edition). The *Chicago Manual of Style*'s note and bibliography formats are the formats followed in this book.

Citation formats for Internet and other electronic references are still evolving; those outlined in the "Electronic Sources" section below are representative of current electronic sources, but these may change as the new media develop. On the job you should check with your organization to learn what reference format it prefers. Whatever style you use, be consistent throughout your report.

NOTES

CHICAGO MANUAL OF STYLE METHOD

The *Chicago Manual of Style*'s notes format includes superscript (raised) figures in the text, as shown in the model report in Chapter 12. These small numbers mark quotations, paraphrased passages, and author references. They tell the reader that the preceding ideas or words originated with someone who is identified in the *Notes* section.

A note identifying each reference may appear as a footnote at the bottom of the page where it was cited or as an endnote at end of the report. Sample *Notes* pages appear in Figure C.1, and at the end of the model report in Chapter 12. Endnote entries are single-spaced with double-spacing between. They are arranged in the order cited in the text, and they are numbered consecutively. They are shown here with full-sized numbers (such as *1.*, *2.*, *3.*, and so forth). Your word processor, however, may show endnotes with superscript figures. Either form is acceptable.

When referring to a previously mentioned footnote, cite the page number along with the author's last name or a shortened form of the title if no author is given. The Latin forms *ibid.*, *op.cit.*, and *et al.*, are rarely seen in business reports today.

Here are some of the most frequently used endnotes, styled in accordance with the *Chicago Manual of Style* format.

BOOK, ONE AUTHOR

1. Sara White, *Profiting in the Knowledge Age: A Canadian Guide to the Future* (Toronto: McKnight Publishing, 1999), p. 25.

BOOK, MANY AUTHORS

2. Manny Colver, Dan Smith, and Jeremy Devport, *Careers in the Twenty-First Century* (Scarborough, ON: ITP Nelson, 1999), 356–358.

JOURNAL ARTICLE

3. John Drovich, "Peace in the Middle East," *Canadian Journal of International Studies* 19, no. 5 (1999): 23–45.

MAGAZINE ARTICLE

4. Bill Safer, "Future Leadership," *Canadian Management*, April 1999, 45.

NEWSPAPER ARTICLE

5. Trisha Khan, "Beyond 2000: Working in the Next Century," *Winnipeg Free Press*, 22 August 1999, B3.

GOVERNMENT PUBLICATION

6. Human Resources Development Canada, *How to Find a Job* (Ottawa: Supply and Services Canada, 1996), 30.

ENCYCLOPEDIA ARTICLE WITHOUT AN AUTHOR

7. *Encyclopaedia Britannica*, 15th ed., s.v. "Great Lakes."

INTERVIEW

8. Izzy Asper, interview by author, 14 June 1999.

PARENTHETIC, OR MLA, METHOD

The style recommended by the Modern Language Association and set out in the *MLA Handbook for Writers of Research Papers* (4th ed., 1995) recommends that citations be given in the text of the paper rather than in footnotes or endnotes. The parenthetic comments include the author's last name and the page in the work on which the reference is found. If the work is anonymous or the author's name is unavailable, an abbreviated title is used to identify the reference. The following excerpt illustrates the MLA method:

> Several private studies on the subject of occupational health are now being conducted (Peters 127). In addition, Health Canada plans to develop its own study at a cost of $600,000 ("Uneasy Silence" 54).

When the author is mentioned in the text, it is unnecessary to include the name again in the parenthetic reference. Just insert the page reference as shown here:

> Peters also notes that stress could be a contributing factor in the health problems reported thus far (135).

BIBLIOGRAPHY

A bibliography is a complete list of all the references cited in a report. It may also include all references consulted by a researcher, particularly for more formal reports. For less formal reports and those with fewer than ten footnotes or endnotes, a bibliography may be omitted. For reports with many references, though, a bibliography is necessary because its alphabetical arrangement helps readers locate items quickly.

Notice in the sample bibliography items shown below—which follow the *Chicago Manual of Style* format—that each segment of an entry ends with a period instead of a comma. The author's full name is followed by a period, the year of publication is followed by a period, and so on. Note, too, that entries are presented in hanging indented form, with the second and succeeding lines indented five spaces from the first line. This placement highlights the first word of each entry, thus enabling readers to locate specific entries quickly. Entries are single-spaced with double-spacing between them. An additional example of a bibliography can be seen in the model report in Figure 12.10.

If using the parenthetic, or MLA, method of documentation, the full citation of works is given in a section entitled "List of Works Cited" or "Works Cited," which is placed at the end of the report. The list gives full publishing information for each of the sources cited in your paper and acts as the bibliography. The MLA style does not require you to list all of the sources consulted, as the *Chicago Manual of Style* prefers, only those you refer to directly in the text. In both the *Chicago* and MLA methods the sources are listed alphabetically by author or editor. If the title has no author, use the first word in the title other than *a, an,* or *the.*

BOOK, ONE AUTHOR

White, Sara. 1999. *Profiting in the Knowledge Age: A Canadian Guide to the Future.* Toronto: McKnight Publishing.

BOOK, SAME AUTHOR

————. 1990. *Life After Your Career.* Winnipeg: Cargo Press.

BOOK, MANY AUTHORS

Colver, Manny, Dan Smith, and Jeremy Devport. 1999. *Careers in the Twenty-First Century.* Scarborough, ON: ITP Nelson.

MAGAZINE OR JOURNAL ARTICLE

Drovich, John. 1999. "Peace in the Middle East," *Canadian Journal of International Studies* 19, no. 5: 23–45.

NEWSPAPER ARTICLE

Khan, Trisha. 1999. "Beyond 2000: Working in the Next Century." *Winnipeg Free Press,* 22 August, B3.

GOVERNMENT PUBLICATION

Human Resources Development Canada. 1996. *How to Find a Job.* Ottawa: Supply and Services Canada.

INTERVIEW

Asper, Izzy. 1999. Interview by author. 14 June.

In general, the objective in citing sources, whether print publications or electronic publications, is to provide enough information that your reader can locate your sources. Your citations for electronic sources will follow the guidelines for print sources given above, but you are required to include additional information in citations for electronic documents. Some of the information required for print sources may be unavailable; if this is the case, simply provide whatever information is available.

The *MLA Handbook* makes the following recommendations for citing electronic sources:

- Give the same information for electronic sources as you would for print publications.
- Be sure to give all relevant dates. Because electronic sources can change or move, cite the date the document was produced as well as the date you received the information. If the electronic publication is or was available in print form (i.e., as a book or in a journal), include the original print publication date before the other dates.
- When citing on-line works, it is important to include the network address or uniform resource locator (URL), which indicates where you found your information. In citing URLs, never use a hyphen to mark a break in the address.
- Because it may be difficult to gain access to information at a later date, it is a good idea to download (print) any citation information for future reference.

The examples of electronic sources outlined below show the styles for bibliographic entries; for samples of endnotes for on-line sources, see Figure C.2.

ARTICLE FROM AN ON-LINE PERIODICAL/PUBLICATION

Generally, citations for on-line publications (for example, journals, newspapers, and magazines) as well as items included in these publications (such as articles, reviews, interviews) will follow the guidelines for print publications. Some of the usual information (for example, page numbers) may not be available; if not, cite whatever is available. At the end of the citation provide the date you accessed the information and the network address.

ARTICLE IN A JOURNAL

Chrisman, Laura, and Laurence Phillips. 1999. "Postcolonial Studies and the British Academy." *Jouvert.* March 3. [on-line]. [cited 10 June 1999]. Available from social.chass.ncsu.edu/jouvert/v3i3/chrisph/htm.

Brown, Ronnie R. 1995. "Photographs That Should Have Been Taken." *Room of One's Own.* February 18. [on-line]. [cited 26 May 1999]. Available from www.islandnet.com/Room/enter/poetry/photos.htm.

ARTICLE IN A NEWSPAPER OR ON A NEWSWIRE

These sites change very frequently—in some cases daily—so it is a good idea to download or record URL and citation information immediately.

Schuss, Deborah Gastfreund. 1999. "Many Top College Students Use Tutors to Keep an Edge." *Boston Globe Online.* June 4. [cited 5 June 1999]. Available from www.boston.com/dailyglobe2/150/ learning/Many-top-college-students-use-tutors-to-keep-an-edge+.shtm.

"Canada's Unemployment Rate Dips." 1999. *CBC News Online*. June 4. [cited 5 June 1999]. Available from cbcnews.cbc.ca/cgi-bin/templates/view.cgi?/news/1999/06/04/unemploy990604.

ARTICLE IN A MAGAZINE

Caragata, Warren. 1999. "Guide to Y2K." *Maclean's Online*. April 19. [cited 5 June]. Available from www.macleans.ca/pub-doc/1999/04/19/Cover/4998.html.

PROFESSIONAL OR PERSONAL SITE

List the publication information in the following order: the name of the creator of the site, the title of the cite (underlined), a description (e.g., *Homepage*, neither underlined nor enclosed in quotation marks), the name of any associated organization or university, the date you accessed the information, and the network address. If some of this information is unavailable, cite whatever is available.

ACCUTE (Association of Canadian College and University Teachers of English). Homepage. Memorial University. 26 May. Available from www.mun.ca/accute/history.htm.

Thompson, Scott. 1998. Scottland. Homepage. July 25. [accessed 5 June 1999]. Available from www.scottland.com/.

ON-LINE BOOK

Many books are now available electronically, either independently or as part of a scholarly project. Follow the general recommendations for citing books in print, but include the additional information as required for electronic citations.

ON-LINE BOOK AVAILABLE INDEPENDENTLY

Give the name of the author first if it's available; if not, give the name of the editor, translator, or compiler, followed by a period and the appropriate abbreviation *(ed., trans.,* or *comp.).* Next give the original publication date, then the title of the work (underscored), the name of the editor, translator, or compiler (if not already given and if relevant), the publication information, the date you accessed the information, and the address. The publication information will vary depending on whether or not the text has been previously published in print form. If it has not been previously published, give the date it was published electronically and the name of any associated organization or university. If it has been previously published in print form, include, if available, the city of publication, the name of the publisher, and the year of publication, followed by the date of electronic publication, and the name of any associated organization or university. In either case, complete your citation with the date you accessed the information and the network address.

Here are two examples:

Montgomery, Lucy Maud. 1908. Anne of Green Gables. 26 April 1999. [cited 30 May 1999]. Available from www.literature.org/authors/montgomery-lucy-maud/anne-of-green-gables.

Dewey, John. 1916. <u>Democracy and Education</u>. London: Macmillan. 22 November 1995. [cited 5 June 1999]. Available from www.ilt.columbia.edu/academic/ texts/ dewey/d_e/contents.html.

OTHER ELECTRONIC SOURCES

The citations for other electronic sources will follow the recommendations for print versions with some additional required information. Be sure to include the type of document you are citing (e.g., transcript, on-line posting, or e-mail) between the date of publication and the date you accessed the information. End your citation with the date you accessed the information and the network address.

TELEVISION/RADIO

Mansbridge, Peter. 1999. "Eaton's Saga." <u>The National</u>. CBC-TV. 4 June. Transcript [cited 5 June 1999]. Available from www.tv.cbc.ca/national/trans/current.html.

E-MAIL COMMUNICATION

Rozoff, Peter (prozoff@oxfam.ca). 1996. "Your Inquiries to Oxfam." E-mail to author. [3 July].

ON-LINE POSTING

Murley, Susan (e-grad@nwe.ufl.edu). 1998. "Technical Writing." On-Line posting. 2 May 1998. [cited 3 May 1998].

CD-ROM AND OTHER DATABASES

Research material is available in electronic form on CD-ROMs from vendors such as SilverPlatter and UMI-Proquest, and on-line from computer services or networks such as Dialog and Lexis-Nexis. For CD-ROMs and other online service citations, give the same publishing information as for other sources and add pertinent information about the electronic source. You may find that some of the information about an electronic source, such as the name of the vendor, is not available. If so, you may omit this information. If the CD-ROM publication you are citing contains more than one disk, specify the total number of disks, or, if you are using only one of a multiple set, specify the disk number of the one you are using.

"United States Banking System." 1994. *Compton's Interactive Encyclopedia*, version 2.0. [CD-ROM]. New Media, Inc.

MATERIAL FROM AN ON-LINE SERVICE

Online services such as Dialog, CompuServe, America Online, ProQuest Direct, and Lexis-Nexis provide a variety of databases that may be revised continually or periodically. For on-line services that provide a URL, cite the relevant information as listed above for electronic publications. Give the name of the service before the date you accessed the information. If the service does not provide a URL, indicate the method by which you retrieved the information. For example, if you used a keyword, write "keyword" (neither in quotation marks nor underlined) at the end of your citation, followed by a colon and the keyword you used to find your information.

"Table Tennis." 1997. *Compton's Encyclopedia Online*. Vers. 2.0. America Online. 4 July 1998. Keyword: Compton's.

FIGURE C.1

Sample Endnotes Page

NOTES

1. Brenda Lynn, "Diversity in the Workplace: Why We Should Care," *CMA Management Accounting Magazine*, June 1996, 9–12.

2. "Firms Gain Competitive Strength from Diversity," *Financial Post,* May 1995, 31.

3. British Columbia Ministry of Education, Skills and Training, *The Impact of Demographic Change* (Victoria: Ministry of Education, Skills and Training, 1996), 35.

4. R. J. Burke, and C. A. McKeen, "Do Women at the Top Make a Difference? Gender Proportions and the Experiences of Managerial and Professional Women," *Human Relations* 49, no. 8 (1996): 1093–1104.

5. *Impact of Demographic Change,* 36.

6. PPG Canada Inc., *1999 Annual Report* (Toronto: PPG Canada Inc., 2000), 2–3.

7. Michael Able and Joan Ryan, *Management Principles*, 2nd ed. (Boston: Bard Press, 1996), 258.

8. Kevin Benson, interview by author, 7 September 1999.

9. "James A. Naismith," *The Basketball Encyclopedia*, Version 1.0. [CD-ROM], Distillation Media Inc., 1998.

10. Daryl Rand, "The Ethics of Handwriting Analysis in Pre-Employment Screening," *The Online Journal of Ethics* 1, 1, 1995 [on-line] [cited 7 June 1997]; available from candor.depaul.edu/ethics/hand.html.

11. John Markoff, "Voluntary Rules Proposed to Help Insure Privacy for Internet Users," *The New York Times*, 5 June 1996, business sec., in *Cyber Times* [on-line] [cited 7 July 1997]; available from www.nytimes/com/library/cyber/week/y05dat.html.

12. Scott Thompson, <u>Scottland</u>, homepage, 25 July 1998 [accessed 5 June 1999]; available from www.scottland.com.

13. Su Park, "Estimation and Prediction of Brand Equities Through Survey Measurement of Consumer Preference Structures" (Ph.D. diss., Stanford University, 1993), 259.

14. Roberto C. Goizueta, "Annual Report to Share Owners," 26 February 1996 [on-line Web site] [cited 15 March 1997]; available from cocacola.com/co/chairman.html. [Note: If no author is given, begin with the name of the page.]

Magazine article

Newspaper article, editorial

Government publication

Journal article, with volume and issue numbers

Subsequent reference

Annual report

Book, two authors, edition

Interview

Encyclopedia article, CD-ROM

Journal article, on-line

Newspaper article, on-line database

Personal site

Unpublished material

World Wide Web site

FIGURE C.2

Sample Bibliography Page

BIBLIOGRAPHY

Able, Michael, and Joan Ryan. *Management Principles*. 1996. 2nd ed. Boston: Bard Press.

Benson, Kevin. Interview by author. 7 September 1999.

Burke, R. J., and C. A. McKeen. 1996. "Do Women at the Top Make a Difference? Gender Proportions and the Experiences of Managerial and Professional Women." *Human Relations* 49, 8:1093–1104.

Financial Post. 1995. "Firms Gain Competitive Strength from Diversity." 9 May 1995, 31.

Goizueta, Roberto C. 1996. "Annual Report to Share Owners," 26 February. [on-line Web site]. [cited 15 March 1997]. Available from cocacola.com/co/chairman.html.

The Impact of Demographic Change. 1996. British Columbia Ministry of Education, Skills and Training. Victoria: Ministry of Education, Skills and Training, 35.

Lynn, Brenda. 1996. "Diversity in the Workplace: Why We Should Care." *CMA Management Accounting Magazine*, June, 9–12.

Markoff, John. 1996. "Voluntary Rules Proposed to Help Insure Privacy for Internet Users." *The New York Times*, 5 June. Business sec. In *Cyber Times* [on-line database]. [cited 7 July 1997]. Available from www.nytimes/com/library/cyber/week/y05dat.html.

"James A. Naismith." 1998. *The Basketball Encyclopedia*, Version 1.0. [CD–ROM]. Distillation Media Inc.

Park, Su. 1993. "Estimation and Prediction of Brand Equities Through Survey Measurement of Consumer Preference Structures." Ph.D. diss., Stanford University, 259.

PPG Canada Inc. 2000. *1999 Annual Report*. Toronto: PPG Canada Inc.

Rand, Daryl. 1995. "The Ethics of Handwriting Analysis in Pre-Employment Screening." *The Online Journal of Ethics*, 1,1. April 24. [on-line]. [cited 7 June 1997]. Available from condor.depaul.edu/ethics/hand.html.

Thompson, Scott. 1998. Scottland, homepage. July 25. [accessed 5 June 1999]. Available from www.scottland.com.

Zimmerman, Troy. 1997. (tzimmerman@aol.com). "Excellent Web Sites for Job Seekers." E-mail to Carla Wagner (cwagner@idbsu.edu). [October 2].

Side annotations:

- Book, two authors, edition
- Interview
- Journal article, with volume and issue numbers
- Newspaper article, editorial
- World Wide Web site
- Government publication
- Magazine article
- Newspaper article, on-line database
- Encyclopedia article, CD-ROM
- Unpublished material
- Annual report
- Journal article, on-line
- Personal site
- E-mail message

Grammar/Mechanics Handbook

The Grammar/Mechanics Handbook consists of three parts:

1. Grammar/Mechanics Diagnostic Test
   - To assess your strengths and weaknesses in eight areas of grammar and mechanics
2. Grammar/Mechanics Profile
   - To pinpoint specific areas in which you need remedial instruction or review
3. Grammar Review with Review and Editing Exercises
   - To review basic principles of grammar, punctuation, capitalization, and number style
   - To provide reinforcement and quiz exercises allowing you to interact with the principles of grammar and test your comprehension
   - To serve as a systematic reference to grammar and mechanics throughout the writing course
   - To be used for classroom-centred instruction or self-guided learning

Grammar/Mechanics Diagnostic Test

Name _____

This diagnostic test is intended to reveal your strengths and weaknesses in using the following:

plural nouns	adjectives	punctuation
possessive nouns	adverbs	capitalization style
pronouns	prepositions	number style
verbs	conjunctions	

The test is organized into sections corresponding to these categories. In sections A–G, each sentence is either correct or has one error related to the category under which it is listed. If a sentence is correct, write *C*. If it has an error, underline the error and write the correct form in the space provided. Use ink to record your answers. When you finish, check your answers with your instructor and fill out the Grammar/Mechanics Profile on page 400.

A. Plural Nouns

branches _____

Example: The newspaper named editors in chief for both <u>branchs</u>.

_____ 1. Three of the dairies in the region qualified for government subsidies.

_____ 2. Four freshmans discussed the pros and cons of attending colleges or universities.

_____ 3. Since the 1980s most companys have begun to send bills of lading with shipments.

396

4. Neither the Johnsons nor the Morris's knew about the changes in beneficiaries. _____
5. The manager asked all of the crews to work on the next four Saturday's. _____

B. POSSESSIVE NOUNS

6. We sincerely hope that the jurys judgment reflects the stories of all the witnesses. _____
7. In a little over two months time, the administrative assistants had finished three reports for the president. _____
8. Mr. Franklins staff is responsible for all accounts receivable contracted by customers purchasing electronics parts. _____
9. At the next shareholders meeting, we will discuss benefits for employees and dividends for shareholders. _____
10. Three months ago several employees in the sales department complained of Mrs. Kwons smoking. _____

C. PRONOUNS

Example: Whom did you ask to replace Tom and I?   me _____

11. My manager and myself were willing to send the copies to whoever needed them. _____
12. Some of the work for Mr. Gagne and I had to be reassigned to Mark and him. _____
13. Although it's motor was damaged, the car started for the mechanic and me. _____
14. Just between you and me, only you and I know that she will be transferred. _____
15. My friend and I applied for employment at Reynolds, Inc., because of their excellent employee benefits. _____

D. VERB AGREEMENT

Example: The list of arrangements have to be approved by Tim and her.   has _____

16. The keyboard, printer, and monitor costs less than I expected. _____
17. A description of the property, together with several other legal documents, were submitted by my lawyer. _____
18. There was only two enclosures and the letter in the envelope. _____
19. Neither the manager nor the employees in the office think the solution is fair. _____
20. Because of the holiday, our committee prefer to delay its action. _____

E. VERB MOOD, VOICE, AND TENSE

21. If I was able to fill your order immediately, I certainly would. _____
22. To operate the machine, first open the CD caddy and then insert the CD. _____
23. If I could chose any city, I would select Vancouver. _____
24. Those papers have laid on his desk for more than two weeks. _____
25. The auditors have went over these accounts carefully, and they have found no discrepancies. _____

F. ADJECTIVES AND ADVERBS

_____ 26. Until we have a more clearer picture of the entire episode, we shall proceed 436cautiously.

_____ 27. For about a week their newly repaired copier worked just beautiful.

_____ 28. The recently elected official benefited from his coast to coast campaign.

_____ 29. Mr. Snyder only has two days before he must complete the end-of-the-year report.

_____ 30. The architects submitted there drawings in a last-minute attempt to beat the deadline.

G. PREPOSITIONS AND CONJUNCTIONS

_____ 31. Can you tell me where the meeting is scheduled at?

_____ 32. It seems like we have been taking this test forever.

_____ 33. Our investigation shows that the distribution department is more efficient then the sales department.

_____ 34. My courses this semester are totally different than last semester's.

_____ 35. Do you know where this shipment is going to?

H. COMMAS

For each of the following sentences, insert any necessary commas. Count the number of commas that you added. Write that number in the space provided. All punctuation must be correct to receive credit for the sentence. If a sentence requires no punctuation, write *C*.

2 _____ **Example:** However, because of developments in theory and computer applications, management is becoming more of a science.

_____ 36. For example management determines how orders assignments and responsibilities are delegated to employees.

_____ 37. Your order Mrs. Tahan will be sent from Toronto Ontario on July 10.

_____ 38. When you need service on any of your pieces of equipment we will be happy to help you Mr. Hamel.

_____ 39. Kevin Long who is the project manager at Techdata suggested that I call you.

_____ 40. You have purchased from us often and your payments in the past have always been prompt.

I. COMMAS AND SEMICOLONS

Add commas and semicolons to the following sentences. In the space provided, write the number of punctuation marks that you added.

_____ 41. The salesperson turned in her report however she did not indicate what time period it covered.

_____ 42. Some interest payments may be tax deductible dividend payments are not.

_____ 43. We are opening a branch office in Kelowna and hope to be able to serve all your needs from that office by the middle of January.

44. As suggested by the committee we must first secure adequate funding then we may consider expansion. _____

45. When you begin to conduct research for a report consider the many library sources available namely books, periodicals, government publications, and databases. _____

J. COMMAS AND SEMICOLONS

46. After our office manager had the printer repaired it jammed again within the first week although we treated it carefully. _____

47. Our experienced courteous staff has been trained to anticipate your every need. _____

48. In view of the new law that went into effect April 1 our current liability insurance must be increased however we cannot immediately afford it. _____

49. As stipulated in our contract your agency will supervise our graphic arts and purchase our media time. _____

50. As you know Mrs. Laurendeau we aim for long-term business relationships not quick profits. _____

K. OTHER PUNCTUATION

Each of the following sentences may require dashes, colons, question marks, quotation marks, periods, and underscores, as well as commas and semicolons. Add the appropriate punctuation to each sentence. Then, in the space provided, write the total number of marks that you added.

Example: Price , service , and reliability – these are our prime considerations.   3 _____

51. The following members of the department volunteered to help on Saturday Kim Carlos Dan and Sylvia. _____

52. Mr Danner, Miss Reed, and Mrs Rossi usually arrived at the office by 8 30 am. _____

53. Three of our top managers Tim, Marcy, and Asad received cash bonuses. _____

54. Did the vice president really say "All employees may take Friday off _____

55. We are trying to locate an edition of Maclean's that carried an article entitled E-mail Beats Office Politics _____

L. CAPITALIZATION

For each of the following sentences, circle any letter that should be capitalized. In the space provided, write the number of circles that you marked.

Example: Ⓥice Ⓟresident Ⓓaniels devised a procedure for expediting purchase orders from Ⓐrea 4 warehouses.   4 _____

56. although english was his first language, he also spoke spanish and could read french. _____

57. on a trip to the east coast, uncle henry visited the bay of fundy. _____

58. karen enrolled in classes in history, german, and sociology. _____

59. the business manager and the vice president each received a new apple computer. _____

60. jane lee, the president of kendrick, inc., will speak to our conference in the spring. _____

M. Number Style

Decide whether the numbers in the following sentences should be written as words or as figures. Each sentence either is correct or has one error. If it is correct, write *C*. If it has an error, underline it and write the correct form in the space provided.

five _____ **Example:** The bank had <u>5</u> branches in three suburbs.

_____ 61. More than 2,000,000 people have visited the Parliament Buildings in the past five years.

_____ 62. Of the 35 letters sent out, only three were returned.

_____ 63. We set aside forty dollars for petty cash, but by December 1 our fund was depleted.

_____ 64. The meeting is scheduled for May 5th at 3 p.m.

_____ 65. In the past 20 years, nearly 15 percent of the population changed residences at least once.

GRAMMAR/MECHANICS PROFILE

In the spaces at the right, place a check mark to indicate the number of correct answers you had in each category of the Grammar/Mechanics Diagnostic Test.

		NUMBER CORRECT*				
		5	4	3	2	1
1–5	Plural Nouns	_____	_____	_____	_____	_____
6–10	Possessive Nouns	_____	_____	_____	_____	_____
11–15	Pronouns	_____	_____	_____	_____	_____
16–20	Verb Agreement	_____	_____	_____	_____	_____
21–25	Verb Mood, Voice, and Tense	_____	_____	_____	_____	_____
26–30	Adjectives and Adverbs	_____	_____	_____	_____	_____
31–35	Prepositions and Conjunctions	_____	_____	_____	_____	_____
36–40	Commas	_____	_____	_____	_____	_____
41–45	Commas and Semicolons	_____	_____	_____	_____	_____
46–50	Commas and Semicolons	_____	_____	_____	_____	_____
51–55	Other Punctuation	_____	_____	_____	_____	_____
56–60	Capitalization	_____	_____	_____	_____	_____
61–65	Number Style	_____	_____	_____	_____	_____

*Note: 5 = have excellent skills; 4 = need light review; 3 = need careful review; 2 = need to study rules; 1 = need serious study and follow-up reinforcement.

GRAMMAR REVIEW

PARTS OF SPEECH (1.01)

1.01 Functions. English has eight parts of speech. Knowing the functions of the parts of speech helps writers better understand how words are used and how sentences are formed.

a. *Nouns:* name persons, places, things, qualities, concepts, and activities (for example, *Kevin, Montreal, computer, joy, work, banking*).

b. *Pronouns:* substitute for nouns (for example, *he, she, it, they*).

c. *Verbs:* show the action of a subject or join the subject to words that describe it (for example, *walk, heard, is, was jumping*).

d. *Adjectives:* describe or limit nouns and pronouns and often answer the questions *what kind? how many?* and *which one?* (for example, *fast* sale, *ten* items, *good* manager).

e. *Adverbs:* describe or limit verbs, adjectives, or other adverbs and frequently answer the questions *when? how? where?* or *to what extent?* (for example, *tomorrow, rapidly, here, very*).

f. *Prepositions:* join nouns or pronouns to other words in sentences (for example, desk *in* the office, ticket *for* me, letter *to* you).

g. *Conjunctions:* connect words or groups of words (for example, you *and* I, Mark *or* Jill).

h. *Interjections:* express strong feelings (for example, *Wow! Oh!*).

NOUNS (1.02–1.06)

Nouns name persons, places, things, qualities, concepts, and activities. Nouns may be classified into a number of categories.

1.02 Concrete and Abstract. Concrete nouns name specific objects that can be seen, heard, felt, tasted, or smelled. Examples of concrete nouns are *telephone, dollar, IBM,* and *apple*. Abstract nouns name generalized ideas such as qualities or concepts that are not easily pictured. *Emotion, power,* and *tension* are typical examples of abstract nouns.

Business writing is most effective when concrete words predominate. It's clearer to write *We need 16-pound bond paper* than to write *We need office supplies*. Chapter 3 provides practice in developing skill in the use of concrete words.

1.03 Proper and Common. Proper nouns name specific persons, places, or things and are always capitalized *(Nortel, Winnipeg, Jennifer)*. All other nouns are common nouns and begin with lowercase letters *(company, city, student)*. Rules for capitalization are presented in Sections 3.01–3.16.

1.04 Singular and Plural. Singular nouns name one item; plural nouns name more than one. From a practical view, writers seldom have difficulty with singular nouns. They may need help, however, with the formation and spelling of plural nouns.

1.05 Guidelines for Forming Noun Plurals

a. Add *s* to most nouns *(chair, chairs; mortgage, mortgages; Monday, Mondays)*.

b. Add *es* to nouns ending in *s, x, z, ch,* or *sh* (*bench, benches; boss, bosses; box, boxes; Schultz, Schultzes*).

c. Change the spelling in irregular noun plurals *(man, men; foot, feet; mouse, mice; child, children)*.

d. Add *s* to nouns that end in *y* when *y* is preceded by a vowel *(jockey, jockeys; valley, valleys; journey, journeys)*.

e. Drop the *y* and add *ies* to nouns ending in *y* when *y* is preceded by a consonant *(company, companies; city, cities; secretary, secretaries)*.

f. Add *s* to the principal word in most compound expressions *(editors in chief, fathers-in-law, bills of lading, runners-up)*.

g. Add *s* to most numerals, letters of the alphabet, words referred to as words, degrees, and abbreviations *(5s, 1990s, Bs, ands, CAs, yrs.)*. Note that metric abbreviations take neither a period nor an *s* to make the *m* plural *(1g, 2g)*.

h. Add *'s* only to clarify letters of the alphabet that might be misread, such as *A's, I's, M's,* and *U's* and *i's, p's,* and *q's*. An expression like *c.o.d.s* requires no apostrophe because it would not easily be misread.

1.06 Collective Nouns. Nouns such as *staff, faculty, committee, group,* and *herd* refer to a collection of people, animals, or objects. Collective nouns may be considered singular or plural depending on their action. See Section 1.10i for a discussion of collective nouns and their agreement with verbs.

REVIEW EXERCISE A—NOUNS

In the space provided for each item, write *a* or *b* to complete the following statements correctly. When you finish, compare your responses with those provided. For each item on which you need review, consult the numbered principle shown in parentheses.

1. Nearly all (a) *editor in chiefs,* (b) *editors in chief* demand observance of standard punctuation.
2. Several (a) *jockeys,* (b) *jockies* were honoured at the banquet.
3. Please write to the (a) *Davis's,* (b) *Davises* about the missing contract.
4. The industrial complex has space for nine additional (a) *companys,* (b) *companies*.
5. That accounting firm employs two (a) *secretaries,* (b) *secretarys* for five CAs.
6. Four of the wooden (a) *benches,* (b) *benchs* must be repaired.
7. The home was constructed with numerous (a) *chimneys,* (b) *chimnies*.
8. Tours of the production facility are made only on (a) *Tuesdays,* (b) *Tuesday's*.
9. We asked the (a) *Jones's,* (b) *Joneses* to contribute to the fundraising drive.
10. Both my (a) *sister-in-laws,* (b) *sisters-in-law* agreed to the settlement.
11. The stock market is experiencing abnormal (a) *ups and downs,* (b) *up's and down's*.
12. Three (a) *mouses,* (b) *mice* were seen near the trash cans.
13. This office is unusually quiet on (a) *Sundays,* (b) *Sunday's*.
14. Several news (a) *dispatchs,* (b) *dispatches* were released during the strike.
15. Two major (a) *countries,* (b) *countrys* will participate in trade negotiations.
16. Some young children have difficulty writing their (a) *bs and ds,* (b) *b's and d's*.
17. The (a) *board of directors,* (b) *boards of directors* of all the major companies participated in the surveys.
18. In their letter the (a) *Metzes,* (b) *Metzs* said they intended to purchase the property.
19. In shipping we are careful to include all (a) *bill of sales,* (b) *bills of sale*.
20. Over the holidays many (a) *turkies,* (b) *turkeys* were consumed.

1. b (1.05f) 3. b (1.05b) 5. a (1.05e) 7. a (1.05d) 9. b (1.05b) 11. a (1.05g) 13. a (1.05a)
15. a (1.05e) 17. b (1.05f) 19. b (1.05f) (Only odd-numbered answers are provided. Consult your instructor for the others.)

PRONOUNS (1.07–1.09)

Pronouns substitute for nouns. They are classified by case.

1.07 Case. Pronouns function in three cases, as shown in the following chart.

Nominative Case *(Used for subjects of verbs and subject complements)*	**Objective Case** *(Used for objects of prepositions and objects of verbs)*	**Possessive Case** *(Used to show possession)*
I	me	my, mine
we	us	our, ours
you	you	your, yours
he	him	his
she	her	her, hers
it	it	its
they	them	their, theirs
who, whoever	whom, whomever	whose

1.08 Guidelines for Selecting Pronoun Case

a. Pronouns that serve as subjects of verbs must be in the nominative case:

   He and *I* (not *Him* and *me*) decided to apply for the jobs.

b. Pronouns that follow linking verbs (such as *am, is, are, was, were, be, being, been*) and rename the words to which they refer must be in the nominative case: It must have been *she* (not *her*) who placed the order. (The nominative-case pronoun *she* follows the linking verb *been* and renames *it*.)

   If it was *he* (not *him*) who called, I have his number. (The nominative-case pronoun *he* follows the linking verb *was* and renames *it*.)

c. Pronouns that serve as objects of verbs or objects of prepositions must be in the objective case:

   Mr. Laporte asked *them* to complete the proposal. (The pronoun *them* is the object of the verb *asked*.)

   All computer printouts are sent to *him*. (The pronoun *him* is the object of the preposition *to*.)

   Just between you and *me*, profits are falling. (The pronoun *me* is one of the objects of the preposition *between*.)

d. Pronouns that show ownership must be in the possessive case. Possessive pronouns (such as *hers, yours, ours, theirs*, and *its*) require no apostrophes:

   We found my diskette, but *yours* (not *your's*) may be lost.

   All parts of the machine, including *its* (not *it's*) motor, were examined.

   The house and *its* (not *it's*) contents will be auctioned.

   Don't confuse possessive pronouns and contractions. Contractions are shortened forms of subject-verb phrases (such as *it's* for *it is, there's* for *there is*, and *they're* for *they are*).

e. When a pronoun appears in combination with a noun or another pronoun, ignore the extra noun or pronoun and its conjunction. In this way pronoun case becomes more obvious:

The manager promoted Jeff and *me* (not *I*). (Ignore *Jeff and*.)

f. In statements of comparison, mentally finish the comparative by adding the implied missing words:

Next year I hope to earn as much as *she*. (The verb *earns* is implied here: . . . *as much as she earns*.)

g. Pronouns must be in the same case as the words they replace or rename. When pronouns are used with appositives, ignore the appositive:

A new contract was signed by *us* (not *we*) employees. (Temporarily ignore the appositive *employees* in selecting the pronoun.)

We (not *us*) citizens have formed our own organization. (Temporarily ignore the appositive *citizens* in selecting the pronoun.)

h. Pronouns ending in *self* should be used only when they refer to previously mentioned nouns or pronouns:

Robert and *I* (not *myself*) are in charge of the campaign.

i. Use objective-case pronouns as objects of the prepositions *between, but, like*, and *except:*

Everyone but John and *him* (not *he*) qualified for the bonus.

Employees like Miss Gallucci and *her* (not *she*) are hard to replace.

j. Use *who* or *whoever* for nominative-case constructions and *whom* or *whomever* for objective-case constructions. In making the correct choice, it's sometimes helpful to substitute *he* for *who* or *whoever* and *him* for *whom* or *whomever:*

For *whom* was this book ordered? *(This book was ordered for him/whom?)*

Who did you say would drop by? *(Who/he . . . would drop by?)*

Deliver the package to *whoever* opens the door. (In this sentence the clause *whoever opens the door* functions as the object of the preposition *to*. Within the clause itself *whoever* is the subject of the verb *opens*. Again, substitution of *he* might be helpful: *He/Whoever opens the door*.)

1.09 Guidelines for Making Pronouns Agree With Their Antecedents. Pronouns must agree with the words to which they refer (their antecedents) in gender and in number.

a. Use masculine pronouns to refer to masculine antecedents, feminine pronouns to refer to feminine antecedents, and neutral pronouns to refer to antecedents without gender:

The man opened *his* office door. (Masculine gender applies.)

A woman sat at *her* desk. (Feminine gender applies.)

This computer and *its* programs fit our needs. (Neutral gender applies.)

b. Use singular pronouns to refer to singular antecedents:

Common-gender pronouns (such as *him* or *his*) traditionally have been used when the gender of the antecedent is unknown. Business writers construct sentences to avoid the need for common-gender pronouns. Study these examples for alternatives to the use of common-gender pronouns:*

Each student must submit *a* report on Monday.

All students must submit *their* reports on Monday.

Each student must submit *his or her* report on Monday. (This alternative is least acceptable since it is wordy and calls attention to itself.)

c. Use singular pronouns to refer to singular indefinite subjects and plural pronouns for plural indefinite subjects. Words such as *anyone, something,* and *anybody* are considered indefinite because they refer to no specific person or object. Some indefinite pronouns are always singular; others are always plural.

Always Singular		Always Plural
anybody	everything	both
anyone	neither	few
anything	nobody	many
each	no one	several
either	somebody	
everyone	someone	

Somebody in the group of touring women left *her* (not *their*) purse in the museum.

Either of the companies has the right to exercise *its* (not *their*) option to sell stock.

d. Use singular pronouns to refer to collective nouns and organization names:

The engineering staff is moving *its* (not *their*) facilities on Friday. (The singular pronoun *its* agrees with the collective noun *staff* because the members of staff function as a single unit.)

Jones, Cohen, and James Inc. *has* (not *have*) cancelled *its* (not *their*) contract with us. (The singular pronoun *its* agrees with *Jones, Cohen, and James Inc.*, because the members of the organization are operating as a single unit.)

e. Use a plural pronoun to refer to two antecedents joined by *and*, whether the antecedents are singular or plural:

Our company president and our vice president will be submitting *their* expenses shortly.

f. Ignore intervening phrases—introduced by expressions such as *together with, as well as*, and *in addition to*—that separate a pronoun from its antecedent:

One of our managers, along with several salespeople, is planning *his* retirement. (If you wish to emphasize both subjects equally, join them with *and:* One of our managers *and* several salespeople are planning *their* retirements.)

g. When antecedents are joined by *or* or *nor*, make the pronoun agree with the antecedent closest to it.

Neither Jackie nor Kim wanted *her* (not *their*) desk moved.

* See Chapter 4, pages 74–75, for addition discussion of common-gender pronouns and inclusive language.

REVIEW EXERCISE B—PRONOUNS

In the space provided for each item, write *a*, *b*, or *c* to complete the statement accurately. When you finish, compare your responses with those provided below. For each item on which you need review, consult the numbered principle shown in parentheses.

_____

_____

_____

_____

_____

_____

_____

_____

_____

_____

_____

_____

_____

_____

_____

_____

_____

1. Mr. Behrens and (a) *I*, (b) *myself* will be visiting sales personnel in the New Brunswick district next week.
2. James promised that he would call; was it (a) *him*, (b) *he* who left the message?
3. Much preparation for the seminar was made by Mrs. Washington and (a) *I*, (b) *me* before the brochures were sent out.
4. The Employee Benefits Committee can be justly proud of (a) *its*, (b) *their* achievements.
5. A number of inquiries were addressed to Jeff and (a) *I*, (b) *me*, (c) *myself*.
6. (a) *Who*, (b) *Whom* did you say the letter was addressed to?
7. When you visit Mutual Trust, inquire about (a) *its*, (b) *it's* certificates.
8. Copies of all reports are to be reviewed by Mr. Khan and (a) *I*, (b) *me*, (c) *myself*.
9. Apparently one of the female applicants forgot to sign (a) *her*, (b) *their* application.
10. Both the printer and (a) *it's*, (b) *its* cover are missing.
11. I've never known any man who could work as fast as (a) *him*, (b) *he*.
12. Just between you and (a) *I*, (b) *me*, the share price will fall by afternoon.
13. Give the supplies to (a) *whoever*, (b) *whomever* ordered them.
14. (a) *Us*, (b) *We* employees have been given an unusual voice in choosing benefits.
15. On her return from Mexico, Mrs. Hamilton, along with many other passengers, had to open (a) *her*, (b) *their* luggage for inspection.
16. Either James or Robert will have (a) *his*, (b) *their* work reviewed next week.
17. Each person who becomes a charter member of this organization will be able to have (a) *his*, (b) *his or her* name inscribed on a commemorative plaque.
18. We are certain that (a) *our's*, (b) *ours* is the smallest wristwatch available.
19. Everyone has completed the reports except Debbie and (a) *he*, (b) *him*.
20. Lack of work disturbs Mr. Thomas as much as (a) *I*, (b) *me*.

1. a (1.08h)   3. b (1.08c)   5. b (1.08c, 1.08e)   7. a (1.09a)   9. a (1.09a)   11. b (1.08f)   13. a (1.08j)   15. a (1.09f)   17. b (1.09b)   19. b (1.08i)

CUMULATIVE EDITING QUIZ 1

Use proofreading marks (see Appendix B) to correct errors in the following sentences. All errors must be corrected to receive credit for the sentence. Check with your instructor for the answers.

Example: Nicholas and ~~him~~ he made all there (ir) money in the 1990's.

1. Just between you and I, whom do you think would make the best manager?

2. Either Stacy or me is responsible for correcting all errors in news dispatchs.

3. Several of the donkies found there way back before sunset.

4. One of the secretarys warned Sharif and I to get the name of whomever answered the phone.

5. The committee sent there decision to the president and I last week.

6. Who should Angela or me call to verify the three bill of sales received today?

7. Several of we employees complained that it's keyboard made the new computer difficult to use.

8. All the CEO's agreed that the low interest rates of the 1990's could not continue.

9. Every customer has a right to expect there inquirys to be treated courteously.

10. You may send you're contribution to Eric or myself or to whomever is listed as your representative.

VERBS (1.10–1.15)

Verbs show the action of a subject or join the subject to words that describe it.

1.10 Guidelines for Agreement With Subjects. One of the most troublesome areas in English is subject-verb agreement. Consider the following guidelines for making verbs agree with subjects.

a.   A singular subject requires a singular verb:

The stock market *opens* at 10 a.m. (The singular verb *opens* agrees with the singular subject *market*.)

He *doesn't* (not *don't*) work on Saturday.

b.   A plural subject requires a plural verb:

On the packing slip several items *seem* (not *seems*) to be missing.

c.   A verb agrees with its subject regardless of prepositional phrases that may intervene:

This list of management objectives *is* extensive. (The singular verb *is* agrees with the singular subject *list*.)

Every one of the letters *shows* (not *show*) proper form.

d.   A verb agrees with its subject regardless of intervening phrases introduced by *as well as, in addition to, such as, including, together with*, and similar expressions:

An important memo, together with several letters, *was* misplaced. (The singular verb *was* agrees with the singular subject *memo*.)

The president as well as several other top-level executives *approves* of our proposal. (The singular verb *approves* agrees with the subject *president*.)

e.   A verb agrees with its subject regardless of the location of the subject:

Here *is* one of the letters about which you asked. (The verb *is* agrees with its subject *one*, even though it precedes *one*. The adverb *here* cannot function as a subject.)

There *are* many problems yet to be resolved. (The verb *are* agrees with the subject *problems*. The adverb *there* cannot function as a subject.)

In the next office *are* several word processing machines. (In this inverted sentence the verb *are* must agree with the subject *machines*.)

f. Subjects joined by *and* require a plural verb:

Analyzing the reader and organizing a strategy *are* the first steps in letter writing. (The plural verb *are* agrees with the two subjects, *analyzing* and *organizing*.)

The tone and the wording of the letter *were* persuasive. (The plural verb *were* agrees with the two subjects, *tone* and *wording*.)

g. Subjects joined by *or* or *nor* may require singular or plural verbs. Make the verb agree with the closer subject:

Neither the memo nor the report *is* ready. (The singular verb *is* agrees with *report*, the closer of the two subjects.)

h. The following indefinite pronouns are singular and require singular verbs: *anyone, anybody, anything, each, either, every, everyone, everybody, everything, many a, neither, nobody, nothing, someone, somebody*, and *something*:

Either of the alternatives that you present *is* acceptable. (The verb *is* agrees with the singular subject *either*.)

i. Collective nouns may take singular or plural verbs, depending on whether the members of the group are operating as a unit or individually:

Our management team *is* united in its goal.

The faculty *are* sharply *divided* on the tuition issue. (Although acceptable, this sentence sounds better recast: The faculty *members* are sharply divided on the tuition issue.)

j. Organization names and titles of publications, although they may appear to be plural, are singular and require singular verbs.

Clark, Anderson, and Horne Inc. *has* (not *have*) hired a marketing consultant.

Thousands of Investment Tips is (not *are*) again on the best-seller list.

1.11 Voice. Voice is that property of verbs that shows whether the subject of the verb acts or is acted upon. Active-voice verbs direct action from the subject toward the object of the verb. Passive-voice verbs direct action toward the subject.

Active voice: Our employees *write* excellent letters.
Passive voice: Excellent letters *are written* by our employees.

Business writing that emphasizes active-voice verbs is generally preferred because it is specific and forceful. However, passive-voice constructions can help a writer be tactful. Strategies for effective use of active- and passive-voice verbs are presented in Chapter 4.

1.12 Mood. Three verb moods express the attitude or thought of the speaker or writer toward a subject: (1) the indicative mood expresses a fact; (2) the imperative mood expresses a command; and (3) the subjunctive mood expresses a doubt, a conjecture, or a suggestion.

Indicative: I *am looking* for a job.
Imperative: *Begin* your job search with the want ads.
Subjunctive: I wish I *were* working.

Only the subjunctive mood creates problems for most speakers and writers. The most common use of the subjunctive mood occurs in clauses including *if* or *wish*. In such clauses substitute the subjunctive verb *were* for the indicative verb *was*:

If he *were* (not *was*) in my position, he would understand.

Mr. Dworski acts as if he *were* (not *was*) the boss.

I wish I *were* (not *was*) able to ship your order.

The subjunctive mood may be used to maintain goodwill while conveying negative information. The sentence *I wish I were able to ship your order* sounds more pleasing to a customer than *I cannot ship your order*, although, for all practical purposes, both sentences convey the same negative message.

1.13 Tense. Verbs show the time of an action by their tense. Speakers and writers can use six tenses to show the time of sentence action; for example:

Present tense:	I *work;* he *works.*
Past tense:	I *worked;* she *worked.*
Future tense:	I *will work;* he *will work.*
Present perfect tense:	I *have worked;* he *has worked.*
Past perfect tense:	I *had worked;* she *had worked.*
Future perfect tense:	I *will have worked;* he *will have worked.*

1.14 Guidelines for Verb Tense

a. Use the present tense for statements that, although they may be introduced by past-tense verbs, continue to be true:

What did you say his name *is?* (Use the present tense *is* if his name has not changed.)

b. Avoid unnecessary shifts in verb tenses:

The manager *saw* (not *sees*) a great deal of work yet to be completed and *remained* to do it herself.

Although unnecessary shifts in verb tense are to be avoided, not all the verbs within one sentence have to be in the same tense; for example:

She *said* (past tense) that she *likes* (present tense) to work late.

1.15 Irregular Verbs. Irregular verbs cause difficulty for some writers and speakers. Unlike regular verbs irregular verbs do not form the past tense and past participle by adding *-ed* to the present form. Here is a partial list of selected troublesome irregular verbs. Consult a dictionary if you are in doubt about a verb form.

TROUBLESOME IRREGULAR VERBS

Present	**Past**	**Past Participle** *(always use helping verbs)*
begin	began	begun
break	broke	broken
choose	chose	chosen
come	came	come
drink	drank	drunk
go	went	gone
lay (to place)	laid	laid

Present	Past	Past Participle
lie (to rest)	lay	lain
ring	rang	rung
see	saw	seen
write	wrote	written

a. Use only past-tense verbs to express the past tense. Notice that no helping verbs are used to indicate the simple past tense:

The auditors *went* (not *have went*) over our books carefully.

He *came* (not *had come*) to see us yesterday.

b. Use past participle forms for actions completed before the present time. Notice that past participle forms require helping verbs:

Steve had *gone* (not *went*) before we called. (The past participle *gone* is used with the helping verb *had*.)

c. Avoid inconsistent shifts in subject, voice, and mood. Pay particular attention to this problem area, for undesirable shifts are often characteristic of student writing.

Inconsistent: When Mrs. Moscovitch read the report, the error was found. (The first clause is in the active voice; the second, passive.)

Improved: When Mrs. Moscovitch read the report, she found the error. (Both clauses are in the active voice.)

Inconsistent: The clerk should first conduct an inventory. Then supplies should be requisitioned. (The first sentence is in the active voice; the second, passive.)

Improved: The clerk should first conduct an inventory. Then he or she should requisition supplies. (Both sentences are in the active voice.)

Inconsistent: All workers must wear security badges, and you must also sign a daily time card. (This sentence contains an inconsistent shift in subject from *all workers* in first clause to *you* in second clause.)

Improved: All workers must wear security badges, and they must also sign a daily time card.

Inconsistent: Begin the transaction by opening an account; then you enter the customer's name. (This sentence contains an inconsistent shift from the imperative mood in first clause to the indicative mood in second clause.)

Improved: Begin the transaction by opening an account; then enter the customer's name. (Both clauses are now in the indicative mood.)

REVIEW EXERCISE C—VERBS

In the space provided for each item, write *a* or *b* to complete the statement accurately. When you finish, compare your responses with those provided. For each item on which you need review, consult the numbered principle shown in parentheses.

1. A list of payroll deductions for our employees (a) *was*, (b) *were* sent to the human resources manager.
2. There (a) *is*, (b) *are* a customer service representative and two salespeople waiting to see you.

3. Increased computer use and more complex automated systems (a) *is*, (b) *are* found in business today. _____

4. Crews, Meliotes, and Bove, Inc., (a) *has*, (b) *have* opened an office in St. John's. _____

5. Yesterday Mrs. Phillips (a) *choose*, (b) *chose* a new office on the second floor. _____

6. The man who called said that his name (a) *is*, (b) *was* Johnson. _____

7. *Office Computing and Networks* (a) *is*, (b) *are* beginning a campaign to increase readership. _____

8. Either of the flight times (a) *appears*, (b) *appear* to fit my proposed itinerary. _____

9. If you had (a) *saw*, (b) *seen* the rough draft, you would better appreciate the final copy. _____

10. Across from our office (a) *is*, (b) *are* the parking lot and the information office. _____

11. Although we have (a) *began*, (b) *begun* to replace outmoded equipment, the pace is slow. _____

12. Specific training as well as ample experience (a) *is*, (b) *are* important for that position. _____

13. Inflation and increased job opportunities (a) *is*, (b) *are* resulting in increased numbers of working women. _____

14. Neither the organizing nor the staffing of the program (a) *has been*, (b) *have been* completed. _____

15. If I (a) *was*, (b) *were* you, I would ask for a raise. _____

16. If you had (a) *wrote*, (b) *written* last week, we could have sent a brochure. _____

17. The hydraulic equipment that you ordered (a) *is*, (b) *are* packed and will be shipped Friday. _____

18. One of the reasons that sales have declined in recent years (a) *is*, (b) *are* the lack of effective advertising. _____

19. Either of the proposed laws (a) *is*, (b) *are* going to affect our business negatively. _____

20. Bankruptcy statutes (a) *requires*, (b) *require* that a failed company pay its debts to secured creditors first. _____

---

1. a (1.10c)   3. b (1.10f)   5. b (1.15a)   7. a (1.10j)   9. b (1.15b)   11. b (1.15b)   13. b (1.10f)
15. b (1.12)   17. a (1.10a)   19. a (1.10h)

REVIEW EXERCISE D—VERBS

In the following sentence pairs, choose the one that illustrates consistency in the use of subject, voice, and mood. Write *a* or *b* in the space provided. When you finish, compare your responses with those provided. For each item on which you need review, consult the numbered principle shown in parentheses.

1. (a) You need more than a knowledge of equipment; one also must be able to interact well with people. _____
   (b) You need more than a knowledge of equipment; you also must be able to interact well with people.

2. (a) Maurice and Jon were eager to continue, but Bob wanted to quit. _____
   (b) Maurice and Jon were eager to continue, but Bob wants to quit.

3. (a) The salesperson should consult the price list; then you can give an accurate quote to a customer. _____
   (b) The salesperson should consult the price list; then he or she can give an accurate quote to a customer.

4. (a) Read all the instructions first; then you install the printer program. _____

(b) Read all the instructions first, and then install the printer program.

5. (a) She was an enthusiastic manager who always had a smile for everyone.
    (b) She was an enthusiastic manager who always has a smile for everyone.

1. b (1.15c)   3. b (1.15c)   5. a (1.14b)

CUMULATIVE EDITING QUIZ 2

Use proofreading marks (see Appendix B) to correct errors in the following sentences. All errors must be corrected to receive credit for the sentence. Check with your instructor for the answers.

1. Assets and liabilitys is what my partner and myself must investigate.

2. If I was you, I would ask whomever is in charge for their opinion.

3. The faculty agree that it's first concern is educating students.

4. The book and it's cover was printed in Japan.

5. Waiting to see you is a sales representative and a job applicant who you told to drop by.

6. Every employee could have picked up his ballot if he had went to the cafeteria.

7. Your choice of mutual funds and bonds are reduced by this plan and it's restrictions.

8. My uncle and her come to visit my parents and myself last night.

9. According to both editor in chiefs, the tone and wording of all our letters needs revision.

10. The Davis'es, about who the article was written, said they were unconcerned with the up's and down's of the stock market.

ADJECTIVES AND ADVERBS (1.16–1.17)

Adjectives describe or limit nouns and pronouns. They often answer the questions *what kind? how many?* or *which one?* Adverbs describe or limit verbs, adjectives, or other adverbs. They often answer the questions *when? how? where?* or *to what extent?*

1.16 Forms. Most adjectives and adverbs have three forms, or degrees: positive, comparative, and superlative.

	Positive	**Comparative**	**Superlative**
Adjective:	clear	clearer	clearest
Adverb:	clearly	more clearly	most clearly

Some adjectives and adverbs have irregular forms.

	Positive	**Comparative**	**Superlative**
Adjective:	good	better	best
	bad	worse	worst
Adverb:	well	better	best

Adjectives and adverbs composed of two or more syllables are usually compared by the use of *more* and *most;* for example:

The Payroll Department is *more efficient* than the Shipping Department.

Payroll is the *most efficient* department in our organization.

1.17 Guidelines for Use

a. Use the comparative degree of the adjective or adverb to compare two persons or things; use the superlative degree to compare three or more:

Of the two letters, which is *better* (not *best*)?

Of all the plans, we like this one *best* (not *better*).

b. Do not create a double comparative or superlative by using *-er* with *more* or *-est* with *most:*

His explanation couldn't have been *clearer* (not *more clearer*).

c. A linking verb (*is, are, look, seem, feel, sound, appear,* and so forth) may introduce a word that describes the verb's subject. In this case be certain to use an adjective, not an adverb:

The characters on the monitor look *bright* (not *brightly*). (Use the adjective *bright* because it follows the linking verb *look* and modifies the noun *characters.* It answers the question *What kind of characters?*)

The company's letter made the customer feel *bad* (not *badly*). (The adjective *bad* follows the linking verb *feel* and describes the noun *customer.*)

d. Use adverbs, not adjectives, to describe or limit the action of verbs:

The business is running *smoothly* (not *smooth*). (Use the adverb *smoothly* to describe the action of the verb *is running. Smoothly* tells how the business is running.)

Don't take his remark *personally* (not *personal*). (The adverb *personally* describes the action of the verb *take.*)

e. Two or more adjectives that are joined to create a compound modifier before a noun should be hyphenated:

The *four-year-old* child was tired.

Our agency is planning a *coast-to-coast* campaign.

Hyphenate a compound modifier following a noun only if your dictionary shows the hyphen(s):

All her purchases were *tax-exempt.* (Include the hyphen because most dictionaries do.)

The tired child was four years old. (Omit the hyphens because the expression follows the word it describes, *child,* and because dictionaries do not indicate hyphens.)

f. Keep adjectives and adverbs close to the words that they modify:

She asked for a cup of *hot* coffee (not a *hot cup of coffee*).

Patty had *only* two days of vacation left (not *Patty only had two days*).

Students may sit in the *first* five rows (not *in the five first rows*).

He has saved *almost* enough money for the trip (not *He has almost saved*).

g. Don't confuse the adverb *there* with the possessive pronoun *their* or the contraction *they're:*

Put the documents *there*. (The adverb *there* means "at that place or at that point.")

There are two reasons for the change. (The adverb *there* is used as an expletive or filler preceding a linking verb.)

We already have *their* specifications. (The possessive pronoun *their* shows ownership.)

They're coming to inspect today. (The contraction *they're* is a shortened form of *they are*.)

REVIEW EXERCISE E—ADJECTIVES AND ADVERBS

In the space provided for each item, write *a, b,* or *c* to complete the statement accurately. If two sentences are shown, select *a* or *b* to indicate the one that expresses the thought more effectively. When you finish, compare your responses with those provided. For each item on which you need review, consult the numbered principle shown in parentheses.

1. After the interview, Krishnan looked (a) *calm*, (b) *calmly*.
2. If you had been more (a) *careful*, (b) *carefuller*, the box might not have broken.
3. Because a new manager was appointed, the advertising campaign is running very (a) *smooth*, (b) *smoothly*.
4. To avoid a (a) *face to face*, (b) *face-to-face* confrontation, she wrote a letter.
5. Darren completed the employment test (a) *satisfactorily*, (b) *satisfactory*.
6. I felt (a) *bad*, (b) *badly* that he was not promoted.
7. Which is the (a) *more*, (b) *most* dependable of the two models?
8. Can you determine exactly what (a) *there*, (b) *their*, (c) *they're* company wants us to do?
9. Of all the copiers we tested, this one is the (a) *easier*, (b) *easiest* to operate.
10. (a) Mr. Aldron almost was ready to accept the offer.
    (b) Mr. Aldron was almost ready to accept the offer.
11. (a) We only thought that it would take two hours for the test.
    (b) We thought that it would take only two hours for the test.
12. (a) Please bring me a glass of cold water.
    (b) Please bring me a cold glass of water.
13. (a) The committee decided to retain the last ten tickets.
    (b) The committee decided to retain the ten last tickets.
14. New owners will receive a (a) *60-day*, (b) *60 day* trial period.
15. The time passed (a) *quicker*, (b) *more quickly* than we had expected.
16. We offer a (a) *money back*, (b) *money-back* guarantee.
17. Today the financial news is (a) *worse*, (b) *worst* than yesterday.
18. Please don't take his comments (a) *personal*, (b) *personally*.
19. You must check the document (a) *page by page*, (b) *page-by-page*.

20. (a) We try to file only necessary paperwork.
    (b) We only try to file necessary paperwork.

1. a (1.17c)   3. b (1.17d)   5. a (1.17d)   7. a (1.17a)   9. b (1.17a)   11. b (1.17f)   13. a (1.17f)
15. b (1.17d)   17. a (1.17a)   19. a (1.17e)

PREPOSITIONS (1.18)

Prepositions are connecting words that join nouns or pronouns to other words in a sentence. The words *about, at, from, in,* and *to* are examples of prepositions.

1.18 Guidelines for Use

a. Include necessary prepositions:

What type *of* software do you need (not *what type software*)?

I graduated *from* high school two years ago (not *I graduated high school*).

b. Omit unnecessary prepositions:

Where is the meeting? (Not *Where is the meeting at?*)

Both printers work well. (Not *Both of the printers.*)

Where are you going? (Not *Where are you going to?*)

c. Avoid the overuse of prepositional phrases.

Weak: We have received your application for credit at our branch in the
              Halifax area.
Improved: We have received your credit application at our Halifax office.

d. Repeat the preposition before the second of two related elements:

Applicants use the résumé effectively *by* summarizing their most important experiences and *by* relating their education to the jobs sought.

e. Include the second preposition when two prepositions modify a single object:

George's appreciation *of* and aptitude *for* computers led to a promising career.

CONJUNCTIONS (1.19)

Conjunctions connect words, phrases, and clauses. They act as signals, indicating when a thought is being added, contrasted, or altered. Coordinate conjunctions (such as *and, or, but*) and other words that act as connectors (such as *however, therefore, when, as*) tell the reader or listener in what direction a thought is heading. They're like road signs signalling what's ahead.

1.19 Guidelines for Use

a. Use coordinating conjunctions to connect only sentence elements that are parallel or balanced.

Weak: His report was correct and written in a concise manner.
Improved: His report was correct and concise.

| **Weak:** | Management has the capacity to increase fraud, or reduction can be achieved through the policies it adopts. |
| **Improved:** | Management has the capacity to increase or reduce fraud through the policies it adopts. |

b. Do not use the word *like* as a conjunction:

It seems *as if* (not *like*) this day will never end.

c. Avoid using *when* or *where* inappropriately. A common writing fault occurs in sentences with clauses introduced by *is when* and *is where*. Written English ordinarily requires a noun (or a group of words functioning as a noun) following the linking verb *is*. Instead of acting as conjunctions in these constructions, the words *where* and *when* function as adverbs, creating faulty grammatical equations (adverbs cannot complete equations set up by linking verbs). To avoid the problem, revise the sentence, eliminating *is when* or *is where*.

| **Weak:** | A bullish market is when prices are rising in the stock market. |
| **Improved:** | A bullish market is created when prices are rising in the stock market. |

| **Weak:** | A flowchart is when you make a diagram showing the step-by-step progression of a procedure. |
| **Improved:** | A flowchart is a diagram showing the step-by-step progression of a procedure. |

| **Weak:** | Word processing is where you use a computer and software to write. |
| **Improved:** | Word processing involves the use of a computer and software to write. |

A similar faulty construction occurs in the expression *I hate when*. English requires nouns, noun clauses, or pronouns to act as objects of verbs, not adverbs.

Weak:	I hate when we're asked to work overtime.
Improved:	I hate it when we're asked to work overtime.
Improved:	I hate being asked to work overtime.

d. Don't confuse the adverb *then* with the conjunction *than*. *Then* means "at that time"; *than* indicates the second element in a comparison:

We would rather remodel *than* (not *then*) move.

First, the equipment is turned on; *then* (not *than*) the program is loaded.

REVIEW EXERCISE F—PREPOSITIONS AND CONJUNCTIONS

In the space provided for each item, write *a* or *b* to indicate the sentence that is expressed more effectively. When you finish, compare your responses with those provided. For each item on which you need review, consult the numbered principle shown in parentheses.

_____ 1. (a) Do you know where this shipment is being sent?
                      (b) Do you know where this shipment is being sent to?
_____ 2. (a) She was not aware of nor interested in the company insurance plan.
                      (b) She was not aware nor interested in the company insurance plan.
_____ 3. (a) Mr. Samuels graduated college last June.
                      (b) Mr. Samuels graduated from college last June.

4. (a) "Flextime" is when employees arrive and depart at varying times.
   (b) "Flextime" is a method of scheduling worktime in which employees arrive and depart at varying times. _____

5. (a) Both employees enjoyed setting their own hours.
   (b) Both of the employees enjoyed setting their own hours. _____

6. (a) I hate when the tape sticks in my VCR.
   (b) I hate it when the tape sticks in my VCR. _____

7. (a) What style of typeface should we use?
   (b) What style typeface should we use? _____

8. (a) Business letters should be concise, correct, and written clearly.
   (b) Business letters should be concise, correct, and clear. _____

9. (a) Mediation in a labour dispute occurs when a neutral person helps union and management reach an agreement. _____
   (b) Mediation in a labour dispute is where a neutral person helps union and management reach an agreement.

10. (a) It looks as if the plant will open in early January.
    (b) It looks like the plant will open in early January. _____

11. (a) We expect to finish up the work soon.
    (b) We expect to finish the work soon. _____

12. (a) At the beginning of the program in the fall of the year at the central office, we experienced staffing difficulties. _____
    (b) When the program began last fall, the central office experienced staffing difficulties.

13. (a) Your client may respond by letter or a telephone call may be made. _____
    (b) Your client may respond by letter or by telephone.

14. (a) A résumé is when you make a written presentation of your education and experience for a prospective employer. _____
    (b) A résumé is a written presentation of your education and experience for a prospective employer.

15. (a) Stacy exhibited both an awareness of and talent for developing innovations. _____
    (b) Stacy exhibited both an awareness and talent for developing innovations.

16. (a) This course is harder then I expected.
    (b) This course is harder than I expected. _____

17. (a) An ombudsman is an individual hired by management to investigate and resolve employee complaints. _____
    (b) An ombudsman is when management hires an individual to investigate and resolve employee complaints.

18. (a) I'm uncertain where to take this document to.
    (b) I'm uncertain where to take this document. _____

19. (a) By including accurate data and by writing clearly, you will produce effective memos. _____
    (b) By including accurate data and writing clearly, you will produce effective memos.

20. (a) We need computer operators who can load software, monitor networks, and files must be duplicated. _____
    (b) We need computer operators who can load software, monitor networks, and duplicate files.

---

1. a (1.18b)   3. b (1.18a)   5. a (1.18b)   7. a (1.18a)   9. a (1.19c)   11. b (1.18b)   13. b (1.19a)
15. a (1.18e)   17. a (1.19c)   19. a (1.18d)

Use proofreading marks (see Appendix B) to correct errors in the following sentences. All errors must be corrected to receive credit for the sentence. Check with your instructor for the answers.

1. If Treena types faster then her, shouldn't Treena be hired?

2. We felt badly that Mark's home was not chose for the tour.

3. Neither the company nor the workers is pleased at how slow the talks seems to be progressing.

4. Just between you and I, it's better not to take his remarks personal.

5. After completing there floor by floor inventory, managers will deliver there reports to Mr. Quinn and I.

6. If the telephone was working, Jean and myself could have completed our calls.

7. Powerful software and new hardware allows us to send the newsletter to whomever is currently listed in our database.

8. The thirteen year old girl and her mother was given hot cups of tea after there ordeal.

9. We begun the work two years ago, but personnel and equipment has been especially difficult to obtain.

10. Today's weather is worst then yesterday.

PUNCTUATION REVIEW

COMMAS 1 (2.01–2.04)

2.01 Series. Commas are used to separate three or more equal elements (words, phrases, or short clauses) in a series. To ensure separation of the last two elements, careful writers always use a comma before the conjunction in a series:

> Business letters usually contain a dateline, address, salutation, body, and closing. (This series contains words.)

> The job of an ombudsman is to examine employee complaints, resolve disagreements between management and employees, and ensure fair treatment. (This series contains phrases.)

> Trainees complete basic keyboarding tasks, technicians revise complex documents, and editors proofread completed projects. (This series contains short clauses.)

2.02 Direct Address. Commas are used to set off the names of individuals being addressed:

> Your inquiry, *Mrs. Johnson*, has been referred to me.

> We genuinely hope that we may serve you, *Mr. Lee*.

2.03 Parenthetical Expressions. Skilled writers use parenthetical words, phrases, and clauses to guide the reader from one thought to the next. When these expressions interrupt the flow of a sentence and are unnecessary for its grammatical completeness, they should be set off with commas. Examples of commonly used parenthetical expressions are:

all things considered	however	needless to say
as a matter of fact	in addition	nevertheless
as a result	incidentally	no doubt
as a rule	in fact	of course
at the same time	in my opinion	on the contrary
consequently	in the first place	on the other hand
for example	in the meantime	therefore
furthermore	moreover	under the circum-stances

As a matter of fact, I wrote to you just yesterday. (Phrase used at the beginning of a sentence.)

We will, *in the meantime*, send you a replacement order. (Phrase used in the middle of a sentence.)

Your satisfaction is our first concern, *needless to say.* (Phrase used at the end of a sentence.)

Do not use commas if the expression is necessary for the completeness of the sentence:

Tamara had *no doubt* that she would finish the report. (Omit commas because the expression is necessary for the completeness of the sentence.)

2.04 Dates, Addresses, and Geographical Items. When dates, addresses, and geographical items contain more than one element, the second and succeeding elements are normally set off by commas.

a. Dates:

The conference was held February 2 at our home office. (No comma is needed for one element.)

The conference was held February 2, 1999, at our home office. (Two commas set off the second element.)

The conference was held Tuesday, February 2, 1999, at our home office. (Commas set off the second and third elements.)

In February 1999 the conference was held. (This alternative style omitting commas is acceptable if only the month and year are written.)

b. Addresses:

The letter addressed to Mr. Jim W. Ellman, 600 Novella St., Winnipeg, MB R2H 1R4 should be sent today. (Commas are used between all elements except the province and postal code, which in this special instance are considered a single unit.)

c. Geographical items:

She moved from Windsor, Ontario, to Truro, Nova Scotia. (Commas set off the province unless it appears at the end of the sentence, in which case only one comma is used.)

In separating cities from provinces and days from years, many writers remember the initial comma but forget the final one, as in the examples that follow:

The package from Edmonton, Alberta {,} was lost.

We opened June 1, 1985 {,} and have grown steadily since.

REVIEW EXERCISE G—COMMAS 1

Insert necessary commas in the following sentences. In the space provided write the number of commas that you add. Write *C* if no commas are needed. When you finish, compare your responses with those provided. For each item on which you need review, consult the numbered principle shown in parentheses.

1. As a rule we do not provide complimentary tickets.
2. You may be certain Mr. Kirchoff that your policy will be issued immediately.
3. I have no doubt that your calculations are correct.
4. The safety hazard on the contrary can be greatly reduced if workers wear rubber gloves.
5. Every accredited TV newscaster radio broadcaster and newspaper reporter had access to the media room.
6. Deltech's main offices are located in Vancouver British Columbia and Regina Saskatchewan.
7. The employees who are eligible for promotions are Terry Evelyn Maneesh Rosanna and Yves.
8. During the warranty period of course you are protected from any parts or service charges.
9. Many of our customers include architects engineers lawyers and others who are interested in database management programs.
10. I wonder Mrs. Stevens if you would send my letter of recommendation as soon as possible.
11. The new book explains how to choose appropriate legal protection for ideas trade secrets copyrights patents and restrictive covenants.
12. The factory is scheduled to be moved to 2250 North Main Street Belleville Ontario L4A 1T2 within two years.
13. You may however prefer to correspond directly with the manufacturer in Hong Kong.
14. Are there any alternatives in addition to those that we have already considered?
15. The rally has been scheduled for Monday January 12 at the football stadium.
16. A cheque for the full amount will be sent directly to your home Mrs. Ivanic.
17. Goodstone Tire & Rubber for example recalled 400,000 steelbelted radial tires because some tires failed their rigorous tests.
18. Alex agreed to unlock the office open the mail and check all the equipment in my absence.
19. In the meantime thank you for whatever assistance you are able to furnish.
20. Research facilities were moved from Montreal Quebec to Fredericton New Brunswick.

1. rule, (2.03)   3. C (2.03)   5. newscaster, radio broadcaster, (2.01)   7. Terry, Evelyn, Maneesh, Rosanna, (2.01)   9. architects, engineers, lawyers, (2.01)   11. ideas, trade secrets, copyrights, patents, (2.01)   13. may, however, (2.03)   15. Monday, January 12, (2.04a)   17. Rubber, for example, (2.03)   19. meantime, (2.03)

2.05 Independent Clauses. An independent clause is a group of words that has a subject and a verb, and that could stand as a complete sentence. When two such clauses are joined by *and, or, nor,* or *but,* use a comma before the conjunction:

We can ship your merchandise July 12, *but* we must have your payment first.

Net income before taxes is calculated, *and* this total is then combined with income from operations.

Notice that each independent clause in the preceding two examples could stand alone as a complete sentence. Do not use a comma unless each group of words is a complete thought (that is, has its own subject and verb).

Net income before taxes is calculated *and* is then combined with income from operations. (No comma is needed because no subject follows *and.*)

2.06 Dependent Clauses. Dependent clauses do not make sense by themselves; for their meaning they depend on independent clauses.

a. *Introductory clauses.* When a dependent clause precedes an independent clause, it is followed by a comma. Such clauses are often introduced by *when, if,* and *as:*

When your request came, we immediately responded.

As I mentioned earlier, Sandra James is the manager.

b. *Terminal clauses.* If a dependent clause falls at the end of a sentence, use a comma only if the dependent clause is an afterthought:

The meeting has been rescheduled for October 23, *if I remember correctly.* (Comma used because dependent clause is an afterthought.)

We responded immediately *when we received your request.* (No comma is needed.)

c. *Essential versus nonessential clauses.* If a dependent clause provides information that is unneeded for the grammatical completeness of a sentence, use commas to set it off. In determining whether such a clause is essential or nonessential, ask yourself whether the reader needs the information contained in the clause to identify the word it explains:

Our district sales manager, *who just returned from a trip to our Prairie region office,* prepared this report. (This construction assumes that there is only one district sales manager. Since the sales manager is clearly identified, the dependent clause is not essential and requires commas.)

The salesperson *who just returned from a trip to our Prairie region office* prepared this report. (The dependent clause in this sentence is necessary to identify which salesperson prepared the report. Therefore, use no commas.)

The position of assistant sales manager, *which we discussed with you last week,* is still open. (Careful writers use *which* to introduce nonessential clauses. Commas are also necessary.)

The position *that we discussed with you last week* is still open. (Careful writers use *that* to introduce essential clauses. No commas are used.)

2.07 Phrases. A phrase is a group of related words that lacks both a subject and a verb. A phrase that precedes a main clause is followed by a comma only if the phrase contains a verb form or has five or more words:

Beginning November 1, Mutual Trust will offer two new combination chequing/savings plans. (A comma follows this introductory phrase because the phrase contains the verb form *beginning*.)

To promote their plan, we will conduct an extensive direct-mail advertising campaign. (A comma follows this introductory phrase because the phrase contains the verb form *to promote*.)

In a period of only one year, we were able to improve our market share by 30 percent. (A comma follows the introductory phrase—actually two prepositional phrases—because its total length exceeds five words.)

In 1999 our organization installed a multiuser system that could transfer programs easily. (No comma needed after the short introductory phrase.)

2.08 Two or More Adjectives. Use a comma to separate two or more adjectives that equally describe a noun. A good way to test the need for a comma is this: mentally insert the word *and* between the adjectives. If the resulting phrase sounds natural, a comma is used to show the omission of *and:*

We're looking for a *versatile, programmable* calculator. (Use a comma to separate *versatile* and *programmable* because they independently describe *calculator. And* has been omitted.)

Our *experienced, courteous* staff is ready to serve you. (Use a comma to separate *experienced* and *courteous* because they independently describe *staff. And* has been omitted.)

It was difficult to refuse the *sincere young* telephone caller. (No commas are needed between *sincere* and *young* because *and* has not been omitted.)

2.09 Appositives. Words that rename or explain preceding nouns or pronouns are called *appositives.* An appositive that provides information not essential to the identification of the word it describes should be set off by commas:

Rozmin Kamani, *the project director for Sperling's,* worked with our architect. (The appositive, *the project director for Sperling's,* adds nonessential information. Commas set it off.)

REVIEW EXERCISE H—COMMAS 2

Insert only necessary commas in the following sentences. In the space provided, indicate the number of commas that you add for each sentence. If a sentence requires no commas, write *C.* When you finish, compare your responses with those provided. For each item on which you need review, consult the numbered principle shown in parentheses.

_____ 1. A corporation must be registered in the province in which it does business and it must operate within the laws of that province.

_____ 2. The manager made a point-by-point explanation of the distribution dilemma and then presented his plan to solve the problem.

3. If you study the cost analysis you will see that our company offers the best system at the lowest price. _____

4. Molly Epperson who amassed the greatest number of sales points was awarded the bonus trip to Hawaii. _____

5. The salesperson who amasses the greatest number of sales points will be awarded the bonus trip to Hawaii. _____

6. To promote goodwill and to generate international trade we are opening offices in the Far East and in Europe. _____

7. On the basis of these findings I recommend that we retain Jane Rada as our counsel. _____

8. Mary Lam is a dedicated hard-working employee for our company. _____

9. The bright young student who worked for us last summer will be able to return this summer. _____

10. When you return the completed form we will be able to process your application. _____

11. We will be able to process your application when you return the completed form. _____

12. Employees who have been with us over ten years automatically receive additional insurance benefits. _____

13. Knowing that you wanted this merchandise immediately I took the liberty of sending it by Express Parcel Services. _____

14. The central processing unit requires no scheduled maintenance and has a self-test function for reliable performance. _____

15. International competition nearly ruined the Canadian shoe industry but the textile industry remains strong. _____

16. Joyce D'Agostino our newly promoted office manager has made a number of worthwhile suggestions. _____

17. For the benefit of employees recently hired we are offering a two-hour seminar regarding employee benefit programs. _____

18. Please bring your suggestions and those of Mr. Mason when you attend our meeting next month. _____

19. The meeting has been rescheduled for September 30 if I remember correctly. _____

20. Some of the problems that you outline in your recent memo could be rectified through more stringent purchasing procedures. _____

---

1. business, (2.05)   3. analysis, (2.06a)   5. C (2.06c)   7. findings, (2.07)   9. C (2.08)   11. C (2.06b)   13. immediately, (2.07)   15. industry, (2.05)   17. hired, (2.07)   19. September 30, (2.06b)

Commas 3 (2.10–2.15)

2.10 Degrees and Abbreviations. Degrees following individuals' names are set off by commas. Abbreviations such as *Jr.* and *Sr.* are also set off by commas unless the individual referred to prefers to omit the commas:

Anne G. Turner, *M.B.A.*, joined the firm.

Michael Migliano, *Jr.*, and Michael Migliano, *Sr.*, work as a team.

Anthony A. Gensler *Jr.* wrote the report. (The individual referred to prefers to omit commas.)

The abbreviations *Inc.* and *Ltd.* are set off by commas only if a company's legal name has a comma just before this kind of abbreviation. To determine a company's practice, consult its stationery or a directory listing:

> Firestone and Blythe, *Inc.*, is based in Canada. (Notice that two commas are used.)

> Computers *Inc.* is extending its franchise system. (The company's legal name does not include a comma just before *Inc.*)

2.11 Omitted Words. A comma is used to show the omission of words that are understood:

> On Monday we received 15 applications; on Friday, only 3. (Comma shows the omission of *we received*.)

2.12 Contrasting Statements. Commas are used to set off contrasting or opposing expressions. These expressions are often introduced by such words as *not, never, but,* and *yet:*

> The consultant recommended tape storage, *not* floppy-disk storage, for our operations.

> Our budget for the year is reduced, *yet* adequate.

> The greater the effort, the greater the reward.

If increased emphasis is desired, use dashes instead of commas, as in *Only the sum of $100—not $1000—was paid on this account.*

2.13 Clarity. Commas are used to separate words repeated for emphasis. Commas are also used to separate words that may be misread if not separated:

> The building is a long, long way from completion.

> Whatever is, is right.

> No matter what, you know we support you.

2.14 Quotations and Appended Questions

a. A comma is used to separate a short quotation from the rest of a sentence. If the quotation is divided into two parts, two commas are used:

> The manager asked, "Shouldn't the managers control the specialists?"

> "Not if the specialists," replied Xiang, "have unique information."

b. A comma is used to separate a question appended (added) to a statement:

> You will confirm the shipment, won't you?

2.15 Comma Overuse. Do not use commas needlessly. For example, commas should not be inserted merely because you might drop your voice if you were speaking the sentence:

> One of the reasons for expanding our operations in the Atlantic region is {,} that we anticipate increased sales in that area. (Do not insert a needless comma before a clause.)

> I am looking for an article entitled {,} "State-of-the-Art Communications." (Do not insert a needless comma after the word *entitled*.)

A number of food and nonfood items are carried in convenience stores such as {,} 7-Eleven and Stop-N-Go. (Do not insert a needless comma after *such as*.)

We have {,} at this time {,} an adequate supply of parts. (Do not insert needless commas around prepositional phrases.)

REVIEW EXERCISE I—COMMAS 3

Insert only necessary commas in the following sentences. Remove unnecessary commas with the delete sign ( ). In the space provided, indicate the number of commas inserted or deleted in each sentence. If a sentence requires no changes, write *C*. When you finish, compare your responses with those provided. For each item on which you need review, consult the numbered principle shown in parentheses.

1. We expected Charles Bedford not Krystina Rudko to conduct the audit. _____
2. Brian said "We simply must have a bigger budget to start this project." _____
3. "We simply must have" said Brian "a bigger budget to start this project." _____
4. In August customers opened at least 50 new accounts; in September only about 20. _____
5. You returned the merchandise last month didn't you? _____
6. In short employees will now be expected to contribute more to their own retirement funds. _____
7. The better our advertising and recruiting the stronger our personnel pool will be. _____
8. Mrs. Delgado investigated selling her stocks not her real estate to raise the necessary cash. _____
9. "On the contrary" said Ms. Mercer "we will continue our present marketing strategies." _____
10. Our company will expand into surprising new areas such as, women's apparel and fast foods. _____
11. What we need is more not fewer suggestions for improvement. _____
12. Randall Clark B. Comm. and Jonathan Georges M.B.A. joined the firm. _____
13. "The world is now entering" said President Saunders "the Knowledge Age." _____
14. One of the reasons that we are inquiring about the publisher of the software is, that we are concerned about whether that publisher will be in the market five years from now. _____
15. The talk by D. A. Spindler Ph.D. was particularly difficult to follow because of his technical and abstract vocabulary. _____
16. The month before a similar disruption occurred in distribution. _____
17. We are very fortunate to have, at our disposal, the services of excellent professionals. _____
18. No matter what you can count on us for support. _____
19. Joan Sandoval was named legislative counsel; Jeremy Freeman executive adviser. _____
20. The information you are seeking can be found in an article entitled, "The Fastest Growing Game in Computers." _____

---

1. Bedford, Rudko, (2.12)   3. have," said Brian, (2.14a)   5. month, (2.14b)   7. recruiting, (2.12)
9. contrary," Mercer, (2.14a)   11. more, not fewer, (2.12)   13. entering," Saunders, (2.14a)
15. Spindler, Ph.D., (2.10)   17. have at our disposal (2.15)   19. Freeman, (2.11)

CUMULATIVE EDITING QUIZ 4

Use proofreading marks (see Appendix B) to correct errors and omissions in the following sentences. All errors must be corrected to receive credit for the sentence. Check with your instructor for the answers.

1. Business documents must be written clear, to ensure that readers comprehend the message quick.

2. Needless to say the safety of our employees have always been most important to the president and I.

3. Agriculture Canada which provide disaster assistance to farmers are setting up an office in Miami Manitoba.

4. Many entrepreneurs who want to expand there markets, have choosen to advertise heavy.

5. Our arbitration committee have unanimously agreed on a compromise package but management have been slow to respond.

6. Although the business was founded in the 1950's its real expansion took place in the 1990s.

7. According to the contract either the dealer or the distributor are responsible for repair of the product.

8. Next June, Lamont and Jones, Inc., are moving their headquarters to Calgary Alberta.

9. Our company is looking for intelligent, articulate, young, people who has a desire to grow with an expanding organization.

10. As you are aware each member of the jury were asked to avoid talking about the case.

SEMICOLONS (2.16)

2.16 Independent Clauses, Series, and Introductory Expressions

a. *Independent clauses with conjunctive adverbs*. Use a semicolon before a conjunctive adverb that separates two independent clauses. Some of the most common conjunctive adverbs are *therefore*, *consequently*, *however*, and *moreover*:

Business letters should sound conversational; *therefore*, familiar words and contractions are often used.

The bank closes its doors at 5 p.m.; *however*, the ABM is open 24 hours a day.

Notice that the word following a semicolon is *not* capitalized (unless, of course, that word is a proper noun).

b. *Independent clauses without conjunctive adverbs*. Use a semicolon to separate closely related independent clauses when no conjunctive adverb is used:

Some interest payments are tax deductible; dividend payments are not.

Ambient lighting fills the room; task lighting illuminates each workstation.

Use a semicolon in *compound* sentences, not in *complex* sentences:

> After one week the paper feeder jammed; we called the service company. (Use a semicolon in a compound sentence.)

> After one week the paper feeder jammed, although we were using it according to instructions. (Use a comma in a complex sentence. Do not use a semicolon after *jammed*.)

The semicolon is very effective for joining two closely related thoughts. Don't use it, however, unless the ideas are truly related.

c.   *Independent clauses with other commas.* Normally, a comma precedes *and, or,* and *but* when those conjunctions join independent clauses. However, if either clause contains commas, change the comma preceding the conjunction to a semicolon to ensure correct reading:

> If you arrive in time, you may be able to purchase a ticket; but ticket sales end promptly at 8 p.m.

> Our primary concern is financing; and we have discovered, as you warned us, that money sources are quite scarce.

d.   *Series with internal commas.* Use semicolons to separate items in a series when one or more of the items contain internal commas:

> Delegates from Brandon, Manitoba; Lethbridge, Alberta; and North Bay, Ontario, attended the conference.

> The speakers were Katherine Lang, manager, Riko Enterprises; Henry Holtz, vice president, Trendex, Inc.; and Margaret Slater, human resources director, Coast Productions.

e.   *Introductory expressions.* Use a semicolon when an introductory expression such as *namely, for instance, that is,* or *for example* introduces a list following an independent clause:

> Switching to computerized billing are several local companies; namely, Ryson Electronics, Miller Vending Services, and Black Advertising.

> The author of a report should consider many sources; for example, books, periodicals, databases, and newspapers.

COLONS (2.17–2.19)

2.17 Listed Items

a.   *With colon.* Use a colon after a complete thought that introduces a formal list of items. A formal list is often preceded by such words and phrases as *these, thus, the following,* and *as follows.* A colon is also used when words and phrases like these are implied but not stated:

> Additional costs in selling a house involve *the following:* title examination fee, title insurance costs, and closing fee. (Use a colon when a complete thought introduces formal list.)

> Collective bargaining focuses on several key issues: cost-of-living adjustments, fringe benefits, job security, and hours of work. (The introduction of the list is implied in the preceding clause.)

b. *Without colons.* Do not use a colon when the list immediately follows a *to be* verb or a preposition:

The employees who should receive the preliminary plan are James Sears, Monica Spears, and Rose Paquet. (No colon is used after the verb *are*.)

We expect to consider equipment for Accounting, Legal Services, and Payroll. (No colon is used after the preposition *for*.)

2.18 Quotations. Use a colon to introduce long one-sentence quotations and quotations of two or more sentences:

Our consultant said: "This system can support up to 32 users. It can be used for decision support, computer-aided design, and software development operations at the same time."

2.19 Salutations. Use a colon after the salutation of a business letter:

Ladies and Gentlemen: Dear Ms. Tsang: Dear Jamie:

REVIEW EXERCISE J— SEMICOLONS, COLONS

In the following sentences, add semicolons, colons, and necessary commas. For each sentence indicate the number of punctuation marks that you add. If a sentence requires no punctuation, write *C*. When you finish, compare your responses with those provided. For each item on which you need review, consult the numbered principle shown in parentheses.

1. A strike in Montreal has delayed shipments of parts consequently our production has fallen behind schedule.
2. Our branch in Burnaby specializes in industrial real estate our branch in Island Lakes concentrates on residential real estate.
3. The sedan version of the automobile is available in these colours Olympic red metallic silver and Aztec gold.
4. If I can assist the new manager please call me however I will be gone from June 10 through June 15.
5. The individuals who should receive copies of this announcement are Jeff Doogan Alicia Green and Kim Wong.
6. We would hope of course to send personal letters to all prospective buyers but we have not yet decided just how to do this.
7. Many of our potential customers are in southern British Columbia therefore our promotional effort will be strongest in that area.
8. Since the first of the year we have received inquiries from one lawyer two accountants and one information systems analyst.
9. Three dates have been reserved for initial interviews January 15 February 1 and February 12.
10. Several staff members are near the top of their salary ranges and we must reclassify their jobs.
11. Several staff members are near the top of their salary ranges we must reclassify their jobs.
12. Several staff members are near the top of their salary ranges therefore we must reclassify their jobs.

13. If you open an account within two weeks you will receive a free cookbook moreover your first 500 cheques will be imprinted at no cost to you. _____

14. Monthly reports from the following departments are missing Legal Department Human Resources Department and Engineering Department. _____

15. Monthly reports are missing from the Legal Department Human Resources Department and Engineering Department. _____

16. Since you became director of that division sales have tripled therefore I am recommending you for a bonus. _____

17. The convention committee is considering Dartmouth Nova Scotia Moncton New Brunswick and Charlottetown Prince Edward Island. _____

18. Several large companies allow employees access to their personnel files; namely Nortel Corel Corp. and Ford Canada. _____

19. Sylvie first asked about salary next she inquired about benefits. _____

20. Sylvie first asked about the salary and she next inquired about benefits. _____

1. parts; consequently, (2.16a) 3. colours: Olympic red, metallic silver, (2.01, 2.17a) 5. Doogan, Alicia Green, (2.01, 2.17b) 7. British Columbia; therefore, (2.16a) 9. interviews: January 15, February 1, (2.01, 2.17a) 11. ranges; (2.16b) 13. weeks, cookbook; moreover, (2.06a, 2.16a) 15. Department, Human Resources Department, (2.01, 2.17b) 17. Dartmouth, Nova Scotia; Moncton, New Brunswick; Charlottetown, (2.16d) 19. salary; (2.16b)

APOSTROPHES (2.20–2.22)

2.20 Basic Rule. The apostrophe is used to show ownership, origin, authorship, or measurement.

Ownership: We are looking for Brian's keys.
Origin: At the president's suggestion, we doubled the order.
Authorship: The accountant's annual report was questioned.
Measurement: In two years' time we expect to reach our goal.

a. *Ownership words not ending in* **s.** To place the apostrophe correctly, you must first determine whether the ownership word ends in an *s* sound. If it does not, add an apostrophe and an *s* to the ownership word. The following examples show ownership words that do not end in an *s* sound:

the employee's file	(the file of a single employee)
a member's address	(the address of a single member)
a year's time	(the time of a single year)
a month's notice	(notice of a single month)
the company's building	(the building of a single company)

b. *Ownership words ending in* **s.** If the ownership word does end in an *s* sound, usually add only an apostrophe:

several employees' files	(files of several employees)
ten members' addresses	(addresses of ten members)
five years' time	(time of five years)
several months' notice	(notice of several months)
many companies' buildings	(buildings of many companies)

A few singular nouns that end in *s* are pronounced with an extra syllable when they become possessive. To these words, add '*s*.

> my boss's desk
>
> the actress's costume

Use no apostrophe if a noun is merely plural, not possessive:

> All the sales representatives, as well as the administrative assistants and managers, had their names and telephone numbers listed in the directory.

2.21 Names. The writer may choose either traditional or popular style in making singular names that end in an *s* sound possessive. The traditional style uses the apostrophe plus an *s*, while the popular style uses just the apostrophe. Note that only with singular names ending in an *s* sound does this option exist.

Traditional Style	**Popular Style**
Russ's computer	Russ' computer
Mr. Jones's car	Mr. Jones' car
Mrs. Morris's desk	Mrs. Morris' desk
Ms. Horowitz's job	Ms. Horowitz' job

The possessive form of plural names is consistent: the Joneses' car, the Horowitzes' home, the Morrises' daughter.

2.22 Gerunds. Use '*s* to make a noun possessive when it precedes a gerund, a verb form used as a noun:

> Mr. Smith's smoking prompted a new office policy. (*Mr. Smith* is possessive because it modifies the gerund *smoking*.)
>
> It was Betsy's careful proofreading that revealed the discrepancy.

REVIEW EXERCISE K—APOSTROPHES

Insert necessary apostrophes in the following sentences. In the space provided for each sentence, indicate the number of apostrophes that you added. If none were added, write *C*. When you finish, compare your responses with those provided. For each item on which you need review, consult the numbered principle shown in parentheses.

1. Your account should have been credited with six months interest.
2. If you go to the third floor, you will find Mr. Londons office.
3. All the employees personnel folders must be updated.
4. In a little over a years time, that firm was able to double its sales.
5. The Harrises daughter lived in Whitehorse for two years.
6. An inventors patent protects his or her invention for several years.
7. Both companies headquarters will be moved within the next six months.
8. That position requires at least two years experience.
9. Some of the companys assets could be liquidated; therefore, a few of the creditors were satisfied.
10. All secretaries workstations were equipped with terminals.
11. The package of electronics parts arrived safely despite two weeks delay.
12. Many nurses believe that nurses notes are not admissible as evidence.

13. According to Mr. Cortez latest proposal, all employees would receive an additional holiday. _____

14. Many of our members names and addresses must be checked. _____

15. His supervisor frequently had to correct Jacks financial reports. _____

16. We believe that this firms service is much better than that firms. _____

17. Mr. Jackson estimated that he spent a years profits in reorganizing his staff. _____

18. After paying six months rent, we were given a receipt. _____

19. The contract is not valid without Mrs. Harris signature. _____

20. It was Mr. Smiths signing of the contract that made us happy. _____

---

1. months' (2.20b)   3. employees' (2.20b)   5. Harrises' (2.21)   7. companies' (2.20b)   9. company's (2.20a)   11. weeks' (2.20b)   13. Cortez' or Cortez's (2.21)   15. Jack's (2.20)   17. year's (2.20a)   19. Harris' or Harris's (2.21)

CUMULATIVE EDITING QUIZ 5

Use proofreading marks (see Appendix B) to correct errors and omissions in the following sentences. All errors must be corrected to receive credit for the sentence. Check with your instructor for the answers.

1. The three C's of credit are the following character capacity and capital.

2. We hope that we will not have to sell the property however that may be our only option.

3. As soon as the supervisor and her can check this weeks sales they will place an order.

4. Any of the auditors are authorized to proceed with an independent action however only the CEO can alter the councils directives.

5. Although reluctant technicians sometimes must demonstrate there computer software skills.

6. On April 6 1998 we opened an innovative fully-equipped employee computer centre.

7. A list of maintenance procedures and recommendations are in the owners manual.

8. The Morrises son lived in London Ontario however there daughter lived in Saint John New Brunswick.

9. Employment interviews were held in Winnipeg Manitoba Calgary Alberta and Victoria British Columbia.

10. Mr. Lees determination courage and sincerity could not be denied however his methods was often questioned.

OTHER PUNCTUATION (2.23–2.29)

2.23 Periods

a. *Ends of sentences.* Use a period at the end of a statement, command, indirect question, or polite request. Although a polite request may have the same structure as a question, it ends with a period:

Corporate legal departments demand precise skills from their workers. (End a statement with a period.)

Get the latest data by reading current periodicals. (End a command with a period.)

Mr. Rand wondered if we had sent any follow-up literature. (End an indirect question with a period.)

Would you please re-examine my account and determine the current balance. (A polite request suggests an action rather than a verbal response.)

b. *Abbreviations and initials.* Use periods after initials and after many abbreviations.

R. M. Johnson	c.o.d.	Ms.
M.D.	a.m.	Mr.
Inc.	i.e.	Mrs.

Use just one period when an abbreviation falls at the end of a sentence:

Guests began arriving at 5:30 p.m.

2.24 Question Marks. Direct questions are followed by question marks:

Did you send your proposal to Datatronix Inc.?

Statements with questions added are punctuated with question marks.

We have completed the proposal, haven't we?

2.25 Exclamation Points. Use an exclamation point after a word, phrase, or clause expressing strong emotion. In business writing, however, exclamation points should be used sparingly:

Incredible! The entire network is down.

2.26 Dashes. The dash is a legitimate and effective mark of punctuation when used according to accepted conventions. As an emphatic punctuation mark, however, the dash loses effectiveness when overused.

a. *Parenthetical elements.* Within a sentence a parenthetical element is usually set off by commas. If, however, the parenthetical element itself contains internal commas, use dashes (or parentheses) to set it off:

Three top salespeople—Tom Judkins, Morgan Templeton, and Mary Yashimoto—received bonuses.

b. *Sentence interruptions.* Use a dash to show an interruption or abrupt change of thought:

News of the dramatic merger—no one believed it at first—shook the financial world.

Ship the materials Monday—no, we must have them sooner.

Sentences with abrupt changes of thought or with appended afterthoughts can usually be improved through rewriting.

c. *Summarizing statements.* Use a dash (not a colon) to separate an introductory list from a summarizing statement:

Sorting, merging, and computing—these are tasks that our data processing programs must perform.

2.27 Parentheses. One means of setting off nonessential sentence elements involves the use of parentheses. Nonessential sentence elements may be punctuated in one of three ways: (1) with commas, to make the lightest possible break in the normal flow of a sentence; (2) with dashes, to emphasize the enclosed material; and (3) with parentheses, to de-emphasize the enclosed material. Parentheses are frequently used to punctuate sentences with interpolated directions, explanations, questions, and references:

> The cost analysis (which appears on page 8 of the report) indicates that the copy machine should be leased.

> Units are lightweight (approximately 500 g) and come with a leather case and operating instructions.

> The IBM laser printer (have you heard about it?) will be demonstrated for us next week.

A parenthetical sentence that is not imbedded within another sentence should be capitalized and punctuated with end punctuation:

> The Model 20 has stronger construction. (You may order a Model 20 brochure by circling 304 on the reader service card.)

2.28 Quotation Marks

a. *Direct quotations.* Use double quotation marks to enclose the exact words of a speaker or writer:

> "Keep in mind," Mrs. Fontaine said, "that you'll have to justify the cost of automating our office."

> The boss said that automation was inevitable. (No quotation marks are needed because the exact words are not quoted.)

b. *Quotations within quotations.* Use single quotation marks (apostrophes on the typewriter) to enclose quoted passages within quoted passages:

> In her speech, Mrs. Deckman remarked, "I believe it was the poet Robert Frost who said, 'All the fun's in how you say a thing.' "

c. *Short expressions.* Slang, words used in a special sense, and words following *stamped* or *marked* are often enclosed within quotation marks:

> Rafael described the damaged shipment as "gross." (Quotation marks enclose slang.)

> Students often have trouble spelling the word "separate." (Quotation marks enclose words used in a special sense.)

> Jobs were divided into two categories: most stressful and least stressful. The jobs in the "most stressful" list involved high risk or responsibility. (Quotation marks enclose words used in a special sense.)

> The envelope marked "Confidential" was put aside. (Quotation marks enclose words following *marked.*)

In the four preceding sentences, the words enclosed within quotation marks can be set in italics, if italics are available.

d. ***Definitions.*** Double quotation marks are used to enclose definitions. The word or expression being defined should be underscored or set in italics:

> The term *penetration pricing* is defined as "the practice of introducing a product to the market at a low price."

e. ***Titles.*** Use double quotation marks to enclose titles of literary and artistic works, such as magazine and newspaper articles, chapters of books, movies, television shows, poems, lectures, and songs. Names of major publications—such as books, magazines, pamphlets, and newspapers—are set in italics (underscored on the typewriter) or typed in capital letters.

> Particularly helpful was the chapter in Smith's *Effective Writing Techniques* entitled "Right Brain, Write On!"

> John's article, "Corporate Raiders," appeared in the *Toronto Star*; however, we could not locate it in a local library.

f. ***Additional considerations.*** Periods and commas are always placed inside closing quotation marks. Semicolons and colons, on the other hand, are always placed outside quotation marks:

> Mrs. Levesque said, "I could not find the article entitled 'Technology Update.' "

> The president asked for "absolute security": all written messages were to be destroyed.

> Question marks and exclamation points may go inside or outside closing quotation marks, as determined by the form of the quotation:

> Sales Manager Martin said, "Who placed the order?" (The quotation is a question.)

> When did the sales manager say, "Who placed the order?" (Both the incorporating sentence and the quotation are questions.)

> Did the sales manager say, "Narwinder placed the order"? (The incorporating sentence asks question; the quotation does not.)

> "In the future," shouted Bob, "ask me first!" (The quotation is an exclamation.)

2.29 Brackets. Within quotations, brackets are used by the quoting writer to enclose his or her own inserted remarks. Such remarks may be corrective, illustrative, or explanatory:

> June Cardillo said, "The CRTC [Canadian Radio Television and Telecommunications Commission] has been one of the most widely criticized agencies of the federal government."

REVIEW EXERCISE L—OTHER PUNCTUATION

Insert necessary punctuation in the following sentences. In the space provided for each item, indicate the number of punctuation marks that you added. Count sets of parentheses and dashes as two marks. Emphasis or de-emphasis will be indicated for some parenthetical elements. When you finish, compare your responses with those provided. For each item on which you need review, consult the numbered principle shown in parentheses.

1. Will you please stop payment on my Cheque No. 233 _____

2. (Emphasize.) Your order of October 16 will be on its way you have my word by _____
October 20.

3. Mr Sirakides, Mrs Sylvester, and Miss Sidhu have not yet responded _____

4. Wanda Penner asked if the order had been sent c o d _____

5. Interviews have been scheduled for 3:15 pm., 4 pm, and 4:45 pm _____

6. (De-emphasize.) Three knowledgeable individuals the plant manager, the con- _____
struction engineer, and the construction supervisor all expressed concern about
soil settlement.

7. Fantastic The value of our stock just rose 10 points _____

8. The word de facto means existing in fact, regardless of the legal situation. _____

9. (De-emphasize.) Although the appliance now comes in limited colours brown, _____
beige, and ivory, we expect to see new colours available in the next production
run.

10. Was it the manager who said What can't be altered must be endured _____

11. The stock market went nuts over the news of the takeover. _____

12. Because the envelope was marked Personal we did not open it. _____

13. Price, service, and reliability these are our prime considerations in equipment _____
selection.

14. The letter carrier said Would you believe that this package was marked *Fragile* _____

15. (Emphasize.) Three branch managers Kelly Cardinal, Stan Meyers, and Ivan _____
Sergo will be promoted.

16. (De-emphasize.) The difference in weight between two different brand name _____
portable computer models see Figure 4 for weight comparisons may be
considerable.

17. All the folders marked Current Files should be sent to Human Resources. _____

18. I am trying to find the edition of Canadian Living, which carried an article enti- _____
tled The Future Without Shock.

19. Martha Simon MD and Gail Nemire RN were hired by Healthnet, Inc _____

20. The computer salesperson said This innovative, state-of-the-art portable sells for _____
a fraction of the cost of big-name computers."

---

1. 233. (2.23a)   3. Mr. Mrs. responded. (2.23a, 2.23b)   5. p.m. p.m. p.m. (2.23b)   7. Fantastic! points! (2.25)   9. (brown ivory) (2.27)   11. "nuts" (2.28c)   13. reliability— (2.26c)   15. managers—Sergo— (2.26a)   17. "Current Files" (2.28c)   19. Simon, M.D., Nemire, R.N., Inc. (2.23b)

CUMULATIVE EDITING QUIZ 6

Use proofreading marks (see Appendix B) to correct errors and omissions in the following sentences. All errors must be corrected to receive credit for the sentence.
Check with your instructor for the answers.

1. Although the envelope was marked Confidential the vice presidents assistant
thought it should be opened.

2. Would you please send my order c.o.d?

3. To be eligible for an apartment you must pay two months rent in advance.

4. We wanted to use Russ computer, but forgot to ask for permission.

5. Wasnt it Jeff Song not Eileen Lee who requested a 14 day leave.

6. Miss. Judith L. Beam is the employee who the employees council elected as their representative.

7. The Leader Post our local newspaper featured an article entitled The Worlds Most Expensive Memo.

8. As soon as my manager or myself can verify Ricks totals we will call you, in the meantime you must continue to disburse funds.

9. Just inside the entrance, is the receptionists desk and a complete directory of all departments'.

10. Exports from small companys has increased thereby affecting this countrys trade balance positively.

STYLE AND USAGE

CAPITALIZATION (3.01–3.16)

Capitalization is used to distinguish important words. However, writers are not free to capitalize all the words they consider important. Rules or guidelines governing capitalization style have been established through custom and use. Mastering these guidelines will make your writing more readable and more comprehensible.

3.01 Proper Nouns. Capitalize proper nouns, including the *specific* names of persons, places, schools, streets, parks, buildings, religions, holidays, months, agreements, programs, services, and so forth. Do not capitalize common nouns that make only *general* references.

Proper Nouns	Common Nouns
Michael DeNiro	a salesperson in electronics
Germany, Japan	two countries that trade with Canada
George Brown College	a community college
Assiniboine Park	a park in the city
Phoenix Room, Delta Inn	a meeting room in the hotel
Catholicism, Buddhism	two religions
Labour Day, New Year's Day	two holidays in the year
Priority Post	a special package delivery service
Lions Gate Bridge	a bridge

3.02 Proper Adjectives. Capitalize most adjectives that are derived from proper nouns:

Greek symbol	British thermal unit
Roman numeral	Norwegian ship
Inuit land claims	

Do not capitalize the few adjectives that, although derived from proper nouns, have become common adjectives, through usage, in expressions like the following. Consult your dictionary when in doubt.

manila folder	diesel engine
india ink	french fries

3.03 Geographic Locations. Capitalize the names of specific places such as cities, provinces, mountains, valleys, lakes, rivers, oceans, and geographic regions:

Iqaluit	Lake Ontario
Rocky Mountains	Arctic Ocean
Cape Breton Island	James Bay
the East Coast	the Pacific Northwest

3.04 Organization Names. Capitalize the principal words in the names of all business, civic, educational, governmental, labour, military, philanthropic, political, professional, religious, and social organizations:

Inland Steel Company	Board of Directors, Teachers' Credit Union
*The Globe and Mail**	The Rainbow Society
Toronto Stock Exchange	Securities and Exchange Commission
United Way	Psychological Association of Manitoba
Child and Family Services	Mennonite Brethren Bible College

*Note: Capitalize *the* only when it is part of the official name of an organization, as printed on the organization's stationery.

3.05 Academic Courses and Degrees. Capitalize particular academic degrees and course titles. Do not capitalize references to general academic degrees and subject areas:

Professor Bernadette Ordian, Ph.D., will teach Accounting 221 next fall.

Beth Snyder, who holds bachelor's and master's degrees, teaches marketing classes.

René enrolled in classes in history, business English, and management.

3.06 Personal and Business Titles

a. Capitalize personal and business titles when they precede names:

Vice President Ames	Uncle Edward
Board Chairperson Frazier	Councillor Herbert
Member of Parliament Ronald Fontaine	Sales Manager Klein
Professor McLean	Dr. Mira Rosner

b. Capitalize titles in addresses, salutations, and closing lines:

Mr. Juan deSanto	Very truly yours,
Director of Purchasing	
Space Systems, Inc.	
Richmond, BC V3L 4A6	Clara J. Smith
	Supervisor, Marketing

c. Capitalize titles of high government rank or religious office, whether they precede a name, follow a name, or replace a name.

the Prime Minister of Canada	Gaston Pelletier, Senator
the Premier's office	the Speaker of the House of
the Lieutenant-Governor	Commons
of British Columbia	an audience with the Pope
J. W. Ross, Minister of Finance	

d. Do not capitalize most common titles following names:

The speech was delivered by Wayne Hsu, president, Inter-Tel Canada.

Lois Herndon, chief executive officer, signed the order.

e. Do not capitalize common titles appearing alone:

Please speak to the *supervisor* or to the *office manager.*

Neither the *president* nor the *vice president* was asked.

However, when the title of an official appears in that organization's minutes, bylaws, or other official document, it may be capitalized.

f. Do not capitalize titles when they are followed by appositives naming specific individuals:

We must consult our *director of research*, Ronald E. West, before responding.

g. Do not capitalize family titles used with possessive pronouns:

my mother   our aunt
your father   his cousin

h. Capitalize titles of close relatives used without pronouns:

Both Mother and Father must sign the contract.

3.07 Numbered and Lettered Items. Capitalize nouns followed by numbers or letters (except in page, paragraph, line, and verse references):

Flight 34, Gate 12	Plan No. 2
Volume I, Part 3	Warehouse 33-A
Invoice No. 55489	Figure 8.3
Model A5673	Serial No. C22865404-2
Rural Route 10	page 6, line 5

3.08 Points of the Compass. Capitalize *north, south, east, west,* and their derivatives when they represent specific geographical regions. Do not capitalize the points of the compass when they are used in directions or in general references.

Specific Regions	**General References**
living in the North	heading north on the highway
Easterners, Westerners	west of the city, western Ontario, southern Saskatchewan
going to the Middle East	the northern part of Canada

3.09 Departments, Divisions, and Committees. Capitalize the names of departments, divisions, and committees within your own organization. Outside your organization capitalize only specific department, division, and committee names:

The inquiry was addressed to the Legal Department in our Consumer Products Division.

John was appointed to the Employee Benefits Committee.

Send your résumé to their human resources division.

A planning committee will be named shortly.

3.10 Governmental Terms. Do not capitalize the words *federal, government, nation,* or *province* unless they are part of a specific title:

Unless *federal* support can be secured, the *provincial* project will be abandoned.

The *Provincial* Employees' Pension Fund is looking for secure investments.

3.11 Product Names. Capitalize product names only when they refer to trademarked items. Except in advertising, common names following manufacturers' names are not capitalized:

Magic Marker	Apple computer
Kleenex tissues	Swingline stapler
Q-tips	3M diskettes
Levi 501 jeans	Sony dictation machine
DuPont Teflon	Canon camera

3.12 Literary Titles. Capitalize the principal words in the titles of books, magazines, newspapers, articles, movies, plays, songs, poems, and reports. Do not capitalize articles *(a, an, the)*, short conjunctions *(and, but, or, nor)*, and prepositions of fewer than four letters *(in, to, by, for*, etc.) unless they begin or end the title:

Jackson's *What Job Is for You*? (Capitalize book titles.)

Gant's "Software for the Executive Suite" (Capitalize principal words in article titles.)

"Performance Standards to Go By" (Capitalize article titles.)

"The Improvement of Fuel Economy With Alternative Motors" (Capitalize report titles.)

3.13 Beginning Words. In addition to capitalizing the first word of a complete sentence, capitalize the first word in a quoted sentence, independent phrase, item in an enumerated list, and formal rule or principle following a colon:

The business manager said, "*All* purchases must have requisitions." (Capitalize first word in a quoted sentence.)

Yes, if you agree. (Capitalize an independent phrase.)

Some of the duties of the position are as follows:

1. *Editing* and formatting Word files

2. *Receiving* and routing telephone calls

3. *Verifying* records, reports, and applications (Capitalize items in an enumerated list.)

One rule has been established throughout the company: No smoking is allowed in open offices. (Capitalize a rule following a colon.)

3.14 Celestial Bodies. Capitalize the names of celestial bodies such as *Mars, Saturn,* and *Neptune*. Do not capitalize the terms *earth, sun,* or *moon* unless they appear in a context with other celestial bodies:

Where on earth did you find that manual typewriter?

Venus and Mars are the closest planets to Earth.

3.15 Ethnic References. Capitalize terms that refer to a particular culture, language, or race, but do not capitalize the words *anglophone* and *francophone*.

Oriental	Hebrew
Caucasian	Indian
Latino	Japanese
Cree	Judeo-Christian

3.16 Seasons. Do not capitalize seasons:

In the *fall* it appeared that *winter* and *spring* sales would increase.

REVIEW EXERCISE M—CAPITALIZATION

In the following sentences correct any errors that you find in capitalization. Circle any lowercase letter that should be changed to a capital letter. Draw a slash (/) through a capital letter that you wish to change to a lowercase letter. In the space provided, indicate the total number of changes you have made in each sentence. If you make no changes, write *0*. When you finish, compare your responses with those provided. For each item on which you need review, consult the numbered principle shown in parentheses.

5 _____

Example: Bill McAdams, currently Assistant Manager in our Personnel Department, will be promoted to Manager of the Employee Services Division.

_____ 1. The pensions act, passed in 1949, established the present system of social security.

_____ 2. Our company will soon be moving its operations to the west coast.

_____ 3. Marilyn Hunter, m.b.a., received her bachelor's degree from McGill university in montreal.

_____ 4. The President of Datatronics, Inc., delivered a speech entitled "Taking off into the future."

_____ 5. Please ask your Aunt and your Uncle if they will come to the Lawyer's office at 5 p.m.

_____ 6. Your reservations are for flight 32 on air canada leaving from gate 14 at 2:35 p.m.

_____ 7. Once we establish an organizing committee, arrangements can be made to rent holmby hall.

_____ 8. Bob was enrolled in history, spanish, business communications, and physical education courses.

_____ 9. Either the President or the Vice President of the company will make the decision about purchasing xerox photocopiers.

_____ 10. Rules for hiring and firing Employees are given on page 7, line 24, of the Contract.

_____ 11. Some individuals feel that canadian management does not have the sense of loyalty to its employees that japanese management has.

_____ 12. Where on Earth can we find better workers than Robots?

_____ 13. The minister of finance said, "we must encourage our domestic producers to compete internationally."

_____ 14. After crossing the sunshine skyway bridge, we drove to Southern British Columbia for our vacation.

15. All marketing representatives of our company will meet in the empire room of the red lion motor inn. _____
16. Richard Elkins, ph.d., has been named director of research for spaceage strategies, inc. _____
17. The special keyboard for the IBM Computer must contain greek symbols for Engineering equations. _____
18. After she received a master's degree in electrical engineering, Joanne Dudley was hired to work in our product development department. _____
19. In the Fall our organization will move its corporate headquarters to the franklin building in downtown vancouver. _____
20. Dean Amador has one cardinal rule: always be punctual. _____

---

1. Pensions Act (3.01)   3. M.B.A. University Montreal (3.01, 3.03, 3.05)   5. aunt uncle lawyer's (3.06e, 3.06g)   7. Holmby Hall (3.01)   9. president vice president Xerox (3.06e, 3.11) 11. Canadian Japanese (3.02)   13. Minister of Finance We (3.06c, 3.13)   15. Empire Room Red Lion Motor Inn (3.01)   17. computer Greek engineering (3.01, 3.02, 3.11)   19. fall Franklin Building Vancouver (3.01, 3.03, 3.16)

CUMULATIVE EDITING QUIZ 7

Use proofreading marks (see Appendix B) to correct errors and omissions in the following sentences. All errors must be corrected to receive credit for the sentence. Check with your instructor for the answers.

1. The Manager thinks that you attending the three day seminar is a good idea, however we must find a replacement.

2. We heard that professor watson invited edward peters, president of micropro inc. to speak to our business law class.

3. Carla Jones a new systems programmer in our accounting department will start monday.

4. After year's of downsizing and restructuring canada has now become one of the worlds most efficient manufacturers.

5. When our company specialized in asian imports our main office was on the west coast.

6. Company's like amway discovered that there unique door to door selling methods was very successful in japan.

7. If you had given your sony camera to she or I before you got on the roller coaster it might have stayed dry.

8. Tracy recently finished a bachelors degree in accounting, consequently she is submitting many résumé's to companys across the country.

9. The Lopezs moved from Edmonton Alberta to Vancouver British Columbia when mr lopez enrolled at the university of british columbia.

10. When we open our office in montreal we will need employees whom are fluent in english and french.

NUMBER STYLE (4.01–4.13)

Usage and custom determine whether numbers are expressed in the form of figures (for example, *5, 9*) or in the form of words (for example, *five, nine*). Numbers expressed as figures are shorter and more easily understood, yet numbers expressed as words are necessary in certain instances. The following guidelines are observed in expressing numbers in written sentences. Numbers that appear on business forms—such as invoices, monthly statements, and purchase orders—are always expressed as figures.

4.01 General Rules

a. The numbers *one* through *ten* are generally written as words. Numbers above *ten* are written as figures:

The bank had a total of *nine* branch offices in *three* suburbs.

All *58* employees received benefits in the *three* categories shown.

A shipment of *45,000* light bulbs was sent from *two* warehouses.

b. Numbers that begin sentences are written as words. If that number involves more than two words, however, the sentence should be written so that the number does not fall at the beginning.

Fifteen different options were available in the annuity programs.

A total of *156* companies participated in the promotion (not *One hundred and fifty-six companies participated in the promotion*).

4.02 Money.
Sums of money $1 or greater are expressed as figures. If a sum is a whole dollar amount, omit the decimal and zeros (whether or not the amount appears in a sentence with additional fractional dollar amounts):

We budgeted *$30* for blank CDs, but the actual cost was *$37.96*.

On the invoice were items for *$6.10, $8, $33.95*, and *$75*.

Sums of less than $1 are written as figures that are followed by the word *cents:*

By shopping carefully, we can save *15 cents* per blank CD.

4.03 Dates.
In dates, numbers that appear after the name of the month are written as cardinal figures (*1, 2, 3*, etc.). Those that stand alone or appear before the name of a month are written as ordinal figures (*1st, 2d, 3d,** etc.):

The Professional Development Committee will meet *May 7*.

On the *5th* day of February and again on the *25th*, we placed orders.

In domestic business documents, dates generally take the following form: *January 4, 2000*. An alternative form, used primarily in military and foreign correspondence, begins with the day of the month and omits the comma: *4 January 2000*.

---

* Some writers today are using the more efficient *2d* and *3d* instead of *2nd* and *3rd*.

4.04 Clock Time. Figures are used when clock time is expressed with *a.m.* or *p.m.* Omit the colon and zeros in referring to whole hours. When exact clock time is expressed with the contraction *o'clock*, either figures or words may be used:

> Mail deliveries are made at *11 a.m.* and *3:30 p.m.*

> At *four* (or *4*) *o'clock* employees begin to leave.

4.05 Addresses and Telephone Numbers

a.   Except for the number *one*, house numbers are expressed in figures:

> 540 Elm Street   17802 Parliament Avenue
> One Desmeurons Boulevard   2 Highland Street

b.   Street names containing numbers *ten* or lower are written entirely as words. For street names involving numbers greater than *ten*, figures are used:

> 330 Third Street   3440 Seventh Avenue
> 6945 East 32 Avenue   4903 West 103 Street

> If no compass direction *(North, South, East, West)* separates a house number from a street number, the street number is expressed in ordinal form (*-st, -d, -th*).

> 256 42d Street   1390 11th Avenue

c.   Telephone numbers are expressed with figures. When used, the area code is placed in parentheses preceding the telephone number:

> Please call us at *(818) 347-0551* to place an order.
> Mr. Sui asked you to call *(619) 554-8923, Ext. 245*, after 10 a.m.

4.06 Related Numbers. Numbers are related when they refer to similar items in a category within the same reference. All related numbers should be expressed as the largest number is expressed. Thus if the largest number is greater than *ten*, all the numbers should be expressed in figures:

> Only *5* of the original *25* applicants completed the processing. (Related numbers require figures.)

> The *two* plans affected *34* employees working at *three* sites. (Unrelated numbers use figures and words.)

> PetroCan operated *86* rigs, of which *6* were rented. (Related numbers require figures.)

> The company hired *three* accountants, *one* customer service representative, and *nine* sales representatives. (Related numbers under *ten* use words.)

4.07 Consecutive Numbers. When two numbers appear consecutively and both modify a noun that follows, readers may misread the numbers because of their closeness. The writer should (1) rewrite the expression or (2) express one number in word form and the other in figure form. Use word form for the number that may be expressed in the fewest number of words. If both numbers have an equal count, spell out the first number and place the second one in figures:

> We need *350 five-page* coloured inserts. (Use word form for the number that may be expressed in the fewest words.)

Please purchase *thirty 4-inch* galvanized nails for the job. (Use word form for the first number since both have an equal word count.)

4.08 Periods of Time. Periods of time are generally expressed in word form. However, figures may be used to emphasize business concepts such as discount rates, interest rates, warranty periods, credit terms, loan or contract periods, and payment terms:

This business was incorporated over *fifty* years ago. (Use words for a period of time.)

Any purchaser may cancel a contract within *72* hours. (Use figures to explain a business concept.)

The warranty period is *5* years. (Use figures for a business concept.)

Cash discounts are given for payment within *30* days. (Use figures for a business concept.)

4.09 Ages. Ages are generally expressed in word form unless the age appears immediately after a name or is expressed in exact years and months:

At the age of *twenty-one*, Elizabeth inherited the business.

Wanda Unger, *37*, was named acting president.

At the age of *4 years and 7 months*, the child was adopted.

4.10 Round Numbers. Round numbers are approximations. They may be expressed in word or figure form, although figure form is shorter and easier to comprehend:

About *600* (or *six hundred*) stock options were sold.

It is estimated that *1000* (or *one thousand*) people will attend.

For ease of reading, round numbers in the millions or billions should be expressed with a combination of figures and words:

At least *1.5 million* readers subscribe to the ten top magazines.

Deposits in money market accounts totalled more than *$115 billion*.

4.11 Weights and Measurements. Weights and measurements are expressed with figures:

The new deposit slip measures *5* by *15 cm*.

Her new suitcase weighed only *1.2 kg*.

Regina is *750 kilometres* from Calgary.

4.12 Fractions. Simple fractions are expressed as words. Complex fractions may be written either as figures or as a combination of figures and words:

Over *two-thirds* of the shareholders voted.

This microcomputer will execute the command in *1 millionth* of a second. (Combination of words and numbers is easier to comprehend.)

She purchased a *one-fifth* share in the business.

4.13 Percentages and Decimals. Percentages are expressed with figures that are followed by the word *percent*. The percent sign (%) is used only on business forms or in statistical presentations:

We had hoped for a *7 percent* interest rate, but we received a loan at *8 percent*.

Over *50 percent* of the residents supported the plan.

Decimals are expressed with figures. If a decimal expression does not contain a whole number (an integer) and does not begin with a zero, a zero should be placed before the decimal point:

The actuarial charts show that *1.74* out of *1000* people will die in any given year.

Inspector Norris found the setting to be *.005* centimetres off. (Decimal begins with a zero and does not require a zero before the decimal point.)

Considerable savings will accrue if the unit production cost is reduced by *0.1* percent. (A zero is placed before a decimal that neither contains a whole number nor begins with a zero.)

QUICK CHART–EXPRESSION OF NUMBERS

Use Words	Use Figures
Numbers *ten* and under	Numbers *11* and over
Numbers at beginning of sentence	Money
Periods of time	Dates
Ages	Addresses and telephone numbers
Fractions	Weights and measurements
	Percentages and decimals

REVIEW EXERCISE N—NUMBER STYLE

Circle *a* or *b* to indicate the preferred number style. Assume that these numbers appear in business correspondence. When you finish, compare your responses with those provided. For each item on which you need review, consult the numbered principle shown in parentheses.

1. (a) 2 alternatives   (b) two alternatives   _____
2. (a) Seventh Avenue   (b) 7th Avenue   _____
3. (a) sixty sales reps   (b) 60 sales reps   _____
4. (a) November ninth   (b) November 9   _____
5. (a) forty dollars   (b) $40   _____
6. (a) on the 23d of May   (b) on the twenty-third of May   _____
7. (a) at 2:00 p.m.   (b) at 2 p.m.   _____
8. (a) 4 two-hundred-page books (b) four 200-page books   _____
9. (a) at least 15 years ago   (b) at least fifteen years ago   _____
10. (a) 1,000,000 viewers   (b) 1 million viewers   _____
11. (a) twelve cents   (b) 12 cents   _____
12. (a) a sixty-day warranty   (b) a 60-day warranty   _____
13. (a) ten percent interest rate (b) 10 percent interest rate   _____
14. (a) 4/5 of the voters   (b) four-fifths of the voters   _____
15. (a) the rug measures one by two metres (b) the rug measures 1 by 2 metres _____
16. (a) about five hundred people attended (b) about 500 people attended _____
17. (a) at eight o'clock   (b) at 8 o'clock   _____
18. (a) located at 1 Broadway Boulevard (b) located at One Broadway Boulevard _____

19. (a) three computers for twelve people   (b) three computers for 12 people
20. (a) 4 out of every 100 licences   (b) four out of every 100 licences

1. b (4.01a)   3. b (4.01a)   5. b (4.02)   7. b (4.04)   9. b (4.08)   11. b (4.02)   13. b (4.13)   15. b (4.11)   17. a or b (4.04)   19. b (4.06)

CUMULATIVE EDITING QUIZ 8

Use proofreading marks (see Appendix B) to correct errors and omissions in the following sentences. All errors must be corrected to receive credit for the sentence. Check with your instructor for the answers.

1. The prime minister of Canada recommended a 30 day cooling off period in the united nations peace negotiations.

2. Please meet at my lawyers office at four p.m. on May 10th to sign our papers of incorporation.

3. A Retail Store at 405 7th avenue had sales of over one million dollars last year.

4. Every new employee must receive their permit to park in lot 5-A or there car will be towed.

5. Mr thompson left three million dollars to be divided among his 4 children rachel, timothy, rebecca and kevin.

6. Most companys can boost profits almost one hundred percent by retaining only 5% more of there current customers.

7. Although the bill for coffee and doughnuts were only three dollars and forty cents Phillip and myself had trouble paying it.

8. Only six of the 19 employees, who filled out survey forms, would have went to hawaii as their vacation choice.

9. Danielles report is more easier to read then david because her's was better organized and had good headings.

10. At mcdonald's we devoured 4 big macs 3 orders of french fries and 5 coca colas for lunch.

ENDNOTES

Chapter 1

1. Interview by author, 20 June 1999.
2. "That West Coast Difference," *Maclean's*, 26 May 1997, 21.
3. Anthony Wilson-Smith, "A Quiet Passion," *Maclean's*, 1 July 1995, 8–12.
4. Jon P. Alston and Theresa M. Morris. "Comparing Canadian and American Values: New Evidence from National Surveys." *Canadian Review of American Studies* 26, no. 3 (Autumn 1996): 301–315.
5. Kathleen K. Reardon, *Where Minds Meet* (Belmont, CA: Wadsworth, 1987), 199.
6. Vivienne Luk, Mumtaz Patel, and Kathryn White, "Personal Attributes of American and Chinese Business Associates," *The Bulletin of the Association for Business Communication*, December 1990, 67.
7. T. Morrison, Wayne Conaway, and George Borden, *Kiss, Bow, or Shake Hands: How to Do Business in Sixty Countries* (Holbrook, MA: Bob Adams Inc., 1994), 44.
8. Susan S. Jarvis, "Preparing Employees to Work South of the Border," *Personnel,* June 1990, 63.
9. Lennie Copeland and Lewis Griggs, *Going International* (New York: Penguin Books, 1985), 12.
10. *Going International*, 108.
11. *Kiss, Bow, or Shake Hands*, 44.
12. Jeff Copeland, "State Less, Listen More," *American Way*, American Air Lines, 15 December 1990.
13. Nancy Rivera Brooks, "Exports Boom Softens Blow of Recession," *Los Angeles Times,* 29 May 1991, D1.
14. Statistics Canada, CANSIM, Matrices 6367, (estimates), 6900 (projections) available from www.statcan.ca/english/Pgdb/People/Population/demo23c.htm and Matrix 3472 available from www.statcan.ca/english/Pgdb/People/Labour/labor05.htm.
15. Patrick Carnevale, quoted in Genevieve Capowski, "Managing Diversity," *Management Review*, June 1996, 16.
16. Joel Makower, "Managing Diversity in the Workplace," *Business and Society Review*, Winter 1995, 48–54, in ABI/INFORM [on-line database] [cited on 7 August 1996]; available from telnet://melvyl.ucop.edu.
17. Anthony Patrick Carnevale and Susan Carol Stone, *The American Mosaic* (New York: McGraw-Hill, 1995), 60.
18. Lee Gardenswartz and Anita Rowe, "Helping Managers Solve Cultural Conflicts," *Managing Diversity*, August 1996; available at: www.jalmc.org/hlp-mgr.htm.
19. Based on Pete Engardio, "Hmm. Could Use a Little More Snake," *Business Week,* 15 March 1993, 53.
20. Based on: "Information and Practice Development, Service on Multiple Disability." Royal National Institute for the Blind, United Kingdom: www.rnib.org.uk/welcome1.htm (last update, 27 August 1998).

Chapter 2

1. Jan Spak, "Rising above the Pack," *Winnipeg Free Press*, 6 June 1998, E1.
2. Albert Mehrabian, *Silent Messages* (Belmont, CA: Wadsworth, 1971), 44.
3. J. Burgoon, D. Coker, and R. Coker, "Communicative Explanations," *Human Communication Research*, 12 (1986): 463–494.
4. Julius Fast, *Subtext: Making Body Language Work in the Workplace* (New York: Viking, 1991), 129.
5. Ray Birdwhistell, *Kinesics and Context* (Philadelphia: University of Pennsylvania Press, 1970).
6. Diane Arthur, "The Importance of Body Language," *HR Focus* 72, no. 6 (June 1995): 22–23.
7. "In Athens, It's Palms In," *Newsweek,* 10 December 1990, 79Q.
8. *Business Week*, 18 October 1993, 6.
9. Dean Allen Foster, *Bargaining Across Borders* (New York: McGraw-Hill, 1992).
10. "What's the Universal Hand Sign for 'I Goofed'?" *Santa Barbara News-Press,* 16 December 1996, D2.

Chapter 3

1. Cathy Chapman, presentation to the Just Language Conference, Vancouver, 1995; available from plainlanguage.com/whatisplain.html.
2. J. Peder Zane, "For Investors, an Initial Public Offering of English," *The New York Times*, 25 August 1996, F7.
3. Cathy Chapman, presentation to the Just Language Conference, Vancouver, 1995; available from plainlanguage.com/whatisplain.html.

Chapter 4

1. Cynthia Selley, interview by author, June 15, 1999.
2. Government of British Columbia, Ministry of Women's Equality, "Communicating Without Bias," 1992 [cited 10 April 1999]; available from www.weq.gov.bc.ca/GENERAL/communicating.bias.html#RTFToC1.
3. Christina Stuart, "Why Can't a Woman Be More Like a Man?" *Training Tomorrow*, February 1994, 22–24.

Chapter 5

1. Eric Nee, "Interview with Microsoft Executives," *Upside*, April 1995, 66–68.
2. See, for example, Mary K. Kirtz and Diana C. Reep, "A Survey of the Frequency, Types and Importance of Writing Tasks in Four Career Areas," *The Bulletin of the Association for Business Communication*, December 1987, 22.
3. Robert Half International, as quoted in Cynthia A. Barnes, *Model Memos* (Englewood Cliffs, NJ: Prentice-Hall, 1990), 4.
4. Interview by author, 29 November 1994.
5. Elizabeth J. Hunt, "Communicating in the Information Age," *Canadian Business Review*, Summer 1996, 23–25.
6. "@ Risk," *The Economist*, 14 November 1998, 73.
7. "Brainstorming E-mail Messages," *Bottom Line/Business*, October 1996, 15.
8. Davis Sheremata, "Caught by the Repair Man," *Alberta Report/Western Report*, February 1998, 42.
9. "@ Risk," *The Economist*, 14 November 1998, 74.

Chapter 6

1. Interview by author, 25 June 1999.
2. Based on Kathleen Sibley, "Survey Ties High-Tech to Unethical Practices," *Computing Canada*, 25 May 1998, *KPMG 1998 Business Ethics Survey*, 4; available from www.kpmg.ca.
3. Brian Banks and David North "Oh, Rats, Why Snitch Lines Aren't Catching on in Canada," *Canadian Business*, February 1995, 17.
4. Ibid.

Chapter 7

1. Elizabeth J. Hunt, "Communicating in the Information Age," *Canadian Business Review* 23, no.2 (Summer 1996): 24.
2. Marcia Mascolini, "Another Look at Teaching the External Negative Message," *The Bulletin of the Association of Business Communication*, June 1994, 46.
3. Saburo Haneda and Hirosuke Shima, "Japanese Communication Behavior as Reflected in Letter Writing," *The Journal of Business Communication* 1 (1982): 29.
4. Elizabeth Tebeaux, "Designing Written Business Communication Along the Shifting Cultural Continuum," *Journal of Business and Technical Communication* 13 no. 1 (January 1999): 49.
5. Wolfgang Manekeller, as cited in Iris I. Varner, "Internationalizing Business Communication Courses," *The Bulletin of the Association for Business Communication*, December 1987, 10.

Chapter 8

1. Vera N. Held, "Banking on Words," *Canadian Banker*, Mar/Apr 1993, 30.
2. Michael Granberry, "Lingerie Chain Fined $100,000 for Gift Certificates," *Los Angeles Times*, 14 November 1992, D3.
3. Based on Gene Sloan, "Under 21? Carnival Says Cruise Is Off," *USA Today*, 29 November 1996; Jill Jordan Sieder, "Full Steam Ahead: Carnival Cruise Line Makes Boatloads of Money by Selling Fun," *U.S. News and World Report*, 16 October 1995, 72.
4. New Brunswick Human Rights Commission, *Sexual Harassment in Employment in New Brunswick*, February 1999. Available at www.gov.nb.ca/hrc%2Dcdp/e/sexharas.htm. Reprinted by permission.

Chapter 9

1. Peter Urs Bender, "The Five Steps to Leadership," *Canadian Manager* 23, no.3 (Fall 1998): 23.
2. E. S. Browning, "In Pursuit of the Elusive Euroconsumer," *The Wall Street Journal*, 23 April 1992, B1.
3. Gabriella Stern, "Heinz Aims to Export Taste for Ketchup," *The Wall Street Journal*, 20 November 1992, B1.
4. Alecia Swasy, "Don't Sell Thick Diapers in Tokyo," *The New York Times*, 3 October 1993, F9.
5. Ron Simmer, Alice Iordache, Brenda Wishart, "PATSCAN Patent and Trademark Searching," [cited June 1999]; available from www.library.ubc.ca/patscan/ funny_trade.html.
6. Raju Narisetti, "Can Rubbermaid Crack Foreign Markets?" *The Wall Street Journal*, 20 June 1996, B1.
7. Neil Morton, "Some Like It Cold," *Canadian Business*, September 1997, 99.

Chapter 10

1. Andrew S. Grove, "The Fine Art of Feedback," *Working Woman*, February 1992, 28.
2. Virginia Shea, "Express Yourself :-)," *Computerworld*, 6 March 1995, 87. Reprinted by permission.
3. Andrew Pollack, "Happy in the East (^_^) or Smiling :-) in the West," *The New York Times*, 12 August 1996, C5. Copyright © 1996 by the New York Times Co. Reprinted by permission.
4. David Angell and Brent Heslop, *The Elements of E-Mail Style* (Reading, MA: Addison-Wesley, 1994), 111.

Chapter 11

1. Jean Pascal Souque and Jacek Warda, "A Winning Formula" [interview with Terence Matthews, Newbridge Networks Corp.], *Canadian Business Review* 23 no. 2 (Summer 1996): 7.

Chapter 12

1. Brian Hutchinson, "Just Do It," *Canadian Business*, December 1996, 75.
2. Herman Holtz, *The Consultant's Guide to Proposal Writing* (New York: John Wiley, 1990), 188.
3. Based on Jane Applegate, "Weigh Freight Expenses Carefully," *Los Angeles Times*, 14 August 1992, D3.
4. Based on Karen S. Sterkel, "Integrating Intercultural Communication and Report Writing in the Communication Class," *The Bulletin of the Association of Business Communication*, September 1988, 14–16.

Chapter 13

1. Marc Belaiche, "Tips on Improving Your Resume," *Canadian Manager* 23 no. 3 (Fall 1998): 17.
2. Paula Fuchsberg, "Effective Resumes: Make It Easy to See Your Best Qualities," *The Philadelphia Inquirer*, 13 May 1996.
3. "Tips on Improving Your Resume," 17.
4. Interview by author, 21 January 1997.
5. *Resumes for Dummies* (Foster City, CA: IDG Books, 1996), 64.
6. "A Good Cover Letter Gives Job Applicants Edge," *Communication World*, January/February 1996, 13.
7. Harriet M. Augustin, "The Written Job Search: A Comparison of the Traditional and a Nontraditional Approach," *The Bulletin of the Association for Business Communication*, September 1991, 13.
8. Jim Carroll and Rick Broadhead, *1999 Canadian Internet Directory and Research Guide* (Scarborough, ON: Prentice Hall Canada, 1998), 9.

Chapter 14

1. Michael Stern, "Dear Sir: You Are an Oaf...," *Canadian Business*, 24 April 1998, 38.
2. Ron Fry, *Your First Interview* (Hawthorne, NJ: The Career Press, 1991), 16.
3. Caryl Rae Krannich and Ronal L. Krannich, *Dynamite Answers to Interview Questions* (Manassas Park, VA: Impact Publications, 1994), 46.
4. J. Kenneth Horn, "Personnel Administrators' Reactions to Job Follow-up Letters Regarding Extending Interviews and Offering Jobs," *The Bulletin of the Association for Business Communication*, September 1991, 24.
5. Julia Lawlor, "Networking Opens More Doors to Jobs," *USA Today*, 19 November 1990, B7.
6. "Dear Sir: You Are an Oaf...," 39.

INDEX

To the owner of this book

We hope that you have enjoyed *Essentials of Business Communication,* Third Canadian Edition, by Mary Ellen Guffey and Brendan Nagle (ISBN 0-17-616759-5), and we would like to know as much about your experiences with this text as you would care to offer. Only through your comments and those of others can we learn how to make this a better text for future readers.

School _____ Your instructor's name _____

Course _____ Was the text required? _____ Recommended? _____

1. What did you like the most about *Essentials of Business Communication?*

_____
_____
_____

2. How useful was this text for your course?

_____
_____
_____

3. Do you have any recommendations for ways to improve the next edition of this text?

_____
_____
_____

4. In the space below or in a separate letter, please write any other comments you have about the book. (For example, please feel free to comment on reading level, writing style, terminology, design features, and learning aids.)

_____
_____
_____

Optional

Your name _____ Date _____

May Nelson Thomson Learning quote you, either in promotion for *Essentials of Business Communication,* or in future publishing ventures?

Yes _____ No _____

Thanks!

You can also send your comments to us via e-mail at
college@nelson.com

PLEASE TAPE SHUT. DO NOT STAPLE.

TAPE SHUT

TAPE SHUT

- - - - - - - - - - - FOLD HERE - - - - - - - - - - -

Nelson
Thomson Learning™

MAIL ➤ **POSTE**
Canada Post Corporation
Société canadienne des postes
Postage paid   Port payé
if mailed in Canada   si posté au Canada
Business Reply   **Réponse d'affaires**
0066102399   **01**

0066102399-M1K5G4-BR01

NELSON THOMSON LEARNING
HIGHER EDUCATION
PO BOX 60225 STN BRM B
TORONTO ON M7Y 2H1

TAPE SHUT

TAPE SHUT